NEW CLASSICS

Photographs by Sîan Irvine

Gary Rhodes
NEW CLASSICS

London, New York, Sydney, Delhi, Paris, Munich, and Johannesburg

Publisher: Sean Moore
Editorial Director: Chuck Wills
Project Editor: Barbara Minton
Art Director: Dirk Kaufman
Production Director: Chris Avgherinos
DTP: Tracy McCord, Russell Shaw

First US edition published in 2001 by
Dorling Kindersley Publishing, Inc.
95 Madison Avenue
New York, New York 10016

New Classics
ISBN 0-7894-8028-X

This book is published to accompany the television series entitled *New British Classics,* first broadcast in 1999.
The series was produced by BBC Features and Events.
Executive Producer: Nick Vaughan-Barratt
Producer: Mandy Cooper

First published, 1999, by BBC Worldwide Ltd,
Woodlands, 80 Wood Lane
London W12 0TT

Reprinted 1999 (twice), 2000 (twice)
© Copyright Gary Rhodes 1999
The moral right of the author has been asserted.
Photographs by Sîan Irvine © copyright BBC Worldwide Ltd

Recipe for mincemeat in *Homemade Mincemeat and Mince Pies* on page 337 taken from *Delia Smith's Christmas* and reproduced by kind permission of Delia Smith.

Commissioning editor: Nicky Copeland
Project editor: Khadija Manjlai
Copy editor: Deborah Savage
Additional research: Susan Fleming
Art director: Lisa Pettibone
Styling by Pippin Britz
Food prepared for photography by Gary Rhodes
Thanks to Divertimente in London, Thomas Goode in London, Villroy & Boch and the Blue Door in London for the loan of items for photography

Typeset in Classical Garamond and Syntax
Printed and bound in Great Britain by Butler & Tanner Ltd, Frome and London
Color separations by Radstock Reproductions, Midsomer Norton
Jacket printed by Lawrence Allen Ltd, Weston-super-Mare

Acknowledgements

This book is the largest collection of recipes that I have written and put together. It's almost impossible to compile such a repertoire without the support and help of others, so I would like to take this opportunity to express my dearest thanks to all, including those not mentioned by name here.

A very special thank you to Sue Fleming for the many hours it took accumulating the vast quantity of research information required. I'd like to thank Borra Garson, Lissanne Kenyon, Gardner Merchant, my team at city rhodes restaurant, in particular Wayne Tapsfield and Michael Bedford, and the BBC books team: Nicky Copeland, Khadija Manjlai; to Andrew Barron, Sarah Miles, and Charlotte Lochhead. Another big thank you to the best home economist in the business – Jo Pratt; to Sîan Irvine for the beautiful photography, Nick Vaughan-Barratt, Mandy Cooper and the rest of the BBC television crew for the many exciting weeks of filming the *New British Classics* series.

And, of course, my wife and sons – Jennie, Samuel and George – who've put up with me for yet another year and will, I hope, for many more to come.

Thank you – simple words that mean so much.

Contents

British cooking has gone through many changes, with different approaches to ingredients resulting in varied tastes and styles. Twenty-five years ago, the UK had a poor reputation and little respect throughout the culinary world. But then an innovative influence, *nouvelle cuisine*, burst onto the scene, affecting restaurants and home kitchens alike. We did not fully understand its style, but it gave us light at the end of the tunnel, inspiring us to find our place in the world of culinary excellence.

It turned out to be a long journey, but we did not lose direction. Two brothers were responsible for this, showing us that classical methods and long-held traditions are the bedrock of new ideas. They showed how to work with tastes, not overwork them, creating complements rather than conflicts.

The brothers have an aura about them: they have given me nothing but inspiration, and continue to do so. I would like to dedicate *New Classics* to the Roux brothers, Albert and Michel, who, for me, are the godfathers of the culinary world.

Thank you.

"The discovery of a new dish is more beneficial to humanity than the discovery of a new star."
Brillat Savarin

Introduction

New Classics is a book of culinary stories and recipes providing us with information of the past, tracing the many flavors that have survived, with many others that have been re-born. British cooking is a long-held passion of mine. While other cuisines have had a large influence the development of British cooking, its worldwide culinary reputation has always been less esteemed than that of France and Italy. I have never quite understood why this was until I started my research on this book. Of course, I had heard various opinions and held many of my own, but the origins and progress of cooking in Britain is more complicated and fascinating than one imagines, and it deserves exploration. In each chapter I have outlined the history of the recipes included. I have also interspersed the chapters with features on ingredients and food occasions (afternoon tea, for example) that I think are particularly, sometimes even uniquely, British.

So, how did the history of cooking start? The first few lines from "The Invention of Cuisine" by Carol Musk set the scene.

Imagine a thin woman
before bread was invented,
playing a harp of wheat in the field.
There is a stone, and behind her
the bones of the last killed,
The black bird on her shoulder
That a century later
Will fly with trained and murderous intent.

They are not very hungry
because cuisine has not yet been invented.
nor has falconry,
nor the science of imagination.

All they have is the pure impulse to eat.

Out of the need to eat for survival came the instinct to put ingredients together and cook them for variety and taste – an impulse that developed in most of the world at the same time.

The principal characteristic of British culinary tradition is the number of influences it has absorbed over the centuries. As a group of islands next to a great continental mass, Britain has always been open to invasion. The invaders came, bringing with them their foods and cooking techniques. The Romans were perhaps of the greatest significance, and during their 400 years of occupation, they introduced many ingredients and ideas to an essentially simple cooking style. Many vegetables, fruits, and meats that are considered British-born were actually brought in by the Romans – from pheasants, guinea fowl, and deer to figs, walnuts, chestnuts, parsley, mint, chervil, onions, leeks, and garlic. The Romans also introduced cabbage and turnips, two vegetables always considered to be purely British.

The Saxons, Angles, and Vikings were also influential, as were the Normans after 1066. These "men of the North" – Normandy was itself originally a Viking stronghold – not only brought in ideas from France and from their own heritage, but from southern Europe, too. Norman forces went on to conquer parts of southern Europe, in particular Sicily, which had been strongly influenced by Arab invaders, and food traditions from there were to spread through Northern Europe. Medieval food in England was rich in many ways that were as much Middle Eastern as northern European, in the use of dried fruits, nuts such as almonds, and a multitude of spices. Cane sugar was another introduction, brought to England by soldiers returning from the Crusades. So rare and expensive were the blocks of refined or brown sugar that they were looked upon as a sweet spice and kept under lock and key.

Food for the rich would not have been dull during and after the Middle Ages, although the many fish days forced on the population by the Church must have made salt fish (most people did not have access to fresh) less than welcome. For ordinary people this simply meant salted and pickled fish, but for the rich there were many more types of seafood available – from basics such as flounder, haddock, herring, and mackerel to the more extravagant oysters, whale meat, sturgeon, crabs, lobsters, and even seals.

It is said that a simpler form of food than that of the medieval style started to creep into Britain during the years of the Commonwealth (1649–60), when the Puritans disapproved of the use of culinary spices, believing them to lead to intemperance and lasciviousness, so much so that they even tried to ban Christmas! British food has always been plain, but, contrary to what is often thought, I don't think it was dull. The majority of the population, denied access to expensive imported fruits, nuts, and spices, cooked and ate very simply, and the traditions of the peasant's table are as important to British culinary heritage as those of the aristocracy. Moreover, the climate and agricultural techniques, in England at any rate, guaranteed adequate grain supplies and lush pastures which produced good-quality meats. So, basically, for those who could afford meat, there was no need to do anything more fancy to a piece of beef than roast it. The majority of people liked foods to taste of what they were, along with "the taste of the fire," and didn't favor rich complementary sauces or tricky combinations of foods as the French might. Then as now, however, sharp and piquant garnish sauces, such as mint or horseradish, were much favored.

Following the great world explorations of the sixteenth century, many foods were introduced to Britain from the New World, among them turkeys, tomatoes, sweet peppers, chilies, and vanilla. The food that was to have the most significance, though, was the potato, which did not take long to become a dietary staple in the British Isles, particularly in Ireland.

The increasing industrialization of the country from the eighteenth century onward, and also the enclosures of land, meant that many people were displaced and rural and culinary traditions began to be eroded. Those who had to seek work in the gradually expanding towns became cut off from their former ways of growing, cooking, and eating. Once again, food became simpler. Eating took second place to work in daily life, playing a smaller part in the family budget, and it became of little general interest. It was at this time that shops selling cooked food became part of the culinary culture, offering some of the dishes that most characterize British cooking to many – such as eels with mashed potatoes, pies and mashed potatoes, and one of the most classic British dishes – fish and chips. With the breakdown of the rural communities resulting in people moving to the cities, some traditions were lost and others replaced with outside influences – notably French cuisine, which dominated "refined" British cooking in restaurants and wealthy private houses in the eighteenth and nineteenth centuries. These dual culinary styles continued until the First and Second World Wars, when food for pleasure became difficult to obtain because of rationing being established.

Later, with the introduction of *nouvelle cuisine* – a new "fashion" in cooking – Britain seemed to lose its way completely. Perhaps I should say *mislay*, rather than *lose*, because in many country districts, those parts of England, Scotland, Wales, and Ireland furthest from the urban centers of influence, great traditions managed to survive. In these regions, I've personally experienced, with nothing but gustatory pleasure, large pots containing all three courses – boiled ham with lots of vegetables and potatoes cooking away with a muslin bag holding a leek dumpling, for instance, where the vegetables are served with the broth for soup, followed by the ham and potatoes, and finished with a wedge of the savory dumpling. In the last few years there has been a more generalized revival of interest in the old ways. Twenty years ago, British cooking was looked upon as having nothing to offer but well-done roast beef and soggy Yorkshire pudding. It was in the mid-1980s that the image of British cooking began to change, and I am proud to have played a small part in this, re-introducing to my menus recipes that I consider to be Great British Classics. Lancashire hotpot, fishcakes, and bread and butter pudding are all part of a huge tradition, north to south and east to west, and are all honest and simple, with real, full, delicious flavors. Why did Britons lose these dishes? Slowly braised oxtail (returning soon, we hope, page 230) is perhaps one of the best foods in the world. It's also exciting and encouraging to see and hear how many of my colleagues in the business are re-thinking their views on British food and exploring complementary culinary roads.

Nothing ever stands still, however, and this is undoubtedly true in cooking. Flavors and tastes have changed in the last twenty years in Britain. Ingredients people hadn't even heard of, such as chilies, pasta, polenta, vanilla beans, and many fresh herbs, are now virtually commonplace. To some people, it seems very adventurous to try out these "new" tastes, but it's almost a replay of what it must have been like in the Middle Ages when these tastes – spices, dried fruits, citrus fruits, and so on – were making their first appearance. It wasn't the years of the Raj that introduced Britain to spices. People had been using them centuries before as essential ingredients in British cooking. Gingerbread, for instance, with ginger as its main component, is an ancient, basic cake; the cloves in apple pie along with the dried fruits, currants, golden raisins, and prunes that appear in so many festive cakes and puddings are a direct survival of a medieval tradition – a British tradition. So, all these new trendy flavors are not so new after all. They have been part of British cuisine for some time and are now playing their part in a revival.

I have always had a strong passion for classics – after all, every new style has been born from them – but putting this book together, taking it from its original idea and researching it, has stirred a new passion within me. Now, my feelings for cooking, in particular British cooking, are "souffléing" larger than I ever imagined. It's a soufflé that won't overcook,

but will keep that gentle, soft texture inside without allowing any flavors to become lost.

The world has become a global village, providing and making accessible to us almost all the food ingredients from different corners of the Earth. With all of these items available, Britons must make sure the basic traditions and classics are not forgotten. I've worked to bring these traditional dishes up to a new level of eating so that they will rate more than comfortably with the best from other countries. The simplest of dishes are often the best: a plate of fish and chips executed well is perfection to eat and can stand up to any international fish dish. British food might have taken on many of its influences from outside, but the end results – what there is today – are as good as those of any other country and this book is a celebration of that fact.

You'll discover many dishes I want to be viewed as new British classics, such as omelette thermidor, scallops with black pudding, braised beef with caramelized onions and turnip purée, and others, including baked egg custard tart, that I've simply brought back to life. And, I've given recipes for historical dishes for which the ingredients are now difficult or impossible to buy. Many readers will not be able to find sources for such wild, natural, or specialty foods as rowan berries, certain kinds of game birds, or pig's blood for black pudding, for example. The recipes are included, however, as historical presentations of British classic foods.

The whole book is about taking British ideas (and there are so many) from yesterday and refining them for tomorrow – for another thousand years. These recipes, with their rejuvenated flavors, are here to be enjoyed and to revive your feelings for good traditional cooking, as well as to give you new culinary inspirations. And, of course, recipes can be adapted to suit your own tastes – as Roger Vergé, one of the great French chefs of the world, says:

"A recipe is not meant to be followed exactly – it is a canvas on which you can embroider."
Cuisine of the Sun (translated by Caroline Conran), 1979

General Information

Included here are a few hints and tips which you might find helpful, some culinary and some about ingredients or products used in my recipes.

Blind-baking Pastry

Line the pan with the rolled-out pastry and let it rest, preferably in the refrigerator, for 20–30 minutes. Now, line the pastry shell with baking parchment, foil, or waxed paper, and fill it with baking beans (kept especially for the purpose) or pie weights. Bake the pastry at the suggested temperature for the recommended time. It is best, when blind-baking, to leave the excess pastry hanging over the edge of the pan, because pastry shrinks as it cooks. After it is baked and cooled, remove the pie weights and trim off the excess pastry for a perfectly neat, even finish.

Butter

The butter I use most is unsalted because it gives greater control over the seasoning of a dish.

Chocolate

Chocolate basically consists of two components: cocoa solids (including cocoa butter) and sugar. Chocolate with a cocoa-solid content of 70 percent or over is considered unpalatable because it is too bitter. Extra-bitter chocolate ranges from to 70 percent cocoa solids, but is palatable. A bittersweet chocolate will be in the 60–70 percent range, when it should hold 30-35 percent cocoa butter. Valrhona "Grand Cru," which falls into this category, is probably the best for cooking. There are also semisweet chocolates and milk chocolates: the semisweet varieties must always include a minimum of 30 percent cocoa butter within the solids, making it easier to work with.

I have always bought my cooking chocolate from the French maker Valrhona or Callebaut, a famous Belgian company. These makes are not always easily obtainable, but the Swiss chocolate Lindt, is readily available, good to work with, and carries a good depth of flavor.

White chocolate is a blend of cocoa butter, sugar, and milk, and, for a quality product, should contain no more than 50 percent sugar.

Crème Fraîche

This is made by pasteurizing milk before the cream has formed. The milk is then separated into cream and skim milk. The cream is pasteurized again, giving it extra shelf life; selected lactic cultures are added to give it acidity. It can be used for both sweet and savory sauces. Heavy or clotted creams contains about 40 percent fat, crème fraîche just 30 percent.

Eggs

All eggs used in the recipes in this book are large.

Fromage Blanc and Fromage Frais

Fromage blanc is a soft, unripened cheese, usually made with a culture and from skim milk. Fromage frais is fromage blanc, beaten to a smooth consistency. Both contain between zero and 8 percent fat, unless they have been enriched with cream. Fromage frais can replace yogurt in ice creams, mousses, and so on.

Game Seasons in the US and Britain

Game seasons vary by state regions in the US. Check with your local government or on the Internet for these regulations and for license requirements.

The hunting game in Britain has been important for rich and poor alike throughout its history. The following table illustrates this continuing tradition:

Grouse – 12 August to 10 December

Mallard (wild duck) – September to January

Partridge – 1 September to 1 February

Pheasant – 1 October to 1 February (best between December and January)

Quail – All year

Venison – March to October

Wild hare – March to July

Butane Torch

A butane gas canister can be used as a torch in the kitchen to give a crisp glaze to many desserts. They are available from most hardware stores and kitchen supply stores. Follow the instructions carefully, and of course, keep them away from children.

Herbs

If you substitute dried herbs for fresh herbs, remember to use only half the amount specified.

Ice Cream Making

I recommend using an ice cream machine for the best results: as it churns, the mixture becomes lighter and the texture smoother. Fill the machine half to two-thirds full, to leave room for the mixture to increase in volume.

If you don't have a machine, you can still make ice creams: freeze the ice cream mixture and whisk it every 20–30 minutes until it is set. It will still taste good, although it may be a bit grainier because of the larger ice crystals.

Medjool Dates

Medjool dates come from India and they are the most delicious. Plump and meaty, they have a natural fudge-toffee flavor that is perfect for many dishes.

Pig's Caul and Sausage Skins

Caul is the lacy lining of a pig's stomach. It is very difficult to obtain but you might be able to order it through your butcher. To make it easier to use, it must be soaked in cold water for 24 hours first and then drained. Use it almost like plastic wrap, rolled around meat or a meaty mixture to which it will cling. If caul is unavailable, cook without a covering or use buttered foil.

Sausage casings, which are the intestines of pigs, can be ordered from your butcher as well. Soak them for several hours and rinse well before use.

Pin Bones

These fine bones are found in round fish fillets, that is, red mullet, trout, salmon, cod, and so on. The bones run down the center of most of these fillets and are easily removed with fine pliers or tweezers. It's worth spending the time to remove them, so that the fish becomes more comfortable to eat.

Seasoning

Unless otherwise stated, "season" or "seasoning" simply means seasoning with salt and pepper – preferably freshly ground black or white pepper.

"It may be that there are some men who seek gold, but there lives no man who does not need salt, which seasons our food." Cassiodorus, AD 468–568

Sour cream

Sour cream is light or heavy cream that has been treated with a culture; it contains about 20 percent butterfat. You can make it at home by simply adding a few drops of lemon juice to heavy cream.

Squeeze Bottles

Small plastic bottles with narrow spouts can be bought in good kitchen supply stores. Filled with something like a sauce or *coulis* (a sieved puréed sauce, usually fruit-related), they can be squeezed to neatly decorate a plate or the food on it.

Stocks, Gravies, and Sauces – Alternatives

There are a number of stock and sauce recipes throughout the book, but many good ready-made alternatives (fresh, granular, or in cubes) are available in supermarkets.

Suet

The hard white fat surrounding beef kidneys which is shredded and floured for use in the kitchen. It is vital in making traditional British suet pastries and puddings. Because it is difficult to find in the US, hardened vegetable shortening, having the advantage of being suitable for vegetarians, can be substituted.

Vanilla

Vanilla beans are the fruit of a tropical vine. When you buy them, they are long, thin, and black. They can be split to allow you to use the tiny seeds inside, or the beans, very fragrant in themselves, can be used whole. Keep the beans in an airtight jar with your superfine sugar, and the sugar will be infused with the vanilla flavor – giving you a constant supply of vanilla sugar for desserts and cakes.

Vegetarian Dishes

All vegetarian dishes in this book have been marked with the symbol Ⓥ.

Vinegars

I use a selection of vinegars in this book. Red-wine vinegar is a favorite. Because many of those available are thin and not very red-wine-flavored, I urge you to spend a little more to buy a vinegar that bears the hallmark of a good wine – a Bordeaux vinegar, say, or my current favorite, Cabernet Sauvignon. Balsamic is the vinegar of the moment; you should spend a little more to get a good-quality product. The older the balsamic vinegar gets, the better it tastes – and the more expensive it is to buy, but because of its strength you won't use it up very quickly. I also like to use good-quality cider vinegar.

Weights and Measures

All the recipes in the book have been given in both American standard and metric. Stick to one system of measurement in using these recipes.

Spoon sizes: Tablespoon measurements are ½ oz (15 g) for solids and ½ fl oz (15 ml) for liquids, and teaspoons are ⅙ oz (5 g) for solids and ⅙ fl oz (5 ml) for liquids. All spoon measurements are level.

Yeast

Three types of yeast are available – fresh, compressed yeast, dried yeast, and easy-blend dried yeast. Fresh is very perishable and should be used quickly, or frozen; the dried yeasts should be stored in a cool place and checked for expiration dates.

Fresh and granular dried yeasts need to be activated in lukewarm liquid before being added to flour; easy-blend yeast doesn't need to be mixed with water first and can be mixed directly the flour. Dried yeast is twice as potent as fresh yeast, so use ½ oz (15 g) dried, for example, when a recipe specifies 1 oz (25 g) fresh yeast. Two level teaspoons is approximately ½ oz (15 g) dried yeast.

Yogurt

Low-fat or skim milk is treated with a culture of selected lactic cultures to make natural yogurt. The butterfat content is between zero and 8 percent, making natural yogurt very healthy.

OPPOSITE
Pressed Tomato Cake with Peppered Goat Cheese (page 66)

Soups

Once man succeeded in making
fireproof containers (saucepans), soup
would probably have been the very
first episode in a long-running cooking
show. Diet no longer consisted, by
necessity, of individual foods such as
grains, seeds, leaves, and berries or
a hunk of meat charred over flames.
Now these ingredients could be mixed
and cooked in water to achieve
different flavors and textures.
Soup was originally known as
"pottage," a name that stuck for
hundreds of years. The principal early
vegetables or "potherbs" used were
leeks and kale, but after the Roman
occupation of Britain, new ingredients
became available, including onions,
cabbage, and legumes such as
beans and peas.

Through the succeeding centuries, pottage remained one of the three main staple foods for all classes of society (the other two being bread and ale). The peasant's one would consist of water with whatever else he could find, grow, or dry for the winter – a little grain, a few root or legume vegetables, some wild herbs or seaweed, and occasionally, a little meat. But quite often it might just be water and the regional grain. A pottage was likely to be the meal of the day for a working man, either for breakfast or supper. The rich would probably include more protein or some nourishing vegetables in theirs and, often, a fine wheat version known as "frumenty" might serve as an accompaniment to meat or fish. Cereal pottage for breakfast still survives now in the Scottish classic, cooked oatmeal, which many of us eat to start our day. And legume varieties were taken to America by early colonists and returned to Britain centuries later as Boston baked beans.

Often the pottage was poured over what were called "sops," pieces of bread or toast served in a tureen or bowl. In France the dish became known as *soupe*, and in the latter seventeenth century, the name soon transferred, to a thinner version enjoyed by the British upper class. Other French influences crept in as well. Meat began to be cooked in and served with sauces (rather than being an integral part of pottage), and vegetables were boiled separately and then buttered. The concept of a meal consisting of individual courses was gradually adopted. The new "soup" became a course by itself at the beginning of a meal, and was known as a "remove" dish because, after the soup was eaten, it was removed from the table to be replaced, usually, by a fish dish.

Soups became even more ambitious in their ingredients. In the eighteenth century, turtle soup – made from green turtles shipped live in tanks from the West Indies – became popular. It was served, on many banquet menus, in several different ways – as thick, clear calipash (the part next to the upper shell), calipee (belly), and fins. (Mock turtle, an infamous English soup, was made from a calf's head simmered in stock and served in an empty turtle shell.) Meanwhile, pottage, or the thicker vegetable, meat, or fish soup, remained a basic food for the poor, as it has always been in more northerly countries.

Soup is one of the very few foods that has a virtually unlimited repertoire. Flavors from everything edible can be cooked, mixed, and mingled; and the end result can range from a clear consommé to a thick, creamed soup. This wonderful variety of consistencies suits different eating times, both of day and year. In the following chapter, you will find a "pottage" to fit almost every category. Here are a few examples of what I suggest: for lunch, *Vegetarian Scotch Broth* (page 31) or *Cullen Skink* (page 27); at a dinner party, the *Clear Ham Soup* (page 20), or *Lobster "Bisque"* (page 23); and for supper on a cold, snowy, winter evening, it would just have to be the *Boiled Bacon and Vegetable "Main Course" Soup* (opposite), served with chunks of bread. How's that for appetizers?

PAGE 14
Lobster "Bisque" Soup (page 23)

Boiled Bacon and Vegetable "Main Dish" Soup

Bacon and vegetables are a common combination all over Great Britain, as they have been for centuries. Bacon was always available throughout the year, and vegetables would be grown at home. I found this dish many years ago while filming in Northumberland. I'll always remember having the vegetables served in a bowl of stock for the first course, which was then followed by the bacon, pieces of potato, and some of the broth. The "pudding" was a chunk of savory leek dumpling, also cooked in the broth. So, basically, all three courses were cooked in the same pot, something that has always been very traditional.

This is a main-dish soup, with the bacon served with the vegetables. The recipe for a leek dumpling is included as an optional extra.

SERVES 6–8 FOR MAIN COURSE OR 10–12 FOR AN APPETIZER

2 lb (900 g) slab bacon soaked in cold water
    for 24 hours
1 bay leaf
Sprig of fresh thyme
12 oz (350 g) pearl onions, peeled
3 large carrots, cut into 1 in (2.5 cm) dice
4 celery sticks, cut into 1 in (2.5 cm) pieces
2–3 large potatoes, peeled and cut into
    1 in (2.5 cm) dice
1 large rutabaga, cut into 1 in (2.5 cm) dice
2–4 tablespoons (25–50 g) butter
Salt and pepper
Chopped fresh parsley, to garnish (optional)

For the Leek Dumpling

2¼ cups (250 g) self-rising flour
9 oz (250 g) leeks, sliced
4½ oz (125 g) shredded suet
2 teaspoons English mustard powder
1 egg, beaten
About ½ cup (100 ml) cold water
Salt and pepper

Once the bacon has been soaked for 24 hours, to remove its excess saltiness, rinse it well and cover with cold water again in a large saucepan. Bring to a boil and then place under cold running water to totally refresh. This will take out any remaining excess salt flavor.

Now cover again with water, adding the bay leaf and sprig of thyme. Bring to a simmer and cook for 1¼ hours. After this initial 1¼ hours' cooking time, the vegetables can be added and cooked for the last 45 minutes. The total cooking time will be approximately 2 hours. This guarantees the vegetables are cooked through completely and they will soak up all of the bacon-stock flavor.

After they are completely cooked, in about 2 hours, turn off the heat and let the soup rest, covered, for 15 minutes.

Remove the bacon and either just break it or carve into slices. Remove the thyme and bay leaf from the stock. Add the butter and stir it in. Check the seasoning, adding pepper and salt only if necessary. Present the meat in large bowls and divide the vegetables and stock among all four. Finish with a sprinkling, if using, of chopped parsley. The one-pot meal is now ready to enjoy.

To make the leek dumpling, mix together the self-rising flour, leeks, and suet. Season with salt, pepper, and mustard. Mix in the egg and enough of the water to create a soft dough. Pour boiling water over a muslin cloth, wring it out until it's almost dry, and dust it with flour. Place the dough on the muslin and tie into a bag. This can now be lowered into the broth one hour before the cooking time is over and served with the finished dish.

Spicy Smoked Haddock and Saffron Soup

Kedgeree became a popular breakfast dish (see page 162) following the years of the British Raj in India. It's made from a blend of rice, smoked haddock, and curry, and this soup brings haddock and curry together again, only omitting the rice (although cooked rice could be added at the end if preferred). The spicy flavor here comes from a medium hot curry powder, and the saffron adds to this taste, working well with the curry and at the same time enriching the color of the soup.

SERVES 4 GENEROUSLY

Butter
1 medium leek, washed and cut into
    rough ½ in (1 cm) dice
1 medium potato, peeled and cut into
    rough ½ in (1 cm) dice
2 small garlic cloves, crushed
1 tablespoon medium curry powder
Good pinch of saffron strands
12 oz (350 g) smoked haddock fillet
1½ cups (350 ml) water (or *Chicken Stock*,
    page 33, for a stronger flavor)
1 cup (250 ml) milk
½ cup (100–125 ml) light cream
    (or heavy, for an extra-rich finish)
Squeeze of lemon juice
Salt and pepper
10–12 cilantro leaves, to garnish (optional)

Preheat the oven to 350°F/180°C.

Melt a teaspoon of butter in a saucepan and when it begins to bubble, add the chopped leeks, the potatoes, and the crushed garlic. Cook for a few minutes on a medium heat without letting the vegetables brown. Add the curry powder and saffron and continue to cook for a few minutes.

While the vegetables are cooking, you can poach the haddock. Lay the fillet in an ovenproof roasting pan or dish; pour the water or stock and milk on top. Add a teaspoon of butter, cover with foil, and bring to a slow simmer. Finish cooking the dish in the oven, for 5–6 minutes.

After it's cooked, remove the fish from the broth and keep to one side. The cooking broth can now be added to the soup vegetables. Bring to a simmer and cook for 15–20 minutes until all the vegetables are completely tender.

The curry soup can now be made into a smooth purée. For a very smooth, silky finish, strain through a sieve. Add the cream along with a squeeze of lemon juice to liven up all the flavors. Season with salt and pepper, if needed.

While the soup is cooking, the haddock fillet can be skinned and all its bones removed; flake the flesh. Add the haddock flakes to the soup and serve. To finish, roughly chop the cilantro (if using) and sprinkle on top.

Note: I like to serve this soup with lots of good crusty bread, for dipping and for wiping the bowl clean.

Leek and Potato Broth ⓥ

Leeks were early pottage vegetables, and even when potatoes were introduced, they tended not to be cooked in the same way. However, throughout Europe this combination has proved long-lasting – in France this soup is the famous *potage bonne femme*.

The classic recipe consists basically of leeks, potatoes, and a white stock. I've added a few more ingredients to enrich the flavors – some onions, a touch of cream, and butter – which will lift the soup, making it a bit more exciting. The heavy cream can be omitted or replaced with crème fraîche for a lighter touch, or even sour cream to give a slightly acidic finish.

SERVES 4–6

4 tablespoons (50 g) butter
1 large onion, sliced
2 large potatoes, cut into ½ in (1 cm) dice
2½ cups (600 ml) *Chicken* or *Vegetable Stock*
    (page 33 or 36)
1 lb (450 g) leeks, shredded or cut into
    ½ in (1 cm) dice
⅔ cup (150 ml) heavy cream
Salt and pepper

ABOVE
Spicy Smoked Haddock and Saffron Soup

Melt a quarter of the butter and add the sliced onion. Cook for a minute or two until softened. Add the diced potatoes and cook them for a minute or two, stirring, before adding the stock. Bring to a simmer and cook until the potatoes have become barely tender. This should take 8–10 minutes.

Increase the heat until the stock is almost boiling. Add the leeks and continue to simmer for 5–6 minutes until the leeks are tender.

Add the heavy cream and remaining butter. Bring back to simmering and season well with salt and pepper.

The leek and potato broth is now ready to serve and it goes beautifully with good crusty bread.

Note: If using crème fraîche or sour cream, take a ladle of the hot broth and whisk it into either choice of cream to emulsify and bring it up to temperature before pouring into the pot. Crisp strips of bacon also work very well in this soup.

Clear Ham Soup with Pea Pancakes

England has always been famous for cured hams, and many counties have developed different cures. There are a lot of ham recipes in eighteenth- and nineteenth-century cookbooks, but the combination of cured pork with peas – not as sophisticated as this recipe, I must admit – is an ancient one.

In the past, such a soup would have been a thick pottage, but here I am making a liquid with the clarity of a consommé. To create this, of course, takes a lot of time. First, the ham stock has to be made (after soaking the hocks for 24 hours); then it has to be chilled. The next step is to clarify the stock, leaving you with a clear soup. Making a good consommé brings a great sense of achievement. If that's what you enjoy, then do try this recipe. It will give you a minimum of 5 cups (1–2 liters) of finished consommé.

Then all you need to do is to make the pea pancakes, which are a wonderful garnish for the soup. They can be served floating in the consommé or as a separate garnish. The pancakes are not essential. But pea and ham is a great British soup

that I've turned around. The ham is the leader this time, with peas close behind. This recipe amount will give you at least 14–18 small pancakes.

For the Ham Stock

1 onion, roughly chopped
2–3 celery sticks, roughly chopped
1 leek, roughly chopped
1 large carrot, roughly chopped
Butter
Sprig of thyme
1 bay leaf
Few black peppercorns
2 raw ham hocks, soaked in
    cold water for 24 hours
1 lb (450 g) chicken wings
At least 3½ quarts (3 liters) water

For the Clarification Crust

1 large chicken breast half
1 small onion, peeled and roughly chopped
1 small carrot, peeled and roughly chopped
1 celery stick, roughly chopped
1 egg white (2 for extra body and security!)
Salt and pepper

For the Pea Pancakes

8 oz (225 g) frozen peas, cooked
1 egg
1 egg yolk
3 tablespoons all-purpose flour
3 tablespoons heavy cream
4 tablespoons (50 g) unsalted butter
2–3 oz (50–75 g) ham, finely shredded
    (optional)
Oil or butter, for frying
Salt and pepper

For the stock, lightly soften the vegetables in a teaspoon of butter in a large pot, without letting them brown.

OPPOSITE
Clear Ham Soup with Pea Pancakes

Add the thyme, bay leaf, peppercorns, ham hocks, and chicken wings and cover with plenty of water.

Bring to a simmer, skimming off any impurities that rise to the top. Allow the stock to simmer on the lowest possible heat, uncovered, for 2 hours. The finished quantity of stock needed for the soup is approximately 2½ quarts (2.25 liters): if the liquid reduces too quickly, simply top up with extra water during the cooking time.

At the end of this cooking time, the flavor of the ham will have become predominant, with the chicken wings helping to create a balance among the flavors. Do not add any salt since the ham will provide enough saltiness on its own.

Strain the stock and then place the ham hocks in the broth to keep them moist. Allow the broth to cool. After it has cooled, the hocks can be removed and trimmed. This involves removing the skin, discarding it, and cutting the meat from the bone. Some of this can be finely shredded to add to the pea-pancake mixture. Any remainder will be delicious to eat in a good homemade sandwich with mayonnaise and crisp Iceberg lettuce.

Now it's time to make the clarification crust. Place all of the ingredients, except the egg white(s), in a food processor. This mixture can now be processed to a pulp. Remove the purée and place in a bowl. Mix in the egg whites and check for seasoning, being careful not to oversalt.

Blend together the stock with the chicken mixture. Place over a low heat, making sure the soup is stirred well and so that it won't stick to the bottom of the pan. Slowly, a pad will start to form, which is the clarification mixture rising to the top.

When the first stage of this appears, increase the heat and whisk quickly. Return the heat to its former temperature. The crust will now begin to form again. The soup can be allowed to cook at a gentle simmer for 1½ hours. During this time, the impurities in the original stock will be absorbed into the crust.

Usually a small gap will form at the top of the crust. It's from here you can taste the soup and test its strength. If the flavor still seems shallow after the cooking time, then just continue to simmer for another 20–30 minutes. Now it's time to strain the consommé.

For the ultimate clear soup, ladle the stock through a double thickness of muslin cloth being careful not to break the crust too much. Don't try to strain every last drop. The last inch of consommé is best poured into a separate pan; if this is totally clear just strain into the rest of the consommé. However, this may have taken on a slight cloudiness from the crust. If so, keep separate. Now take a look at the beautiful amber-colored consommé you have made. Your moment of pride begins.

To make the pea pancakes, place the peas, egg, egg yolk, flour, and cream in a food processor and process to a smooth consistency. Heat a frying-pan and add the butter, allowing it to brown to the nut-brown stage. Add the butter to the mixture and season with salt and pepper. If making pea and shredded ham pancakes, stir in the shredded ham at this stage. The mixture is now ready to cook.

Heat a frying-pan over a medium heat and add a trickle of oil or a teaspoon of butter. The pancake mixture can now be dropped in, a tablespoon at a time. This will spread slightly, giving you small pea pancakes; you'll probably have room to cook 3–4 together, depending on the size of your pan. Cook until golden, 3–4 minutes, and then turn over and brown the other side for 1–2 minutes. Remove and keep warm while the remaining mixture is cooked.

The pancakes can be made well in advance and allowed to cool. To re-heat, take a ladleful of consommé and warm the cakes gently in a saucepan or, if serving separately, in warm melted butter. Now, re-heat the soup and garnish with the pea pancakes. The results are worth every minute of the effort in this recipe.

Note: The pancake mix can be spooned into small stainless-steel buttered rings in a frying-pan for perfectly round results.

Lobster "Bisque" Soup

From Elizabethan times onward, many French culinary techniques and recipes were adopted by the British gentry. One of these was the bisque, a soup with a broth foundation combined with pieces of meat or poultry, and regarded as the king of all soups. From the eighteenth century, a bisque was usually associated with puréed crustaceans, often crayfish. Lobster, then as now, would have been the most extravagant and valued of the lot.

In order to get the maximum flavor from the shells, cooking bisque does take time, so it's worth making a larger quantity and freezing some (the soup freezes well). Broken lobsters can be found at a reasonable cost, or if you eat a lot of lobster, simply save and freeze any cooked shells until you reach the quantity required. This recipe can also be adapted to crab or shrimp, simply by replacing the quantity of lobster shells with those of the appropriate seafood.

MAKES 1¼ - 2 QUARTS (1.2–1.75 LITERS)

1 lb (450 g) lobster shells or a 1½ lb
    (675 g) lobster
5–8 cups (1.2–1.75 liters) *Fish Stock*
    (page 35)
2 tablespoons (25 g) butter
1 tablespoon olive oil
1 large carrot, roughly diced
2–3 shallots or 1 large onion, roughly diced
2 celery sticks, roughly diced
1 small leek, roughly diced
1 fennel bulb, roughly diced
1 garlic clove, crushed
1 star anise (optional)
Strip of orange zest
Few basil leaves
Few tarragon leaves
Pinch of saffron, soaked (page 397)
2 tablespoons (50 ml) brandy
4 large ripe tomatoes, quartered
1 teaspoon tomato purée
½ of a liter bottle white wine
⅔ cup (150 ml) light cream (optional)
Few drops of lemon juice
Salt and pepper
Pinch of cayenne pepper

If you are using a live lobster, bring the fish stock to a boil and drop in the lobster. Cook for 3–4 minutes, then remove from the heat. Leave the lobster in the stock until completely cooled. This will help flavor the stock and keep the lobster meat moist.

Break off the claws and crack them open with the back of a heavy knife to release the meat. The joints connecting the claw to the body should also be cracked open and the meat removed. Split the body and tail through the middle, lengthwise, and remove the tail meat.

Reserve all of the lobster meat in a little of the cooking liquid to keep it moist. The meat can be used either as a garnish for this soup or in another recipe, such as *Lobster Omelette "Thermidor"* (page 75). All of the shells, whether you're using ones from the live lobster or frozen/broken shells (see recipe introduction), can now be crushed as finely as possible. This can be achieved relatively easily with a rolling pin, hitting the shells to break them up in a saucepan.

To make the soup, melt the butter with the olive oil. Add the diced carrot, shallots or onion, celery, leek, and fennel, with the crushed garlic, star anise, orange zest, basil, and tarragon leaves. Add the pinch of saffron and cook over a medium heat for 10–15 minutes, without browning. The vegetables will now begin to soften.

Add the crushed lobster shells and cook for another 10 minutes. Add the brandy and, if possible, flame (*flambé*) the contents of the pan. Boil until almost dry. Add the quartered tomatoes and tomato purée and continue to simmer for 6–7 minutes. Pour in the white wine and reduce the liquid by half. Add 5 cups (1.2 liters) of fish stock and bring to a simmer; cook for 25–30 minutes.

The soup, with the shells and all vegetables included, can now be puréed in a food processor to a smooth consistency. Strain through a fine sieve to remove any shells, pushing all the flavor through.

The bisque, if too thick, can now be thinned with extra fish stock until it reaches the correct consistency. Season with salt, pepper, and a pinch of cayenne pepper. The lobster bisque soup is now ready to serve.

For a creamier finish, add the light cream, a splash at a time, to suit your taste. A drop or two of lemon juice can also be added to lift the total taste (or add an extra splash of brandy).

Note: If making the *Lobster Omelette "Thermidor"* (page 75) take ⅔–1¼ cups (150–300 ml) of finished bisque and reduce by half to two-thirds. This can now be used to enhance the cheese sauce for the "Thermidor."

The soup can also be enhanced with a trickle of Lobster/Shellfish Oil (page 386).

Almond and Celery Soup ⓥ

Soups and dishes that were "white" were very popular in the early Middle Ages, the white coming from pounded chicken or other pale meat, or from almonds. These nuts were introduced from the Mediterranean, becoming an essential ingredient, added whole to dishes as a garnish, made into a milk (as we use coconut today), or pounded for a white thickening in a dish. In the past, cooks would have had to pound the whole shelled almonds in a mortar, but today we can buy them already ground.

A nice garnish is to toast a few flaked almonds and sprinkle them on top. Using chicken stock gives a meatier flavor to the almond and celery combination, but you can, of course, make it vegetarian by using vegetable stock.

SERVES 4–6

2 tablespoons (25 g) butter
1 lb (450 g) celery sticks, roughly diced
½ small onion, roughly chopped
1 small potato, peeled and roughly diced
⅔ cup (150 ml) dry white wine
1 cup (100 g) ground almonds
2 cups (500 ml) *Chicken* or *Vegetable Stock* (page 33 or 36)
1 cup (250 ml) milk
1 cup (250 ml) light cream (this can be replaced by extra milk)
Salt
Pepper

Melt the butter in a large saucepan. Add the vegetables and cook on a low heat, turning them in the butter until all are coated. Cover with a lid and simmer for 10–15 minutes until the vegetables begin to soften.

Add the white wine and increase the heat without the lid. This will allow the wine to reduce. After it has reduced, add the ground almonds, stock, and milk. Season with the salt and pepper, bring to a simmer, and cook for 20 minutes. Check that all of the vegetables are cooked through.

Add the light cream and return to a simmer; the soup can now be removed from the heat and puréed until smooth.

For a smoother finish without the grainy texture from the almonds, strain through a fine sieve, pushing all flavors through with a ladle. Re-check for seasoning and the soup is ready to serve.

Note: A small squeeze of lemon juice will help lift all of the flavors.

Chopped fresh chives and a trickle of cream are also good for garnishing the soup.

This soup will also tastes good cold. It may be slightly too thick when it cools, so just thin with a drop more milk.

Chunky Tomato Soup

Following their introduction in England from the New World in the sixteenth century, tomatoes did not gain acceptance as a food until almost two centuries later. They were usually cooked into soups or made into an acid pickle with garlic, ginger, and vinegar, so British tomato soup and tomato ketchup (page 49) have a long history. But people were so suspicious of them that it was only in the twentieth century that people began to eat tomatoes raw.

This soup can be served as either an appetizer or a main course, but one of my favorites is to offer this soup warm from a large flask at picnics. Its real beauty is how easy it is to make, and its chunky nature makes it a pleasure to eat. I like to serve it with bread croûtons, fried or baked in olive oil, and flaked Parmesan cheese sprinkled over the top. As illustrated, this soup also makes a great vegetarian dish – simply omit the bacon and replace the chicken stock with a vegetable stock.

SERVES 6–8

3 onions, chopped
3 carrots, cut into ¼ in (5 mm) dice
3 celery sticks, cut into ¼ in (5 mm) dice
¼ cup (50 ml) olive oil
2 tablespoons (25 g) unsalted butter
1 bay leaf

1 large garlic clove, crushed
6 strips of bacon
2 lb (900 g) ripe tomatoes, preferably plum
2½–4 cups (600–900 ml) *Chicken* or *Vegetable Stock* (page 33 or 36)
Small bunch of fresh basil, chopped
Small bunch of fresh tarragon, chopped
Tomato purée (optional, to taste)
Salt and pepper

Sweat the chopped onions, carrots, and celery in the olive oil and butter for a few minutes. Then add the bay leaf and garlic and cook for a few more minutes. Add the bacon, if using, and continue to cook for about 5 minutes until the vegetables are slightly softened.

BELOW
Chunky Tomato Soup

Cut the tomatoes into eight pieces. Add them to the vegetables, cover the pan, and cook gently for about 15 minutes. The cooking will create its own steam and slowly cook the tomatoes. The mixture must be stirred occasionally, helping the tomatoes to break down and starting to create the soup.

When the tomatoes have softened, add the stock, a ladle at a time, until you have a thinner consistency. This brings us to personal choice. The soup can be as thick or as thin as you like. Let it cook for another 20 minutes. Add the chopped herbs and check for seasoning; you may find that a little tomato purée will help the strength of taste. The soup is now ready to serve.

Roast Parsnip Soup, Glazed with Parmesan and Chive Cream ⓥ

Parsnips are native to Britain, and they fulfilled the function of potatoes before the latter were introduced. They were served with roast beef and eaten with salt fish on Ash Wednesday and other fast days. It was their sweet flavor that was valued mainly and, in Elizabethan times, they were even included in sweet dishes. They could also stay in the ground over the winter without spoiling making them an extremely useful food.

I love roast parsnips. I hated parsnips when I was a child, but I could eat truck loads now. The idea for this soup came from trying a wonderful Delia Smith recipe, her roast Parmesan parsnips – great as a vegetable, so why not a soup? The soups packed with flavor, and when the cream is spooned on top and glazed, it gives the whole dish a new look, taste, and finish.

SERVES 4

4 tablespoons (50 g) butter
1 lb (450 g) parsnips, peeled, quartered and
    woody centers removed
2 shallots or 1 onion, finely chopped
2½–3 cups (750 ml) *Chicken* or *Vegetable Stock*
    (page 33 or 36)

½ cup (125 ml) light cream (optional)
Salt and pepper

For the Parmesan Cream (optional)

1 medium egg yolk
4 tablespoons heavy cream
1 heaping tablespoon freshly grated Parmesan
1 teaspoon chopped fresh chives
Pinch of salt

Preheat the oven to 425°F/220°C. Heat a roasting pan on top of the stove. Melt 2 tablespoons (25 g) of the butter, and once it's bubbling, add the parsnips. Allow to reach a golden color, turning them in the pan. The parsnips can now be roasted in the oven for 15–20 minutes.

Toward the end of roasting, melt the remaining 2 tablespoons (25 g) of butter in a saucepan. Add the chopped shallots or onion and cook, without browning, for a few minutes, until softened. Transfer the parsnips to the saucepan. Add the stock and bring to a simmer. The soup can now be gently simmered for 15 minutes.

Now it's time to pour in the light cream, if using. Season with salt and pepper and in a food processor to a smooth consistency. For a guaranteed smooth finish, push through a fine sieve. The roast parsnip soup is ready to serve.

Here's the Parmesan cream, if using, to finish the dish. Add the egg yolk to the heavy cream and lightly whisk until it begins to form soft peaks. Fold in the grated Parmesan with the chives and a pinch of salt.

Once the hot soup has been ladled into bowls, spoon the Parmesan chive cream over each. These can now be glazed under a preheated broiler. The cream will become golden brown and ready to serve.

Note: Another nice garnish, if serving the soup without glazing it, is toasted French bread, topped with lots of melting Parmesan.

Cullen Skink

A Gaelic word meaning "essence," "soup," or "broth," "skink" can be made with meat or fish, and is the Scottish version of pottage. Traditionally it could feature beef, or for those who could not afford that, grain simmered with a sheep's head. Along the coastlines of Britain, soup-stews made with fish were more common. This is my version of one that originated in Cullen, a small village in the north-east of Scotland. How "Skink" and Cullen met and stayed together I'm not quite sure, but they have had a long-lasting relationship.

Basically, this soup simply consists of smoked haddock (preferably Finnan haddock), onions, and potatoes cooked in milk with some butter. I like to add a leek to the soup, as well, giving it a fuller and fresher finish, and lifting all the other flavors. Cullen skink can stand as a complete meal on its own, with simply the addition of some good crusty bread for dunking.

SERVES 4–6, DEPENDING ON HOW HUNGRY YOU ARE

2 large potatoes, peeled
1 small leek (optional)
Butter
1 onion, finely chopped
9 oz (250 g) smoked haddock fillet
1 bay leaf
4 cups (750 ml) milk
¼ cup (50 ml) heavy cream (single for a looser finish)
Squeeze of lemon juice
Salt and pepper

Chop the potatoes and then the leek. I like to cut one of the potatoes into neat ½ in (1 cm) dice to use as a garnish. The other can be cut into rough ½ in (1 cm) dice. The leek, if using, should first be split, separating the white from green. Wash both parts well to make sure they are free of soil and grit. Chop the white part into rough ½ in (1 cm) dice. The green can now be cut into neat ½ in (1 cm) dice (*brunoise*); this will be used as part of the finished garnish.

Melt a teaspoon of butter in a saucepan big enough to accommodate the fish. Cook the onion on a medium heat for a few minutes, without browning it, until soft. Place the smoked haddock in the pan along with the bay leaf. Pour in some of the milk, barely covering the fish.

This can now be brought to a simmer and cooked for 4–6 minutes, depending on the thickness of the fish. Remove the fish from the pan and keep to one side. Add the roughly chopped potato, leek, and remaining milk. Bring to a simmer and cook until the potato has cooked through. This will take 15–20 minutes.

While the skink is cooking, remove any skin and bones from the haddock fillet. This can now be flaked, revealing the moist translucent flesh. The other garnishes, the potato dice and leek *brunoise*, can be blanched. Simply cook the potato in salted water until cooked completely through (10–15 minutes). The leeks will take literally a few minutes. Once cooked, drain through a sieve, and keep to one side.

When the soup is ready, remove the bay leaf and process to a smooth purée. Add the heavy or light cream and season with salt, pepper, and a squeeze of lemon juice.

Add the garnishes, haddock flakes, diced potatoes, and leeks and bring back to a warm temperature. Add a teaspoon more of butter for an even richer finish. The Cullen skink is ready to enjoy.

Note: The potatoes and leek can be roughly chopped and cooked in the soup for a thicker finished consistency, leaving the haddock flakes for garnish.

Freshly chopped parsley is a nice finishing touch, adding lots of flavor and color.

Crème fraîche can be added in place of heavy cream for a lower fat content.

For a real classic Cullen, use Finnan haddie. This will contain more bones, but carries a flavor other types of haddock cannot quite match. Well worth the extra work.

Creamy Bubble and Squeak Soup with Crisp Bacon

Bubble and squeak is reputed to have been given its name because it echoes the sound the ingredients make when frying. Usually thought of as a nineteenth-century dish of leftover potatoes and cabbage, the dish was originally made with beef and cabbage, without potatoes. Here, I have taken the potatoes and mixed them with onions and Brussels sprouts, the alternative to cabbage. This version has been puréed to a smooth, creamy-soft finish, but it can, if preferred, be left in its rustic, brothy consistency. The flavors and texture can be enhanced by a last-minute addition of slivers of crisp bacon.

This recipe is perfect at Christmas time if you have leftover sprouts, potatoes and crisp bacon rashers from Christmas lunch that you want to use up.

SERVES 4–6

Butter
2 large onions, roughly diced
2 large potatoes, peeled and cut in rough ½ in (1 cm) dice
4 cups (1 liter) *Chicken* or *Vegetable Stock*, (page 33 or 36)
9 oz (250 g) Brussels sprouts, finely shredded and rinsed
½ cup (125 ml) light cream
6–8 strips of bacon, cut into thin strips
Cooking oil
Salt, pepper, and freshly grated nutmeg

Melt the butter in a saucepan. When it starts bubbling, add the onions and potatoes. Cook without browning for 5–10 minutes, until they begin to soften. The stock can now be added. Bring to a simmer and cook for 20–25 minutes, until the vegetables are totally cooked.

Season the soup with salt, pepper, and a pinch of nutmeg. Bring to a boil and add the shredded sprouts. Allow the soup to simmer vigorously for 6–8 minutes until the sprouts become tender.

The soup can now be completely puréed and then pushed through a sieve for a smooth, creamy finish. Add the light cream and check the seasoning.

Cook the bacon strips while the soup is simmering, by heating a non-stick frying-pan with a drop of cooking oil. Begin to cook the bacon on a fairly high heat. This will seal the individual strips. After a minute or two, reduce the cooking temperature so the bacon is just bubbling. As the bacon cooks, its natural fat will melt, letting it "deep-fry" in its own oil. Continue until the strips are a deep color and have become very crisp, almost like crackling. Strain off the fat and place the bacon pieces on paper towels to absorb any remaining oil. You now have crisp bacon, which tastes very good sprinkled over the bubble and squeak soup.

Note: For vegetarians, omit the bacon strips and cook the vegetables in vegetable stock. The soup can also be served as a bubble and squeak broth. Simply cut the onions and potatoes into neat ½ in (1 cm) dice, and follow the recipe, adding the shredded sprouts. After all the vegetables are cooked, add 4 tablespoons (50 g) butter in place of the light cream. The bacon can be an optional extra.

Frozen-pea Soup ⓥ

The most famous pea soup was called "The London Particular" because it was as thick as a London fog – which was called, in its turn, a "pea-souper." Peas, in fact, are one of man's oldest vegetables. Dried, they were an ingredient of the earliest pottages in Britain – and of the famous pease pudding and mushy peas – but it was not until the sixteenth century, when Italian gardeners developed tender varieties, that they could be eaten fresh. For this recipe I'm using frozen peas. This will give you a version that is quicker, greener, and just as fresh-tasting as the historic dish.

SERVES 4–6

1 large onion, finely chopped
Butter
2 cups (450 ml) *Vegetable* or *Chicken Stock*, (page 36 or 33) or alternative (page 11)

OPPOSITE
Creamy Bubble and Squeak Soup with Crisp Bacon

ABOVE
Vegetarian Scotch Broth

1 lb (450 g) frozen peas
Pinch of sugar
⅔ pint (150 ml) light cream (optional)
Salt and pepper

Cook the onion in the butter for a few minutes, without letting it brown, until softened. Add the stock and bring to a rapid simmer. Add the peas now and cook on a fast heat for 3 minutes. Once the peas are soft and tender, season with salt, pepper, and sugar and then purée in a food processor to a smooth consistency. For an even smoother finish, push the soup through a sieve. For a creamier consistency, add the light cream. The pea soup is now ready to eat, preferably with lots of crusty bread.

Note: A sprig or two of fresh mint can be added to the soup during the cooking of the onion for some extra taste. The soup can be garnished with toasted bread croûtons and small, crisp-cooked strips of bacon.

Vegetarian Scotch Broth ⓥ

This is the classic pottage, a nourishing country soup that can be made with whatever is in season, the only essentials being barley, vegetables, and a little meat (usually lamb or mutton). Traditionally, the meat would be boiled with the barley for an hour before adding the vegetables, then cooked for another hour. It would be left in a cold place overnight for the fat to set and be removed. After re-warming, a little butter and parsley were added and the soup was ready. However, I thought we would make a vegetarian version, with lots of vegetables and pearl barley in a vegetable stock. The soup will take about an hour to make – no waiting overnight – and it is packed with fresh flavors.

The famous Dr Johnson was rather dismissive of Scotland and the Scots but less so about Scotch broth: his companion, James Boswell, recorded in 1776 that the great man ate several platefuls and "seemed very fond of the dish. I said, 'You never ate it before?' – Johnson, 'No, sir; but I don't care how soon I eat it again.' "

SERVES 4–6

2 oz (50 g) pearl barley
6 cups (1.5 liters) *Vegetable Stock* (page 36)
2 onions, cut into ¼ in (5 mm) dice
2 carrots, cut into ¼ in (5 mm) dice
1 large turnip, cut into ¼ in (5 mm) dice
1 small rutabaga, cut into ¼ in (5 mm) dice
2 celery sticks, cut into ¼ in (5 mm) dice
1 potato, cut into ¼ in (5 mm) dice
1 leek, finely shredded
Butter
Salt and pepper
2 teaspoons chopped fresh parsley

Wash the pearl barley well. Place in a saucepan with the vegetable stock. Bring to a simmer, skimming off any impurities. The barley can now be gently simmered for 30– 40 minutes, until tender. At this point, add the onions and carrots and cook for another 8 minutes.

Now it's time to add the turnips, rutabaga, celery, and potato. Return to a simmer and continue to cook for 20 minutes; check all the vegetables are cooked.

To finish, add the finely shredded leeks; the soup will just take 5 more minutes to be finished. Season with salt and pepper. Add a heaping teaspoon of butter and chopped parsley.

The vegetarian Scotch broth is now ready to serve, and it will be at its best with lots of crusty bread.

See also

Cheddar cheese Soup (page 70)
Pan-fried Red Mullet with a Tomato and Leek Soup
(page 149)

Basic Stocks

Soups and stocks have always had a close relationship, the soup always needing a helping hand from stock. In the strictest culinary terms, the two are completely different. A soup is a finished dish, complete in itself, while stock is used as the base or foundation for finished dishes, and if it is clarified, it stands on its own as the ultimate clear soup – consommé.

A stock is water in which meat or fish plus vegetables, or vegetables alone, have simmered until the water takes on their flavor. This would have been an essential and daily part of the diet after the introduction of cooking pots, when the first pottages – or soups – were created and enjoyed. Very many different vegetable and herb flavorings would be added to make the liquid more interesting and flavorful to the palate. As the liquid warmed, it softened the often tough meat (if any was used) and hard grains, whose starches would swell and thicken the liquid. As well as being practical and nourishing, stocks would have been economical – and they still are – in that tough pieces of meat and bone could be used along with trimmings, carcasses, and leftovers that might otherwise be thrown away.

From very early times throughout the Middle Ages and almost to the present day, stocks have been made in the same way and used in pottages, soups, and as the foundation of sauces. Interestingly, in French culinary terms, *fond* or "foundation" is the name for stock. In 1651, the first great French cookbook, *Le Cuisinier François* by François Pierre de la Varenne, was published, and it began with a stock – as most cookbooks, French, American, or British, have since that time. A cookbook published not much later in England mentioned a basic sauce called "cullis," which was a stock boiled down until sticky and intense in flavor, which was used to enrich other sauces – in much the same way as meat glazes (in professional chefs' kitchens) and stock cubes are used today. (The word "cullis" comes from the French *coulisse*, something that slides easily, possibly related to the current menu word, *coulis*.) In fact, stock or soup cubes were known in the eighteenth century. Gelatinous meat stocks would be boiled down to a "glue" which could be chopped into squares and added to sauces, or the squares could be carried by travelers and added to water for an instant soup. The cubes were even used to prevent sea-sickness.

The nutritional importance of rich stocks and broths has always been appreciated. In the late nineteenth century, however, the London-based French chef Alexis Soyer (working at the Reform Club, Pall Mall) uncovered a scandal. Famous for his social reform in the culinary field (he had designed soup kitchens and created soups for the Irish during the famine of the 1840s), he arrived in the Crimea in 1855 and found that meat for the men in the hospital was being cooked in water for a set length of time, unrelated to the size of the cut of meat. The consequent stock/broth, which would have nourished the sick more efficiently than undercooked solids, was being thrown away. What a waste! Strict instructions followed, with the chef himself visiting all the hospitals, tasting the various individual broths personally.

Today, stocks remain at the heart of the professional kitchen, but it is less easy for the domestic cook to have a huge stockpot simmering away on a back burner, the broth absorbing every scrap of flavor from bone, root, and herb. It seems the three witches from *Macbeth* understood the importance of ingredients, too, as we see with this recipe of theirs:

> Fillet of a fenny snake,
> In the cauldron boil and bake;
> Eye of newt, and toe of frog,
> Wool of bat, and tongue of dog,
> Adder's fork, and blind-worm's sting,
> Lizard's leg, and howlet's wing –
> For a charm of pow'rful trouble,
> Like a hell-broth boil and bubble.

If all of Shakespeare's ingredients aren't available, there are, however, some very good stock cubes available in supermarkets, as well as stocks in cans and cartons, which are almost as authentic as homemade (see page 11). So, you're not under any pressure to make the stocks featured in this chapter. But if you feel inspired, the following recipes form a basic guide to the classic types and flavors.

OPPOSITE
Chicken Pot Roast (page 244) made with *Chicken Stock*

Chicken Stock

Chicken stock is one of the most important bases in the professional and domestic kitchen. It's used for most soups and many cream sauces, the latter because it is pale in color – it is often known as "white" (rather than "brown") stock. It's very easy to make but you need to use raw chicken bones. Your butcher should be able to supply you with some chicken bones, or you can take the breasts off a whole chicken, saving them for another dish, and use the carcass for the stock.

Or, if you can find one, cook a whole stewing hen with vegetables in water and you will have a quick, tasty stock along with the bird to serve as well. Chicken wings also give you an equally flavorful result.

If you do not have a large stockpot, you can easily reduce the quantities listed below. For information on ready-made alternatives, see page 11.

MAKES 2½ QUARTS (2.25 LITERS)

2 onions, chopped
2 celery sticks, chopped
2 leeks, chopped
2 tablespoons (25 g) unsalted butter
1 garlic clove, crushed
1 bay leaf
Sprig of thyme
Few black peppercorns
4 lb (1.8 kg) chicken carcasses, chopped
3¾ quarts (3.4 liters) water

In a large stockpot (about 9 quarts/8.5 liter capacity), lightly soften the vegetables in the butter without browning. Add the garlic, bay leaf, thyme, peppercorns, and chopped carcasses. Cover with the cold water and bring to a simmer, skimming all the time. Allow the stock to simmer for 2–3 hours, then drain through a sieve. The stock is now ready to use and will keep well chilled or frozen.

Veal or Beef Stock or Jus

This brown stock is the basis of many dishes and sauces, particularly in the professional kitchen, and often contributes the defining flavor and richness – the essence – of a good dish. It takes a long time to achieve, particularly if you make the *jus* after the stock, but it's very satisfying, and, of course any left over will keep well in your freezer for later. The stock should be started in the morning so that you can allow it to cook throughout the day. Your butcher will be able to supply you with raw veal or beef bones and trimmings if you request them in advance.

Good, ready-made stocks and *jus* gravies can also be bought in supermarkets.

MAKES 5–6 QUARTS (4.5–6 LITERS) STOCK OR 2½–5 CUPS (600 ML–1.2 LITERS) JUS/GRAVY

3 onions, halved
2–3 tablespoons water
5 lb (2.25 kg) veal or beef bones
8 oz (225 g) veal or beef trimmings
    (from the butcher)
8 oz (225 g) carrots, coarsely chopped
3 celery sticks, coarsely chopped
1 leek, chopped
3–4 tomatoes, chopped
1 garlic clove, halved
1 bay leaf
Sprig of thyme
Salt

Preheat the oven to 250°F/120°C. Place the onion halves down flat in a roasting pan and sprinkle them with the water. Put the pan into the oven and allow the onions to caramelize slowly until they have totally softened and browned. This process will take 1–2

hours. The sugars in the onions will cook slowly and produce a wonderful taste.

Place the onions into a large stockpot and leave to one side. Increase the oven temperature to 400°F/200°C. Place all the bones and trimmings in the roasting pan and roast for about 30 minutes until well browned. Roast the chopped carrots and celery in another roasting pan (without adding any oil) for about 20 minutes until lightly browned.

When the vegetables are ready, add the roasted bones, trimmings, and vegetables to the onions in the pot along with the leek, tomatoes, garlic, bay leaf, and thyme. Fill the pot with cold water – you'll need about 6–7½ quarts (6–7.2 liters). Bring the stock to a simmer, season with salt and skim off any impurities. Allow to cook for 6–8 hours for the maximum flavor. If it seems to be reducing too quickly, add cold water to cover.

Then, drain and discard the bones and vegetables. The liquid that remains is your veal stock, and you can cool it and freeze it in conveniently sized containers.

Alternately, make a veal or beef *jus*/gravy with the stock. Allow the liquid to boil down to 2½–5 cups (600 ml–1.2 liters), skimming all the time. The stock should be thick and of a sauce-like consistency. Make sure that you taste frequently during the reduction process. If the sauce tastes right but is not thick enough, add a little cornstarch to thicken it. (Of course, I hope that won't be necessary.) You now have a veal or beef *jus*/gravy, a classic sauce.

Game Stock

In Britain, people use wild (wood) pigeons for this stock. In the US, you can purchase squabs – young pigeons – at gourmet butcher shops or order them via the Internet. You can buy whole squabs and use the breasts for roasting and the rest of the carcasses for stock. For this recipe, I suggest that you buy frozen birds. These obviously won't give you the fullest flavor, but since the whole birds will be used, a good stock can be made. Red wine will give the stock a rich, all-round flavor. Armagnac, Cognac, Madeira and port can also be used.

There are two versions here. Using chicken stock will give you a thin game stock to work with. Using the basic veal *jus* will provide an instant game sauce.

1 tablespoon cooking oil

3 wood pigeons or 3 squabs, thawed, if frozen, and
    chopped into small pieces

1 large onion or 2 shallots, roughly chopped

1 large carrot, roughly chopped

2 celery sticks, roughly chopped

4–5 mushrooms, quartered

1 liter bottle of red wine

1 garlic clove, chopped

Sprig of thyme

5 juniper berries, crushed

Few black peppercorns

2–3 tomatoes, chopped

5 cups (1.2 liters) *Chicken, Veal* or *Beef Stock* or *Jus*
    (page 33 or 34)

1¼ cups (300 ml) water, if using gravy/*jus*

Heat the oil in a large frying-pan. Add the chopped
pigeons/squabs and cook on a medium heat until well
browned and caramelized/roasted. This will take
approximately 20 minutes on top of the stove.

Transfer the pigeons/squabs to a suitably sized
saucepan. Add the onions, carrot, celery, and mushrooms
to the frying-pan and cook until they begin to soften
and brown, but do not let them get too dark because
this will create a bitter finish. Increase the heat and add
a third of the red wine to lift all the flavors from the
bottom of the pan. Transfer all to the saucepan
containing the pigeons. Add the garlic, thyme, juniper
berries, black peppercorns, and tomatoes. Cook until
the tomatoes have reduced into the red wine. Add the
rest of the wine from the bottle, bring to a fast simmer,
and allow to reduce by three-quarters. Add the stock
or *jus* (plus water, if using *jus*). Return to a simmer.
If making a stock, simmer for 1–1½ hours. For the
gravy, simmer for 45 minutes–1 hour. Strain through
a fine sieve or, for a guaranteed smooth finish, twice
through a muslin cloth.

The stock/sauce is now ready to use.

Fish Stock

To make a delicious fish stock, use white fish bones – in
particular, turbot and sole bones. These give a good
flavor without an oily texture. Ask at your fishmarket
for a supply of bones. Using white bones will produce
a strongly flavored stock, with a a good, full taste and a
clear, jelly-like finish which is perfect for poaching and
making fish soups and sauces.

For information on ready-made alternatives,
see page 11.

1 large onion, sliced

1 leek, sliced

2 celery sticks, sliced

4 tablespoons (50 g) unsalted butter

Few fresh parsley stalks

1 bay leaf

6 black peppercorns

2 lb (1 kg) turbot or sole bones, washed

1¼ cups (300 ml) dry white wine

2½ quarts (2.25 liters) water

Salt

Sweat the sliced vegetables in the butter without
browning them. Add the parsley stems, bay leaf, and
peppercorns. Chop the fish bones, making sure there
are no blood clots left on them. Add to the vegetables
and continue to cook for a few minutes. Add the wine
and boil to reduce until almost dry. Add the water,
season with salt, and bring to a simmer. Allow the
mixture to simmer for 20 minutes, then drain through
a sieve. The stock is now ready to use, or you can store
it for a few days in the refrigerator or in the freezer for
up to 3 months.

Court Bouillon ⓥ

Court Bouillon is described in the new *Larousse
Gastronomique* (a cooking encyclopedia) as an aromatic
cooking broth for fish, meat, and vegetables. And that's
exactly what it is, but it is mostly used for fish – in
particular, shellfish. It's quite powerful, adding flavor
when cooking lobsters (overleaf), crab, and mussels.
It's a joy to make because in cooking it releases a
wonderfully aromatic perfume. (Making a *court
bouillon* for vegetables and meats may require a slightly
different percentage of wine and vinegar.)

This recipe can be halved to fit a smaller saucepan,
making a smaller finished quantity.

1 carrot, sliced
1 onion, sliced
1–2 celery sticks, sliced
1 garlic clove, sliced
½ oz (15 g) fresh ginger, peeled and sliced
½ teaspoon each fennel seeds and white peppercorns
1 star anise
1 tablespoon sea salt
1 cup (250 ml) white wine
2 tablespoons white-wine vinegar
Grated zest of 1 orange
Bouquet garni of tarragon leaves, bay leaf and
    thyme, tied in muslin or a strip of leek
2 quarts (2 liters) water
Juice of 1 lemon

Place all the ingredients in a suitably sized saucepan and bring to a boil. Cook on a fast simmer for 15–20 minutes.

Remove the pan from the heat and leave to infuse for 2–3 hours before using.

The liquid can now be used as it is or strained through a sieve. To cook live lobsters, crab, and other shellfish, the bouillon will need to be re-boiled.

To Cook Live Lobsters in a Court Bouillon

If you have fresh lobsters, all you will need to cook them is a large pot of boiling *court bouillon*. Drop in the lobsters and return to a boil. After the stock is boiling, cook for 3–5 minutes, depending on size. Now, remove the pot, leaving the lobsters in. They will continue to cook and their meat will become very relaxed. After the lobsters are at room temperature, they are ready to open.

Note: For even softer and barely cooked lobster, bring back to a boil and remove the pot from the heat immediately.

A quicker way to cook lobster is simply to use boiling salted water and follow the instructions above. Of course, cooked lobsters are also available from most good fishmarkets and supermarkets.

Vegetable Stock ⓥ

This is a great alternative to chicken and fish stock in many recipes, particularly if making vegetarian soups. This is a basic recipe, but it can be adapted in any number of ways simply by adding or substituting other vegetable or herb flavors for a subtle difference. Never use starchy root vegetables, such as potatoes, parsnips, or turnips, however, as they will make the stock cloudy.

For information on ready-made alternatives, see page 11.

MAKES APPROX. 5 CUPS (1.2 LITERS)

8 oz (225 g) carrots (optional)
2 onions
4 celery sticks
2 leeks, white part only
1 fennel bulb
1–2 zucchini
1 tablespoon vegetable oil
1 bay leaf
Sprig of thyme
1 teaspoon each coriander seeds
    and pink peppercorns
½ lemon, sliced
6 cups (1.5 liters) water
Pinch of salt

Cut all the vegetables roughly into ½ in (1 cm) dice. Warm the vegetable oil in a pan, then add all the diced vegetables, the herbs, coriander seeds, peppercorns, and lemon slices. Cook, without browning, for 8–10 minutes, allowing the vegetables to soften slightly. Add the water and a pinch of salt, and bring to a simmer. Once at simmering point, cook for 30 minutes, without a lid. During this time the stock should reduce, increasing the flavor and depth.

The stock can now be strained through a sieve, leaving you with about 5 cups (1.2 liters). If you find there is more than this, simply boil rapidly to reduce. You can also reduce the stock if you find that the flavor is not full enough.

OPPOSITE
Pan-fried Red Mullet (page 149) made with *Fish Stock*

Sauces
and
Dressings

It was during the eighteenth century
that a foreign visitor directed his
criticism at English culinary traditions
with his remark that the natives had
sixty different religious sects but only
one sauce. Perhaps he encountered one
too many of the white sauces made
with butter and flour alone that were
very common at the time. But the
history of sauces in Britain is actually
of much greater depth and variety
than his remark suggests.

When the Romans controlled much of Europe, including England, they would have introduced their strong-tasting garnish and seasoning sauces, *liquamen* and *garum*, made from fermented salted fish. (The anchovy and Worcestershire sauces sold today are probably not unlike *garum*; the fish sauces of Asia, such as *nam pla*, are very similar.) This may have created a taste in the British for strong flavors, for many of the medieval sauces were extremely piquant. They consisted predominantly of vinegar with other ingredients added, or of ale and/or wine alone. Another alternative was a sweet and sour mixture, usually consisting of vinegar or verjuice (the juice of sour grapes, sorrel, or crab apples) and sugar and/or pounded dried fruit.

The earliest "sauce" was the flavored liquid in which soup or pottage ingredients were cooked. It would be thickened with cereal grains or bread, or by adding wheat flour (but this was expensive), egg yolks, or cream. Breadcrumbs were popular, always giving a sauce a thick consistency and texture. This thickened sauce would rest perfectly on the bread trencher (a piece of bread used as a plate), without being absorbed too quickly or running off.

After the Conquest of 1066, the Normans introduced more elaborate ways of preparing foods, particularly sauces. Their ideas were partly French, but also partly Arab, for the Normans had also conquered the Arab-ruled Sicily not long before. This might explain the Middle Eastern components of much medieval saucing – the use of almond milk, the incorporation of ground almonds, the mixing in of dried fruit with sweet spices. Soldiers returning from the Crusades also brought back spices in the eleventh and twelfth centuries, and these were gradually incorporated into many sauces, often in order to disguise meat that was beginning to rot.

In the sixteenth century, sauces began to be thickened with "fried flour." This was a flour and lard liaison, a technique that has come down through culinary history as the roux (from the French for "reddish-brown") and which marked the beginning of gravy. In the eighteenth century, many sauces became simpler, and this is when the white or butter sauce grew in popularity. A Swiss visitor, Carl Moritz, wrote about the food he encountered in lodging houses on his travels through England in the 1780s: "To persons in my situation, [it] generally consists of a piece of half-boiled or half-roasted meat; and a few cabbage leaves boiled in plain water; on which they pour a sauce made of flour and butter, the usual method of dressing vegetables in England." Hannah Glasse, one of the century's most famous cooking writers, actually prided herself on the simplicity of many of her sauces and gravies, and she was highly critical of the intricate and complicated French recipes: ". . . So much is the blind folly of this age, that they would rather be imposed on by a French booby than give encouragement to a good English cook."

The sauces I've chosen for this chapter are mostly accompaniments to savory dishes, such as Cumberland sauce, salad dressing, and so on. You'll find the sauces particular to recipes, i.e. accompaniments to fish or meat dishes, featured along with the recipes themselves. I feel we have room to recognize and appreciate both the British sauce-making tradition, which has come a long way since its "heavy" days, and the influences of the French style.

PAGE 38
Cumberland Sauce (page 42)

Classic Hollandaise Sauce ⓥ

This is a classic French sauce, listed by Escoffier as one of the five basic sauces. It is of Dutch origin, though, and was also known in England as Dutch sauce. It goes very well with fish. It can be bought ready-made, but here are two ways of making it, both very good.

MAKES APPROX. 1¼ CUPS (300 ML)

16 tablespoons (225 g) unsalted butter
2 tablespoons malt or white wine vinegar
6 white peppercorns, lightly crushed
1 tablespoon water
2 egg yolks
Salt and cayenne or pepper
Squeeze of lemon juice

Melt the butter in a pan, then let cool slightly so that it is barely warm. If it is too hot when added, the sauce will curdle. The warmed butter will separate, leaving all its solids in the bottom of the pan. Pour off and save the butter oil which is now clarified butter. Discard the milky solids.

Boil the vinegar with the peppercorns until reduced by half. Add the water to cool, and strain the reduction through a sieve into a bowl. Add the egg yolks and whisk together. Place the bowl over a pan of hot water and whisk to a *sabayon*. A *sabayon* is created by the cooking and thickening of the egg yolks. As they are whisked, they increase in volume to a cream consistency. When the yolks have reached this stage, remove the bowl from the heat and continue to whisk, slowly adding the warm, clarified butter. When all the butter has been whisked in, the sauce should have reached a thick consistency which can now be seasoned with salt and cayenne or pepper and finished with the lemon juice.

If the hollandaise curdles, make a one-egg yolk *sabayon* and slowly whisk in the separated sauce. This should bring the sauce back to the right consistency.

Note: To increase the flavors of this sauce, a pinch of dried tarragon, chopped onion, or shallot can be added to the reduction leaving you with a béarnaise-flavored sauce, which goes well with meat dishes and even a plain broiled steak. The sauce can also be finished with freshly chopped tarragon or parsley.

Simple Hollandaise Sauce ⓥ

The classic way of making Hollandaise Sauce involves a flavored reduction, but this quicker version tastes just as good.

MAKES APPROX. ⅔ CUP (150 ML)

8 tablespoons (100 g) unsalted butter
1 egg yolk
½ tablespoon warm water
Squeeze of lemon juice
Salt and cayenne pepper or white pepper

Make clarified butter by melting the butter in a pan and then letting it cool slightly so that it is barely warm when added to the sauce; the sauce will curdle if it is too hot. The butter should have separated so that you add only the clarified butter to the sauce, not the milk solids that will have collected at the bottom of the pan.

Add the egg yolk to the water in a bowl set over a pan of hot water and whisk until light in color and thickened. Remove from the heat and slowly add the clarified butter, whisking until the sauce is thick and all the butter is used. Add the lemon juice and season with salt and cayenne or white pepper.

Note: A teaspoon of Dijon or English mustard will bring a warmth and extra body to the finished flavor.

Cider Vinegar Dressing ⓥ

We tend to think that dressings made with oil and vinegar, or oil, vinegar, and eggs were imported from France, but from very earliest times, British cooks were dressing salads and other dishes in a similar way. Cider vinegar is English, of course.

This dressing works very well with the recipe for *Seared, Cured Salmon Cutlets with Leeks, Bacon, and a Cider-vinegar Dressing* (page 167). It will also go well with a simple tossed salad. I have included raw egg and egg yolk in the recipe, so if you don't want to use raw eggs, I've presented a version using commercially-made mayonnaise. So no excuse, you've got to try it.

MAKES 1–1¼ CUPS (250–300 ML)

1 heaping teaspoon sugar
1½ tablespoons cider vinegar
1 egg yolk
1 egg
2 teaspoons Dijon mustard
1 cup (250 ml) peanut oil
Salt and pepper

Warm the sugar with the vinegar and allow the mixture to cool. Mix the egg yolk and whole egg with the mustard and sweetened vinegar. Gradually add the peanut oil, a drop or two at a time, and whisk vigorously until it has amalgamated to create the dressing. Season with salt and pepper and the dressing is finished.

Mayonnaise-based Cider Dressing Ⓥ

This recipe is an alternative to the one above, replacing the eggs with mayonnaise. It's always nicer to make your own mayonnaise (see page 49), but good commercially-made varieties can be bought.

1½ tablespoons cider vinegar
1 heaped teaspoon sugar
2 teaspoons Dijon mustard
¾–1 cup (200–250g) mayonnaise (bought)
Salt and pepper

Mix together and warm the vinegar and sugar. Let the mixture cool. Mix the vinegar with the mustard and add the mayonnaise; check for seasoning, adding salt and pepper to taste. If the dressing is too thick, thin it with a few teaspoons of warm water.

Cumberland Sauce Ⓥ

Queen Victoria's relative, the Duke of Cumberland, who became the last independent ruler of Hanover, is said to be the person honored by this sauce, though nobody seems to know why. The sauce has become an essential and inseparable partner to all game dishes, as well as to cold meats, meat pies and terrines – he must have enjoyed the hunt!

There have been many variations of Cumberland sauce, but the foundation has always been the same – red currant jelly. Cumberland sauce takes on a consistency of a loose jam, usually garnished simply with orange and lemon rind. In many recipes, fresh and glacé cherries have also been used, but I'm sticking to the orange and lemon rind, with the addition of chopped shallots.

Most recipes suggest the sauce be strained through a sieve to give a smoother finish, but I prefer a coarser texture as a good balance to the accompanying dish, particularly is a meat to be served cold. For maximum flavor, always check the fruit content of the red currant jelly before you buy it. Many contain a minimum of fruit and lots of additives.

SERVES 6–8

Juice of 1 lemon plus 2 strips of peeled zest
Juice of 1 orange plus 2 strips of peeled zest
1 shallot, finely chopped
4 tablespoons red-wine vinegar
¼ teaspoon mustard powder, preferably English
¼ teaspoon powdered ginger
4 tablespoons port
6 heaping tablespoons red currant jelly (use one
    with a high fruit content – with red currants
    listed as the first ingredient)
Salt
Pinch of cayenne pepper

The peeled strips of lemon and orange zest should have the white pith scraped away, leaving the rich, pure zest. Cut this into very thin strips, even thinner than matchsticks. Place the strips (both orange and lemon together) in cold water and bring to a boil. Now allow to cook for 5 minutes before straining.

Place the chopped shallots in a saucepan along with the vinegar. Bring to a simmer and then cook and reduce them until they are almost dry.

Strain both of the fruit juices into the saucepan and reduce by half.

Mix the mustard and ginger together, adding 1 tablespoon of the port to create a paste.

Add the red currant jelly to the vinegar reduction, along with the remaining 3 tablespoons of port. The sauce can now be warmed over a moderate heat until the jelly has completely melted. Add the mustard and ginger paste and season with a pinch of salt and cayenne pepper.

If you prefer a smoother finish, strain the sauce through a sieve to remove the shallots before adding the blanched lemon and orange zest.

The sauce tastes best served cold. If kept refrigerated in a screw-top jar, it will last up to 2 weeks.

Note: I find this sauce goes well with the cold meats and pâtés that are served at the Christmas season.

If you are not a fan of ginger, simply omit it from the recipe. The mustard quantity can then be doubled for extra bite.

A splash of Worcestershire sauce can be added to also sharpen the flavors.

Tartar Sauce ⓥ

Fish and chips is a British favorite, and it is perfectly complemented by tartar sauce. The flavor and acidity of capers, gherkins, and onions work so well with the crisp batter and succulent fish, and the sauce creates a lovely dip for homemade "chips." It can also be used a spicy dip for crudités.

The sauce is not British, however, but a French classic. In France, it is traditionally made by pounding hard-boiled egg yolks to a fine paste before adding olive oil to make a mayonnaise-like consistency, then mixing in a touch of vinegar, lemon juice, and chopped chives. I'm not really sure how all the extras – the capers, gherkins, and so on – found their way into the sauce, but I'm glad they did. I've also added a little chopped green olives for extra flavor, but if you're not a fan, simply omit them.

There is actually a British sauce that is not too dissimilar to tartar called Cambridge sauce.

MAKES APPROX. 1¼ CUPS (300 ML)

1¼ cups (300 ml) mayonnaise (bought or see the recipe, page 49)
1 oz (25 g) gherkins, chopped
1 oz (25 g) capers, chopped
1 oz (25 g) green olives, chopped
1 oz (25 g) shallot or onion, finely chopped
2 teaspoons chopped fresh parsley (optional)
Squeeze of lemon juice
Salt and pepper

Simply mix all the ingredients together, seasoning with salt, pepper, and a squeeze of lemon juice.

Bread Sauce ⓥ

This is one of the oldest of sauces, but it's not made as often as it used to be. Its image is of a thick, lumpy sauce with a bland flavor. In fact, it has a creaminess and a spiciness that lends itself very well to poultry and game dishes. Bread or breadcrumbs were used in the Middle Ages to thicken basic sauces to accompany meat, fish, and game. Many were made with milk, usually almond milk, and spiced with a sprinkling of something such as saffron, pepper, or ginger. This recipe, with the inclusion of an onion spiked with cloves and dustings of nutmeg and mace, is an echo of those medieval flavors.

It looks like quite a long list of ingredients for a sauce that has a simple bread and milk image. Some of these can be omitted from the recipe. The spices are part of the milk infusion which will lift the complete flavor. However, using the onions studded with cloves, a few black peppercorns, and the bay leaf will still give a good result.

The finely chopped onion will be left in the finished sauce, giving a coarser texture. Again, it can be left out if you prefer.

1 onion
2–3 cloves
½ small onion, very finely chopped (optional)
Few black peppercorns
1 bay leaf
Pinch of ground mace
Pinch of freshly grated nutmeg
1 allspice berry (optional)
1¼ cups (300 ml) milk
1 cup (50 g) white breadcrumbs (taken from
    slightly stale bread)
2–3 tablespoons heavy cream
2 tablespoons (25 g) butter
Salt and freshly ground white pepper

Stud the whole onion with the cloves and place it along with the chopped onion, peppercorns, bay leaf, and all the spices in a saucepan with the milk.

Bring to a rapid simmer and then remove from the heat. The milk can now be left to infuse for 45 minutes–1 hour (longer for even more flavor). Remove the whole onion, peppercorns, allspice berry, and bay leaf.

Add the breadcrumbs and return to the heat. Allow to cook on a medium heat for 15–20 minutes, until the crumbs have swollen and thickened the sauce.

Add the heavy cream and butter. Season with salt and pepper and remove from the heat. The sauce is ready to serve. If keeping warm, cover with waxed paper or plastic wrap to prevent a skin from forming.

Applesauce ⓥ

In the Middle Ages, it was believed that an animal should be cooked and/or served with something that it fed on, since pigs are extremely fond of windfall apples, the association between sharp fruit and sweet meat probably was made very early. Applesauce was also served with goose, roast duck, and game dishes. Slow-roasted duck, cooked until so well done that it's falling off the bone, goes beautifully with a cinnamon-flavored applesauce. (Similar matchings of meat and accompaniment, traditionally called "tracklements," are horseradish

with beef, mint sauce with lamb, and red currant jelly with mutton and venison.) For a vegetarian option, you can serve applesauce with a simple cheese and onion flan that's finished with a sprinkling of toasted chopped almonds.

In many old recipes, quince was also added, usually mixed with cooking apples. The apples I'm using here are Stayman Winesap, but you can go half-and-half with Granny Smith apples. This will give a sharper edge to the finished flavor.

SERVES 8

450 g (1 lb) Stayman Winesap apples
¼ cup (25 g) sugar
Juice of ½ lemon
4 tablespoons water
½ cinnamon stick or pinch of ground
    cinnamon (optional)

Peel, core, and cut the apples into rough small dice. Place in a heavy-bottomed saucepan with all the remaining ingredients. Now, cook over a medium to low heat covered with a lid for approximately 15 minutes. During the cooking time, stir to guarantee even cooking.

After the apples are cooked and tender and beginning to form a purée, remove the pan from the heat, discarding the cinnamon stick, if using. The apples can now be whisked to a sauce consistency. The more you whisk, the smoother the finish. I like to leave some texture in the apples, because this keeps more of the natural apple taste. It's also possible to purée the sauce in a food processor for the ultimate smooth finish – the decision is yours. Applesauce is best served warm for maximum taste.

Note: After the applesauce is done, a teaspoon of butter can be added while whisking. This will enrich the finished flavor, also giving a silky consistency.

Fresh herbs can also be added. A teaspoon of chopped sage goes very well with crispy crackling roast pork.

White Sauce ⓥ

The foundation for this sauce was first introduced in the seventeenth century, becoming very popular in Britain in the eighteenth century. It goes by the name béchamel, and is made with a roux base, a combination of butter cooked with flour. This is a French influence that has become a regular British culinary term. The word roux derives from the French for "reddish-brown." For this recipe, however, the roux is kept at its white stage early in the cooking process, maintaining a creamy white finish to the sauce.

Béchamel is a "mother" sauce to many others, including parsley, mustard, capers, onions, and cheese. It's important when cooking a béchamel sauce that it's over a low heat and kept moving from time to time in the pan. If left to simmer on its own for too long, the flour will stick and begin to burn. This flavor then infuses and spoils the sauce.

MAKES APPROX. 2⅔ CUPS (750 ML)

1 onion
1 bay leaf
1–2 cloves (optional)
1¼ cups (600 ml) milk
2 tablespoons (25 g) butter
¼ cup (25 g) all-purpose flour
⅔ cup (150 ml) heavy or light cream (optional)
Salt, pepper, and freshly grated nutmeg

BELOW
Slow Honey-roast Pork Belly (page 184) with *Applesauce*

Pierce the onion with the cloves and the bay leaf. Place in a saucepan with the milk and bring to a simmer. Simmer for a few minutes before removing from the heat and set aside to infuse for 1 hour; this is not essential but it gives the milk some body and flavor.

Melt the butter in a heavy-bottomed pan. When it has completely melted, add the flour. Stir the two together over a low heat to create the roux. Cook for 3–4 minutes, stirring to make sure it cooks evenly.

While the roux is cooking, the milk can be re-heated, leaving in the onion to increase the flavor.

The milk can now be stirred into the butter and flour a little at a time. This will emulsify with the roux and become very thick. Continue this process until all the milk has been added. The sauce now needs to cook over a gentle heat for a minimum of 20 minutes. During the cooking time, stir or whisk constantly to prevent it from sticking. After 20 minutes, add the cream you've chosen to loosen and enrich the consistency. Obviously, light cream will make the sauce thinner than heavy.

Season with salt, pepper, and nutmeg. Strain the béchamel through a sieve to guarantee a smooth finish.

If you are not using the sauce immediately, cover it with buttered waxed paper or plastic wrap. This basic white sauce can quickly be turned into a parsley sauce with the addition of the freshly chopped herb, or perhaps into a mustard sauce, adding English, Dijon, or wholegrain mustard to suit your taste.

Note: A teaspoon of butter will enrich any of these sauces.

Cheese Sauce (Sauce Mornay) ⓥ

The idea of adding grated cheese to a white sauce doesn't seem to have occurred to anyone until sometime in the eighteenth century when vegetables and macaroni began to be topped with cheese and then toasted. The sauce is great invention, and it has so many uses, working well with other flavors. Cauliflower, macaroni, lasagna, leeks, and many other foods have a relationship with cheese sauce.

Here, I add the cheese to a basic white sauce, which makes a larger quantity of cheese sauce, but you can make less by halving both the white sauce and the ingredients below. I also like to add mustard because I find it lifts the flavor of the cheese.

MAKES APPROX. 3½ CUPS (900 ML)

1 × *White Sauce* (page 45)
1 heaping teaspoon English or Dijon mustard (optional)
4–6 oz (100–175 g) Cheddar cheese, grated
Salt and pepper

Warm the white sauce. Add the mustard, if using, along with 4 oz (100 g) of the grated Cheddar. Stir until melted.

Now, it is time to taste and season with salt and pepper. If you prefer a stronger flavor, then add the remaining cheese.

Cook for 2–3 minutes, making sure the sauce does not over-heat. Boiling any cheese sauce will separate the fat content from the cheese itself, creating an almost curdled consistency.

For a guaranteed smooth consistency, strain through a sieve.

The rich cheese sauce is now ready and waiting for cauliflower, leeks, broccoli, spinach, macaroni, or lasagna, etc.

Note: A squeeze of lemon juice will always lift the flavors.
For a richer finish, whisk in a mixture of 2 egg yolks and 4 tablespoons of heavy cream after the sauce is ready. Make sure the sauce does not boil or the egg yolks will scramble.

Cumberland Applesauce ⓥ

This sauce – nothing to do with the Duke of Cumberland this time – is a classic accompaniment to the famous Cumberland sausage (page 368). It also goes very well with about any sausage, ham, or terrine, plus roast pork, goose, lamb chops, and poultry; you can also use it as a dressing for simple vegetarian salads or as an accompaniment to savory tarts. The spicy flavor and the lemon juice lift the apples, giving them a sweet but sharp zing. I use Granny Smith apples here because their strong flavor is exactly what the Cumberland sausage needs.

MAKES APPROX. 1 LB (450 G)

1 lb (450 g) Granny Smith apples, peeled and cored
Butter
⅓ cup (50 g) light brown sugar (more can be added for those with a sweet tooth; superfine sugar can also be used for a "whiter" finish)
½ teaspoon ground cinnamon
¼ teaspoon ground nutmeg
Juice of ½ lemon
2–3 tablespoons water

Dice the apples into rough ½ in (1 cm) pieces. Melt a teaspoon of butter in a saucepan. Add the apples and cook, covered with a lid, for a few minutes over a moderate heat. The apples will now begin to break down. Add the sugar, spices, lemon juice, and water, stirring them in well. Replace the lid and continue to cook for 10 minutes. The apples will have become very tender. The "sauce" can now be whisked to break down its texture. For a totally smooth finish, continue cooking for a few more minutes. The sauce can now be puréed to a smooth paste.

Note: The juice from the remaining ½ lemon can be added for a slightly more acidic finish.

Basic White Wine or Champagne Fish Sauce

This is the perfect sauce for most kinds of fish – creamy, rich in flavor, but still light on the palate.

MAKES APPROX. ¾–1 CUP (200–250 ML)

Butter
2 shallots, finely sliced
1 bay leaf
2 oz (50 g) button mushrooms, finely sliced
1 cup (225 ml) white wine or champagne
1 cup (225 ml) *Fish Stock* (page 35)
⅔ cup (150 ml) heavy cream
Salt and pepper

Melt a teaspoon of butter in a saucepan. Add the shallots and bay leaf and cook over a medium heat without browning for 1–2 minutes. Add the mushrooms and continue to cook and soften for a further 2–3 minutes.

Add the white wine or champagne and bring to a rapid simmer over a medium heat, cooking until the wine has reduced by two-thirds. Pour in the fish stock and again reduce by two-thirds.

Add the heavy cream and return to a slow simmer. Allow to cook, the cream taking on all of the flavors and slightly thickening, for 6–8 minutes.

Season with salt and pepper and strain through a fine sieve.

Before serving the sauce, quickly whiz it in a food processor; the consistency will become lighter and very frothy, making the sauce less intense without an over-cooked flavor.

Note: For a richer finish, whisk in 2–4 tablespoons (25–50 g) of butter. It's important not to boil the sauce after the butter has been added so that you don't separate the fat content.

A squeeze of lemon juice will lift the flavor of almost any cream sauce.

I prefer not to make cream sauces too thick because thick ones tend to leave a film around the palate instead of giving a fresh, light and lively flavor.

Tarragon leaves can also be added to the sauce reduction. After the sauce is cooked and strained, a few more torn leaves can be added before serving.

Red Wine Sauce

This sauce tastes good with almost any meat – chicken, beef, pork, veal – and even goes well with baked fish.

MAKES APPROX. 5 cups (1.2 LITERS)

4 shallots, chopped
1 large carrot, chopped
2 celery sticks, chopped
2 tablespoons (25 g) unsalted butter
1 garlic clove, crushed
1 bay leaf
1 sprig of fresh thyme
8 oz (225 g) beef skirt or beef trimmings (optional)
1 tablespoon olive oil (optional)
1 bottle red wine
5 cups (1.2 liters) *Veal Jus* (page 34) or bought
    alternative (page 11)
Salt and pepper

In a large pan, cook the chopped vegetables in a little butter with the garlic and herbs, allowing them to brown. If you are using the meat, brown it on all sides in a frying pan in the oil, then take the meat out and add it to the vegetables. Pour the red wine into the frying-pan to dissolve any flavors left from the browned meat. Scrape and stir, then pour the wine onto the meat and vegetables and boil to reduce until almost dry.

Add the veal *jus* and bring to a simmer; skim off any impurities, then simmer the sauce gently for 30 minutes. Pass through a sieve, squeezing all the juices from the vegetables and meat. Check for seasoning and you now have a rich, glistening red-wine sauce.

Homemade Salad Dressing ⓥ

This is the sauce that many of us remember scooping a spoonful out of a jar and placing on the side of a plate of salad. I always liked it, I must admit, and often wondered how it was made. It's not a mayonnaise since it is a "cooked" sauce, but has a very similar texture. After searching for, finding, cooking, and tasting many recipes, this is the one I have settled on. It has a sweet and slightly sour taste with a creamy finish. It's worth making because it tastes good, it's easy to make, and homemade accompaniments are always nice to offer.

MAKES 200–300 ML (7–10 FL OZ)
DEPENDING ON THE QUANTITY OF DRESSING

1 tablespoon all-purpose flour
4 teaspoons superfine sugar
2 teaspoons mustard powder, preferably English
Pinch of salt
2 eggs
½ cup (100 ml) white wine vinegar
⅔ cup (150 ml) heavy cream
Squeeze of lemon juice

BELOW
Homemade Salad Dressing

Mix together the flour, sugar, mustard, and salt. Beat in the eggs and white wine vinegar. Place the bowl over a pan of simmering water and stir until warmed and thickened, taking about 4–5 minutes. Then remove the bowl from the heat and let it cool.

Now, it is time to add the cream. With this, you can be as generous as you wish. A minimum of ½ cup (100 ml) will be needed. Finish with a squeeze of lemon juice and the salad dressing is ready. If refrigerated, the sauce will keep for a minimum of 1–2 weeks.

Note: The salad dressing is delicious served as an accompaniment to Scotch eggs – preferably the homemade ones (page 73).

Mayonnaise ⓥ

No one seems to be sure where this cold sauce comes from, but it may be a modern example of the medieval mixing of eggs and verjuice (the sour juice of crab apples or unripe grapes). It's more likely that it is from the Minorcan town of Mahon, which was said to have very good eggs. Whatever the origination, mayonnaise is useful in any number of ways – in potato salad, as a foundation for other sauces, in sandwiches, and many more.

MAKES APPROX. 1¾ CUPS (450 ML)

3 egg yolks
1 tablespoon white wine vinegar
1 teaspoon English or Dijon mustard
Salt and pepper
1¼ cups (300 ml) olive oil
1 teaspoon hot water
Few drops of lemon juice (optional)

Whisk the egg yolks, vinegar, mustard, and seasonings together, then slowly add the olive oil, whisking continuously. When all the oil is added, finish with the water and correct the seasoning. A few drops of lemon juice can be added to enhance the taste.

If refrigerated, the mayonnaise will keep for up to 1 week.

Note: Peanut oil can be used instead of the olive oil for a milder flavor.

A quick mayonnaise can be made that is a lower fat alternative. Take a scant ²/₃ cup (140 g) of fromage frais (fromage blanc, a really low fat version can be found in gourmet food shops), 1 teaspoon of Dijon mustard, and 1 teaspoon of lemon juice. Mix all three ingredients together, season with salt and pepper, and the healthy mayo is finished. An egg yolk can be added for a richer color and flavor. This recipe can be used in place of any commercially-made mayonnaise called for throughout the book.

Homemade Tomato Ketchup ⓥ

The tomato was not really accepted as a food until the latter part of the eighteenth century, and even then, it was cooked and puréed for a soup or made into a piquant pickle with vinegar and spices. The word "ketchup" comes from the Chinese, meaning "brine of pickled fish," and refers to a sauce similar to the Thai *nam pla* we have recently become familiar with. The nearest to the original "ketchup" in Britain would actually have been an anchovy sauce or essence.

Despite this confusion, tomato ketchup, tomato sauce, and tomato soup, as well, have become very popular. Ketchup for me has always been that classic, bought one, Heinz, but there's nothing like homemade. Its flavor is fresher and the spicy ingredients add a new edge that livens up the whole experience. I'm not trying to compete with that famous ketchup company, but try making your own – just once.

MAKES APPROX. 2¹/₂ CUPS (600 ML)

1 clove
1 bay leaf
½ teaspoon ground coriander, or a few
    coriander seeds
½ teaspoon ground cinnamon, or ½ cinnamon
    stick (optional)
1 cup (250 ml) cider or white wine vinegar
8 tablespoons demerara or superfine sugar
3 lb (1.5 kg) ripe tomatoes (net weight after
    quartering and seeding)
½ teaspoon sea salt

½ tablespoon mustard powder, preferably English
1 garlic clove, crushed
Dash of Tabasco sauce
1 tablespoon tomato purée

Tie the clove, bay leaf, coriander, and cinnamon stick, if using, in a piece of muslin. Place the vinegar and sugar in a heavy-bottomed pan and bring to a simmer. Add the tomatoes and all other ingredients and bring to a boil, stirring to prevent any sticking. When it is boiling, reduce the temperature and simmer, stirring occasionally, for 40 minutes. Be careful that the mixture doesn't stick to the bottom of the pan. Discard the muslin bag, purée the mixture in a food processor, and then push it through a sieve.

If you find the sauce to be thin after it cools, then simply re-boil and thicken with a little cornstarch or arrowroot mixed with water to form a paste, being careful not to make it too starchy. This will prevent the tomato water separating from the sauce. The sauce will keep, if refrigerated, for a minimum of 1 month.

So that's how tomato ketchup is made. Whether it's for dunking your French fries or topping your hamburger, the taste experience is worth every minute of preparation time.

I've also used this recipe to flavor the tomato cakes on page 66. The sauce works like a seasoning, lifting all of the flavors.

Basic Vinaigrette ⓥ

This may be a French name, but the British have been dressing their salads and vegetables with oil and vinegar for centuries. This particular dressing is very basic, but has lots of flavors, particularly from the infusion of the fresh basil, tarragon, and thyme.

MAKES APPROX. 2½ cups (600 ML)

1¼ cups (300 ml) extra-virgin olive oil
(French or Italian)
1¼ cups (300 ml) peanut oil
¼ cup (50 ml) balsamic vinegar

Bunch of fresh basil
Small bunch of fresh tarragon
3–4 sprigs of fresh thyme
12 black peppercorns, lightly crushed
3 shallots, finely chopped
2 garlic cloves, crushed
1 bay leaf
1 teaspoon coarse sea salt

Warm the olive and peanut oils together. Place all the remaining ingredients in a jar holding 3 cups (750 ml). Pour the oil into the jar and close with tightly fitting lid. For the best results, let the mixture marinate for a week, which allows all the flavors to enhance the oils. To help the dressing along, shake the bottle once a day. Taste for seasoning before using.

For a quick basic vinaigrette, mix 1 teaspoon of balsamic vinegar and 2 tablespoons olive oil. Season with salt and pepper and the dressing is finished.

Onion Gravy

The first "gravy" was a sweet, spicy sauce. By Elizabethan times it had become a sauce made by browning beef in fat before stewing it. For a classic onion gravy, use a reduced beef stock (*jus*) and slowly caramelized onions, capturing all of their natural sweet-savoriness which increases in strength as the gravy cooks.

This method requires fewer ingredients, and at the same time, carries a lot more depth and flavor than the "poor man's gravy" of times past, which consisted of "A glass of beer, a glass of water, an onion cut small, some pepper and salt, a little lemon peel grated, a clove or two, and a spoonful of mushroom, or pickled walnut liquor."

This gravy is perfect with liver, sausage, and mashed potatoes, *Toad in the Hole* (page 370), and *Yorkshire Pudding* (page 237), and is a vital component of the recipe *Faggots in Onion Gravy*, page 228.

MAKES APPROX. 2–2½ CUPS (450–600 ML)

4 large onions, thinly sliced or finely chopped
2 tablespoons water
1¼ cups (300 ml) *Veal* or *Beef Jus*
     (page 34) or alternative (page 11)

Place the onions in a pan with the water and cook over a very low heat. This will slowly draw the natural sugar content from the onions, and along with the juices, the onions will caramelize. This is a slow process, possibly taking up to 2 hours. It is very important that the onion does not burn because this creates a bitter taste. When a golden caramel flavor has been achieved, add the *jus*.

For a quicker caramelizing method, cook the onions to a golden brown color in a teaspoon of butter. Add a teaspoon of brown sugar and cook for 1–2 minutes. Taste the onions for sweetness. If you decide they need to be a little sweeter, repeat with the same quantity of sugar until the flavor you are after is achieved. Now, simply add the *jus* and cook for 6–8 minutes before serving.

BELOW
Faggots with Onion Gravy (page 228)

Green Pepper Butter ⓥ

This butter works well with almost all fish, meat and poultry, from broiled sole or roasted sea bass to broiled steak, cutlets, or chicken breasts.

10 tablespoons (150 g) butter
2 shallots, finely chopped
1 heaping teaspoon chopped green peppercorns
2 tablespoons brandy
4 tablespoons white wine
Squeeze of lemon juice
Salt

Melt a teaspoon of butter, adding the chopped shallots and green peppercorns. Cook for a few minutes before adding the brandy. Boil and reduce until almost dry. Add the white wine, also reducing until almost dry. Allow the mixture to cool. Mix the shallots into the remaining butter, and add a squeeze of lemon juice and pinch of salt.

The butter can now be wrapped in plastic wrap and rolled into a cylinder shape. Refrigerate or freeze until needed.

Note: Chopped parsley or onions can also be added to this recipe.

Green Lemon Butter ⓥ

This is an old recipe that is very close to a basic parsley butter. The difference that interested me, and which does work well, is the addition of onion juice. This gives the butter a much fuller flavor. For any mustard fans, a teaspoon of toasted and lightly crushed mustard seeds can also be added. This butter recipe goes particularly well with *Broiled or Pan-fried Dover Sole* (page 141).

FOR 8 TABLESPOONS (100 G) BUTTER

2 oz (50 g) parsley (4 oz/100 g if you want
    extra green)
1 medium onion, peeled
Juice of 1 lemon
8 tablespoons (100 g) unsalted butter, at room
    temperature
Salt and pepper

Pour 1¼ cups (300 ml) of boiling water over the parsley and let it stand for 1–2 minutes. Drain and squeeze out the excess liquid. The parsley must now be chopped until very, very fine. This can be most easily done in a food processor or coffee grinder. It is important that the parsley has a moist, almost puréed consistency.

The onion can now be cut into eight pieces and mashed using a mortar and pestle. This will begin to release the natural onion juices, but finish squeezing the onion pieces by hand until all the juices have been released. The onion solids can be discarded because all their flavor has been squeezed away. Quickly boil the lemon juice and reduce it by half. Let it cool.

Mix the lemon juice with the onion and parsley. The butter can now be beaten in. The flavors will spread throughout the butter and turn it to a green color. Season with salt and pepper.

Now, spoon the butter onto a square of plastic wrap and roll into a cylinder shape. The green butter can be refrigerated or frozen until needed (this will keep for up to 3 months).

When serving the butter, simply unwrap it, cut into slices, and place them on top of the fish.

Note: The onion juices can be replaced by finely chopping ½ a medium onion and cooking it, without browning, to a soft stage. Now, process it to a purée before adding.
Green lemon butter also goes very well with chicken, pork, veal, and vegetarian dishes.

Basic Butter Sauce ⓥ

This sauce is better known among chefs as *beurre blanc*. It is a very simple, very buttery sauce that works with many dishes, whether they're fish, meat, or vegetarian. The basic ingredients are normally white wine vinegar, water, chopped shallots, and butter. I have added a few more ingredients to this recipe to incorporate much more flavor. I have also given four "stocks" as alternatives, starting with water and then fish, chicken, and vegetable. Your choice depends on which dish you are serving the sauce with. Two variations in flavorings follow the basic recipe.

8 tablespoons (100 g) butter, chilled and cubed
1 shallot or ½ small onion, finely chopped
1 bay leaf
½ star anise (optional)
2 cardamom pods (optional)
2 tablespoons white wine vinegar
4 tablespoons white wine
6 tablespoons water or *Chicken Stock*, *Fish Stock*
    or *Vegetable Stock* (page 33, 35 or 36)
    or alternative (page 11)
2 tablespoons light cream
Salt and pepper

Melt a teaspoon of the butter and add the shallot or onion, the bay leaf, and a grinding of black pepper, and if using, the star anise and cardamom pods. Cook the vegetables for a few minutes until softened without letting them brown. Add the vinegar and reduce by three-quarters; add the wine and again reduce by three-quarters. Pour in the water or stock of your choice and reduce by half. Add the light cream to help emulsify the butter.

Bring the reduction to a simmer and whisk in the remaining butter, a few pieces at a time. Season with salt and pepper and strain through a sieve. If the sauce is too thick, thin it with a few drops of water or lemon juice. The basic butter sauce is now ready to use.

Note: For a soft, creamy, frothy finish, simply beat with a electric hand mixer.

Cilantro Butter Sauce ⓥ

1 recipe *Basic Butter Sauce* (page 52)
½ bunch cilantro
½ teaspoon lightly crushed coriander seeds

Reserve a quarter of the cilantro leaves for chopping and adding to the finished sauce. Roughly chop the remaining leaves and stems and add them to the basic butter-sauce reduction with the crushed coriander seeds. After the sauce has been cooked and strained, add the chopped cilantro just before serving.

Mustard Butter Sauce ⓥ

1 recipe *Basic Butter Sauce* (page 52)
1 tablespoon whole wheat mustard

Warm the butter sauce and then add the mustard. I like the sauce to have a fairly strong flavor, and 1 tablespoon of whole wheat mustard will give you exactly that. Add more if you prefer a stronger flavor.

See also

Curry Cream Sauce (page 393)
Broiled or Pan-fried Dover Sole (page 141)
Horseradish Sauce (page 55)
Mint Sauce (page 55)
Radish and French Bean Salad with Seared Scallops
(page 109)
Whole Roast Sea Bass (page 160)

Herbs

Herbs can be used to influence many tastes in a dish and to add flavors of their own. Originally, many flavors were taken from plants we recognize today but which we certainly wouldn't eat. In prehistoric times, for example, a variety of native wild plants would have been used as herbs to add different tastes to foods. An onion-garlic flavor could be obtained from the leaves and shoots of hedge garlic or garlic mustard, along with the leaves and bulbs of wild garlic (ramsoms). Peppery flavors came from wall pepper (*Sedum acre* or biting stonecrop), watercress, and lady's smock (a meadow flower); a vinegary, lemony tang came from sorrel; and a nutmeg-cinnamon bitterness from all parts of the tansy (a pretty plant, with a taste that wouldn't be considered so pleasant today).

Things changed when the Romans arrived, for it is believed they brought with them some 200 varieties of herbs native to the Mediterranean. They planted gardens with whatever seeds were needed for medicines and for food flavorings. Many hardy herbs, such as dill and fennel, became naturalized, growing as escapees along the coastlines and close to houses and towns. You can still find many herbs growing along the ancient roadsides of Britain, probably marking the routes taken by the Roman legions. These herbs include chervil, dill, fennel, rue (an aromatic and bitter perennial herb used mainly in medicine), sage, savory (a spicy herb used in slow-cooking dishes), marjoram, lemon balm (a strongly perfumed, lemon flavor), borage (with its mild, cucumber-like flavor), hyssop (with a minty but bitter and used in the making of Chartreuse), lavender, mint, parsley, rosemary, and thyme. During the 400 or so years of Roman occupation, these herbs were used both in cooking and medicine, and remain familiar to this day.

After the establishment of the Christian church, herbs were grown mainly by monks. The monks were the "conventional" healers of the day, practicing in medicine from their infirmaries. But throughout the Middle Ages, herbs were also grown by rich and poor for medicinal purposes and for use in cooking. Many early pottages (soups) were flavored with two of today's favorite herbs – parsley and sage. Also many other herbs we now consider to be weeds, such as chickweed (a common annual herb), nettles, and easterledge (or bistort – a tannin-rich perennial plant of the knotweed family), were used not only in pottages and salads but also to purify the blood. These were particularly welcome in the early spring after a winter of eating nothing but dried and salted foods.

By Tudor times, the poet and chronicler Thomas Tusser wrote that no kitchen garden was complete unless it grew at least 40 herb varieties. Herbs were used in many ways other than the culinary. The strongest, most aromatic and antiseptic were mixed with the reeds and rushes strewn across the floor to keep rooms smelling sweet and to keep illness at bay. Many other herbs were used to flavor ales, wines, teas, scents, aromatic posies, pomanders (which consisted of aromatic substances to protect against disease), and cosmetics and were even included in insect repellents and furniture polish.

Herbs were still being used in sauces and soups, and also in forcemeat, a ground meat stuffing for poultry, beef, or veal. Often the herbs used would have sour and strong flavors – tansy or rue, for instance – which had the strength to disguise off flavors or lift tasteless, insipid ones. Horseradish, previously used as a medicine, began to be appreciated as a condiment in the early seventeenth century, and it was served with fish as well as meat, a tradition that has continued with its accompaniment to smoked salmon or classic roast beef.

The medicinal and culinary uses of herbs reached their climax in Europe during the sixteenth and seventeenth centuries. The discovery of America and other world explorations led to a great interest in new plants. More people began growing medicinal herbs themselves, particularly once the infirmaries of the monks no longer existed. The wealthy always preferred herbs of Mediterranean origin, and these were described in seventeenth-century French cook books as "sweet" or "fine" (French cuisine had begun to have considerable influence on English cooking). The "faggot of sweet herbs" (our modern bouquet garni) is said to have been adopted by English cooks at this time, along with many other flavorings that have become traditional in our cooking.

The use of herbs declined in Britain during the eighteenth and nineteenth centuries because of the Industrial Revolution. As people were obliged to move from the countryside to the towns, the growing of herbs dwindled, as did many other traditions.

From the mid nineteenth century onward, the only herbs commonly used were the famous four, the "parsley, sage, rosemary, and thyme" of the folksong "Scarborough Fair."

I like to think that the new British style of cooking and the new classics in this book will reintroduce us to some of the wonderful tastes there are in herbs. Over the last twenty years, herbs have become very fashionable, appearing in many, often too many dishes. Before adding an herb to a sauce, dressing, or stuffing, its full potential flavor should be understood and appreciated. Often, I feel that the herb's addition is purely to make use of its rich, usually green, color. Remember when flavoring a sauce or oil with an herb that it's to infuse, not to *con*fuse.

Horseradish Sauce ⓥ

Native to west and Southeast Asia, horseradish is a root with an ancient history. It was very popular with the Egyptians and Romans, since both cultures always enjoyed and appreciated strong flavors. The hot taste was first offered from its extracted juice and then over the years, the white grated root began to be used instead.

Horseradish is easily recognizable – a large thick root with an outer skin of a deep yellow/bronze color, white, hot flesh lying underneath, and a central core which is inedible and very tough. If refrigerated, the root keeps for many weeks; it also freezes well.

The strange name came about, according to Jane Grigson, because of a misspelling. The Germans, who loved the plant, called it *Meerettich*, "sea root," because it came from across the sea. The British adopted and adapted the name, but mistakenly used the word *Mähre*, or "mare," which sounds the same as *Meer*, thus "horse."

Horseradish sauce goes very well not only with beef but also with ox tongue, terrines, and some fish dishes. The heavy cream used in this recipe can be replaced with crème fraîche or equal quantities of crème fraîche and natural yogurt. Lemon juice can also replace the vinegar.

MAKES APPROX. 1 CUP (200 ML)

2 oz (50 g) fresh horseradish, finely grated
1 teaspoon Dijon or English mustard
1 tablespoon white-wine vinegar
1 teaspoon caster sugar
⅔ cup (150 ml) heavy cream
Pinch of salt

Place all of the ingredients in a bowl and whisk together to a soft-peak consistency. The sauce is best served chilled.

Note: Using English mustard will give a hotter finish to the sauce. Dijon is slightly milder. To calm the sauce even more, omit the vinegar, replacing it with a squeeze of lemon juice and a pinch more sugar. For a slight oniony flavor, add chopped chives, especially if using crème fraîche.

Another version of this sauce can be made with part homemade mayonnaise (page 49) or the commercial variety. This gives the sauce a good depth and also turns it into a horseradish dip that can be served with many other dishes. Follow the above quantities for *Horseradish Sauce* and stir in 2 tablespoons of mayonnaise. Add a teaspoon of English mustard with the juice of ½ lemon. Pour in ½– ⅓ cup (100–150 ml) of heavy cream and stir to a sauce consistency.

Mint Sauce ⓥ

One of the most famous medieval sauces was "green sauce," which called for pounding together parsley, sage, a couple of varieties of mint perhaps, garlic, pepper, and salt, plus breadcrumbs, vinegar, or ale. This was the recommended accompaniment to fish. Often the mixture was simpler – an herb mixed with vinegar and perhaps some sugar. Our present-day mint sauce to accompany lamb is a direct descendant of this. The association between lamb and mint is a reflection of the medieval belief that an animal's best accompaniment or "tracklement" was a plant that it ate or that grew near where it grazed.

This is probably the easiest recipe in the book. The amount here is more than you need for one lamb meal, but the vinegar acts as a preservative, so keep the jar chilled and it will last indefinitely. Apart from using this as a straight mint sauce, I also use it as an enhancer for gravies and other sauces. A teaspoon in a lamb stew or in the gravy for a lamb roast will lift all the flavors.

ABOVE
Sage Fava Beans with Bacon and Tomato

MAKES APPROX. ⅔ CUP (150 ML)

⅔ cup (150 ml) malt vinegar
Small bunch of fresh mint
1½–2 heaping tablespoons light brown sugar
Fresh mint leaves, chopped

The mint for the sauce needn't be chopped, just left as it is.

Pour the vinegar onto the mint in a small pan. Add the light brown sugar. Using 2 tablespoons will make the sauce sweeter, which some people prefer. Simply bring to a boil and the sauce cook for a few minutes until the sugar has dissolved. Let it cool. After it has cooled, it's best to simply store it in a tightly closed jar with all the mint leaves left in to increase the mint flavor. In time the mint will completely discolor due to the acidity of the vinegar.

To finish the sauce, strain off some of the vinegar through a tea strainer and add chopped fresh mint.

Sage Fava Beans with Bacon and Tomato

Sage is an herb that has always been popular in Britain. It's use in stuffings dates from the seventeenth century, when Sir Kenelm Digby, a diplomat, writer, and amateur man of science, proposed that a simple sage and onion stuffing would be better for wild duck than the complicated, rich stuffings common at the time. His suggestion became widely accepted and has been used up to today for duck, turkey (see page 327), and pork.

Here I've used sage in a dish that goes well with many others. The sage butter flavor, helped along by tomato, makes the fava beans a perfect accompaniment to almost any lamb dish (or chicken, beef, veal, pork, and game). For a good simple roast leg of lamb in search of a tasty garnish, this is it.

The best bacon for this is *Preserved (Confit) Bacon* (page 192); it has just the right texture after it's warmed. Or buy a piece of ham and cut into ¼ in (5 mm) dice.

4 oz (100 g) *Preserved (Confit) Bacon* (page 192)
    or bought cooked ham, diced
2–3 large tomatoes, blanched and peeled
1 teaspoon chopped fresh sage
4 teaspoons (50 g) unsalted butter, at room
    temperature
12 oz–1 lb (350–450 g) fava beans, cooked and
    skinned (page 96)
Squeeze of lemon juice (optional)
Salt and pepper

Warm the preserved bacon or the ham in a few tablespoons of water or stock. Simply warm gently on a low heat. This softens the texture. The tomatoes, after being peeled, need to be cut into ½ in (1 cm) cubes.

Mix the chopped sage with the butter. (You can be made the butter in larger amounts and then freeze it, using whatever is needed when you need it.)

After it is mixed, let the butter harden in the refrigerator. When it's added to the beans, the cold butter emulsifies with the juices, creating an almost butter-sauce consistency. If it's too warm, it will melt like butter and the oils will separate from the solids.

Take 2–3 tablespoons of water or liquid from the bacon warming and place in a saucepan (a wok works very well with this dish). Add the fava beans and re-heat/steam for 2–3 minutes. When they are hot, add the diced bacon, drained of the liquid. Stir gently before adding the tomatoes.

The butter can now be added, warming and stirring into the mixture. Season with salt and pepper. The beans are ready. To lift the butter flavor, a small squeeze of lemon juice can be added just before serving.

Stuffed Herrings with Apples and Tarragon

Tarragon is probably used more in French cooking than in British, but it can lend its unique flavor to so many of Britain's best-loved dishes – to chicken, to omelettes, to mushrooms, fish, sauces, and salad dressings (see page 50). Here, I use it, along with apples for their slight acidity in a stuffing for herring, a fish that has long been a British favorite, both fresh and smoked. To add extra spiciness, there is a touch of horseradish too. This is not essential, but does heighten flavor of the dish.

I also use pig's caul in this recipe; again it's not essential, but it does guarantee that the fish holds together. An alternative is to wrap the herrings in buttered foil and bake them, before finishing under a hot broiler. Another important point to remember in order to make the fish more enjoyable to eat is to remove as many of the fine bones as possible from the flesh itself. This can be done easily using pliers or tweezers.

Creamy *Mashed Potatoes* (page 124) and watercress salad will go very well with this dish.

4 tablespoons (50 g) unsalted butter
1 onion, finely chopped
1 teaspoon chopped fresh tarragon
½–1 teaspoon horseradish cream (optional)
4 apples, peeled, cored, and cut into ½ in
    (1 cm) dice
1 cup (50 g) fresh white breadcrumbs
4 herrings, cleaned and filleted, with pin bones
    removed (page 11)
4–6 oz (100–175 g) pig's caul, soaked in water
    overnight (page 11) (optional)
2 teaspoons vegetable oil
1 tablespoon all-purpose flour
Salt and pepper
Lemon slices and watercress, to garnish

Preheat the oven to 375°F/190°C.

Melt 2 tablespoons (25 g) of the butter in a frying-pan and fry the onion for a few minutes until softened but not browned. Add the tarragon and apples and fry for a few minutes. The horseradish cream, if using, can now be added. Mix in the white breadcrumbs and season to taste. Stir the mixture thoroughly. Remove from the heat and allow to cool.

Divide the mixture into four and place on top of four of the fillets. Cover with the remaining four fillets. Squeeze any excess water from the pig's caul, if using, and cut into four pieces. Wrap the pig's caul, or buttered foil, around the herring packages.

On the stove-top, heat the remaining butter and the oil in a roasting pan. Add the herring packages, dust with flour, and fry until golden. Transfer to the oven and cook for 10–12 minutes. To serve, spoon the juices on top and garnish with lemon slices and watercress.

Lemon and Thyme Dumplings

Dumplings have a long history dating back to the one-pot cooking days, when a ball of flour and fat plus some flavorings, usually herbs, were dropped into the pot along with the boiling meat or vegetable pottage. Dumplings not only made the meal go further, but they also added considerable nutritional value and flavor – as these dumplings add to a roast chicken for Sunday dinner, to boiled bacon, and many of the braised beef or lamb dishes. So next time you are making a stew, try these.

SERVES 4

4 oz (100 g) fresh veal bone marrow for
    the best flavor, or shredded suet
1 cup (100 g) white breadcrumbs
2 tablespoons heavy cream
3 egg yolks
Pinch of freshly grated nutmeg
1 heaping teaspoon chopped fresh thyme
Finely grated zest and juice of 1 lemon
Salt and pepper
Chicken Stock (page 33) or water, for cooking

Mix all the ingredients together, except for the stock or water, and season to taste with salt and pepper. Using 2 tablespoons, shape into four large or eight small ovals, or roll into balls. Drop these into a simmering stock or water and cook for 10–15 minutes, depending on the size. Any excess dumpling mixture can be left refrigerated and used for another dish.

Sage Fritters Ⓥ

Most pork dishes and many lamb and poultry ones go well with sage.

These sage fritters can be made by two methods. The first is coated and fried in a beer batter for a complete souffléd finish. The second is simply coated in milk and flour for a thinner but still crisp finish.

MINIMUM OF 6 PORTIONS

3–4 sage leaves per portion
Cooking oil, for deep-frying
1 cup (100 g) self-rising flour
⅔ cup (150 ml) lager
Salt

Heat the oil to 350°F/180°C. Lightly coat each leaf in the flour. Whisk the remaining flour with the lager. Dip the leaves into the batter and carefully place in the oil. (The oil needs to be at least ¾ in/2 cm deep.) These will take only a few minutes to become golden and souffléd. Turn them over and complete the cooking.

After they're completely golden, lift from the oil, drain on paper towels, and season with salt. Place on the finished dinner plates.

For simple flour and milk frying, simply dip the leaves in milk and then into flour and deep-fry them until golden. Remove from the fat and season with salt. These can now also be used to garnish the finished plate.

Both variations can be fried 10 minutes before serving; they will keep their crisp finish.

BELOW
Lemon and Parsley Carrots

Lemon and Parsley Carrots ⓥ

Lemon works very well with carrots. The natural sweetness of the vegetables, especially if you've bought young carrots, is delicious with the wonderful lemon acidity, but is also helped by a pinch of sugar, which lifts all the flavors.

Parsley has been a favorite herb since medieval times, when it was used as a major ingredient in a green sauce (more like today's salsa), served mostly with the fish eaten on non-meat days. It's delicious with vegetables as well, and I use the flat variety here, which holds more flavor than the curly. Instead of chopping it, which never works well with flat parsley – bruising as it cuts – I merely tear it into pieces.

SERVES 4

1 lb (450 g) carrots, preferably baby, peeled
    (if using baby carrots, leave ½ in/1 cm of
    stalk on top to give a new color to the dish)
1 teaspoon sugar
2 tablespoons (25 g) butter
juice of ½ lemon
Salt and pepper

Few sprigs of fresh flatleaf parsley, stems
    removed and leaves torn

If baby carrots are not available, larger ones can be sliced ¼ in (5 mm) thick or cut into matchsticks. Baby vegetables can be split lengthwise.

Whatever carrots are being used, barely cover them with water. Add a pinch of salt, the sugar, and half the butter and cover with waxed paper. Bring to a simmer and cook until the carrots are just tender. This will take from 3 to 10 minutes, depending on size. After they're tender, use a slotted spoon to remove the carrots and keep to one side.

Now, bring the cooking liquid to a boil and reduce by three-quarters. This should now be approaching a syrup consistency. Add the lemon juice and increase the heat to a simmer for another minute. Check the flavor: a sweet lemony carrot, almost butter sauce, is what you should have. Return the carrots to the pan and re-heat in the sauce. Season with salt and pepper. Add the remaining butter. The carrots are now lemon glazed and waiting for the addition of torn parsley. Sprinkle in the parsley and stir. The carrots are ready to serve.

See also

Calves' Liver Steak and Kidney, with Red Wine Carrots, and Rosemary Butter (page 218)
Chicken Fillet "Steaks" with Chestnut Mushrooms, Sage, and Lemon Sauce (page 248)
Coriander Butter Sauce (page 53)
Broiled Lamb with "Irish" Cabbage and Mashed Potato Sauce (page 187)
Parsleyed Cod with Mustard Butter Sauce (page 168)
Slow-roast Shoulder of Pork with Pearl Barley and Sage Stuffing (page 209)
Spicy Tomato and Mint Relish (page 381)

Cheese and Eggs

Cheese and eggs are two very basic
foods that have been with us for
thousands of years. When primitive
man settled down, one of his first
tasks was to domesticate animals for
food use. Among them were the
ancestors of today's cows, sheep,
goats, and chickens, producing milk
and eggs that became major foods.
Because milk would have soured fairly
quickly, much of it would have been
"eaten" as curds and whey – and this
is how the idea for making cheese
from sour milk was born.

Slices of bacon with a cooked, new-laid egg would have been a rare and special meal – a combination that continues, forming part of a traditional British breakfast.

In the Middle Ages, "white meats" – as milk, milk products, and eggs were known – were the daily basic food of the better off peasants. The family who had a cow, a pig, and a couple of hens or geese would have enough to keep them going. The cow alone could provide milk, curds, whey (thought very nourishing), cheese, butter, sour milk, and buttermilk. The pig would be killed in the autumn and salted to supply meat throughout the winter. Slices of bacon with a cooked new-laid egg would have been a rare and special meal – a combination that continues, forming part of a traditional British breakfast.

These foods were also enjoyed by the rich but were less important in their diets, since meat was the main feature of their diets. For both the rich and the peasantry, though, cheese and eggs would have been useful foods on the many religious fast days, although eggs as well as meat were forbidden during Lent. A variety of cooking methods was soon found for eggs, with roasting in their shells in the ashes of a wood fire becoming one of the first. Next followed the basics, boiling and frying in butter or lard. In the early fifteenth century, eggs were made into a version of scrambled eggs, the predecessor in England of the French omelette. "Herbolace" was a mixture of eggs and herbs, often enriched with cheese, while "tansy" was a mixture of raw eggs flavored with the sour juice of tansy leaves. Both were turned over heat to make a scrambled egg-type mixture. Eggs were also used, mostly by the wealthy, to make pancakes, fritters, nourishing "caudles" (drinks), and as a foundation ingredient for tart fillings.

Cheese was developed in a number of forms and textures during medieval times, the main ones being soft, hard, and new or "green." The soft would have resembled cream cheese; the hard was a Cheddar type made from renneted milk and firmed by pressing; and the green was a very new soft cheese. The richer and more digestible soft cheeses would have been eaten by the wealthy. The hard cheese was a fairly cheap food which soon became a feature of the poorer man's diet. His everyday meal of bread and cheese has come down to us virtually unchanged as the plowman's lunch that appears on almost every pub menu.

It wasn't until the late-seventeenth century, though, that the different types of local cheeses that had evolved became known to the majority of people. The fact the cheeses from the West Country were different from those in the north was only known to people who might have encountered them in their travels, or who could afford to have them brought to them. When transport by road, sea, and canal improved, perishable goods including cheeses could be appreciated across the country. By the end of the century, cheese names famous today, such as

PAGE 60
Macaroni, Artichoke, and Mushroom Cheese Pie (page 64)

Stilton, Gloucester, Cheddar, and Wiltshire, had become familiar to many. It is interesting, too, that many foreign cheeses were known as well, at least to those in the larger cities. As early as 1577, Parmesan was highly praised, followed by Dutch and Norman cheeses, with English cheeses last.

Nearer the present, both eggs and cheese have remained important features of the diet, although cheese was slightly looked down upon because of its association with the working classes. Mrs Beeton herself, although giving many "receipts" or recipes for cheese dishes, wrote: ". . . cheese, in its commonest shape, is only fit for sedentary people, as an after-dinner stimulant, and in very small quantity. Bread and cheese, as a meal, is only fit for soldiers on march or laborers in the open air, who like it because it 'holds the stomach a long time.' " Mrs Gaskell, in her novel *Wives and Daughters*, gently mocked the pretensions of Mrs Kirkpatrick, just before she remarried; on being told by his daughter that her husband-to-be, Dr Gibson, ate toasted cheese, she declared, "Oh! but my dear, we must change all that. I shouldn't like to think of your father's eating cheese; it's such a strong-smelling, coarse kind of thing. We must get him a cook who can toss him up an omelette, or something elegant." How about a perfectly cooked cheese omelette? Now that sounds very elegant to me.

In the nineteenth century, cheese, despite its coarse and indigestible reputation, was eaten mostly after dinner as a separate course or as a savory such as a "rabbit" (or rarebit, page 178). In the last twenty years, however, English cheeses have improved vastly. Britain may not have the variety of cheeses that France does, but the flavors and textures provided by British cheese, I believe, can stand up to those of almost any other country.

Eggs gained a new pride of place for the first meal of the day in the nineteenth century. Having been used very generously in puddings and pies –

especially after the power of egg whites to make a mixture rise was recognized – they became a special and unique part of the Victorian breakfast. No breakfast sideboard was complete without a little dish of boiled eggs, or a special warmer containing fried, scrambled, or buttered eggs. Eggs have contributed to so many dishes, whether savory or sweet. They hold textures and flavors together, lending the silky finish of the yolk and the strength of the white to almost all other ingredients. This chapter gives you some recipes to start with, but you'll find plenty more throughout this book.

Eggs have contributed to so many dishes, whether savory or sweet. They hold textures and flavors together, lending the silky finish of the yolk and the strength of the white to almost all other ingredients.

Macaroni, Artichoke, and Mushroom Cheese Pie ⓥ

Macaroni, originally known as "macrows," was introduced to Britain from Italy in the fourteenth century. It was not until the eighteenth century, though, that the idea of toasted, grated cheese was allied with vegetables and, by extension, macaroni. The macaroni was boiled, then drained and tossed in cream before being sprinkled with cheese and browned. It became a very popular supper dish in Victorian times – and it is still delicious.

This vegetarian recipe takes it a bit further. The flavor and texture are extended by the addition of artichokes and mushrooms, and the whole dish is served in a pastry case – hence the name "pie." I've given a recipe for cooking artichokes (page 96), but if this all seems too much, then simply use canned (these can be found in gourmet stores), or simply add extra mushrooms (wild for real extravagance). I use two cheese sauces in this recipe, again, not essential, but the classic cheese or Mornay is there to create the glaze. If you choose to use only the Parmesan cream sauce, then top with either grated Cheddar or Parmesan to give the melted finish.

SERVES 4 AS A MAIN COURSE

1 lb (450 g) *Quick Puff* or *Flaky Pastry* or
    Shortcrust Pastry, rolled 2 mm thick
    (page 365 or 364)
2 medium-sized globe artichokes, cooked
    (page 96) or 7 oz (200 g) canned
    artichoke hearts
Butter
4 oz (100 g) button or cremini mushrooms,
    quartered
1¼ cups (150 g) macaroni, cooked (follow
    instructions on the package)
Salt and pepper

For the Mornay Sauce

Cheese Sauce (page 46); make only ⅓ of the
    total recipe
2 egg yolks or ⅔ cup (150 ml) *Simple Hollandaise
    Sauce* (page 41)
2 heaping tablespoons softly whipped cream

For the Parmesan Cheese Sauce

1¼ cups (300 ml) heavy cream
3 oz (75 g) Parmesan cheese, freshly grated
2 tablespoons crème fraîche
Squeeze of lemon juice

Preheat the oven to 400°F/200°C.

The metal pastry rings I use for this recipe are 4 in (10 cm) in diameter and 2½ in (6 cm) high. If these are unavailable, substitute with mini 4 in (10 cm) flan rings, placing one on top of another to get the same depth. The rings should first be buttered and placed on a waxed-paper-lined baking sheet. Roll out the pastry and cut out four 4 in (10 cm) circles, one for the bottom of each ring. Roll the remaining pastry and cut into strips wide enough to line the sides of the rings. After the pastry is in place, press it along the bottom edge, so that it makes a good seal with the bottom, and then all the way around the sides so that it comes a little above the ring. Line each pastry with waxed paper or foil and fill with baking beans or pie weights. Let the pastry rest in the refrigerator for 20 minutes.

Bake the pastry cases blind for 15–20 minutes to a light golden brown. This will guarantee a crisp finish.

To make the Parmesan cheese sauce, bring the heavy cream to a boil. Whisk in the Parmesan cheese and crème fraîche and reduce the heat. Add lemon juice to taste, some salt, and pepper, and the sauce is now ready to use.

To finish the dish, warm the pie shells in a medium oven. Cut each cooked artichoke into 8-12 pieces. Melt a teaspoon of butter in a frying-pan and fry the mushrooms to a golden brown. Add the artichokes and gently fry. The warm macaroni can now be mixed with the artichokes, seasoning all with salt and pepper. Remove from the heat and bind with the Parmesan cheese sauce. Divide the mixture among the pie shells.

Make the Mornay sauce after the pies are ready. Either add the egg yolks or the amount of hollandaise sauce to the cheese sauce, and gently fold in the whipped cream. To check for the perfect golden glaze, spoon a little onto a baking sheet and brown under the broiler. Add a tablespoon or so more cream if it doesn't glaze properly.

Spoon the finished Mornay sauce on top of each pie and place under a hot broiler, coloring to a rich golden glaze. These wonderfully rich macaroni cheese, artichoke, and mushroom pies are now ready to serve.

Note: These pies are particularly delicious with a tossed green salad flavored with *Basic Vinaigrette* (page 50), with the addition of tiny sliced red onions, watercress, and chopped walnuts.

One to two tablespoons of cooked spinach can be placed in the bottom of each pastry case to create another flavor and texture in the complete dish.

Steamed Leek and Cheddar Cheese Casserole ⓥ

This is a vegetarian answer to steak and kidney pudding. It has the very rich flavors and the pleasant pudding texture. I've kept this recipe simple, with the two main flavors of leek, an early pottage vegetable, and of Cheddar, the very British cheese. But the dish is also a reflection of the old English dumpling tradition which, I'm glad to say, lives on. The dumpling has taken on many more roles, starting as a simple meal extender, moving onto an accompaniment, and now, as here, a dish that stands on its own.

Many other ingredients can be added – mushrooms, sweet peppers, onions, and so on. I also include a cream sauce that is quick and easy to make. It can be left "plain" or finished with grated Parmesan for cheese sauce, or English or Dijon mustard for a mustard sauce.

SERVES 4

8 oz (225 g) leeks, sliced
2 cups (225 g) self-rising flour
½ teaspoon salt
¾ cup (100 g) vegetable shortening

6 oz (175 g) Cheddar cheese, grated
    (extra can be placed in the center of
    the pudding for a gooey middle)
About ⅔ cup (150 ml) water
Black pepper

For the Cream Sauce

4 tablespoons heavy cream
4 tablespoons crème fraîche
4 tablespoons (50 g) unsalted butter
1–2 tablespoons finely grated Parmesan cheese or
    1–2 teaspoons English or Dijon mustard
1 tablespoon water
Salt and pepper

The leeks should first be blanched in boiling, salted water for 30 seconds–1 minute. After they're blanched, drain the water from them and allow to cool on a dish towel.

Sift together the flour and salt. Add the vegetable shortening, cheese, and a grinding of pepper. Mix well together. Add the leeks and enough water to give a soft dough texture.

Butter and lightly flour a 1¼ quarts (1.2 liter) baking dish and fill with the leek mixture. Press down and cover with buttered foil, pleated to allow for expansion. The dish can now be placed in a steamer or on a trivet in a covered pan and steamed for 1½–1¾ hours until firm to the touch. Keep checking the water level to make sure it doesn't boil dry.

Meanwhile, make the sauce. Place the heavy cream, crème fraîche, and butter in a small saucepan. Bring to a boil, whisking continuously. Sprinkle in the cheese, if using, and whisk it in. Remove from the heat and season with salt and pepper. The cheese sauce is ready. If it is too thick, add the water.

Repeat the same process to make the mustard sauce, adding the amount of mustard that suits your taste buds.

After the pudding is cooked, remove the foil and turn out; the pudding is ready to enjoy. Extra grated Cheddar cheese can be sprinkled on top and gratinated under a preheated broiler.

Pressed Tomato Cake with Peppered Goat Cheese

Although it was viewed with suspicion for hundreds of years, the tomato has become one of the most popular fruit/vegetables in the country, particularly when used in soups and ketchup. Here, I've brought together tomatoes and cheese – goat cheese would have been much more common in the past – in a dish that makes a wonderful appetizer or main course. The flavor of the homemade tomato ketchup heightens the taste of the finished dish. It's not essential to use the ketchup, but the flavor is so powerful that it's worth the time. (The other bonus is having the rest of it to serve with other dishes; you won't want to buy it again.) All the flavors blend very well: the tomatoes, cheese, and shallots make a classic combination, but one that gives you a totally different finish.

You will need four 3 × 2 in (8 × 5 cm) metal cooking rings.

SERVES 4 AS AN APPETIZER

For the Cakes

12 ripe tomatoes, preferably plum, blanched
    and skinned and cored
6–8 tablespoons *homemade Tomato Ketchup*
    (page 49)
Salt and pepper

For the Goat's Cheese

7–8 oz (200–225 g) soft goat cheese,
    rind removed
½–⅔ cup (100–150 ml) heavy cream
1 teaspoon freshly ground black pepper
Squeeze of lemon juice

For the Dressing and Garnish

6 tablespoons olive oil
1 teaspoon Dijon mustard
Squeeze of lemon juice
2 teaspoons chopped fresh flatleaf parsley
4 large shallots, cut into rings, to garnish

Quarter the tomatoes, discarding the seeds. The tomato quarters can now be seasoned with salt and pepper before being layered in the rings. After each layer has been placed in the ring, spread with a teaspoon of tomato ketchup before adding the next layer. After all the rings have been filled, cover them with plastic wrap and place a baking pan with cans for weights on top to press them down. These are best left refrigerated for several hours.

Beat the goat cheese until softened. Add the heavy cream and black pepper and mix to a smooth, peppery paste. Add a pinch of salt along with the lemon juice. Both of these flavors will heighten the complete taste of the cheese and pepper. The mixture needs to be soft enough to be piped. The peppered goat cheese is now ready to use. This can be made several hours in advance, along with the tomato cakes. When needed, remove from the refrigerator and allow it to soften.

BELOW
Pressed Tomato Cake with Peppered Goat Cheese

To make the dressing, whisk all the ingredients together, except for the shallots, checking for seasoning with salt and pepper. More Dijon mustard can be added for a "hotter" and richer finish.

The tomato cakes can be pushed from the rings. Place the cakes in the center of the plates, and garnish with the shallot rings around the outside.

The best way to serve the goat cheese cream is to use a piping bag with a plain ½ in (1 cm) tube and pipe it on top of the cakes. You can simply shape the mixture between spoons to make quenelles, if you prefer, and place them on top.

To finish, spoon the mustard and parsley dressing over and around the cakes.

Cherry tomatoes with peppered goat cheese

The above recipe can also be used to make 35–40 canapés. This variation is easier because it uses cherry tomatoes rather than cakes. Simply cut off the bottom of the tomatoes and spoon out all the seeds. Now, pipe in the cheese, leaving a "spiked" finish. Just before serving, finish with a trickle of dressing. The tasty canapés are ready to serve.

Apple and Blue Cheese Tart ⓥ

Apple pie is a British classic, popular all over the country. Apparently, apples used to be transported up north from Kent – the Garden of England from very early days – on the coal barges, because they loved apple pie in Yorkshire and other northern counties. There, the pie was served with cheese, and this recipe is an adaptation of that idea. You can use the classic Stilton, as here, or a Wensleydale, or even an Irish Cashel Blue.

The pie is made in the classic French *tarte tatin* style. Basically, the apple halves are caramelized before being covered with puff pastry, then baking and glazing the pie with a blue cheese. It's a great savory pie with tastes to suit everyone. You could serve it for lunch, for a picnic, and it's perfect with a basic green salad and a spoonful of crème fraîche or sour cream.

SERVES 4

2 tablespoons (25 g) butter
4 medium Granny Smith apples, peeled, cored and halved crosswise through the middle
2 tablespoons (25 g) superfine sugar
8 oz (225 g) *Quick Puff* or *Flaky Pastry* (page 365), rolled into a 11 in (28 cm) diameter circle
4¾–5 oz (120–150 g) Stilton or other blue cheese, thinly sliced
Pepper

Preheat the oven to 425°F/220°C.

Melt the butter in a 10 in (25 cm) frying-pan with an ovenproof handle, or in a flan ring. Add the apples, flat side down, and cook slowly on the stove for a few minutes, making sure the butter doesn't burn. Turn the apples over and continue to cook for another minute or two.

The apples can now be turned flat side down once more. Increase the heat. The apples will begin to become a rich golden brown. Sprinkle the superfine sugar over them. Reduce the heat slightly and allow the sugar to caramelize onto the apples in the pan. It's at this point that you might need to add one or two *drops* of water to the pan. This will help the sugar to caramelize.

Remove the pan from the stove. Arrange the apple halves neatly in it and allow them to cool. After they're cool, fit the pastry disk on top. Place the tart in the preheated oven and bake for 18–20 minutes until it is golden. Remove from the oven after it is cooked and allow it to rest for 2–3 minutes before placing a plate or serving dish on top and carefully turning the whole pan over.

The tart is now resting on its presentation plate and ready for the cheese.

Place the thin blue cheese slices on top, just enough to cover, and place under a preheated broiler. Allow the cheese to warm and begin to melt over the apples. Finish with a twist of pepper.

The Apple and Blue Cheese Tart is ready to serve; it goes very well with a glass of port or red wine.

Cauliflower Cheese with Crisp Parmesan Crumbs ⓥ

Cheese began to be used as a topping for vegetables in the eighteenth century. The cardoon, a vegetable that's a very close relative of the globe artichoke and uncommon now, was among the first to be treated in this way, the recipe coming from France where it was known as *chardons à la fromage*. The cardoons were covered with Cheddar or Parmesan and browned with a hot cheese iron or under a salamander. The idea was soon adopted in England for the more familiar cauliflower, but the original plain grated cheese topping soon became the popular and versatile white or cheese sauce.

Cauliflower cheese is one of my childhood favorites. I always considered it a treat to be eating that (probably lumpy) cheese sauce with the tender cauliflower. Good dishes will always live on and this one certainly has. The crisp Parmesan crumbs are an optional extra, but they do give the dish another texture and flavor to be enjoyed.

The first question always asked is – which is the best cheese to use?

Well, it usually is made with strong, aged Cheddar, and why not? Cheddar is a cheese that gives a good result every time. If you wish, however, you can replace it with Gruyère and Parmesan; I call this version "the three Cs" – "continental cauliflower cheese." The flavors of Gruyère and Parmesan (I use equal quantities) together are powerful, so 2 oz (50 g) less of each cheese will be plenty for the recipe.

This dish is a perfect alternative for a vegetarian Sunday dinner.

SERVES 4

1 large cauliflower, divided into florets
Butter
Salt and pepper

For the Cheese Sauce

1 clove
1 bay leaf
1 small onion
2½ cups (600 ml) milk
2 tablespoons (25 g) butter
¼ cup (25 g) all-purpose flour

⅔ cup (150 ml) light cream (optional)
1 teaspoon English mustard (optional)
6–7 oz (175–200 g) Cheddar cheese
    (or Gruyère with Parmesan), grated
Salt, pepper and freshly grated nutmeg

For the Crisp Parmesan Crumbs (optional)

4 slices of white bread, crusts removed
Butter
1 tablespoon grated Parmesan cheese,
    or more to taste
Salt and pepper

To make the sauce, first, stud the clove through the bay leaf and into the onion. This can now be placed in a saucepan with the milk. Warm the milk slowly, allowing the flavors of the onion to impregnate the milk. When you've brought it up to a simmer, cover with a lid and let it stand for 15 minutes.

Now it's time to make the roux. Melt the butter in a suitable saucepan. After it has melted, add the flour and cook on a low heat for a few minutes, stirring from time to time.

The milk can now be added, a ladle at a time. While the milk and roux are cooking, they will emulsify and can be blended to a smooth "béchamel" sauce. This can now be cooked, adding the onion from the milk, for approximately 20–25 minutes.

The sauce will be quite thick. Remove the onion and season the sauce with salt, pepper, and nutmeg. Add the light cream, if using. This will thin the sauce slightly, and give it a richer finish. Add the mustard and 6 oz (175 g) of the grated Cheddar. After the cheese has completely melted into the sauce, re-taste for seasoning and strength. It is important that the sauce does not boil because this will cause the cheese to separate. Strain the sauce through a sieve.

To cook the cauliflower florets, bring a pan of salted water to a boil and drop in the cauliflower. Bring it to a gentle boil. Cook until barely tender; this will take only a few minutes, leaving a slight bite. Drain off the water. Warm a teaspoon of butter in a frying-pan and add the florets. Toss them in the

ABOVE
Cauliflower Cheese with Crisp Parmesan Crumbs

butter without browning and season them with salt and pepper. You can do this ahead of time and refresh the cauliflower in ice water. To re-heat, either microwave or plunge it back into boiling water.

To finish, preheat the oven to 400°F/200°C or preheat the broiler. Spoon a little of the cheese sauce into an ovenproof dish, arrange the cauliflower on top, and coat with more of the sauce. Sprinkle the last 1 oz (25 g) of grated Cheddar on top and place under the broiler or in the oven to melt and brown for 10–15 minutes.

To make the Crisp Parmesan Crumbs, the bread can either be blitzed in a food processor or broken down by hand into rough crumbs. The "rough" basically means maintaining large and small sizes throughout. These crumbs can now be pan-fried in a teaspoon of butter to a golden brown and a crisp finish. At this stage, add the Parmesan cheese which will start to melt instantly, creating a sticky consistency among the crunchy crumbs. Now, sprinkle the crumbs over the finished cauliflower dish.

All you have to do now is serve it. This is superb as a complete dish on its own, accompanied by a tossed green salad.

Note: It's not essential to glaze the cauliflower cheese under the broiler or in the oven – it can be served simply with the cheese sauce poured over it and Crisp Parmesan crumbs to finish.

It's also not essential to break the cauliflower into florets. The vegetable can be kept whole and boiled. This will take approximately 10–15 minutes, depending on the size of the cauliflower. Make sure the central core has been cut away. After it has cooked, cut it, and serve as per the florets.

Cheddar Cheese Soup ⓥ

Cheddar cheese is a British classic, the ultimate farmhouse cheese. It was made in and around Somerset, and it was the cheese tourists ate when they visited the Cheddar Gorge – so the name stuck. A farmer's published account of how his wife made her cheese in the mid-nineteenth century brought Cheddar cheese to the world. The word spread, and his children took the recipe and the name to Denmark, Canada, Ireland, Scotland, and Australia.

Mature Cheddar is delicious on its own, and it enhances other textures and tastes, whether as a sauce, a rarebit, or an accompaniment to fruit and nuts.

This soup is extremely delicious – one of those you taste and then just can't stop eating. This recipe is for a vegetarian version, but I also like to serve it with flakes of smoked haddock and a diced tomato (to remind you of the *Smoked Haddock with Welsh Rarebit*, page 163), or I add some cooked macaroni for a macaroni and cheese soup.

SERVES 4 AS AN APPETIZER

Butter
2 onions, finely chopped
2 potatoes, cut into rough ½ in (1 cm) dice
1 quart (1 liter) *Vegetable Stock* (page 36)
½ cups (125 ml) heavy cream (optional)
⅔ cup (150 g) mature Cheddar cheese (or more
    if you prefer an extra-cheesy flavor),
    finely grated
English or Dijon mustard (optional)
Salt and pepper

Melt a teaspoon of butter and cook the onions for a few minutes over a medium heat without browning. Add the diced potatoes and continue to cook, with a lid on the pan to create steam and to prevent the potatoes from browning. Cook for a few minutes. Add the vegetable stock and bring to a simmer. The soup can now be left to cook for 20–25 minutes until the vegetables are soft.

Purée and push through a sieve for a smooth consistency.

Place back over a medium heat, add the heavy cream, if using, and bring to a simmer. The grated cheese can now be added, stirring it in well. The cheese will thicken the soup, so it's best to grate and add only 4 oz (100 g) before checking the consistency and flavor. If you prefer it to be stronger in cheese taste, then grate and add more. It's important that the soup be brought only to a very low simmer, you boil it, the cheese will begin to separate. Season with salt and pepper and the soup is ready.

To heighten the flavor even more I like to add a touch of English or Dijon mustard, giving it an extra bite.

Variations

Here are a few alternatives to give the soup different flavors.

As mentioned in the introduction, cooking some macaroni to garnish the soup gives you a macaroni and cheese soup.

Diced cooked leeks also go very well combined with any of the variations.

Cook 4 oz (100 g) of natural smoked haddock in ½ cup (125 ml) of milk and a teaspoon of butter. The milk and butter can be added to the soup, replacing, or in addition to, the heavy cream. The cooked haddock can now be flaked and added, along with diced tomato and/or the diced leeks.

The Great British Omelette ⓥ

Omelettes have been known in Britain since the sixteenth century, and many centuries before that in France. The name derives from the Latin *lamella*, meaning "thin plate," and that's how the omelette was first cooked, almost in pancake fashion. In Britain it was first known as "amulet."

Making an omelette involves simply the setting of eggs with an added flavoring of your choice. It's not really a cooking process, more of a "warming" to thicken the egg, giving you a set, scrambled effect with a soft finish and no color.

SERVES 1

2–3 eggs (3 small or 2 large)
Butter
Salt and pepper, preferably black

It is very important to have a good non-stick, 6 in (15 cm) omelette pan.

Warm the pan on the stove. While the pan is heating, crack the eggs into a bowl and whisk with a fork. Do not season the eggs until the omelette is about to be made; if eggs are salted too early, they break down and become thin, runny, and slightly discolored, giving the omelette a dull look.

The omelette pan should now be hot enough to add a teaspoon of butter. As the butter melts and becomes bubbly, season the eggs and pour them into the pan. They will now take only 3–4 minutes to cook. To make sure they're light, keep the eggs moving by shaking the pan and stirring the eggs with a fork. This prevents them from sticking and browning. You will soon have a scrambled look to the eggs. Now cheese or any other flavoring can be added. Allow the eggs to set on the bottom for 5–10 seconds; the eggs will still be moist and not completely set in the center. Holding the pan at a downward angle, slide and tap the omelette toward the edge, folding it over as you do so.

This can now be turned out onto a plate and shaped under a cloth to give a half-moon shape. The omelette is now ready. It will have no color but be filled with an almost soufflé texture. This makes it a dream to eat, simply melting in your mouth.

Omelette Arnold Bennett ⓥ

This omelette has its own history. The famous novelist and theater critic, Arnold Bennett, was a frequent visitor to the Savoy Hotel Grill. In his great hotel novel *Imperial Palace*, published in 1930, Bennett based his fictional chef, Roho, on Jean-Baptiste Virlogeux, then *chef de cuisine* at the Savoy Grill. In tribute, Virlogeux created this omelette, and Bennett is said to have ordered it on every one of his visits to the restaurant. The dish has since been immortalized and has become a regular feature on the Savoy Grill menu and on many other restaurant menus, too.

It is simply a smoked haddock and cheese omelette. In the original recipe, the haddock was poached, flaked, and mixed with Parmesan cheese. The omelette was kept flat, sprinkled with the haddock, the cream poured on top, and then it was glazed under the broiler. The method hasn't changed too much since then, but chefs of today, myself included, take the classic idea and adapt it to suit their own style. My version is a basic three-egg omelette topped with flakes of haddock and then glazed with a cheese (Mornay) sauce flavored with English mustard. To help the glaze, add some hollandaise sauce which is extra work but worth every minute of it. You can make a quicker sauce to use by folding in an egg yolk together with lightly whipped cream. The glaze will still work.

Otherwise, the only difference is that I serve the omelette in the pan in which it was cooked. The pans being used are small, non-stick 4 · ¾–1¼ in (10 · 2–3 cm), or, alternatively, you can make 1 or 2 large omelettes using an 8 in (20 cm) pan and 6 eggs for each large omelette.

The Mornay sauce is a basic milk, flour- and butter-based sauce, with the addition of Cheddar cheese. I suggest you make this in a minimum amount of 1¼ cups (300 ml); any less and you will be chasing the sauce around the pan. After the recipe is made and before adding the cheese, measure the amount of cheese sauce required for this recipe. The remainder can be refrigerated for up to 1 week – for your next glazed omelette.

It's for this reason that I have listed 1¼ cups (300 ml) of milk to poach the haddock in. After the fish is poached, the milk can be strained and used to make the cheese sauce recipe following the basic method. This adds extra flavor; the slight smokiness in the milk transfers to the sauce.

After you've made and tasted this dish (and you can even have it for breakfast), you'll know why someone would want to order it on every visit to the Savoy. So here's my homage to both Arnold Bennett and Jean-Baptiste Virlogeux.

MAKES 1–4 OMELETTES

8–10 oz (225–300 g) smoked haddock fillet
    (2–3 oz/50–75 g per portion)
1¼ cups (300 ml) milk
Butter
⅔ cup (150 ml) *Cheese Sauce* (page 46),
    made with the haddock-poaching milk
2–3 tablespoons *Simple Hollandaise Sauce*
    (page 41) or 1 large egg yolk

5–6 tablespoons heavy cream, whipped
1–2 teaspoons English mustard
3 eggs per serving
Salt and pepper
1 tablespoon olive oil, mixed with a squeeze of
    lemon juice and seasoned to serve (optional)

Stage one is to poach the fish. Preheat the oven to 350°F/180°C. Grease an ovenproof dish or saucepan. Lay the smoked haddock fillet in the dish, with the skin left on, and cover with the milk, adding a teaspoon of butter. Cover with a lid and bring the haddock slowly to a low simmer. This can now be cooked in the oven for 4–5 minutes or very gently poached on top of the stove for just a few minutes. Remove from the heat. If the fish is particularly thick and has been protruding above the milk, turn the fillet over and let it stand for a further 2–3 minutes.

Lift the fish from the milk. The milk can be strained and used to make the cheese sauce.

While the cheese sauce is cooking, make the hollandaise (or use an egg yolk). When whipping the heavy cream, it's important not to whisk it past the thickening stage, but still light and creamy.

The fish can now be carefully flaked, saving any juices to add extra flavor to the sauce. The flakes will softly fall away from the skin, with a slight translucent center to each one. This will tell you just how moist they are.

After the cheese sauce is made, the English mustard can be added. Stir in 1 teaspoon and taste, before adding the other, if needed.

Before cracking the eggs to make the omelette, it's important that the sauce is ready to glaze. Fold 2 tablespoons of hollandaise sauce or the egg yolk, along with the whipped cream, into the warm cheese sauce. To test if it will glaze, place 2 teaspoons of sauce on a suitable baking sheet under a preheated broiler. The sauce should slightly rise under the heat and glaze with an all-round golden finish. If it appears to be taking too long and almost boiling before browning, stir in more of the hollandaise sauce and cream before re-testing.

Melt a small teaspoon of butter in an omelette pan. While melting on a medium heat, crack and whisk

3 eggs together well, creating an emulsion between the yolk and white. After the butter begins to bubble but hasn't reached the nut-brown stage, season the egg with a grinding of pepper and a pinch of salt. Now, it is time to pour the eggs into the bubbling butter. If the eggs are seasoned too early and left out in the air, the mixture becomes very thin and takes a slight discoloration. So, for a maximum bright-yellow finish, season just before cooking.

The eggs can now be gently stirred with a fork in the pan. Keep the pan moving so that the eggs will not actually set and become over-cooked. This stage is really just a scrambling. After they are thickened, but still slightly liquid and soft, in about 2–3 minutes, remove the pan from the heat. The smoked haddock flakes can be sprinkled on top. The bottom of the omelette will set and the eggs will continue to cook in the heat remaining in the pan.

Spoon the finished cheese sauce on top and finish under a hot broiler. Within 45 seconds–1 minute, a rich golden brown Omelette Arnold Bennett will be ready to serve. The olive oil and lemon juice can be mixed together, seasoned, and spooned over each omelette as it is finished.

This process can now be repeated to make the remaining omelettes.

Note: Two omelettes can always be made at the same time. But don't prepare more than two at once; they will over-cook because you won't have time to attend to each one.

The finished sauce, with the hollandaise and cream added, can be kept for a maximum 1–2 hours at room temperature covered with plastic wrap. After this time, the sauce tends to separate.

Scotch Eggs

It doesn't take much to work out where Scotch eggs originated. Becoming very much a part of English eating habits, they are a Scottish speciality. They were originally part of the Scottish breakfast, but they were also served hot at high tea with gravy. The British know them today as a pub snack, a picnic feature, or a cold buffet selection, usually displaying that unlovely gray border surrounding the center – as if the sausage has had an argument with the egg! The crumbs are often soggy as well.

But these can be quite delicious with a flavored, well-seasoned sausage and the eggs cooked perfectly, and I'm trying to give you the way to achieve that here. These Scotch eggs are delicious as a snack, a picnic, lunch, or supper dish, or with a mixed green salad, baked potato, and lots of homemade *Piccalilli* (page 385) or *homemade Salad Dressing* (page 48).

MAKES 4

4 eggs, boiled for 7 minutes (page 81), and refreshed under cold running water
Butter
1 shallot or ½ small onion, very finely chopped
Finely grated zest of 1 small lemon
Pinch of ground mace
2 teaspoons chopped fresh sage
8 oz (225 g) pork sausage
2 medium eggs, for coating
2 cups (100 g) dried white breadcrumbs, for coating
Peanut oil or sunflower oil, for deep-frying
Salt and pepper

Peel the shells from the eggs and keep the eggs to one side.

Melt a teaspoon of butter in a frying-pan. After it is bubbling over a medium heat, add the finely chopped shallot or onion. Cook for a few minutes without browning until softened. Remove from the heat and allow the mixture to cool. When it is cool, add the grated lemon zest, mace, and chopped sage. Add the cooked shallot/onion to the sausage and season with salt and pepper.

Divide into four and mold around the eggs, creating an even layer. This can be made easier by lightly flouring a sheet of plastic wrap. Place the sausage on top of the sheet and also lightly dust the sausage with flour. Top with another sheet of plastic wrap and roll out. This will ensure an even thickness. Remove the top layer of plastic wrap and place the egg on top of the sausage mixture. Lift and wrap it around the egg, and when the egg is covered,

remove the plastic wrap. If you dampen your hands to do this, you will achieve a perfectly smooth finish. Repeat the process to form the other three.

Beat the raw eggs. Pass the "balls" through the eggs and then roll in the crumbs. For an extra crispy finish, which I prefer, pass through the eggs and crumbs again. Refrigerate to relax and set the mixture.

When ready to cook, heat the oil to 350°F/180° and cook two eggs at a time. These will take 5–7 minutes to cook and become golden and crispy.

Remove and drain them on paper towels; then repeat the cooking process for the last two.

These can now be served immediately or served cold. Simply split in two before serving.

Variation: Whiskey Scotch Eggs

Follow the Scotch egg ingredients, omitting the lemon zest and sage. As the chopped onions cook and become softened, add 1–2 measures of Scotch whiskey. Bring to a boil and reduce until almost dry. Now, complete the dish using the Scotch Egg recipe.

A good sauce to serve with the whiskey eggs is to take ½ teaspoon of light brown sugar and bring to a simmer with ¼ cup (50 ml) whiskey. Reduce by half and cool. Mix with 4–6 tablespoons of mayonnaise and a teaspoon of English mustard. The whiskey dip is ready.

Note: The breadcrumbs can be mixed with half and half coarsely ground oatmeal for a stronger Scottish effect.

OPPOSITE
Scotch Eggs

Lobster Omelette "Thermidor"

This dish is certainly not British; in fact, it's very French. So why is it featured in this book? The reason is I would like this to become a British Classic of the future. After all, the best lobsters are found in Scottish waters, and the sauce is flavored with classic English mustard.

The basic idea has been taken from the French. The "real" thermidor consists of halved lobsters with their meat presented in the shell, then glazed with a cheese sauce flavored with English mustard and bound with a sauce Bercy, a basic fish and whitewine sauce flavored with shallots and parsley. An outstanding dish.

This, however, is a simple three-egg omelette with poached lobster meat scattered on top. It is then glazed with a rich cheese sauce – enhanced by the addition of English mustard and reduced lobster bisque (soup). The sauce, lifted and strengthened by the bisque, packs the palate with lobster flavors.

There might seem to be too many components to the dish, but this can all be made more simply. The hollandaise sauce to help the glaze can be replaced by an egg yolk whipped into the cream. The lobster bisque recipe is a large amount to make for an omelette, but if you're making the soup to serve as a part of a meal, then save some to freeze for future omelettes. If you prefer, you can buy a good-quality canned soup to use. Half a pan, boiled and reduced by a third to half (about ½ cup/100 ml), will give you the strength needed. An optional extra to finish the dish is the *Lobster Oil* (page 386).

The amounts of sauces in the ingredients are for a minimum of four servings.

The four omelette pans used are 4 in (10 cm) wide × ¾–1¼ in (2–3 cm) deep, as per *Omelette Arnold Bennett* (page 71). Two 8 in (20 cm) pans can be used instead (with 6 eggs per large omelette). Serve larger omelettes from the pans at the table.

SERVES 4

1 lb (450 g) cooked lobster (page 154)
Butter
3 eggs per serving

For the Sauce

⅔ cup (150 ml) *Lobster "Bisque" Soup* (page 23)
    or canned lobster bisque
1–2 teaspoons English mustard
⅔ cup (150 ml) *Cheese Sauce* (page 46)
2–3 tablespoons *Simple Hollandaise Sauce*
    (page 41) or 2–3 egg yolks
5–6 tablespoons heavy cream, lightly whipped
Salt and pepper
Lemon juice
Lobster or *Shellfish Oil* (page 386), to serve (optional)

The lobster meat is best kept "whole," leaving the shell and claws as taken from the shell in some of the cooking liquid until needed. This will keep them moist and succulent. When ready to use, simply cut into ½ in (1 cm) pieces, mixing with the lobster meat trimmings. The meat can be gently warmed in the liquid, when needed. It's important not to boil cooked lobster – this toughens the texture.

Bring the lobster bisque (homemade or canned) to a boil and allow to reduce by half. It will now have a thick consistency and a very strong flavor. Add the English mustard to the cheese sauce, a teaspoon at a time, along with adding the bisque a tablespoon at a time, giving a rich mustard and lobster flavor and color. If using hollandaise, add 2 tablespoons along with three-quarters of the whipped cream (if not using hollandaise, add the egg yolk).

The sauce can now be tested by pouring a tablespoon onto a suitable baking sheet and glazing under a hot broiler. Within 1 minute, the sauce should have taken on a rich golden finish. If not, add another tablespoon of hollandaise, along with the remaining whipped cream. Check the sauce for seasoning with salt, pepper, and a squeeze of lemon juice. The sauce will now keep for 1–2 hours at room temperature covered with plastic wrap.

To make the omelettes, melt a teaspoon of butter in the pan(s). Crack 3 eggs into a bowl and whisk them to a smooth emulsion of yolk and white.

After the butter is bubbling, but not at the nut-brown stage, season the eggs with salt and pepper. Pour the eggs in the butter and gently stir and move the pan over a medium heat.

The eggs should not be allowed to set on the bottom. They need a soft scrambling in the pan. After 2–3 minutes when barely beginning to set, remove the pan from the heat. The heat in the pan itself will seal the bottom, without browning the eggs. The omelette will have a soft bottom, rather than a golden brown, leathery finish. Now, sprinkle a portion of the warmed lobster on top, spoon the sauce over it, and glaze under a preheated broiler.

The Lobster Omelette "Thermidor" will now have a beautiful golden shine, just waiting to be eaten. After it's ready, sprinkle with a few drops of the lobster oil, if using.

Note: It's best, if making individual omelettes, not to make more than two at a time. Spoon the sauce on top and place to one side while the last two are made. After all have the sauce added, glaze all four under the broiler.

Eating these omelettes is a complete experience that, I promise you will never forget.

Crab meat and soup can also be used in this recipe instead of lobster. Shrimp will also work, making the sauce with a reduced lobster bisque soup to enhance their flavor.

See also

Boiled Eggs (page 81)
Cheese Sauce (Sauce Mornay) (page 46)
Classic Scrambled Eggs (page 79)
Curried Eggs (page 394)
Egg and Bacon Salad (page 114)
The British Fried Egg (page 79)
Gruyère Cheese, Leek, and Mushroom Flan
    (page 279)
Hollandaise Sauce (page 41)
Homemade Pancakes (page 82)
Mayonnaise (page 49)
Poached Eggs (page 82)
Simple Hollandaise Sauce (page 41)
Smoked Haddock with Welsh Rarebit
    (page 163)
Spicy Scrambled Eggs (page 81)
Yorkshire Pudding (page 237)

ABOVE
Lobster Omelette "Thermidor"

The Great British Breakfast

The classic breakfast is probably the most famous of all British "dishes" around the world. It has become a standard feature on almost every hotel breakfast menu to be found. To me, this is not surprising. The combination of ingredients work together so well – pork sausages, crispy bacon, mushrooms, tomatoes, black pudding, fried bread, all balanced with the soft creamy yolk of a fried egg – this meal has become a treat. But the breakfast offers so much more, with the famous cooked oatmeal, other grains, and stewed prunes all playing a big part.

The novelist Somerset Maugham once said that to eat well in Britain you had to eat breakfast three times a day. He must have been referring to the lavish spreads mentioned above, which were introduced by the Victorians. Before the Victorian era, the first meal of the day was usually a rather uninspired affair. Until late in the seventeenth century, the majority of people, rich and poor, rose at dawn and broke their night's fast – hence "break-fast" – with foods such as ale, soft cheese, and bread, or some ale and salted fish, or a soup made from the local grain. The custom still survives in the north, particularly in Scotland, where many think the only way to start the day properly is with a bowl of oat porridge. Robert Burns was very flattering about his national dish, calling it "the chief o' Scotia's food." The Englishman Dr Johnson was less enthusiastic, describing oats in his *Dictionary of the English Language* as "A grain which in England is generally given to horses, but in Scotland supports the people."

By the beginning of the eighteenth century, the upper and middle classes preferred a lighter breakfast and at a later hour; they ate spice-bread (plain bread dough enriched with spices or seeds), with one of the new drinks of the time – chocolate or coffee. By the end of the century, these classes were breakfasting on plain bread or on toast and butter and were drinking the third new drink to be introduced – tea. Already being served at other times of the day, tea became more economical to buy than coffee and chocolate. People began to drink it at other meals during the day (including, later, the entirely new and uniquely British ritual of afternoon tea). It had probably would have been served plain until then, but at this time, a little cream or milk was added to the teacup along with some sugar.

It was not until Edwardian and Victorian times that the British breakfast as it is known today became established. Since most people had only a snack or small meal in the middle of the day, a larger meal than before was thought necessary to keep them going until the dinner hour. It was Mrs Beeton herself who suggested that for "the comfortable meal called breakfast," her readers should offer a selection of cold meats and game, potted meats, brawn, and pies, along with hot fish dishes, chops, and steaks, kidneys, sausages, bacon and eggs, muffins, toast, marmalade, and butter. To one such lengthy breakfast menu listing, she added, "etcetera, etcetera..." I'm glad I wasn't the breakfast chef on duty for that menu!

It was at this time that "collops" of bacon and fried eggs – a rare treat for the working man – became a dish for the middle and upper classes. Now, too, eggs that were scrambled, poached, shirred (baked), coddled, and boiled became an important part of the breakfast table. Queen Victoria is supposed to have eaten one small boiled egg every day, a modest meal, but it was said the egg was then served with a golden egg-cup for her to eat with a golden spoon. Ancient and new foods were soon to appear on the breakfast menu, most of which are included in this collection of British classics. Black puddings, made since medieval times, were enjoyed mainly in the north. Kippers – smoked herrings – were broiled, buttered, jugged, or potted. Smoked haddock – Finnan haddie or Arbroath smokies – was poached in milk or flaked into rice for kedgeree.

The taste for hot foods introduced from the Indian subcontinent revealed itself in "deviled" foods, among them game, chicken legs, livers, and kidneys. Toast was spread with the relatively new preserve made of bitter Seville oranges – marmalade. Potted meats and fish were also popular. George Borrow, in his book *Wild Wales* (1862), describes a breakfast at the White Hart Inn: "Pot of hare: ditto of trout; pot of prepared shrimps: can of sardines; beautiful beefsteak; eggs, mutton, large loaf, and butter, not forgetting capital tea. There's a breakfast for you!" And curry itself made an appearance on many an ex-colonial's table. It is said that Merchant Navy seamen were once offered a different curry for breakfast every day of the week.

With such excess, the invention of "brunch" at the beginning of the twentieth century, when breakfast and lunch were brought together into one meal, must have appeared rather more sensible, at least to those watching their weight. "Brunch" is generally thought of as American, but it may well have originated at Oxford, where the students were notoriously late risers. A great meal for a weekend, brunch allows you to take your time and serve some British breakfast classics.

This section might not give you the lengthy variety of Mrs Beeton-style breakfast recipes, but what it does include are useful tips and hints to help you achieve the perfect breakfast.

The Great British Fried Egg ⓥ

One of the first ways people cooked eggs was by baking them whole in the ashes of the fire. Or they were fried in fat in a container of some sort, probably much as they are today. But what makes the perfect fried egg? Every book you read will give you a different recipe, some telling you just to use lard for frying, or peanut oil, bacon fat, butter, or a combination of oils. Some like their eggs sunny side up, others like them turned over – it's your choice.

Cooking a fried egg to perfection is actually scientific. If the oil or fat is not hot enough, the albumen in the egg white will not coagulate quickly enough, and, consequently, the white spreads, to cover the bottom of the pan. The egg is then almost poached or boiled in oil. If the fat is too hot, the egg coagulates too quickly, causing a very crisp bottom and edge while the rest is still too raw. Apparently the perfect temperature of oil for frying an egg is 225–280°F/124–138°C, which sounds great, but you aren't really going to use a thermometer to measure the temperature of the oil.

The following recipe contains butter, which will always give you better-flavored results.

1 large egg
1 tablespoon (15 g) of butter

A small pan works best. A non-stick 6 in (15 cm) omelette pan for one egg is ideal. This will give you a good depth of butter, not spreading it too thinly over the bottom. Heat the butter in the pan and bring to a bubbling stage. This is the important point. The "perfect" temperature will be found by not quite allowing the butter to reach a nut-brown stage. The temperature is then just right.

Another point to remember is to keep the egg in the shell until absolutely the last minute. Now, crack the egg into the pan and give it 30 seconds to set before basting with the butter. This will guarantee even cooking. Now, cook the egg to your taste and lift it out carefully with a spatula.

Classic Scrambled Eggs ⓥ

Eggs cooked in this basic method have been part of the British tradition since medieval times, when herbs were added to make "herbolaces" and "tansies." The eggs were whisked together, then "scrambled" in butter; they are still made in virtually the same way today.

After beating yolks and whites together, there's the option of adding liquid to the eggs, which will break down the coagulating mass, giving you a softer and moister finish. Milk, water, or cream can be used. But using water doesn't excite me, and cream will give you a too rich result, so milk is probably the best choice to suit everybody's tastebuds. The only problem is the amount. Too much liquid results in it separating from the eggs during and after cooking, leaving puddles of eggy "cream." The best proportion for each egg is a maximum of 1 tablespoon of liquid. For myself, I prefer to make a perfect scrambled egg with no additional ingredients (apart from salt and pepper).

2 large eggs, per person
Butter
Salt and pepper

Put a teaspoon of butter in a saucepan and let it bubble away, making sure it doesn't reach a nut-brown stage. Put the eggs in a bowl, season them, and beat well, then pour into the butter. Now, turn them with a wooden spoon, fairly vigorously, capturing every corner of the pan. When the eggs are starting to set and have a "lumpy" look but still soft, remove the pan from the stove. The eggs are best slightly under-done because they always continue to cook after they've been taken off the heat. The scrambled eggs are ready to serve.

Note: Something I am very strict about when cooking scrambled eggs or omelettes is the seasoning. It's not so much the quantities – a "pinch and a grinding" is plenty – but *when* it's added. Eggs should always be broken at the last minute. After the butter is bubbling in the pan and the eggs are broken and beaten, *now* is the time to season the eggs, and then immediately pour them into the bubbling butter. The reason has to do with the salt itself! Freshly beaten eggs have a wonderful thick and bright yellow color. If salt is added too early, the egg will become very thin and watery and at the same time lose their bright yellow color, exchanging it for a dull orange tinge, and the eggs won't be as light and fluffy in texture or color. So season at the last second.

Variations

Here are a few extras that can be added to scrambled eggs, creating completely new dishes.

They can simply be served on hot buttered toast or on bread toasted in a skillet. One variety of French toast is made by buttering bread and then frying it until golden on both sides, or broiling it, allowing the butter to melt through the bread. It's said that this traditional bread foundation for eggs is an echo of the medieval bread trencher, and is why the British – and it is only the British – eat things like baked beans or canned spaghetti on toast.

Smoked salmon goes beautifully with scrambled eggs, either as thin slices on top or cut in strips stirred in at the last minute. For an extra taste, just as the eggs are setting, add a spoonful of crème fraîche, giving you a lighter finish and at the same time a slightly sour cream taste. Sprinkling in chopped chives also tastes good.

Try fresh oysters lightly poached and placed on top, along with sour cream.

Add Parmesan cheese and sliced scallions that have been cooked in butter before adding the eggs.

Caviar with sour cream and toast.

The ultimate: a slice of pan-fried *foie gras* placed on top of the eggs.

OPPOSITE
Full English Breakfast with
Sautéd Potatoes (page 121)

Spicy Scrambled Eggs Ⓥ

These spiced eggs hold a lot of the flavors the British learned about and loved during the years of the Raj in India, and they are wonderful as an appetizer or a snack.

SERVES 1–2

½ heaping teaspoon crushed garlic
½ heaping teaspoon crushed fresh ginger
Unsalted butter
1 tablespoon finely chopped onion
½ teaspoon chopped fresh red chili
½ teaspoon ground turmeric
1 tomato, seeded and diced
3 eggs, beaten
Salt and pepper
½ teaspoon chopped cilantro (optional)

Pound the garlic and ginger together to a paste. Heat a frying-pan and add a teaspoon of butter. After the butter is bubbling, add the garlic and ginger paste, the chopped onion, chili, turmeric, and tomato. Cook for a few minutes until lightly softened. Add the beaten eggs and stir over the heat until the eggs have softly scrambled. Taste and season with salt and pepper, if necessary, stir in the chopped cilantro, if using, and serve.

Boiled Eggs Ⓥ

Eggs have been served boiled since very early times, and were once a basic food, eaten out of hand or cut up and added to salads. They became popular as a breakfast food in Victorian times. They are very easy to do, but if you take note of the following methods, I can guarantee you better results.

How long one boils an egg is really up to the individual. A very, very soft-boiled egg (rare) will take only 2½ minutes. A medium-rare (very soft) will take 3½ minutes. And what I think most people prefer, a medium egg, with that just-soft yolk, will take 4 minutes. But what's the secret?

First, it's to have your eggs at room temperature. A cold egg cooked straight from the refrigerator will have such a change in pressure that it will crack. This then releases some albumen (the egg white), which creates uneven cooking. Water that is boiling will also create turbulence, jiggling the eggs around so that they could easily bump into one another and crack.

For Soft-boiled Eggs

The easiest way to soft boil eggs is to bring your saucepan of water to a gentle simmer. Using a tablespoon, carefully lower the egg or eggs into the water. After the water has returned to the simmering point, cook for 2½–4 minutes – rare to medium.

Or you can place the eggs in a saucepan of cold water, bring to a fast simmer, and then lift the pan from the heat. Place a lid on the pot and leave the egg standing in the hot water for 3–4 minutes (a minute longer for very large eggs). The egg is now ready to enjoy (with toast).

Alternately you can carefully place the egg in simmering water and cook for 1 minute. Remove from the stove and complete as for the cold water method, leaving it standing in the pot covered with a lid.

For Hard-boiled Eggs

In many recipes you're told to boil the eggs for 10–12 minutes. Surely that can leave nothing but a very dry, crumbly yolk with that "delicious-looking" black border between yolk and white! The best way to hard-boil eggs is to place them in a saucepan of boiling water and bring to a fast simmer. Cook for 7–8 minutes and then remove the eggs, running them under cold water for 1–2 minutes to calm the cooking. Now, let them cool to room temperature. After they are cooled, peel and cut one of them to see if the egg is totally cooked but with a slightly soft and moist center.

Poached Eggs ⓥ

Eggs have always been important in British cooking and eating, and poaching them would have been an early technique. You'll find a few poached eggs uses throughout the book. There's something about the consistency of poached eggs that makes a wonderful dish – the warm soft yolk spilling out and mixing with and enriching other flavors is enticing.

I'm using a cooking liquid that is two-thirds water to one-third cider or white-wine vinegar. This may sound expensive, but vinegar costs very little, and the

results are worth every penny. The vinegar doesn't affect the flavor of the eggs, but what it does is make the white set instantly around the yolk, creating a neater poached egg. If you are concerned about the quantity of vinegar, then simply add only a few tablespoons; the complete, round poached egg will probably not be achieved, but the egg will still poach.

> 4 eggs
> Water
> White-wine or cider vinegar

Fill a saucepan with two-thirds water and a third vinegar. Don't add salt because this tends to break down the egg-white consistency. Bring the water and vinegar mixture to a boil and stir. Now, crack one egg at a time into the center of the liquid and poach for 3–3½ minutes. The eggs are then ready to serve, or they can be poached in advance and plunged into iced water immediately.

Trim off any untidy whites to give you the perfect poached egg. To re-heat, simply plunge into boiling water for 1 minute.

The eggs are now hot and ready to serve.

Homemade Pancakes ⓥ

Pancakes were among the very early enriched breads cooked on the griddle, and they have become one of our favorite for breakfast and afternoon teas. They have a long-standing association with Shrove Tuesday, otherwise known as Pancake Day, which is when all the eggs must be used up before Lent.

Pancakes are a Sunday treat in my home, with my sons and me whisking away to make the batter. And then I cook the pancakes while they eat them: I'm making a mistake somewhere! But they are so easy to make and simply delicious with a pancake syrup poured on top. They could also be served with honey, jam, or ice cream. For a savory dish, they can be filled with ratatouille, fish stew, mussels, chicken, and so on.

This recipe will make 16–24 pancakes, depending on the size of pan used. It's best to use a 8 in (20 cm) or 6 in (15 cm) frying-pan.

MAKES 16–24 PANCAKES

2 cups (225 g) all-purpose flour
Pinch of salt
2 eggs
2½ cups (600 ml) milk
4 tablespoons (50 g) unsalted butter, melted
Vegetable oil, for frying

Sift the flour and salt into a bowl. Whisk the eggs and the milk into the flour. Add the melted butter and whisk. At this stage, the mixture can be used for sweet or savory pancakes.

For a savory flavor, chopped fresh parsley or mixed herbs can also be added.

To cook the pancakes, preheat the frying-pan. Lightly oil the pan and pour in some of the pancake batter, making sure the pan has only a thin layer of mixture by tilting and rotating the pan to make it spread out.

Cook for 30–40 seconds, until golden brown. Turn the pancake over and cook for a further 20–30 seconds.

The pancake is now cooked. Keep warm between squares of waxed paper while you cook the remainder. Two or three pancakes per person should be plenty.

If made well in advance, the pancakes can be microwaved for 30–40 seconds to re-heat.

Breakfast Tomatoes Ⓥ

A breakfast "extra" that we all enjoy. Broiled tomatoes garnish a breakfast plate so beautifully, giving more color, texture, and, of course, flavor. I'm not certain when tomatoes found their way onto the British breakfast menu, but it was probably in the early twentieth century. After many hours of research, the only tomato addition I found was in Mrs Beeton's *Household Management*, in a recipe for tomato sausage made from a large quantity of tomato purée, cooked rice, breadcrumbs, chopped onion, and mixed herbs, all filled into skins and pan-fried. I don't think I'm going to try that recipe. So here's an alternate idea or two.

SERVES 4

4 plum or small round tomatoes
Dribble of olive oil

2 tablespoons (25 g) butter
Small sprinkling of coarse sea salt
Freshly ground black pepper

The tomatoes can be either pan-fried or broiled. Whichever method you choose, core the tomatoes by inserting the point of a small knife to the stem end and then turning and twisting the tomato while the knife cuts, angled towards the center; the core will simply fall out.

If using plum tomatoes (which will hold their shape better when they are cooked than standard tomatoes), then cut lengthwise to give two halves. Cut round tomatoes through the middle.

To Broil

Place the tomatoes, skin-side down, on a greased baking sheet. Divide the butter among the tomatoes, placing less than a teaspoon on top of each. Dribble all with a drop or two of olive oil and season very lightly with salt and a grinding of pepper. Place them under a hot broiler and cook to a golden finish. This should take no longer than 5–7 minutes, depending on the size of the tomatoes. After they have cooked, arrange on the breakfast plates, pouring any juices released from the tomatoes on top.

To Pan-fry

Heat a tablespoon or two of olive oil in a large frying-pan with. Season the tomatoes with the sea salt and pepper. After the pan is hot, place the tomatoes in it, flesh-side down. It is important not to shake the pan so that the juices aren't released from the tomatoes, causing them to boil and stew rather than fry. After 2–3 minutes, check the color of the tomatoes. They should have begun to soften and turn golden brown. At this point, add the butter to the pan. The butter will begin to bubble. Allow it to reach its nut-brown stage before turning the tomatoes over. They can now be cooked for a further 2–3 minutes, basting with the nutty butter and olive oil. The tomatoes are ready to serve, pouring excess liquid on top.

Breakfast Mushrooms ⓥ

Mushrooms became part of the breakfast menu a little earlier than tomatoes. They weren't often served on their own at breakfast but more often as part of a fish dish, such as a pie.

I serve whole button, cremini, or portobello mushrooms for breakfast. Portobello mushrooms can be either sliced ¼–½ in (5 mm–1 cm) thick if frying or left whole and broiled.

Portobello Mushrooms

SERVES 4

4 large portobello mushrooms
25 g (1oz) butter, melted, or 2 tablespoons olive oil
Salt and pepper

I don't like to wash any mushrooms (apart from wild) because I always feel that I am washing away flavor and at the same time filling the vegetable with water. It's best to simply wipe them clean with a damp cloth and trim off any excess stems. For broiling, place the mushrooms, top-down, on a buttered baking sheet. Divide the butter among them, brushing each mushroom. Season with salt and pepper. The mushrooms can now be cooked under a hot broiler. They will take 6–8 minutes to cook, depending on their thickness.

To shallow fry, heat a large frying-pan and add the olive oil. Add the mushrooms and allow to cook for 1–2 minutes before turning them in the pan. Season with salt and pepper and continue to cook for a few minutes until tender.

Large portobello mushrooms can also be cut into thick slices before frying.

Button and Cremini Mushrooms

10 oz (300 g) button or cremini mushrooms, stems trimmed and wiped clean
2 tablespoons olive oil
4 tablespoons (50 g) butter
Salt and pepper

Mushrooms always tend to soak up the fat used for frying. For this recipe, the butter has been doubled to account for the soaking.

Heat a large frying-pan with the olive oil. With the oil at the point of smoking, add the mushrooms. These can now be seasoned with salt and pepper and left for a few minutes before turning them in the pan. Continue to cook, adding the butter. As the butter heats, it will turn to a nutty brown color and flavor, heightening the taste of the mushroom. The mushrooms should take 6–8 minutes to fry and become tender. Large button mushrooms will take 10–12 minutes.

If you are worried about the fat content, then here's a way to almost dry-fry/roast, using a minimum of fat. Simply heat a teaspoon of oil in a frying-pan, roasting pan or broiler pan. Add the mushrooms and cook over a moderate heat, turning from time to time. As they cook, they will become browned with small burned tinges. This gives a great bitter edge to the finished flavor.

Mushrooms tend to take longer to cook by the dry-fry/roast method, approximately 8–10 minutes for small and 12–15 for large. They can also be roasted in a hot oven at 425°F/220°C for about 12–15 minutes. Season with salt and pepper and serve.

Breakfast Bacon

In early recipes for bacon and eggs going back to the sixteenth century, the instructions were to take the whitest and youngest bacon and cut it into thin slices. These slices were placed in a dish, hot water was poured over them, and they were left to stand for an hour or two, thus taking away the extreme saltiness. The next stage would be to thread them on a long metal skewer and hold them to the heat of the fire to toast them. Today cooking bacon doesn't need all that preparation. If you want to boil a slab of bacon or ham, however, it needs to be pre-soaked.

The bacon slices that are common for breakfast are streaked with lean, giving you the best of both worlds. Canadian bacon can be bought smoked or unsmoked; the difference can be found in the "aroma." Smoking always give the flesh a rich pink color, with the rind taking on a golden-edged orange. The unsmoked Canadian bacon, is a lot paler, with its rind more of an "off-white." The flavor is up to you. Smoked bacon is richer and stronger as well as saltier.

The unsmoked will have a "leaner," less salty flavor, but still be very "bacony."

Slab bacon can be bought with its rind on or off, and thinly or thickly sliced. If you are buying bacon with rind on, it's always best to trim this away before cooking for easier serving. To achieve really crispy bacon, slicing it thinly will give you the best results.

Strips of bacon, use 2–3 slices per serving.

To Broil

Broil the bacon slices under a preheated hot broiler for 2–3 minutes on each side, a little longer for extra crispness.

To Pan-fry

Heat a dry frying-pan. The bacon can now be cooked over a medium heat; this will draw the fat from the strips, leaving crispy bacon. Frying will also take 2–4 minutes on each side, depending on the crispness required. After it has cooked, lift the bacon from the pan, leaving any excess fat. The strips can now be kept warm in a preheated oven. This will also help crisp the bacon.

The fat in the pan can now be used for frying bread (*Fried Bread*, below). The taste of bacon on the bread is delicious. And if you're not using the fat for bread, then you can pan-fry mushrooms in it.

Fried Bread ⓥ

The British passion for crisp fried bread must be a holdover from the days when we ate our meals from trenchers of bread before plates were used. I think fried bread is a must for a "modern" English breakfast.

Any bread can be used for frying, from either thin, medium, or thick-sliced, and the bread can be any flavored with a soft or crusty texture. The bread will fry at its best if it is about 48 hours old. If it is too fresh, it will soak up far too much fat and be far too greasy. Simply make sure that the frying-pan has barely enough fat to cover the bottom. The bread slices can then be pan-fried until golden brown before turning and completing the frying. If the pan becomes dry, simply add a trickle more fat.

Fried bread will take 2–3 minutes on each side.

If it is cooked too quickly, the bread becomes burned on the edges and turns a very patchy color. About 2–3 minutes on each side will give you a crisp, evenly browned slice. A teaspoon of butter can also be added after the slice is turned for a nutty flavor to finish.

For the ultimate fried bread, shallow-fry the bacon first, not too quickly, but with barely enough heat to draw excess fat from the strips, leaving you with very crisp bacon and a pool of bacon fat for cooking the bread. The flavor is immense. Simply follow the same method as frying in oil, adding a teaspoon of butter after you turn the slices. You now have crisp bacon-flavored fried bread – a pleasure to eat.

Classic Cooked Cereal ⓥ

Oats probably arrived in Britain mixed in with other seeds brought by immigrants. They grew very easily in more northerly, colder, and wetter parts of the country where few other cereals would survive. Oats became – and remain – a major crop in the north of England, in Ireland, and in Scotland, and oatmeal porridge – cooked cereal – still survives, as do a number of other oat dishes.

Cooked cereal is eaten all over Scotland and in many other parts of the world. Traditional cooking of oatmeal for cereal involved boiling the water and then sprinkling in the oats with your left hand while you stirred, clockwise, with your right. And it wasn't a spoon you would be stirring with; it was always a straight wooden stick. Some people would add the oats in stages to create different textures, leaving "crunchy bits" in the finished dish. The pot would slowly simmer away for 30–40 minutes before it was ready. The pinch of salt would be added toward the end of cooking in order not to toughen the oats.

Cooked cereal was often served with cold milk or cream, which you dipped your spoon into before every mouthful of cereal. Traditionally, many a Scotsman would have a glass of beer to go with it.

Oats are probably the most nutritious of all cereal grains, being very rich in oils. Rolled oats are the main form of oats sold in supermarkets. These will take a maximum of 10 minutes to cook, sometimes as little as 6–7 minutes. Most varieties of oats come with the

ABOVE
Fried Bread (page 85)

cooking instructions printed on the container, usually ½ cup (50 g) of oats per 1¼ cups (300 ml) of milk. (Notice I say milk. Traditionally, cereal is cooked with all water.) Full-milk cooked cereal will be quite rich, but can be thinned by using half water and half milk, for a milder flavor.

Now, cream, brown or white sugar, honey, syrup, jam, or marmalade can all be passed to spoon on top.

SERVES 2, GENEROUSLY

2½ cups (600 ml) water
⅔ cup (60 g) porridge oats
Pinch of salt

To Serve

Cold milk or cream
Sugar

Bring the water to a boil, preferably in a non-stick pan. Sprinkle in the oats while stirring or whisking, making sure to stir any from the corners of the saucepan. After all the oats have been added to the water, continue to whisk/stir until the water has returned to a boil. Cover the pan with a lid and reduce the heat to a slow simmer. The cereal can now cook for 25–30 minutes until completely tender. Add a pinch of salt and the classic porridge is ready. Cream, milk, and sugar can be passed separately to sprinkle in to taste.

Note: To make sure the oats will not burn when returned to a boil, you can transfer the mixture to a double boiler, cover it, and place over simmering water. This will take about 30 minutes to cook.

Wayne's Cereal ⓥ

This second cooked cereal recipe was given to me by a fellow chef and friend, Wayne Tapsfield. He often makes this for the kitchen staff during the winter months, and it's now become a favorite. The recipe breaks every tradition, but gives loads of flavor.

SERVES 4–6

2 cups (225 g) cooked oatmeal
2½ cups (600 ml) milk
1¼ cups (300 ml) water (the water can be doubled
    and milk halved for a milder finish)
⅓ cup (50 g) superfine or light soft brown sugar
Pinch of salt
½ cup (100 ml) evaporated milk
½ cup (100 ml) heavy cream
    (light for a less rich finish)
1–2 tablespoons golden syrup, to serve

Bring the milk and water to a boil. Pour in the oats, whisking continuously. When the mixture comes back to a boil, add the sugar and salt, reducing the heat to a slow simmer and stirring occasionally. After 8–10 minutes, add the evaporated milk and heavy cream. Continue to cook gently to warm the milk and cream for the final 2 minutes.

Remove from the heat and add the golden syrup to taste. The super rich cereal is ready to enjoy. This cooked cereal really is worth a try and since it is delicious to eat. (Wayne tells me he sometimes finishes it with grated nutmeg, clotted cream, and butter. I just didn't have the nerve to include them.)

Broiled Kippers

In the mid eighteenth century a mild smoked cure for herring was introduced in Yarmouth, which involved the whole herring being smoked. Because the fish were only half-dried before being smoked over an oak fire, they remained plump and puffed out, for which reason they were called bloaters. They're still considered a delicacy today.

Some years after this, in the late nineteenth century, another smoke cure for herring was found. It was invented on the Northumberland coast by a Mr Woodger, who got the idea from an old system of curing salmon called kippering. Herrings were so cheap and plentiful then that another means of preserving them was very welcome. Before this, herring had been eaten fresh, salted, or salted and dry-smoked; in this last form they were the means of survival of thousands of families throughout the centuries. They were soaked overnight and then boiled and served with potatoes, the potatoes removing the excessive saltiness. As the years passed, extremely salty flavors became less popular so many of the fishing ports around the coasts of Scotland and England worked on milder cures for herring. Today the best kippers – smoked herring – come from Loch Fyne in Scotland and still use Mr Woodger's method of smoke curing.

The fish are split down the back before salting and then smoked over oak chips. A short soaking in strong salt brine is used to form a sticky solution of protein on the herring flesh, which then dries during the smoking process to give that rich, deep shine. As the years passed, the curing became lighter, keeping the fish plumper but at the same time making them more anemic in color. As a result, most kippers today are dyed during the curing process. There are, however, still some undyed kippers to be found, mostly in Scotland and the Isle of Man.

Kippers can be bought on or off the bone. With bone-in fish, always cut away the head and tail with scissors before cooking.

1 kipper per person
Butter

To Serve

Lemon wedges
Brown bread and butter

Using a sheet of buttered foil guarantees that a strong kipper smell is not left on your broiler pan. Place the kipper, flesh-side up, on the foil and put it on the broiler pan. Top the kipper with a teaspoon of butter. Place under a preheated broiler and cook for 4–5 minutes until the butter is bubbling. The kipper is now ready to be enjoyed. Remove from the broiler. Pull away the central bone and place the kipper on the serving plate. Pour any butter and juices left on the foil over the fish.

Serve with a wedge of lemon plus brown bread and butter to mop up the juices.

Note: Kippers also go very well with poached or scrambled eggs.
If you feel that kippers are too salty, before broiling simply place them head first in a pitcher and pour boiling water over them. Leave for 2–3 minutes before pouring off the water.

Smoked Haddock

Haddock is a smaller member of the cod family. When bought fresh, it's mostly found whole, filleted, or cut into haddock steaks. The reputation that has grown worldwide over the years concerns the smoked versions, and smoked haddock is one of the finest British breakfast ingredients. Naturally smoked haddock fillets, which I much prefer to the yellow-dyed versions (many of which are chemically flavored to create the smoky taste), have even been accepted in France as a great speciality. The French name for haddock is *aiglefin*, but over the years the smoked fish has become known as "haddock." So if you have ever seen this listed on a French menu, it means smoked, not fresh.

In the eighteenth century, Finnan haddies, named after the village of Findon in Aberdeenshire, were haddock beheaded, split, and smoked over seaweed or peat and sphagnum moss. The result was quite hard, dry, and black. When the peat ran out, oak chips were introduced, and the fish took on and maintained, their beautiful golden lemon color. They are cold smoked, and have a more subtle flavor than the smokies.

Arbroath smokies are unique, small fish which are beheaded and gutted but left whole, hung in pairs high on wooden spits or over whisky barrels, then dry salted and hot-smoked in pairs over oak or silver birch chips. It is said they originated in the early nineteenth century when fishermen from Auchmithie moved to Arbroath, taking with them their practice of hanging fish inside the chimneys to smoke. The commercial possibilities were spotted very quickly by the locals, and Arbroath smokies were born. They have since become one of the most respected smoked fish worldwide. The skin has a lovely rich, copper color which, after it is removed, reveals a golden crust working into a much paler flesh. The fish has a very savory flavor and a creamy texture.

Smoked haddock fillets are wonderful simply lightly poached in milk and butter and served with buttered toast for breakfast. I don't think that anything else is needed, apart from perhaps a poached egg. For any other meal there's plenty that can be added – a spinach and cheese sauce, eggs in an *Omelette Arnold Bennett* (page 71), or a tomato salad with *Welsh Rarebit* (page 178).

Finnan Haddie

For a classic *Cullen Skink* soup (page 27), Finnan haddie should be used, bones and all, to get the maximum flavor from the fish. After the fish has cooked in the soup, all the skin and bones are removed, and the flesh is flaked and returned to the liquid. The *Cullen Skink* then has a very delicate and detailed flavor, something a straightforward smoked fillet cannot match.

To cook Finnan haddie, simply place it in a dish in the oven preheated to 325°F/160°C, with milk and lots of butter. This will then create a steam, softening the flesh. Serve with the bones removed and some of the rich cooking liquid poured on top.

Arbroath Smokie

Split the fish and place some butter with a grinding of pepper in the center. Close the fillets. Brush the outside skin with butter as well and warm the fish under a preheated broiler or in a low oven (325°F/160°C). The smokie doesn't need to be cooked because its complete smoking has already done this, so it's simply a warming process. After it is warmed, remove the skin, open the fish, and then pull away the bones. If it becomes too cold, lightly warm again, pour the butter on top and serve.

Arbroath Smokie and Cream Cheese Pâté

Pastes of fish or meat were once made as a means of preservation, and these were very popular at breakfast. This pâté is rather more sophisticated, good for an appetizer, for a snack or savory, or in sandwiches for tea – or, of course, for breakfast.

SERVES 4–6

1 pair of Arbroath smokies, boned and skinned
Juice of ½ lemon
Pinch of cayenne pepper
8 oz (250 g) cream cheese
¼ cup (50 ml) light cream
¼–½ teaspoon Dijon or English mustard
1 tablespoon chopped fresh chives (optional)
Salt and pepper

The smokies must first be puréed in a food processor along with the lemon juice and cayenne pepper. Add the cream cheese, light cream, and mustard and process to a smooth paste. Check for seasoning. While at this soft stage, the chopped chives, if using, can be stirred in.

The pâté can now be spooned into a suitable dish and refrigerated for at least 1 hour to set. A little melted butter can be poured over the dish to prevent a skin from forming. This pâté goes very well with thick, hot, crisp toast.

Stewed Prunes ⓥ

At the beginning of this century, the health and daily diet of children – and of adults – was considered very seriously. In winter, children would be encouraged to have some cooked cereal for breakfast followed by stewed fruit; in summer they might start with some fresh fruit, followed by one of the then new cereals introduced from America, pioneered by a man named Kellogg. Stewed prunes were considered particularly valuable, and it was at this time – perhaps to encourage reluctant small eaters? – that chant originated "Tinker, Tailor, Soldier, Sailor," counting out the pits along the edge of the bowl.

Until the nineteenth century, prunes were more popular in Britain than plums. The best prunes today come from Agen in France and from California. The French believe the U.S. prunes can't beat theirs because their methods of drying the plum would be hard to match.

Soak the prunes before use – for flavor, the best soaking medium is tea – and do so overnight. In this recipe, the sugar can be omitted; without it, however, the natural sugars from the prunes will be drawn into the soaking liquid.

2 cups (500 ml) water
2 tea-bags
8 oz (225 g) prunes
¼ cup (50 g) sugar

Bring the water to a boil and pour onto the tea-bags in a suitable bowl. Add the prunes. Stir in the sugar, cover and let them stand for several hours, preferably overnight. Remove the tea-bags and the prunes are ready to serve.

Note: The bags can be left in just for a few hours and then removed. This will prevent the tea flavor from becoming too strong. The sugar can be stirred in, if needed, after the prunes have been soaked.

See also

Deviled Kidneys (page 178)
Orange Marmalade (page 390)
Strawberry Jam (page 387)
Smoked Eel Kedgeree (page 162)

Vegetables and Salads

One of the pleasures of cooking fresh vegetables is having so much natural flavor just waiting to be enjoyed. One of the most criticized aspects of British, however, food has been our general treatment of vegetables – it's said that we undervalue and over-cook them. This may have been the norm in the past but it's certainly not so now, nor was it so, perhaps surprisingly, in the more distant past, when vegetables received the respect they deserved.

Wild vegetables, herbs, seeds, and leafy greens would probably have been the most important element, apart from the occasional meat kill, of prehistoric man's diet. After cooking vessels were introduced and after the Romans brought in several new vegetable varieties, both wild and cultivated vegetables would have been used in the vegetable soup-pottages which were so important in the diet of poor and rich alike from very early times up to the eighteenth century. Some favorites used were early types of onions, leeks, turnips, carrots, peas, fava beans, and cabbage. Possibly this close relationship among the vegetables and an over-cooked soupy consistency contributes to the bad reputation of the British treatment of vegetables. For many centuries in Britain, vegetables were not seen as something to eat fresh but as inevitable additions to dishes such as stews which were always cooked for hours in large amounts of water.

Another factor would have been the long association of vegetables, herbs, and leaves with medicine. Also, the agricultural year itself would have contributed to the public's view of vegetables. In the summer there would be plenty to eat, followed by feasting after the harves, and then the lean months of winter. Winters would be dominated by salted meats and dried legumes; then spring would bring fresh green leaves again. Even today in the north of England, it is believed that easterledge (a plant with tannin-sour leaves used to counter smallpox and snake bites in medieval times), dandelion, and nettle leaves should be eaten in spring to cleanse the body after the heavy food of winter. Growers of watercress say that, despite the fact that it is available year-round, it is most in demand in the early spring of the year.

The great explorations of the sixteenth century introduced many new varieties of vegetables to Europe and eventually to Britain. Among them were potatoes, tomatoes, beans (kidney, French, haricot, and green beans), peppers, chilies, and pumpkin. Continual trials by Continental gardeners, particularly the Italians,

French, and Dutch, resulted in the improvement of many wild varieties of vegetables, among them celery (developed from the wild smallage), cauliflower, Jerusalem artichoke, and spinach. The wealthy started to spend lavishly on their gardens and farms, and they would grow a huge variety of vegetables for their tables. Market gardens, too, began to spring up around larger towns and cities. Those around London, at Wanstead and Blackheath, were fertilized by London "night soil." In the mid-seventeenth century, the main vegetable market in London, beside St Paul's, was moved to the roomier garden and orchard of the convent of St Peter in Westminster, a venue that became the famous old Covent Garden market (now located at Nine Elms).

Many English cookbooks, which began appearing in the sixteenth and seventeenth centuries, list all the new vegetables then available, and carefully detail how these vegetables should be cooked and sauced. Not long after, vegetables began to be thought of as "Vegetables," a distinct category of food to be eaten in its own right, and with respect. At this time many of the classic British combinations, such as boiled beef with carrots and duck with green peas, became common. But there was still a general tendency to boil vegetables for far too long. The people of the time did, however, get the simple accompaniment right – melted butter rather than the infamous "heavy" English butter sauce. And because meat had established itself as the most desirable type of food, particularly in the towns, vegetables rarely found their way onto menus. After the Industrial Revolution, vegetables were associated in many minds with poverty, and this may be another reason why so few memorable vegetable cooking techniques and dishes developed in Britain.

The goal of the recipes featured here emphasize the natural flavors of the vegetables themselves and to give you the right perfect cooking times to achieve the best results. Whenever you cook vegetables, acknowledge what they will be accompanying. For a

PAGE 90
Roasted Parsnips (page 95)

poached/steamed piece of fish, it's better to cook the vegetables until barely tender than have them fighting against the softness of the fish.

After the Victorian idea of vegetables being "good for you" – a saying still used in most households – in the last two decades we seem to have rediscovered the joys of vegetables. There is a certain sense of this being the reverse as far as salads are concerned, though. We may have cooked vegetables to death in the past, but we have eaten leaves and herbs raw since at least the fourteenth century – and usually dressed with oil and vinegar. In many early books, salad plants are listed which later disappeared from sight until the last few decades. Corn salad or *mâche* and arugula, for instance, were grown and enjoyed in salads as long ago as the sixteenth century. Many of these simple green salads were eaten for health, but they developed over the centuries into compound "grand salads," similar to those we associate now with America. These would often include fresh greens, cooked vegetables, meat, fish, hard-boiled eggs, nuts, raisins, and citrus fruit, a mixture that became known as, variously, Salamagundy, Solomon Grundy, or Salmagundi. One of the beauties of salad-making is having an almost unlimited choice of ingredients, whether creating a simple leaf salad or a great salmagundi.

A salad can appear at almost any meal, and in almost any course – as an appetizer, a main dish, and even to replace a dessert. It is possibly most associated with appetizers because the Romans believed the milky juices of lettuce leaves lined the stomach, enabling them to drink more with their meals. But a salad can also be served as a simple accompaniment or side dish. Salads are a perfect excuse to use your culinary license, to express your personality, but you must always remember not to over-flavor. This could hade the beautiful fresh flavors of the leaves themselves. Various salads and dressings are featured in this book for you to choose from, but sometimes for me, a trickle of good olive oil and a squeeze of lemon juice are enough to please the palate.

First of all, here is a list of salad ingredients, followed overleaf by a selection of salad greens.

Artichokes – bottoms or hearts
Asparagus – peeled and blanched
Broccoli florets – blanched
Capers – left whole or chopped
Carrots – thinly sliced, shredded, or grated
Celery – trimmed and sliced
Chilies – finely chopped or thinly sliced
Cucumber – preferably peeled and seeded
Eggs – hard-boiled or poached
Fava beans – blanched and peeled
Fennel – raw and thinly sliced
Fine French beans – blanched
Fresh picked herbs – flat parsley, basil,
    tarragon, mint, cilantro, etc.
Garlic – used in dressings or roasted
New potatoes – cooked and sliced
Olives – black or green, pitted
Red onions – thinly sliced
Sesame seeds – toasted
Scallions – chopped or thinly sliced
Shallots – thinly sliced into rings
Snow peas – blanched
Sweet bell peppers – red, green, or yellow
Tomatoes – plum, round, or cherry
Walnuts, hazelnuts, almonds – shelled

And there are plenty more. Often, simply salad greens and dressing together are enough without other additions.

When shopping for salad greens, try using *mesclun*. This is not an actual lettuce but, instead, a name for a mixture of young tender greens, usually consisting of baby spinach, lamb's lettuce, arugula, or *mizuna* and small curly endive leaves from the heart.

Always choose good crisp leaves, not bruised ones. To store them and to keep them in the best possible condition, store them in a plastic bag, refrigerated. This will help maintain their natural crispness. If the greens become slightly limp, simply refresh in ice water, carefully shaking away the excess. Always pick and tear the leaves by hand – a knife will bruise the leaves. Here's a list of salad greens, with their descriptions.

Arugula – Often called *arugula* or *roquette*. The long thin stem and leaves vaguely resemble dandelion greens. It has a peppery, bitter flavor, sometimes almost too bitter. It is, however, an attractive leaf to use in almost any salad or as a garnish.

Butterhead – An open, light, loose-leafed lettuce.

Curly endive – Curly leaved endive has become very fashionable – but it's a trend that will last. As the leaves grow, they become less bitter, giving a more comforting flavor. Choose one with a yellow heart; these leaves have a better flavor than the very crinkly, deep green leaves.

Dandelion – Known as *piss-en-lit* in France, its thin long leaves range from a yellow/white to almost deep green. Similar flavor to arugula, but it must be picked young.

Escarole – Similar in flavor to curly endive and not too different in appearance. Rather than the complete curly look, escarole has more of a gathered crinkly look.

Iceberg – These lettuces have the crispest leaves of all, and the flavor is good and fresh.

Lamb's lettuce – Also known as *mâche* or corn salad. Very much a winter salad that carries a nutty flavor in its small, deep golden leaves.

Little Gem – This is a smaller and equally crisp version of Romaine. Delicious to use in a common green salad or in the world-famous Caesar salad.

Lollo rosso – A crinkly red-and-green-leaved lettuce, which doesn't have much flavor, but which lends a nice texture and color to a salad. Oakleaf lettuce is very similar with a softer leaf and deeper red color. Both of these come into the "loose-head" lettuce category.

Mizuna – A Japanese leaf, very attractive, small arugula-like leaves, carrying a mild pepper flavor.

Purslane – This grows wild in many areas and is sometimes and presented and served in small sprigs. It was grown and used in salads in Britain in the Middle Ages, but somehow went out of fashion, almost being looked on as a garden weed. In France it's known as *pourpier* and is still considered an important salad item.

Radicchio – An Italian member of the chicory family. Its color ranges from a deep ruby red to pink, finishing with a creamy white. It comes as a round head and in a long, Romaine-like shape. It has a peppery flavor with a pleasant bitterness as well. A wonderful leaf for simply mixing with other greens along with a drop of dressing.

Romaine/Cos – Cos is the English name for it. Romaine is a long, crisp, and nutty-flavored lettuce.

Spinach – Mostly associated with vegetable dishes, the young tender leaves go beautifully in a good green salad, or a salad tossed with bacon pieces and walnuts.

Watercress – Mostly used in garnish form, but it works in salads as well. Rich, dark green sprigs will add a peppery bite to almost any green salad.

Roasted Parsnips ⓥ

This sweet root vegetable has been used in many recipes over the years. It was the traditional accompaniment for roast beef before the potato was introduced, and it was also often served with boiled salt cod on Ash Wednesdays. Its sweetness has been turned into honey, jams, and even wine. It has been featured in puddings, stews, and soups, puréed for mousses and vegetable accompaniments, and the most classic of all, roasted. In Italy the pigs for Parma ham are fed on parsnips to give their flesh a rich and slightly sweet flavor. The French don't care much of parsnips, preferring turnips instead. But parsnips were once valued so highly in Britain that they were used to cure toothache, to keep adders away, to serve as an aphrodisiac for men, and even to reduce swollen testicles.

Parsnips are at their best during the winter months. The smaller they are, the more tender they'll be and the less preparation they'll need. The core of baby parsnips need not be cut out; with cooking will become very tender. They also don't need to be peeled, just well scrubbed before cooking. Larger parsnips, from 6–8 oz (175–225 g) upward, will need to be peeled and the core cut away.

From roasted to creamed, the flavors are totally different, but you must give them some attention – plain boiling just isn't very exciting. Here, I show you how to roast them without making them over-sweet. The addition of honey will give the parsnips a bitter–sweet edge of flavor, but I leave that option to you. As you know by now, my style of cooking is about understanding and balancing tastes.

Preheat the oven to 400°F/200°C. If the parsnips have woody centers, cut these out before cooking.

The parsnips can be boiled in salted water for 2 minutes before roasting. I don't think this is essential; however, if you prefer them very soft with a crispy skin and almost hollow but creamy center, then the par-boiling will help.

Preheat a roasting pan on top of the stove and add the oil. Fry the parsnips in the oil until golden brown on all sides, allowing burned tinges on the edges. The tinges will give a slightly bitter flavor that will balance the sweetness.

Roast in the oven, turning occasionally for 20–30 minutes, depending on their size. (If you want them very soft, leave in for 35–40 minutes.) Remove from the oven and season with salt and pepper. Add the butter to enrich the finished flavor and the honey, if using. Cook for another 5–10 minutes.

Place them in a serving dish, spooning any remaining caramelized juices over them.

SERVES 6

2 lb (900 g) parsnips, peeled and quartered (if you have found small parsnips that do not need to be quartered, then 1¼ lb/750 g should be enough)
2 tablespoons olive or cooking oil
2–4 tablespoons (25–50 g) butter
2 tablespoons honey (optional)
Salt and pepper

Creamed Parsnips ⓥ

Parsnips can be prepared like mashed potatoes, that is, boiled, and then mashed with butter and cream. Boiling alone simply gives a watery taste with the real depth and flavor of the vegetable lost. So here below is a method that will retain the natural flavor of the parsnip.

You can serve these creamed parsnips as a vegetable accompaniment, but they can also be served in other ways. I use them in *Steamed and Braised Mallard with a Parsnip Tart* (page 261) and they can also be made into a parsnip ravioli.

SERVES 4–6

1 lb (450 g) parsnips, peeled and roughly diced (core removed)
Squeeze of lemon juice
4 tablespoons (50 g) butter
½ cup (100 ml) water
¼ cup (50 ml) heavy cream
Salt and pepper

Place the diced parsnips in a bowl and squeeze the lemon juice over them, making sure all of them are covered well.

Melt the butter in a heavy-bottomed saucepan until it begins to foam. Add the parsnips and stir them before adding the water.

Now, they can be cooked slowly for 15 minutes or until they are completely tender and have broken down.

Place in a food processor. Gently boil the heavy cream and add to the parsnips, season with salt and pepper, and process to a fine purée.

For an even smoother finish, push through a fine sieve. The creamed parsnips are now ready to enjoy.

Braised Globe Artichokes Ⓥ

Although we think of them as rather exotic, globe artichokes used to be a familiar sight in British gardens, introduced from Italy (as so many vegetables were) in Elizabethan times.

They can have a variety of uses. The outside leaves can be cooked and used as garnishes or in salads. There is a small bite of flesh to be eaten at the bottom of them. The small, younger leaves attached to the artichoke bottoms in the center can be cooked still attached and then used in salads, or as complete vegetarian dishes. For me the artichoke bottom is the best and most succulent part.

To cook them and to keep their natural color, I like to make a tomato and lemon stock. The acidity from the lemon and sweetness of the tomato give the artichoke even more flavor without masking its own.

SERVES 6

6 globe artichokes
Juice of 1 lemon

For the Stock

4 very ripe tomatoes, roughly chopped
Juice of 1 lemon
1¼ cups (300 ml) water
Salt
1 teaspoon coriander seeds (optional)
1 bay leaf (optional)

To make the stock, place all the ingredients together in a pan and bring to a simmer. The stock is now ready to use. (If cooking just 2 artichokes, then reduce the tomatoes to 2 and the coriander seeds, if using, by half.)

Remove the stems from the artichokes and then cut around the bottom, removing the leaves. Now, cut across about 1½ in (4 cm) from the bottom and cut off any excess stem. The center of the bottom will still be intact. Rub with lemon juice.

Place the artichoke bottoms and the remaining lemon juice in the stock and simmer for 20–30 minutes until tender. When cooked and cooled, remove and discard the bristly centers. The artichokes are now ready to use.

Note: The artichoke-flavored stock can be reserved, strained, and refrigerated and used for cooking artichokes once more. After that it will have taken on too many bitter flavors and should be discarded.

Fava Beans Ⓥ

The fava bean has been around since at least the Bronze Age, and it has been eaten both fresh and dried; in fact, the dried variety sustained people throughout the long winter months, perhaps cooked along with bacon. The Egyptians had a love-hate relationship with the bean. Many loved the vegetable but priests felt that the hollow stems were used by the souls of the dead as a passageway to life after death. Despite this, the bean was soon enjoyed by the masses. In fact, until Columbus arrived in America, when the kidney bean and all its relations were introduced to Europe, the fava bean was as important to daily eating as the potato is now.

Cooking with fava beans seems to have declined in Britain nowadays, which I find difficult to understand because they are so delicious,

Broiled Baby Leeks Ⓥ

particularly when fresh. The season for the fresh beans is extremely short, lasting only through the first few months of summer. Take advantage of this and eat as many as you can – they really are superb, simply lightly buttered. Look for them very early in the season; if you're able to find the small beans in 3–4 in (8–10 cm) pods, they can be eaten pod and all, so no flavor is lost – and no weight either. Later, of course, you have to buy a large quantity of them unshelled to get a reasonable amount of beans.

It's best to cook fava beans as soon as they are picked. Otherwise they tend to become limp and their sugar content will turn to carbohydrate, which inevitably changes the texture and flavor. This simple recipe uses the average kidney-shaped bean which needs to be shelled before it's cooked.

I insist on serving fava beans with their gray skin removed. This way the deep, rich green color shows, and they are perfectly tender. For another recipe that uses these beans, see *Sage Fava Beans with Bacon and Tomato* (page 56).

SERVES 4

1 lb (450 g) shelled fava beans
Butter
Salt and pepper

Bring a large saucepan of well salted water to a boil. Remove the lid and add the beans; it's now important the lid stays off to maintain the intense green color of the vegetable.

Cook medium-sized beans for approximately 1–2 minutes, 5 minutes maximum. After they are tender, lift them from the pan and drop into ice water. When the beans are cold, they can have their skins removed. To re-heat, melt a rounded teaspoon of butter and add a tablespoon or two of water. Bring to a simmer and add the skinned, cooked beans. Season with salt and pepper. The beans will be hot within a minute or two and ready to eat.

After they are cooked and skinned, they can be seasoned and rolled in the melted butter and microwaved when needed.

Baby leeks are the young, thin variety, which are sometimes called "pencil" leeks. Eating them broiled gives the young leeks quite a sweet flavor and a slightly bitter edge.

Before broiling, the leeks need to be pre-cooked in boiling salted water. This will tenderize the texture prior to cooking under a hot broiler. If you are serving them as a vegetable accompaniment, 2–3 leeks per serving will be plenty.

SERVES 4

8–12 baby leeks, washed and the tops and bottom trimmed
Butter, melted
Salt and pepper

Plunge the leeks into boiling salted water and cook without a lid for 2–3 minutes. If they're slightly thicker, cook for 4–5 minutes. After they are tender, the leeks can be removed from the pan and left to cool naturally, or quickly plunged into ice water. If cooled in the ice water, leave in for only the same period as the cooking time: 2–3 minutes. Dry the leeks and brush them with the butter. The leeks can be prepared to this stage well in advance and refrigerated until needed.

To finish, simply place the leeks under a hot broil and cook for a few minutes, turning them over occasionally to mark and brown all around. Season with salt and pepper before serving.

Note: These leeks go very well with most dishes, but in particular, with the *Roast Loin of Pork with an Apricot and Sage Stuffing* (page 330).

Leeks with Prunes Ⓥ

The combination of leeks and prunes is an old one, both being popular pottage ingredients. Together they are a perfect accompaniment to pork and poultry dishes. Prunes have a long relationship with duck, with pork in a stuffing form, and with chicken and Armagnac in that classic French style. Leeks, too certainly go well with all of those foods,

so it was a question of trying to bring the two together, and they've "married" well.

The prunes must be pitted and ready to eat. Soaking them first would create a stewed finish to the dish and everything might become overcooked and soggy. With a shredded leek, I prefer them with a bite left in. A squeeze of lime is not essential but does lift all the other flavors.

SERVES 4

1 lb (450 g) leeks, split lengthwise,
    washed and shredded
4 oz (100 g) pitted prunes
Butter
Salt and pepper
Squeeze of fresh lime juice (optional)

It's best to shred the leeks finely (about ⅛ in/2–3 mm); they will then cook very quickly. The prunes can be split lengthwise and cut into pieces.

Melt a rounded teaspoon of butter in a large frying- or braising pan. After it bubbles, add the leeks. Any water from them will prevent the butter from becoming burned. Season with salt and pepper.

Cook on a high heat for 2–3 minutes. The leeks will now be quite tender. While still on a high heat, add the prunes and toss into the leeks. After they've warmed through, add another rounded teaspoon of butter and a squeeze of lime, if using, and serve.

Note: The prunes can be given an almost scorched effect by throwing them into a very hot, dry pan. Stir for just 30–40 seconds and then add to the leeks. This brings out a richer prune flavor.

OPPOSITE
Leeks with Prunes

Stilton and Red Onion Salad with Peppered Beef Fillet

Basically, nothing could be more British than this combination of the very English Stilton cheese and beef. It harks back to the great compound salads of the seventeenth and eighteenth centuries. The dish is very lively, full of amazing flavors – one of those dishes you just can't get enough of.

The "pickled" red onions are delicious in themselves and can be served as part of any salad to accompany a "plowman's lunch'.

This is a great dish for a dinner party. It goes well as an appetizer, but I would be happy to serve just large plates of this dish for a main course with a good bottle of red. This helps you get away from the standard three courses that cause you far too much pressure, and your friends will have more than enough flavors to enjoy. A lot of the work can also be done well in advance – the beef fillet can be prepared and peppered, the red onions cooked and pickled, the Stilton crumbled, and the dressing made.

SERVES 4 AS AN APPETIZER

For the Beef

12 oz–1 lb (350–450 g) beef fillet
1 tablespoon crushed black peppercorns
Oil or butter

For the Salad

3 red onions
2 tablespoons olive oil
2 tablespoons peanut oil
2 tablespoons balsamic vinegar
Squeeze of lemon juice
10 very thin slices of French bread, halved
8–12 oz (225–350 g) mixed green leaves
4 oz (100 g) Stilton cheese, broken (more can be
    added for blue-cheese lovers, or Roquefort
    can be substituted)
Salt and pepper

For the Dressing

3 tablespoons port
2 teaspoons Dijon mustard

2 tablespoons red wine vinegar (preferably
    Cabernet Sauvignon)
4 tablespoons walnut oil
4 tablespoons peanut oil
Salt and pepper

First, roll the beef in the crushed black peppercorns. The meat will start to take on the pepper flavor and can be left until needed. The onions and dressing can now both be prepared and kept until you are completing the dish.

Start with the onions. Cut them into 6–8 wedges, keeping the root of the onion in place to prevent them from falling apart. Bring a pan of water to a boil, add the cut onions, and cook for 2 minutes.

Warm together the oils, the balsamic vinegar, and lemon juice. Drain the onions and add them to the oil/vinegar mixture. Remove this from the heat, season with salt and pepper and let the onions marinate at room temperature, turning every so often to ensure an even flavor. The onions will be at their best after a minimum 1–2 hours, so these can easily be prepared in the morning for an evening meal.

To make the dressing, boil and reduce the port by half and allow it to cool. Mix the mustard with the red wine vinegar. Whisk together the oils and pour slowly into the mustard and vinegar mixture, while continuing to whisk vigorously. After all has been added, whisk in the reduced port and season with salt and pepper.

BELOW
Stilton and Red Onion Salad with Peppered Beef Fillet

The French bread slices can be crisped by drizzling them with oil and either toasting or baking them in a hot oven.

To roast the beef fillet, preheat the oven to 425°F/220°C. Heat an ovenproof frying-pan and drizzle with a drop of oil or rounded teaspoon of butter. Add the fillet and brown to a deep evenly seared effect. Now, finish by roasting in the hot oven for about 10–12 minutes. This will keep the beef nice and pink in the center. Up to 20 minutes will make it medium-well to well done.

After the meat is cooked, remove it from the oven and let it rest for another 10–12 minutes. This will totally relax the meat and it will still be warm enough for serving.

To finish the dish, mix the red onions (spooned out of the marinade) with the salad greens and the blue cheese. Add some of the red wine/port dressing to bind. Slice the beef, allowing three thin slices per serving, and overlap the slices on each plate. Divide the salad, placing it towards the top of the plate. Drizzle on some more of the dressing and place the crispy toasts on top.

Note: The port and mustard dressing can be excluded from this recipe and the marinade used to replace it. A splash or two of port can be added to the marinade, along with mustard, if preferred.

One egg yolk can be added to the vinegar and mustard before adding the oils to the dressing. This will give a creamier finish.

Bubble and Squeak Artichokes with Mushrooms ⓥ

That old favorite, bubble and squeak, was originally a mixture of fried beef and cabbage, the potato addition coming much later. Here I use the basic idea of bubble and squeak in a vegetarian main course. The "squeak" ingredients are formed into packets and then served in an artichoke bottom with the almost dry-fried mushrooms.

These are helped along and enriched by a red wine dressing. Red wine and mushrooms have always had a close relationship. This is a perfect recipe for using up any leftover mashed potatoes. I've suggested using about 4 cups (350 g) of potatoes, but a minimum of 3 cups (225 g) will also work.

A lovely optional extra is to finish the dish with *Hollandaise Sauce* (page 41).

SERVES 4 AS A MAIN COURSE

1 medium Savoy cabbage
2 onions, sliced
4 tablespoons (50 g) butter
4 cups (350 g) *Mashed Potatoes* (page 124)
    (no cream added)
Oil, for frying
4 large globe artichokes, cooked (page 96)
28 small button mushrooms
⅔ cup (150 ml) *Hollandaise Sauce* or *Simple Hollandaise Sauce* (page 41)
2 tablespoons olive oil
1 teaspoon chopped fresh chives
Salt and pepper
Lime juice (optional)

For the Red Wine Vinegar Dressing

2 tablespoons Dijon mustard
2 tablespoons red wine vinegar (preferably Cabernet Sauvignon)
4 tablespoons walnut oil
4 tablespoons peanut oil

Remove four of the outer leaves from the Savoy cabbage by first cutting away some of the stalk. The leaves will now fall away easily. The thick stalk veins can now be cut out from the leaves without cutting the leaf in half. These leaves will be used to wrap the bubble and squeak packets. A medium cabbage is the best size to buy, so that the outer leaves are large enough for wrapping. Wash them well.

Split the remaining cabbage in half and then cut one half into quarters. These two quarters should be plenty for four servings. The remaining half can be kept for another meal. Cut any stalk away from the quarters and shred the leaves very finely.

Bring a large pot of salted water to a boil. After it's boiling, add the washed large leaves. Cook for a few minutes until the leaves are very tender. Refresh in ice water. When they are cold, spread the leaves out to dry on a cloth. The shredded cabbage can now be blanched in the boiling water. Drop in the cabbage, return to a boil, and the shredded cabbage will be cooked almost immediately. Drain through a colander and then spread the hot cooked cabbage on a baking sheet. Let it cool, then refrigerate.

The sliced onions can now be cooked in 2 tablespoons (25 g) of the butter. Fry to a rich golden caramel brown. Season with salt and pepper. Let them cool. The mashed potatoes can also be used cold.

Mix together the shredded cabbage and the onions. Add enough of the potatoes to bind and create a good texture, you will probably need all of the mashed potatoes. Season with salt and pepper.

Quarter the mixture and shape it into balls. Season the blanched cabbage leaves and lay them on a cutting board, season them with salt and pepper. Where the stalk vein has been cut away, overlap the cabbage by ½ in (1 cm). Place the balls in the center and wrap the leaf around. Because the cabbage is tender it should shape easily. Then, wrap each one in plastic wrap, twisting it firmly at the bottom to give a full, round, ball shape. The wrapped balls can now be refrigerated to set.

Melt half the remaining butter with a trickle of cooking oil and pan-fry the artichokes. These will take 4–5 minutes to acquire a golden edge.

BELOW
Bubble and Squeak Artichokes with Mushrooms

Cabbage

While these are cooking, the mushrooms can also be browned. Heat a frying-pan with a drop of cooking oil. Add the mushrooms and cook over a medium heat until they begin to very slightly burn and become tender. The mushrooms will take about 6–8 minutes to cook. During the last minute of cooking, add the remaining rounded teaspoon of butter. Season with salt and pepper.

The hollandaise sauce, if using, and the red wine dressing can be made between 30 minutes and 1 hour before serving the dish.

To make the dressing, mix the mustard with the red wine vinegar. Whisk the oils together and pour slowly onto the mustard and vinegar while whisking vigorously. After all has been added, season with salt and pepper. The addition of 1 egg yolk or a heaping teaspoon of mayonnaise to the vinegar and mustard will guarantee the emulsion of the oils.

The chopped chives can be added to the olive oil and seasoned with salt and pepper. A drop of lemon or lime juice can also be added to this oil for an extra bite.

Re-heat the bubble and squeak packets, preferably in a microwave for about one minute. They can also be placed in a steamer for 6–8 minutes to heat through.

Place an artichoke bottom in the center of each plate. Pour two teaspoonfuls of hollandaise sauce into each one. Place the mushrooms, seven each, around the artichoke. Peel away the plastic wrap and place a bubble and squeak packet on top of each artichoke.

The red wine dressing can now be spooned around and over the mushrooms. You can do this quickly and easily by piping from a squeeze bottle (page 11). The chive olive oil can now also be drizzled around the mushrooms.

A tablespoon or two of hollandaise sauce, if using, can now be spooned over each packet top.

Note: A large Portobello mushroom can be broiled and used to place the packets on. These could be used to replace the artichoke and button mushrooms.

If desired, freshly grated truffles can be added to the hollandaise sauce. To increase the truffle flavor, truffle vinegar can be added along with a little truffle oil.

Cabbage has a history that is actually longer than that of potatoes. It has been part of the British diet since the time of the Celts, and it was an early pottage vegetable. But it was was a tough, wild variety that apparently is still grown in Europe and northern Britain around the sea coasts. It was very different from the more tender cabbages we now know, very bitter and, consequently, with a bad reputation. It was eaten for medicinal purposes, especially while drinking because it was believed to prevent drunkenness. The Romans developed the plant, taking away some of that bitterness, but the vegetable was still an open-leaved variety similar to kale, not a tight-packed ball as we have today. It wasn't until centuries later that European gardeners mastered the art of cabbage-growing. From the Dutch came the white cabbage (and coleslaw). A late seventeenth-century gardener's book was quoted in *Food in England* by Dorothy Hartley: " 'Tis scarce 100 years since we had Cabbages out of Holland, Sir Arthur Ashley of Wilburg St Giles, in Dorsetshire, being the first who planted them in England. Cabbage is not so greatly magnified by the rest of the doctors, as affording but a gross and melancholy juice. Yet loosening, if moderately boiled. It is seldom eaten raw, except by the Dutch." From the kingdom of Savoy (now part of France) came the Savoy cabbage, probably the most common variety in Britain today.

Over the years, the simple cabbage has developed into a very large family: green, Savoy, white, red, then the cabbage family – kale, cauliflower, broccoli, Brussels sprouts... Most of these have become popular in Britain, particularly in Ireland, where so many traditional dishes – champ and colcannon, for instance – utilize cabbage. That these still exist and are still enjoyed demonstrates how simple, delicious dishes will never die.

One of the beauties of cabbage is that it is an all-year-round vegetable which can stand up very well to cold and even icy conditions. The vegetable does, however, present one or two problems: the first is the unsavory smell caused by sulphur in the leaves if it is overcooked. Overcooked cabbage has a dull, almost yellow color along with the bad odor. That leads to the second problem – understanding the cooking of cabbage so that it can be enjoyed at its best. The much earlier Roman variety needed several hours of rapid boiling before becoming tender and edible, with its bitter flavor mellowed. This traditional way of cooking it obviously lasted hundreds of years, extending to the new, more tender variety. Cabbage, in fact, takes only minutes to cook to its best, keeping all its natural tastes and colors, and presenting an inviting aroma rather than an odor.

The Dutch white cabbage tastes at its best as sauerkraut, or raw in coleslaw (probably what it was developed for in its native country). White cabbage must be shredded or grated very finely, though, if you are serving it raw. Shredding prevents it from being too tough to eat. Sweet and sour cabbage can also be made. Bring 1 tablespoon sugar and 4 tablespoons of white wine vinegar to a boil and pour over the finely shredded cabbage. Season with salt and let it cool.

Green and Savoy cabbages can also be finely shredded or grated and used in salads. It is important to serve them immediately; otherwise the acidity of vinegar or citrus fruit (limes work very well with ginger and cabbage) will discolor the leaves.

The golden rule whenever cooking any variety of green cabbage – any green vegetable for that matter – is to always cook in plenty of boiling salted water *without a lid*. Bring the water to a boil, remove the lid, and add the shredded cabbage. This will take only about 1–2 minutes to cook, or until the water just begins to boil again. Drain the cabbage, re-season with salt and pepper, and add a rounded teaspoon of butter to finish. Serve the vegetable immediately.

Another method for cooking cabbage is by heating a few tablespoons of water with a rounded teaspoon of butter, then adding the cabbage and stirring for a few minutes over a high heat until tender. Sliced onions and strips of bacon can be tossed in butter before adding the raw or pre-cooked shredded cabbage. This gives you a flavorful vegetable dish or one that can be used as an accompaniment for meat or fish.

If cabbage has been quickly blanched in boiling water to take out the rawness, it can be sautéed to an almost golden brown tinge in butter or perhaps in a flavored oil. (Sesame oil works very well, and sesame seeds, shrimp, and a squeeze of lemon go with it beautifully.)

Pieces of *Pork Cracklings* (page 179) mixed with sautéed cabbage also go very well. And stir-fry dishes using many other flavors along with the cabbage give you delicious vegetarian appetizers, main courses, or side dishes. When cooking with other ingredients, the cabbage must be shredded very finely, then added at the last moment. Ingredients that go well with cabbage are mushrooms, onions, sweet bell peppers, leeks, bean sprouts, chilies, herbs, ginger, garlic, lemon, limes, tomatoes – the list goes on and on.

Try *Colcannon* (page 126), *Bubble and Squeak* (page 126), *Steamed Halibut and Cabbage with a Salmon Gravlax Sauce* (page 132), *Broiled Lamb with "Irish" Cabbage and Mashed Potatoes Sauce* (page 187), and you'll see that cabbage need never be boring.

Creamed Cabbage and Bacon

The "creamed" in the recipe title doesn't mean puréed, but refers to the cream I have added. This collects all the bacon and onion flavors, creating a sauce for the cabbage.

This creamed cabbage goes particularly well with the roast beef dishes on pages 232 and 238.

SERVES 4–6

1 Savoy cabbage
2 tablespoons (25 g) butter
2 onions, sliced
6 strips of bacon
2 tablespoons water
6 tablespoons heavy cream, more if necessary
Salt and pepper

Remove the large, tough, outer leaves from the cabbage. Quarter the cabbage head and cut out the stalk. The cabbage can now be finely shredded.

Melt a rounded teaspoon of butter in a large pan. When it begins to bubble, add the onions. Cook over a medium heat for 6–7 minutes until slightly softened and with tinges of golden color. The bacon can be fried separately at the same time on a high heat until crisp.

Add the 2 tablespoons of water to the onions along with the cabbage. It's important to cook over a fairly high heat and to keep the cabbage moving for an even cooking. Season with salt and pepper. Cook for a few minutes. Check the cooked stage of the cabbage. It should be barely tender. If not, continue to cook until it reaches that stage. Add the crisp bacon and the cream and bring to a simmer. During this time, the cream will slightly thicken and will take on the taste of the bacon and onions.

The cabbage will now be very tender and just right for serving. Re-check the seasoning and adjust with salt and pepper.

Note: The cabbage can first be blanched in boiling water until tender. Drain it and let it cool. Cook the onions and bacon as above and allow them to cool. These can now both be refrigerated until needed. To re-heat, warm the onions and bacon in a hot pan. Add the cabbage and when it has warmed, add the cream. Now, finish as above. This method allows you to do part of the work ahead of time, giving you more stove space when needed.

Cabbage with Bean Sprouts and Onions ⓥ

In this recipe I've blanched the cabbage to take out its rawness and flavored it very simply with olive oil. The bean sprouts give a light, crunchy taste.

SERVES 4

½ green cabbage, shredded
8 oz (225 g) bean sprouts
2 onions, sliced
2 tablespoons (25 g) butter
1 tablespoon olive oil
Salt and pepper
A pinch of five-spice powder

Blanch the cabbage and bean sprouts separately in boiling, salted water, then refresh under cold water and drain well. Melt the butter and olive oil in a frying-pan and fry the onions until softened and golden brown. Add the cabbage and bean sprouts and season with salt, pepper, and five-spice powder. Now, stir-fry for 2–3 minutes and the dish is ready.

Curly Kale ⓥ

Kale, a green vegetable of the cabbage family grown in the winter and early spring, has been cultivated and eaten in Britain for hundreds of years. It is similar to cabbage in flavor, with a thicker and firmer texture, and it keeps both when cooked, as well as maintaining its amazing deep green color. When raw, it has a "curly" parsley look about it. I like to eat it simply tossed in butter and seasoned. It can also be used in stir-fries (after blanching) and mixed with spices, pasta, or potatoes. It also goes very well with *Pan-fried Cod with Carrots, Parsley, and Bacon* (page 143).

SERVES 4

1½–2 lb (750–900 g) kale
Butter
Salt and pepper

Remove the stems from the kale, wash well, and cook the leaves in boiling, salted water for 3–4 minutes without a lid. Don't overcrowd the saucepan with the kale because it will take longer for the water to return to a boil, causing the kale to lose its rich color. Drain well in a colander, removing excess water. Season with salt and pepper and stir in a rounded teaspoon of butter.

The kale can also be cooked ahead of time and refreshed in ice water. Season and butter it when cold and refrigerate until needed. Now, all you need to do is microwave it and serve.

Broccoli ⓥ

Broccoli is another member of the cabbage family. Originating in Italy, it was popularized in Britain in the early eighteenth century by a man named Stephen Switzer who ran a seed business, importing exotic species such as cardoons, celeriac, and Florence fennel. Broccoli comes in various sizes and varieties. My favorite is Calabrese. This is the broccoli that grows in individual florets with a thick stem. This variety really keeps its color and it is very tender to eat, requiring very little cooking. There is also purple sprouting broccoli, which was apparently the original form of the vegetable. It is also very tender when cooked but never quite keeps that rich purple color.

SERVES 6–8

2 lb (900 g) broccoli
Butter
Salt and pepper

Boil some salted water in a deep pan. Trim off the stems of the broccoli florets (these can be kept to be cooked as another vegetable dish). After the water is boiling, drop in the florets, making sure the lid is left off. These will take only 2–5 minutes to become tender but still with a little bite, depending on the size of the florets. After they are cooked, remove them from the water, and if not using immediately, plunge into ice water to stop the cooking and retain their green color. These can simply be re-heated by dropping once again into boiling water for 1 minute, or by microwaving.

The broccoli can now be seasoned with salt and pepper, buttered, and served.

Variations

You could vary this basic "buttered" recipe. After the broccoli has cooked, you could top it with Stilton rarebit (see *Port and Stilton Cheese Toasts*, page 172) and finish it under the broiler; sprinkle it with grated Parmesan and brown under the broiler; fry it in some garlic butter or in butter with some flaked almonds; or finish it with some *Hollandaise* or *Simple Hollandaise Sauce* (page 41).

Buttered Brussels Sprouts ⓥ

Brussels sprouts were one of those vegetables I didn't like at school, with their disgusting sulphur smell, their pale greenish yellow color, and the soggy texture. Was it the vegetable itself or the cooking that was to blame? Of course, I blamed the vegetable, but years later I realized it was, in fact, the cooking that ruined them.

The true botanical history of this vegetable is not well documented, although it was said to be around Brussels (in Belgium) that it was first grown. A member of the cabbage family, it has become a favorite British vegetable, especially in the winter. Eliza Acton was the first to include a recipe for cooking the sprouts in her *Modern Cooking*, published in 1845. Alexis Soyer, a great chef who cooked in the Reform Club, Pall Mall, also included a recipe for them in his *Modern Housewife* of 1849. So Brussels sprouts are a comparatively recent passion.

There are a few golden rules to choosing and buying. To appreciate the great flavor – quite different from cabbage – and the slightly nutty crunch after they are cooked, it's important to buy them as small and tight-leaved as possible. These signs indicate freshness and such sprouts will require minimal cooking. Never buy yellow sprouts, those whose color is fading, or with too much loose leaf. All these indicate the sprouts are old and they'll taste pretty old too.

Here's a very simple recipe, with a few alternate ideas to enjoy. There are even more options for cooking Brussels sprouts; they can be finely shredded raw in salads, or boiled, pan-fried or roasted.

SERVES 4

1 lb (450 g) small Brussels sprouts
2–4 tablespoons (25–50 g) butter
Salt and pepper

The first stage is to bring a large pot of salted water, three-fourths full, to a boil.

While waiting for the water to boil, remove any damaged outer leaves (there should be very few if small, tight sprouts have been chosen). A small criss-cross incision can now be made in the bottom of each stem end; this speeds up the cooking process.

After the water is boiling, remove the lid of the pan and add the cleaned sprouts. It's important not to replace the lid. For perfect Brussels sprouts that keep their bite and rich green color, cook for 2–3 minutes only. If you prefer well-done sprouts, then cook for 2 minutes more. Don't overfill the pan since this causes the temperature to drop and takes longer for the water to return to a boil, resulting in the sprouts losing their rich green color.

After they're cooked, lift or drain them from the pan. Melt the butter in the saucepan and roll the sprouts in it. Season with salt and pepper and serve.

Variations

Here are a few alternatives. For sautéed (pan-fried) sprouts, melt 2–4 tablespoons (25–50 g) butter in a large frying-pan or wok. After it is bubbling, add the cooked Brussels sprouts. These can now be pan-fried in the hot butter, allowing them to take on a golden edge. This method brings out a nutty flavor from the bubbling butter.

Flavored oils can also be used for lightly coating and cooking or pan-frying the vegetables. Walnut, hazelnut, or olive oil work very well.

Fry strips of bacon before sautéing; this would be good for a Christmas holiday dinner, particularly if you add chopped chestnuts.

Diced onions or pearl onions also taste very good with Brussels sprouts.

Finely shred the sprouts and turn into a stir-fry. Many other ingredients can be added, creating interesting flavors, e.g. bean sprouts, onions, sweet bell peppers, chilies, and so on.

Cheese and Onion Zucchini ⓥ

The zucchini is a member of the same family as squash and pumpkin, and the vegetable originated in the Americas. Also in the same vegetable family is the marrow, a type of squash very much associated with Britain where people compete to see who can grow the largest. Marrows were very popular in the nineteenth century, and were grown in kitchen gardens. The zucchini itself was probably not appreciated until, some say, Elizabeth David inspired us with her memories of the Mediterranean in the 1950s.

They have now become part of British cooking. They work very well with many other flavors – garlic, tomatoes, or simply tossed in butter – and are superb in a ratatouille. There is a slight bitterness in their flavor. This can be drawn out by lightly placing slices in a colander salting them, and draining them for 30 minutes, allowing the bitter juices to be released.

This recipe can be made with English Cheddar as suggested, but for a slightly more Continental flavor, use Parmesan.

BELOW
Cheese and Onion Zucchini

1 lb (450 g) zucchini
2 tablespoons (25 g) butter
1 small onion, peeled
2–3 oz (50–75 g) Cheddar or Parmesan cheese,
    preferably finely grated
Salt and pepper

When choosing zucchini, make sure they are very firm. If they have softened and the skin is slightly leathery, the flavor will be bitter. Very small zucchini will not need to be salted.

Trim off the ends and slice the zucchini. If sliced about ¼ in (4–5mm) thick, they will cook quickly while still retaining a texture. Also, if you slice at a slight angle, an attractive oval shape is achieved. Lightly salt the zucchini and place them in a colander above a bowl.

After 30 minutes, they need to be dried on a cloth unless you are worried about the salt content; if so, rinse the slices under cold water and dry.

Heat a frying-pan or wok and add the butter. When it's bubbling, add the zucchini. Fry for 2–3 minutes before grating the onion on top. Season with salt and pepper. Cook on a high heat for another 2 minutes. Sprinkle in half the cheese and then transfer to an ovenproof dish. Top with the remaining cheese and gratinate under a hot broiler.

The cheese and onion zucchini are now ready to serve.

Note: Chopped tomatoes can also be added with the onions. It's important that all the juices and seeds are removed. This will prevent the vegetables from stewing.

Mushrooms with Shallots, Crisp Bacon, and Red Wine

Mushrooms have been used as food for centuries, but have been cultivated in Europe and the US for only about 150 years. Japan cultivated them beginning in the first century AD. All cultivated mushrooms have been developed from the wild field mushroom, *Agaricus campestris*. For this recipe, you can use common button mushrooms, crimini mushrooms with their slightly nutty flavor, or one of the many wild mushrooms varieties now in the markets. The wild ones will give a much stronger flavor and a "meatier" texture.

An almost burned flavor created by almost dry-frying gives a bitter edge to the dish. Mushrooms absorb almost any amount of fat added to a pan, resulting in an oily finish. That doesn't happen with this dish; instead, preparing them this way gives them a drier border which holds all of the mushroom juices.

4 strips of streaky bacon
1 tablespoon olive oil
2 shallots, sliced
Butter
1 lb (450 g) button mushrooms, wiped
½ cup red wine
Salt and pepper

Cut the bacon strips into small dice. Heat a frying-pan or wok. Warm a tiny dribble of the olive oil, add the bacon, and cook on a medium heat. This will take 7–8 minutes to fry. After any juices have been released and then reduced in the pan, the bacon will become dry. Increase the heat and cook until it is totally crisp. Remove from the pan and keep to one side.

Add the shallots and fry for 1–2 minutes with a small touch of the butter. Also remove and keep to one side.

Continue heating the pan and add the remaining oil. After the pan is hot, add the mushrooms. Cook on a medium heat. The oil will be quickly absorbed and the mushrooms will begin to darken in the pan. Allow them to take on almost burned tinges and continue to cook until tender. This will take 8–10 minutes. Now, return the shallots to the pan. Add half of the red wine, season with salt and pepper, and increase the heat, reducing until almost dry. Add the remaining wine and also reduce until almost dry.

The crisp bacon, along with a rounded teaspoon of butter, can now be tossed into the mushrooms to finish the dish.

Note: The red wine can be omitted from this recipe.
   Chopped tarragon adds another flavor that works very well.

Radish and French Bean Salad with Seared Scallops

This is a lovely summer dish, which can be offered as an appetizer, a snack lunch, or a main course at dinner.

   The radish is a member of the mustard family, obviously the reason for the bite they carry. There are many varieties, the most common of which are the round scarlet globe and the milder long red and white. The latter is known as the French breakfast radish, though why I'm not quite sure since I've yet to see a Frenchman eating them for breakfast.

   Scallops, despite breeding naturally around Britain's northern coasts, were always more of a rarity – and thus a treat in Britain. Always choose fresh scallops, not frozen. Frozen scallops are soaked in water before freezing. This "soufflés" the meat so that the scallops look bigger and weigh more, giving a better deal to the seller instead of to the buyer. The ultimate scallops to buy are the ones picked by hand and they couldn't be any fresher. With all of my scallop recipes, I prefer to use large ones for a rich, sweet, and meaty texture.

SERVES 4 AS AN APPETIZER

1 teaspoon sesame seeds
6 oz (175 g) fine French beans, preferably extra fine
12 large fresh scallops, trimmed (if there is roe attached, clean it off and use it to make roe butter, see Note)
1 tablespoon olive oil
Butter
12 French breakfast radishes, quartered lengthwise

For the White Wine Dressing

2 shallots, finely chopped
½ cup sweet white wine, preferably Sauternes
1 heaped teaspoon Dijon mustard
Juice of 1 lime
6 tablespoons walnut oil
1 tablespoon olive oil
Salt and pepper

For the Yogurt and Sour Cream Dressing

¼ cup (50 ml) natural yogurt
¼ cup (50 ml) sour cream
Juice of ½ lime
Salt and pepper

To make the white wine dressing, cover the chopped shallots with the sweet white wine and bring to a simmer. Cook on a medium heat until the wine has reduced almost completely. Let it cool. Spoon the Dijon mustard into a small bowl and mix with the lime juice. Slowly whisk in the two oils. Add the shallots and season with salt and pepper. That's the first dressing made.

   For the second dressing, mix the first three ingredients together and season with salt and pepper.

   The sesame seeds can be quickly toasted under a hot broiler, turning from time to time to give a complete golden color.

   The beans should be cooked in plenty of salted boiling water without a lid. After the water is boiling rapidly, add the beans. Cook for a few minutes until the beans have become tender but still have a slight bite. Remove from the water or drain through a colander, steeping the beans in ice water. After they're cold, remove from the water and drain well.

   To cook the scallops, heat a frying-pan with a tablespoon of olive oil. The scallops should be dry. This will prevent them from "poaching" in the pan. When the oil is almost smoking, place the scallops in the pan, making sure the maximum heat is maintained. It's important the scallops are seared, taking on a slightly burned tinge around their edges. Cook for 1–1½ minutes and then add a rounded teaspoon of butter. Cook for another 30 seconds;

the scallops will now have a rich golden color and are ready to be turned. After you've turned them, cook for another 1–2 minutes. The scallops can now be seasoned with salt and pepper and removed from the pan.

While the scallops are searing, mix together the beans, radishes, and sesame seeds. Spoon 2–3 tablespoons of the white wine dressing into the bean mixture and stir in well, making sure plenty of shallots have been included. Spoon some of the yogurt and sour cream dressing toward the top of each plate. The bean and radish salad can now be divided among the four plates, building a "bonfire effect" salad. After shaping the salads, spoon any dressing left in the bowl on top.

The scallops, three per serving, can now be arranged in a semi-circle in front of the salad. The dish is now ready to serve.

Note: I very rarely use scallop roes in my recipes, but I hate to throw flavors away. So, if the scallops you buy come with roe, turn them into a scallop-roe butter by simply puréeing the roe in a food processor with an equal amount of unsalted butter. To guarantee a smooth finish, push the purée through a sieve. Now, simply wrap in plastic wrap and freeze until needed. The butter can enhance the flavor of a fish sauce, soup, or stew – literally just a tablespoon whisked into four servings of a basic fish sauce (see *Basic White Wine or Champagne Fish Sauce,* page 47) will be enough to enrich the finished taste. The butter also slightly thickens a sauce or soup. Just remember not to re-boil the liquid because this will separate the butter.

Dandelion and Bacon Salad

A dandelion and bacon salad is a well-known French dish, but I'm sure we have been eating something similar has been prepared in Britain for years. Dandelion greens were valued in country areas as spring greens after the dried legume diet of the winter months, and they were used medicinally as a diuretic (the French name *piss-en-lit* graphically

describes this property). Food writers in the seventeenth century mentioned that the greens were good to eat, and because dandelion is related to wild chicory, the roots have been used to make a coffee substitute. Green dandelion grows wild and has been picked for many years. It was a tough and bitter leaf and was cooked mostly as a vegetable, boiled for 20–30 minutes before being tossed in butter. People began to cover them before harvesting to blanch them, which keeps them tender and less bitter to eat.

The dandelion greens can be mixed with other salad greens, but this one we'll keep as a straight dandelion salad. Another ingredient I'm adding is diced bread, which will be fried in the bacon fat. A sprinkling of finely grated Parmesan can also be added. The dressing is simply a well-flavored oil: olive, walnut, or hazelnut will all complement the other flavors.

SERVES 2 AS AN APPETIZER

2 large bunches of dandelion greens
2 slices of thick bread (white, whole wheat, or multi-grain)
6 strips of bacon cut into ¾ in (2 cm) pieces
2–4 tablespoons olive, walnut, or hazelnut oil
1 tablespoon finely grated Parmesan cheese (optional)
Salt and pepper

The dandelion leaves can first be washed and drained in a colander.

Cut the slices of bread into ½ in (1 cm) dice. Fry the bacon in a hot frying-pan; the bacon will create its own fat, cooking the pieces until very crisp. Remove the bacon with a slotted spoon and keep to one side. The bread can now be fried in the fat left in the pan until it is golden and crisp. Return the bacon pieces, mixing them with the bread croûtons.

Place the greens in a bowl and sprinkle with the bacon and bread. Season with salt and pepper and trickle with the oil. If using the freshly grated Parmesan, sprinkle it on top and serve.

Note: A squeeze of lemon or lime juice or a teaspoon of red wine vinegar can also be added.

OPPOSITE
Radish and French Bean Salad with Seared Scallops

Gratin of Grated Turnips ⓥ

Turnips are root vegetables, members of the cabbage family, and have been around in Europe for hundreds of years; they were probably spread northward by the Romans. Their closest relative is the rutabaga, which only came upon the vegetable scene in the seventeenth century, the name being a contraction of "Swedish turnip." Before the potato was introduced, turnips were probably the staple carbohydrate food of the poor.

The turnips here are cooked using a concept vaguely like that of dauphinoise potatoes. It is a very simple dish to make, and the turnips will go very well with many dishes featured in this book, lamb and game in particular.

SERVES 4–6

1¼ cups (300 ml) heavy cream
1 large garlic clove, crushed
Sprig of fresh thyme
1½ lbs (675 g) peeled turnips, coarsely grated
    (about 1 lb 14 oz/850 g unpeeled weight)
Butter
Salt and pepper

Warm the cream, garlic, and thyme all together. Infuse for 10 minutes before adding the grated turnips and then seasoning with salt and pepper.

Cook over a medium heat, gently simmering until the turnips are tender. This will take just 15–20 minutes. Remove the sprig of thyme and add a rounded teaspoon of butter to the mixture. The cream will have reduced in this time and become slightly thicker.

Spoon into a greased vegetable dish and gratinate under a hot broiler until golden brown.

Note: Freshly grated Parmesan cheese can be sprinkled on top before glazing. Also, a quarter or half an onion can be grated and mixed with the turnip.

Asparagus with Melted Butter or Hollandaise Sauce ⓥ

Asparagus, a member of the lily family, was eaten by the Ancient Egyptians, Greeks, and Romans, and was probably introduced to Britain – as were so many vegetables – by the Romans during their 400-year-long occupation. Thereafter, it wasn't until the Elizabethan age that asparagus began to be grown again, but it was always a rare and special vegetable for a variety of reasons. An asparagus bed takes three or four years to establish, and although the shoots are available only from May to early July, the dormant vegetable monopolizes that bed for the remainder of the year. This is not a very practical arrangement for most vegetable gardeners, but for those who do the two short months of freshly picked asparagus bring nothing but sheer paradise.

The accompaniments here are the most traditional – melted butter or a hollandaise sauce. To the melted-butter version, I add a tablespoon or two of water, which will then emulsify the butter into a sauce consistency. I also season the spears with coarse sea salt, which is very exciting to eat with asparagus and many other green vegetables: when you bite and crunch on the salt, the flavors become even more alive.

For an appetizer I like to offer 6–8 medium spears per serving.

SERVES 2 AS AN APPETIZER

12–16 medium asparagus spears

To Serve with Melted Butter

6 tablespoons (75 g) unsalted butter
2–3 tablespoons water
Freshly ground black or white pepper
Pinch of sea-salt

To Serve with Hollandaise

⅔ cup (150 ml) *Hollandaise Sauce* or *Simple Hollandaise Sauce* (page 41)

If serving with hollandaise, make the sauce first.

Cut away the tough ends of the asparagus stalks, about of the gray/white bottom stalk ¾–1¼ in (2–4 cm), keeping the spears a uniform length.

The asparagus can now be plunged into a large saucepan of rapidly boiling salted water. Twelve to

Buttered Spinach ⓥ

sixteen spears is the maximum that should be cooked at one time, any more and the water will lose its heat and begin to stew the spears.

Cook, with the lid off, for 2–3 minutes (4 is the absolute maximum), and lift from the pot.

Arrange the servings on hot plates. To glaze and shine the asparagus, lightly brush with melted butter. Sprinkle with the coarse sea-salt. While the asparagus is cooking, bring the 2–3 tablespoons water to a boil in a small saucepan. Add the butter in chunks, whisking in vigorously. Add a twist of pepper and the sauce is ready to serve.

Hollandaise sauce, if using, can be offered separately.

Note: A squeeze of lemon juice can be added to the butter sauce, with a teaspoon of chopped fresh chives for a slight oniony bite.

BELOW
Asparagus with Melted Butter or Hollandaise Sauce

Spinach, originally from Persia, didn't reach Britain until the fourteenth century, and was one of the first vegetables to be cooked by itself, rather than being boiled in a pottage. It was simply braised and served with a little oil and spices or sugar sprinkled on top as a cooked salad.

Fresh spinach is one of my favorite vegetables. Cooked with a rounded teaspoon of butter and plenty of seasoning and served straight from the pan – you just can't beat it. It's also a vegetable that can be cooked in advance, however. Simply drop into boiling, salted water and cook for just a few minutes until tender; lift or drain from the pan and plunge into ice water to immediately stop the cooking process. After it is cold, any excess water can be squeezed gently from the tender leaves. To have it totally ready to re-heat in a frying-pan or microwave, add a rounded teaspoon or two of butter along with a sprinkling of salt, pepper and freshly grated nutmeg. The spinach will keep well like this, refrigerated, until needed.

Here's the recipe if you'd rather serve this delicious vegetable straight from the pan.

SERVES 4–6

2–4 tablespoons (25–50 g) butter
2 lb (900 g) spinach leaves, picked and washed
Salt and pepper
Freshly grated nutmeg

Heat a large saucepan with the butter. After it's bubbling, add the spinach leaves. The water still clinging to the leaves after washing will create enough steam in the pan to cook the spinach. The heat can now be increased. Stir the leaves in the pan. These will begin to wilt and within a few minutes, will have become tender. Season with the salt, pepper, and nutmeg. The spinach is now ready to serve.

If a lot of excess water has collected after cooking, then drain the spinach in a colander before serving.

Spinach Dumplings ⓥ

These dumplings make a lovely vegetarian main course or a delicious appetizer, served with a very easy and quick tomato sauce.

SERVES 4 AS A MAIN COURSE
AND 8 AS AN APPETIZER (MAKES 16)

1 onion, finely chopped
4 tablespoons (50 g) unsalted butter
1¼ lb (550 g) fresh spinach, stalks removed
8 oz (225 g) mascarpone or cream cheese
8 oz (225 g) all-purpose flour
1 egg
1 egg yolk
Pinch of freshly grated nutmeg
Salt and pepper
4 oz (100 g) Parmesan cheese, grated, to serve

For the Sauce

3 tablespoons olive oil
10–12 tomatoes, blanched in boiling water for
    10 seconds and skinned, or 1 × 400 g (14 oz)
    can chopped tomatoes
1 small garlic clove, crushed
1–2 teaspoons tomato ketchup (optional)

Sweat the chopped onion in the butter for a few minutes until softened, then allow to cool.

Wash the spinach well to remove any grit, then shake off any excess water. Blanch the spinach in boiling, salted water for about 30 seconds, then refresh in ice water. Squeeze the spinach until all the liquid is removed and then chop it finely.

Mix the spinach and onion together and then fold in the cheese and flour. Lightly beat the egg and egg yolk together, then add them to the mixture and season with salt, pepper, and nutmeg. Let the mixture to rest for about 30 minutes and then mold the mixture into dumplings with floured-dusted hands.

The dumplings can now be cooked in simmering salted water for 10–15 minutes. Meanwhile, preheat the broiler and make the tomato sauce.

Seed the tomatoes and chop the tomato flesh into a ¼ in (5 mm) dice. Heat a tablespoon of olive oil with the clove of garlic and add the tomatoes. Cook them until tender and almost reduced to a pulp, allowing the natural juices to reduce. After reducing, season with salt and pepper and add the remaining olive oil. For a sweeter, spicy finish, add the ketchup, if using.

Arrange the dumplings in a flameproof dish and cover with the grated Parmesan. Finish under a hot broiler, until the cheese is lightly browned. The dumplings are now ready to serve with the tomato sauce.

Egg and Bacon Salad

A British egg salad holds the reputation of limp salad greens, tomatoes, cucumber, radish, and beets that stain everything else, all mixed with salad dressing from a jar. I think the British have moved on from those days.

Salads were once a great feature of British cooking. Hard-boiled eggs have been used in salads since Elizabethan times, as the forerunners of the great composite salads of the seventeenth century. The foundation of the salads would be flowers and greens, perhaps some cucumber, dressed with oil and vinegar, then the eggs placed on top. Often slices of cold cooked poultry or meat or pieces of fish would be added as well.

This egg salad is accompanied by bacon, making it a traditional British combination. Within the recipe, various cooking alternatives are given: poaching or boiling the eggs, frying or broiling the bacon, and toasting or frying the bread. Variety is obviously the spice of this dish. This salad is a delicious dish to serve for brunch.

OPPOSITE
Egg and Bacon Salad

4 slices of thick-sliced white, whole wheat, or
    multi-grain bread, crusts removed
4 poached or 4–6 "soft" hard-boiled eggs (page 81)
4 strips of bacon
4 small butterhead lettuces, leaves separated and
    rinsed (Romaine can also be used; tear the
    leaves into suitable strips)
3–4 tablespoons red wine vinegar
2–3 tablespoons olive or peanut oil
4 scallions, washed and finely shredded
Salt and pepper

Cut the slices of bread into ½ in (1 cm) dice, unless broiling. In this case, leave the slices whole. Cut the "soft" hard-boiled eggs into quarters. The ingredients list suggests 4–6 eggs; 4 should be enough but 6 eggs will obviously provide more generous servings.

The bacon can now be pan-fried or broiled until crisp. If pan-frying, a dry pan can be used. Any fat content from the bacon will be released into the pan. This will also happen if broiling. Whichever method you choose, keep the bacon fat for frying the bread. After it's cooked, remove the bacon from the pan and keep it warm. Now add the bread and fry until golden and crisp. You might need extra oil to achieve a golden finish. If the bacon has been broiled, simply brush each slice of bread with the fat released, and toast. Now, it can be diced.

Season the salad greens with salt and pepper. It's best, whenever making salads, to sprinkle salt around the bowl and not directly on the leaves. This prevents the salt from falling onto wet leaves and sticking in lumps. Cut the bacon into small pieces and mix it into the greens, with the scallions and fried or toasted bread. Mix together the red wine vinegar and the olive or peanut oil. This mixture can be spooned on top of the greens, adding just enough to coat. Arrange on four plates or present as one large salad. The hard-boiled egg quarters can now be seasoned with salt and pepper and placed among the leaves.

For poached eggs, re-heat in simmering water for 1 minute before placing on top of the salads.

Note: Extra red wine vinegar can be mixed with olive or peanut oil with the addition of mustard to taste. This can be kept in a jar to be shaken when ready to use.

A pinch of sugar can be added to the red wine vinegar to sweeten the finish, slightly reducing the piquant acidity.

It's always nice to offer homemade *Salad Dressing* (page 48) or *Mayonnaise* (page 49) with this dish.

Fresh Peas

Fresh green peas were not eaten in Europe until Italian gardeners developed the garden pea as opposed to the field pea, which was dried, in the sixteenth century. They have become a classic vegetable since then to be "buttered" in the British vegetable tradition. I've added a few more flavorings here, making the dish more like the classic French pea dish called *petits pois à la française*.

1 lb (450 g) fresh peas, weighed out of their pods
4 tablespoons (50 g) unsalted butter
2 onions, sliced
4 strips of bacon
¼–⅓ cup (50–85 ml) *Chicken* or *Vegetable Stock*
    (page 33 or 36), or water
Salt and pepper

You can cook the peas in advance and finish preparing the dish later right before serving. Bring a large pan of salted water to a boil. Drop in the shelled peas, return the water to a boil, and boil until tender, keeping the lid off throughout and the water boiling all the time. This takes from 4–7 minutes, depending on the size of the pea. If the peas are not tender by then, simply keep boiling until they are ready. Drain the peas, and keep to one side. (If you are serving them immediately, simply toss in some butter and season.)

When you wish to serve the peas, melt 2 tablespoons (25 g) of the butter and cook the onions and bacon until slightly softened. Add the stock or water and bring to a boil. Add the remaining butter and season with salt and pepper. Quickly re-heat the peas in a microwave or in a pan of boiling water for 30 seconds, then drain. Toss the peas in the reduced bacon and onion liquid, and serve immediately.

Braised Split Peas ⓥ

The legumes that became so important in the British diet (the small Celtic bean of the fava bean family and the pea introduced by the Romans) were brought in from the Continent. The pea was particularly prized because it could be eaten fresh (although nothing like as sweet and tender as the garden peas cultivated centuries later in Italy). It could also be dried for grinding into a bread meal or lengthily simmered in a meat or vegetable soup, adding bulk, flavor, and texture. An early Great British dish was bacon and peas, both of which were cooked in the pot together. This was popular with rich and poor alike and something that I re-introduced to my menus fifteen years ago. Later, after the invention of the pudding cloth, dried peas were wrapped in the cloth and boiled in the bacon pot producing the famous pease pudding. This was then cut into pieces to be served with the bacon.

I think split peas are delicious slowly braised until barely tender. They go well with many other dishes too, from the *Boiled Bacon with Pearl Barley* on page 224, to *Pork* or *Cumberland Sausages* (pages 367 and 368), or fish and chips. For a really softened finish, cook for another 10–15 minutes with a little more stock.

SERVES 6–8

4 oz (100 g) carrots
2 celery sticks
2 onions
1 garlic clove, crushed (optional)
1 tablespoon olive oil
2 tablespoons (25 g) unsalted butter
1 lb (450 g) dried green split peas

1 quart (900 ml) *Vegetable* or *Chicken Stock*
    (page 36 or 33)
Salt and pepper

Preheat the oven to 400°F/200°C.

Cut the carrots, celery and onions into ¼ in (5 mm) dice. Sweat with the garlic, if using, in the olive oil and butter for a few minutes in a flameproof casserole dish. Add the split peas and cook for 1–2 minutes, stirring. Cover with 2½ cups (600 ml) of the stock and bring to a simmer. Cover and cook in the preheated oven for 20–25 minutes or until tender. The peas will need stirring during cooking and, possibly, more stock will need to be added. Season with salt and pepper before serving.

BELOW
Braised Split Peas

Green Beans and How to Cook Them

There are many varieties and sizes of green beans, which are sometimes known as haricots verts in the food industry. The most popular type served in restaurants is the extra-fine French bean, which is considered to be a first-class vegetable. The beauty of cooking this bean is the minimum preparation needed; it simply needs the ends trimmed, although I prefer to leave the spiky, pointed end attached for better visual presentation.

Another favorite of mine is the runner bean. These beans are usually found as a flat, smooth form or a coarser and fatter variety. You can cut the flat beans in two ways: either shredded at an angle to give 1½–2 in (4–5 cm) thin strips, or as larger diamonds. The coarse bean string needs to be pulled away from both sides before finely shredding; a thicker cut can often result in a tough result.

A major advantage to using these vegetables is that you can par-boil them well in advance and re-heat when needed. After they've cooked using the method that follows, simply drain from the saucepan and plunge into ice water. This immediately stops the cooking and also allows the beans to keep their rich green color. After they're cold, remove from the cold water and plunge back into boiling water for 30–45 seconds when you're ready to serve them.

There are a few golden rules that should never be broken when cooking these or, indeed, any green vegetables. Always use a large saucepan up to three-fourths full of boiling salted water and never use a lid at any time during the cooking; even when the water has boiled and the beans are cooking, don't cover the pan with a lid. By using this method, the vegetables' rich color is kept. One more small point: try not to cook too many green vegetables at once. If you do, the water temperature decreases and it will take too long to return to the boiling point, which often results in the loss of color.

On the opposite page is a guide to cooking times for beans. Having prepared them for cooking, plunge them in boiling, salted water first and cook according to the times listed below:

Extra-fine beans – very thin beans should be finish cooking as soon as the water returns to a boil. It's best to test the beans first, which should always keep a good bite to them. Extra-fine beans should otherwise

take no more than a minute to cook.
Fine French beans (a more common size) – these take 2–3 minutes after the water returns to a boil.
Runner beans, finely shredded – after 45 seconds–1 minute, they should be done.
Runner beans, cut into diamond shapes – they should take 1–2 minutes after the water returns to a boil.

Note: The coarser variety of runner bean will always take a little longer to cook.

Roast Mushroom and Leek Shepherd's Pie Ⓥ

Since shepherd's pie is such a classic of British cooking, it would be a shame to leave out a vegetarian variety. This is an easy recipe, which becomes almost "meaty," using the large Portobello mushrooms. The dish is layered like a lasagna with the mashed potatoes piped or spread across the top.

SERVES 4–6

Olive or cooking oil
2 lb (900 g) flat or open-cup mushrooms, wiped and stalks removed
3–4 leeks, finely shredded
Butter
1 onion, sliced
1½–2 lb (750–900 g) *Mashed Potatoes* (page 124)
Juice of ½–1 lemon
Salt and pepper
1 teaspoon each chopped fresh parsley, tarragon and basil (optional)

Preheat the oven to 450°F/230°C.
Heat a frying-pan or roasting pan with a tablespoon or two of olive or peanut oil. Season the mushrooms with salt and pepper and place in the pan. Fry the mushrooms over a high heat, browning

them well. After a minute, turn them in the pan and repeat the browning (another teaspoon of oil may be needed). Now, roast the mushrooms in the hot oven for 5–6 minutes. After they've cooked, remove them and keep to one side. Because of the fast frying and roasting, the mushrooms will have kept all of their juices, giving a richer flavor.

Heat a tablespoon of olive oil with a rounded teaspoon of butter and add the sliced onion. Cook over a moderate heat for a few minutes until softened but with very little color. Increase the heat, add the shredded leeks and season with salt and pepper. Stir for 3–4 minutes, and the leeks should now be tender.

Using a buttered ovenproof vegetable or shepherd's pie dish, cut the mushrooms into slices and place them on the bottom of the dish. Spoon some leeks, on top and then repeat with the mushrooms; continue to layer the ingredients until all are used.

The mashed potatoes can now be finished with the lemon juice and chopped herbs, if using. Spread or pipe the potatoes on top. Brush with butter and place in a hot oven for 10 minutes before serving. For an extra golden brown topping place under a preheated broiler.

Note: If using plain mashed potatoes to top the "pie," grated Cheddar or little pieces of Gorgonzola can be sprinkled on top and broiled for a cheesy finish.

See also
Sage Fava Beans with Bacon and Tomato (page 56)
Breakfast Mushrooms (page 84)
Breakfast Tomatoes (page 83)
Lemon and Parsley Carrots (page 59)
Macaroni, Artichoke, and Mushroom Cheese Pie (page 64)
Pressed Tomato Cake with Peppered Goat Cheese (page 66)
Steamed Leek and Cheddar Cheese Pudding (page 65)
Vegetarian Scotch Broth (page 31)

OPPOSITE
A selection of green vegetables

Potatoes

Over the years, potatoes have become a main feature in many of my dishes, in particular, for soft and creamy mashed potatoes, every Briton's favorite. In fact, potatoes are one of the staple foods in Britain, and they are much loved. But it may surprise you to know that they have been around in Western Europe for only about 400 years.

Native to South America, the potato was discovered by the conquering Spanish in Peru, and it was brought to Europe in about 1536. Sir Francis Drake is thought by many to have been responsible for the potato's introduction to Britain, but Sir Walter Raleigh was probably the more likely person since it was he who first cultivated this root vegetable at his Irish estate in County Cork, in about 1590. Another theory maintains that potato tubers were washed ashore in western Ireland from the wrecked Spanish Armada, and became established in their new home. The first recorded mention of the potato – and an illustration – was in John Gerard's *Herbal* of 1597, where it was wrongly described as being "of Virginia, the American state." This mistaken attribution remained for some time, mainly to distinguish it from *batatas* or the sweet potato (oddly enough, an earlier introduction). It wasn't until about 1710 that the potato became known as the "common," or more significantly, the "Irish" potato.

The potato was disliked for centuries in Europe, for many reasons. Its appearance was unpleasant, slightly warty and scabby, and it was thought to be related to leprosy, the dreaded skin disease of the time. The fact, too, that the potato was a relative of highly poisonous plants such as the deadly nightshade was not in its favor. It was also the first plant in Europe to be cultivated from unfamiliar tubers rather than from seed.

In Ireland, however, the potato did manage to become established and much more rapidly and completely than elsewhere in the British Isles. In a country with an impoverished peasantry and a soil and climate suitable for little else in an agricultural sense, the potato was ideal: it could survive in poor soil; it needed little cultivation; it could be harvested by hand, only a small plot was needed for a crop sufficient to feed a family; and it didn't need to be threshed, ground, or roasted. Once it was planted, it simply grew. From that, the potato became an essential part of the diet for the mass of the Irish population within about a century of its introduction, a fact illustrated by the number of Irish potato dishes. These include colcannon, boxty, champ, Irish stew, and a legion of potato cakes, breads, and soups, some of which you'll find in this book. And when the killer potato blight hit the whole of Europe in 1845–6, it was Ireland, the sole country reliant on this one crop, that was the most tragically devastated. It has been estimated that up to one million people died of starvation at that time, and another million emigrated, principally to England and North America.

The potato was also grown in Scotland and the north of England, welcomed where wheat was hard to grow because of climate, soil, and cost, as in Ireland. The tuber's soft flesh made a change from the oats and barley commonly grown for human consumption. But there was never the same enthusiasm for it as that shown by the Irish, and the fact that they were the major food of the immigrant Irish didn't help either. There are a number of traditional Scottish and northern English recipes, among them the oddly named kailkenny, stelk, panhaggerty, and rumbledethumps. Bubble and squeak in its present-day form is related to these Irish and Scottish recipes – basically a mixture of mashed potatoes and green vegetables – but originally it was made with meat and cabbage leftovers, without the potato. It couldn't have been the same.

Over the years, bad harvests and grain shortages led to the potato's gradual adoption and appreciation. By the end of the eighteenth century it was the most important vegetable crop in Britain. Potatoes became a very popular street food. They were baked (beginning about 1835) in the bakehouse, then sold by street vendors to be eaten warm with butter and salt. Later they were sold fried to accompany flounder or other fish, marking the beginning of the fish and chip trade. Mashed potatoes with eels and parsley broth – "Eels and Mash" – was a dish sold by London's fish stalls in the later years of the nineteenth century. Gradually, potatoes were eaten at home – boiled, mashed, fried, or roasted – to accompany all main courses, whether fish or meat. This was probably when the British reliance on potatoes as an integral part of a meal (meat and two vegetables) originated. Interestingly, if they had been introduced earlier, they would probably have become a soup vegetable, such as onions or leeks; they arrived later, though, falling into the category of roots to be boiled and buttered or fried, to be served as a "vegetable."

There are hundreds of potato varieties known, but only a few are commonly available in Britain, which is a pity. Some of the British favorites are Maris Piper, Estima, Wilja, and King Edward. In the US, the most commonly used varieties are Russet, Idaho, Yukon Gold, various reds, and Fingerling potatoes. All of these make a good mashed potatoes, the potato texture breaking down to give quite a light, creamy finish. Russets and Idahos work well for with their thin skin and superb flavor.

Try these recipes and peel back the natural flavors of this wonderful vegetable.

Sautéd Potatoes ⓥ

More or less any potato can be used for sautéing, but for a perfectly shaped sauté, it's best to use a waxy variety. The Yukon Gold variety will give you that waxiness, as will most new potatoes and small round red ones.

The potatoes should always be cooked before sautéing. Some recipes will tell you to keep them slightly underdone so that during the process of pan-frying they will not break down and will keep their perfect shape.

That's not really what I'm after. I like the potatoes to be boiled or steamed until almost overcooked, then lifted from the water or steamer and allowed to cool naturally. Even standard baking potatoes like the Idaho can be used. These will crumble around the outside, and when they are peeled, will have a fluffy edge. When they are pan-fried (sautéd), they will become very crisp and sometimes actually burn, giving contrasts of flavors. They might not look perfect, but they will taste sensational.

By the way, the word sauté comes from the French verb *sauter*, "to jump" – and that's exactly what the potato pieces should be doing in the pan.

1½ lb (750 g) potatoes, cooked in their skins
Olive or peanut oil, to give a ⅛ in (2 mm) covering of pan
4 tablespoons (50 g) unsalted butter
Salt
1 teaspoon chopped fresh parsley, to serve (optional)

Peel the potatoes and carefully cut them into ¼ in (5 mm) slices; many potatoes will break, but don't worry, the small pieces will become crisp. If you have used new potatoes, then halve them lengthwise. Warm the oil in a frying-pan over a medium heat. Place the potatoes in the oil and cook for 6–8 minutes, shaking softly from time to time. The potatoes will take on a golden edge. Slightly increase the heat and continue to cook for 2 minutes. Unless you have a particularly large frying-pan, cook the potatoes in two batches using half the butter for each. When this begins to bubble, turn the potatoes over and continue to fry until completely golden and crisp. These can now be kept warm in a preheated oven while you cook the other half. After all of the potatoes are completely sautéed, season with salt and sprinkle with chopped parsley, if using.

Note: Other fats can be used for sautéing potatoes. One of the most flavorful is goose or duck fat. Both of these will give you a rich flavor. Lard or bacon fat can also be used.

Sautéd Sea-salt Potatoes ⓥ

Sautéd potatoes are considered a French classic, but they have become very a much part of British tradition. Often, with extra new potatoes cooked, it is the practice to halve them and sauté them in butter. My recipe follows this idea but adds sea salt as well as chopped parsley.

New potatoes or the baking variety can be used, but both will first have to be boiled or steamed until cooked. For the very best results, sauté them while still warm, giving the potato a flaky edge that will become golden and very crisp.

These potatoes go very well with fish or meat. Try them with simple broiled Dover sole (see *Broiled or Pan-fried Dover Sole*, page 141), will go very well.

1 lb (450 g) new or baking potatoes, cooked
1–2 tablespoons cooking oil (olive oil can be used
    for a richer finish)
4 tablespoons (50 g) unsalted butter
1 teaspoon coarse sea salt
1 tablespoon chopped fresh parsley (flatleaf parsley
    will give more flavor)
Pepper

While the potatoes are still warm, peel them. For new potatoes, peeling is not essential but it will give a more crumbled finish. After they are peeled, cut the new potatoes in half lengthwise or the baking potatoes into ¼ in (5 mm) slices. When the potatoes have been peeled

BELOW
Sautéd Sea-salt Potatoes

and sliced, shake the bowl they are in to break up the edges of the potatoes slightly.

Heat a frying-pan or wok with the cooking oil. For this amount of potatoes, it's best to fry them in two batches, creating more room for browning instead of steaming.

Add half of the potatoes to the frying-pan and cook over a medium heat until golden brown on both sides. This will take 8–10 minutes.

Remove the potatoes and keep them warm. Repeat the frying process with the remaining half. When ready, add to those set aside and toss again to completely mix and re-heat. At this point, add the butter and begin to stir/shake the potatoes in the pan. Continue to cook for several minutes to give them a crisp edge. Add the coarse sea salt, chopped parsley, and a grinding of pepper. Toss in the pan.

The potatoes are ready to serve. Some of the sea salt will have dissolved and released its flavor into the potatoes, while some still has a crisp texture.

Note: For extra taste, squeezing in the juice of a lime brings a great finish to the potatoes, particularly if serving with fish.

Potato Cakes ⓥ

These are disks of potato that are poached in butter. As they soften, the potatoes absorb a rich butter flavor. They can be made well in advance and kept refrigerated. To finish, the potatoes are pan-fried to a golden brown. For an alternative, I'm including a recipe for roasted potato disks. These are quickly blanched, fried, and roasted.

While disks -shaped potatoes look good, they can still be cooked very simply by splitting lengthwise in two and then cooking by either method.

MAKES 6 CAKES

3 medium to large potatoes
16 tablespoons (225 g) butter (½ lb block)
Salt

Preheat the oven to 300°F/150°C.

Peel the potatoes and cut them in two. Now cut the disks using a 2¾ in (7 cm) cutter. Trim the potato top and bottom to a neat ½–¾ in (1.5–2 cm) thick.

Dice the block of butter and place the pieces in a suitable saucepan or small roasting pan. Place the potatoes on top in a single layer, and then place the pan over a medium heat and heat to melt the butter, bringing the contents to a soft simmer. The pan can now be placed in the slow oven for 40–45 minutes until the potatoes are tender.

After they're cooked, remove the cakes from the butter. The butter can be kept and strained to use for cooking to cook other vegetables. If not serving the potatoes immediately, then let them cool. They can now be refrigerated until needed.

To finish, melt a rounded teaspoon of butter in a frying-pan and, after it bubbles, pan-fry the potatoes until golden brown. This will take 5–6 minutes. Turn the potatoes over and finish browning. Season with salt and the potato cakes are ready to serve.

Note: Crushed garlic, thyme, and bay leaf can help flavor the potatoes. Simply add 2–3 cloves of crushed garlic, 2–3 sprigs of thyme, and 1 bay leaf to the butter.

Variation: The Roast Alternative

Preheat the oven to 400°F/200°C. Peel and cut the potato disks as above. Blanch in salted, boiling water for 4 minutes. Now, lightly coat in all-purpose flour. Heat a thin layer (2 mm) of oil in a suitable pan for roasting in the oven. Place the potatoes in the oil and fry over a medium heat until rich and golden. Turn the potato disks over and continue to fry until browned. This process will take 6–7 minutes on each side. Now place the pan in the oven and roast for 20–25 minutes. The potato will have a good soft center with a crispy finish. Season well with salt before serving.

Parsnip Potato Cakes ⓥ

This vegetarian dish has many variations. Lots of other tastes and flavors can be added, such as fresh herbs, mustard, or other vegetables. Vegetable hot-pot potato cakes could also be made, cooking a selection of carrots, turnips, and rutabegas as well as the parsnips and potatoes. This recipe can also be adapted to use up the leftover cooked vegetables and potatoes from your Sunday dinner. Mash the roast potatoes and roughly chop whatever vegetables have been left.

The parsnips are simply cooked in butter, without browning, until tender. They can also be pan-fried until golden for a roasted finished flavor.

The cakes can be shallow-fried or deep-fried. This recipe will give you eight cakes – two per person – to serve as an appetizer or to accompany the main course.

SERVES 4

1 lb (450 g) parsnips
4 tablespoons (50 g) butter
1 small shallot or ½ small onion, finely chopped
2⅔ cups (225 g) *Mashed Potatoes*, without milk,
     cream, or butter (page 124)
6 fresh sage leaves, chopped
Oil, for frying
Butter
Salt, pepper, and freshly grated nutmeg

For the Breadcrumb Coating

2–3 tablespoons all-purpose flour
2 eggs, beaten with 2–3 tablespoons milk
3 cups (200 g) fresh or dried breadcrumbs

Peel and quarter the parsnips lengthwise, and cut away the center core. Now cut the vegetable into ½ in (1 cm) dice. Melt 2 tablespoons (25 g) of the butter in a pan and add the parsnips. These can now be cooked covered with a lid over a medium heat for 10 minutes until they become tender. The steam created from being covered will have created some liquid in the pan. Remove the lid and continue to cook for 2–3 minutes. The juices will now be absorbed back into the parsnips. Remove from the heat. Mash with a potato masher, leaving a slightly chunky texture. For a creamier finish, process in a food processor. I prefer a chunkier consistency; mixing them with mashed potatoes will create the creaminess.

In the remaining butter, cook the shallots for 1 minute to take away their rawness, still retaining their texture and acidic bite.

Mix together the mashed parsnips with the potatoes, shallots, and chopped sage. Season with salt, pepper, and grated nutmeg. The mixture can now be shaped into eight disk-shaped cakes or balls. These can be placed on plastic wrap and refrigerated for 30 minutes to set.

To coat the potato cake with breadcrumbs, first season the flour with salt and pepper. Lightly coat each cake with the flour. Pass the cakes, one at a time, through the egg and milk mixture and then through the crumbs, shaping and patting neatly with a spatula. To ensure a good coating, pass the covered cakes through the egg mixture and the crumbs once more. After they're shaped, refrigerate again to set.

To cook, warm a tablespoon or two of cooking oil in a frying-pan. Add a rounded teaspoon of butter and, when it bubbles, place the cakes in the pan. Shallow-fry for 6–7 minutes on each side until golden brown.

For deeper-frying, warm ¼ in (5 mm) of cooking oil in a frying-pan over a low–medium heat. Place the cakes in the oil and cook them for 6–7 minutes. After they become golden, turn them over and repeat the same cooking time. When they are done, remove from the pan and dry on paper towels. The cakes are ready to serve.

Note: A wedge of lemon can be served with the cakes; the acidic lemony flavor heightens the taste.

Mayonnaise (page 49) flavored with either mustard or *Horseradish Sauce* (page 55) can also be offered.

Simple nut-brown butter mixed with a squeeze of lemon also goes very well, particularly if finished with chopped capers, lemon segments, and chopped parsley, for a nut-brown tartar finish.

Garlic Cream Potato Cakes ⓥ

These potatoes will lend themselves to many dishes. I have featured them with fish (see *Pan-fried Red Mullet with a Tomato and Leek Soup*, page 149), but they will also go with almost any meat dish, from sausage to roast lamb or game, stews, and braised dishes.

The concept has been adapted from the French *pommes dauphinoise*, made from sliced, layered potatoes baked in the oven in a garlic cream sauce. The little oval shapes (round will also be fine), approximately ¾ in (2 cm) deep, are cooked in the garlic cream on top of the stove; 40–45 minutes later, they are ready to serve. They can also be made in advanced.

One more tip: infuse the milk and cream overnight with the garlic and thyme. This will intensify and maximize the finished flavor.

SERVES 6

3 large potatoes, peeled

For the Garlic Cream

1¼ cups (300 ml) heavy cream
1¼ cups (300 ml) milk
1 teaspoon coarse sea salt
1–2 thyme sprigs
2 garlic cloves, crushed

Mix together the cream, milk, sea salt, thyme, and garlic. For best results, let the mixture infuse overnight.

Split the potatoes in half lengthwise. These can now be trimmed by hand into oval shapes or cut, using an 3–4 in (8–10 cm) oval cutter.

To cook the potatoes, place in a saucepan and cover with the garlic cream. Bring to a simmer and cook on a minimal heat until the potatoes become tender; a little extra milk can be added if the sauce is becoming too thick. This cooking will take 40–45 minutes. They can now be left to stay hot until the main course is ready, or you can remove them from the pan, and allow them to cool; then refrigerate them until needed. To re-heat, simply microwave.

Note: If more garlic cream is needed to cover the potatoes, barely cover the potatoes with milk and add an extra clove of garlic.

Mashed Potatoes ⓥ

Mashed potatoes have been around for a long time and used to be served with eels from street vendors in the nineteenth century. Soft, creamy, buttered, mashed potatoes are my favorite potato dish of all time – a classic that will definitely see its way through the next millennium.

Mashed potatoes are looked upon as a simple, straightforward dish using any kind of potato for the recipe. During the seasons, various potatoes are available, but Idaho potatoes are easily obtained all year and they purée very well. The rest, of course, is being careful in the cooking and finishing of the dish.

2 lb (900 g) large floury potatoes, preferably
    Idaho, peeled and quartered
8 tablespoons (100 g) unsalted butter
½ cup (120 ml) light cream or milk
Salt, pepper, and freshly grated nutmeg

Boil the potatoes, covered, in salted water until cooked, approximately 20–25 minutes, depending on size. Drain off all the water and replace the lid. Shake the pan vigorously, which will start to break up the boiled potatoes. Add the butter and light cream or milk a little at a time while mashing the potatoes. Season with salt, pepper and some freshly grated nutmeg according to taste. The potatoes will now be light, fluffy, and creamy and ready to serve.

Mashed Potatoes Sauce

This thinner and creamier version of the recipe on the left works as a perfect accompaniment to many meat and fish dishes, in particular the *Broiled Lamb with "Irish" Cabbage* (page 187) and the *Slow-honey-roast Duck* (page 268).

To achieve the "sauce" consistency, simply double the amount of cream or milk. If the "sauce" is made in advance, when re-heating it you may find it has thickened and will need more warm milk or cream to thin it.

BELOW
Mashed Potatoes

Hazelnut Mashed potatoes Ⓥ

This alternate flavor gives the mashed potatoes a completely new face. I like to serve these rich potatoes with the *Roast Loin of Pork with an Apricot and Sage Stuffing* (page 330), but they go well with almost any of the meat dishes and, also, with quite a few of the fish ones.

There are two ingredients I add to the basic mashed potatoes: hazelnut oil and chopped roast hazelnuts. The amounts are really up to personal taste, but a simple guide is to add 1 teaspoon each of oil and chopped nuts for every serving. For a cleaner taste, the hazelnuts should be completely skinned before chopping.

Note: Hazelnuts can be bought already shelled and skinned, saving you preparation time. Then they can be "roasted" with a trickle of oil in a frying-pan. The nuts will brown very quickly, producing a rich flavor.

Chopped parsley can also be added at the end.

Colcannon Ⓥ

Not only did the potato became a staple food in Ireland, but cabbage did as well, and they were combined to make colcannon, a dish traditionally served at Halloween. Often the mixture would contain four symbols – a gold band for marriage, a sixpence for wealth, a thimble to indicate spinsterhood and a button for bachelorhood. Champ is another similar dish served at Halloween, a much more buttery mixture of mashed potatoes and green vegetables, usually scallions.

Colcannon is delicious as a totally vegetarian dish, perhaps with a poached egg on top, or it makes a great accompaniment to something like boiled bacon, ham, or sausage. You can use kale, as is traditional in some parts of Ireland, or white or green cabbage.

SERVES 4

1 lb (450 g) potatoes, peeled
⅔ cup (150 ml) milk or light cream
Pinch of ground mace
1 lb (450 g) kale or cabbage, shredded
2 small leeks or scallion tops, chopped
10 tablespoons (150 g) unsalted butter
Salt and pepper

Boil the potatoes, covered, in salted water until cooked, about 20–25 minutes depending on size. Drain off all the water and replace the lid. Shake the pan vigorously, which will start to break up the potatoes, then mash them until they are light and fluffy. Season with the salt, pepper, and mace and stir in the milk or cream.

Blanch the shredded kale or cabbage in boiling water for 2–3 minutes, until softened. Drain well. Fry the chopped leeks or scallion tops in 2 tablespoons (25 g) of the butter for a few minutes, until softened, then add the cabbage and continue to cook for a few more minutes before spooning them into the mashed potatoes. Melt the remaining butter and add it to the mixture. Check for seasoning and serve.

Bubble and Squeak Ⓥ

Bubble and squeak is a strange name for a vegetable dish, but it's probably so called because of the noises the vegetables make while being fried in the pan. Originally the dish was made with meat and cabbage only, but at some time potatoes were introduced, and they have remained.

As you can see from the recipe, I have given one or two alternatives. This is because bubble and squeak can be creatively varied, and either mashed or cooked potatoes with sprouts or cabbage will taste delicious. I prefer using mashed potatoes because they give a cake-like consistency, but if you're using plain boiled potatoes, simply peel them and cut into thick slices. The dish is usually made from leftovers, so the sprouts or cabbage should be pre-cooked.

SERVES 6–8

2 large onions, sliced
4 tablespoons (50 g) unsalted butter
1½ lb (750 g) potatoes, cooked and sliced, or 1½ lb (750 g) leftover *Mashed Potatoes* (page 124)
1 lb (450 g) green cabbage or Brussels sprouts, cooked (page 103 or 106)
2–3 tablespoons vegetable oil
Salt and pepper

Cook the sliced onions in half the butter until softened and mix with the potatoes and sprouts or cabbage and season with salt and pepper.

Preheat a frying-pan (one large or two small) and add the remaining butter and the oil. Fry the bubble mixture for 6–8 minutes, pushing it down with a spatula to create a cake shape. The pan should be kept hot to create a crisp bottom.

To turn over the bubble, cover the pan with a plate or baking pan, invert the pan so the cake falls onto the plate or pan, then slip it, uncooked side down, back into the pan and repeat the cooking process.

The bubble and squeak is now ready and can be cut into six or eight wedges before serving, or left whole as a cake.

Chips and French Fries ⓥ

Fish and chips is one of our most famous national dishes, but the combination has only been around for about 150 years. Some people say that the fish was cooked and sold in the street by expatriate Italians, and that the fried potatoes were introduced by Belgians, who, of course, are well known for their *frites* or French fries. Who knows?

Chips and French fries come in all shapes and sizes. There are some good-quality frozen French fries around but I don't believe you can find any that can beat homemade ones. I use large potatoes, which will cool after pre-cooking and become tender without losing their potato texture. For each portion 1–1½ potatoes will be plenty. You really need a deep-fat fryer to make these and to guarantee the right temperature.

If you don't have one, the fries will have to be treated with even more care and attention to give you a fluffy, tender, crisp result.

SERVES 4–6

Oil, for deep-frying
4–6 large peeled potatoes, about 3 lb (1.5 kg)
Salt

Heat the oil in the deep-fat fryer or deep, heavy-bottomed pan to 200°F/95°C for blanching.

For making the larger chips, trim the potatoes into rectangles. Now, cut into ½ in (1 cm) thick slices, then cut again to give slices ½ in (1 cm) thick and 2½–3 in (6–7.5 cm) long. If you want the thinner French fries, then simply halve the thickness, making them ¼ × 2½–3 in (5 mm × 6–7.5 cm).

The potato strips now need to be blanched in the preheated fryer. This is very important to guarantee that they will be totally cooked before serving. Frying them at 200°F/95°C will cook them without browning. The large chips will take up to 10–15 minutes before becoming tender. The smaller fries will need only 6–8 minutes. After they are cooked, check by piercing with a knife. When ready, remove from the oil and drain. The chips or fries can be left to cool on waxed paper and or chill them before finishing in the hot fryer.

To finish, preheat the oil in the fryer to 350°F/180°C. Once hot, place the chips in the fat. These will now take 2–3 minutes to become golden brown and crispy. Shake off any excess fat and sprinkle with salt before serving.

See also:

Bubble and Squeak Artichokes with Mushrooms (page 101)
Classic Roast Potatoes (page 238)
Creamy Bubble and Squeak Soup with Crunchy Bacon (page 29)
Leek and Potato Broth (page 18)

Fish and Shellfish

Despite the fame of
British fish and chips, it is only
recently that seafood has become a
British passion again. This reborn
interest was brought about to a great
extent by chefs, most of whom have a
natural passion for cooking fish and
shellfish. Seafood is so versatile,
lending itself to many different
cooking methods – the simplest of
which usually produce the best results.
Creating dishes with fish has become
an enjoyable one in most kitchens.
Britons once virtually survived on fish
and ate it as much as, if not more
than, they did meat.

Fish and shellfish have always been abundant around the islands that form Britain. Very early on, fishermen caught them from the shore and from primitive boats; many fish bones and sea shells have been found in middens (domestic refuse dumps) attached to prehistoric sites. Because the catch could be vast but would quickly spoil, ways of preserving it had to be explored, and fish and shellfish were among the first foods to be salted and wind-dried. (Smoking is thought to have been introduced later by the Viking invaders, and, interestingly, many of the locations of British fish-smoking – a technique for which the country is famous throughout the world – are on the coast facing Scandinavia.) During their rule in Britain, the Romans were hugely enthusiastic about British seafood, so much so that they transported oysters from Colchester (still the center of the oyster industry) back to Rome. They also introduced the technique of sousing, preserving fish in brine, vinegar, and oil, along with their highly flavored fish sauces, *liquamen* and *garum*.

During the Middle Ages, the Church forbade people to eat meat on several days in the week throughout the year, during Lent and on Ember days (certain Wednesdays, Fridays, and Saturdays). There was great religious importance attached to the effect that food had on body and soul, and meat, coming from warm-blooded animals, was thought to induce intemperance and excessive self-indulgence. Fish, on the other hand, being basically cold-blooded, would have the opposite effect, perhaps promoting spirituality. This meant, literally, that on more than half the days in the year the people had to eat fish. For those living near the sea, this might have been no hardship, but for those inland it was not as easy, for they had to rely on salted or dried fish, mainly cod and herring. Country people could have eaten freshwater fish, but often inland ponds and rivers – – belonged to the wealthy or to monasteries. At this time, in their attempts to find lawful "meat," people ate barnacle geese and puffins (because it was said they were born at sea) and beavers (because they had a "fishy" tail). One commentator has suggested that this medieval eating of beavers was probably responsible for the animals becoming extinct in Britain.

Until the Reformation, when the rise of Protestantism reduced the influence of the Catholic Church, wealthy Anglo-Normans ate fish in soups, heavily herbed and spiced to mask the saltiness. The poor ate them in simple stews, often with root vegetables or grains, and later with potatoes and a few herbs added for flavor (the expression "kettle of fish" may have developed around this time). An early relationship was that between fish and parsley, and the herb was a principal ingredient in the famous medieval green fish sauce. When available, and affordable, fresh pike, eel, oysters, and small river and sea fish were also roasted, spitted, and broiled, or fried in butter. They were served on bread trenchers (plates), and later melted butter was poured over them. Sharp fruit garnishes or sauces were often added – mackerel with gooseberries, for example, is an ancient combination and one that still works well. Hot and cold pies in the British tradition used fish, often with clarified butter poured into them as a preservative. Potting fish in butter became a popular means of preservation in the sixteenth century: the Morecambe Bay potted shrimp and potted char (trout) from Lake Windermere are still famous today.

Meat, more commonly available by the seventeenth century, became the most popular protein source, although shellfish were still eaten in

PAGE 128
Lobster Casserole (page 154)

considerable quantities, notably cockles in Wales, and oysters, principally, in southern England. There were such huge numbers of the latter that they were put in meat pies and other dishes as a means of flavoring (particularly the famous steak and oyster pie). It wasn't until the mid nineteenth century when the oyster beds stopped producing because of over-fishing and pollution, that oysters became the province of the rich. And it was at this time, too, due to faster means of transportation – steamships and the railways and the arrival of more sophisticated ways of fishing such as trawling – that fresh fish suddenly became much more accessible to all. Seafood became the main eating habits of the working classes, particularly in Victorian London. Because flounder , mackerel, sprats, fresh and "red" (salted and dried) herrings were cheap and quick to cook – and shellfish such as oysters, cockles and winkles hardly needed cooking at all – seafood was eaten for most meals. At this time, the smell of stale fish was said to be associated with poverty.

Salmon was now sold fresh (for years it had been available from Scotland, salted, dried, or smoked), and plenty of it too – the story goes that London apprentices complained if they had to eat it more than once a week. (A gentler process of curing and smoking salmon would have developed in London at this time.) Cooked eels (with mashed potatoes) and many shellfish were also sold by vendors from street stalls, and in the mid 1850s, this led to the establishment of shops offering fried cod or flounder along with bread or a baked potato. Some years later the accompanying potato was "chipped" (cut into chunks) and fried, rather than baked, and this phenomenon spread throughout the country in the form of what are now famous as British fish and chip shops. The recipe for *Deep-fried Cod in Batter* on page 169 will explain just why this dish became so famous.

Now, in the new millennium, people have learned to love seafood again. Everyone is well aware of its health benefits, not forgetting, of course, its delicious flavors. But most of the British catch goes abroad – have you ever tried to get a local langoustine or scallop in Scotland? Also, because of over-fishing and polluted waters, there are worldwide shortages of fish, indicating the world needs to catch and to cook fish with more care.

Here are some recipes for you to enjoy, offering a complete range of methods and styles of cooking fish. Happy fishing!

During the years of Roman rule, the Romans were hugely enthusiastic about British seafood, so much so that they transported oysters from Colchester back to Rome.

Steamed Halibut and Cabbage
with a Salmon Gravlax Sauce

In the nineteenth century, halibut wasn't thought much of in England, but it's certainly appreciated now. The largest of the flat fish, the wild variety is increasingly rare, but the fish is now being farmed.

Steamed fish with buttered cabbage is a basic recipe very British in concept, and I have added a few details to lift it a little out of the ordinary. It will taste very different with a salmon gravlax sauce and sesame seeds along with the accompanying cabbage. This is an instance of how to bring traditional flavors up to date.

There are quite a few components to this recipe, but it's not difficult if you plan ahead. All of the flavors work well together, with the lemon oil heightening and blending them all.

SERVES 4

4 × 6–8 oz (175–225 g) halibut fillet servings
Butter
1 small Savoy cabbage, finely shredded
1–2 teaspoons sesame seeds, toasted
4 tablespoons olive oil
1 tablespoon lemon juice
Salt and pepper

For the Salmon Gravlax

1 tablespoon (15 g) coarse sea salt
1 tablespoon (15 g) superfine sugar
Pepper
Splash of brandy
1 lb (450 g) salmon fillet, skinned

BELOW
*Steamed Halibut and Cabbage with a
Salmon Gravlax Sauce*

Butter
2 tablespoons finely chopped shallots
2–3 tablespoons brandy
1 teaspoon light brown sugar
3 tablespoons white wine
2 teaspoons white wine vinegar
⅔ cup (150 ml) *Fish Stock* (page 35)
⅔ cup (150 ml) heavy cream
2–3 teaspoons Dijon mustard
1 teaspoon chopped fresh dill

The salmon gravlax needs to be made at least 6 hours in advance. This creates the curing process. Simply mix together the coarse sea salt, sugar, and pepper and moisten with the brandy. Spread the mixture over the salmon fillet, wrap with plastic wrap, refrigerate while it cures. As the fish cures, the salt and sugar are absorbed by the fish.

After it's ready, the salmon can be cut into ¼ in (5 mm) dice. You will probably find you will need no more than 4–5 oz (100–150 g) for the garnish. The rest can be thinly sliced and enjoyed at another meal with a squeeze of lemon. It's best to cure 1 lb (450 g) as a minimum amount to achieve the best results.

To make the sauce, melt a heaping teaspoon of butter in a saucepan, along with the shallots. After the butter is melted, cook the shallots in it for a few minutes without browning. Add the brandy and brown sugar and allow to reduce until you have a syrupy consistency. The white wine and white wine vinegar can also now be added, reducing to the same stage. Pour in the fish stock and boil until reduced by half. Add the heavy cream along with the Dijon mustard. Season with salt and bring to a simmer.

Season the halibut with salt and pepper. Place on a buttered paper and steam above boiling water for 8–10 minutes.

While steaming, melt a heaping teaspoon of butter in a large pan and add the shredded cabbage. Stir well and add 1–2 tablespoons of water. This will create steam and cook the cabbage within a few minutes. Season with salt and pepper, adding the toasted sesame seeds. Divide the cabbage among four plates, placing the halibut on top.

Add the diced gravlax to the sauce, along with the chopped dill, and spoon the sauce over the fish. Mix together the olive oil and lemon juice and season with salt and pepper. To finish the dish, drizzle the lemony olive oil over the halibut and around the dish. The fish is now ready to enjoy.

Steamed Turbot on Cabbage with "Truffle" Sauce

Steamed fish with buttered cabbage couldn't be more British. Turbot has always been rare, highly esteemed, and very expensive, and many look upon it as the best fish in the world. I, for one, wouldn't argue with that. The natural savor of fish, in particular that of turbot, goes very well with a green vegetable, but I've added a few more flavors to create another new classic.

The "truffle" sauce couldn't be more French. I've put the "truffles" in quotation marks here because, as you'll no doubt notice, there are no truffles listed in the ingredients. Instead, the sauce is made with mushrooms and onions, which together give a truffle-like flavor and aroma (truffles are related to mushrooms).

I have, however, included truffle oil as an optional extra. A few dots on top of the fish enhance the taste even more. This oil can be found in gourmet food shops and some large supermarkets. And if you are lucky enough to have a fresh truffle (a black one from the Périgord perhaps), a fine grating added at the last moment creates an even bigger explosion in the mouth.

SERVES 4

1 small Savoy or green cabbage
Butter
4 × 6 oz (175 g) turbot fillet servings, skin left on
Salt and pepper

2 cups (450 ml) Noilly Prat (French dry vermouth)
1¼ cups (300 ml) white wine, preferably
    Gewürztraminer
Juice of ½ lemon
6 oz (175 g) button mushrooms, finely sliced
2–4 tablespoons (25–50 g) butter
4 large shallots, finely sliced
½–⅔ cup (100–150 ml) heavy cream
Salt and pepper
Truffle oil (optional), to serve

To make the sauce: pour the Noilly Prat and white wine into two separate saucepans. Bring each one to a boil and reduce the Noilly by half and the wine by a third. Remove both from the heat and mix the reductions together. Squeeze the lemon juice onto the sliced mushrooms. Melt 1 tablespoon (25 g) of the butter in a saucepan and add the sliced shallots. Cook, without browning, for a few minutes until beginning to soften. Add the sliced mushrooms and continue to cook for another 2–3 minutes.

The alcohol mixture can now be added. On a low heat, simmer for 10–15 minutes. Add ½ cup (100 ml) of the cream, return to a simmer, and cook for another minute before pushing through a sieve.

This is a very important stage. The sauce must be completely squeezed from the shallots and mushrooms, leaving them totally dry. This will then extract every last drop of juice and flavor. If you have any muslin cloth, once the shallots and mushrooms have been pushed through a sieve, take a double layer of cloth and squeeze them once more. The sauce can now be checked for seasoning with salt and pepper. The taste now has an amazing truffle edge. The remaining cream may be needed if the flavor is too acidic. Whisk in a heaping teaspoon or two of butter along with a trickle of truffle oil, if using. The sauce is best processed with a food processor just before serving.

Quarter the cabbage, discarding any bruised outside leaves and cut away the core from each quarter. It's best now to pull away three or four layers of cabbage at a time before cutting, making the job a lot easier. Cut into ½–¾ in (1–2 cm) thick slices. Wash and drain well in a colander.

Melt a heaping teaspoon of butter in a large pan. Add the cabbage and cook over a medium heat, turning the cabbage carefully to ensure an even cooking. Any water from the cabbage will help create steam that will cook the vegetable. After it is tender, season with salt and pepper.

While cooking the cabbage, the turbot can be steamed. Cut four pieces of waxed paper into suitable sizes, butter the pieces, and season them with salt and pepper. Place the fillets on the papers, skin-side up. These can now be steamed over simmering water and cooked for 6–8 minutes, depending on the thickness of the fish. The fillets should be just firm to the touch. If you do not have a steamer, then place the fillets on a baking pan. Add a heaping teaspoon of butter and a sprinkling of white wine to the pan. Cover with foil; bring to a slow simmer and cook in a preheated oven (400°F/200°C) for 6–8 minutes.

To present the dish, divide the cabbage among four plates or bowls. The sauce can now be processed in a food processor, and, if using a truffle, grate it and add before spooning the sauce over and around the cabbage.

Remove the skin from the turbot; this pulls away easily, revealing a beautifully moist fillet. Present the turbot placed on top of the cabbage. Trickle with truffle oil, if available.

Note: If fresh or canned truffles are available, a black slice sitting on top of the turbot is a beautiful garnish.
    Without using truffles or truffle oil, it's still a beautiful dish to serve.

OPPOSITE
Pan-fried Fillet of Red Mullet with Seared Oranges and Scallions

Pan-fried Fillet of Red Mullet with Seared Oranges and Scallions

Red mullet is one of my favorite fish. It's the most prized fish of the Mediterranean (Mullus barbatus), with a rich crimson skin and a delicate flavor. A variety of red mullet which is not quite so delicate (Mullus surmuletus) can also be found in the Atlantic, around the south coast of Britain. Whichever fish you use, the mullet has always been prized. The Romans paid vast sums for it, and the English did too if this quote from Mrs Roundell's *Practical Cookery Book* (1898) has any truth to it: "Fifty years ago gourmands used to spend the summers at Weymouth, on purpose to eat Red Mullet, and would give as much as two guineas for a fine fish."

This dish is very refreshing, with the sweet acidity of the oranges and lemon working with the savory flavor of the scallions. The dressing can be made well in advance, making it a simple dish to finish. The addition of soft, creamy mashed potatoes balances all of these flavors and goes beautifully with the crisp pan-fried red mullet fillets.

SERVES 4 AS AN APPETIZER

all-purpose flour
4 fillets of red mullet from 2 × 12 oz (350 g) fish,
    scaled and pin-boned (page 11)
Butter
Drop of olive oil

Salt and pepper
9 oz (250 g) *Mashed Potatoes* (page 124, optional),
 to serve

For the Garnishes

1 large orange, segmented
Superfine sugar (optional)
8 scallions, sliced into ¾ in (2 cm) strips
Drop of olive oil

For the Dressing

3 tablespoons white wine vinegar
3 tablespoons water
Juice of 3 oranges and 1 curl of zest
Juice of 1 lemon and 1 curl of zest
1 small shallot, chopped
2–3 coriander seeds
1 star anise
Pinch of saffron strands (optional)

To make the dressing, mix the white wine vinegar and water together, boil, and reduce by half. The juices, zests, chopped shallot, coriander, star anise, and saffron, if using, can now all be boiled together and reduced by one half to two-thirds. This will increase the flavor and consistency of the liquid to a thick, rich, syrupy juice.

Mix with the white wine vinegar reduction and then push through a fine sieve. The dressing is now ready.

Now, make the garnishes. After the orange has been segmented, it's best to allow the segments to dry on a cloth. This will soak up the excess juices, and the segments will not steam and break down while searing. You will need three segments per serving.

There are a couple of alternatives for searing. The segments can be placed on a baking pan, sprinkled with a little superfine sugar and then browned under a hot broiler, or you can use a butane torch to give the oranges a slightly burned tinge either with or without sprinkling them with sugar. Another method is to sear the segments in a very hot, dry frying-pan.

After they've browned, cut each segment into thirds and arrange these around the plate.

The scallions are best cut at an angle to give "sharp" little strips. Quickly blanch them in boiling, salted water for 1 minute before draining and allow them to cool, refrigerated, but not in ice water which would simply be absorbed and make them soggy.

To finish the cooking, heat a frying-pan until very hot. Add a splash of olive oil and pan-fry the scallions until golden brown. Season with salt and pepper and keep them warm.

To cook the fish, season the flour with salt and pepper. Lightly coat the skin of the mullet and then brush with butter.

Heat a frying-pan with a drop of olive oil. The fillets can now be placed in the skillet, skin-side down over a medium heat. Allow them to fry without shaking the pan. If the pan is shaken, the heat tends to be reduced and the fish will steam instead of frying. The fillets will only take 3–4 minutes to become crisp and golden. Turn the fillets over and cook for another minute.

The mashed potatoes are optional, but they turn this dish into a dream. They can either be piped or spooned into the center of the plate, sprinkled with the scallions.

Now, simply place the crisp red mullet fillet on top of the mashed potatoes. Spoon or pipe the citrus dressing using a squeeze bottle (page 11), and sprinkle a few drops of the dressing over the fish.

What we have is a pan-fried fillet of red mullet, placed on mashed potatoes with scallions, oranges, and a citrus dressing. How does that sound?

Deviled Whitebait

No-one else eats these tiny fish, heads, tails, and guts included as people do in Britain. Neither do whitebait really exist as fish in a distinct scientific sense, for they are minnows of the herring family, usually sprats or herrings, or sometimes shad. Greenwich became the venue for whitebait dinners in the eighteenth century, and fashionable Londoners would go there in the summer months to eat vast platefuls of deep-fried fish, caught in shoals in the Thames off Blackwall.

And delicious they are still, very crisp and hot. If you eat one, you suddenly want the whole batch. They are available frozen, but are also in season, fresh, between February and August. They are worth looking for.

This recipe is for the well-known classic – deviled whitebait, which is just deep-fried with a bite.

SERVES 4

1 lb (450 g) whitebait, fresh or frozen and
    defrosted
Oil, for deep-frying
Milk
¼–½ cup (25–50 g) all-purpose flour, seasoned with
    salt and cayenne pepper
Salt
Lemon wedges, to serve

For hot and crisp whitebait, they must be deep-fried. Heat the oil to 375°F/190°C; this will guarantee a quick cooking time. The whitebait, whether fresh or frozen, will first need to be sorted; discard any that are bruised or broken. Gently wash and then dry them on a dish towel. The fish can now be dipped in milk and then lightly coated with the seasoned flour. This can be easily achieved by placing a handful of whitebait into a paper bag containing the flour and shaking it. Remove the whitebait and drop into the hot fat. While cooking, the next handful can be dipped in milk and floured.

Cooking the fish at such a high temperature will crisp and brown them in approximately 1 minute. Lift with a slotted spoon and drain on paper towels. While still hot, sprinkle with a pinch of salt. Continue until all are cooked.

Serve with lemon wedges and the little devils are now ready to eat.

RIGHT
Deviled Whitebait

Shrimp (or Lobster) Cocktail

A genuine British classic. Or is it? We have been eating this dish for decades, but where does it come from and when? It might have originated in America, but no one is very sure. The "history" of the shrimp cocktail is only about 30 years old in Britain, dating from the beginning of the 1970s, although still very much with us today. It was so popular then that it became the most featured dish on any menu, along with its close friends – steak and French fries and Black Forest cake. It consisted of frozen watery shrimp, limp lettuce, over-ketchuped mayonnaise, and that ubiquitous twisted lemon slice!

All history has to start somewhere, so I like to think that we are re-writing the shrimp cocktail here. This dish has more components than the original (not all essential, but they do work), each one with its own balanced flavor. And of these, the most important is the shrimp. Second-rate shrimp will never make a first-rate cocktail.

There are many different shrimp available to use. The most basic is the small, pink, ready-cooked variety. These can be found frozen in almost any supermarket or fishmarket. The very best of this sort can be bought in a marinating liquor. They are very moist and full of flavor.

There are also the jumbo shrimp (under 8 per lb/17 per kg), which can be bought frozen – cooked or raw – and can also be found fresh, ready to be cooked. If they need to be cooked, lightly poach or steam them for 2–3 minutes and then let them cool naturally before peeling.

If using jumbo, 2–3 per serving will be plenty. If using small fresh or frozen shrimp, allow 2–3 oz (50–75 g) per person.

Rouille is a spicy "mayonnaise" sauce with red bell pepper and garlic flavored with fresh chilies. It is famous for serving with the great French "bouillabaisse" fish stew and soups. In my recipe, it works as an enhancer to the sweet pepper disks and the total shrimp-cocktail flavor. The recipe makes approximately 1¼ cup (300 ml) of sauce. You can make lees by omitting the can of red peppers.

You will need six 2½ × 2 in (6 × 5 cm) stainless-steel cooking rings for the "cakes." These are available in most kitchen supply stores. If unavailable, then plastic piping can be bought and cut to size.

SERVES 6 AS AN APPETIZER

8 tablespoons olive oil
1 lemon, cut into fourths
4 large red bell peppers or 6 small ones
1 lb 2 oz–1 lb 5 oz (500–600 g) shelled, cooked
    small shrimp or 12–18 jumbo shrimp
1 large iceberg lettuce, finely shredded (the finer
    the better)
12 heaping tablespoons Cocktail Sauce (recipe
    below)
6–8 tablespoons Rouille Sauce (recipe right)
Coarse sea salt and pepper

For the Cocktail Sauce (makes about ⅔ cup/150 ml)

10 tablespoons *Mayonnaise* (page 49)
3–4 tablespoons *Homemade Tomato Ketchup*
    (page 49)

Squeeze of lemon juice
Splash (or two) of brandy
Salt and pepper

For the Rouille Sauce (makes about 1¼ cups/300 ml)

14 oz (400 g) can of red peppers (optional)
2 slices of white bread, crusts removed
Red bell pepper trimmings from cutting disks
2 garlic cloves, crushed
1 medium fresh red chili, very finely sliced,
    with seeds removed
4 tablespoons olive oil
Salt

First, make the cocktail sauce. Whisk together the mayonnaise and 3 tablespoons of tomato ketchup. Add one more spoonful of ketchup if you prefer a sweeter flavor. Add a squeeze of lemon juice and season with salt and pepper.

The brandy can now be added. About 2 teaspoons will be plenty to finish the flavor. To ensure the right consistency, it's important the mayonnaise is thick.

Whisk together the olive oil with the juice of 3 lemon quarters. Season with salt and pepper.

The peppers are going to be cooked, peeled, and cut into disks, using the rings, to create the tops and bases for the "cakes."

Rub the peppers with a little olive oil and place on a baking sheet. Place the peppers under a preheated medium–hot broiler not too close to the heat. The peppers must now be allowed to broil and start to burn. When they begin to burn, turn them, and continue until they are blackened all around. After they've cooked, remove from the heat and place in a bag, close it, and cool for a few minutes. The skin will now be easy to peel away.

OPPOSITE
Shrimp Cocktail

After all the peppers are peeled, cut them open through one side. They will now spread out into one flat red strip. Carefully remove the stem and scrape away all seeds. The rings can now be used to cut 12 disks.

It is important to save all the red pepper trimmings; these will be used to make the rouille. The peppers can be cooked and prepared one to two days in advance. This also gives you time to make the rouille well in advance.

To make the rouille, strain the liquid from the canned peppers, if using, over the slices of bread and let the bread soak for 10–15 minutes.

If not using the canned, simply soak the bread with water. Then squeeze out excess liquid, leaving the bread barely moist. Remove any seeds from the peppers and roughly chop the flesh.

Place all the ingredients except the olive oil in a food processor and process to a purée. While the machine is still running, slowly add the olive oil which will emulsify, creating a sauce consistency. After all the oil is added, season with salt and push the purée through a sieve to create a smooth finish. The rouille sauce is now ready.

To build the shrimp-cocktail "cakes," season the pepper disks and place one in the bottom of each ring. Then peel the shrimp. Dice four to six of the shrimp to mix with the lettuce, creating more flavor and more texture.

Mix the diced shrimp with the finely shredded iceberg. Season with coarse sea salt and pepper. Squeeze the juice from the remaining lemon quarter over and add 2–3 tablespoons of cocktail sauce. Stir all the flavors in together. Add enough sauce to bind the mixture.

Divide the lettuce between the six rings, pushing down to create a firm base, but not breaking the lettuce. After the lettuce is packed in, place the remaining pepper disks on top.

Now, I like to decorate around the serving plates with drizzles of the sauces (cocktail, rouille, and lemon dressing). They can be spooned around or, for the perfect finish, fill small plastic squeeze bottles (page 11) and pipe the sauces to decorate,

alternating all three. With a spatula, lift the cakes in their rings carefully into the center of each plate.

The shrimp can now be placed on top, overlapping to create a pyramid finish and seasoned. Now, it is time to carefully lift off the rings. A trickle or two more cocktail sauce and lemon oil can be drizzled over the shrimp. The shrimp cocktail is re-born!

Note: The mayonnaise can be a good-quality bought-in variety. The ketchup can also be a store-bought variety.
The homemade ketchup can be re-heated and reduced by a third. This will thicken the sauce and also increase its flavor. Cool before adding.
Instead of buying fresh peppers, simply cut disks from canned or in jars (two cans will be needed for six servings). All the trimmings will then make the rouille sauce.

The Lobster Alternative

Lobster cocktail is wonderful to eat, but expensive to make. For a real treat, be sure to try it. The flavors are immense. Lobster holds so much flavor and is so much moister than shrimp. For the ultimate extravagance, small (1 lb/450 g) lobsters can be bought, giving you one per serving. This will be a very generous serving, but what an experience! Using very small lobsters means that you will have one tail per serving, with the trimmings and some of the claw meat to chop for the lettuce. Alternatively, three large (1½–2 lb/700–900 g) lobsters will give you half a tail and one claw per serving, with all trimmings going into the lettuce.

If you have lobsters that are already cooked, then simply break off the tail and tear away the shell. The tails can now be split lengthwise, if large. To open the claws, crack the shell with the back of a heavy knife. This will reveal the fresh lobster meat; pull away the shell and the claws are ready. It's also very important not to miss the rich meat held in the "legs" that connect the claws to the body. These can be cracked or cut open with scissors. This meat can then be cut and added to the lettuce.

If you have fresh lobsters, then see page 154 for how to cook them, either in a court-bouillon or in salted boiling water.

To build the lobster-cocktail "cakes," dice the lobster claw and leg meat, season, mix with the lemon dressing and toss with the lettuce. Then assemble the cakes exactly as for the shrimp ones, topping each one with a small lobster tail or half a tail and a claw.

Broiled (or Pan-fried) Dover Sole with Lemon and Nut-brown Butter

The Dover sole picked up the "Dover" part of its name many years ago, because it was caught in abundance in the Channel and landed at Dover, the main port of supply for London. The range of the fish actually is from the Mediterranean to the north of Scotland. Today the best fish are found in the North Sea and Bay of Biscay. The fish's Latin name, **Solea**, is from the Greek, and the Greeks thought the shape of the fish would make a perfect sandal for an ocean nymph!

Dover soles are the best "sole" in terms of total texture and flavor, much better than the lemon and slip soles, for example. The difference among all of these fish lies predominantly in the texture. The Dover is the firmest, the flesh being almost meaty and very flavorful, which is why it is the most expensive to buy. The others may have a similar shape, but are much softer in texture.

Flounder, one of the most popular fish in Britain these days, can be cooked in the same way as Dover or lemon sole. This is less expensive fish that can be easily found at any fishmarket. For me, there is no better way to eat broiled sole (or flounder) than with a squeeze of lemon and some nut-brown butter. Pan-frying is a good, basic method for cooking fish, and I give you the method here as an alternative to broiling. Pan-frying a 1½ lb (675 g) Dover sole will need a pretty big frying-pan, so I suggest that you broil large fish and make the butter separately, if desired, adding any juices from the broiler pan.

SERVES 2

2 × 1–1½ lb (450–675 g) Dover soles, prepared, or lemon sole or flounder
2 tablespoons (25 g) butter, melted
Salt and pepper
1 small lemon, halved

For Pan-frying

All-purpose flour, seasoned, for coating
1 tablespoon cooking oil

BELOW
Broiled (or Pan-fried) Dover Sole with Lemon and Nut-brown Butter

4 tablespoons (50 g) butter
Salt and pepper
½ teaspoon chopped fresh parsley (optional)
1 lemon, halved

To broil or pan-fry the fish, it first has to be prepared. With any flat fish, I like to leave the white skin on. This becomes almost crisp and it protects the flesh, keeping it moist during the cooking time.

To remove the dark skin, simply make a cut at the tail and scrape a little of the skin away. After you've freed enough skin to grip, then pull it toward the head. The skin will come away cleanly.

The white skin must be scraped clean of all scales. Cut away the side fins and trim the tail. The head can now also be cut away.

Any roe inside the fish can easily be pushed to the head and pulled away. Now, wash away any blood along the main bone and the fish is ready to cook.

To Broil

(This first step applies to either recipe.) Place the two fish, white-skin-side up, on a lightly buttered baking pan. Brush each with the remaining butter and season with salt and pepper.

Place under a preheated broiler and cook for 10 minutes (if using 1 lb/450 g fish, 8 minutes should be enough).

The fish can now be presented on serving plates with a half lemon offered. Pour any juices left on the baking pan over the fish, or add to the butter, if using.

To Pan-fry

If you have a super-large frying-pan and love the taste of pan-fried fish, here are some guidelines, including cooking times.

Lightly flour the white-skin side of the fish, then brush with butter and season. Heat the frying-pan with a tablespoon of cooking oil. Place the fish in the pan, buttered-side down, and pan-fry until golden brown before turning in the pan. For a 1–1½ lb (450–675 g) fish, this will take approximately 5–6 minutes on each side.

Remove the fish from the pan. Add the 4 tablespoons (50 g) of butter and finish as for the pan-fried, nut-brown butter below.

Make the butter when the fish is 2 minutes from being done. Heat a small frying-pan. When it's hot, drop in the 4 tablespoons (50 g) of butter; this will instantly begin to bubble and it will acquire a nut-brown color and a nutty flavor. At this point, season with salt and pepper, add the chopped parsley, if using, and squeeze in some lemon juice.

Adding the lemon juice causes an instant reaction with the butter, creating an almost fizzy, bubbly, soufflé effect. Add any juices from cooking the fish. Now, it's time to pour over the plated fish and serve.

Note: The Dover sole is delicious served with the *Green Lemon Butter* (page 52).

A broiled or pan-fried fish also goes well with simple buttered new potatoes and a green salad or green vegetable.

The *Sautéd Potatoes* on page 121 are also a great accompaniment.

Here's a list of average cooking times for whole or filleted fish giving you simple guidelines for cooking the fish of your choice.

TO BROIL

- Whole flat fish, sole, flounder , etc., weighing 1–1½ lb (450–675 g), as featured, 8–10 minutes, white-skin-side only.
- Fillets of flat fish, 3–4 minutes, one side only.
- Whole round fish, such as mackerel and trout, weighing 12 oz–1 lb (350–450 g), 5–6 minutes on each side.
- Round fish steaks, such as salmon, 6–8 oz (175–225 g), 6–8 minutes on one side only.
- Round fish supremes (i.e. small, thick slices of fillet) 6–8 oz (175–225 g), 6–8 minutes on one side only.

TO PAN-FRY

- Fillets of fish, sole, flounder, etc., 1–2 minutes on each side.
- Whole round fish, mackerel, trout, etc., 12 oz–1 lb (350–450 g), 6–7 minutes on each side.
- Round fish, salmon, cod, etc., 6–8 oz (175–225 g), 4–5 minutes on each side.
- Round fish supremes (i.e. small, thick slices of fillet), 6–8 oz (175–225 g), 4–5 minutes on each side.

Pan-fried Cod with Carrots, Parsley, and Crisp Bacon

Cod has been a favorite fish in Britain for centuries. The British fishing fleet once traveled to Newfoundland to take advantage of the huge shoals of big fish they found there on the Grand Banks. They were salted on land both for the home market and for selling to countries eager for salt cod, primarily Spain and Portugal. In the Middle Ages, salt cod in Britain was traditionally served with mashed parsnips on Ash Wednesday. Fresh cod is probably the most popular fish for coating with batter and deep-frying in fish and chip shops.

Once again, I've combined a traditional British fish with some other familiar flavors. The crisp bacon is quite important to the finished total texture of this dish. The bacon then tastes like crackling and replaces the skin on the cod.

The carrots are cooked in the style of a famous French carrot dish, à la Vichy. Vichy is a region of France where the water is non-chalky and therefore considered perfect for cooking vegetables. While the carrots are cooking, the water reduces with the sugar and butter, which thicken and coat the carrots to make a glaze. To get as close as possible to Vichy, use bottled mineral water rather than that from the tap – it does make a difference.

BELOW
Pan-fried Cod with Carrots, Parsley, and Crisp Bacon

8 slices of bacon
1½ lb (675 g) carrots, sliced ¼ in (5 mm) thick
Natural bottled mineral water
6 tablespoons (75 g) butter
1 teaspoon superfine sugar
2 teaspoons roughly chopped fresh parsley
4 × 6 oz (175 g) cod fillets, skinned
    (cut from a large fillet)
1 tablespoon all-purpose flour
1–2 tablespoons cooking oil
Squeeze of lemon juice
Salt and pepper

The bacon can be cooked in many ways. Under a slow broiler, the strips will cook and become very crisp. The crispiness should really be at the "snapping" stage. It can also be pan-fried until all juices have reduced into the meat, and then finished under the broiler to crisp. Another way is to bake it. This will take 30–40 minutes. Preheat the oven to 400°F/200°C. Place the strips in a baking pan and place another pan on top to keep the bacon flat. Place in the preheated oven and cook for 30 minutes. After a half an hour, remove the top sheet. Pour off any excess fat and then increase the temperature of the oven to 450°F/230°C. Return the bacon and within 10 minutes it will have browned and become very crisp.

Place the carrots in a saucepan and add enough bottled water to cover. Add a pinch of salt, 2 tablespoons (25 g) of the butter and the sugar. Bring to a simmer and cook for 15–20 minutes, until tender. During this time, the cooking liquid will have reduced a little. For the last 2–3 minutes of cooking time increase the heat so the liquid can reduce by half to two-thirds. Add 2 tablespoons (25 g) butter and shake into the carrots. Add the chopped parsley and the carrots are ready.

While the carrots are cooking, the cod can be pan-fried. Season the fish with salt and a grinding of pepper. The presentation side will be the skinned side. This gives a flat, well-browned finish, showing off the lines of the cod flakes. It's best to salt this side only, not dotting with pepper. Lightly dust the skinned side with flour. Heat a frying-pan with the cooking oil, and when it's hot, place the fillets in, floured-side down. They can now be cooked for 5–6 minutes until golden. Add the remaining butter and cook for another minute before turning over and continuing for 2–3 minutes.

The carrots can now be finished with a squeeze of lemon juice. Divide among four plates, placing the cod on top. To finish the dish, place the crisp bacon strips on top of the fish.

Note: Tarragon also works very well with this dish.

Baked Halibut with a Pumpkin Crust

This dish is certainly one full of flavor, and the pumpkin, seeds and all, gives a selection of tastes and textures to compliment the fish. The pumpkin is also helped along by wholegrain mustard. (If you're not fond of mustard, then simply omit it from the recipe.)

Cod fillet can also be used in this recipe, but halibut is certainly first choice, having a close-flaked flesh that holds together very well while cooking.

I like to serve this dish with a white wine cream sauce and leeks, which create a lovely foundation for the halibut.

1 small golden (orange-fleshed), pumpkin
    (1 lb/450 g of flesh will be needed; any
    remaining can be used for soup)
2 tablespoons (25 g) butter
2 oz (50 g) dried pumpkin seeds
1–2 tablespoons wholegrain mustard
6–8 oz (4 × 175–225 g) halibut fillet servings,
    skinned
8 baby leeks or 3–4 medium leeks
Butter
2 tablespoons water
Salt and pepper
About 1 cup (250 ml) *Basic White Wine Fish Sauce*
    (page 47), to serve

Preheat the oven to 400°F/200°C.

Cut the pumpkin in half and scoop out the seeds and save them. Remove the tough peeling from

1 lb (450 g) of the vegetable and cut into rough ¾–1½ in (2–3 cm) dice.

Melt the butter in a roasting pan and when it bubbles, add the chopped pumpkin. Cook for a few minutes, and when it becomes rich and golden in color, cover with foil and cook in the preheated oven for approximately 30 minutes until tender. After the pumpkin is cooked and soft, blend to a purée in a food processor. For an extra-fine smooth purée, pass through a fine sieve. Let it cool.

While the pumpkin is roasting, the fresh seeds can be washed and dried on a cloth. These can now be toasted until golden brown. This will give the seeds a nutty flavor. To guarantee an extra-crunchy topping, toast the bought dried seeds with the fresh ones.

These can now also be ground in a food processor to a fine, almost powdery, consistency. Pass through a fine sieve, to achieve a "ground nutmeg" texture. Season with salt and pepper.

After the pumpkin purée has cooled, add the mustard to taste and season.

Next, grease a baking pan or dish. Season the pan with salt and pepper. On the skin side of each serving of the fish, spread with the pumpkin and mustard purée. A maximum of about ¼ in (4–5 mm) of topping will be plenty. The fish can be topped hours in advance and kept refrigerated until needed.

If using baby leeks, cut at an angle into ½–¾ in (1–2 cm) pieces. If using larger ones, split them in half lengthwise and finely shred. The leeks can now be washed and left to drain prior to cooking.

To cook the halibut, bake it in the preheated oven for 10–12 minutes until beginning to firm. After the fish has cooked, sprinkle the pumpkin purée with a generous layer of the finely ground seeds. To finish, toast the halibut fillets under a hot broiler for a crusty topping.

While the fish is baking, melt a heaping teaspoon of butter in a large saucepan. After it bubbles, add the leeks. Cook for a minute or two, without browning. Add the 2 tablespoons of water and stir. This will create a steam that will cook the shredded leeks in 2–3 minutes. If cooking the pieces of baby leek, add an extra tablespoon or two of water. These will take 3–5 minutes, depending on the size of the leeks.

The white wine fish sauce can now also be warmed and puréed in a food processor.

Add a few tablespoons of sauce to the leeks, making sure any excess water has been strained off, and spoon onto four plates. Pour on more of the sauce and place the pumpkin and mustard crust halibuts on top. The dish is ready to serve.

Note: The champagne version of the sauce can also be served with this dish.

Broiled Trout Fillets with Sautéd Lime Pickle Potatoes and Zucchini

For those who lived far from the sea, brown trout from freshwater rivers and ponds would have been one of the principal sources of fresh fish during the Middle Ages and thereafter. Most trout now is farmed-raised, imported, rainbow trout, but you might also try a sea trout, a fish like the salmon, that lives and feeds in salt water and spawns in fresh.

The foundation for this particular eastern-inspired trout recipe is potatoes pan-fried in butter, mixed with zucchini. The potatoes should be new ones. Yukon Gold is another suitable potato to use. The potatoes and zucchini work very well together, and the flavor is heightened with the sliced pickled limes and finished with a cilantro butter sauce. This dish is featured here as an appetizer, but it could also be served as a main course.

You can make the cilantro butter sauce 20–30 minutes in advance and simply heat and whisk it (an electric hand-mixer works very well), at the last minute, adding the chopped fresh cilantro just before serving.

SERVES 4 AS AN APPETIZER AND 2 AS A MAIN COURSE

2 × 1 lb (450 g) trout, filleted, skin left on
12 oz (350 g) new potatoes or Yukon Gold
   potatoes
9 oz (250 g) zucchini (2–3 medium)
6 tablespoons olive oil
Squeeze of lime juice
4–6 tablespoons (50–75 g) butter
8–10 large fresh cilantro leaves for the sauce
   (see below), shredded
1–2 wedges of Pickled Limes (page 381),
   cut into thin triangular slices
2–3 handfuls of arugula leaves
   (other salad greens can also be used)

Coarse sea salt
Salt and pepper
About ⅔ cup (150 ml) *Cilantro Butter Sauce*
   (page 53), to serve

Make the cilantro butter sauce.

The trout are best bought filleted from your fishmarket. Season with salt and pepper and lay on a lightly buttered baking pan; brush the skin with butter, ready to broil.

Scrub the potatoes clean and cook in boiling, salted water. Almost any new potato will take about 20–25 minutes. After the potatoes have cooked,

BELOW
*Broiled Trout Fillets with Sautéd Lime Pickle Potatoes
and Zucchini*

drain. If not using them immediately, let them cool, then peel and cut into ½ in (1 cm) thick slices.

The zucchini can now be cut into a ½ in (1 cm) dice. Blanch the zucchini in boiling, salted water for 30 seconds to 1 minute. Drain and let them cool on a cloth.

To make the lime oil, mix 4 tablespoons of olive oil with a teaspoon or two of lime juice. Season with salt and pepper.

Warm a heaping teaspoon of butter plus the remaining 2 tablespoons of olive oil in a frying-pan. Add the potatoes and cook on a fairly high heat to give a well-browned golden edge. Add the blanched zucchini and brown them, too. After both are golden and the potatoes are crisp, season with salt and pepper. Add the shredded cilantro leaves to the potatoes.

The triangular slices of pickled limes can now be added along with a trickle of the juices. The sharp flavor and bite of the limes is now calmed by the sautéed potatoes and zucchini, but still gives the whole dish a more lively finish.

Place the seasoned and buttered trout fillets under a hot broiler. These will take just a few minutes to begin to firm and gently cook. Arrange the lime potatoes and zucchini on four plates. Season and dress the arugula (or other salad greens) with a spoonful of the lime oil.

Re-heat and whisk the cilantro butter sauce, adding the fresh cilantro, and spoon some over the potatoes. Arrange the arugula leaves on top. After the trout is barely cooked, still pink in the center, peel off the skins and place the fillets on top of the leaves. Sprinkle with a few sea-salt granules and finish with a trickle of lime juice. The dish is now ready to serve.

Scallops with Broiled Black Pudding à l'orange

Sauce à l'orange became very much part of British food, particularly in the 1970s, usually as a garnish for roast duck. The sauce may have come from France, but mixing fruit of all varieties with fish and meat had been a British custom since the Middle Ages. It became a very fashionable combination again in the 1980s, during the *nouvelle cuisine* rage that hit Britain, here again influenced by France.

Most fruit and fish or meat combinations don't appeal to me. (Chicken and kiwi fruit simply don't work.) But citrus fruit is very different. Once the lemon and orange were introduced in Britain, they became traditional as well. Simply using their juices and bittersweet taste will often heighten a dish, giving it a completely new face. Lemon is used throughout this book to enhance other flavors, and lime works in a similar fashion. Orange? Well, with this dish orange is perfect. The strong flavor of black pudding takes kindly to the taste, and so does the slight bitter edge of the seared scallop. (Apparently, a dish of stewed scallops with orange sauce was very popular in the eighteenth century.)

The combination may sound and look a little "*nouvelle*," but the blending is there. I've also included a tarragon butter sauce, because tarragon and orange work together well, and the buttery, creamy consistency helps balance the total flavors.

As a garnish for this recipe, I have included candied orange peel. Placing some small dice of candied peel on top of each scallop is a tasty garnish to finish the dish. It's not essential to make these – but they do give a new texture to the finished result.

SERVES 4 AS AN APPETIZER

Cooking or olive oil
12 medium–large scallops, cleaned
12 × ¼–½ in (5 mm–1 cm) slices of black pudding
Heaping teaspoon of butter
Salt and pepper
Candied Oranges (page 389), cut in ⅛ in (3 mm)
    dice, to garnish (optional)

For the Orange Sauce (makes 1¼ cup/300 ml)

Butter
3 shallots, sliced
5–6 green peppercorns, crushed
1 small garlic clove, quartered
1 bay leaf

1 small star anise (or 2–3 broken pieces)
2 strips of orange zest
3 tablespoons brandy
⅔ cup white wine
About ¾ cup (150–200 ml) orange juice
⅔ cup (150 ml) *Chicken Stock* (page 33)
1¼ cups (300 ml) *Veal or Beef Jus* (page 34) or
    alternative (page 11)
red wine vinegar (optional)
Salt and pepper

For the Tarragon Butter Sauce

6–8 tablespoons (75–100 g) unsalted butter, cubed
1 small shallot, finely chopped
Sprig of tarragon, plus ½ teaspoon chopped/torn leaves
1 tablespoon white wine vinegar (or tarragon
    vinegar for extra flavor)

⅓ cup white wine
½ cup (100 ml) water or *Fish, Chicken or Vegetable
    Stock* (page 35, 33 or 36)
1 tablespoon heavy cream
Salt and pepper

First, make the orange sauce. Melt a heaping teaspoon of butter in a saucepan. Add the shallots and allow to cook on a medium heat until softened, taking on a good rich caramel color and flavor.

Add the green peppercorns, garlic, bay leaf, star anise, and orange zest with the brandy. Cook until dry. Add the white wine, return to a boil, and reduce by three-fourths.

Add ⅔ cup (150 ml) of the orange juice. Bring to a simmer and again reduce by three-fourths.

BELOW
Scallops with Broiled Black Pudding à l'orange

Pour the chicken stock into the pan and cook until the quantity has reduced by one-third to a half. The jus can now also be added and reduced by a third. Then strain the sauce through a sieve.

The sauce has undertaken a lot of reductions. It's this method that increases the individual flavors, creating the finished sauce. Without being overpowering, the consistency should be just thick enough to coat the back of a spoon. To thin and enliven the sauce, if needed, add a few drops of the remaining orange juice. Season with salt and pepper. A splash or two of red wine vinegar will also help heighten the flavor of the orange sauce.

To make the tarragon butter sauce, melt a heaping teaspoon of the butter and add the chopped shallot and sprig of tarragon. Cook for a few minutes, without browning, until softened. Add the vinegar and reduce until almost dry. Now, add the white wine and reduce by three-fourths. Pour in the stock or water and reduce by two-thirds.

Add the heavy cream, and when it is at the simmering point, whisk in the rest of the butter, a few pieces at a time. After all the butter has been added, season with salt and pepper. Strain through a sieve.

If the sauce is too thick, thin with a few drops of water or lemon juice.

The butter sauce can now be processed in a food processor to lighten the flavor and consistency. Just before serving, add the chopped or torn tarragon leaves.

Heat a frying-pan with a trickle of olive or cooking oil. When it is very hot, place the scallops in the pan. It's important not to disturb the scallops too much in order not to take the heat from the pan, causing the scallops to steam rather than fry.

The black pudding slices can be cooked in a separate pan or brushed with butter and placed under a hot broiler. Whatever you chose, the pudding will take approximately 1½–2 minutes on each side.

After the scallops have seared for 1–1½ minutes, a heaping teaspoon of butter can be added to the pan. Continue to cook for another 30 seconds.

The scallops will now have a deep golden color with a slightly burned edge. It's at this point they can be turned in the pan, seasoned with salt and pepper and cooked for another 1–2 minutes, depending on the size of the scallop.

Remove the scallops from the pan along with the black pudding.

Place a scallop on top of each slice of black pudding and arrange in a row, three per serving, on the plates. If using the diced candied orange, warm in a tablespoon of the rich orange sauce and divide among the scallops, placing 3–4 pieces on top of each. Pour a tablespoon or two of the orange sauce across each scallop with the same quantity of the tarragon butter sauce in between each pile. The dish is ready to serve.

Note: The rich orange sauce is best made in this quantity for maximum flavor. Any remaining amount can be frozen.

Pan-fried Red Mullet with a Tomato and Leek Soup

Red mullet have been called "the woodcock of the sea" because, like the woodcock game bird, they are traditionally cooked whole, not gutted, which lends flavor. Here, though, they are filleted, and the fillets are pan-fried, then placed on top of a potato cake and served with tomato and leek soup. This makes a wonderful main course.

The recipe is not quite as simple as it sounds. The tomato and leek soup is made from a long, slow-cooking, mullet soup base. The ingredients are similar to those for a lobster or crab bisque, with a very distinctive tang of the fish's own flavor.

SERVES 6

3 × 1 lb (450 g) red mullet, filleted, scaled, and boned (page 11)
All-purpose flour, for coating
Butter
2–3 tablespoons olive oil
Salt and pepper
6 × *Garlic Cream Potato Cakes* (page 124), to serve

2–3 tablespoons olive oil
2 medium carrots, finely sliced
1 small fennel bulb, finely sliced
2 celery sticks, finely sliced
4 shallots, finely sliced
Red mullet bones from fillets, and the heads
¼ teaspoon crushed coriander seeds
1 star anise
2 strips of orange peel
¼ teaspoon dried chili flakes
Pinch of saffron strands
Few sprigs of basil
Few sprigs of tarragon
2 measures of Pernod
6 ripe large tomatoes, preferably plum, cut into
    eigths
2 teaspoons tomato purée
⅔ cup of white wine
5 cups (1.2 liters) *Fish Stock* (page 35)
Salt and pepper
Lemon juice

For the Soup Garnish

4 plum tomatoes, blanched and peeled
1 large leek, cut into ½ in (1 cm) dice
2 tablespoons (25 g) butter (optional)

First, make the garnish. After the tomatoes have been blanched and peeled, halve lengthwise and remove all seeds. The flesh can now be cut into ½ in (1 cm) dice to match the leeks. Any trimmings from the tomatoes and leeks can be used in the soup.

The diced leek can now be blanched in boiling, salted water. When the wate boils, drop in the leeks, and cook without a lid for 30–45 seconds. Drain in a colander and let the leeks cool. After they are at room temperature, refrigerate, along with the tomatoes.

To make the soup, preheat the oven to 300°F/150°C. Warm the olive oil in a suitable braising pan. Add the carrots, fennel, celery, shallots, and any leek trimmings. Over a low heat, cook for 20 minutes to soften but not brown.

Chop the mullet bones and heads, and add them to the vegetables, along with the coriander seeds, star anise, orange peel, dried chili, saffron, and herbs. Continue to cook for another 5–6 minutes. Now, add the Pernod and half of the tomatoes. Stir well, place in the preheated oven, and cook without a lid for 1½–2 hours.

It is important during this slow cooking time that the mixture is stirred every 20–30 minutes; this guarantees an even cooking.

After 1½ hours, add the rest of the tomatoes, tomato purée, white wine, and fish stock. Cook for 30 minutes more.

Remove the mixture from the oven and bring to a simmer. Season with salt and pepper and remove from the heat. The soup can now be totally puréed (including bones), then pushed through a coarse sieve and then a fine one.

After being sieved, the soup will have a rich, smooth, full-flavored finish. Re-season with salt and pepper, adding a squeeze of lemon juice, if needed, to heighten the taste even more.

To pan-fry the mullet, season the fish with salt and pepper. Very lightly flour the skin side and then brush with butter.

For six servings, heat two large frying-pans with 2–3 tablespoons of olive oil. When the oil is hot, place the fish in the pans, buttered- (skin-) side down. Cook for 3 minutes by which time the skins will have become golden and crisp. Turn the fish over and continue to cook for 1–2 minutes.

Add the reserved leeks and tomatoes to the finished soup (butter can also be added, if desired).

The garlic cream potato cakes, if hot, can now be placed in the bowls. If made previously, then simply microwave them to heat through. Spoon the soup over them and garnish generously and finish by presenting the mullet on top of the potato.

This recipe involves a lot of cooking time, but you will have great pleasure in eating it.

Note: If you have more soup than you need, it can be frozen, keeping it for another meal.

The soup is also lovely to serve as a soup instead of as a garnish.

Many other fish can also be used in place of the red mullet: sea bass, sea bream, or tuna will all work very well.

Smoked Salmon Terrine with Warm Potato Salad

Because salmon did not keep well, the fish was more commonly available in a smoked form, and the Scottish smoke cure was quite strong. With the arrival of the railways, salmon could be sent fresh to London, and it is probably at this time that the milder London cure was developed. Both Scottish-cured and London-cured are much-loved forms.

This recipe seems very expensive, as 2¼–3¼ lb (1–1.5 kg) is a large amount of smoked salmon. But set in a 6 cup (1.4 liter) terrine, this recipe will give you 12–16 servings. The perfect appetizer for Christmas Eve or dinner for New Year's Day, it is simply thin slices of smoked salmon layered with a butter flavored with anchovies, lemon, and dill.

The anchovies used here are the marinated variety, not the canned. The latter have too high a salt content, which just wouldn't work with smoked salmon. Marinated anchovies are available from most gourmet food shops and supermarkets.

The dressing is delicious, simply crème fraîche, sour cream, and mustard bound around the potatoes, with a squeeze of lemon to finish, all contributing flavors that complement the smoked salmon.

SERVES 12–16

For the Terrine

12 tablespoons (175 g) butter
2 oz (50 g) marinated anchovies
Finely grated zest of 1 lemon
Juice of ½ lemon
2 tablespoons chopped fresh dill
2¼–3¼ lb (1–1.5 kg) sliced smoked salmon
Salt and freshly ground black pepper

For the Potato Salad (serves 4–6)

2 large potatoes, cut into ½ in (1 cm) dice
⅔ cup (150 ml) crème fraîche
⅓ cup (85 ml) sour cream
2–3 teaspoons Dijon mustard
Juice of 1 lemon
4 tablespoons olive oil
2 tablespoons chopped fresh dill
Salt and pepper

Line a 6 cup (1.4 liter) terrine dish or a 2 lb (900 g) loaf pan with plastic wrap. Soften the butter. Cut the anchovy fillets into small ⅛ in (2–3 mm) dice and stir into the butter along with the finely grated lemon zest. Add the lemon juice and season with salt and pepper. To finish, simply fold in the chopped dill. This will now need to be used at room temperature, making it easy to spread.

Place 3–4 slices of the salmon crosswise in the terrine, creating a lining for the filling. It's important to make sure large slices are used, leaving a 1½–1¾ in (3–4 cm) overhang on each side.

Spread a very thin layer of butter over the bottom and cover with slices of salmon. Now, repeat until the terrine is completely full.

This will use most, if not all, of the sliced smoked salmon, and it will be held together with the butter. When the terrine is full, fold over the original slices to cover the top. Cover with plastic wrap and refrigerate, using something heavy as a weight to press the layers of the terrine together. Leave the terrine for several hours, preferably overnight, until ready to turn out.

When the butter is cold, it will set, making the terrine easier to slice.

When it is set, simply turn out, and while it is still wrapped in plastic wrap, the terrine can be servinged. This guarantees that the slices keep their shape. To serve this dish at its best, the terrine can be put on a plate, plastic wrap removed, and allowed to become lightly chilled, giving the butter spread a softer texture.

Now, make the potato salad. This is best served warm, so it should be cooked about 30 minutes before serving the dish.

Cook the diced potatoes in salted water until tender, about 10–12 minutes. While the potatoes are cooking, the dressings can be made.

Whisk together the crème fraîche, sour cream, and Dijon mustard to taste. Add the juice of half the lemon and season with salt and pepper. Mix the 4 tablespoons of olive oil with a squeeze of lemon juice, and season with salt and pepper.

After the potatoes are cooked, drain off the water, and place the potatoes in a bowl. Squeeze the

remaining lemon juice over them and season while still warm. While the potatoes are warm, they will absorb any flavors added to them.

After the potatoes have cooled slightly but still have plenty of warmth, add the crème fraîche dressing and the chopped dill. Place the salad on plates with the terrine slices.

To finish, drizzle a teaspoon or two of the lemon oil over the potatoes and a little around the plate.

The dish is now complete.

Note: The terrine recipe can be halved using a smaller terrine mold.

Sides of smoked salmon can be bought totally trimmed and cleaned of all the pin bones that run down the center of the fillet. If you are slicing the smoked salmon yourself, it's important to use a long, sharp knife to ensure an even cut.

Steamed Slice of Smoked Salmon on a Potato Cake, with Seared Lemons and a Caper Dressing

Smoked salmon has the classic reputation of simply being thinly sliced across the plate and then served with a lemon wedge, or a chopped boiled egg, or shallots, capers, and lemon. All work well, but steaming the fish, as here, shows the range of cooking that can actually be applied to smoked salmon.

You'll notice that some of the classic accompaniments and their flavors are being used in this dish. That's exactly what I'm trying to do with the recipe: I don't want to ignore the traditions but, instead, give them a new face and identity.

The lemon dressing recipe is very different from a basic lemon oil. It's made using a stock syrup, usually associated with sorbets and desserts, but the other flavors manage to calm the sweetness. The quantity of dressing made will be more than what

OPPOSITE
Smoked Salmon Terrine with Warm Potato Salad

you need immediately but it will keep refrigerated for up to a month. Later, you can use it for a mixed green salad.

SERVES 4

4 × 3–4 oz (75–100 g) slices of smoked salmon (approx. ½ in/1 cm thick)

For the Dressing

3 tablespoons (40 g) sugar
½ cup (100 ml) water
2 sticks of lemon grass, cut into ½ in (1 cm) pieces
1 star anise
5 pink peppercorns
Juice of 3 medium lemons (more can be added for extra bite)
Grated zest of 1 lemon
¾ cup (200 ml) olive oil
Champagne or white wine vinegar, to taste
Pinch of salt

For the Potatoes

4–6 peeled potatoes, preferably Cara
Peanut oil
Salt and pepper

For the Garnish

12 lemon segments
3 tablespoons crème fraîche
3 tablespoons natural yogurt
1 teaspoon capers, roughly chopped
1 teaspoon chopped chives
Salt and pepper

The dressing tastes best made 24 hours in advance to infuse all of the flavors. To make the syrup, dissolve the sugar in the water, bring to a boil, and simmer for a few minutes. Allow the syrup to cool.

Place all the dressing ingredients except the vinegar in a saucepan and taste. Add 1–2 tablespoons of vinegar to increase the acidity in order to balance the sweetness. Bring to a boil. Remove from the heat and let it cool. After 24 hours, strain it.

Trim the peeled potatoes into cylinder shapes and cut them into ⅛ in (2 mm) slices.

To cook the disks, I use 4 in (10 cm) non-stick frying-pans. If only one is available, the potato disks can be "built" and browned one at a time, being finished on a baking sheet.

Warm 2 teaspoons of peanut oil in the frying-pan. Before cooking the potatoes it's important the slices are dried on paper towels. Place a slice in the center of the warmed pan and overlap more around it. Season with salt and pepper before placing a second layer on top, finishing with another slice in the center. As the potato begins to brown, lightly press. The starch from the potatoes will help stick the two layers together. After the potatoes become golden, carefully turn them over with a spatula and brown the other side.

When all four servings have been sealed and browned, place them on a buttered baking pan. This stage can be completed many hours before serving. To finish cooking and crisp the potatoes, place in a preheated oven at 425°F/220°C. Cook for 10–15 minutes. The potatoes are now ready to serve.

The lemon segments can be seared quickly in a very hot dry pan, allowing them to brown on one side only, giving a burned edge. An alternative is to brown them with a butane torch (page 11).

Mix together the crème fraîche and yogurt. Season with salt and pepper. Spoon the mixture among four plates, creating a circle, and leaving enough room for the potato cake to be placed in the center.

Cut the lemon segments into two or three pieces and place around them and on top of the crème fraîche.

Mix 8 tablespoons of the lemon dressing with the capers and chives. This mixture can now be spooned around the plate, drizzling the lemons and the cream.

Place the smoked salmon slices on buttered waxed paper and steam over lightly simmering water. The slices will take just a few minutes to warm.

Because smoked salmon is a cured fish and does not need to be cooked, the steaming method is used to simply warm the slices. If cooked through, the flavor and texture will be dry. After steaming, each slice should still have a pink look, with a lightly opaque finish.

Place the potato cakes in the center of each plate and place the smoked salmon on top. Half a teaspoon of dressing can now be trickled over each slice. The dish is now complete.

Note: Fresh salmon can also be used, again steaming or pan-frying for 2–3 minutes.

Lobster Casserole

Fish and shellfish have always been cooked in pottages, the forerunners of our thick soups and casseroles, but lobster would not have been used often since it would always have been rare and expensive. Lobster was very popular for special occasions in Edwardian and Victorian times. It was sometimes served for breakfast, usually cold with a clarified butter, sometimes hot with a spiced sauce for a gentleman's dinner at his London club, or in rich patties or pies.

This particular lobster dish can only be described as sublime. The natural flavor of lobster is one I love, and this dish does nothing but enhance it. The recipe takes a little planning and work – cooking and shelling the lobsters, preparing the vegetables and so on – but the results absolutely warrant it. This dish is a complete meal in itself and it is quite a sensation.

SERVES 4

4 x 1 lb (450 g) lobsters
4–6 tablespoons (50–75 g) butter
3 shallots, roughly chopped
1 carrot, roughly chopped
1 small leek, roughly chopped
1 small fennel, roughly chopped
2 celery sticks, roughly chopped
1 garlic clove, crushed
1 star anise
1 bay leaf
Few fennel seeds
Sprig of tarragon

Pinch of cayenne pepper

2 teaspoons tomato purée

4 tomatoes, seeded and roughly chopped

4 tablespoons brandy

½ cup (125 ml) white wine

1 quart (900 ml) Fish Stock (page 35)

1–2 tablespoons heavy cream (optional)

12 new potatoes

2–3 large carrots, peeled

12 small pearl onions, peeled

12 tarragon leaves, torn or lightly cut

8–12 flat parsley leaves, torn or lightly cut

Squeeze of lemon juice

Salt

Shellfish Oil (page 386, optional)

This dish can be prepared and almost completed several hours before cooking. The lobsters will first be blanched in boiling, salted water, then cracked from their shells. The casserole sauce/liquid can then be made from the shells. While the sauce is cooking, the vegetables can be prepared.

Bring a large pot of boiling, salted water to a boil. Drop the lobsters into the water, keeping the pot on a high heat. Return to a boil and cook for 2 minutes. Remove the shellfish from the pan. When it has cooled, the shells can be cracked and the lobster meat removed, including the meat in the joints between the claws and the tail. The meat can now be wrapped gently in plastic wrap with a heaping teaspoon of butter and kept refrigerated. The lobster meat will later be heated through by steaming.

Break the lobster shells (or crush them) into small pieces. Melt a heaping teaspoon of butter in a large saucepan. Add the shallots, carrot, leek, fennel, and celery. Cook for 10–15 minutes, browning them a little. Add the crushed garlic, star anise, bay leaf, fennel seeds, tarragon, and cayenne pepper. Cook for another 5 minutes before adding the tomato purée and chopped fresh tomatoes. The mixture can now be cooked until the water from the tomatoes have reduced. This will take about 5–10 minutes.

Add the brandy and reduce the liquid by half. Add the white wine and also reduce by half. Now, it is time to add the broken shells, cooking them into the sauce for 5 minutes before topping with the fish stock.

Bring to a simmer and cook for 45 minutes. The sauce can now be processed in a food processor, including shells. Push the mixture through a coarse sieve and then through a fine one.

The vegetables will have thickened the liquid, creating a thin sauce consistency. A few tablespoons of heavy cream can also be added to finish the sauce, along with 2 tablespoons (25 g) of butter. If the sauce tastes a little shallow, a few tablespoons of canned lobster bisque can be added. Season with a pinch of salt and cayenne pepper. Finish with a squeeze of lemon juice.

The potatoes can be boiled and left in their natural shape, peeling them before serving. If this is your choice, then it is best to buy small new potatoes, allowing 3–4 per serving. Large potatoes can be "turned" with a small knife into barrel shapes, allowing three per serving.

The carrots can also be cut to the shape of your choice – diced or sliced. I prefer to "turn" them into barrel shapes, making them similar in size to the potatoes, allowing three pieces per serving. Both the potatoes and carrots can now be simply boiled until tender.

The pearl onions must first be blanched in boiling water for 2 minutes. Remove from the water and allow them to cool.

Split the onions in half and melt a heaping teaspoon of butter in a frying-pan. When it bubbles, place the onions in the pan, cut-side down. Cook for a few minutes until golden brown. Turn the onions and repeat the same cooking time.

To serve the casserole, place the lobsters in a steamer, fitted over lightly simmering water; heat and cook for 5–6 minutes. In this time the lobster meat will have completely warmed through. It is very important the steaming is not too rapid since this would toughen the meat.

Warm the sauce and add the torn herbs. The potatoes, carrots, and pearl onions can also be added to the sauce.

Arrange the lobsters and vegetables in individual bowls, spooning the sauce on top.

After the dish is complete, I like to beat any remaining sauce with an electric hand-mixer to create a frothy finish. The tasty froth can now be spooned over the lobsters, finishing with a drizzle of shellfish oil, if using.

Fish, Mussel, and Leek Cider Pie

Fish pies were a poor man's meal. Almost any fish could be cooked and served in a liquid or sauce topped with pastry, crumble toppings, or mashed potatoes. I prefer the mashed potato topping, which simply needs to be finished under the broiler for a golden crust. Pastry toppings will often lead to overcooked fish underneath.

These pies can be inexpensive to make. It depends on what fish is cooking underneath. I'm going to be extravagant here by using halibut, which holds together well. Cod, haddock, hake, and monkfish can be substituted, as can many other fish. The mussels can be replaced by shrimp, and the leeks by mushrooms or sweet bell peppers.

The sauce is made with the cidery mussel cooking liquid, which will hold all the flavors and maintain a good consistency.

SERVES 4 AS AN APPETIZER OR 2 AS A MAIN COURSE

- 1½–2 lb (675–900 g) fresh live mussels, bearded, washed and scrubbed
- 1 lb (450 g) halibut fillet
- 4 small young leeks, cut into ½ in (1 cm) pieces, or 2 medium leeks, split lengthwise and sliced
- Butter
- 1½–2 lb (675–900 g) *Mashed Potatoes*, including butter and cream (page 124)

OPPOSITE
Fish, Mussel, and Leek Cider Pie

Mussel Cooking Liquid

- Butter
- 1 onion, sliced
- Leek trimmings (from leeks above)
- 1 garlic clove, peeled
- Few tarragon leaves
- 1¼ cups (300 ml) cider
- 2½ cups (600 ml) *Fish Stock* (page 35) or water

For the Sauce

- 3 tablespoons (35 g) butter
- ⅓ cup (35 g) all-purpose flour
- Mussel cooking liquid (above)
- ⅔ cup (150 ml) heavy cream (optional)
- Squeeze of lemon juice
- Salt and pepper

To cook the mussels, melt a heaping teaspoon of butter in a large saucepan. Add the onions, leek trimmings, garlic, and tarragon leaves. Cook for 8–10 minutes until the vegetables have softened. Pour in the cider, boil, and reduce by three-fourths. Add the mussels and fish stock, cover with a lid, and cook on a high heat. Shake the pan and stir the mussels until they open, taking only a few minutes.

Remove all of the mussels and reduce the cooking liquid by a fourth. Any mussels that don't open should be discarded; then take out the cooked mussels from the open shells, removing any bits of shell or grit in the flesh. Strain the cooking liquid through a sieve and cover the mussels with a ladleful to keep them moist.

For the sauce, melt the butter in a small saucepan and add the flour. Cook for a few minutes, until the mixture takes on a sandy color and texture. Add the stock, a ladle at a time, stirring it into the flour mixture (roux) until all of it has been added.

Bring the sauce to a slow simmer and cook for 35–40 minutes. It is important to stir the sauce from time to time to prevent it from sticking. The sauce can be finished with the heavy cream and a squeeze of lemon juice for a richer finish. Extra cider can be boiled, reduced, and added to the sauce to give a stronger cider flavor. Check and adjust the seasoning with salt and pepper.

Preheat the oven to 400°F/200°C. The halibut can now be lightly poached in some of the liquid that is keeping the mussels moist. Place the fish fillet on a buttered ovenproof dish and add a few tablespoons of the cooking liquid. Cover with buttered waxed paper and cook in the preheated oven for just a few minutes to firm the fillet. Remove from the oven. The fillet can now be broken into large flakes.

Melt a heaping teaspoon of butter and cook the leeks for a few minutes until softened and tender.

Mix together the leeks, fish, and mussels, checking that the mussels have been properly bearded and no shell or grit is left in the flesh.

Take half of the sauce and mix it in to bind the mussels, leeks, and fish. More may be needed to thin the sauce slightly but don't make the mixture too moist. (Any extra sauce can be served separately.) Spoon the mix into a suitable ovenproof dish. If you are preparing to serve it later, then let it cool. If not, then spoon or pipe the hot mashed potatoes on top. The pie can now be lightly brushed with butter and glazed in a hot oven at 425°F/230°C. This will take only 8–10 minutes. The dish can also be finished by browning under a hot broiler. It is now ready to serve.

If the pie mixture has been allowed to cool, pipe the potatoes on top and refrigerate until needed. To re-heat and glaze, place in a preheated oven at 375°F/190°C for 25–30 minutes. To glaze, finish under the broiler.

Note: This dish goes very well with *Buttered Spinach* (page 113). Brushed egg, or melted cheese, or white breadcrumbs can also be used to glaze the potato topping.

Mussel, Leek, and Tomato Casserole, with Spinach and a Warm Poached Egg

Mussels have been eaten since prehistoric times in Britain, and a number of recipes for them exist from the fourteenth century onward. In the very early days, they used to be baked on hot stones beside the sea, and a little butter was inserted as the shells opened. They were also baked in pies, boiled and served with parsley, or packed into rolls or baked potatoes in Ireland.

This recipe is quite simple, with the mussel cooking liquid becoming the foundation of the sauce. Once everything is in the bowls except the egg, the sauce can be glazed to a golden finish. Place the egg in the center and coat with a spoonful of frothy sauce, drizzle with lemon oil, and then serve. Breaking into the egg yolk and eating it with the seafood and vegetables is delicious.

SERVES 4 AS AN APPETIZER OR 2 AS A MAIN COURSE

2¼ lb (1 kg) fresh live mussels, bearded, washed and scrubbed
1¼ cups (300 ml) white wine
1¼ cups (300 ml) Fish Stock (page 35) or water
1¼ cups (300 ml) heavy cream
1 leek, cut into ½ in (1 cm) dice
3 tomatoes, blanched and peeled
Lemon juice
2 tablespoons crème fraîche
6–8 oz (175–225 g) Buttered Spinach (page 113)
1 large egg yolk
4 poached eggs (page 82)
2 tablespoons olive oil
Salt and pepper

When washing and scrubbing fresh mussels you will notice the beard protruding from the shell. Cut this away using a small knife.

In a large saucepan, boil the white wine reducing it by half. Add the fish stock or water and bring to a boil. Add the mussels and cook on a high heat, turning the mussels in the pan. After a few minutes, the mussels will open. Remove them from the pan. Reduce any mussel liquid by three-fourths. When it has reduced, add 1 cup (250 ml) of the heavy cream. Cook for 10 minutes, allowing the sauce to reduce and thicken slightly, then strain through a fine sieve.

While the sauce is cooking, the mussels can be removed from their shells, discarding any that haven't opened.

The leek can now be blanched in boiling water for 1–2 minutes until tender. Drain the leek and spread out to cool. Halve the tomatoes and deseed them, then cut into ½ in (1 cm) dice.

Check the mussel sauce for seasoning and add a squeeze of lemon juice along with the 2 tablespoons of crème fraîche. Place a fourth of the sauce into a small saucepan. To the remaining sauce add the mussels, diced leek, and tomatoes and warm it. The spinach can now be microwaved or pan-fried.

Divide the spinach into small mounds in the center of four ovenproof serving plates. Whisk the remaining ¼ cup (50 ml) heavy cream to a very soft peak. Add the egg yolk and whipped cream to the mussel sauce containing the diced leek and tomatoes.

Spoon the mussels, leek, and tomatoes around the spinach, finishing with enough sauce to cover. Each plate can now be placed under a hot broiler to glaze the sauce to a golden brown.

While glazing, heat the poached eggs in simmering water. Poached eggs will take 1 minute to re-heat.

When all the servings are glazed, place the eggs on top of the spinach mounds. Beat the separate sauce with an electric mixer to a frothy consistency. Spoon 1–2 tablespoons on top of each egg.

Mix the olive oil with a squeeze or two of lemon juice, season with salt and pepper, and trickle the mixture over the egg. The dish is ready to serve.

Note: The sauce does not have to be glazed to finish. If you would prefer not to, then simply omit the egg yolk and whipped cream.

Soused Mackerel

Sousing as a means of preserving fish (and meat) dates back to Roman times, the Romans having borrowed the technique from the Greeks and introduced it to northern Europe. In the Middle Ages in Britain, many fish, usually herring, were soused in extremely powerful liquids, presumably to counter the extreme saltiness of the fish or to disguise the rotting process.

Most fish were soused raw, but this recipe is slightly different. The mackerel is heated briefly in its spicy liquid, which is given a thin sauce consistency with the addition of butter, then it is served warm with potatoes.

SERVES 4 AS AN APPETIZER OR A LIGHT LUNCH

4 mackerel fillets, all bones removed
Salt and pepper
½ quantity *Mashed Potatoes* (page 124) with lemon
    and shallots (see Note), to serve
4 tablespoons (50 g) butter
1 tablespoon chopped fresh parsley

For the Sousing Liquor

1 small fennel bulb, very thinly sliced
2 carrots, thinly sliced
2 celery sticks, thinly sliced
1 leek, thinly sliced
2 shallots or 1 onion, thinly sliced
Bouquet garni of 1 bay leaf, 1 star anise, a few
    fresh basil leaves, 2 sprigs each of fresh thyme
    and tarragon, tied in a square of muslin or a
    strip of leek leaves, or a bouquet garni sachet
6 black peppercorns
¼ cup (50 ml) olive oil
4 tablespoons (50 g) unsalted butter
⅔ cup (150 ml) dry white wine
⅔ cup (150 ml) white wine vinegar
2½ cups (600 ml) water

Cook all the vegetables in a pan with the bouquet garni, peppercorns, olive oil, and the butter for a few minutes. Add the white wine, wine vinegar, and water and simmer for about 10–12 minutes, until the vegetables are tender. This is the sousing liquid. Allow it to cool and remove the bouquet garni.

Place the fillets in a lightly buttered flameproof dish and cover with the liquid and vegetables. Season with salt and pepper. Bring slowly to a simmer then remove from the heat. The fish is now ready.

Spoon some of the hot mashed potatoes into serving bowls and place the mackerel on top. Stir the butter and the parsley into the cooking liquid. Ladle the vegetables and sauce around the fish and serve.

Note: For mashed potatoes with lemon and shallots, fry a finely diced shallot in a heaping teaspoon of butter until softened, without browning. Add to the mashed potatoes along with a squeeze of lemon juice.

Whole Roast Sea Bass

Whole fresh fish would once have been roasted beside the fire and served with a sharp or spicy sauce or relish, perhaps not too unlike the sweet pepper butter offered below and the *Green Pepper Butter* on page 52.

Roasting a whole fish and presenting it at the table is such a pleasure. Cutting through the crisp skin to find succulent, almost steamed fish underneath makes you very hungry. As far as preparation is concerned, ask at your fishmarket to have the bass gutted, trimmed, and sealed, making sure the blood clot line is scraped and washed.

The fish can also be stuffed with many flavors – lemons, garlic, thyme, and basil are common. I'll be using some of these to help enhance the juices released from the fish. Serve either buttered new potatoes or creamy mashed potatoes with the fish.

SERVES 4

3¼ lb (1.5 kg) sea bass, cleaned and scaled
2 tablespoons (25 g) butter, softened
Coarse sea salt
Pepper
All-purpose flour
½ lemon
2 garlic cloves, peeled and split
Few basil leaves
Cooking oil

For the Sweet Red Pepper Butter

10 tablespoons (150 g) butter, softened
1 large red bell pepper, finely diced
Pepper (or dash of Tabasco sauce)

To make the red pepper butter, melt a heaping teaspoon of the butter in a small saucepan. Add the sweet bell pepper and cook on a gentle heat for 7–8 minutes until tender. Remove from the heat and let it cool. Mix the remaining butter with the sweet bell peppers, including all pepper juices and seasoning. This can now be left as a coarse butter, puréed in a food processor, or pushed through a sieve for a smooth consistency.

The butter can be rolled into cylinders, wrapped in plastic wrap or presented in a small bowl. Refrigerate until needed.

To cook the fish, preheat the oven to 400°F/200°C. Brush the inside of the fish with butter and season. Dust the outside skin with all-purpose flour and then brush with butter and season. Cut the lemon into four wedges and place inside the bass along with the garlic and basil leaves. Heat a roasting pan with a few tablespoons of cooking oil.

BELOW
Whole Roast Sea Bass

Place the fish in the pan on a medium–high heat and fry gently to a golden brown; carefully turn the fish over and brown it also. This process will take only 2–3 minutes on each side.

Place in the preheated oven and roast for 20–25 minutes, basting with the juices as the bass cooks.

Remove the fish from the roasting pan, allowing any juices to collect in the pan.

Present the sea bass on a large serving plate, topping it with slices of the sweet red pepper butter. Offer any accompanying vegetables separately.

Any juices left in the pan can be thinned with 3–4 tablespoons of water, strained through a sieve or tea strainer, and poured over the bass.

Salmon Fish Cakes

Fish cakes were originally an economical dish, using up leftover scraps of cooked fish with nothing wasted. Potatoes were the usual foundation, as they are here, but egg and breadcrumbs were sometimes used, particularly with cockle fritters, and especially in Wales. Any fish would be suitable, but blander fish need boosting in flavor (adding a little smoked fish to it, as you might to a fish pie).

Salmon is the perfect fish for cakes, holding its moistness with a rich "fat" content that helps spread the flavor. If salmon is unavailable, fresh cod or haddock can be used, making sure the fish is slightly undercooked before mixing with the potatoes. This guarantees a moist rather than dry or cakey finish.

SERVES 4–6

1 tablespoon unsalted butter
2 shallots, finely chopped
1 lb (450 g) salmon, filleted and skinned
⅔ cup (150 ml) dry white wine
1 tablespoon chopped fresh parsley
12 oz (350 g) *Mashed Potatoes*, without cream
    or butter (page 124)

2 tablespoons all-purpose flour, for coating
2 eggs, beaten, for coating
4 cups (225 g) fresh or dried breadcrumbs,
    for coating
Salt and pepper
Vegetable oil, for deep-frying

For the Lemon Butter Sauce

12–16 tablespoons (175–225 g) unsalted butter
Juice of 1 lemon
¼ cup (50 ml) *Chicken or Vegetable Stock*
    (page 33 or 36)
Salt and pepper

BELOW
Salmon Fish Cakes

Preheat the oven to 400°F/200°C and use the butter to grease a baking pan. Season the pan. Sprinkle the finely chopped shallots onto the prepared baking pan, place the salmon on top, and season again with salt and pepper. Add the white wine, cover with foil, and cook in the preheated oven for about 8–10 minutes until the fish is barely cooked. Very thick fillets may need a few minutes more. The salmon will be barely firm on the outside and still pink in the middle.

Place the salmon in a colander over a pan to collect all the cooking juices. When all the juices have been collected, boil them to reduce to a syrupy consistency.

Break up the salmon with a wooden spoon, then add the syrupy reduction and the chopped parsley. Fold in 8 oz (225 g) of the potato, adding it a spoonful at a time until you have a binding texture. Check for seasoning, then roll the mixture into 12 to 18 balls about 1½ in (4 cm) in diameter. Three cakes per serving will be enough. Lightly dust a cake with the flour, dip it into the beaten eggs, and then roll it in the breadcrumbs; repeat the process of egg and breadcrumbs once more.

The fish cakes are now ready for deep-frying. Heat the vegetable oil to 350°F/180°C, then fry the fish cakes for about 4–5 minutes until golden brown. Drain well on paper towels.

To make the sauce, chop the butter into ½ in (1 cm) pieces and put into a pan with the lemon juice and stock. Bring to a simmer, whisking all the time. Do not allow the sauce to boil or the butter will separate. If it's too thick, add more stock, and if you like a sharper taste add more lemon juice. Season and serve immediately. To give a creamier texture, simply beat the sauce with an electric hand mixer.

To serve, pour the warm lemon butter sauce into individual serving dishes or bowls and place three fish cakes in the center of each one.

Note: Lemon butter sauce is one of the simplest possible sauces with a silky texture and barely enough acidity for the salmon fish cakes. This sauce works well with almost any fish.

Smoked Eel Kedgeree

The word "kedgeree" is an Anglo-Indian adaptation of the Hindi *khicharhi or chichri*, a spicy dish consisting of onions, rice, lentils, and fish or meat. It was encountered by the British during the years of the Raj and brought back to England. It is now usually made with smoked haddock without the lentils. Because they are so flavorful, I have used eels in this dish. Eels, too, have played a large part in Britain's culinary history; they were once almost the only fresh fish available to people in the country, and in the tenth century, live eels were used as currency to pay rents to the Abbots of Ely.

This dish could almost be called a risotto, because it's made by the risotto method, but it still holds all the flavors of a good old-fashioned kedgeree. I serve it as an appetizer, but it can be a total meal in itself – for breakfast or for a great lunch or supper. Hard-boiled eggs are traditionally used, but having a warm poached egg placing on top of the rice and just breaking the yolk over it is a dream. If you really cannot find smoked eel, you can make the dish with smoked haddock.

SERVES 4

1 lb (450 g) smoked eel

For the Eel Stock

1 onion, chopped
1 leek, chopped
2 celery sticks, chopped
6 mushrooms or 2 oz (50 g) mushroom
    trimmings
1 bay leaf
1 fresh thyme sprig
2 fresh tarragon sprigs
Few black peppercorns
4 tablespoons (50 g) unsalted butter
1¼ cups (300 ml) dry white wine
5 cups (1.2 liters) Fish Stock (page 35), fish stock
    cube or water

For the Kedgeree

2 onions, finely chopped
8 tablespoons (100 g) butter

2 oz (50 g) veal bone marrow, chopped (optional)
1¼ cups (225 g) arborio or long-grain rice
Approx. 1¼ cups (300 ml) *Curry Cream Sauce*
    (page 393), or ready-made

To Serve

4 eggs, poached (page 82)
3 tablespoons olive oil
2 teaspoons minced fresh chives

Smoked eel is one of my favorite smoked fish. It has to be skinned and filleted first; you can probably have this done at your fishmarket. To do it yourself, simply cut off the head and position the knife against the top half of the central bone. Carefully cut along the bone, removing the fillet of fish. Turn the fish over and repeat the same process on the other side. Now, the skin can be removed: slide your finger or thumb under the skin at the head end and it should tear off all the way along. The fillets may need a little trimming down the sides to remove any excess skin.

After the eels are skinned, turn the fillets onto their backs to show the center. From the head end to half-way down there will be some bones. Simply position the knife under these bones and cut away from the flesh. You now have two long fillets of eel. Cut these into ½ in (1.5 cm) pieces and refrigerate until needed.

To make the eel stock, chop all the bones, skin, and trimmings. Place the chopped vegetables, herbs, and peppercorns in a large pan with the butter and cook them gently for 10 minutes without letting them brown. Add the bones and trimmings and continue to cook for another 5 minutes. Add the white wine and boil to reduce until almost dry. Add the fish stock, stock cube, or water. (Fish stock will give you a stronger and better taste. If you are using water, ask at your fishmarket for some fish bones to cook along with the eel.) Bring the stock to a simmer and cook for 20 minutes. Strain through a sieve and the stock is ready.

For the kedgeree, cook the chopped onions in the butter with the bone marrow, if using, for 5–6 minutes until softened. Stir in the rice and cook for 2 minutes, then start to add the hot eel stock a ladle at a time, stirring continuously. This will create steam and help the cooking process. Wait for the stock to be absorbed before adding more; keep adding the stock and stirring until the rice begins to soften – this will take about 15–20 minutes. The rice should be tender and the mixture still moist.

When the rice is cooked, stir in half the curry sauce and taste. At this stage it becomes a matter of personal choice; some more or all of the curry sauce can be added if you want a stronger taste.

Add the pieces of chopped eel to the kedgeree and stir in to warm them through. Warm the poached eggs in boiling water, then drain well. Spoon the kedgeree into four bowls and place a poached egg on top of each one. Spoon a little olive oil over the eggs and sprinkle with the snipped chives. The dish is now ready.

Smoked Haddock with Welsh Rarebit

This has become my signature dish, and I must say it is one of my favorites. It's very British in concept, using wonderful smoked haddock – choose a natural fish, not one that has been dyed bright yellow – with a Welsh rarebit topping. To crown the flavors and textures, I serve it on a fresh tomato salad, presenting hot and cold tastes together. It's lovely as an appetizer, a supper, or as a light meal.

SERVES 4 AS AN APPETIZER OR A LIGHT LUNCH

6 ripe plum or salad tomatoes
Salt and pepper
4 × 4 oz (100 g) slices of natural
    smoked haddock
6 oz (175 g) *Welsh Rarebit* mixture (page 178)
1 tablespoon finely snipped fresh chives
⅔ cup (150 ml) *Basic Vinaigrette* (page 50)

Preheat the oven to 350°F/180°C and preheat the broiler to medium.

First, core the tomatoes, then blanch them in boiling water for 10 seconds. Cool them quickly in ice water, and the skins should peel off easily. Slice the tomatoes and arrange overlapping on the center of individual plates. You'll need about 1½ tomatoes per serving, and this amount should make enough for four circles. Sprinkle with a little salt and a grinding of pepper.

Arrange the haddock slices in a buttered flameproof dish. Split the rarebit into four pieces and pat out on your hands to about ⅛ in (2–3 mm) thick (the mix should be quite pliable and easy to use), trimming to give a neat finish. Lay the pieces on top of the haddock. Brown under the broiler until golden, then finish the haddock in the preheated oven for 4–5 minutes.

Add the chives to the vinaigrette and spoon it over the tomatoes. Place the haddock on top and serve.

Smoked Haddock and Welsh Rarebit Tartlets

For this variation of the recipe above, it's best to buy small pastry canapé tartlet cases. This will save a lot of time and work.

This is a great recipe to try, especially if you've made the above recipe and have rarebit left over. If you have any smoked haddock fillet tails, use them here. One small haddock fillet will fill a lot of tartlets, so the quantities are up to you.

¼ *Welsh Rarebit* mixture (page 178)
1 small fillet (12 oz–1 lb/350–450 g) smoked
     haddock, preferably natural
1¼ cups (300ml) milk
Butter
2–3 large tomatoes, blanched in boiling water,
     peeled, seeded and diced into ¼ in
     (5 mm) pieces
1 heaping teaspoon chopped chives
2 tablespoons olive oil
1 teaspoon balsamic vinegar
40 canapé pastry tartlets
Olive oil, to finish (optional)

The Welsh rarebit mixture can be melted into balls and patted by hand into disks about ⅛ in (2–3mm) thick – big enough to cover the tartlet cases.

To cook the smoked haddock, place the fillet into a suitable dish. Bring the milk and a heaping teaspoon of butter to a boil and pour over the fish. Cover and let it stand for a few minutes. The fish is now cooked. Break the fish into flakes and mix with the diced tomatoes and chopped chives. Mix together the olive oil and vinegar (extra vinegar can be added for a more piquant flavor) and pour over the filling. Divide among the tartlet cases and top with the Welsh rarebit disks.

Place the tartlets under a preheated broiler and cook until golden brown. For a shiny finish, lightly brush with a drop of olive oil. The rarebit tartlets are ready to serve.

Broiled Herrings with Braised Lentils

Herrings in one form or another, usually salted and dried, formed the staple diet of many people in Britain almost until the twentieth century. The tough and dark "red" herring was very strong in taste but managed to keep hunger at bay. Over the years, we have continued to salt and smoke herring, but now for pleasure rather than necessity, and today the bloater (a closed herring, lightly smoked so that it is still plump and "bloated") and the kipper (a split, brined and smoked herring) are famous British specialities.

Fresh herrings are eaten, too. In Scotland, they are coated with oatmeal and fried in bacon fat. Herrings broiled whole on the bone with a separate hot English mustard sauce – a very traditional British combination – was one of the first dishes I was taught to make as a young chef. They were delicious to eat, but because of the bones, hard work. So, to simplify everything for the eater, I take them off of the bone and serve them simply with the sauce. To serve with them, mashed potatoes go very well, and lentils are even tastier.

ABOVE
Smoked Haddock with Welsh Rarebit

ABOVE
*Seared, Cured Salmon Cutlets with Leeks, Bacon, and
a Cider Vinegar Dressing*

8 large herring fillets
Butter, melted

For the Braised Lentils

4 tablespoons (50 g) unsalted butter
1 oz (25 g) carrot, finely diced
1 oz (25 g) celery, finely diced
1 oz (25 g) onion, finely diced
1 oz (25 g) leek, finely diced
1 small garlic clove, crushed
4 oz (100 g) green lentils (*lentilles de Puy*)
2 cups (450 ml) *Chicken or Vegetable Stock*
    (page 33 or 36)
Salt and pepper

For the Mustard Seed Sauce

2 shallots, finely chopped
1 celery stick, chopped
½ leek, chopped
1 bay leaf
4 tablespoons (50 g) unsalted butter
1 cup dry white wine
1¼ cups (300 ml) Fish Stock (page 35)
⅔ cup (150 ml) heavy cream
2 teaspoons wholegrain mustard, to taste

Preheat the oven to 400°F/200°C and butter and season a small flameproof baking pan.

To cook the lentils, melt the butter in a small ovenproof braising pan. Add the diced vegetables and garlic and cook for a few minutes. Add the lentils, stirring well. Cover with the stock and bring to a simmer. Cover with a lid and braise in the preheated oven for about 30–35 minutes until the lentils are tender and all the stock has been absorbed. Make sure they are tender before taking them from the oven. Season with salt and pepper.

To make the sauce, sweat the vegetables and bay leaf in the butter for a few minutes. Add the white wine and boil to reduce until almost dry. Add the fish stock and continue to boil until reduced by three-fourths. Pour in the cream and cook slowly until the sauce is thick enough to coat the back of a spoon. Strain through a fine sieve. Stir in the

mustard a teaspoon at a time until the right taste is achieved, spicy but not overpowering.

To cook the herring fillets, place them on the greased baking pan and brush with butter. Cook under the hot broiler for about 5–6 minutes. As soon as the fillets have browned they will be ready to serve.

To serve, spoon the lentils onto the center of four hot plates, pour the mustard sauce over them and place the fillets on top of the lentils. The dish is now complete.

Seared, Cured Salmon Cutlets with Leeks, Bacon, and a Cider Vinegar Dressing

Salmon is the king of freshwater fish – although, of course, it spends a lot of its life in the sea. Salmon was once eaten much more often than it is now, when the rivers in which it spawned were cleaner, and when pollution and overfishing were not taking their toll on the Atlantic fishing grounds. If wild salmon is not available, farmed-raised salmon are a good value.

This particular salmon dish has lots of good British flavors, with leeks, bacon, and cider among the classic ingredients. You'll notice that I've used the word "cured" in the title of the recipe. This curing is an optional extra, but an absolutely beautiful one. It gives the dish and the salmon a whole new texture and flavor. It's not essential so don't be put off by it. Fresh salmon cutlets can also be used.

SERVES 4 AS AN APPETIZER

For the Salmon

1 tablespoon (15 g) coarse sea salt
1 tablespoon (15 g) superfine sugar
Splash of brandy or whiskey
1 lb (450 g) salmon fillet, skinned and boned
    (page 11)
Pepper

6 strips of bacon
Cooking oil
1 lb (450 g) leeks, shredded
Butter
Salt and pepper
Cider Vinegar Dressing (page 41)

Mix together the sea salt and sugar; bind with the brandy or whiskey to a consistency that will go through a squeeze bottle.

Lay the salmon fillet on a piece of plastic wrap, big enough to wrap around it, grind pepper over the salmon, and then spread with the salt and sugar mixture.

Wrap the plastic wrap around the fillet, place on a pan and refrigerate it. It should now be left to cure for 4–6 hours, giving enough time for the salt to dissolve with the sugar and impregnate the salmon flesh. The salmon can be left for 24 hours. The texture will then become slightly firmer as a "raw cooking" process takes place.

After it has cured, the salmon can be cut into eight cutlet pieces, two per serving, ready to pan-fry.

For the garnish, fry the bacon strips in a drop of cooking oil over a medium heat until completely crisp, almost like a fine bacon crackling. Other methods of cooking the bacon are to broil it until crisp, pouring off excess fat, or bake in a hot oven, also pouring off any excess fat. These strips can be cooked in advance; they will stay crisp and reheat well when mixed with the hot leeks.

For the leeks, heat a heaping teaspoon of butter in a large pan or wok. When it bubbles, add the washed leeks. Cook on a high heat until tender; this will only take 2–3 minutes. The slightly moist leeks will create steam, helping to cook them quickly.

Add the bacon and season with salt and pepper. Also add 2–3 tablespoons of cider dressing to bind and hold the garnish together.

Spoon the mixture onto four plates. Trickle with more of the cider dressing (squeeze bottle piping can be used for a more decorative finish, see page 11).

The salmon pieces can be shallow-fried while the garnish is cooking. It's best to heat the pan very hot with a drop of cooking oil. Place the "cutlets" in the pan and cook for 1–2 minutes to brown the edges on one side until slightly burned. Turn them over to seal them. It's important that the fish is only cooked medium-rare to medium, bearing in mind it has been cured.

The fish pieces can now be placed on top of the leek and bacon garnish.

The dish is now ready to serve.

Note: I also like to add a few drops of lemon oil. Simply mix a few tablespoons of olive oil with a teaspoon or two of lemon juice and season with salt and pepper.

Parsleyed Cod with Mustard Butter Sauce

Parsley has been associated with fish since the Middle Ages as one of the principal herbs used in the famous green sauce. I have changed this classic cod and parsley combination to give a purée of parsley mixed with spinach, which is spread over the fish so that the parsley flavor comes through in every bite. If you serve this with some curly kale, roast potatoes, and a mustard butter sauce, you will have a complete meal.

If pig's caul (page 11) is unavailable, wrap the cod in buttered aluminum foil and steam it instead of pan-frying, or you can pan-fry the cod and put it on top of the warm purée or vice versa.

I use two varieties of parsley here because I want to add the stronger flavor from the flat parsley into the curly parsley, which has a thicker texture.

SERVES 4

Small bunch of fresh flatleaf parsley
Small bunch of fresh parsley
4 oz (100 g) spinach, picked and washed
4 × 6–8 oz (175–225 g) servings of cod fillet, skinned and boned
8 oz (225 g) pig's caul, soaked in cold water overnight

1 tablespoon cooking oil
Butter
Salt and pepper

To Serve

Curly Kale (page 105)
Butter
Mustard Butter Sauce (page 53)
"Banana" Roast Potatoes (page 239)

Preheat the oven to 400°F/200°C. The two parsleys and the spinach should be plunged into salted, boiling water for 2–3 minutes until cooked and tender. Drain in a colander and refresh with cold water. When the spinach is cold, squeeze out any excess water and process in a food processor to a smooth purée. Season with salt and pepper.

This purée can now be spread ⅛ in (3 mm) thick on the presentation (skinned) side of the cod. Then cut the pig's caul into four pieces. Use these to wrap around the cod servings. Refrigerate until firm.

To cook the cod, warm the tablespoon of cooking oil in a frying-pan. Put the cod servings in the pan, parsley-side down, and add a heaping teaspoon of butter. Cook and brown for 3–4 minutes until golden with the rich green coming through. Turn the fish over and transfer to an ovenproof dish, if necessary. Complete by cooking in the oven for 8–10 minutes.

While the cod is cooking, warm the curly kale in a little butter and season. Warm the mustard sauce and add one or two spoonfuls to the curly kale.

After the cod is cooked, remove it from the pan and place at the front of the plate. Arrange a small pile of roast potatoes, allowing four pieces per serving, along with a few spoonfuls of curly kale. Pour the mustard sauce over and around the kale and serve.

Deep-fried Cod in Batter

One of the most famous fish dishes in the whole of the British Isles, it's almost always bought wrapped in paper from the local food shop.

Battering cod fillets is not difficult at all, providing you have either a deep fat fryer or a very large saucepan. This cooking method for fish was first introduced using the batter simply to protect the fish during its cooking time. After the fish was deep-fried and golden brown, it was presented on the plate and the person eating it would cut away and discard the batter to enjoy only the fish.

Eventually, the batter became an edible and enjoyable component of the dish. The batter has to be flavorful and crisp, but, equally important, should be thick enough to protect the fish itself.

If a thick batter is used and it is slowly and carefully submerged into the preheated fat (beef dripping is the most classic cooking fat, but a good-quality cooking oil will work just as well), it will form a protective casing around the fish itself. While the fat cooks the batter, it will begin to soufflé into a crisp armor, while the heat steams the fish.

The cod fillet will now have the most beautiful natural flavor with near-translucent flakes to enjoy, surrounded by crisp fried almost crackling-style batter. It is certainly delicious.

If a very thin batter is used, it will not soufflé. Instead, it will wrinkle all over the fish, sticking to the flesh and without holding a crispness. After you remove it from the fryer, the fish juices will run out, moistening the already softening batter so that by the time you are home the fish will have stuck to the paper it's wrapped in. After you've eaten your own battered cod, I doubt if you'll buy the ready-made stuff again.

A wedge of lemon goes well with the fish along with *Tartar Sauce* (page 43) and homemade *Chips* (page 127) for the perfect supper.

SERVES 2

2 × 6–8 oz (175–225 g) cod fillet servings, boned
Squeeze of lemon juice
Salt and pepper

2 cups (225 g) self-rising flour, sieved
1¼ cups (300 ml) lager

Preheat the fat-fryer oil to 350°F/180°C.

Leaving the skin on the cod fillets holds the fillet together when it's dipped into the batter and placed in the oil. Squeeze a little lemon juice over each fillet and season with salt and pepper. These can now be lightly floured before making the batter.

To make the batter, place the sifted flour into a large bowl. Whisk in three-fourths of the lager. At this point check the consistency of the batter: it should be very thick, almost too thick to beat. If it appears to be over-gluey, whisk in a little more lager to thin slightly. Season with a pinch of salt. The cod fillets can now be dipped, one at a time, into the batter mixture. It's best to hold the fillet at the thin end (in one corner) between thumb and forefinger. Coat the fish in the batter and lift from the bowl. Some of the batter will begin to fall away slowly. If the batter falls away quickly, it means it's too thin, in which case add a tablespoon or two more of flour.

Don't allow too much of the batter to fall off before placing in the deep hot oil. Submerge only an inch at a time, and after three-fourths of the fish is

in, the batter will lift the fillet, floating the fish. Submerge the remaining fillet in the same way, being careful not to burn your fingers.

Allow the fish to cook for 2–3 minutes before turning it over. At this point the fish will not be golden brown but the batter will have sealed and souffléd. Cook until golden brown all over. A thick slice of cod will take up to 12 minutes to cook, an average fillet 9–10 minutes.

After it has cooked, remove from the oil and drain on paper towels. Sprinkle with salt and serve.

Note: The batter quantities can be doubled to give enough for 4–6 servings.

For an extra garnish, deep-fry curly parsley in the oil. Plunge the parsley carefully into the hot fat as the oil tends to spit. When this calms down after a minute or two, remove the parsley from the pan and lightly salt it.

See also

Angels on Horseback (page 175)
Arbroath Smokie and Cream Cheese Pâté
(page 89)
Cullen Skink (page 27)
Broiled Kippers (page 87)
Lobster "Bisque" Soup (page 23)
Lobster Omelette "Thermidor" (page 75)
Seared Scallops with Radish and French Bean
Salad (page 109)
Smoked Haddock (page 88)
Soft Herring Roes on Caper Toasts (page 177)
Spicy Smoked Haddock and Saffron Soup
(page 18)
Stuffed Herrings with Apples and Tarragon
(page 57)

ABOVE
Deep-fried Cod in Batter

Savories and Snacks

The savory, when served as a separate course at a meal, is unique to Britain. Originally the word would have simply referred to an unsweetened, piquant dish rather than a sweet one, and in the seventeenth century could have been offered before the meal as an appetizer or at the end of the meal. In Victorian times, though, the savory developed into a course that was offered, usually at dinner, *before* the dessert. (And today, this is when a cheeseboard, the modern equivalent of the savory course, is correctly served.)

A savory was considered both as a digestive (probably necessary after a huge Victorian meal) and as a means of cleansing the palate before the sweetness of a dessert. It is just as likely, though, that having a little savory mouthful or two offered a chance of finishing up the dinner wines which accompanied the main course, and this traditionally was up to the men. Since then, the savory has somehow become associated in our minds with men, just as sweet things are often thought to be more to satisfy the taste of women. It could simply be that women didn't have the room for a savory – after some seven or so courses! – or that the men preferred to skip the dessert in anticipation of the port. Whatever is true, Queen Victoria is said to have defied convention and enjoyed bone marrow on toast as a savory each evening after dinner.

The most popular, and often the only combination contemplated, was cheese on toast. It took on many names and had the advantage of a foundation with many possible variations.

Today, cheese is very frequently associated with savories, but this is no surprise, for a savory, although small, needs to be strongly flavored. Cheese usually contains a great deal of taste in itself, and it was often combined with other strong flavorings. Toasted cheese – or a Welsh "rabbit" or "rarebit" (known sometimes in "polite" circles as *Bonne-bouche à la galloise*) – started off fairly simply. But over the years it could have added to it: Worcestershire sauce, cayenne pepper, anchovy sauce, anchovies, ham, mustard, onions, horseradish, or capers (when the latter is added, the rarebit is known as *Bonne-bouche à l'irlandaise*). Many mixtures for Welsh, Scottish, and Irish rarebits included ale with the cheese. English rarebit called for soaking the bread in red wine first. I believe that my recipe for *Welsh Rarebit* (page 178)

has become a new British classic. The rarebit mixture itself can simply be spooned onto toast, but when it is served on top of a piece of smoked haddock that has been placed on a tomato and chive salad, it is a completely different experience (see *Smoked Haddock with Welsh Rarebit*, page 163). That dish has become one of the most popular I've ever featured on a menu. The rarebit is freezes well, so if you make it in quantity, you can freeze the remainder for future meals, snacks, or savories.

Other favorite piquant ingredients included anchovies, here used in what might be the most savory of all, *Scotch Woodcock* (page 176), as well as bloaters, sardines, fish roe, and smoked salmon. Chicken wings, livers, kidneys, and fish roe were "deviled" in spicy, hot sauces which were particularly popular in the nineteenth century. *Devils on Horseback*, for example, another famous savory, was given its name due to the heat of the spices rather than the black color of the prune.

Most savories consist of a piece of toast or fried bread spread with a topping – perhaps another reminder of the medieval bread trencher. Although the popularity of the savory course seems to have now declined, many savory recipes can be served as snacks, as canapés (if small enough), as light lunches if served with salads, or part of a high tea or a light supper, the latter a late-evening light meal that became common in Georgian times.

I think we should revive the idea of savories. If you don't care for dessert, then don't deprive yourself – have a savory instead. They're easy to prepare and cook, and most importantly, they are exceedingly flavorful.

Port and Stilton Cheese Toasts Ⓥ

The village of Stilton in Huntingdonshire gave its name to this most famous of English cheeses. It was not originally made there, but the recipe was acquired in the late eighteenth century by the landlord of the Bell Inn in Stilton, which was a stage on the main road from London and northward to Scotland. The landlord sold the cheese to the stagecoach passengers who stopped there, and the cheese proved so popular that it became famous as "Stilton" over the whole country.

A piece of good Stilton and a glass of rich port is a real British Classic for rounding off a meal. This

ABOVE
Port and Stilton Cheese Toasts

recipe gives this "classic" a totally different feel, though, serving it hot, and with the flavors of Stilton and port working together. With every bite, you have the Stilton and port experience in one. Serve as a savory instead of a dessert. It is also good for lunch or supper with a salad of watercress, apple, and grapes (see Note). And for the ultimate experience with this recipe, use toasted walnut bread – the crisp, nutty flavor underneath the Stilton will excite every one of your tastebuds.

This recipe will be enough for 6–8 slices of bread.

SERVES 6–8

1 teaspoon finely chopped shallots (optional)
¼ cup (50 ml) port
8 oz (225 g) Stilton cheese, crumbled and at room
    temperature
1 tablespoon (15 g) all-purpose flour, plus extra
    for dusting
1 teaspoon English mustard
1 egg
Pepper
6–8 slices of bread, preferably walnut

Place the shallots (if using), in a small saucepan with the port. Bring to a simmer and reduce until almost dry. If you are not including the shallots, then simply boil and reduce the port by half. Let the shallots cool. The Stilton cheese should be crumbled and left at room temperature. This will make the cheese soft and workable without it breaking down.

Now, place all of the ingredients except the bread, in a food processor and process to a paste. The Stilton and port rarebit can now be refrigerated for at least half an hour to set.

To finish the dish, toast the walnut bread. Now, the cheese paste can be spread, molded by hand, or rolled on a flour-dusted surface to a thickness of ⅛ in (3– 4 mm) and cut into rectangles. Top each slice of toast and place under a hot broiler until golden.

Note: For a watercress, apple, and grape salad, mix the leaves of washed watercress with halved, seeded grapes. Peel, core, and slice Granny Smith apples and add to the salad. For a quick dressing, mix 2–3 tablespoons of olive oil with a teaspoon or two of red wine vinegar and a grinding of pepper.

The Stilton and port mixture also works well on toast cut into squares or strips for canapés. It can also be used as a topping or glaze for cauliflower, broccoli, spinach, baked potatoes, chicken breasts, fish fillets, and so on.

Angels on Horseback

Probably the finest of all savories. The "angels" are oysters, wrapped in bacon and then broiled or shallow-fried and presented on strips of warm toast. You can use scallops instead of oysters; the savory then becomes *Archangels on Horseback.*

There are mixed opinions about "angels" and "devils" (see introduction to next recipe). Some say that angels should be chicken livers instead of oysters, which I do not agree with, and others say that devils should be chicken livers instead of prunes. I'm sticking to what I believe is correct – oysters for angels and prunes for devils. Chicken livers can be spiced and deviled on toast, but that happens without the bacon.

Two oysters per serving of savory are the right size, each oyster wrapped in half a slice of bacon. For super-plump angels, two oysters per half slice of bacon can be used.

SERVES 6

12 medium oysters (or 24 for super-plump angels)
6 slices of bacon, unsmoked if possible
Cayenne pepper
3 thick slices of white bread
Butter

For the Oyster Sauce (optional)

Oyster juice
1 heaping teaspoon finely chopped shallots
1 tablespoon heavy cream
2 tablespoons (25 g) butter
Squeeze of lemon juice
Pepper

The oyster sauce is an optional extra. It's such a good way to use all those tasty juices.

OPPOSITE
Devils and Angels on Horseback

Ask at your fishmarket to have the oysters opened, making sure all of the juices are saved for you. After they've been opened, check over the oysters for any bits of shell. Rinse them under cold running water.

Place the oysters in a small saucepan with their juices. Bring to a slow simmer (this should take under 1 minute) and then remove, put the oysters on a plate, and allow them to cool. If you are making the sauce, the juices can now be strained through a sieve. Add the finely chopped shallots and bring to a simmer. Allow the liquid to reduce by half. The heavy cream can now be added and the sauce returned to a simmer. Season with a grinding of pepper and then whisk in the butter and a squeeze or two of lemon juice; the sauce is ready. The acidity of lemon juice and shallots are a classic accompaniment to oysters.

After the oysters have cooled, halve each slice of bacon. Lightly sprinkle the oysters with cayenne pepper and wrap the bacon around them. Pierce with a toothpick to hold the bacon and then place the wrapped oysters on a greased baking pan.

Cook under a preheated broiler until they are golden and crisp, turning them over for an even cooking. This should take 2–3 minutes, provided the broiler is preheated. It's important not to cook the oysters for too long or they will become dry.

The bread can be toasted, buttered, and the crusts removed before cutting into strips or disks. Or, pan-fry the bread in butter before cutting. Serve the angels with or on top of the toasts.

If you have made the sauce, simply pour it around each "angel" or pass it separately.

Note: Try to find unsmoked bacon to use for the "angels;" smoked is strong and salty and might overpower the oysters.

Devils on Horseback

No, they're not chicken livers, they're prunes. The "devil" has nothing really to do with being the opposite of "angel," but is a reference to the piquant flavor, denoting the dish has been seasoned with mustard, cayenne, and/or Worcestershire sauce. It's the spice that is the "devil."

The prunes are pitted and stuffed before being wrapped with the bacon. The pit can be replaced either with a roasted and skinned almond, or with a little chutney. The almond will be easier to use, but I prefer using chutney. To go with the other flavors (mustard and cayenne) I use mango chutney, selecting the coarser pieces to stuff the prunes. If you're a real "devil" fan, use a much hotter and stronger chutney.

High-quality pitted prunes are readily available. To plump them up and for extra flavor soak them in warm tea with the addition of a splash of brandy or Armagnac.

SERVES 6

12 soaked prunes, pitted
¼–½ teaspoon English mustard
1–2 oz (25–50 g) *Mango Chutney* (page 388) or
 bought chutney
6 thin strips of bacon
6 thick slices of bread
Butter, for toast
Cayenne pepper (optional)

When the prunes have been soaked, drain them well. Starting with a ¼ teaspoon, mix the mustard with the mango chutney. Add extra if you want a more "devilish" finish.

Fill each prune with the chutney. Cut the bacon slices in half crosswise and wrap half a slice around each prune, piercing with a toothpick to hold the bacon in place.

Now, cook the wrapped prunes on a buttered baking pan under a hot preheated broiler. Broil until the bacon is golden and crisp on both sides.

While the "devils" are cooking, the toast can be made and buttered or pan-fried in the butter. Remove the crusts and divide into 12 triangles.

The "devils" can now be placed on the toast triangles and served. If using cayenne pepper, dust a little over each one.

Note: The mustard can be mixed with the butter and spread on the toasts. Prunes keep very well soaked in neat Armagnac or Cognac.

Scotch Woodcock

This savory was a favorite with Victorian gentlemen. It's believed the name is a facetious reference to the supposed Scottish meanness with money (!), for woodcock is one of the most expensive game birds. Otherwise, the only resemblance is that both woodcock and the savory – traditionally consisting of scrambled eggs with anchovies (and sometimes capers as well) – are served on toast.

I use marinated anchovies here, which are usually sold in gourmet food shops or in large supermarkets. Basically, the recipe consists of anchovies on toast that are then topped with scrambled egg. There's an element of surprise as you fork through the egg and encounter the savory fish on top of the crisp toast.

SERVES 4

4 thick slices of bread (onion bread is very good
 with this, or use olive bread)
12–16 single marinated anchovy fillets
4 tablespoons (50 g) butter, softened
2 tablespoons heavy cream (milk can also be used)
6 eggs, beaten
Salt and pepper
1 teaspoon chopped fresh chives or parsley
 (optional), to garnish

Toast the bread and remove the crusts. Place the anchovy fillets, side by side three or four to a serving, on each toast.

Brush with a heaping teaspoon of the butter. These can now be warmed under a preheated broiler. Add the heavy cream to the eggs. Melt the remaining butter in a saucepan. When it starts to bubble, season the eggs with salt and pepper. Pour the eggs into the butter and stir, preferably with a wooden spoon, until scrambled but still moist and loose.

Place the anchovy toasts on plates and spoon the scrambled eggs on top.

The dish can be given extra taste and color by sprinkling it with chives or chopped parsley, if desired.

Soft Herring Roe on Caper Toasts

Cod roe with bacon used to be a popular breakfast dish in the south-west of England and in Ireland; herring roe was served for breakfast and high tea. In this recipe roe is briefly fried in butter before being served on hot toast that has been spread with a delicious caper butter.

SERVES 4

8 soft herring roe
All-purpose flour, for dusting roe
4 tablespoons (50 g) butter
½ teaspoon capers, chopped
1 teaspoon shallots, finely chopped
4 slices of toast, crusts removed
Lemon juice
Salt and pepper

Season the roe with salt and pepper and lightly dust with flour. Melt a third of the butter and when it bubbles, add the roe. Quickly pan-fry it to a golden brown.

Mix the remaining butter with the capers and shallots, season with salt and pepper, and spread on the hot toast. When the roe is cooked, arrange it on the toast. Add a squeeze of lemon to the butter in which the roe has been fried (a heaping teaspoon to heighten the taste). Bring the butter to bubbling and simply pour it over each roe toast and serve.

Peppered Mushrooms ⓥ

A favorite topping for many savories in Victorian times, mushrooms were often deviled as well – simply spread some mustard, either English or French Dijon, on top of the toast to heighten the flavor.

SERVES 4

2–3 medium-sized mushrooms per serving
4 tablespoons (50 g) butter
4 slices of toast, crusts removed (onion bread works well)
Salt and pepper
1 teaspoon chopped fresh chives, to garnish

Wipe and cut off the stems of the mushrooms. Season with salt and a grinding of black pepper, being as generous as your taste buds will allow. Melt three-fourths of the butter in a large frying-pan. Add the mushrooms and cook for 7–8 minutes until tender.

Place the mushrooms on the toast, pouring the rest of the butter over them, and sprinkle with the chopped chives.

Sardine and Tomato Toasts

Sardines provide opportunities for many delicious savories. They can simply be boned and served on toast, or broiled with grated Parmesan on top, sprinkled with chopped olives, stuffed, deviled, or deep-fried in batter. Canned sardines can be used, but for this recipe, fresh sardines are best. Ask at your fishmarket to have them filleted for you.

SERVES 4

8 sardines, each cut in half lengthwise
1 small garlic clove
4 slices of onion bread (if unavailable, multi-grain bread can be used)
2 plum or round tomatoes
Coarse sea salt and pepper
Olive oil

Place the 16 fillets, skin-side up, on a lightly greased baking pan. For each serving, arrange four fillets almost overlapping, head to tail. After they have cooked, you will be able to lift each one with a spatula.

Split the garlic clove lengthwise and rub the fillets gently with its cut edges. This will just give the serving a light garlic aroma. Brush the fish with olive oil. Also brush the bread slices with the oil and toast them under a preheated broiler on both sides. Slice the tomatoes and divide the slices, overlapping, among the toasts. Season with coarse sea-salt and a grinding of pepper.

The sardines can now be lightly seasoned with salt and pepper and cooked under the broiler until golden. This will only take 2–4 minutes, depending on the size of the fillets.

While the sardines are cooking, the tomato toasts can be warmed under the broiler. To serve, carefully lift the sardine servings and place them on the tomato toasts. The dish is now ready to serve.

Note: Add a squeeze of lemon juice to a teaspoon of olive oil. This "dressing" can now be spooned over the savory toasts.

Deviled Kidneys

"Deviled" dishes became extremely popular throughout the nineteenth century, both for breakfast and for dinner savories. Herring roe, kidneys, chicken livers, and pieces of meat and poultry were all deviled; the devil sauces were also used to add flavor to leftovers.

Deviled Kidneys is one of the best-known Victorian and Edwardian breakfast dishes, often to be found on a country-house sideboard, sizzling gently in a silver chafing dish.

The kidneys can be cooked in a number of ways, some shallow-fried, some broiled or even baked. Basically, the idea was to zest them up with things such as cayenne, mustard, Worcestershire sauce, lemon juice, and sometimes vinegar. The kidneys could also just be cooked and served with a deviled sauce. The "devil" (below) is quick and easy to make.

SERVES 4

8 lambs" kidneys
2 tablespoons (25 g) butter, melted
1 tablespoon English mustard
2 teaspoons white wine vinegar
1 teaspoon Worcestershire sauce
Drop of peanut oil, if pan-frying
Salt and cayenne pepper
4 thick slices of hot buttered toast, to serve

The outer skin of the kidneys should first be removed, cutting away any gristle.

For broiling, simply split the kidneys open, cutting three-fourths of the way through. The open shape can now be held by threading with a toothpick. Soak the toothpicks in water before using to prevent them from burning. For sautéing, cut the kidneys in two, giving you four halves per serving.

To Broil

Brush the eight kidney pieces with the melted butter and season with a pinch of salt and cayenne pepper. Place under a preheated broiler and cook for 3 minutes on each side.

While they are cooking, mix together the mustard, vinegar, and Worcestershire sauce. Half of this mixture can now be brushed on the kidneys and they can be cooked for another 1–2 minutes. Turn the kidneys and brush with the remaining mustard mixture. Replace them under the broiler and cook for 1 minute.

The deviled kidneys can be presented on the toasts, removing the toothpicks before serving.

To Pan-fry

Season the kidneys with salt and cayenne pepper. Heat a frying-pan to a medium heat with the peanut oil. When the oil is close to smoking, place the kidneys in the pan. These will seal very quickly in the hot oil. Turn after 2 minutes and continue to fry. After approximately 3–4 minutes of cooking, add the butter. Continue to pan-fry, turning the kidneys. After 5–6 minutes the mustard, Worcestershire sauce, and vinegar dressing can be added. Roll the kidneys in the dressing so they are totally covered. Cook for another minute and place them on the warm buttered toasts.

Note: If you are a kidney fan, but prefer them simply broiled or pan-fried, then simply omit the mustard, Worcestershire sauce, vinegar, and the cayenne pepper. Season just with salt and pepper and then follow the cooking methods and times as for deviled.

Welsh Rarebit ⓥ

The origin of the name "rarebit" or "rabbit" has been disputed for centuries. Some say the former comes from the dish's position in the meal, as a "rear-bit" (rather as an hors d'oeuvre was known at one time as a "fore-bit") Another story of the rarebit's origin reflects the patience of the Welsh huntsman's wife when he came home empty-handed from the hunt; the wife had to prepare cheese instead …

There are also many different recipes. Toasted cheese recipes appear in cook books throughout the centuries, and there are English Rabbits, Welsh Rarebits, Buck Rarebits, and Scotch Rabbits, all of them subtly different. Here is my version. This recipe is really the minimum amount you can make for a successful mixture. It will keep in the refrigerator for up to ten days and it also freezes well, so you will have some to use in plenty of other dishes, not least my favorite, *Smoked Haddock with Welsh Rarebit* (page 163). It's also delicious as a simple cheese on toast. When I make it at home,

I divide it into two portions and freeze one of them for use later.

COVERS 8–10 PORTIONS

SMOKED HADDOCK (PAGE 163)

12 oz (350 g) mature Cheddar cheese, grated
⅓ cup (85 ml) milk
¼ cup (25 g) all-purpose flour
½ cup (25 g) fresh white breadcrumbs
½ tablespoon English mustard powder
A few shakes of Worcestershire sauce
1 egg
1 egg yolk
Salt and pepper

Put the Cheddar into a pan and add the milk. Slowly warm them over a low heat, but do not allow the mixture to boil because this will separate the cheese. When the mixture is smooth and just begins to bubble, add the flour, the breadcrumbs, and the mustard and cook for a few minutes more, stirring, over a low heat until the mixture comes away from the sides of the pan and begins to form a ball shape. Add the Worcestershire sauce, salt, and pepper and let it cool.

When the mixture is cold, place it into a food processor, turn on the motor, and slowly add the egg and egg yolk. (If you don't have a processor, simply beat it vigorously with a wooden spoon.) When the eggs are mixed in, chill for a few hours before using. After it has rested in the refrigerator, you will find the rarebit is very easy to handle and ready for many uses.

Pork Crackling and Scratchings

Roast pork is delicious to eat, but one of the best parts of it is the crackling – good, crunchy, salted pork flavor. Irish pubs used to serve salted pigs" trotters to increase the thirst of their customers. Pork scratchings have much the same effect.

To get good, crisp crackling, the skin has to be scored with a sharp knife deep enough to break through. Brush the skin lightly with cooking oil or lard, then sprinkle liberally with salt before roasting. The salt will draw any water from the skin and leave a very crisp finish.

I also like to make crackling without any meat attached. Ask the butcher for some pork rind, preferably from the loin, and cut off any excess fat. Score and salt the skin and roast in a preheated oven at 400°F/200°C. The rind will take 30–40 minutes (or longer for thicker pieces) to become crunchy.

To make pork scratchings, instead of scoring the rind, remove the fat and cut it into ¼ in (5 mm) strips, and then sprinkle with salt. Bake in the preheated oven, again for about 30–40 minutes.

Pork scratchings are good served with pre-dinner drinks or use them in an appetizer for a meal.

I also like to make a pork scratching and apple salad. Simply quarter some apples and cut them again into eigths. Fry and toss them in butter, browning them a little, for 2–3 minutes. Place them around the plate with the warm pork scratchings and mix some snipped fresh chives with *Basic Vinaigrette* (page 50) to spoon on top. Dress the center of the plates with mixed salad greens tossed with dressing.

At Christmas, if you have leftover roast pork and crackling, use the crackling for this salad. You can also spoon some cranberry sauce into the center of the plate along with the dressing and the salad greens.

See also

Classic Scrambled Eggs (page 79)
Coarse Pork Pâté (page 275)
Egg Sandwiches (page 372)
Poached Eggs (page 82)
*Pressed Guinea Fowl Terrine with Shallots,
Mushrooms, and Bacon* (page 260)
Roast Chicken Sandwiches (page 274)
Sausage Rolls (page 277)
Smoked Salmon Rolls (page 374)
Smoked Salmon Terrine with Warm Potato Salad
(page 151)
Spicy Scrambled Eggs (page 81)
Vegetarian Cheese and Onion "Sausage" Rolls
(page 278)
Watercress and Cream Cheese Sandwiches
(page 373)

Meat

Meat is probably the overall favorite food in Britain, with roasts, stews, casseroles, pies, steaks, chops, and ribs all being part of it. But British meat-eating habits have shocked quite a few people over the years. After a visit to England in 1748, a visiting Swedish diplomat, one Per Kalm, recorded his surprise at the amount of meat eaten in England: "… I do not believe that any Englishman who is his own master has ever eaten a dinner without meat." The association of the British with meat-eating is so great that there is actually a corps of yeomen called Beefeaters. The term was also applied, with little respect, to over- or well-fed servants in the seventeenth century.

With the development of mining salt, meat could be preserved, and it was discovered very early that pork was the meat required the least salt to cure it successfully – and it tasted best.

Primitive man would have eaten the meat and organs of animals which were native to the British Isles – deer, wild oxen, pigs, and small game such as hare and beavers. These early people would have followed the herds of meat animals and eaten the flesh warm from the kill or roasted it on a spit over a fire. The internal organs were baked in the fire packed inside the intestines in much the same way as haggis and sausages have been prepared and cooked over the centuries. The only forms of preservation would have been air-drying and basic smoking.

When man began to settle, and to cultivate crops, he began to breed the kinds of animals he liked to eat, most of which – in Britain, cows, goats, and sheep – would also supply milk. The pig was domesticated too, although it was not an animal for milking. The fact, however, that the pig could find food for itself much more efficiently than the others made it extremely valuable. With the development of mining salt, meat could be preserved with salt, and it was discovered very early that pork was the meat requiring the least salt to cure it successfully – and it tasted best. Our passion for salt-cured pork has lasted. Thin slices of cured pork, or "collops" as they were known (usually cooked and served with eggs – our breakfast bacon and eggs) – comprise a dish that was and still is unique in Europe. Great traditions never die.

When the cooking pot was introduced, meat cooking changed dramatically. Now, many cuts of meat that had been too tough to enjoy fresh can be cooked in water along with other flavorings – a technique that was to lead to the great, classic British dishes such as boiled beef and carrots and Irish stew. During the Roman occupation, Britons learned to pen their animals to deliberately fatten them. The Romans and later the Normans introduced many new ideas to basic British cooking, including the making of sausages – smaller animal casings stuffed with meat or organ meats, and black puddings, made from blood (which would always have been used when an animal was killed – it was too nutritious to waste).

Until the seventeenth century, when crops began to be grown specifically to feed animals intended for food, the British meat-eating year would have been dominated by the inability to feed livestock through the winter. This meant that most food animals would be killed in the fall, with only a

PAGE 180
Roast Guinness Lamb (page 194)

few kept for breeding. The fall season was therefore, a time of feasting, of eating organ meats, blood, and marrow (which wouldn't keep), and perhaps some fresh meat. Most of the meat, however, would have been salted, cured, or smoked as appropriate ("corned" in Ireland), to preserve it for the winter. Most people would have no fresh or roasted meats until after Lent, and often, the wealthy might feed a sheep or bullock throughout the winter in order to prepare it for a celebratory meal at Easter (lambs and calves were not usually eaten). The poor would have little to fall back on throughout the winter months except what they could catch or trap, feeding themselves on salted fish and meat, usually bacon, which they would cook in pottages with grains and legumes along with available flavorings.

From the Middle Ages on, fresh meat was roasted and broiled, salted and smoked. Roasting was the most popular cooking method, especially of beef, which had been the favorite meat since Roman times. Preserved meat would be boiled (something we do rarely now, although it is extremely traditional). Meat and organ meats were still boiled in the cooking pot inside animal "plucks," or intestines, (as in making haggis, sausages,and black puddings). When the pudding cloth made its appearance, animal casings could be ignored and a dough of some sort could be used, such as the suet pastry which encloses a steak and kidney pudding (although this dish is now cooked in a bowl).

The wealthy also baked meat in pies, enclosing it in a casing of raised pastry, known as a "coffin." The filling was sometimes sweet, with dried fruit, as well as savory and very flavorful, for the Middle Ages was the heyday of English spicing. In the days before the fork came into use, the pastry was often not eaten, considered merely a convenient wrapping for the meat and gravy.

Meat became cheaper and more readily available from the seventeenth century onward because of improved stock and feed. Its quality improved as well, and meat became part of everyone's diet. French influences crept into the cooking for the wealthy, and meat was cooked in "made" dishes such as fricassees and hashes. In the towns, cookshops flourished, selling pies and puddings, sheep and lamb trotters, and in the north, tripe, faggots, black puddings, boar meat, and ground pork organ meats. With limited facilities for roasting or baking, people would take their meats to the public baker to cook it for them. Possibly because there began to be so much good "flesh" meat to enjoy, the appetite for the "off-falls" ("offal") diminished in most parts of the country. A true appreciation of the delights and variety of organ meats appear to be returning. I have included a few good recipes for it here, using it in pies, stews, casseroles, roasts, and more.

Roasting was the most popular cooking method, especially for beef, which has been the favorite meat in Britain since Roman times.

Slow-honey-roast Belly of Pork

While the prime cuts of leg and loin are so popular, people tend to forget about what is to me one of the tastiest cuts of pork – the belly. Its high fat content often puts people off, but I think the fat adds flavor and gives a more succulent finish. The slow roasting – over about 3 hours – helps to reduce that fat, and the juices bleed into the onions underneath the meat. The slow roasting also helps tenderize the meat so that it can almost be carved with a spoon.

I like to serve a peas and mashed potatoes with this pork dish, two traditional British vegetablee together in one. The *Applesauce* (page 44) makes a perfect accompaniment to the pork.

SERVES 4–6

2¼–2½ lb (1–1.3 kg) piece of pork belly, boned,
    with rind left on
5 large onions, sliced
Cooking oil
1 teaspoon white peppercorns, crushed
Coarse sea salt
2–3 tablespoons honey
2 tablespoons water
Salt and pepper

To Serve

8 oz–1 lb (225–450 g) peas (fresh or frozen)
1 lb (450 g) hot *Mashed Potatoes* (page 124)

Preheat the oven to 350°F/180°C.

Score the pork belly rind with a sharp knife ½ in (1 cm) apart. Place the sliced onions in a roasting pan and place the belly, rind-side up, on top. Trickle it with a little cooking oil and lightly press on the crushed white peppercorns and a sprinkling of coarse sea salt. Place in the oven and cook for 1 hour.

After the first hour, remove the belly from the oven and baste with any fat and juices. If the onions are dry, then add a few tablespoons of water to the pan. Continue to cook for another 1½ hours, basting every 15–20 minutes.

The honey can now be poured over the belly and the oven temperature increased to 400°F/200°C. Cook for another 30–40 minutes, basting every 5–10 minutes. As the honey becomes hotter, it will start to caramelize and leave a rich, golden glaze over the pork.

After the pork belly is cooked and tender (test the meat by piercing with a knife), remove the belly from the oven and let it rest for 10–15 minutes.

While the pork is resting, heat the pan with the onions and add the 2 tablespoons of water on top of the stove. This will lift any residue from the pan and create a moist cooking liquid.

For the mashed peas and potatoes, cook the peas and while hot, purée them in a food processor. Add the purée to the hot mashed potatoes.

Season the onions with salt and pepper and divide among four plates. The pork belly can now be cut into four servings, carved or simply broken, and served on top of the onions. Pour any remaining liquid over the meat and serve with the mashed peas and potatoes. With the vegetables, the pork belly becomes a complete meal – nothing but simplicity on a plate.

Shepherd's Pie or Cottage Pie

This dish is as much of a classic as the British steak and kidney pie. It began, like bubble and squeak, as a way of using up leftovers. The pieces of cooked meat – usually tough mutton – would be cut up small and pounded in the mortar to soften them before being topped with stock and mashed potatoes. Cold lamb is often used nowadays, with chopped onions, carrots, a splash of Worcestershire sauce, and then mashed potatoes or even sliced cooked potatoes on top. Shepherd's pie reminds me of my childhood suppers.

I prefer to use raw lamb, coarsely ground, because it spreads its flavor throughout the sauce while cooking. I like to use *jus* but you could replace it with *Chicken Stock* (page 33) or a bought version of either (see page 11).

For a cottage pie, use beef instead of lamb.

1½ lb (675 g) lamb, coarsely ground (shoulder is a good cut for this recipe)

1 oz (25 g) lamb or beef dripping or 2 tablespoons cooking oil

Butter

3 onions, finely chopped

3 carrots, cut into ½ in (1 cm) dice

4 celery sticks, cut into ½ in (1 cm) dice

½ teaspoon ground cinnamon

½ teaspoon chopped fresh thyme

½ teaspoon chopped fresh rosemary

2 teaspoons tomato purée

2 teaspoons *Tomato Ketchup* (page 49)

1–1½ cups (250–350 ml) red wine

¼ cup (25 g) all-purpose flour

1 cup (200 ml) *Veal or Beef Jus* or *Chicken Stock* (page 34 or 33)

Salt and pepper

2 teaspoons Worcestershire sauce

2 lb (900 g) *Mashed Potatoes* (page 124), made with very little butter and cream or milk

Season the ground lamb with salt and pepper. This should now be fried in the dripping or the oil in a very hot pan to seal the meat and to brown it, rather than letting it stew or boil. For the best results (and it's probably quicker), fry the lamb in small batches. When it browns, pour it into a colander to drain.

In a separate saucepan, melt a heaping teaspoon of butter. Add the vegetables and season them with salt, pepper, and cinnamon. Then add the chopped herbs.

Cook this mixture for 5–6 minutes until it begins to soften. Add the browned lamb and cook over a medium heat for a few minutes. Add the tomato purée, the ketchup, and the Worcestershire sauce, and stir into the mixture. Now, add the red wine. For a really rich finish, it is best to use 1½ cups of wine, but add only ¼ cup at a time, reducing by three-fourths and repeating the process until all has been added. This method prevents the sautéd flavor of the lamb becoming boiled away in too much wine. Sprinkle the flour into the pan and cook for 2–3 minutes.

Pour in the *jus* or stock and bring to a slow simmer. For a rich shepherd's pie, this needs to cook for 1–1½ hours. During the cooking time, the sauce may become too thick; if this happens, add a little water to thin it. Be sure not to allow the sauce to become too thin, however, because mashed potatoes will be spread on top.

During the last 30 minutes of the cooking time, the mashed potatoes can be prepared. Reduce the amounts of butter and cream or milk given in the recipe to give a slightly firmer topping.

After the ground lamb is ready, spoon into an ovenproof serving dish. The mashed potatoes can now be spooned on top, brushed with a little butter, and finished in a very hot oven or under the broiler until golden. Another method is to allow the meat to become cold in the dish before covering with the potatoes. This can now be refrigerated until needed and then re-heated in a hot oven (400°F/200°C) for 35–40 minutes.

Another popular finish is a topping of grated cheese, melted and glazed.

Shepherd's Pie Fritters

Here is a related shepherd's pie recipe which combines the ideas of shepherd's pie with the conventional fritter. The classic shepherd's pie mixture must be thickened to hold up to being rolled and deep-fried. This variation of shepherd's pie is also slightly spicy.

If shaping into balls, the fritters will need to be dipped in egg and breadcrumbs two times to give a neat finish. All they need then is to be deep-fried for a crisp, golden result. A great accompaniment for the fritters is *Spicy Tomato and Mint Relish* (page 381), forming a perfect snack.

This dish is very easy and worth every minute of its cooking time.

Butter
2 onions, cut into very small dice
2 carrots, cut into very small dice
2 celery sticks, cut into very small dice
1 lb (450 g) ground lamb
Pinch of fresh or dried marjoram
Pinch of ground cumin (optional)
1¼ cups (300 ml) *Chicken Stock* or ⅔ cup (150 ml)
   Veal Jus or *Beef Jus* (page 33 or 34)
Worcestershire sauce
10–12 oz (275–350 g) *Mashed Potatoes* (page 124),
   without milk, cream or butter
All-purpose flour, for rolling
1–2 eggs, beaten
8–10 slices from a fresh white bread loaf, crusts
   removed and slices crumbed, or approx. 8 oz
   (225 g) purchased breadcrumbs
Salt and pepper
Oil, for deep-frying

Melt a heaping teaspoon of butter in a saucepan.
When it bubbles, add the chopped onion, carrot, and
celery. Increase the heat and fry quickly, allowing a
golden color to develop. Cook for a few minutes
until beginning to soften.

Now, the ground lamb can be added to the
vegetables, along with the marjoram and cumin
(if using). Cook for 5–10 minutes until the lamb is
sealed. Season with salt and pepper and add half of
the stock or *jus*. Cook over a low heat. The ground
lamb will take 30–40 minutes to become tender. As
the meat is cooking it may need a spoonful of the
remaining stock or *jus* to keep it moist.

After it's cooked, increase the heat to reduce
any excess liquid in the pan. It's important the meat
mixture is not too thin because this would keep it
from binding the mashed potatoes.

When the lamb has reduced, check for seasoning
and add a dash of Worcestershire sauce to finish the
spicy taste. Let it cool.

Next, add the mashed potatoes. Adjust the
seasoning with salt and pepper. The mixture can
now be refrigerated, firming the texture to make

it easier to work with. Dust your hands with flour
and roll the mixture into balls ready to be coated
with breadcrumbs.

Lightly dust the balls with the seasoned all-
purpose flour again and then dip into the beaten egg
and roll in the breadcrumbs. When all the balls are
coated, repeat the egg and breadcrumb passes for a
firmer finish. The shapes can now be patted into neat
fritters. Refrigerate them again to set the shapes firmly
before frying.

To cook the fritters, heat the cooking oil to
325–350°F/170–180°C and deep-fry until golden
brown. Drain well before serving.

Note: The number of fritters made will really depend on the
size and shape that you have made them; if you go for just 1
in (2.5 cm) diameter balls, you'll probably be able to shape up
to 30 pieces.

The fritters can be made into "classic" fish cake shapes,
giving you eight pieces, i.e. four large servings.

Boiled Leg of Lamb with Caper Sauce

This is probably one of the most classic of lamb
dishes, although traditionally it would have been
made with mutton, the meat of a sheep that is older
than a year. Mutton, now difficult to buy, has a
stronger flavor than lamb, a deeper red color, and
contains less fat. You can use lamb for this recipe,
and it works very well.

Capers, the flower buds of a Mediterranean
plant, have been a favored accompaniment
to boiled mutton since medieval times, when they
were presumably imported. The two strong flavors of
the meat itself and the acidity of the capers work
together very well. Nasturtium seeds can be picked
and used in the sauce instead of capers.

I've included potatoes and vegetables with the
lamb, giving you a complete meal from one pot.

3¼ lb (1.5 kg) leg of lamb
9 cups (2 liters) *Chicken Stock* (page 33) or water
Sprig of thyme
1½ lb (675 g) new potatoes, washed
1 lb (450 g) baby carrots, peeled
1 lb (450 g) pearl onions, peeled
12 baby turnips, peeled
4–6 celery sticks, cut into 2 in (5 cm) lengths
Salt and pepper

For the Sauce

2 tablespoons (25 g) butter
¼ cup (25 g) all-purpose flour
⅓ cup (85 ml) heavy cream
Squeeze of lemon juice
1 tablespoon capers, chopped
Salt and pepper

Place the leg of lamb in a large saucepan and add the chicken stock or water. Season with a pinch of salt. Bring to a boil, skimming off any impurities. Add the sprig of thyme and allow the meat to simmer fairly rapidly, skimming from time to time, for 2 hours. During this time the lamb flavor will take over the chicken stock, almost producing a lamb soup.

Now, add the potatoes and other vegetables. Return to a simmer and cook for another 20 minutes. The vegetables will all now be cooked and will have taken on the rich taste. Turn off the heat. Now it's time to make the sauce.

Melt the butter, adding the flour. Cook over a medium heat for 3–4 minutes. While the roux is cooking, drain off 2½ cups (600 ml) of the stock from the lamb. Gradually add the stock to the roux, stirring well after each addition. After all of the liquid has been added, simmer gently for 20 minutes.

Add the heavy cream to the sauce and season it with salt and pepper. Squeeze a drop or two of lemon juice into the sauce to lift the lamb flavor. If the sauce is smooth, simply add the chopped capers, and it is now ready.

During this cooking of the sauce, the lamb will have rested and relaxed, giving you a very tender finish. The vegetables will also by now be slightly

overcooked, something which always works well in a stew. They will have softened and absorbed even more flavor.

Now, divide the vegetables among the plates. Remove the boiled lamb and carve it. The lamb texture will be soft and it will almost tear rather than slice. Finish each serving with a spoonful or two of the caper sauce.

Note: It's not necessary to use baby vegetables: the same weight of carrots and turnips can be cut from larger pieces. Extra capers can be added for a sharper flavor.

Broiled Lamb with "Irish" Cabbage and Mashed Potato Sauce

The "Irish" cabbage basically takes the flavors from my version of a traditional Irish stew – onions, cabbage, carrots – and fries them all as a foundation for the lamb. To me, one of the beauties of cooking is being able to use the flavors of one recipe and present it in a totally new form, introducing different cooking methods that will then give different flavors. I like to add a parsley purée to this recipe, to give it an extra touch (although it's not essential). Parsley, of course, is another classic with Irish stew.

The lamb tastes at its best in this recipe when cooked in a grill pan. It can, however, be pan-fried or roasted.

SERVES 4

1 lb (450 g) *Mashed Potato Sauce* (page 125)
½ of a 1 liter bottle red wine
250 ml (8 fl oz) *Veal or Beef Jus* (page 34)
Salt and pepper
2 boned loins of lamb, with fat removed and the bones reserved
1 tablespoon cooking oil

For the "Irish" Cabbage

1 small Savoy cabbage, finely shredded
1 large carrot, peeled and thinly sliced
Butter
2 onions, sliced
4 slices of bacon, cut into thin strips
Salt and pepper

Small bunch flatleaf parsley, picked and washed
Small bunch curly parsley, picked and washed
2 oz (50 g) *Buttered Spinach* (page 113), omitting
    the butter
1 tablespoon peanut oil
2 tablespoons water
Salt, pepper and freshly grated nutmeg

Preheat the oven to 400°F/200°C.

For the parsley purée, blanch both kinds of parsley in boiling, salted water for a few minutes until tender. Drain and mix them with the spinach. Purée the mixture in a food processor, adding the oil, water, and seasonings. Push through a fine sieve to give a smooth parsley purée. If the purée is too thick, then simply thin with a little more water.

Make the mashed potato sauce. The consistency for this dish needs to be flowing so if it's still too thick, add a little light cream or milk.

The red wine needs to be boiled to reduce it by three-fourths. Add the *jus* and simmer for a few minutes. Season with salt and pepper.

To cook the lamb, season it with salt and pepper and brush with oil. The loins can now be broiled on a hot grill pan, turning from time to time to seal in the juices. It is best to allow the meat to brown richly, with almost burned edges. The burned

Corned Beef

edges go very well with the natural sweetness of the lamb itself. It will take 8–10 minutes to broil to a medium stage. If pan-frying to seal and then roasting, the lamb will need 8–10 minutes' roasting for a medium finish.

After it's cooked, leave the lamb to rest for 6–8 minutes before carving.

For the "Irish" cabbage, blanch the finely shredded cabbage in salted, boiling water for 30 seconds– 1 minute until just tender. Drain. The carrots can be left raw, sliced very thin, or they can be blanched for a minute to take the raw taste away.

Heat a wok or frying-pan and add the butter. After it bubbles, add the onions and carrots. Fry them to a light golden color and to a barely soft texture. In a separate pan, fry the bacon. The bacon will create its own fat and quickly become crisp. Add the bacon to the onions and carrots. It is now time to add the cabbage. Fry, allowing the cabbage to take on some golden-edged tinges, and season with salt and pepper.

Each loin provides two servings. Just before carving, the loins can be brushed with the red wine sauce to give a finished shine. Carve the lamb, allowing 4–5 slices per serving.

Spoon the "Irish" cabbage into the center of the plates. The mashed potato sauce can now be spooned around the cabbage, creating a border. Trickle some parsley purée around, along with the red wine sauce, passing any extra sauce separately.

Place the lamb slices on top of the cabbage. The new Irish classic is now ready to serve.

Note: This dish has many components that make it a complete meal in itself.

The lamb can be served with the "Irish" cabbage, leaving out the potato sauce and parsley purée, if you wish.

OPPOSITE
Grilled Lamb with "Irish" Cabbage and Mashed Potato Sauce

Corned beef is a prepared meat that most people enjoy made into a sandwich with pickles or sliced tomatoes (I do, anyway). People don't think about how it's made; it's almost as if it's just a natural product that appears and is sliced.

Corned beef is basically salted beef. The "corning" usually refers to the large "corns" of salt that were once used. It is particularly associated with Cork in Ireland, which supplied corned beef to England and her colonies for 200 years until the mid-nineteenth century.

If you haven't made corned beef before, you'll be surprised to find out how easy it is to make. Simple, yes, but it does take time. The beef is soaked in brine, and after three days, the texture and color change along with the flavor. The meat is then cooked and cut into slices. In my recipe the end result is more like the textured meat you buy in cans. It's inexpensive, very tasty, and definitely worth a try. The pig's trotters are not essential. I've added them because they help the dish to set firmly.

This is quite a large recipe that will fill a big (10–12 in/25–30 cm) terrine, enough to feed 12–15 people or more.

SERVES AT LEAST 12

5 lb (2.25 kg) beef flank
2 quarts (1.75 liters) cold water
3–4 oz (75–100 g) salt
2 pig's trotters (optional)
1 oz (25 g) gelatine leaves or powdered gelatin

Trim the beef flank of all visible sinews but leave it as a whole piece. Mix the water and 3 oz (75 g) of salt to create a brine. To test the strength of the brine, place a raw new potato in the water; if it doesn't float, simply add more of the remaining salt until it floats. Place the beef in the brine and chill for 3 days.

Remove the meat from the brine and rinse it; discard the salt water. Place the meat in a clean pan with the pig's trotters, if using. Cover the meat with fresh water. Bring to a boil, then simmer for 2½–3 hours, skimming any impurities from the liquid.

After the meat has cooked, remove it from the liquid. Drain the liquid through a fine sieve and taste; it should have a good beef flavor. Discard the trotters, if using. Bring the stock to a boil and boil to reduce it by about a third to half to increase its flavor and jelly content. Test the stock/jelly by spooning a little onto a small plate and chilling it in the refrigerator. The jelly must set very firmly to enable it to hold the beef together. If it doesn't become firm enough, or if you have not used pig's trotters, add some or all of the gelatine to the mixture. Make sure you test the firmness because the dish is better if not set using gelatine. Only about 2½–3¼ cups (600–900 ml) of finished jelly stock will be needed.

While the beef is still warm, break it down into pieces. The meat will almost separate itself between the sinew strips. Any extra sinews can be removed, but make sure that all fat content is kept. The meat can now be pushed through the large disk of a meat grinder (¼–½ in/5 mm–1 cm) or chopped by hand along with the fat. Mix the meat with 2½ cups (600 ml) of reduced liquid and check the consistency. The meat should absorb the liquid and be somewhat loose. If the mixture is too firm, add another 1¼ cups (300 ml) of stock. Taste the corned beef and correct the seasoning with salt and pepper. The mixture can now be pressed firmly into a terrine or bowl and placed in the refrigerator overnight.

After the corned beef has set, turn it out of the terrine or bowl and serve with a salad and pickles, or fried for breakfast, or make it into corned-beef hash.

Refrigerated, this dish will keep for 5–6 days.

Rack on Black

This sounds very British and classic. And it *is* British, but classic? Well, not yet but I hope this recipe will achieve that status.

A butcher in Yorkshire gave me the idea. He was selling it as a cut to be bought and then, obviously, taken home and enjoyed. As soon as I saw the beautifully rich lamb posing intimately with a deep black pudding, I was excited. The possible combinations of textures and flavors working together raced through my mind – a bed of parsnips, bubble and squeak, scallions, creamy potatoes – they'd all work (but not all together, of course). Here's the recipe for the lamb and its sauce; the accompaniment is up to you.

SERVES 4

2 × 6–8 bone section racks of lamb, boned
1 × 6–8 in (12–16 cm) black pudding (1–1½ in
    diameter/2.5–3 cm), weighing 9–10 oz
    (250–300 g), skinned and split lengthwise
2 tablespoons cooking oil
½ bottle red wine
About 1 cup (200–250 ml) *Veal or Beef Jus*
    (page 34)
Salt and pepper

The rolling and tying (see below) is best finished several hours (preferably 24) in advance, giving the meat plenty of time to "set."

The racks should be boned but have the flap of skin/fat still attached. The skin/fat should be trimmed to ⅛ in (2–3 mm) thickness, leaving 4 in (10 cm) to wrap around. If the fat is too thick, it will not cook completely, and consequently become tough. Also, trim away any sinews found around the lamb fillets.

Now, place the flat side of the black pudding halves next to the lamb. Season the lamb with a grinding of pepper. At this stage, do not salt the meat or the juices will be drawn from it.

Fold the skin over the pudding and lamb, firmly shaping them into a cylinder.

Now, it's time to tie the cylinder with string. It's best to tie at both ends first. To prevent it from becoming misshapen during the tying process. After both ends are secure, tie at ½–¾ in (1–2 cm) intervals. Now, wrap the cylinder tightly in plastic wrap to create an even smoother finish and refrigerate it until you plan to cook it.

OPPOSITE
Rack on Black

When it's ready to cook, preheat the oven to 400°F/200°C. Season the cylinders with salt and pepper. Heat a roasting pan over a medium heat with the cooking oil. Place the lamb racks in the pan and allow to brown slowly. As the fat browns it is also cooking: you'll notice more fat in the roasting pan. Continue to cook until completely browned. The racks can now be roasted in the preheated oven. For rare lamb, roast for only 8–10 minutes; for medium meat, cook for 15–18, and for well done, 20–25. Remove the meat from the oven when it is roasted to your liking. As with all roasts, it is important to let the meat rest and relax.

While the lamb is resting, pour away the excess fat from the roasting pan. Heat the pan and add the red wine. This will heighten any lamb flavors (and black pudding spices). Boil and reduce by three-fourths and add the *jus*. Bring to a simmer before straining through a sieve into a clean saucepan. Skim off any impurities that have risen. Season with salt and pepper and the sauce is ready.

Remove the string from the cylinders. They can now be cut into six slices each, allowing three thick slices per serving. These slices guarantee a good texture in both types of meat. Now, serve it on plates with your chosen vegetable accompaniments and pour the sauce around the slices.

Note: This dish goes very well with *Roast Potatoes* (page 238), *Mashed Potatoes* (page 124), *Colcannon* (page 126), *Bubble and Squeak* (page 126), *Buttered Spinach* (page 113) or with many other recipes featured in the book.

The *jus* can be replaced with *Chicken Stock* (page 33). This is then reduced by half with the red wine and 2–4 tablespoons (25–50 g) of butter added to thicken the consistency.

Preserved (Confit) Bacon

Bacon is preserved pork; here the bacon is further presered, taking the idea from the French – although it is similar to British potted meat. *Confit* is the French word for "preserved," and the most usual *confit* is of duck – duck which is cooked and then set in its own fat. This technique allows it to be kept almost indefinitely, and it is a good cooking method if you want to work ahead of time.

But it's not the preserving I'm after here. As the bacon cooks slowly in its own fat, the meat and fat become very tender, breaking down any sinews. I'm sure the thought of cooking any meat slowly in deep fat gives the impression that the meat will absorb the fat and taste strongly of it. That really couldn't be further from the truth. The meat becomes so succulent, soft, and flavorful, you just can't stop eating it. This confit of bacon can be used in many dishes. I include it in *Sage Fava Beans with Tomato* (page 56).

To finish the recipe, I either glaze the bacon with honey, or coat it with a mixture of light brown sugar and black pepper. The perfect accompaniments to this rich dish are *Mashed Potatoes* (page 124) and a buttered green vegetable – preferably cabbage. Any leftover bacon pieces can be used to garnish soups, served with macaroni and cheese, or added to stews.

SERVES 4–6

2¼ lb (1 kg) slab (unsliced) bacon, smoked or
   unsmoked, rind removed, trimmed
1 quart (900 ml) cooking oil or pork fat
2–4 tablespoons clear honey or ¼–½ cup (50–100 g)
   light brown sugar and freshly ground black
   pepper, for glazing

The piece of bacon must be soaked for 24 hours in cold water to remove excess salty flavor.

Preheat the oven to 350°F/80°C. In a small roasting pan deep enough to let the piece be immersed, put a drop of the cooking oil/fat and heat on top of the stove. This next stage of browning the meat is not essential if using as part of a stew or for the fava beans (go straight to the simmering stage). If being served as an appetizer or main dish, the flavor and finish works well. Fry the bacon, fat-side down, to a golden brown. Turn the bacon in the pan and cover it with the remaining oil/fat. Bring to a slow simmer. Cover and cook in the oven for about 1–1½ hours.

After an hour, check the tenderness of the meat by piercing with a knife. The meat should feel totally tender; if it's slightly firm, continue to cook for the remaining half-hour.

After it has cooked, you can use the bacon immediately by removing it and draining off the excess fat. Or, you can save it until needed. Transfer everything to a bowl making sure the meat is totally covered in fat and let it set in the refrigerator.

When you need it, lift the meat from the fat and heat it in a roasting pan, without the preserving fat. Place in a preheated oven (same temperature as when cooked), fat-side down, and heat for 20–25 minutes. The preserved bacon will now be returned to its former glory.

To glaze the bacon with honey, after it is reheated, lightly pat it dry with paper towels. On the top (fat-side down), spoon 2–3 tablespoons of clear honey over it. Place it under a hot broiler and allow the honey to caramelize to a bubbly, sticky finish.

For the peppered brown sugar glaze, mix 1 teaspoon of freshly ground black pepper with each heaping tablespoon of brown sugar. Sprinkle on top of the bacon placed on the broiler pan. Broil the bacon to slowly caramelize the sugar and, at the same time, to cook the black pepper. When it has caramelized and become rich deep golden color, the bacon is ready to carve.

Baked Pork, Prune, and Apple Meatballs

Finely chopped meat (either raw or leftovers that are cooked) is used frequently in traditional British cooking – in shepherd's pie, bubble and squeak, rissoles, and as sausage stuffing – but in this recipe, the meatballs are meatballs with a difference. The flavor of the apples, always a natural with pork, works so well along with the prunes and suggests the many medieval British savory dishes containing the sweetness of dried fruit. The cooking liquid takes on all of these tastes, and when it is reduced, leaves a good, rich finish to the meatballs.

These go well with soft, creamy *Mashed Potatoes* (page 124) and simple buttered cabbage, peas, or, perhaps, runner beans (pages 104, 116 and 118).

SERVES 4

Butter
1 large onion, finely chopped
Pinch of freshly grated nutmeg and ground
    cinnamon
6 soft prunes, chopped
1 teaspoon chopped fresh sage
2 apples, peeled, cored, and cut into a ½ in (1 cm)
    dice
4 oz (100 g) shredded suet
1 egg, beaten
1 lb (450 g) ground pork meat

BELOW
Baked Pork, Prune, and Apple Meatballs

⅔ cup (150 ml) white wine or cider
1¼ cups (300 ml) *Chicken Stock* (page 33)
Arrowroot or cornstarch, if necessary
Salt and pepper

Preheat the oven to 350°F/180°C.

Melt a heaping teaspoon of butter in a frying-pan. Add the chopped onion and fry for a few minutes without browning. Season with the nutmeg and cinnamon and add the prunes. Cook for 1 more minute and remove from the heat. Add the chopped sage and let the mixture cool. When it has cooled add the diced apples, suet, egg, and ground pork. Mix well, seasoning with salt and pepper.

The mixture must be well blended to distribute all the flavors, particularly the suet. Divide into twelve meatballs. A light dusting of flour on your hands will make this job easier. These can now be shallow-fried, turning gently, in another heaping teaspoon of butter to seal and to become a golden brown. The meatballs can now be placed in a roasting pan to one side.

Pour the white wine or cider into a saucepan and boil until reduced by three-fourths. Add the chicken stock. Pour the stock mixture over the meatballs and cook in the oven for 45 minutes until tender.

Lift the "balls" from the pan and keep them warm. Strain off the liquid. Pour the liquid in a small saucepan where the fat will rise to the top. The fat can be skimmed off. The remaining liquid can be left at its natural consistency or thickened with one tablespoon of arrowroot or cornstarch whisked in and then brought to a boil. Another method is to reduce by a third and then whisk in 2–4 tablespoons (25–50 g) of chilled, diced butter. This will give the sauce a silky finish. Now, serve the meatballs with the sauce poured over them.

Note: A splash of Armagnac or Calvados can be added to the finished sauce for extra flavor.

Roast Guinness Lamb

Beer has been used as a meat-cooking broth all over Europe for centuries, particularly in the Low Countries of Holland and Belgium. Hops were introduced to Britain from these countries in the early sixteenth century, and were cultivated in Kent by Flemish *émigrés*, thus initiating the British **beer** industry (as opposed to **ale**, which was unhopped). It may be that the concept of cooking beef in beer stemmed from that time. The idea was later adopted enthusiastically in Ireland, probably because of the unique stout, Guinness, brewed in Dublin since 1759. The rich reduction of this dark malty stout is a delicious foundation for a very powerful gravy. Finishing the lamb with a caramelizing of sugar helps counteract the bitterness of the beer.

Crisp *Roast Potatoes* (page 238) go well with this dish, along with most other vegetables. My favorite is a bowl of *Buttered Spinach* (page 113).

SERVES 6–8

3¼ lb (1.5 kg) leg of lamb, boned, rolled, and tied
1 tablespoon cooking fat or oil
Sprig of rosemary
1¼ cups (300 ml) Guinness or other stout
¼ cup (50 g) light soft brown sugar
1–1¼ cups (200–300 ml) *Veal or Beef Jus* (page 34)
Salt and pepper

Preheat the oven to 400°F/200°C. Season the lamb with salt and pepper. Place it in a roasting pan with the cooking fat/oil and brown over a medium heat until it is totally sealed and has become a rich golden brown color.

Add the sprig of rosemary and the Guinness. Place the lamb in the oven. Baste the lamb every 15–20 minutes and roast for 1 hour.

After the hour, remove the lamb from the oven and gently sprinkle with the sugar. Return to the oven, basting every 3–4 minutes for the next 15 minutes. This cooking time of 1¼ hours will leave the lamb at a medium rare stage. For well done, cook for another 20 minutes. When it has roasted, remove the lamb from the oven and baste once more. The roast can now be moved from the roasting pan.

Gently pour away any fat floating on top of the reduced Guinness and lamb juices. Add the *jus* and bring to a simmer, skimming off any impurities. The sauce will have a very rich, slightly sweetened, caramel stout flavor. The roast lamb, which should always be left to rest and relax for at least 15–20 minutes, making it a lot more tender, will have a deep, glossy color – almost the color of a good rich stout.

When the roast potatoes and vegetables are ready, the meat can be carved, to reveal a pink center surrounded by a deep glaze.

Stewed Red Wine Beef with Anchovy Scones

When cooking pots were invented, slow-cooking of vegetables, grains, and less tender cuts of meat became possible. The earliest meat soups were the forerunners of our various famous stews. This dish is a variation of two classics: the beef stew itself, which was often cooked with a few fillets of anchovies in place of salt as a seasoning, and the beef cobbler. The term "cobbler" originally described a type of pie with a thick dough lining and with a filling. Over the years, the dough lining has turned into scones, which are baked on top of the meat. The dish is a great alternate to that other British classic, beef stew and dumplings.

The best beef cut to use for stewing or braising is chuck steak. This has an open texture that will absorb all of the juices in which it is cooked. A close-textured cut, such as topside, will become tender, but will not absorb any liquid and will be dry. I use some *jus* in this recipe for the absolute maximum taste, but see the alternate (see page 196).

SERVES 4

1½ lb (675 g) chuck steak, cut into ¾ in (2 cm) dice
1 tablespoon (15 g) beef drippings or cooking oil

4 carrots, peeled and quartered lengthwise
3 onions, cut into ½–¾ in (1–2 cm) dice
1 bay leaf
Bottle of red wine (½ bottle can be used, but the whole amount will give a fuller flavor)
2½ cups (600 ml) *Veal or Beef Jus* (page 34)
Salt and pepper

For the Scones

4 tablespoons (50 g) butter
2 cups (225 g) self-rising flour
8–10 canned anchovy fillets, diced
½ teaspoon chopped fresh thyme
1 egg, beaten
2–3 tablespoons milk
Pepper

Preheat the oven to 325°F/160°C. Season the beef with salt and pepper. Heat the dripping or oil in a braising pan or flameproof casserole. Fry the beef, browning and sealing on all sides.

While the beef is frying, cut the carrot quarters into ½–¾ in (1–2 cm) slices. Add the vegetables to the pan along with the bay leaf. Cook for 2–3 minutes before pouring the red wine over them. The mixture can now be cooked until reduced by half. This increases the wine flavor. Add the *jus* and bring to a simmer. It's important the meat is barely covered by the liquid: add some water if needed. When it has reached a simmer, skim off any impurities and cover with a lid; cook the meat in the preheated oven for 1½ hours. This cooking temperature is perfect for braising. It provides a gentle heat that will not boil the meat, instead creating a soft motion that allows the beef to absorb all the flavors.

Check the stew after 1½ hours, skimming any impurities. If it's too thick, add more water. The beef may well need another 30 minutes before you cook the scones. Return the meat to the oven.

To make the scones, rub the butter into the flour to a coarse crumb texture. Season with black pepper. Add the diced anchovy fillets (which will replace salt), along with the chopped thyme. Stir in the egg to create a scone dough, adding milk, if necessary. The mixture can now be divided into four pieces and molded into scone shapes.

When the beef is ready, increase the oven temperature to 180°C/350°F. Remove the lid from the beef and place the scones on top. Return the pot to the oven. The scones will take 25–30 minutes. As the stew simmers and gently bubbles, the scones will bake, absorbing the flavor of the red wine gravy, while becoming golden and crisp on top.

Simply serve the beef on a plate or in a bowl, with the scones placed on top.

Note: Other flavors can also be added to the stew – mushrooms, celery, or strips of bacon all work very well.
The scones can also be flavored with mixed herbs, bacon pieces, or perhaps Parmesan or Cheddar cheese.

Alternative

This method uses water and a stock cube in place of *jus*. The ingredients list is almost identical, with 2½ cups (600 ml) of water and a beef stock cube replacing the *jus* with the addition of one heaping tablespoon of all-purpose flour. The red wine should be boiled and reduced by half in a separate pan. After all the beef has been browned in the beef fat/oil, add the vegetables and continue to cook for 2–3 minutes. Add the flour and stir in. Cook for a few minutes before adding the water a little at a time. As it comes to a simmer, the mixture will thicken. When it thickens, add the stock cube and pour in the red wine. Now, return to a simmer, skim, cover with a lid and cook in the oven. Continue according to the recipe. You'll still have a rich finish to the dish. This technique can be used in many similar stews.

Braised Beef "Olives" with Black Pudding, Pearl Onions, and Mushrooms

Beef "olives" have been appearing on menus since medieval times, when they were known as "allowes" or "aloes." (The name "olive" is probably a corruption of this, and virtually the first veal "olive" recipe appeared in a Gervase Markham book of 1660.) These slices of beefsteak are wrapped around a seasoned forcemeat (mutton and veal can be used as well). Whole pieces of beef can also be braised for "olives" by simply filling with a stuffing. Anchovies were a regular seasoning in most forcemeats, having a strong influence on the finished flavor, but with this recipe the stuffing creates a taste of its own.

The black pudding is roughly chopped and added to ground pork or chicken; these flavors work very well together, helped along with red wine. The garnish of pearl onions and mushrooms also heightens all the tastes, and almost makes this into a beef "olive" *bourguignon* dish.

SERVES 4

4 × 6 oz (175 g) slices of topside or rump of beef (smaller 4 oz/100 g slices can also be used)
½ bottle of red wine (a whole bottle can be used for a stronger taste)
2½ cups (600 ml) *Veal or Beef Jus* (page 34) or water with stock granules
1 tablespoon all-purpose flour
1 tablespoon beef dripping or cooking oil
Sprig of thyme
1 bay leaf
Salt and pepper

For the Stuffing

Butter
1 onion, finely chopped
1 garlic clove, crushed
6 oz (175 g) finely ground pork or chicken
1 egg, beaten
Salt and pepper
6 oz (175 g) black pudding, skinned and roughly chopped

For the Garnish

20 pearl onions, peeled
Butter
20 button mushrooms, cleaned
1 teaspoon chopped fresh parsley (optional)

Place the beef slices between two sheets of plastic wrap; pound them with a rolling pin to a ¼ in (5 mm) thickness.

To make the stuffing, melt a heaping teaspoon of butter in a saucepan and when it bubbles, add the chopped onion and crushed garlic. Cook without browning for a few minutes. When they are tender, remove from the heat and allow to cool.

Season the ground pork or chicken with salt and pepper. Beat in the egg. The cooked onion mixture can now also be added. Add the black pudding, mixing it in well to break down the texture slightly and spreading the flavor through the forcemeat. Check for seasoning.

The stuffing can now be spread among the four steak slices. Roll the slices up and hold them together with two toothpicks per "olive", or simply tie with string. These are best left to firm and set for at least 30 minutes, refrigerated.

While the "olives" are setting, the pearl onions can be blanched in boiling water for 2–3 minutes to release their rawness. Drain and let them cool.

Bring the red wine to a boil in a suitable saucepan or braising pan. Boil and reduce by half before adding the *jus* or water and the stock granules, if using. This dish can be simmered on top of the stove on a low heat, allowing the liquid to barely simmer, or braised in the oven at 325°F/160°C.

Heat a frying-pan with the beef drippings or the cooking oil. Sear the beef "olives" until golden brown. Place them in a braising dish with the red wine sauce, the thyme, and bay leaf. Roll each "olive" in the flour before pan-frying. Season the stuffed "olives" and sear, browning on all sides in the hot pan. After they have browned, place them in the pan with the red wine gravy, the thyme, and bay leaf. Now, bring to a very gentle simmer, making sure the "olives" are barely covered in red wine sauce. If not, then add water to cover. Cook covered with a lid on the stovetop or in the oven for 1½–2 hours, skimming from time to time. The beef "olives" will be very tender.

Toward the end of the cooking time for the "olives," melt a heaping teaspoon of butter in a large frying-pan. When it bubbles, add the pearl onions.

Cook over a medium heat and fry, allowing them to become golden brown and tender. This will take 8–10 minutes. After 6–7 minutes, add the mushrooms, season and continue to cook and brown until both garnishes are ready. Place to one side.

Remove the "olives" from the sauce and keep them warm. Bring the sauce to a simmer and skim off any impurities. Strain through a sieve.

If the flour and water were used, the sauce will probably need to be reduced by a third to give a good consistency. The most important thing is to make sure the flavor does not become too strong. If it is too thin, then thicken with a tablespoon of cornstarch mixed with red wine. It's not important always to have thick, heavy sauces; simply a flavorful cooking liquid will be fine.

Remove the toothpicks or string from the "olives" and divide among four plates. Pour the sauce back over the "olives" and add the pearl onions and mushrooms. Sprinkle each plate with chopped parsley, if using.

These beef "olives" will go very well with a bowl of *Mashed Potatoes* (page 124).

Note: Pan-fried strips of bacon will also work very well with the garnish.

Braised Beef with Slowly Caramelized Onions and Turnip Purée

Braised beef and onions served with a turnip purée certainly isn't an unusual combination to British tastes. The difference in this dish, however, is that the onions are caramelized. They are halved (skin left on) and then cooked, flesh-side down, for 2–2½ hours. This releases all of their natural juices and sugars which begin to caramelize as they cook. No extra stage is needed to caramelize the onions; they simply cook while the beef simmers.

The turnip purée is cooked very simply and, when it's finished is stuffed into the onions. Served with the beef placed on top, the three separate components become one happy family.

SERVES 4

2 large onions, skin left on, halved through the
    middle
1 tablespoon beef dripping or cooking oil
4 × 6–8 oz (175–225 g) pieces of chuck steak,
    tied to keep shape
Salt and pepper

For the Sauce

Butter
1 onion, chopped
1 carrot, chopped
Sprig of thyme
1 bay leaf
2 tomatoes, each one quartered

1 bottle of red wine
2½ cups (600 ml) *Veal or Beef Jus* (page 34) or
    alternative (page 11)

For the Turnip Purée

1 lb (450 g) peeled turnips, cut in ¼ in (2 cm)
    rough cubes
1 cup (200 ml) milk
1 cup (200 ml) water
1–2 tablespoons heavy cream (optional)

Preheat the oven to 275°F/140°C.

Place the onions flesh-side down in a roasting
pan. These can now be placed on the bottom shelf of
a preheated oven. They will slowly begin to

caramelize and should be left alone for 30 minutes before the beef joins them.

To make the sauce, melt a heaping teaspoon of butter in a braising pan. Add the chopped onion, carrot, sprig of thyme, and bay leaf. Cook for 5–10 minutes, allowing them to slightly brown and begin to soften. Add the tomatoes and continue to cook for a few minutes. Pour in the bottle of red wine and bring to a boil. When it is boiling, reduce it by half. Add the *jus* and bring to a simmer.

While the sauce is being put together, season the beef pieces with salt and pepper. Heat a frying-pan with the dripping or cooking oil. When it is hot, add the beef. Sear and brown on all sides before adding it to the sauce in the braising dish.

Bring to a simmer, cover with a lid, and place the dish in the middle of the oven above the onions. Increase the oven temperature to 325°F/160°C. The beef will now take 2 hours to become totally soft and tender. During this cooking time, the onions should be checked to make sure they do not burn. If the sauce is becoming too thick, thin with water. This will prevent the flavor from becoming too strong.

While the meat and onions are cooking, the turnips can also be cooked. Place the turnip chunks in a saucepan and cover them with the milk, water, and a pinch of salt. If not quite covered, add extra milk. Bring to a simmer and cook until tender. This will only take 10–15 minutes. Drain. Cooking the turnips in milk and water will have left them with a beautiful white finish. They can now be puréed in a food processor or pushed through a sieve to a smooth purée. Season with salt and pepper. A tablespoon or two of heavy cream can also be added, if desired, to enrich the creamy finish.

The meat and onions can now both be removed from the dish and kept to one side, cutting away the string from the beef. Strain the sauce through a sieve, check the seasoning, and pour it back over the meat.

OPPOSITE
Piece of Braised Beef with Slowly Caramelized Onions and Turnip Purée

To serve the dish, remove the skin and tough outside layer of onion. Some of the center can also be removed; this creates a caramelized onion "case." Season with salt and pepper.

To create a glaze for the beef, take ⅔ cup (150 ml) of the sauce and boil it to reduce by at least half. This will now give you a very thick, shiny finish which can be brushed over each serving of meat.

Fill the center of each onion with the turnip purée. Present the filled onion halves on plates, placing the shiny, glazed servings of beef on top. Pass the remaining sauce separately. The beef pieces are ready to serve.

It's really quite a simple dish that gives the impression of a lot of work when presented. So if you're hoping to impress as well as create delicious flavors, then this is the dish for you.

The Classic Steak and Kidney Pie

This version is called "the classic" because it's being made and cooked to the recipe we all know. The "new classic" is on page 202 (see *Steak and "Kidney Pie"*), which will bring you a totally different result, with the "pie" placed next to the steak.

In fact, the combination of steak and kidney doesn't seem to be all that old. It wasn't until about the mid-nineteenth century that the essential kidneys were added to a steak pie or pudding – only about 150 years ago.

Around Britain, steak and kidney pie has many different possible pastries – shortcrust, flaky, puff, or suet. Many contain flour or Worcestershire sauce, some with mushrooms and vegetables, some without. People in the West Country pour up to 1¼ cups (300 ml) of clotted cream into the pie before it is served! I like to top the pie with puff pastry, but the suet paste normally used for a steak and kidney pudding (such as the one on page 200) can also be used. It works very well as a topping and, as a bonus, has a good beef flavor from the suet. In this recipe I use vegetables, mushrooms, and Worcestershire sauce – hopefully keeping everybody happy.

Steak and kidney pies are usually straightforward combination of steak, kidneys, onions, water, and Worcestershire, all mixed, topped with pastry, and baked for 2–2½ hours – job done. I've never been able to understand or accept that method. It's purely cooking by chance, to me, there is no certainty that the right flavors, seasonings, or any depth of texture or consistency will be found using this method. I always stew the meat and vegetable filling first, then place it in the pie dish, top it with pastry, and bake it in the oven. You then know exactly what to look forward to. My method also carries the bonus of allowing you to make and refrigerate the filling the day before needed. Cover it with the pastry the following day and bake for 45 minutes to 1 hour and dinner is ready!

BELOW
The Classic Steak and Kidney Pie

SERVES 4–6

1 tablespoon beef dripping or cooking oil
1½ lb (675 g) chuck steak, cut into 1 in (2.5 cm) dice
8 oz (225 g) ox or lamb kidneys, trimmed and diced
12 oz (350 g) *Puff Pastry* (page 365) or *Suet Pastry* (page 204)
2 onions, chopped
3 carrots, peeled and cut into rough ⅝ in (1.5 cm) dice
Butter
4 large Portobello mushrooms, cut into thick slices
2 tablespoons all-purpose flour
1 teaspoon tomato purée
1 bay leaf
2½ cups (600 ml) *Veal* or *Beef Stock* (page 34) or water and stock cube or granules
Worcestershire sauce
Salt and pepper
1 egg, beaten, for glazing

Heat a large frying-pan with a little of the dripping or oil. Season the diced beef with salt and pepper. Fry in the pan until well browned and completely sealed. Lift out the meat and transfer to a large saucepan. Add a touch more oil to the frying-pan, if necessary. Season the kidneys and fry them quickly to seal and brown in the hot pan. Then transfer the kidneys to the saucepan.

The onions and carrots can now be placed in the frying-pan along with a heaping teaspoon of butter; the vegetables can be cooked for 2–3 minutes. In this time they will heighten any flavors left from the meat. Transfer the vegetables to the saucepan. Then, fry the mushroom slices in a little more butter, turning them in the pan for a minute or two; place to one side.

With the saucepan over a medium heat, stir the flour into the meat and vegetables and allow to cook for 2–3 minutes. Add the tomato purée, bay leaf, and mushrooms. It's now time to add the stock. Bring to a simmer, skimming off any impurities. The meat should be barely covered with it; if not, add a little more stock or water. Now, simmer the meat gently, not quite completely covering with a lid, for 1½–2 hours. During the cooking time, the "stew" may need to be skimmed.

After 1½ hours check the meat for tenderness. If it isn't quite soft enough, continue to cook it for another 30 minutes. If the meat is cooking gently, more water will not be needed. The sauce will slowly have reduced, which thickens its consistency and increases its flavor.

After it is cooked, taste for seasoning. Add a dash (or two) of Worcestershire sauce to heighten the beef flavor. The meat and sauce can now be transferred to a 5 cup (1.2 liter) pie dish.

Preheat the oven to 425°F/220°C.

The pastry of your choice can now be rolled out. If using puff pastry, roll it out ¼ in (5 mm) thick; if suet pastry, then a little thicker – approximately scant ½ in (8 mm). Cut a strip of pastry so that will fit around the rim of the dish. This guarantees that the top stays on. It's best to cool the stew to barely warm before covering it with the pastry. Let the pastry top rest after rolling it out and before topping. Brush the rim of the dish with beaten egg, place the strip of pastry on top and brush again.

Make sure the pastry top is bigger than the dish and place it over the top. The pastry can now be pushed down around the sides, trimmed, and crimped for a neat finish. Brush with egg and place in the preheated oven. This will now take 30–40 minutes and then it will be ready to serve.

Note: It's important that the pastry rests after being rolled out, before topping the pie to prevent shrinkage.

Steak and Kidney Pudding

Everybody's favorite, a rich, moist suet pastry steamed around soft, succulent, and tasty chunks of beef. In this recipe, cook the meat first, including carrots, mushrooms, and celery. The sweetness of the carrots heightens the flavor of the sauce.

Eliza Acton, in her *Modern Cookery* of 1845, calls a steak pie or pudding "John Bull's Pudding' (which suggests it was thought of as a very British dish). Mushrooms were used instead of kidneys, which were introduced a little later. (Another steak and suet pudding was known as Bedfordshire Clangers, and what a clanger – included both beef and fruit or jam – a complete meal all in one.)

The recipe for the suet pastry recipe is on page 204. The amount there is for a 5 cup (1.2 liter) pudding mold, as required here.

SERVES 4–6

1–2 tablespoons beef dripping or cooking oil
1 lb (450 g) chuck steak, cut into 1 in (2.5 cm) cubes
8 oz (225 g) ox or lamb's kidneys, cut into 1 in (2.5 cm) dice
2 carrots, cut into rough dice ½ in (1 cm) thick
2 onions, cut into rough dice ½ in (1 cm) thick
2 celery sticks, cut into rough dice ½ in (1 cm) thick
6 oz (175 g) button mushrooms, quartered
1¼ cups (300 ml) stout (optional)
2½ cups (600 ml) *Veal or Beef Jus* (page 34) or alternative (page 11)
1 bay leaf
1 quantity *Suet Pastry* (page 204)
Salt and pepper

Heat a frying-pan with the dripping or oil and fry the beef and kidneys, browning well.

While the meat is being fried in one frying-pan, the carrots, onions, celery and mushrooms can all be fried in a separate large pan in a touch of oil. Cook for a few minutes before adding the stout, if using. Bring to a boil and reduce by two-thirds. Add the *jus* and bring to a simmer. Add the bay leaf.

The beef and kidneys can now be added and brought to a gentle simmer. Cover and cook for

1–1½ hours until the meat becomes barely tender. The meat should only be approaching its tender stage. It will finish its cooking during the steaming of the pudding. Adjust the seasoning with salt and pepper and let it cool.

While the meat is cooking and then cooling, the suet pastry can be made and the deep-dish pie pan lined as explained on page 204.

When the stewed beef and vegetables and cool they can be drained in a colander, reserving the cooking liquid. Remove the bay leaf, spoon the meat and vegetables into the pastry-lined dish, and add enough sauce to barely cover. Brush the rim of the suet pastry with water and cover the filling with a circle of pastry. Top with folded, buttered foil, wrapping it around as you would parchment paper, and twisting it to hold. Place the pudding dish in a steamer (a trivet or colander with a lid will also do the trick; see Note, below) filled with hot water. This will now take approximately 1½ hours to cook the suet pastry and to finish the pudding.

While the pudding is steaming, the remaining steak and kidney liquid can be brought to a simmer and strained through a sieve to make a gravy.

Remove the foil and turn the pudding out. Pour the sauce over and serve.

Note: If you do not have a steamer, a trivet or colander can be used, placing it in a saucepan of boiling water and tightly covering with the pan lid or foil. Or, you can put a plate on the bottom of a large saucepan, place the pudding on top, and pour in hot water to halfway up the side of the dish. Now, briskly simmer the pudding for the 2 hours.

Steak with "Kidney Pie"

Steak and kidney pie, probably the most classic of British dishes, can be found almost anywhere in Britain. But never quite like this! That's quite a statement because there are so many excellent steak and kidney pies and puddings. The reason this dish is unique is that it is made up of a piece of braised steak served with a little kidney and onion pie, so that two separate dishes are presented together to create one new British classic.

6 × 6 oz (175 g) chuck "steaks" (individually trimmed and tied)
Butter
Salt and pepper

For the Kidney Pies

8 oz (225 g) *Shortcrust Pastry* (page 364)
3 onions, sliced
Butter
Light brown sugar
⅔ cup (150 ml) heavy cream
1 egg
8 lamb kidneys or 10–12 oz (225–350 g) veal kidneys, cut into ½ in (1 cm) dice
8 oz (225 g) *Quick Puff Pastry* (page 365), rolled and cut into six 3½–4½ in (8–11 cm) circles
1 egg yolk, beaten, to glaze

For the Sauce

Butter
1 onion, roughly chopped
1 carrot, roughly chopped
2 celery sticks, roughly chopped (optional)
Fresh thyme sprig
3 tomatoes, roughly chopped
1 bottle of red wine
1 quart (900 ml) *Beef Stock* (not too strong, page 34), or water
3–4 lamb kidneys, roughly diced
1¼ cups (300 ml) *Beef or Veal Jus* (page 34) or alternative (page 11)

To make the sauce, melt a heaping teaspoon of butter with the chopped vegetables and the sprig of thyme. Cook for 3–4 minutes until softened and then add the chopped tomatoes. Continue to cook for another 3–4 minutes. Add the red wine, bring to a boil, and reduce by three-fourths. This should take 5–6 minutes. Now, add the beef stock and bring to a simmer.

While the sauce is being made, season the chuck "steaks" with salt and pepper. Heat a frying-pan with a heaping teaspoon of butter and brown the steaks on all sides. Add them to the simmering stock. The beef will take approximately 2½ hours to become completely tender and slightly "overcooked." After 2 hours, check the texture of the meat. When you press it, the meat should almost fall apart with tenderness; if not, continue to cook for another 30 minutes (or more). When it is completely cooked, remove the steaks and cover them with plastic wrap.

To finish the sauce, sauté the roughly diced kidneys in some butter for 3–4 minutes. Add to the beef cooking liquid and reduce it by half, skimming off any impurities. This increases the strength and flavor of the sauce, the kidney giving it extra flavor. When it has reduced, add the *jus*. Bring to a simmer and then strain through a sieve. You should have a well-flavored liquid with a sauce consistency. Now, pour off ⅔ cup (150 ml) and reduce it by at least half again to a very thick shiny, sticky consistency. This will be used to brush or roll the finished steaks before serving. The sauce glistens the meat.

Season the remaining sauce. (If the sauce is too thin but strong enough in taste, it can be lightly thickened with cornstarch or arrowroot.)

The pies can be made while the steaks are cooking. Preheat the oven to 400°F/200°C. Butter six 2½–3 in (6–7 cm) tartlet pans. Roll out the shortcrust pastry, cut into large disks, and use to line the tartlet pans, leaving any excess pastry hanging over the edges of the pans. Line with waxed paper or foil, fill with baking beans or pie weights, and bake blind for 15–20 minutes. When they are cool, remove the waxed paper or foil and the beans or weights. Trim away any excess pastry to leave a neat finish.

Meanwhile, fry the onions in a heaping teaspoon of butter over a high heat. Fry until well softened and on the point of being burned, which will take 5–6 minutes. The burned tinges will give us a bitter edge to this dish which I find adds a good flavor. When they are browned, add a sprinkling of light brown sugar to caramelize the onions and to add a note of sweetness. Now, mix together and season with salt and pepper. Reduce the heat to low. Whisk the cream and egg together and combine with the onions while they are still on the stove. Stir for a few minutes until thickened but not scrambled. Remove from the heat and check for seasoning.

Taste the mixture (it will be coffee-colored) for the depth and balance of bitterness and sweetness. If you feel it is too bitter, add another small sprinkling of sugar. Let it cool.

The ½ in (1 cm) diced kidneys can now be pan-fried very quickly in a hot pan with butter (or cooking oil). This takes about 1–2 minutes and the process seals the kidneys. Season with salt and pepper and let them cool. Then stir in some of the bittersweet onion mixture with the kidneys to bind. Spoon some of the onion mixture into the bottom of the pastry cases and then top the onions with the sautéed kidney mixture.

Brush egg yolk around the edge of the pastry cases and top with the puff pastry circles, pressing and sealing all round. Let the pies rest in the refrigerator for at least 20 minutes. When they are set, trim off any excess pastry around the sides, and brush the tops with egg yolk.

To finish the dish, bake the pies for 15–20 minutes until golden. Warm the steaks in the finished sauce. Remove them and roll or brush with the reduced sticky sauce. To serve, place the steaks and the kidney pies side by side on plates and pour some sauce around them.

Note: The components of this dish can be made well in advance. The steaks will take 30–40 minutes to re-heat in the sauce. The pies will keep, refrigerated, for 24 hours before being baked.

Layered Steak and Onion Pudding

This is another classic combination of beef and onions in a main course that is very easy to make. Put its few ingredients in the steamer and 2 hours later, dinner is ready. The ingredients are baked in the same suet pastry used for the *Steak and Kidney Pudding* (page 201).

The basic idea can be varied in a couple of ways. Thin slices of lamb could be layered with the onions – use thin slices from a breast of lamb along with a touch of chopped mint and another dish is made. Venison is also a good variation particularly if seasoned with a pinch of crushed juniper berries and the accompanying onions lightly sweetened with red currant jelly.

For the beef version, a few crushed green peppercorns can be added for pudding *au poivre*. A homemade *jus* (page 34) can be made to serve with the pudding as a gravy.

SERVES 4

1 recipe *Suet Pastry* (right)

For the Filling

3 onions, sliced
4 tablespoons (50 g) butter
2 teaspoons light brown sugar
1¼ lb (600 g) chuck steak, cut into thin strips
Worcestershire sauce
Salt and pepper
Approx. ⅔ cup (150 ml) water

Butter and line a 5 cup (1.2 liter) charlotte mold with the pastry as explained on page 206.

The onions can now be fried in batches, using the butter. It's important to fry them well, allowing the onions to almost burn; this will create a natural bitter caramelizing. As each batch comes to that stage, season well with salt and pepper and add a sprinkling of the sugar for a slightly sweet finish. Let the onions cool.

The meat must be lean so trim off all visible fat as you cut into thin strips. One of the important stages of this dish, as with a Cornish pasty, is to season it well. The sharp pepper bite heightens the whole dish. After all of the beef is cut, season it well and sprinkle it with a tablespoon of Worcestershire sauce.

Now, the pie can be filled, spooning the onions in first. Place thin slices of beef in one layer on top. Repeat the same process until the dish has been completely filled. Pour in the water. More can be added to bring it almost level with the top layer. Brush the edge with water and cover with the pastry. Cover with buttered and folded foil. The pudding can now be cooked in a steamer (or a colander

inside a large saucepan, see Note, page 202), for 2 hours.

During its cooking time, you can prepare if you are serving it.

After the 2 hours, remove the pudding from the steamer and let it rest for 10–15 minutes before turning out of the dish.

The water in the pudding will have taken on the juices from the meat and onions to give a well-flavored liquid. This dish goes well with simple accompaniments such as buttered carrots, cabbage, or greens.

Suet Pastry

This pastry is most famous for the part it plays in the Great British steak and kidney pudding (such as the one on page 201). It takes on all of the flavors happening inside, when coated with a rich gravy, it is unbelievably delicious to eat. It can also be used as a topping for many baked dishes, *The Classic Steak and Kidney Pie* (page 199) being one of them. With this dish, it has the bonus of the beef flavor contained in the suet.

Dried suet can be used, but fresh can never be beaten for its texture and flavor. If using fresh suet, simply pull away the thin outer skin and chop by hand. You could also grate it.

The quantity here will be enough to fill and top a 5 cup (1.2 liter) charlotte mold. This is the size used in the steak and kidney pudding recipe. To top *The Classic Steak and Kidney Pie*, only 2 cups (225 g) of self-rising flour, 4 oz (100 g) of suet and ⅔ cup (150 ml) of water will be needed.

2½ cups (300 g) self-rising flour
5 oz (150 g) shredded suet
1 cup minus 1 tablespoon (200 ml) water
Salt

Sift the flour and salt together into a mixing bowl.

OPPOSITE
Layered Steak and Onion Pudding

Add the suet, crumbling it into the flour. Stir in the water to form a fairly firm dough. Wrap in plastic wrap and allow to rest for 20 minutes.

The pastry is now ready to use. Lightly flour a surface for rolling the pastry. For the steak and kidney pudding, roll it about ¼–½ in (.5–1 cm) thick.

When lining a mold with pastry, always leave ½–¾ in (1–2 cm) hanging over the edge. When the mold has been filled, the overhanging pastry can be folded in to create a border on which to place the pastry lid. Brush the border with water before sealing the top circle of pastry.

Alternately, is to leave the pastry hanging over. Place the lid on top of the filling, moisten with water, and then fold the border in.

Note: Whatever mold you use, it must always be well buttered.

Heatproof plastic bowls work perfectly with steamed puddings. Butter well, and when the pudding is cooked, invert the bowl, gently squeeze it, and the pudding will fall out.

Steak and Oyster Pie

Here is what I hope will be another long-lasting, new British classic. Its concept is similar to that of the *Steak and "Kidney Pie"* on page 202, with the "pie" becoming a separate feature on the plate. The beef is cooked in red wine, and the oyster pie is finished with a glaze of red wine béarnaise sauce.

Oysters were once an inexpensive food for everyone, so much so that in the nineteenth century, they were included in steak and kidney puddings, mixed into them just before the pastry tops were added and the pies went into the oven to be cooked. Since then, because of pollution, they have become rare and are now mostly raised in fisheries.

There are two main types of oysters: rock oysters, which are farmed, and native oysters, which are wild. Rock oysters are also known as Pacific oysters, but are now more commonly and generically known by their French name *fines de claires*. Rock oysters are produced in several countries, including Ireland and France, where they are graded according to their quality, so you'll find ones referred to as *fines de claires, spéciales,* and *label rouge*. The seed for rock oysters are bred in hatcheries and then put out to sea on platforms called trestles. Here they grow by feeding on the plankton that grows naturally in the sea. It takes two to three years for them to reach their market size, which is 3–4 oz (80–100 g). If they are grown in inlets of the sea where there is a certain element of fresh water coming in, their flavor is sweeter.

Native oysters are produced predominantly in the shallow bays on the south coast of England, Holland, France, and around the west coast of Ireland. They also feed on plankton in the sea but take four to six years to reach the same weight (3–4 oz/80–100 g) as rock oysters. They are fished by dredging, generally from small boats, between September and April, which is the season for them.

Whichever of the two types you choose and despite the cost, oysters are worth including because of their amazing flavor.

Opening oysters is not the easiest of jobs. Ask at your fishmarket to have them opened for you. It is important that all of the juices are saved because they will be used to spread the oyster flavor through the red wine sauce. Here are a few tips on how to open an oyster.

1   Hold the oyster in a thick cloth. This will help grip the shell and prevent it from slipping and cutting your hand.

2   The oyster must be held cup-side down. The knife (oyster knives can be easily obtained from kitchen supply stores) can now be inserted in the "pointed" end of the oyster. This is where the hinge holding the shell will be found.

3   Holding tightly, push the knife against and into the hinge point, twisting slightly as you do. The hinge will break, loosening the lid.

4   Lift the top lid of the shell. Be careful not to lose the juices from the cup base. Now, cut away the muscle connecting the flesh to the top shell.

5   Run the knife underneath the oyster, releasing it from the base.

6   Always check that no shell splinters have been

caught in the flesh before serving. For this dish, keep the oysters separate and pass the juices through a tea strainer to remove any grit.

For the Pastry Cases

Butter
1 lb (450 g) *Shortcrust* or *Puff Pastry* (page 364
    or 365)

For the Beef

6 × 8 oz (225 g) chuck steaks,
    trimmed of all sinews and tied
Cooking oil
1 onion, roughly chopped
1 carrot, roughly chopped
½ leek, roughly chopped
2 celery sticks, roughly chopped
1 small garlic clove
Sprig of thyme
1 bay leaf
Bottle of red wine, preferably claret
4–5 cups (900 ml–1.2 liters) *Veal or Beef Jus*
    (page 34), not too thick and strong; the flavor
    will develop while braising
Butter
Salt and pepper
3–4 tomatoes, chopped (optional)

For the Béarnaise Sauce

8 tablespoons (100 g) unsalted butter
Few white peppercorns, crushed
1 teaspoon chopped shallots
2 tablespoons red wine vinegar
2 egg yolks
⅔–1¼ cups (150–300 ml) red wine, reduced by
    three-fourths
Squeeze of lemon juice
1 teaspoon chopped fresh parsley
½ teaspoon chopped fresh tarragon
Salt and pepper
4–5 tablespoons lightly whipped heavy cream,
    to glaze

For the Pies

8–10 oz (225–300 g) *Buttered Spinach* (page 113),
    cooked weight
Butter
2–3 shallots, finely chopped
18 large rock oysters, opened, with their juices

Preheat the oven to 400°F/200°C.

Butter six 3 × 2 in (5 × 8 cm) metal cooking rings. Roll out the shortcrust or puff pastry, cut into large disks and use to line the metal rings, leaving any excess pastry hanging over the edges of the pans. Line with waxed paper or foil, fill with baking beans and bake blind for 15–20 minutes. When they are cool, remove the waxed paper or foil and the beans or weights. Trim away any excess pastry to leave a neat finish.

Turn the heat down to 350°F/180°C.

While the pastry is baking, season the beef with salt and pepper. Heat an ovenproof braising pan on top of the stove with some cooking oil. When the pan is hot, seal the beef pieces, browning the meat completely. Remove the beef and add the vegetables to the pan. Cook for 10–15 minutes until the vegetables have also browned, caramelizing them. Add the garlic, thyme, and bay leaf and continue to cook for a few minutes. Pour the wine over the mixture and bring to a simmer. Cook, reducing the wine by three-fourths. The *jus* can now be added.

Return the meat to the pan and bring to a simmer. Cover with a lid and braise slowly in the oven for 2½–3 hours. The meat will now be totally soft and tender. During the cooking time, it is important to check each hour, skimming away any impurities that collect on the surface. Also, if the sauce is becoming too thick and strong, thin it slightly with water. Three or four chopped tomatoes can also be added to the vegetables. These will give a slight sweetness to the finished result.

When they are cooked, remove the beef pieces and place to one side. Strain the sauce through a sieve. Pour half of the sauce on top of the meat, reducing the remaining amount to a rich red wine sauce consistency. While it is reducing, check that the flavor does not become too strong. If the sauce is too thin, mix a teaspoon of cornstarch with a little red wine and add to thicken. About ½–1 cup of red wine can also be reduced and added to give an even stronger red wine flavor. The steaks can now be kept warm in the liquid and re-warmed in when needed. If refrigerating and re-warming at a later date, the beef will need at least 45 minutes to 1 hour of gentle simmering before it will have returned to its former glory of softness and succulence.

To create a glazed finish on the beef, reduce ½–⅔ cup (100–150 ml) of liquid by two-thirds to three-fourths. This will now be very shiny and sticky to "paint" on the pieces of meat before serving.

This basic recipe method will stand as a dish completely on its own, but the pie is really delicious served with oysters, spinach, and béarnaise sauce.

Make the béarnaise sauce next. Melt the butter and let it stand. The solids will sink to the bottom of the pan, leaving clarified butter.

Place the peppercorns, chopped shallots, and vinegar together in a saucepan. Bring to a simmer and reduce by two-thirds; let it cool. Mix the egg yolks and vinegar reduction together in a bowl. Over a pan of lightly simmering water, whisk to a sabayon, lifting the mixture to at least twice its volume. Remove the bowl from the heat and slowly add the clarified butter, whisking vigorously. The butter will now emulsify with the egg yolks, leaving a thick, creamy sauce. It is important to add the butter slowly. When all the butter has been added and the sauce is thick, pour in the red wine reduction, a little at a time until the mixture coats a spoon. Season with salt and pepper. Strain through a sieve, adding a squeeze of lemon juice and the chopped herbs.

When the beef is completely warmed through, add a few tablespoons of the oyster juice at a time to the finished red wine sauce. These juices have a rather high salt content, so do not adjust the seasoning until the oyster juice has been added.

Warm the pastry cases in a preheated oven. While they warm, heat the spinach and season with salt and pepper. Divide the spinach among the pastry cases. Melt another heaping teaspoon of butter in a hot pan, add the chopped shallots, and cook for 1 minute. Increase the heat in the pan and add the oysters. Cook the oysters for literally only 20–30 seconds before placing three of them into each pastry case on top of the spinach.

Fold the whipped cream into the béarnaise sauce. Spoon the sauce over the oysters, covering the tops of the pies. These can now be glazed to a golden brown under a preheated broiler.

For each serving, place one of the pies and a piece of glazed steak next to one another on the plates and pour the red wine oyster sauce around them. The dishes are complete.

This really does taste like a dream, the warm oysters topped with the red wine béarnaise. When the pie is cut, the sauces mingle with every flavor in the dish.

White Lamb Stew

Many dishes were "white" in medieval times, usually flavored and "browned" by pounded almonds and almond milk. This white lamb stew is similar to the French *blanquette*, which is usually associated with the "white" meats veal, pork, and chicken. It's a variation of stewed lamb finished with a cream sauce.

The meat I use is shoulder of lamb, which is very flavorful. Ask your butcher to give you a lean shoulder, diced large. Pieces of 1½–1¾ in (3–4 cm) will be just right.

Blanquettes, classically, are simply garnished with button mushrooms and onions. I thought we would add some carrots too, for extra flavor and color. This will definitely be a full meal but, if you prefer to serve an accompaniment with the dish, a bowl of buttered pasta would be ideal.

SERVES 4–6

2–2¼ lb (900 g–1 kg) shoulder of lamb, cut into
1½–1¾ in (3–4 cm) dice
1 onion, sliced

Sprig of thyme (rosemary and marjoram are good
   alternatives)
1 large garlic clove, crushed (optional)
1 bay leaf
2½ cups (600 ml) *Chicken Stock* (page 33) or water
2 glasses of white wine
2 large carrots, cut into ½ in (1 cm) dice
8 oz (225 g) button mushrooms, cleaned (wiped
   rather than washed)
⅔ cup (150 ml) heavy cream
Lemon juice
Salt, pepper and freshly grated nutmeg

To Garnish

8 oz (225 g) pearl onions, peeled
Cooking oil

The diced lamb should first be placed in a saucepan
and covered with cold water. Bring it to a boil and
then refresh it in cold water. This method lifts any
impurities from the meat.

Season the lamb with salt, pepper, and nutmeg
and place it in the clean saucepan with the sliced
onion, thyme, garlic, and bay leaf. Pour in the
chicken stock and white wine on top to cover the
meat. If the two liquids have not quite covered the
meat, then top up with water.

Bring to a simmer. This will now take 1½–2
hours of slow cooking, possibly even 2½ hours for
large pieces. During the cooking, skim from time to
time, keeping the liquid clean.

After 1 hour of cooking, add the carrots. The
mushrooms can be added to the stew during its final
30 minutes. This will keep their natural flavor.

To make the garnish, place the pearl onions in a
saucepan and cover with cold water. Bring to a
simmer and cook for 4–5 minutes. Drain and dry the
onions on a cloth. Heat a frying-pan with a drop of
cooking oil and shallow-fry until the onions are
golden brown.

When the meat is tender and cooked, strain off
the liquid, keeping the meat with the mushrooms
and carrots covered with plastic wrap. The sprig of
thyme and bay leaf can be discarded.

The liquid can now be brought to a boil and
allowed to reduce by a half or two-thirds. This will
increase the lamb flavor. Add the heavy cream and
return to a simmer; cook for 4–5 minutes and season
with salt and pepper, if needed.

One or two squeezes of lemon juice can now
be added to liven up the sauce. Add the lamb and
the pearl onions and mushrooms and return to a
simmer. The dish is ready to serve.

Note: Adding chopped fresh parsley or torn leaves of tarragon
is a nice way to finish the dish.

Slow-roast Shoulder of Pork with Pearl Barley and Sage Stuffing

Shoulder of pork is an inexpensive cut of meat.
It can be boned, rolled, and tied, which is how
you'll find it in most butcher shops. The pork will
need to be cooked for 4 hours, so you can do
something else while your piece of pork is roasting
away nicely.

The "stuffing" is actually going to be cooked
separately in an ovenproof dish because the long
meat cooking time would do nothing but spoil it. A
forcemeat to accompany meat is very traditional in
Britain, but it is an optional choice. Remember that
none of these recipes is "carved in stone." The
stuffing is a great addition, though; the pearl barley
gives it a new texture and flavor. But if you have a
favorite sage and onion stuffing, then serve that.

The gravy presented here is flavored with
prunes. Again, this is not essential, but it does go
beautifully with the pork. *Applesauce* (page 44)
would also be a delicious accompaniment.

I use a large pork shoulder here, so it will
probably go even further than the six servings I have
specified.

SERVES 6

3¼–4¼ lb (1.5–1.8 kg) boned and rolled shoulder
   of pork, rind scored
Cooking oil
Salt

3 oz (75 g) pearl barley
Heaping teaspoon of butter
2 onions, chopped
2–2½ cups (500–600 ml) *Chicken Stock*
        (page 33) or water with stock granules
        or cube
3 strips of bacon, cut into small dice
2 teaspoons chopped fresh sage
1 apple, peeled and chopped
1 egg, beaten
¼ cup (50 g) white breadcrumbs
Salt and pepper

For the Sauce

1 heaping tablespoon finely chopped, cooked
        prunes
1–2 tablespoons prune juice
Splash of Armagnac, brandy or Calvados (optional)
1¼ cups (300 ml) *Veal or Beef Jus/gravy* (page 34)
        or *Chicken Stock* (page 33)

Preheat the oven to 325°F/160°C.

When buying the pork, ask for three or four pork bones to rest the meat on while it cooks. If unavailable, then a wire rack will do the trick. This is basically to prevent the meat from becoming burned or dry, which it does if it's in contact with the roasting pan. Also, fat will collect in the bottom, and it can be used for basting.

Oil the pork skin and sprinkle well with salt. Rest the meat on the bones or rack and place in the middle of the preheated oven. Leave for an hour before basting with the pork fat that has collected. Continue to cook for another 3 hours, basting from time to time.

During that first hour the stuffing can be made. Rinse the pearl barley under a cold running water. Melt the butter in a saucepan. When it bubbles, add the chopped onions. Cook for a few minutes until softened but without browning. Add the barley and continue to cook for 2–3 minutes. Add 2 cups (500 ml) of the chicken stock and bring to a simmer. Cover with waxed paper and gently simmer, stirring from time to time, for 45–50

minutes, until tender. If the barley becomes dry during the cooking time, add the remaining stock. When it has cooked, remove from the heat and let it cool.

The bacon can now be fried in a non-stick frying-pan; if the pan is hot enough it will not need any fat. Just cook for a minute or two to seal the pieces. Let it cool.

When all the ingredients are cool, mix together the barley, bacon, sage, apple, and egg. Season with salt and pepper. The breadcrumbs can also be added to the mixture. Spoon into a buttered ovenproof dish. This can now be put into the oven to bake 40–45 minutes before the pork is ready.

After the 4 hours of roasting and basting, the pork should have a good, crisp crackling. Take from the oven and let it rest for 15–20 minutes. During this resting time the oven temperature can be raised to 400°F/200°C. The stuffing will take on a crisp topping if left for another 10 minutes.

The gravy can also be made while the pork is resting. Pour off excess fat from the roasting pan, leaving behind any juices. Heat the pan on top of the stove. Add the prunes and the tablespoon of prune juice. Bring to a simmer, stirring them around. This will lift any flavors left behind. If using Armagnac, or one of the other spirits, then add a spoonful or two now, allowing it to reduce in the pan. The gravy or stock can now also be added and simmered for 10 minutes. Strain through a sieve, pushing all of the prune flavor through. The gravy is now ready to serve.

Remove the crackling from the pork and break into pieces. Gently carve the pork; it will almost simply break into slices. Arrange the meat and crackling on plates, along with a spoonful of stuffing and gravy.

Note: Classic *Roast Potatoes* (page 238), along with greens, *Cabbage, Kale,* or *Sprouts* (page 103, 104 or 106), will all go very well with this dish.

If made with stock, the gravy will obviously have a much thinner consistency but will still have picked up all of the flavors, which is certainly the most important aspect.

Boiled and Baked Ham

Hams are the hind legs taken from pigs that have been raised to become heavier but less fat than those raised to produce fresh pork. These hams are usually salted by soaking in brine and then air-dried and/or smoked. Air-dried and cold-smoked hams are raw, and hot-smoked ham is cooked. Italian Prosciutto, or Parma ham, is dry-cured and air-dried, for instance. Most of the hams in Britain are cooked – hot-smoked or boiled. Legend has it that the original York hams – renowned for their excellent flavor – were smoked over shavings from all the wood needed to build York Minster.

Whole brined hams can be bought cooked or uncooked, and here I use an uncooked ham. It's best to order this ham well in advance from your butcher. The ham can then be soaked to reduce the salt flavor before you cook it. Soak the hams at home for 24 hours, changing the water a few times to get rid of as much salt as possible.

You might be offered a ham that has a slight mold developing on the skin. This simply proves how well the meat has been cured. Make sure the mold is scraped away before cooking it.

Many years ago lots of flavors were added to the boiling liquid, including chopped onions, carrots, celery, turnips, rutabegas, parsnips, as well as fresh herbs, peppercorns, cider, sugar, grated

BELOW
Boiled and Baked Ham

apples, and molasses. The cooking liquid must have been delicious.

In this recipe I use a whole ham, which weighs about 12–16 lb (5.5–7.2 kg). If you decide to cook a whole ham, ask your butcher to remove the aitch bone and trotter. You will need a large saucepan for cooking the ham. You'll probably want to cook this at Christmas or for a summer barbecue since the amount is very large. Otherwise, smaller cured pork cuts can be ordered; a pork shoulder, called a "picnic ham" in the US, weighing about 3–7 lb (1.4–3 kg) pieces would be ideal. Simply follow the cooking time of 20 minutes per 1 lb (450 g).

There are several different ways of glazing hams: the traditional cloves and brown sugar, or honey flavored with dried English mustard, or honey and molasses. I've even found a recipe for a ground coffee, mustard, and brown sugar glaze. Here, I use a glaze of English mustard and light brown sugar.

If you're serving the ham hot, buttered new potatoes and fresh peas are the perfect accompaniment.

SERVES 20–25 AS PART OF A BUFFET

12–16 lb (5.5–7.2 kg) ham, soaked in cold water
    for 24 hours, changing the water occasionally
2 onions, quartered
Few cloves
Few black peppercorns
1 bay leaf
4 tablespoons English mustard
Approx. 1 cup (225 g) light brown sugar
1¼ cups (300 ml) *Chicken Stock* (page 33, optional)

Place the soaked ham in a large saucepan with the onions, cloves, peppercorns, and bay leaf. Cover with water and bring to a boil, skimming away any impurities. The ham can now be left to simmer, allowing 20 minutes per 1 lb (450 g).

Preheat the oven to 375°F/190°C.

When the ham has cooked, remove it from the stock and let it stand for 10–15 minutes before peeling away the skin. The fat can now be left as it is or it can be scored, creating a diamond pattern.

Brush the ham with the mustard and sprinkle well with the brown sugar.

The ham can now be placed in the preheated oven and baked for 30–45 minutes. During this time, the sugar will caramelize. Any glaze collecting in the pan should be basted back onto the ham. When the ham is golden, remove it from the oven and let it rest for 15–20 minutes before carving and serving, or leave it until cold.

The chicken stock, if using, can be poured into the roasting pan and brought to a simmer. This will dissolve any residue left in the pan. Simmer, allowing it to reduce by a third to a half. Strain through a sieve and offer as a ham gravy.

Haslet

Haslet is an early English terrine or loaf made from cooked, ground pork organ meats. It is traditional in the north of England, and it is still found in many butcher shops, delicatessens, and supermarkets there. Haslet was usually made using the pig's heart, liver and lungs mixed with ground pork belly and pork back fat. This is almost impossible to find as a complete "pluck" (sheep's may be easier to find, for homemade haggis), but the separate organ meats should be readily available to buy individually. To keep this recipe simple, I will be using pig's liver and heart mixed with pork shoulder meat and back fat.

Haslet is also classically made with sage, which gives it quite a distinctive flavor.

12–16 SERVINGS

1 pig's heart
12 oz (350 g) pig's liver
1 lb (450 g) pork shoulder
8 oz (225 g) pork back fat
3 large onions, finely chopped
1 tablespoon chopped fresh sage
4 slices of white bread (crusts removed), soaked
    in milk
¼–½ teaspoon freshly grated nutmeg
Salt and pepper
4 tablespoon (50 g) butter or pork fat, for basting

For this recipe, a buttered terrine (12 × 3 × 3 in/30 × 8 × 8 cm) or a 2 lb (900 g) loaf pan can be used. Preheat the oven to 375°F/190°C.

All of the meat and fat can either be hand chopped or ground. If grinding, use a medium blade. After the meat is chopped or ground, add the chopped onions and sage. Remove the bread slices from the milk and squeeze them out. Add to the meats along with the seasonings.

Place the meat mixture in the terrine or loaf pan and dot with the butter or pork fat. Cover with a lid or foil before cooking in the preheated oven for 50–60 minutes.

Uncover the meat for the last 15 minutes of cooking time; this will give the haslet a golden brown finish. To check that the haslet is cooked with a texture firm to the touch, insert a skewer. If the terrine is cooked, the skewer will come out clean.

When the Haslet is cooked, remove it from the oven. It will have slightly shrunk away from the sides of the mold, releasing some of its juices. Another terrine or pan can be placed on top to press it lightly, giving the loaf a firmer texture. It is important that any fat and juices are kept in the terrine, since these will create a good, moist finish to the haslet.

When it is cool, refrigerate until completely set.

To turn out, dip the mold in warm water, releasing the haslet. Slice thinly before serving.

A spoonful of homemade *Piccalilli* (page 385) will go very nicely, or serve with a well-flavored English mustard.

Calves' Liver Steak with Blue Cheese Dumplings and Blue Cheese Butter Sauce

Calves' liver is one of the most tender and tasty types of organ meats. Here, I use a slice from the whole liver, more thickly cut than usual. It is not essential to cut it this way, since many people prefer the classic thin slice that just takes seconds to cook when flashed in a hot pan and flipped over. The difference lies in the finished texture. The thicker-cut steak, which can be cooked to your preference, will hold a lot of good succulent juice providing it's served medium-rare to medium.

Dumplings are a long-established accompaniment to meat and organ meats in the Britain, but these potato dumplings are more like the Italian *gnocchi*. I've simply added English Stilton to the potato, all-purpose flour, and some eggs to create a delicious accompaniment for the liver. For a classic combination, pan-fry or broil thin slices of liver and serve with creamy *Mashed Potatoes* (page 124), *Onion Gravy* (page 50) and crisp bacon.

SERVES 6

6 × 6–8 oz (175–225 g) calves' liver steaks
All-purpose flour, seasoned, for dusting (optional)
Cooking oil
Butter
Salt and pepper

For the Dumplings

2¼ lb (1 kg) large potatoes, with skin left on
6 oz (175 g) Stilton or other blue cheese, chopped
1½–2 cups (175–200 g) all-purpose flour, sifted
1 egg
1 egg yolk
Salt, pepper, and freshly grated nutmeg
Butter and "olive" or cooking oil, for pan-frying (optional)

For the Blue Cheese Butter Sauce

8 tablespoons (100 g) unsalted butter, chilled and diced
1 shallot or ½ small onion, finely chopped
1 bay leaf
1 tablespoon white wine vinegar
1 glass of white wine
½ cup (100 ml) water or *Chicken Stock* (page 33)
2 tablespoons light cream
2 oz (50 g) Stilton or other blue cheese, chopped
Pepper

The dumplings can be made well in advance, so let's start with these.

Cook the potatoes whole in salted, boiling water until tender (generally about 20 minutes,

depending on size.) Peel the warm potatoes and mash them to a smooth texture. At this point, the cheese can be added. While the potato is still warm, the cheese will melt and spread through the mixture. Add the flour, egg, and egg yolk. Season with salt and pepper, being careful not to add too much salt since most blue cheeses have a strong, seasoned flavor. Add a touch of grated nutmeg.

The dumpling mixture can now be rolled into ½–¾ in (1–2 cm) balls. Simply take a rounded tablespoon of the mixture and roll it with floured hands or roll on a floured surface. After they are rolled, the dumplings are ready to poach in simmering water for 3–4 minutes; 5 minutes is the maximum time they will need. Cook a handful at a time by dropping them carefully into the water; as the cooking time passes, they will rise to the top of the pan. It's at this point that they are ready. If you aren't using them immediately, refresh them in ice water. They can be made to this stage in advance.

After the dumplings have cooled, refrigerate them on baking sheets and cover with plastic wrap. They can be re-heated by pan-frying whenever needed. To pan-fry, melt a heaping teaspoon of butter along with a drop of "olive" or cooking oil in a frying-pan. When the butter begins to bubble, add the dumplings. Fry on a medium heat until golden brown. This will have created another texture in the dumplings and completely warm them through. They are now ready to serve.

Next, make the blue cheese sauce. This is a basic butter sauce flavored with blue cheese. If the amount of butter is excessive for you, it can be halved, but an extra 4–5 tablespoons of light cream will be needed to give the same quantity of sauce.

Melt 2 teaspoons of the butter, and add the chopped shallot or onion with the bay leaf. Cook for a few minutes without browning, until softened. Add the white wine vinegar, allowing it to simmer

and reduce by three-fourths. Add the white wine and also reduce by three-fourths. Pour in the water or stock and reduce by half. The light cream can now be added. Return to a simmer. The remaining butter, best if you have chilled it, can be whisked in a little at a time. The chopped blue cheese can now be added. Allow the sauce to simmer only slightly so the cheese doesn't separate. Season with a grinding of pepper and, once the cheese has melted, strain through a sieve. If the sauce is too thick, add a drop or two more water or stock.

The sauce is now ready to serve. For a light, creamy effect and taste, beat with an electric hand-mixer. This puts air into the sauce and lightens it.

Now, for the liver. If broiling or pan-frying, the liver can first be lightly coated in seasoned flour. This will create a thin, crisp texture, and it also helps prevent the liver from sticking to a pan or broiler.

Heat a frying-pan with a little cooking oil. When it is hot, place the steaks in the pan. It's best not to salt and pepper directly onto raw liver; the salt draws blood from the liver and also burns the meat. Cook for 3–4 minutes before adding a heaping teaspoon of butter. Continue to cook for another minute before turning the steaks over. Now, season with salt and pepper on the seared side. Continue to cook over a medium heat for another 4–5 minutes. Season the other seared side and place on the plates. The steaks are now ready to serve.

The dumplings can simply be placed next to the steak and the sauce drizzled over them. The dumplings can also be passed separately, allowing people to help themselves. If you've "poached" the steaks, as explained below, then just pour a little of the sauce over the meat.

Note: Buttered spinach, kale, mustard greens, or leeks all go very well with this dish. If using one of these leafy green vegetables, then why not arrange it on the plates, placing the liver steak on top?

After it has been quickly sealed on both sides, a calves' liver steak can be "poached" in warm stock or *jus*. It's a "soft" way of cooking liver steaks. Simply take some stock (perhaps flavored with red wine) and warm it to almost a simmer. The liver can be dropped in and allowed to warm and cook through. Literally 7–8 minutes will give you a medium-rare

---

OPPOSITE

Calves' Liver Steak with Blue Cheese Dumplings and Blue Cheese Butter Sauce

stage – that's for an 8 oz (225 g) steak approximately ¾ in (2 cm) thick. If poaching the liver in gravy, an extra sauce can quickly be made from it. After the meat is cooked, some of the gravy can be reduced to a rich and shiny consistency.

Pressed Ox Tongue

Ox tongue is a substantial, tender, and tasty meat. It used to be boiled, or boiled then roasted (spiked with cloves), potted, and made into sausage along with ox cheeks and palates.

Most ox tongues bought these days will have been previously pickled in a sweet brine. The tongues are rubbed with salt and then left to pickle in a mixture of water, salt, and sugar. This pickling process takes from four to six days. It's at this stage that you'll probably buy it. Unsalted or unpickled tongue can be used as well, but it tends to take a fair bit longer to poach.

It's best to buy the tongue 48 hours before you are going to serve the dish. This then allows 24 hours of soaking in cold water and the following day for cooking and pressing. After the tongue has been cooked, it can also be set in its own jelly. To achieve a better flavor, one or two split calves' feet can be added to the liquid. This will help the liquid with its jelling (see opposite).

Cold tongue goes very well with many of the pickles and chutneys featured in this book, or after being cooked and trimmed, could be served hot with homemade gravy and *Mashed Potatoes* (page 124). A *Mustard Butter Sauce* (page 53) is a traditional accompaniment.

This amount of ox tongue will give 6–8 generous servings for a main course or will provide many thin slices for a cold buffet.

3½–4 lb (1.6–1.8 kg) ox tongue, pre-soaked
    in water for 24 hours
1 large onion, thickly sliced
2 carrots, thickly sliced
4 celery sticks, thickly sliced
1 bay leaf
Sprig of thyme
8 black peppercorn
Powdered gelatin, if necessary

Cover the tongue with water and bring to a boil. Cook for 6–7 minutes and then refresh under cold water. This will lift impurities from the tongue.

Wipe the saucepan clean and replace the tongue. Cover with 3½ quarts (3 liters) of water and again bring to a boil, skimming away any further impurities. Simmer, skim, and cook for 30 minutes more before adding the vegetables, bay leaf, thyme, and peppercorns. The tongue can now be gently simmered for another 3–3½ hours.

After it has cooked, remove the tongue and quickly dip into cold water to calm its fierce heat and make it easier to peel off the skin. After peeling, any tiny bones at the root end of the tongue can be pulled away and the meat neatly trimmed.

While it is still hot, the tongue can be fitted into a 6 in (15 cm) soufflé dish. Press with a suitable weight on top and let it set in the refrigerator.

If you would prefer to make a jelly, strain one quart (1 liter) of the cooking liquid into the pan, boil it, and reduce by at least half. This will strengthen the flavor of the jelly. It's important to taste the liquid, making sure it isn't becoming too salty. If the flavor seems shallow, add 2 teaspoons of chicken or beef stock granules. This will add body. The jelly can be tested for setting on a side plate. If it's not setting, add 2–3 teaspoons of powdered gelatin or a leaf of gelatine (following instructions on the package.) If using stock cubes and gelatine, strain again before pouring onto the tongue. Allow to set, pressing lightly as above, preferably overnight.

The tongue tastes delicious and maintains a moist finish when set in jelly. Simply slice and serve.

Black Pudding

Black pudding is an acquired taste, but what a taste that is! Good-quality black pudding is so delicious to eat, whether as part of your breakfast or as part of another recipe. You'll find several recipes in this book that include it, which I think demonstrates how much I love this culinary treat.

A good friend of mine, Jack Morris, runs his own butcher shop in Bolton. He has become renowned throughout the world for his homemade black pudding, a recipe that has won many international titles, often leaving the French *boudin noir* way behind. As much as I tried to twist his arm, he wouldn't release the famous recipe (and I don't blame him), so here's a recipe that's almost as good. It contains many flavors and ingredients, making it quiteadventurous. The recipe specifies fresh pig's blood, which may be difficult to buy (dried blood can be substituted), but I thought I would include an original recipe to give you an idea of how the puddings were once made.

A basic black pudding recipe would, classically, be made from pearl barley, rice, or groats (these are unprocessed oats, which look similar to birdseed, available from pet shops or health-food stores), fine oatmeal, pork fat, onions, pig's blood, and seasonings.

Jack told me a little story of the "other Black Beauties," as he calls them, and of how they came to England. Here's the story. The black pudding started its life in Europe. Monks, who kept their own livestock, also grew their own herbs and cereals. When the pig was slaughtered, they collected the blood, added cereal, herbs, seasonings, and diced fat and mixed them together very much as the precess is done today. The intestines were then filled and boiled in a large pan. The name was "Blut Wurst," blood sausage. The monks travelled through Europe and then arrived in England, settling in Yorkshire, where the name was changed to "blood pudding." Eventually they crossed the Pennines into Lancashire, where the sausage became famous and was known as "black pudding."

Here's the recipe for a new "Black Beauty," which makes a large number of sausages. If pig's head is unavailable, substitute with three or four pig's trotters, cooked for 2–3 hours.

MAKES 25–30 BLACK PUDDINGS

For the Pig's-head Liquid

1 boned pig's head, rolled and tied
1 onion, studded with 2 cloves
1 large carrot, chopped
Green from diced white leeks, chopped (see method)
1 teaspoon crushed black peppercorns
1 heaped teaspoon cayenne pepper
Salt
Sprig of thyme
1 bay leaf
About 3½ quarts (3 liters) water

For the Black-pudding Mixture

9 oz (250 g) pinhead oats
Butter
12 oz (350 g) chopped onions
12 oz (350 g) white of leek, cut into ¼ in (5 mm) dice
2 garlic cloves, crushed
12 oz (350 g) bacon, cut into ¼ in (5 mm) dice
12 oz (350 g) pork back fat, cut into ¼ in (5 mm) dice
1 tablespoon chopped fresh thyme
1 tablespoon chopped fresh tarragon
About 3½ quarts (3 liters) pig's blood, or dried blood equivalent
Salt, pepper, cayenne pepper, and ground mace
5 yards (5 meters) sausage casing, soaked in cold water for several hours

To cook the pig's head, place all ingredients for the liquid in a large saucepan and bring to a simmer. Cook for at least 3 hours, then check that the head has become tender. If not, continue to simmer for a total of 4 hours.

Remove from the heat, placing the head in a suitable container, and pour the strained stock over it. Allow it to cool and the jelly to set. The head can now be removed and the meat cut into ½–¾ in (1–2 cm) dice.

Toast the pinhead oats until golden brown to achieve a nutty texture and flavor.

In a large pan, melt a heaping teaspoon of butter, adding the chopped onions. Cook for 5 minutes until softened before adding the diced white leek and the crushed garlic. Add the bacon and continue to cook for 5–6 minutes. The diced pig's-head meat can now also be added, reducing the heat to a gentle simmer. Blanch the back fat in boiling water and drain. Add to the sausage ingredients. The fresh herbs and pinhead oats can now be added to the mixture.

Stir the blood well and pass it through a sieve. Pour it into the sausage mixture. It is now important to stir the blood in the pan, checking its temperature as you heat it to 104°F/40°C. At this point it will begin to coagulate and thicken. The blood must not rise above this temperature or it will start to spoil. The absolute maximum it can reach is 122°F (50°C). Remove from the heat and season generously with salt, pepper, cayenne, and ground mace.

The sausage casing can now be filled. To make sure the fat content is equally distributed, use a funnel or piping bag with a plain nozzle, stirring the mixture to maintain the even spreading of flavors. As the sausages are piped, tie the casings at about 6 in (15 cm) intervals.

The sausages can now be poached in the stock already made or in salted water, heating to no more than 170°F (80°C). Poach for 15 minutes, then remove from the heat and let them stand for another 15 minutes in the liquid.

The black puddings can now be removed and refrigerated after being cooled.

To serve, the sausages can be re-heated in warm water, split, and broiled, or sliced and pan-fried, or broiled.

Even if you don't make black pudding, at least now you know how this recipe is made.

Calves' Liver Steak and Kidney with red wine Carrots and Rosemary Butter

Liver and kidneys together are always a good combination. This dish is a favorite with organ meat-lovers, the kidney roasted on top of the stove with a lump of rosemary butter melting inside, the liver pan-fried and served on the red wine carrots, topped with pan-fried scallions. All of these ingredients provide wonderful flavors.

In this recipe, the kidney is presented on a roast potato disk, which are very easy to make. Everybody enjoys roasted potatoes.

This recipe serves four, but one large cut of veal kidney will sometimes give you five servings. If you can find a source for pig's caul, wrap the kidney pieces in it. But caul is not the easiest product to obtain so you can make the dish without it.

SERVES 4

1 medium-sized veal kidney
4 oz (100 g) pig's caul, soaked for several hours (page 11, optional)
4 × 6 oz (175 g) calves' liver steaks, approx. ½ in (1 cm) thick
All-purpose flour, for coating
Cooking oil
Butter
Salt and pepper
Bunch of scallions, cut into ¼ in (5 mm) pieces

For the Butter Sauce

1 tablespoon chopped rosemary
8 tablespoons (100 g) butter, softened
2 tablespoons white wine vinegar
1 glass of white wine
½ cup (100 ml) *Chicken Stock* (page 33)
1 tablespoon heavy cream
Squeeze of lemon juice

For the red wine Carrots

2–3 large carrots, peeled
½ cup (100 ml) *Chicken Stock* (page 33) or water

Butter
Pinch of sugar
1–1½ cups of red wine

For the Roasted Potatoes

2 large Russet potatoes, peeled
All-purpose flour, for coating
Cooking oil
Butter

For the Red Wine Sauce

1–1½ cups of red wine
⅔ cup (150 ml) *Veal or Beef Jus* (page 34) or
    alternative (page 11)

First, make the butter sauce. Mix the rosemary with the butter. Refrigerate to set. When it is cold, form 2 tablespoons (25 g) of it into four small lumps. These will be used to fill the kidney pieces.

The kidney can be bought separately or in suet fat, in which case, the fat will need to be removed. The inner fat and veins should be cut away carefully, leaving an open, cleaned kidney. Divide the kidney into four pieces. Season them inside and place a rosemary butter lump in the center of each. Wrap the kidney around the butter, creating four meatball-sized shapes. If using pig's caul, squeeze it dry and open it into a large net. Cut into four pieces and wrap each kidney piece. Refrigerate until needed.

If caul is unavailable, simply leave the four kidney pieces without the butter lumps. After they've been cooked, the rosemary butter can be added, rolling the kidneys in the butter to coat them.

For the red wine carrots, cut the carrots into thin sticks (2¼ × ¼ in/6 cm × 5 mm). Place the stock or water and carrots in a saucepan with a heaping teaspoon of butter and pinch of sugar.

Bring to a simmer and cook for 6–8 minutes until the carrots are tender. Remove the carrots from the liquid and place to one side.

Boil and reduce the cooking liquid by three-fourths to a syrupy consistency. In a separate pan, reduce the red wine also by three-fourths. The two can be mixed together. This is the red wine liquid to be used to re-heat the carrots when needed.

Preheat the oven to 400°F/200°C. Cut two disks (2½ × ¾ in/6–7 × 2 cm) from each potato. These can now be poached in salted water until barely cooked through. This will take 12–15 minutes. When they are cooked, drain and lightly coat them with flour while still warm. Heat a thin layer (2 mm) of cooking oil in a frying- or roasting-pan and place the potatoes in it. Fry until golden brown and crisp. Turn the potatoes over and repeat to the same stage.

Add a heaping teaspoon of butter and finish by roasting in the preheated oven for 5–6 minutes. Remove and season with a pinch of salt. The golden, crisp potatoes are ready.

Now, heat the white wine vinegar in a small saucepan and reduce it by half. Add the white wine, boil and reduce by three-fourths. Add the chicken stock and reduce by half. This reduction can now be kept until the sauce is needed. To finish, re-heat the reduction, adding the heavy cream. The remaining rosemary butter can now be whisked in, keeping the sauce from boiling again. Season with salt and pepper. Add a squeeze of lemon juice to heighten the flavors and finish the sauce.

Now, make the red wine sauce. Boil and reduce the red wine by three-fourths. Add the *jus* and cook for a few minutes. Adjust the seasoning with salt and pepper. The sauce is now ready.

To finish the dish, heat two frying-pans. Season the kidneys with salt and pepper. Add a drop of cooking oil to both pans. Place the kidneys in one of the pans and fry, until brown. Cooked on top of the stove, the kidneys will take approximately 5 minutes, maintaining a slightly pink center.

Dust the liver with a little flour and also begin to pan-fry it. After it has browned on one side (2 minutes), add a heaping teaspoon of butter and turn the liver over. Continue to cook for another 2 minutes, seasoning with salt and pepper.

While the liver and kidneys are cooking, the carrots can be re-heated in the red wine liquid. As they heat, the liquid will reduce, coating the carrots. Season with salt and pepper.

Heat the red wine sauce. After it is warm, place to one side, reducing 2–3 tablespoons to a thicker consistency. The sauce can now be brushed over the kidneys and the liver to give them a rich glaze.

The potatoes can now be placed on one side of the plates, arranging the red wine carrot sticks on the other. While arranging the plate, quickly pan-fry the scallions in a heaping teaspoon of butter, without browning, and season them. Place the roasted kidney on top of the roasted potatoes. Spoon 2–3 tablespoons of red wine sauce over the carrots, placing the liver on top. Now, simply finish the dish with the scallions spooned on top of the liver and the rosemary butter sauce around the kidney. The dish is complete.

Note: There are quite a few components to this dish, but if you prepare as much as possible in advance, it becomes quite simple. Here are a few tips on how to make the finishing easier.
1 Cook and glaze the carrots early with the red wine reduction. These can now be refrigerated and microwaved when needed.
2 Brown the potatoes on one side only. Finish on the other side in a hot oven when needed.
3 Have both sauces ready, the butter sauce needing the butter to be whisked in, the separate red wine glaze reduced and ready.

Pigs' Trotters Bourguignon

This dish is one I hope to become the ultimate "new classic." Trotters are amazing to eat. They need some care and attention, and a fair bit of work is involved, but the results merit all that – and more.

Eating pigs' trotters is a very British thing to do. In the eighteenth century, trotters were sold for "street eating" and in Ireland, they were a traditional pub food until not so long ago. Salted pigs' trotters, or "Crubeens," are a speciality of Cork.

This trotter dish is well up to date, though. I've taken the *bourguignon* garnishes from France, usually button onions, mushrooms, and bacon, which are served with braised meat and a red wine sauce. I'm doing exactly that here, the difference being that I put the onions, mushrooms, and bacon *inside* the

actual trotters. These are bound with a rich pork stuffing flavored with *foie gras* (optional). So as you eat this delicious dish, you experience many flavors.

This recipe will fill 6–8 trotters. Ask your butcher to bone the trotters for you. Hind trotters have a better shape and more meat. They might need to be singed to remove any hair, and then soak them in water for 24 hours. Make them a day before you wish to serve them, starting the preparation 48 hours in advance. This gives the stuffing time to become firm in the trotters, and allows them to hold their shape and texture perfectly.

SERVES 6

6 boned pigs' trotters, preferably hind, singed and soaked in cold water for 24 hours

For the Cooking Liquid

Butter
1 onion, chopped
1 carrot, chopped
2 celery sticks, chopped
Sprig of thyme
1 bay leaf
Few black peppercorns
Bottle of red wine (for maximum flavor)
2½ cups (600 ml) *Chicken Stock* (page 33)
1¼ cups (300 ml) *Veal or Beef Jus* (page 34)

For the Stuffing

3–4 oz (75–100 g) *foie gras*, chilled (if unavailable, increase the amount of ground pork)
8 oz (225 g) finely ground lean pork meat, chilled
4 oz (100 g) finely ground pork fat, chilled
1 egg
Heaping teaspoon of butter
2 tablespoons finely chopped shallots

OPPOSITE
Pigs' Trotters Bourguignon

1 large garlic clove, crushed

1 teaspoon chopped fresh thyme

4 oz (100 g) chicken livers, soaked in milk for
    24 hours

1 cup (200 ml) heavy cream

Splash each of Armagnac and Madeira (or brandy,
    if neither is available)

2–3 tablespoons of thick *jus* (take 5–6 tablespoons
    of cooking liquid and reduce by half before
    chilling and adding)

Salt and pepper

For the Garnish

3–4 oz (75–100 g) button onions

4 tablespoons (50 g) butter

3–4 oz (75–100 g) button mushrooms, quartered

3 oz (75 g) unsmoked bacon or cooked ham, cut
    into ¼ in (5 mm) dice

To cook the trotters, preheat the oven to 325°F/160°C.

Melt a heaping teaspoon of butter in a braising pan large enough to hold the trotters. Add the vegetables, thyme, bay leaf, and peppercorns. Cook, allowing them to take on a little color, for 4–5 minutes. Add the red wine, a fourth of the bottle at a time. Reduce by two-thirds before adding more wine; continue to add and reduce until all is added.

The stock and *jus* can now be added, along with the raw trotters. Bring to a simmer, cover with a lid, and place in the oven. These can now gently braise for 2½–3 hours until completely tender. To check, simply lift and pinch the trotter skin. This should give and tear very easily. After they are cooked, let them rest in the liquid for 20 minutes.

Butter six large squares of foil. Place a trotter on each square and fill them with the stuffing.

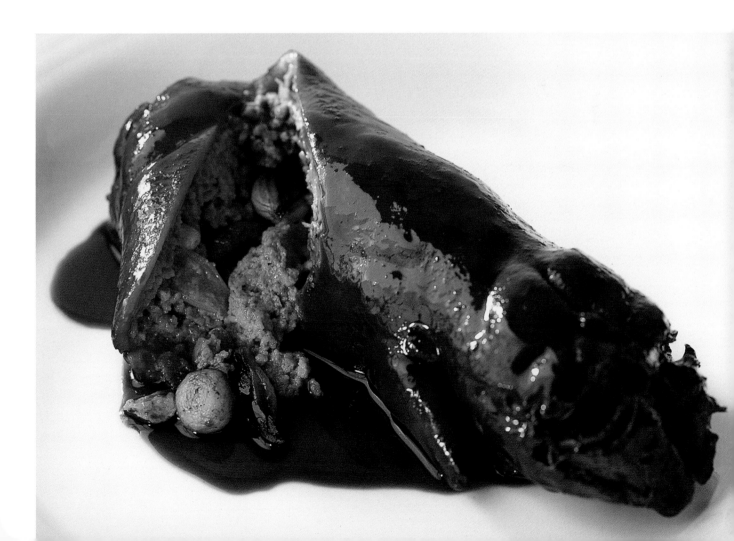

The cooking liquid can now be strained through a sieve. Bring to a simmer and skim off any impurities; also check the consistency and the seasoning. The flavor should be quite powerful. Reduce to strengthen it and thicken if needed. After it's ready, take 10–12 tablespoons of this sauce and boil it to reduce by half. This gives you a glossy glaze to paint the trotters with just before serving.

For the stuffing, process the *foie gras*, if using, in a food processor and mix with the ground pork meat and the fat. Purée them to combine and season well with salt and pepper. Blend in the egg.

The mixture is best placed in a stainless-steel bowl or equivalent over a bowl of ice. This will keep the filling firm. Or you can make sure the food processor and all of the ingredients are cold.

Melt a heaping teaspoon of butter in a frying-pan. When it is hot, add the chopped shallots, garlic, and thyme. Remove the livers from the milk and dry them on paper towels. Add the livers to the shallots, increase the heat, and pan-fry for 2–3 minutes. Let them cool. These can now also be puréed and stirred into the pork mixture. Now it's time to stir in the heavy cream a little at a time, mixing well to hold a good consistency. When all of the cream has been added, season again with salt and pepper. Add a splash each of Armagnac and Madeira (or brandy) and pour in the reduced *jus*.

The stuffing is now ready. To test, a spoonful can be poached in lightly simmering water. This will only take 2–3 minutes to cook. From this you can check its seasoning and texture. If very firm, a drop of two more cream can be added, but be careful because too much will spoil the mixture.

For the garnish, blanch the pearl onions in boiling water for 2–3 minutes. Drain and allow them to cool naturally. When cooled, cut each in half.

Melt some of the butter, add the onions, cut-side down, and fry them until they become golden with tinges of caramelizing. This will take 6–7 minutes. Turn the onions over and continue to cook for another 4–5 minutes. Remove and cool them.

After wiping the pan clean, melt another heaping teaspoon of the butter. When it bubbles, add the mushrooms. Fry until golden brown and tender. This will take only 4–5 minutes on a high heat.

Over a low heat, melt the remaining butter and add the bacon. This can now be gently fried, without browning, for 2–3 minutes. (If using cooked ham, simply leave it in its cooked state.) After all of the garnish has chilled, fold gently into the stuffing.

Divide the stuffing among the trotters. It's best to shape the stuffing cylindrically, creating a shape to fold the trotter skin around. The trotters are best made reasonably plump, keeping the size and shape of the original trotter. When all have been filled, the foil can be rolled around, twisting at either end. For extra firmness, wrap them again with another square of foil.

The trotters are best if refrigerated for 24 hours before heating for serving.

To serve, steam the trotters for 18–20 minutes. While the trotters are steaming, the sauce and glaze can be re-heated.

When they are cooked, allow the trotters to rest for 5 minutes before carefully removing the foil. Brush each with the glaze and present on plates or in large bowls. The sauce can now be poured over them or passed separately. These trotters taste wonderful with *Mashed Potato Sauce* (page 125).

Note: If a steamer is unavailable, then place the trotters in a roasting pan in ¼ in (5 mm) of hot water. These can now be baked in a preheated oven at 375°F/190°C, for 15–18 minutes. Let them rest before serving.

Irish Stew

This famous Irish meat and potato stew is a classic example of the dishes that were prepared when most households had only one cooking pot to be heated over a fire. The stew has a combination of ingredients that would have been easily available – some lamb or mutton, lots of onions, and inevitably in Ireland, lots of potatoes.

It is a dish that can be prepared and cooked in many different ways. You can look in a dozen cookbooks and find a dozen varying recipes. Some people add carrots; others think this is sacrilege. Some put potatoes on the bottom to create a sauce and thicken the juices and then top with more potatoes. A few recipes include a handful of pearl barley, which would make the dish more substantial. Here's my version for you to try.

SERVES 4

1½ lb (675 g) neck of lamb, cut into cutlets
8 tablespoons (100 g) unsalted butter
4 onions, sliced
1 lb (450 g) potatoes, peeled and cut into rough dice
1 garlic clove
1 bouquet garni (1 bay leaf, 1 sprig each of fresh rosemary and thyme tied in a square of muslin or strip of leek) or bouquet garni sachet
6 cups (1.5 liters) *Chicken Stock* (page 33) or water
6 oz (175 g) carrots, sliced
6 celery sticks, cut into 1 in (2.5 cm) pieces
8 oz (225 g) Savoy cabbage, shredded
Salt and pepper
2 teaspoons chopped fresh parsley, to garnish

Cover the meat with cold water in a large pan and bring to a boil. Drain off the water and cover the meat again with cold water. Drain well.

Melt the butter in a large braising pan and add the sliced onions, half the diced potatoes, and the garlic. Add the bouquet garni to the pan and sweat it for 2 minutes. Add the lamb cutlets and cover with the chicken stock. Bring the stock to a simmer, cover, and cook for 30 minutes. The meat will be partially cooked and the potatoes will have started to purée and thicken the stock.

Add the diced carrots and continue to cook for another 10 minutes. Add the remaining potatoes and the diced celery and cook for 15–20 minutes. At this stage the potatoes should not be puréed but simply cooked until soft. Add the cabbage and cook for another 2–3 minutes until the meat and vegetables are tender. Season with salt and pepper, remove the bouquet garni, and serve in individual bowls or one large bowl. Finish with the chopped parsley. You now have a complete meal.

Boiled Bacon with Pearl Barley and Lentils

After killing the pig in the fall, most households would have a barrel of salted or pickled pork to last through the winter. There would also be a barrel of dried beans, and the combination was the dietary mainstay of most of the British throughout the centuries.

There are many alternate ways of serving boiled bacon. It still goes well with dried beans – which would have been the fava bean variety before kidney beans were introduced from America – with other

BELOW
Irish Stew

legumes or grains, such as pearl barley and lentils, and even with parsley sauce. It could be made into a winter soup. The bacon can also be served with *Braised Split Peas* (page 117), along with a little stock spooned over them. Any leftover stock can be frozen for soup-making, for sauces, or even for your next boiled bacon.

SERVES 6–8

4 lb (1.8 kg) unsmoked rolled bacon collar, rind removed
5 carrots
4 onions
2 celery sticks
1 leek
Sprig of thyme
1 bay leaf
2–2½ cups (1.75–2.25 liters) *Chicken Stock* (page 33)
3 oz (75 g) pearl barley
1 large rutabaga
2 large parsnips
8 tablespoons (100 g) unsalted butter
1 tablespoon chopped fresh parsley
Salt and pepper
Mashed Potatoes (page 124), to serve

For the Braised Lentils

Butter
1 onion, finely diced
2 oz (50 g) green lentils, preferably *lentilles de Puys*
⅔ cup (200 ml) *Chicken Stock* (page 33) or *Vegetable Stock* (page 36)

Soak the bacon in water for 24 hours before cooking. This will reduce the salt content.

Put the bacon in a large pot. Coarsely chop two of the carrots, one of the onions, the celery, and the leek and add to the pot with the herbs. Pour on the chicken stock, bring to a simmer, skim off impurities, cover, and cook gently for about 1½ hours. Allow the bacon to rest in the stock for 30 minutes.

To cook the lentils, melt a heaping teaspoon of butter in a small ovenproof braising pan. Add the diced onion and cook for a few minutes. Pour in the lentils, stirring well. Cover with the stock and bring

to a simmer. Cover with a lid and braise in the preheated oven for about 30–35 minutes until the lentils are tender and all the stock has been absorbed. If the stock is absorbed before they become tender, simply add a little more water. When the lentils are ready, season with salt and pepper.

Cook the pearl barley in approximately 2 cups (400 ml) of the cooking liquid for about 15–20 minutes until soft. Meanwhile, cut the remaining carrots and onions, the rutabaga, and the parsnips into ½ in (1 cm) dice and sweat in half the butter. Add the pearl barley and a little more stock, if necessary, to form a soup consistency. Allow this to simmer for about 15 minutes until all the vegetables are tender. Add the cooked lentils, the remaining butter, and the chopped parsley to create a barley, lentil, and vegetable stew. Check for seasoning.

To serve, place the warm mashed potatoes in the center of the serving plates and spoon some of the stew around them. Slice the bacon, allowing two slices per serving, and place the slices on top of the potatoes. Finish with a spoonful of stock on top of the meat and serve.

Boiled Brisket of Beef and Vegetable Stew

Boiled meat" used to be much more common than it is now. Meat that had been salted, as most meats were from the Middle Ages up until the nineteenth century, had to be "boiled" (or stewed); cooked in any other way it would be hard and unpalatable. This recipe will reintroduce you to a traditionally British cooking technique which results in meat that is extremely tender.

Brisket is a cut of beef taken from the forequarter. It is normally pickled in brine, which is a combination of salt, saltpeter, and water. The beef can be kept in brine for up to ten days. This will help tenderize the cut. If buying brisket already salted, I suggest you soak it in fresh water for 24–48 hours to release some of the salty taste. This goes very well with *Mashed Potatoes* (page 124).

2 lb (900 g) brisket, soaked in fresh water
1 carrot
1 onion
1 bay leaf
2 celery sticks
1 leek
Fresh thyme sprig

For the Vegetable Garnish

2 onions, cut into ½ in (1 cm) dice
3–4 celery sticks, cut into ½ in (1 cm) dice
Butter
1 small rutabaga, cut into ½ in (1 cm) dice
2 large carrots, cut into ½ in (1 cm) dice
2 leeks, cut into ½ in (1 cm) dice
2–3 tablespoons heavy cream
1 teaspoon each chopped fresh parsley and thyme
Salt and pepper

Cover the brisket with fresh cold water in a large saucepan and bring to a boil. When it boils, pour the water off and refresh the beef in cold water. Cover with with more cold water, adding the whole vegetables and the thyme. Cover and bring to a simmer, skimming away any impurities. The beef will take 2½–3 hours to become totally tender.

While the beef is cooking, prepare the garnishing vegetables, cooking them separately. Cook the onions and celery without browning in a heaping teaspoon of butter. Blanch the rutabaga, carrots, and leeks in water or some of the brisket cooking liquid until tender.

When the beef is cooked, drain off two-thirds of the cooking liquid and reduce to 1¼ cups (300 ml). Add the cream and all of the garnishing vegetables. Warm through and season with salt and pepper. Add a heaping teaspoon of butter and stir in. Add the chopped herbs. Carve the brisket and place the slices in bowls or on plates. I prefer to serve this dish in large bowls and treat the sauce as a beef and vegetable soup. If the "soup" is too thick, thin it with more of the stock. Spoon the garnishing vegetables and sauce on top and serve.

Note: You could use whole, small vegetables for the garnish (you will need to cut the rutabaga in chunks and the celery sticks in half). Simply stew the beef in water and add the vegetables toward the end of cooking, serving them as the garnish.

Lancashire Hot-pot

This is the English version of Irish stew. It's one-pot cooking again and was traditionally put into the oven at the end of a busy baking day to cook slowly until done. Some versions contain mushrooms and, occasionally, oysters were placed under the potatoes for the last half hour (as they were in a steak and kidney pie).

Lancashire hot-pot usually consists of neck of lamb, kidneys, onions, potatoes, and stock (usually water), but I've refined it by adding more textures and tastes, showing how good ordinary lamb shoulder chops can be. The chops should be lean with the little bone and fat left on them. The vegetables have to be chopped into very small dice, which may sound tiresome but it's worth doing. You will need a shallow flameproof braising dish to hold the chops in one layer.

SERVES 4

2 carrots, finely diced
2 celery sticks, finely diced
2 onions, finely diced
1 leek, finely diced
4–6 tablespoons (50–75 g) unsalted butter
½ garlic clove, crushed
2 large sprigs of fresh rosemary
4 thick, lean lamb shoulder chops
⅔ cup (150 ml) dry white wine
2½ cups (600 ml) *Veal or Beef Jus* (page 34)
    or alternative (page 11)
4 large potatoes, peeled
1 tablespoon lamb fat or beef dripping
Salt and pepper
Good pinch chopped fresh parsley, to garnish

Preheat the oven to 400°F/200°C.

Lightly cook the diced vegetables in the butter with the garlic and rosemary for a few minutes until softened. Drain and keep to one side. Fry the chops in the butter remaining in the pan for about 3–4 minutes on each side until golden. Remove and drain. Add the white wine to the pan and boil to reduce until almost dry. This will help release all the flavors into the sauce. Add the *jus*, bring just to a simmer, then strain through a sieve.

Shape the potatoes into cylinders and slice them ⅛ in (3 mm) thick. You will need about ten slices per chop. Quickly pan-fry the potatoes in the fat or dripping until golden and barely tender, then drain them well.

Place the chops in the braising dish and spoon the vegetables over them. Season with salt and pepper. Layer the potatoes on top of the vegetables, overlapping them. Pour the *jus* around and bring to a simmer. Place in the preheated oven and braise them for about 40–50 minutes.

Remove the chops with the vegetables and potatoes still on top. Bring the sauce to a boil,

skimming off any impurities. It should be rich and dark, thick enough to coat the back of a spoon. Place the chops in hot bowls, pour the sauce around them and sprinkle with chopped parsley.

Homemade Haggis

This is not a recipe to make on a daily basis, but if you've never eaten it before and you feel like trying it, you will be more than pleasantly surprised.

Haggis is probably the earliest example of the Great British sausage/pudding; it used to be made wherever oats were grown in Britain, although now it is associated mostly with Scotland. It is traditionally eaten at Hogmanay (New Year) and on Burns Night (25th of January). The poet Robert Burns called haggis "Great chieftain o' the puddin' race," devoting a whole poem to it, and Queen Victoria was taken with it as well. Visiting the Atholls of Blair Castle, she wrote, "There were several Scotch dishes, two soups, and the celebrated "Haggis" which I tried last night and really liked very much. The Duchess was delighted with my taking it." I personally love to eat a good haggis with mashed potatoes or "tatties," and mashed turnips or "neeps," the real Scottish way. (The mashed "turnips" in Scotland are, in fact, mashed "rutabagas" to the English.) Mixing the rutabagas with the mashed potatoes is a good idea because it gives the haggis more flavor.

Haggis has a ground meat-like consistency that certainly isn't short of flavor. I like to make individual serving haggises (traditional haggises are cooked in the sheep's paunch or stomach). It can also be made into a steamed haggis pudding by simply making the recipe, placing the mixture into two 2 quart (1.75 liter) pudding molds, covering them with buttered foil, and then steaming for 3½ hours. Alternatively, you can use individual 1¼ cups (300 ml) pudding molds and steam them for 1½–2 hours. The haggis can be served with gravy made from the cooking liquid.

BELOW
Lancashire Hot-pot

2½ lb (1.1 kg) sheep heart and liver, combined
Chicken Stock (page 33) or water
Carrot, onion, celery, and leek, chopped (optional)
6 large onions, finely chopped
2 tablespoons (25 g) unsalted butter or a little
    cooking oil
6 oz (175 g) steel-cut oats
4 oz (100 g) shredded suet
½ teaspoon chopped fresh thyme
½ teaspoon chopped fresh sage
2 teaspoons salt
Pinch of cayenne pepper
Pinch of black pepper
Finely grated zest and juice of 1 lemon
    (optional)
8–16 oz (225–450 g) pig's caul to wrap the haggis
    (page 11, optional, needed if not using
    pudding molds), soaked overnight in cold
    water
Mashed Potatoes (page 124), to serve

Wash the sheep heart and liver, place in a pan, and cover with chicken stock or water. (Chicken stock will give you a stronger flavor and more of a jellied finish.) It's best to add some chopped carrot, onion, celery, and leek to the stock or water to increase the flavor. The organ meat can now be simmered for 12 hours. After the meat has cooked, let it cool in the pan, then set in stock overnight. The heart and liver can now be ground in a meat grinder with a medium blade. Because liver has a very powerful taste, I prefer to use only half of one to balance the flavors.

The cooking liquid should be tasted for flavor and seasoning. If it tastes a little weak, then simply return to a boil and reduce it to increase the depth of flavor. Up to 2½ cups (600 ml) of stock will be needed for the haggis mixture to give a moist texture.

The chopped onions can be lightly softened in the butter or a drop of oil, without browning, then allowed to cool. The steel-cut oats can be toasted to a golden brown color. All the ingredients can now be mixed together, including the meat, herbs, salt,

cayenne, and pepper, plus the stock to finish the mixture. It should be well seasoned, giving a full flavor with a bite from the cayenne pepper. Lemon zest and juice can also be added to this mixture to lift the other flavors. Divide the mixture into 8–10 servings.

If you are using pig's caul, drain the soaked caul, squeeze out excess water, and place it on a chopping board. Cut into 8–10 evenly sized pieces. Wrap each serving of the haggis mixture in the caul to make oval shapes. To keep the shape and prevent the caul from splitting, also wrap each serving in buttered foil. If pig's caul is unavailable, then simply wrap each serving in plastic wrap twice, then again in foil.

To cook, simply boil any remaining stock with the addition of water to reach the amount needed to cover the haggis. The haggis servings can now be cooked in the simmering liquid for 45–60 minutes. After they have cooked, they will keep hot in the stock. Some stock can be strained off and made into a gravy for the haggis. I always like to serve them straight from the stock, the mixture being moist enough because of the added stock. Of course, while it the haggis cooks the mashed turnips/rutabagas will also be cooking on the stove along with mashed potatoes to finish the dish.

Variation

Very late one evening when I was staying in a hotel in Glasgow, I became restless and decided to pop into a fish and chip shop for a bite to eat. To my surprise I ended up having the speciality of the house. It was battered deep-fried haggis with curry sauce – certainly a dish I hadn't tried before and I was surprised that I really loved it!

So there's another option, if you have any haggis left over. After the haggis is cold, just lightly flour it, dip in batter (lager mixed with self-rising flour to a thick consistency makes a delicious batter), and deep-fry until golden. Now, simply serve it with a curry sauce.

Faggots in Onion Gravy

The word "faggot" means a bundle, as of twigs for kindling a fire, so almost anything can be brought together to make that bundle. I make these "faggots" with beef and organ meats in this recipe, and also with pigeon in *Rich Ground Squab on a Potato Cake with Mustard Cabbage*, page 252.

I usually use trimmings from cuts of beef when making these "faggots." Pig's caul is the classic wrapping for them. Your butcher might be able to get some for you; if so, soak it in cold water for 24 hours before using. Or, you can fry the "faggots" without the caul, as you would brown meatballs, but the finish and flavor won't be quite the same.

The best dishes to serve with "faggots" are *Colcannon* (page 126) or *Mashed Potatoes* (page 124).

SERVES 4

2 onions, finely chopped
1 garlic clove, crushed
½ teaspoon fresh thyme leaves
½ teaspoon chopped fresh sage
½ teaspoon chopped fresh parsley
4 tablespoons (50 g) unsalted butter
⅔ cup (150 ml) *Veal or Beef Jus* (page 34)
6 oz (175 g) lean beef rump or topside, well trimmed
6 oz (175 g) ox heart, trimmed
6 oz (175 g) ox kidney, trimmed
6 oz (175 g) lamb's liver, trimmed
Salt and pepper
1 egg
1 lb (450 g) pig's caul, soaked in cold water for 24 hours (page 11)

To Finish

5 cups (1.2 liters) *Veal or Beef Stock* (page 34)
1 oz (25 g) beef drippings
Onion Gravy (page 50)

Cook the chopped onions, garlic, and herbs in the butter until soft. Add the veal or beef *jus* and boil to reduce by half. Let the mixture cool, then allow it to set in the refrigerator.

Grind the various meats in a meat grinder with a medium blade. Place all the ground meat in a mixer and beat slowly, adding salt and pepper to taste. The salt will also thicken the meat, giving a gelatinous texture. Add the egg and the reduced, cooled onion mixture. The meat mixture is now ready, and is best left chilled for 2–3 hours to allow it to become firm.

To form the "faggots," squeeze any excess water from the caul and cut it into eight 8 in (20 cm) squares. Spoon about ½ cup (3 oz) of the meat mixture into the center of each square and wrap, turning the caul around the meat to form firm ball shapes.

When you are ready to cook the "faggots," warm the veal or beef stock. Fry the "faggots" in the drippings until brown on all sides, then place them in the stock and simmer very gently for 12–15 minutes until beginning to firm up. Remove the pan from the heat and let the "faggots" rest. Allow them to cool in the cooking liquid and then chill them. The liquid will set like a jelly and will preserve the "faggots" for up to a week in the refrigerator.

When you want to serve the "faggots," warm them gently in the jelly for 15–20 minutes until tender. To serve, lift them from the liquid. Pour the onion gravy on top and serve.

Note: When they are cooked, the "faggots" can be frozen for up to 1 month. The freezing process softens and improves the texture.

Bolognese Sauce or Beef Fillet, Bacon, Chicken Liver, and Red Wine Ragu

Spaghetti Bolognese, which has become so much part of British diets, is a great Italian dish – or is it? In fact, Bolognese sauce doesn't really exist in Italy. The only sauce that resembles the British one is the *Ragù Bolognese*, a sauce that must contain at least two kinds of meats, beef and pork being the classics. The recipe I present here has three kinds of meat – beef, bacon, and chicken livers.

From reading and researching through many books and recipes, and having had the pleasure of eating many bowls of spaghetti (with a glass of red wine to help them along), this recipe has become my favorite. The ingredients work very well together. If you are not a fan of bacon or chicken livers, simply replace them with extra beef. An extravagant ingredient, you'll notice, is the beef fillet, the most expensive cut of beef. The results are so delicious that it's money well spent. I use only beef fillet end pieces, though, which you'll sometimes find at half the price of the prime cut. The meat can be either coarsely ground or shredded by hand to give a meatier texture.

Please don't be put off by these extras. The recipe can still be made using everyday ground beef with red wine and canned Italian puréed tomatoes, or "passata," available in almost every supermarket). The flavors are full and the consistency is very saucy, rather than simply a moist ground meat.

The pasta to go with this sauce is really up to you. Homemade linguine, fettuccine, or tagliatelle would be great, but packaged dried spaghetti or other pastas will go with the sauce perfectly.

The method might sound like a lot of work, but it isn't really: we use only two pans and do a bit of chopping. The result is exceptional and once you've tried it you won't want to make your Bolognese any other way.

SERVES 4–6

6 oz (175 g) chicken livers, cut into rough ½ in
    (1 cm) dice
Butter
6 strips of bacon, finely diced
1 large or 2 medium onions, finely chopped
1 large or 2 medium carrots, finely chopped
2 celery sticks, finely chopped
1 large garlic clove, finely chopped or crushed
1–1½ cups (225–350 ml) red wine
1 lb (450 g) beef fillet trimmings, coarsely ground
    or shredded
Olive oil
8 oz (225 g) tomato "passata"
1 teaspoon tomato paste
6 tomatoes, blanched, peeled and cut into ½ in
    (1 cm) dice (or a 400 g/14 oz can of chopped
    tomatoes, drained of all liquid)

⅔–¾ cup (150–200 ml) *Veal or Beef Jus* (page 34)
Salt, pepper, and freshly grated nutmeg

Whenever using chicken livers for any recipe it's best to soak them for 24 hours in milk. This helps release excess blood from the livers, making them less bitter. After they've been soaked, dry them on a cloth and cut into ½ in (1 cm) dice.

Melt a heaping teaspoon of butter in a frying-pan and when it bubbles add the diced bacon. Fry until golden before transferring it to a saucepan.

Now, place the onions, carrots, celery, and garlic in the frying-pan. The vegetables heighten any bacon flavor left in the pan. Cook for a few minutes until slightly softened and browned. Add to the bacon. Stir them together and add ½ cup (125 ml) red wine. Over a medium–high heat, allow this mixture to reduce by at least three-fourths until almost dry. Add another ½ cup (125 ml) and continue with the same process until all the wine has been added and reduced.

While the wine is reducing, the beef can be seasoned with the salt, pepper, and nutmeg. Heat the frying-pan with some olive oil until very hot. Fry the beef, a handful or two at a time, until well sealed and browned. Place to one side. Season the chicken livers and fry them in olive oil very quickly to seal. Also place them aside. Add the "passata," the tomato purée, half of the diced tomato, and the *jus* to the vegetables. Bring to a simmer. The beef can now be added, still keeping the liver separate.

Return to a simmer and cook for 45 minutes. At this point, if the sauce is too thick then simply thin it with water. Add the chicken livers, return to a simmer, and cook for another 15–20 minutes. Add the remaining tomato dice for an extra texture. Check the consistency and the seasoning, and the Bolognese *Ragù* is ready to serve.

Try a spoonful of this over some delicious buttered pasta with freshly grated Parmesan cheese – and you're actually very English.

Note: For an even richer finish, add an extra ½ cup (125 ml) red wine and a dash of Worcestershire sauce. Fresh oregano or basil can be added for a herby *ragù*.

Braised Oxtail

This traditional British dish has become my "signature dish." Although it's not possible to buy oxtail at the time of publication, Oxtail is so delicious and such a Great British classic that I find it exciting to cook and even more exciting to eat. You can pick up the tails and eat them with your fingers and simply dip your bread in the bowl to mop up the sauce. The oxtails are also very good served with creamy *Mashed Potatoes* (page 124).

SERVES 4–6

4 oxtails, trimmed of fat
4 oz (100 g) beef drippings
8 oz (225 g) carrots, chopped
8 oz (225 g) onions, chopped
8 oz (225 g) celery sticks, chopped
8 oz (225 g) leeks, chopped
1 lb (450 g) tomatoes, chopped
Sprig of thyme
1 bay leaf
1 garlic clove, crushed
2½ cups (600 ml) red wine
2½ qts (2.25 liters) *Veal Stock* (page 34)
Salt and pepper

BELOW
Bolognese Sauce

1 carrot, finely diced
1 onion, finely diced
2 celery sticks, finely diced
½ small leek, finely diced
4 tomatoes, peeled, seeded and diced
1 heaping tablespoon chopped fresh parsley

For this recipe, the veal stock should be very liquid, not reduced to a sauce consistency (*jus*), so that it won't become too strong when braising the tails. Oxtails can be used in place of veal bones when making the stock for extra beef flavor.

Preheat the oven to 400°F/200°C.

First, separate the trimmed tails between the joints and season with salt and pepper. In a large pan, fry the tails in the drippings until brown on all sides, then drain them in a colander. Fry the chopped carrots, onions, celery, and leeks in the same pan, collecting all the residue from the tails. Add the chopped tomatoes, thyme, bay leaf, and garlic and continue to cook for a few minutes. Place the tails in a large braising pan with the vegetables. Pour the red wine into the first pan and boil to reduce until almost dry. Add some of the stock then pour onto the meat in the braising pan and cover with the remaining stock. Bring the oxtails to a simmer and braise them in the preheated oven for 1½–2 hours until the meat is tender.

Lift the pieces of meat from the sauce and place to one side. Push the sauce through a sieve into a pan, then boil to reduce it, skimming off all impurities, until it reaches a sauce consistency.

While the sauce is reducing, quickly cook the diced garnish carrot, onion, celery, and leek in a tablespoon of water until soft. When the sauce is ready, add the oxtails and the diced vegetable garnish and simmer until the tails are warmed through. Add the diced tomato and spoon into hot bowls, allowing three or four oxtail pieces per serving. Sprinkle with chopped parsley and serve.

See also

Boiled Bacon and Vegetable "Main-course" Soup
(page 17)
Coarse Pork Pâté (page 275)
Cornish Pasty (page 273)
Homemade Pork Pie (page 280)
Individual Roast Beef with Bitter Onions
(page 232)
One-piece Roast Pork with Caramelized Apple and Chestnut Brussels Sprouts (page 234)
Stilton and Red Onion Salad with Peppered Beef Fillet
(page 99)
Roast Leg of Lamb (page 234)
Roast Rib of Beef (page 236)
Sausage Loaf (page 276)

Sunday Dinner Roast

It was in the nineteenth century that taking a meal in the middle of the day – a lunch – became the norm. And it is probably since then that the Sunday afternoon dinner has turned into a Great British institution. Presumably it developed because Sunday was generally a day of rest, when the family could go to church together and then come home and eat together. And in the country renowned for its meat, what better for that meal than a cut of meat?

Originally, roasting meant cooking meat over a fire. This would have been what primitive man did, spearing pieces of his kill with sticks and holding them over fire. Roasting was also the most logical process in the days of huge open fires when food was revolved above or beside the fire by means of a spit. As the meat revolved over the fire, the fat in it melted and basted the meat. However, this all changed in about the nineteenth century when the enclosed fire – or the domestic oven – was developed. Meat cooked in an oven is sometimes said to be baked rather than roasted, but I don't entirely agree. The meat is exposed to all-round heat but, as with good roasting, it is always basted during the cooking time. "Baking" indicates an almost dry form of cooking – and I certainly am not fond of a dry roast. Whatever the truth, traditionalists and perfectionists keep the argument going, but the two terms – roasted and baked – have become virtually interchangeable in relation to oven-cooked meat.

That England became so well known for its roasts was primarily due to the fact that fuel was available. England had plenty of trees which, when burned, gave off the high heat necessary for roasting, while elsewhere only slower cooking methods, such as simmering or stewing, were possible (done over furze or peat fires). Another reason roasting became so particularly English lies in its agriculture. England's pasture lands are particularly lush because of the mildness of the weather and the amount of rain, and this produces lots of grass and hay which, in turn, makes animals fat and flavorful. The British have farmed animals specifically for eating at the table from the earliest times, while the French tend to cook animals that have worked for years on the land, and these are older, tougher, and stringier. This partly explains a fundamental difference in culinary styles. The French generally have to bone, roll, and braise or stew meats with other ingredients to make them taste good. The quality of British meat, which I think is far and away the best in the world, meant that Britons could excel at "plain roasts."

Roasting meat in a conventional modern oven is, on the surface, very straightforward, yet it arouses great controversy – should meat be roasted at high heat, a low heat, or a combination of both? Those in favor of high-heat roasting claim that meat cooked this way is the best in flavor, and because of the initial searing, that it has a wonderfully browned outside crust. Lovers of slow-roasts criticize the way in which meat shrinks at higher temperatures, and boast of the tenderness of meat cooked by their favored process. Fans of the combination method sear their roasts first at a very high temperature, then reduce the heat for the rest of the cooking time.

Nobody is completely right or completely wrong for each of the methods is correct if applied to a particular cut of meat. The thing to remember with almost all roasts is to sear and seal the meat before placing it in the oven. This will hold in all of its natural juices and flavors, resulting in a much tastier and succulent roast.

A Swedish diplomat in the 1690s, Per Kalm who was always eager to comment on British cooking, observed the English dining habits on one of his visits to England: "The Englishmen understand almost better than any other people the art of properly roasting a joint, which also is not to be wondered at; because the art of cooking as practiced by most Englishmen does not extend much beyond roast beef and plum pudding." Things have changed since then, as we know – but roasting is still one of the classic Great British ways of cooking and always will be.

Individual Roast Beef with Bitter Onions

Roasts were always big cuts of meat in the past, placed on the spit and roasted in front of the fire. Here, you can keep the meat as a whole roast, but occasionally I do like to cut bigger roasts into separate servings. First, they cook a lot quicker, and it's nice to have your own individual "roast."

It's best to buy a 2 lb (900 g) piece of sirloin. This will guarantee a virtually sinew-free cut. You should also trim away any excess fat to keep the meat lean. All you need to do now is split the meat lengthwise and then each in half again. You now have four mini sirloin cuts. The bitter onions give a slightly sweet-sharp flavor, and when served with the gravy, they balance well with the taste of the roast.

The beauty of this dish is that a few basic ingredients result in lots of flavor. The onions can be fried in advance and then simply re-heated.

SERVES 4

Butter
4 large onions, sliced
Pinch of light brown sugar (optional)
4 × 6–8 oz (175–225 g) trimmed individual sirloins
    (as above)
Cooking oil
1 cup of red wine
1¼ cups (300 ml) *Veal or Beef Jus* (page 34) or
    alternative (page 11)
Salt and pepper

Melt a heaping teaspoon of butter in a frying-pan and add the onions. With this amount of onions it may be best to cook them in 2–3 batches. Allow the onions to cook fairly rapidly, taking on a deep color while also becoming tender. As onions cook, the natural sugar content almost caramelizes. Yellow Spanish onions are good ones for roasting. When all are fried, place them in a single pan and season with salt and pepper. If when you taste them they are slightly too bitter, then the brown sugar can be added. It's important not to add too much or the onions will taste artificial.

To roast the beef, season each individual "cut," and in a roasting pan, cook the meat on a medium heat in a small amount of oil, fat-side down. As the meat becomes hot, it will also cook, tenderize, and release the fat so it won't have a "raw" taste.

When it's well browned, turn the beef and brown the other sides. The cuts can now be roasted to your specification. For a good medium-rare pink finish, roast at 400°F/200°C for 8–10 minutes. Medium will take 10–12 minutes and well done, 12–15 minutes.

When they are roasted, it's important let the cuts rest for 5–10 minutes; this relaxes the meat, giving it a more tender finish.

While the beef is resting, pour off any excess fat from the pan, re-heat the pan, and add the red wine. This will heighten any flavors. Reduce by three-fourths before adding the *jus*.

Bring the liquid to a simmer and cook for a few minutes before straining through a fine sieve. Any excess oils/fat will now rise to the top and can be spooned off.

To serve, divide the bitter onions among four plates, carve each roast into three slices, and place the slices either at the side or on top of the onions. The red wine gravy can now either be poured around the meat or served separately.

I serve the *Classic Roast Potatoes* on page 238 with this dish. To make them even richer and to finish with a shine, the potatoes can be brushed with some of the red wine gravy. It's best to take a third of the sauce and reduce it by half to increase its strength and flavor, leaving the right consistency to brush over the potatoes.

BELOW
Individual Roast Beef with Bitter Onions

Roast Leg of Lamb

With the introduction of potatoes, daily meals changed to become "a meat with two veggies," and long may this continue. It makes for a great Sunday afternoon dinner, with a gathering of family and friends enjoying very simple foods. Lamb wasn't part of this tradition until well into the eighteenth century, since sheep were valued primarily for their wool, and young sheep, or lamb, was only available occasionally.

This is a recipe for a simple leg of lamb with no other flavorings apart from salt and pepper – two of my favorites – but I have included some variations at the end of the method. There are also plenty of recipes throughout the book for vegetables to accompany the roast.

SERVES 4–6

1 leg of lamb on the bone (usually 3¼ lb/1.5 kg)
Cooking oil
Salt and pepper
1¼ cups (300 ml) *Chicken Stock* (page 33), or
    2½ cups (600 ml) for gravy lovers

Ask your butcher to remove the pelvic bone from the cut. This will help when carving the meat. Preheat the oven to 400°F/200°C. Heat a roasting pan with a few tablespoons of cooking oil.

Season the leg with salt and pepper and place in the pan, presentation-side down. This can now be fried over a medium heat and "browned" until completely golden.

Place in the preheated oven and roast, basting from time to time, cooking the meat as you like it. Here are the times to watch:
Medium-rare – 15 minutes per 1 lb (450 g) + 15 minutes
Medium – 20 minutes per 1 lb (450 g) + 20 minutes
Well done – 25–30 minutes per 1 lb (450 g) + 25–30 minutes

When it is roasted, remove the leg of lamb from the oven and let it rest for 15–20 minutes before carving.

While the lamb is resting, pour away any fat from the pan, leaving in any cooking residue. Heat it on top of the stove, adding the chicken stock. Cook and simmer, allowing the stock to reduce by a third. You will now have a very loose gravy full of natural lamb flavors. This can be lightly thickened with arrowroot or cornstarch. Either thickener can be thinned with water, or red or white wine.

The lamb is now ready to serve.

Note: *Veal Jus* (page 34) can be used in place of the chicken stock for an instant, thick gravy.

Variations

Here are some other flavors that can be used to give the lamb flavor an extra dimension.
1   Simply rub the leg with a cut clove of garlic before browning.
2   Make small incisions across the leg and fill with thin slices of garlic and small sprigs of rosemary.
3   Pour honey over the leg for the last 20 minutes of roasting, basting every 5 minutes to leave a glaze.
4   Mix 2 tablespoons of clear honey with 2 tablespoons of teriyaki marinade and 2 tablespoons of soy sauce. Boil all three together until thick and sticky. When the meat has cooked, brush the leg with the spicy, sticky glaze.
5   Mix 2–3 cloves of crushed garlic with the finely grated zest of 1 lemon and a tablespoon of chopped mint. Cover the leg after it has been browned and roast it. The gravy will also pick up all of these flavors.
6   Brush the leg with red currant or mint jelly 10–15 minutes before the end of its cooking time.

Roast Pork with Caramelized Apple and Chestnut Brussels Sprouts

The relationship between pork and apples is one that has lasted for hundreds of years and will continue for many more. A pig always eats windfall apples if it gets the chance, and the story goes that, in medieval days, the residue of dry, mashed apples left after pressing crab-apples for verjuice would be cooked with a piece of pork. Both apples and pork working together set the tradition, which the British have continued.

The pork featured here is cut into individual servings, similar to *Individual Roast Beef with Bitter Onions* (page 232). If you're not sure about cutting the loin, then simply leave it as a whole roast. The apples are caramelized in halves, giving a more solid texture.

(For the classic *Apple Sauce*, see page 44.) The garnish of apples and Brussels sprouts will work with just about any roast pork – and the sprouts are also particularly good served with a holiday roast turkey. For an extra garnish, which tastes good and creates another interest on the plate, try *Sage Fritters* (page 58).

SERVES 4

2 lb (900 g) pork loin, boned weight, skinned
    (keep the bones, chopped, to make the gravy)
2 apples, peeled, cored, and halved
1¼ cups (300 ml) dry cider
Sugar
8–12 oz (225–350 g) Brussels sprouts
2 large onions, sliced
Butter
2–3 oz (50–75 g) chopped chestnuts (if using fresh,
    check cooking times on page 332)
Salt and pepper

For the sauce

Pork bones, chopped
Small bunch sage
About 1 cup (200–250 ml) *Chicken Stock* (page 33)
4 tablespoons (50 g) butter, chilled and diced

When buying the loin, it's best to ask for the skin to be removed with some fat along with it. This is what you will use for the crackling. The crackling, apples, and gravy can be made in advance, at least 1 hour before roasting the pork loin.

For the crackling, preheat the oven to 400°F/200°C. Score the skin with a sharp knife and season it with a sprinkling of salt. The skin can now be placed on a wire rack in a baking pan. Bake in the preheated oven for 40–50 minutes. During this time, excess fat will run through the wire rack, leaving you with a crisp piece of crackling. The excess fat left in the can can now be used for roasting the pork loin pieces so that no flavors are wasted.

BELOW
*Roast Pork with Caramelized Apple and
Chestnut Brussels Sprouts*

Place the four apple halves in a saucepan and cover with the cider. Bring to a simmer, cook for 1 minute, and allow to cool. During this time the apples will continue cooking. To finish, remove the apples and reserve the cider.

To make the gravy, roast the chopped pork bones in the oven while the crackling is cooking. At that temperature they should only take 20–30 minutes. (For extra flavor, also roast with the bones a mixture of 1 onion, 1 carrot, 1 small leek, and a few sticks of celery, all chopped.) When all are roasted, transfer them to a saucepan. Add the cider from the apples with a few sage leaves. Bring to a boil and reduce by three-fourths. Now it's time to add the chicken stock and bring it to a simmer. The roasted bones will give the stock a deeper color. Cook for 20–30 minutes, allowing the stock to reduce by a third.

Strain the stock. This can now be thickened by whisking in the butter to create a flavorful gravy. It can also be thickened with cornstarch mixed first with a little water. Set to one side.

Shred the Brussels sprouts. Sweat the sliced onions in a heaping teaspoon of butter for a few minutes, allowing them to soften and take on a golden color. Remove and allow them to cool. While the onions are cooking, blanch the sprouts in boiling, salted water for 30 seconds–1 minute. Remove them from the pan and allow them to cool, refrigerated, spread on a dish cloth. These two operations can be done well in advance.

To cook the pork, cut the loin into four mini loins like small but thick sirloin steaks. Season with salt and pepper. Begin browning them in a roasting pan on top of the stove over a medium heat, fat-side down (using the pork fat from the crackling). This process will now slowly cook away the fat and, at the same time, leave a rich golden color. Brown the pork completely.

Place the roasting pan in the oven at 400°F/200°C and cook the pork, fat-side down, for 12–15 minutes. After the individual roasts have cooked, remove from the oven and let them rest for 12–15 minutes before carving. If you'd prefer to serve the pork loin whole, simply follow the instructions for the individual loins, but roasting the whole loin for 30–40 minutes.

While the pork is roasting, finish the apples and sprouts. Melt a heaping teaspoon of butter in a frying-pan, place the apples in it, presentation-side down, and pan-fry until golden. Turn them over and cook for another minute or two. To finish, sprinkle them with sugar and glaze under a hot preheated broiler. The apples are now golden, glazed, and ready to serve.

Melt a heaping teaspoon of butter in a wok or frying-pan. Add the onions, sprouts, and chestnuts. Simply fry for a few minutes, seasoning with salt and pepper (a pinch of nutmeg also works well) until hot.

Spoon the mixture onto the plates. Place a glazed apple beside it. Each roast can now be carved into three slices and arranged beside the Brussels sprouts in a fan shape. Break the crackling into pieces and place it on top. Now, simply pour the sauce around the meat.

Note: The dish is now complete. If you are serving it with your Christmas dinner then, obviously, *Classic Roast Potatoes* (page 238) would be wonderful. Otherwise, I suggest good, creamy *Mashed Potatoes* (page 124).

Roast Rib of Beef

This book was written in Britain when beef was not allowed to be sold on the bone – the classic British way over the centuries. The British people are told it will return, and I do hope so, because the beef prepared this way maintains a much sweeter flavor and more juices are created to give a better gravy. Good Scottish beef was always the best to choose.

If meat on the bone is available, select a three rib roast. This will weigh approximately 8 lb (3 kg) including bones. The same rib piece can be bought off the bone. Buy it "oven-ready" (this means the beef will be chined, leaving the rib bones attached; ask your butcher to give you the bone trimmings to rest the roast on while it cooks.

Serve your roast beef with roast potatoes and Yorkshire pudding. A vegetable that goes particularly well with the roast beef is *Parsnip Purée* (from *Steamed and Braised Mallard with Parsnip Tart*, page 261): its creamy texture served with the moist and tender rib is sensational (double the amount for this recipe). Other good accompaniments to a roast rib, very much along French lines, are *French Fries* (page 127) and a simple green salad. Offer a mayonnaise mixed with horseradish cream and a touch of mustard. We know this will work well with the beef and you can also dip your fries in it.

Cooking oil

1 × 3-rib-bone forerib of beef, oven-ready, approximate weight 8 lb (3 kg), or a boned and rolled rib from the same-sized cut, approximate weight 4½–5½ lb/2–2.5 kg)

4 shallots, peeled and roughly chopped

2 garlic cloves, halved

Sprig of thyme

½ bottle of red wine

1¼ cups (300 ml) *Veal Jus* (page 34)

Salt and pepper

Preheat the oven to 375°F/190°C.

Heat a roasting pan with 2–3 tablespoons of cooking oil. Season the beef rib generously with salt and pepper. Place in the hot pan and brown and seal on all sides. Any bone trimmings, if available, can now be put into the pan, placing the beef on top of them. Roast in the preheated oven, allowing 15 minutes per 1 lb (450 g), whether on or off the bone, for a medium-rare finish.

Baste the beef every 15 minutes to guarantee an all-round flavor and seasoning. Half-way through the cooking time, turn the roast over, sprinkling the shallots, garlic, and thyme around the meat in the pan.

When the cooking time is complete, remove the beef from the oven and roasting pan. Cover with foil and let it rest for 20–30 minutes before carving.

Pour any excess fat from the roasting pan, leaving in the shallots, garlic, and thyme, which will have collected much of the beef juices and flavor. Heat the pan on top of the stove and add a third of the wine. This will instantly dissolve the residue left in the pan. Reduce until almost dry. Add another third of the wine, and repeat the boiling and reducing until almost dry and you have used the remaining wine. Add the *jus* and return to a simmer. Cook for 5–10 minutes before pushing through a sieve, extracting the juices from the shallots, garlic, and thyme. The red wine gravy is now ready. Adjust the seasoning with salt and pepper.

After letting the beef rest, it will be ready to carve. If serving "à meat and two veggies," *Classic Roast Potatoes* (page 238) and almost any two vegetables featured in the vegetable section (pages 95–127) will complete your meal.

Note: Chicken or beef stock or water can be used in place of the *jus* to create the gravy. A sprinkling of flour in the roasting pan before adding the liquid will help thicken it.

The recipe for traditional *Horseradish Sauce* to accompany the beef can be found on page 55.

Yorkshire Pudding

The most renowned classic of all Great British dishes is probably Roast Beef and Yorkshire Pudding. Why Yorkshire? It must have been a thrifty cook in the north of England who originally devised a way of utilizing the fat that dripped into a pan under the spit-roasting meat. A batter pudding that collected the flavors of the beef fat and juices was a perfect answer. The original Yorkshire would have been ¾–1½ in (2–3 cm) thick, and it was turned during its cooking time to give you a crisp top and bottom with the rich pudding inside. It's often cooked this way today.

The pudding was then cut into squares and served as a separate course before the roast, with lots of gravy poured over it. (The idea was that it fill the diner up a bit, so that the roast beef would serve more people.) These days, Yorkshire tends to be lighter, crisper, and quite often cooked in individual molds. The puddings are then served, usually two a serving (but most people will eat even more), *with* the beef instead of as a separate course.

The recipe will give you a well risen, crisp pudding. It can be cooked as one thick pudding, but it will need to be turned over halfway through its cooking time. This only works if you bake it in a roasting pan. Another classic recipe using this batter is *Toad in the Hole* (page 370). There the batter has been reduced to accommodate the amount required.

You'll notice I've included an egg white in this recipe which gives the batter even more of a lift, for a lighter, crisper finish.

MAKES UP TO 24 PUDDINGS

2 cups (225 g) all-purpose flour

Pinch of salt

3 eggs

1 egg white (optional)

1¼– 2 cups (300–450 ml) milk

Oil, lard, or dripping, for cooking

Preheat the oven to 425°F/220°C. This amount will fill 10–12 4 in (10 cm) individual pans, approximately two 12-cup muffin pans or 1 medium roasting pan, approximately 8 ¥ 10 in (20 ¥ 25 cm). Muffin pans can also be used for the individual puddings.

The batter can be made to be used immediately, but I recommend at least ½–1 hour of resting time. For absolute perfection I let it rest, refrigerated, for 24 hours and then re-whisk just before baking. Any resting time relaxes the batter, creating a different consistency.

Sift the flour with the salt. Add the eggs and egg white, if using. Whisk in 1¼ cups (300 ml) of the milk. This gives you a thick batter that works very well. To check for the perfect consistency, simply lift a spoon in and out. The batter should hold and coat the back of a spoon. If it seems to have congealed after resting, then simply add some of the remaining milk until the right consistency is reached. The batter is now ready to cook.

Oil or grease your chosen pan(s) generously. Then heat these in the oven until they are almost smoking.

Now it's time to add the batter. For individual pans or muffin pans, fill each to almost full. For the medium roasting pan, just add all of the batter. Bake in the preheated oven for 25–30 minutes (individuals and muffin pans). An extra 5–10 minutes may still be needed for a crispy finish. A roasting pan will take 45 minutes to 1 hour.

Note: The *Onion Gravy* (page 50) is a great accompaniment.

Classic Roast Potatoes

Roast potatoes are a weekly institution in most British families and households. When it's time for that Sunday afternoon dinner, it's time for roast potatoes. For the very best results it's important to use the right kind of potato. Almost any potato can be roasted, but if you love that crisp edge with a light, fluffy, and creamy interior, then floury potatoes are needed. Russet or Idahos are the varieties that will always give you the

BELOW
Yorkshire Pudding

ABOVE
Classic Roast Potatoes

right result. These potatoes will take at least 1 hour to achieve the right finish; for extreme crispiness, cook for 1½ hours.

SERVES 4–6

6–9 medium potatoes (allowing 3 halves each)
Salt
Cooking oil or lard
All-purpose flour, seasoned

Preheat the oven to 400°F/200°C. Peel the potatoes and halve them lengthwise. The peeling side of the potatoes can now be scraped with a knife to give a smooth domed shape to all the halves. Place in a saucepan and cover with cold, salted water. Bring to a boil and then simmer for 5–6 minutes. Drain in a colander and let them stand for 2–3 minutes before shaking the colander gently. This will begin to break down the edge of the potatoes. These slightly rough edges will become crisp and crunchy during the roasting process.

Heat a frying-pan with ¼ in (5 mm) of oil or melted lard. When it's hot, the potatoes can be lightly rolled in flour, shaking off any excess and fried in the oil, turning them occasionally until completely golden brown.

Now, transfer the potatoes to a roasting pan. Pour some of the cooking oil into the pan (approximately ⅛ in/2–3 mm deep), sprinkle the potatoes with salt, and roast them in the oven for 30 minutes before turning in the pan. Roast for another 30 minutes. Remove the crisp roast potatoes from the pan and serve.

A heaping teaspoon of butter can be melted over the potatoes to enrich the crisp roast taste. For an ultra-crispy finish, increase the cooking time to 1½ hours, turning the potatoes in the pan half-way through.

"Banana" Roast Potatoes

To make these you need large potatoes. Peel them and cut them lengthwise. Shape them to look like bananas by cutting away the edges at each end, leaving sharp points and creating a curved edge in the center with a knife. Four "bananas" make one up one serving.

To roast the potatoes, par-boil them for 3–4 minutes before draining and allowing them to cool for 10 minutes. Heat olive or cooking oil in a roasting or frying pan and fry the potatoes to a golden brown. Before placing them in the oven, add a heaping teaspoon of butter. The potatoes will take 20–30 minutes to become rich in color and texture with the points almost burned. Season with coarse or table salt and serve.

See also

Rack on Black (page 190)
Roast Chicken Legs with Sea Salt and Thyme
(page 246)
Roast Grouse (page 247)
Roasted Parsnips (page 95)
Roast Guinness Lamb (page 194)
Roast Partridge on Toast with Wild Mushrooms
(page 255)
*Roast Pheasant with Bacon-braised Barley and a
Whiskey Cream Sauce* (page 258)
Slow-honey-roast Belly of Pork (page 184)
*Slow-roast Shoulder of Pork, with Pearl Barley and
Sage Stuffing* (page 209)
*Traditional Roast Turkey with Sage, Lemon, and
Chestnut Stuffing with all the Trimmings* (page 327)

Poultry
and Game

"Poultry," wrote the nineteenth-century French gastronome Brillat Savarin, "is for the cook what canvas is to the painter. It is served to us boiled, roasted, fried, hot or cold, whole or in pieces, with or without sauce, boned, skinned, stuffed, and always with equal success." I don't think anyone who cooks would disagree with him, since poultry, especially chicken, is incredibly versatile. Game, too, is one of my favorite ingredients, intense in flavor, and so versatile that it can be cooked in many ways – and it's very British.

"Poultry is for the cook what canvas is to the painter."

Brillat Savarin

Wild birds – which are now considered "game" – would have been an important part of the early Britons' diet, and they ate a wider variety of them than we would dream of today – seabirds such as guillemots, gannets, and puffins, as well as more familiar birds such as ducks, geese, herons, blackbirds, thrushes, and so on. Wild ox and wild pig would have been other sources of meat before the idea of domesticating animals was introduced. After this time, primitive man settled down to tend fields and to raise cattle, sheep, goats, and pigs – and, occasionally, chickens. It is thought that by the late Iron Age, the red jungle fowl from India had already been introduced and become naturalized. This bird arrived via Persia, Greece, and Rome, and was the ancestor of the domestic chicken, perhaps one of the most important introductions of all.

Many Roman techniques of animal raising became familiar in Britain during the 400 years of Roman occupation. The Romans liked to eat domestic fowl, and in special enclosures, they raised many more delicate varieties, among them pheasants, peacocks, partridges, and guinea fowl. (Romans did not care for quail, apparently believing the birds fed on poisonous herbs). They also built unique structures in which wild pigeons could nest and breed – *columbaria* – and these became blueprints for the medieval dovecotes still to be seen near or adjacent to very old houses. Also kept in special quarters near the kitchen were three other kinds of animals introduced by the Romans for food. Rabbits were brought from Spain (new-born rabbits were a particular delicacy), and collected dormice and snails were fed until they were fat and succulent, the latter too plump to be able to get back into their shells.

Throughout the Middle Ages, poultry and game were important to everyone, although there were many severe game laws which, at different times, forbade most people from hunting birds. The wealthy hunted on horseback for deer and boar in specially designated park areas, and they used trained falcons to catch wild birds. Trapping rabbits and native hare was more the province of the peasants and probably represented the major fresh meat part of the peasants' diet, along with any wild birds they could shoot. Chickens were far too valuable as egg layers to be killed and eaten before they were old and stringy, fit only for the cooking pot. (And other meat animals were usually slaughtered only in the fall). The wealthy, however, could roast the younger, better fed chickens on spits in front of the fire, as they did their large cuts of meat or venison. Smaller birds were roasted too, basted with butter and flour or breadcrumbs to protect them from the heat and then served on sops (croûtes) of bread to absorb the juices (much as the partridge – see *Roast Partridge on Toast with Wild Mushrooms*, a new British classic, on page 255 – and other game birds still are today). Over the years, thrushes, plovers, larks, finches, rooks, and blackbirds would all have been fattened, roasted, and eaten and many were sold in London at shops in the area still known as "Poultry" (near the heart of the City area) from the end of the thirteenth century.

Roast birds in medieval times were served with a black sauce (similar to a giblet gravy today), made

PAGE 240
Roast Pheasant with Bacon-braised Barley and a Whiskey Cream Sauce

with the offal (organ meats), or a white sauce (almonds and spices then, a bread sauce now). Saucing has always been important, and applesauce for goose, cranberry for turkey, and red currant for venison are very ancient and respected combinations. Older chickens, wild birds, and game meats were also boiled in pottages, the ancestors of our many game stews, and steamed in game and chicken pudding, and baked for pie fillings. British game pies are famous but none so famous – or perhaps infamous – as the Yorkshire Christmas pie once was. This consisted of boned turkey stuffed with a goose, then a chicken, followed by a partridge, and then a pigeon. These are placed in a thick pie crust and tucked around with chunks of hare, venison, wild birds, and masses of butter before being baked. The whole idea sounds awesome and not one I'm eager to try! In the eighteenth century, game and birds were potted, as was fish, and preserved with melted butter.

Birds, domestic or wild, were for many years a special food associated with celebrations. They were given as presents during the twelve days of Christmas (perhaps the origin of the "partridge in a pear tree"). Geese were traditionally roasted and served at Michaelmas, probably because the young birds would have eaten well throughout the summer, and become plump ("Christmas is coming, and the goose is getting fat"). It is also said that Queen Elizabeth I was eating goose on September 29, 1588, when she was told of the Spanish Armada's defeat, and she decreed that it be eaten on that day thereafter. (Geese were also given as part payment of rent in a bad year, for Michaelmas is one of the farming community's quarter days, when rent was due.)

Large birds such as swans, herons, and peacocks were always the centerpiece of feasts, but despite their splendor, they were all rather tough and stringy, so they were soon replaced by the succulent turkey, after its introduction from America in the sixteenth century.

This chapter includes many dishes that will stand as the centerpiece of our dinner tables, not merely to look at but, more importantly, to eat and enjoy. Several chicken dishes and various cooking methods are featured, along with a selection of game, including quail, grouse, pigeon, partridge, wild duck, venison, and hare. While the length of the ingredients list for many of the recipes might be long, most of them are everyday pantry items.

This chapter started with a Brillat Savarin quotation, so I thought I'd finish with one too: "Game," he writes, "is a healthy, warming, and savory food, fit for the most delicate palate and easy to digest. In the hands of an experienced cook, game can provide dishes of the highest quality which raises the culinary art to the level of science."

"Game is a healthy, warming, and savory food, fit for the most delicate palate and easy to digest."

Brillat Savarin

Chicken Pot Roast with Carrots and Potatoes

Pot roasting is a style of cooking that has been ignored far too long. It's actually a method of steaming, though done in an oven in a pot with a tight-fitting lid.

Many years ago the chicken would have been cooked with lashings of butter to create the steam. After the bird was cooked, stock would be added to the dish. My method turns that around, cooking the chicken in the steam created by the stock and then finishing it with butter.

This excerpt from Mark Strand's poem, "Pot Roast," sums up my feelings nicely – hopefully you'll feel exactly the same.

> I gaze upon the roast,
> that is sliced and laid out
> on my plate
> and over it
> I spoon the juices
> of carrot and onion.
> And for once I do not regret
> the passage of time.

SERVES 4

2 large onions, cut into ½ in (1 cm) dice,
    or 12 oz (350 g) pearl onions
1 lb (450 g) carrots, peeled
6 medium potatoes
3½ lb (1.6 kg) chicken
1 lemon
Olive oil
Bouquet garni of sage and thyme sprigs wrapped
    and tied in muslin or cheesecloth
1¼ –2½ cups (300–600 ml) *Chicken Stock*
    (page 33)
4 tablespoons (50 g) butter
Salt and pepper
Paprika (optional)

Preheat the oven to 400°F/200°C.

The choice of onions is up to you. The pearl onions work very well; if using them, before adding to the pot roast, place them in a pan of cold water and bring to a boil. Now, refresh them in cold water. This will take the rawness and acidity away.

A chopped large onion will also work with the flavors without needing to be blanched.

The carrots should be quartered lengthwise and then cut at an angle into ½–¾ in (1–2 cm) thick pieces.

As for the potatoes, I like to cut them at an angle lengthwise from "end to end," then simply trim a flat base at the thick ends and the potatoes will stand up in the pan, exposing the tops. These will turn a rich golden brown.

To season the chicken, first rub it with lemon and then squeeze the remaining juice into a cup and keep it to one side. Now, sprinkle the chicken with salt, black pepper, and paprika, if using. The paprika gives extra flavor to the bird and imparts a pink/red color. To sprinkle paprika evenly, here's a quick tip: simply place ½ teaspoon in a tea strainer and dust it across the skin. Heat a large frying-pan with a trickle of olive oil. The chicken can now be cooked all over to a rich golden brown.

After it has browned, place the bird in a large, deep braising pan. If you don't have a braising pan then use a roasting pan; this can then be covered with foil after all the other ingredients are added. Stand the potatoes around the the chicken and add the bouquet garni. Stir in half to three-fourths of the stock – the amount depends upon the size of the pan. The potatoes should be in at least 1 in (2.5 cm) of stock. You might need to add the full 2½ cups (600 ml). Brush the potato tops with butter, bring the pot to a simmer, and cover with a lid. The dish can now be placed in the preheated oven.

After 20 minutes, remove the lid and baste the chicken and potatoes with the stock. Add the carrots and onions and replace the lid. Continue to cook for another 20 minutes and then baste the bird and potatoes again. The lid can now be left off.

The last 20 minutes of cooking without a lid will help brown the bird and potatoes. During this time, baste once or twice more. After 1 hour total cooking time, the bird will be ready to remove. Cover with foil to keep warm while it relaxes.

The potatoes can now also be removed, brushed with some of the butter, and finished under the broiler to create a slightly burned tinge on the tops.

Skim excess fat from the remaining liquid and pour it off into a separate dish; you can use a spoonful or two of the liquid to keep the carrots and onions warm. You might find the stock will need to be reduced for a more intense flavor. Add the remaining butter for a softer finish. The vegetables (onions and carrots) can now be added. Pour in a teaspoon or two of the lemon juice to heighten the flavors and to give a very fresh lemony edge.

Divide the chicken into four servings, a part of a breast half with either the thigh or drumstick per serving. Arrange in bowls with three potatoes and a spoonful of carrots and onions. The rich lemony liquid can now be spooned over the vegetables and chicken and the dish served. It's a delicious dish that gives so many complex flavors from one pot – simple but good.

Note: An extra touch that also works very well is to finish the liquid with a little chopped fresh sage. Sage and lemon go very well together, especially when served with chicken.

Roast Chicken with Liver-thickened Gravy

This is a simple roast chicken, cooked as it would have been centuries ago – but in the oven instead of on a spit. It almost creates its own gravy in the pan while the vegetables roasted with it take on all the flavor and juices. Some white wine and chicken stock are added to the pan and reduced. Butter is mixed with the pounded chicken liver and added in turn, which enriches, thickens, and flavors the liquids, creating a sauce not unlike the black one served with chicken in the Middle Ages.

For the very best flavor, select a free-range chicken. Chicken livers will be included with the giblets of the bird.

SERVES 4

3–4 lb (1.5–1.75 kg) free-range chicken
4 tablespoons (50 g) butter, softened
Cooking oil
2 onions, peeled and quartered (root left on)
2 large carrots, peeled and quartered lengthwise
4 celery sticks, halved
Sprig of thyme
1 bay leaf
1¼ cups white wine
1¼ cups (300 ml) *Chicken Stock* (page 33) or water
1 oz (25 g) chicken livers
Salt and pepper

Preheat the oven to 375°F/190°C. Brush the chicken with some of the butter and season with salt (preferably sea-salt) and pepper. Heat a roasting pan or flameproof casserole dish with a spoonful of cooking oil. Place the chicken breast-side down and brown over a medium heat. When each breast and leg become a light golden brown, remove the bird from the pan. Scatter the vegetables, thyme, and bay leaf in the pan. Place the chicken breast-side down on top of the vegetables and roast for 25 minutes. Now, the bird can be turned over and basted. Continue to roast for another 35–40 minutes.

The chicken should now be beautifully roasted, with a deep golden finish. To test that the bird is cooked, press the thigh or drumstick between forefinger and thumb. The flesh should feel tender and give when it is pressed. Remove the chicken from the pan, cover with foil, and let it rest.

Pour off all the juices from the pan, leaving in the vegetables. Add the white wine to the pan, bring to a simmer and allow the liquid to reduce by half.

While the wine is reduces, skim off any fat from the juices saved. Add the chicken stock or water, bring to a boil, and reduce by half. If using water, a stock cube or some stock granules can be added for extra flavor.

While the sauce is reducing, purée the raw liver in a food processor with the remaining butter. This will take on a smooth texture.

When the sauce has reduced, lower the heat to a simmer. Cut up the chicken, into four servings. Arrange on plates with the onions, carrots, and celery.

Whisk the liver butter into the simmering gravy. Return to a gentle simmer and strain through a sieve. Spoon the liver gravy over the chicken.

The dish is now ready to serve. It really is delicious: the vegetables have become almost over-cooked, but they contain so much flavor from the chicken and from the stock it creates. The liver taste doesn't become too strong – it simply heightens the overall flavor of the dish.

Note: After the servings have been cut from the chicken, the carcasses can be pressed in a sieve, releasing even more juices into the sauce.

Red wine can be used in place of the white. Chopped chives can also be added to the sauce after it is strained.

Roast Chicken Legs with Sea Salt and Thyme

The sea salt in this recipe is used simply as a seasoning along with the thyme. It gives a crunchy texture to the skin when cooked, and at the same time, it sharpens all the other tastes.

The legs can simply be served roasted with a green salad, but I like to add even more flavors – mustard which has always been popular in British cooking, a little heavy cream, and a squeeze of lemon.

SERVES 4

4 large chicken legs
1 tablespoon olive oil
2 teaspoons coarse sea salt
1 teaspoon fresh thyme leaves
Butter
Squeeze of lemon juice
4 tablespoons heavy cream or crème fraîche
1 teaspoon English, Dijon, or wholegrain mustard
Pepper

Preheat the oven to 400°F/200°C.

The thigh bones from the legs can be removed, although this is not essential. If you do wish to take them out, simply turn the legs, skin-side down. Cut along the thigh bone, which will become exposed. Now, cut on either side against the bone, pulling the flesh away. Cut beneath the bone and then twist to remove it. (You may need to cut at the joint to free the bone.)

Heat a roasting pan or ovenproof frying-pan with the olive oil. Sprinkle the sea salt and thyme over the chicken legs, skin-side up. Lightly press the seasonings onto the skin to keep them attached.

Place the chicken pieces in the pan, skin-side down, and cook over a moderate heat for 5–6 minutes. During the cooking time, add a heaping teaspoon of butter; this will develop a nutty flavor. When the pieces are deep golden in color, turn the chicken legs over and continue to cook for another minute or two before placing in the preheated oven. The legs will now need to cook for a maximum of 20 minutes.

BELOW
Roast Chicken Legs with Sea Salt and Thyme

When they are cooked, remove the pan from the oven and take the legs from the pan, keeping them warm. I prefer to leave all the residue in the pan, but if you want a less buttery finish, you can pour the fat away. Add a squeeze of lemon juice to the pan along with a tablespoon or two of water. Bring to a simmer, adding the cream and mustard. When all is melted, mixed, and heated, strain through a tea strainer over the rich chicken pieces. Check the seasoning and add pepper to taste (you won't need any salt). The chicken is ready to serve.

A bowl of pasta goes very well with this dish.

Note: For extra thyme flavor, mix together 4 tablespoons (50 g) butter, ½ teaspoon chopped fresh thyme, zest of ¼–½ lemon, salt, and pepper. Rub the thyme butter underneath the skin of the chicken pieces. Cook as before.

Roast Grouse

You can order Scottish grouse on the Internet (see Suppliers, page 400). Several states in the US have hunting seasons for ruffed grouse; consult your state's hunting and game commission for dates and regulations. Red grouse (*Lagopus lagopus Scoticus*) are said by many to be the finest game birds in the world. They are unique to Britain, being found only in Scotland and the very north of England. (They are closely related to the willow grouse of Scandinavia and North American grouse and ptarmigans.) Their hunting season in Britain runs from August 12th to December 10th. The birds taste best until the end of October; after that time they seem to be drier in texture. They also need little hanging to develop their flavor – no longer than two or three days, or they will become too powerfully gamey in flavor.

Grouse are not usually stuffed, but in Scotland where the berries grow, a few wild mountain raspberries or rowanberries are often put inside the birds. Here, I use a few juniper berries and some thyme for flavoring. The traditional accompaniments are *Bread Sauce* (page 43) and *Rowan Jelly* (page 386) or *Red Currant Jelly* (page 386 or 389), all tasting delicious with the birds.

SERVES 4

4 young, grouse
4 strips of bacon
8 juniper berries
4 sprigs of thyme
Cooking oil
1 onion, roughly chopped
1 carrot, roughly chopped
1 celery stick, roughly chopped
1–2 cloves
1 bay leaf
2 tablespoons (25 g) butter
1¼ cups (300 ml) red wine
1¼ cups (300 ml) *Chicken Stock* (page 33) or water
Cornstarch, thinned with a little red wine (optional)
Salt and pepper
Watercress, to garnish (optional)

Preheat the oven to 425°F/220°C. Untie the birds and season with salt and pepper inside and out. Wrap a strip of bacon around each one. Place two juniper berries and a sprig of thyme inside each carcass and re-tie.

Heat a little oil in a roasting pan. Add the chopped onion, carrot, celery, cloves, and bay leaf. Cook for 10–15 minutes, allowing the vegetables to brown a little and to become partially softened. Make space in the pan to put in the birds on one side. Add the butter and cook for 2–3 minutes. Turn the birds onto the other side and continue to cook for another 2–3 minutes.

Now, turn the birds onto their backs and roast in the preheated oven for 8–9 minutes. Take the pan from the oven and remove the grouse, allowing them to rest for a minimum of 10 minutes.

Place the baking pan on the stove over a medium heat. Add the red wine and bring to a boil. Allow to reduce by two-thirds. Add the stock or water and return to a boil.

Untie and remove the bacon. Remove the legs and breasts from each roasted bird and keep them warm. Chop all of the carcasses and add to the roasting pan. The stock must now be reduced by half. During this time, the gravy will have absorbed all of the roast grouse taste.

Check for seasoning and then strain the sauce through a fine sieve. If you prefer a thicker gravy, mix in cornstarch or arrowroot thinned with a little red wine. A few tablespoons of the gravy can be reduced to a shiny glaze. This can then be brushed over the birds.

Re-warm the grouse in the oven for only a minute or two. The bacon strips can be crisped under a hot broiler. Present the grouse on four plates topped with the bacon strips, the watercress, and the gravy.

Note: *Classic Roast Potatoes* (page 238) or simple buttered new potatoes go well with this dish as will *Creamed Cabbage and Bacon* (page 104).

Any grouse bought in November and December taste best made into game casseroles or stews (see page 263).

Chicken Fillet "Steaks" with Chestnut Mushrooms, Sage, and Lemon Sauce

A great dish to make for a dinner party, these fillet steaks are guaranteed to surprise your friends. They will all be wondering from what sort of chicken they came. The chicken breasts are cut and shaped to look exactly like a beef fillet steak, otherwise known as *tournedos*. It is best to prepare these 24 hours in advance so that the chicken will have plenty of time to hold its shape.

The sauce is made like the recipe for *Basic White Wine or Champagne Fish Sauce* (page 47). Simply replace the fish stock with chicken stock and include any trimmings from the chestnut mushrooms. A few sage leaves can also be added to help flavor the finished sauce.

This dish goes very well with *Buttered Spinach* (page 113).

SERVES 4

6 × 6 oz (175 g) boneless, skinless chicken
     breast halves
3–4 fresh sage leaves, chopped
4 oz (100 g) pig's caul, soaked in cold water
     overnight (page 11, optional)
2 tablespoons (25 g) butter, softened
Salt and pepper

For the Sauce

8 oz (225 g) chestnut or button mushrooms
1 cup (250 ml) *Basic White Wine or Champagne Fish
     Sauce* (page 47), made with chicken stock
     instead of fish
Lemon juice
2–3 fresh sage leaves, chopped
Salt and pepper

To make the "fillet steaks," take a large rectangle of
foil and cover it with a similarly sized sheet of waxed
paper. Brush the paper with butter.

Squeeze excess water from the pig's caul. This
can now be totally spread out on top of the buttered
paper. (If not using caul, check the Note at the end
of the recipe.)

Remove all of the small "fillets" attached to the
underside of the chicken breasts. These can now be
diced and puréed in a food processor. Mix with the
chopped sage leaves and season with salt and pepper.
The breasts can now be cut into strips. Place the
strips side by side on top of the caul, making sure
the length is between 8–9 in (20 and 22 cm). This
will give you enough to cut into four "tournedos"
(fillet steaks). When all are in place, the sage-
flavored puréed chicken can be spread across the top
using a wet spatula. Just a thin layer covering all will
guarantee they hold together.

Now, keeping the caul on the outside, roll the
chicken into a cylindrical shape. Wrap the caul

OPPOSITE
*Chicken Fillet "Steaks" with Chestnut Mushrooms,
Sage, and Lemon Sauce*

---

around it along with the paper and foil. When it's
rolled, twist the foil at either end for a firmer finish.
Refrigerate for several hours, preferably overnight.

Preheat the oven to 400°F/200°C. The roll can
now be cut into four "steaks." After they've been cut,
carefully remove the foil and paper, leaving the caul
wrapped around them. For extra security, tie one or
two lengths of string around them loosely.

To cook, melt a heaping teaspoon of butter in a
frying-pan. Season the steaks with salt and pepper,
place them in the pan, and fry to a golden brown.

Now, place the pan in the preheated oven and
cook for 10–12 minutes. After the "steaks" are
cooked and firm, remove them from the oven and
let them rest for 5–6 minutes.

To make the sauce, trim the stems from the
chestnut mushrooms, slice them, and sauté in a hot
pan with the remaining butter. Season with salt and
pepper. When they are tender and well browned,
remove them from the pan and dry on paper towels.
Warm the white wine sauce and flavor with lemon
juice and chopped sage leaves. The mushrooms can
now also be added to the sauce.

Remove the string from the "steaks" and serve
with the mushroom sauce spooned over the top.

Note: If pig's caul is unavailable, place the chicken strips on
the waxed paper-covered foil. Wrap and roll as described.
When they are set, cut into steaks. These can now be
seasoned top and bottom, leaving the foil wrapped around
them. Cook in the frying-pan sealing the on both sides. Finish
in the preheated oven for 12–15 minutes. When the "steaks"
have rested, peel away the foil and paper; they will still
hold together.

If you are serving buttered spinach with this dish, the
chicken makes an attractive presentation resting on top of it.

Rabbit Leg Casserole with Marjoram and Mustard

Rabbit and mustard have enjoyed a long-lasting
relationship in recipes from all over Europe. The
flavors work wonderfully together, and this dish
using the combination along with the sweet, herby
perfume of the marjoram, is very delicious.

Wild or domestic rabbits are usually sold whole, but I prefer using only the large, plump legs which finish with a rich moistness. The saddle can be quite dry. You can remove the thighbone, if you like, to make serving the rabbit a little easier, but it's not essential (see *Roast Chicken Legs with Sea Salt and Thyme*, page 246, for how to do this). Remember to include the bones in the cooking.

It's interesting that when people used to cook goose in the old days, they would put a "stuffing" of rabbit legs into the cavity along with the flavorings and butter. When the goose was cooked, the rabbit legs were given to the children because they were less rich and there would be more of the goose to feed the hungry men. The dish was known as "six-legged goose."

SERVES 4

4 large or 8 small rabbit legs
All-purpose flour, for dusting
2 tablespoons (25 g) butter
2 large onions, sliced
1 garlic clove, peeled
Sprig of fresh marjoram
1 cup white wine
⅔ cup (150 ml) *Chicken Stock* (page 33)
⅔ cup (150 ml) heavy cream
1 tablespoon prepared English mustard
1 teaspoon chopped fresh marjoram
Salt and pepper

Preheat the oven to 375°F/190°C.

Season the rabbit legs with salt and pepper. Lightly dust them with the all-purpose flour. Melt the butter in a large frying-pan. Place the legs in the pan and fry to a golden brown, turning them over to brown both sides. Add the onions, the garlic clove, and a sprig of marjoram and continue to cook for about 5–6 minutes until the onions have begun to soften.

OPPOSITE
Rabbit Leg Casserole with Marjoram and Mustard

Transfer all the contents of the frying-pan to a suitable braising dish. Add the white wine and chicken stock and bring to a simmer. The dish can now be placed in the preheated oven and cooked for 45–50 minutes.

When the rabbit has cooked, pour through a colander, capturing the cooking liquid in a suitable saucepan. The stock can now be boiled and reduced by half. Add the heavy cream and simmer for 5–6 minutes. Now, add the mustard to finish the sauce. After it's whisked in, taste for strength: if you are a big mustard fan, add more for that extra bite. Season with salt and pepper, if necessary. Strain the sauce through a sieve. Discard the sprig of marjoram and garlic clove from the rabbit legs.

Return the legs and onions to the sauce, adding the chopped marjoram to finish the dish.

The casserole is ready to serve. This dish goes very well with greens such as *Buttered Spinach* (page 113). For a complete change, serve it with buttered noodles.

Note: Button mushrooms (4–5 oz/100–150 g) can be added with the onions for a fuller finish.

Strips of bacon also work well if fried with the onions.

A squeeze of lemon juice is always a great addition to any cream sauce – this one included.

Rabbit, Pork, and Cider Potato Pie

Rabbit with pork is an old combination in the British tradition, just as rabbit with winter savory is a classic in Europe, particularly in France. The combination of all three, moistened with English cider and topped with potatoes instead of pastry, creates a traditional dish with a fresh outlook.

What I like about this pie is that after all the ingredients have been added, you don't have very much more to do except place the dish in the oven and leave it for a couple of hours. As the pie slowly cooks, it creates its own sauce for the finished dish.

It's best to use boned rabbit legs, ask your butcher to help you out with this.

4 rabbit legs, boned, bones reserved
1¼ cups (300 ml) water
2½ cups (600 ml) dry cider
1 lb (450 g) pork belly, skinned
4 celery sticks, well washed
1 Granny Smith apple, grated
3 onions, sliced
2 sprigs of savory
2–3 carrots, peeled and cut into ½ in (1 cm)
    thick slices
Small pinch of ground cinnamon
2 bay leaves
2–3 potatoes, peeled and cut into ½ in (1 cm)
    thick slices
2–4 tablespoons (25–50 g) butter
Salt and pepper

After the rabbit legs have been boned, separate the thigh meat from the drumstick. The bones can now be placed in a saucepan. Pour in the water with half the cider (1¼ cups/300 ml) and bring the mixture to a simmer. This can now be left to cook on a very low heat while the pie is being put together.

Preheat the oven to 350°F/180°C. Slice the pork belly into six slices. After the celery is washed, peel it to remove the strings, or simply pull them away with the tip of a knife. The celery sticks can now be cut at an angle into ½ in (1 cm) pieces. They will then spread out more easily.

Mix the grated apple with the sliced onions and season with salt and pepper. Sprinkle a third of the apple and onion mixture onto the bottom of a buttered ovenproof casserole (a round, lidded Le Creuset-style dish is perfect) along with 1 sprig of the savory. Half of the sliced celery can now also be added. Season the pork slices and place three of them in the dish. Place all of the carrots on top. Season the rabbit legs with salt and pepper and place them in the dish, pushing all of the ingredients down as you do so.

Scatter with another third of the onions, the sprig of savory, the cinnamon, and the remaining celery. The last three slices of pork belly can now be placed on top.

Now, add the remainder of the onions. Strain the cider and water stock, which will have picked up some of the rabbit flavor. Add the remaining cider to the stock and pour it over the vegetables and meats. The liquid should barely reach the level of the onions. If it doesn't, add more water or, for an even richer flavor, use cider. Place the two bay leaves on top and then overlap with the potato slices to totally cover the surface.

Season with salt and divide 2 tablespoons (25 g) of the butter into small pieces and dot them on top of the potatoes. Bring the ingredients to a simmer, cover with a lid, and place in the preheated oven. This can now be left to cook for 1½ hours before removing the lid. The potatoes will have softened and all of the juices will be strengthened in flavor.

Brush the potatoes with more butter and return the pan to the oven (without the lid) for another 30 minutes. If, after this time, the potatoes have not browned, simply increase the temperature of the oven to 400°F/200°C, brush the potatoes with butter once more, and cook for another 15–20 minutes. The pie is now ready to serve.

Allow the dish to stand for 10 minutes after it is removed from the oven so that all the ingredients will relax. Now, it's time to serve. The cider will have been mellowed by the stock created from both meats, but it will still have its distinctive flavor.

Note: After an hour of the cooking time, it's a good idea to check and lightly press on the potatoes. This will give you an idea of how much liquid is in the pan. If it appears a lot has been absorbed by the vegetables, simply pour another ⅔ cup (150 ml) of water or cider on top. Replace the lid and continue to cook.

Rich Ground Squab on a Potato Cake with Mustard Cabbage

Extremely popular in the past as a means of using up pieces of organ meats left over after a pig had been killed, "faggots" are a cross between a pâté and a sausage – a pâté mixture bound up in caul fat (all sausages used to be encased in animal entrails) formed into sausage shapes.

This dish has a gamey flavor, bound and balanced with pork and chicken livers, which give the moist texture needed for a succulent finish. It's important but not essential to freeze the "faggots" in their liquid – not a traditional technique, I must admit, but it breaks the meats down, giving a softer finish. So, plan ahead with this dish by defrosting the amount needed, allowing it to warm through slowly. You'll then have the richest, moistest meat you could hope for. This recipe will make approximately twelve "faggots." For an ultimately rich flavor, a *Game Stock* (page 34) will be needed. This can be made from the carcasses of the squab used here. (The British use wood pigeon for this dish; use squab in the US. See Suppliers, page 400)

Serve the ground squab "faggots" with *Potato Cakes* (page 122), or use *The Roast Alternative* (page 123). For the cabbage, use either green or Savoy, boiled and flavored with a mustard sauce.

MAKES 12 FAGGOTS

1 quart (900 ml) *Game Stock* (page 34), made from squab legs and carcasses
6 squab breasts (use the legs and carcasses from the whole birds for the stock, above)
2 small chicken breasts, skinned
8 oz (225 g) pig's caul, soaked in cold water overnight (page 11)
Cooking oil
Salt and pepper

BELOW
Rich Ground Squab on a Potato Cake with Mustard Cabbage

6 oz (175 g) pork meat, trimmed (belly or leg
    can be used)
2 oz (50 g) *foie gras* (optional)
3 oz (75 g) pork back fat
3 oz (75 g) chicken livers
1 tablespoon chopped shallots
1 garlic clove, crushed
½ teaspoon lightly chopped thyme leaves
2–3 tablespoons Armagnac or brandy
4 tablespoons Madeira
1 egg white
¼ cup (100 ml) heavy cream (1–2 tablespoons
    more may be needed)
Salt and pepper

For the Squab Reduction

Sprig of thyme
2 juniper berries, crushed
½ garlic clove
3 tablespoons Madeira
3 tablespoons port
6 tablespoons squab *jus*, made from game
    stock (above)

For the Garnishes (to serve 6)

½ small green or Savoy cabbage, cut into wedges
⅔ cup (150 ml) *Mustard Butter Sauce* (page 53),
    using English mustard
Butter
6 *Potato Cakes* (page 122), pan-fried

Reduce 1¼ cups (300 ml) of the game stock by three-fourths. This will leave you with a thick game *jus* to use for the squab reduction.

To make this squab reduction, place the thyme, juniper berries, and garlic in a small pan along with the Madeira and port. Bring to a boil and reduce by three-fourths before adding the game *jus*. Strain through a sieve and let it cool.

Remove the skin and meat from the squab breasts; grind the meat twice through a coarse blade of meat grinder. The chicken breasts can be ground once through a fine blade. If the meat is diced and well chilled, along with the grinding blades, it will be easier to grind.

For the stuffing, the pork meat, *foie gras* (if using), pork back fat, and chicken livers can now be ground twice through coarse blade and once through a fine blade. Or they can be puréed in a food processor to a fine paste as an alternate to grinding.

Place the shallots, garlic, and thyme in a small saucepan with the Armagnac or brandy and Madeira. Bring to a simmer and then reduce until almost dry. Let them cool.

Working in a bowl placed over a pan of ice, mix the shallots with the pork mixture. Season with salt and pepper and mix in the egg white. The mixture will now become quite firm. Stir in the heavy cream. To check that it has the right consistency and flavor, poach a teaspoon of the mixture in simmering water. After 2–3 minutes, the mousse will be cooked. Now, check for seasoning and consistency. The mixture should barely set and not be tough or overfirm. If it has become too firm, then add a tablespoon more heavy cream, checking until you have a soft-cooked consistency. Season with salt and pepper. It's important when testing that the mixture is well chilled; if not, the mousse will separate in the pan.

Now, the pork mixture can be added to the ground squab and chicken. Stir in the squab reduction and check the seasoning again. The meat mixture should be left for 2–3 hours to chill and set in the refrigerator. This will make it a lot easier to roll in the caul.

After the meat mixture has set, it can now be shaped. Take a heaping tablespoon of it and roll by hand, forming balls the size of large plum tomatoes.

Squeeze any excess water from the pig's caul and open it out flat across a board. The "faggots" can now be well wrapped individually, making sure they are totally encased in the caul.

To cook, heat a frying-pan with a little cooking oil. Season the balls with salt and pepper. These can now be pan-fried until completely sealed and golden. Place the remaining 2½ cups (600 ml) of warm stock in a saucepan, carefully add the balls, and simmer very gently for 15–20 minutes. Remove the pan from the stove and allow the balls to cool in their sauce.

Now, for the very best results, place the balls in a pan. Strain and pour the sauce over them. At this point, you can freeze the "faggots"; it's not essential, but freezing does help the texture.

When you want to re-heat the balls, defrost and warm them at a gentle simmer until heated through. This will take 20–25 minutes. Strain off some of the sauce and skim off any impurities and fat. The sauce will have a rich squab flavor. (A splash of red wine might help to liven it up some more.) To give the balls a shiny glaze, reduce 1¼ cups (300 ml) of the sauce to a thicker glazing consistency. Some of this can now be brushed over the balls.

For the garnishes, blanch the cabbage wedges in plenty of well-salted boiling water until barely tender. This will take 4–5 minutes. As with all green vegetables, it is important that the cabbage be boiled without a lid. Refresh in iced water. Use the outer 3–4 layers of each wedge of cabbage with the stalk/core attached. Cut away the remainder. (The extra cabbage can simply be buttered and served as a vegetable for another meal, or shredded and used in a stir-fry.) Butter and season the outside layers. When you are ready to serve the "faggots," microwave them for 30–40 seconds.

To present the dish, place a potato cake in the center of a plate or bowl. Place the glazed "faggot" on top. Pour a tablespoon or two of the remaining reduced squab sauce over the "faggots." Place the cabbage leaves on top, giving an arched shape. Now, finish by spooning mustard sauce over the cabbage. The "faggots" are now ready to serve.

Roast Partridges on Toast with Wild Mushrooms

The Romans used to cage and raise partridges, and they roasted them over or in front of a fire – a practice continued in Britain for centuries. The British season for shooting partridge runs between September 1st and February 1st. During the nineteenth century, partridges were one of Britain's most common game birds. The gray-legged variety is native to Britain, and many years ago were found in abundance. Now, the gray-legged bird is not so common and has to be bred. A red-legged variety was introduced in the seventeenth century from France; it is reasonably easy to find, larger than the gray-legged, but lacking in the gray-legged's intense flavor. The red are, however, beautiful-looking birds and a joy to cook and serve. (See Suppliers, page 400)

The history of accompaniments in Britain, as it does elsewhere, relates to the seasons. Partridges are best in the fall, when most wild mushrooms are found, so it is almost culinary law that the two go well together. For a good combination of flavor and color, choose a mixture of black trumpets, which have a strong earthy flavor; chanterelles, which are a rich orange color and have a sort of apricot and pepper aroma; morels, which have a nutty flavor and are a scarce wild mushroom only available during the spring; and oyster mushrooms, which are now cultivated. They range from an oyster-gray color to a yellowish brown. They are best eaten young, for a bitter flavor takes over as they age. Alternately, you can buy a bag or two of mixed wild mushrooms. It's important that the mushrooms are well washed.

Dried morels are sometimes available in gourmet markets, and after they've been soaked, they come back to life very well. The water they have been soaked in can be strained through a sieve or muslin and used as a wild mushroom stock in making the sauce. If using dried mushrooms instead of fresh, 2 oz (50 g) will be sufficient.

The toast foundation for the partridge is an echo of the medieval bread slice or trencher which acted as a plate for pieces of meat or bird (and was sometimes given to the poor). These slices of toast are topped with a mixture made from the liver and heart of the bird along with one or two other flavors for a delicious finish. The *Game Stock* from page 34 can be used as the sauce. I prefer to cook the stock with no alcohol for this particular dish and add the neat Madeira at the end. I also like to add one more flavor to this dish, an expensive one – *foie gras*. It's not essential but it completely lifts the dish.

A high-quality chicken liver *pâté* or canned *foie gras* can be substituted if fresh is unavailable. Both *foie gras* and chicken liver *pâté* can be bought at gourmet food shops.

SERVES 4

6 oz (175 g) black trumpet mushrooms
6 oz (175 g) chanterelle mushrooms
3–4 oz (75–100 g) morels (optional)
5 oz (150 g) oyster mushrooms
4 plump partridges, including livers
    and hearts, preferably red-legged
    with a thin slice of pork back fat
4 fresh thyme sprigs
1 large garlic clove, quartered
4 tablespoons (50 g) butter
1–2 tablespoons peanut oil
1¼ cups (300 ml) *Game Stock* (page 34)
2–3 tablespoons Madeira
Salt and pepper

For the Toast and the Pâté

Butter
2 large shallots, finely chopped
2–3 oz (50–75 g) *foie gras* or chicken-liver *pâté* or
    tinned *pâté de foie gras*
4 thick slices of whole grain bread

Preheat the oven to 425°F/220°C.

First, prepare the mushrooms – whatever varieties you're using. Wash them well by wiping a with damp paper towels two or three times, removing any grit found inside. Wipe them carefully and let them drain them on a dish towel.

For black trumpet, split the mushrooms lengthwise, cutting away the bottom of the stem. Clean as instructed, above.

Large chanterelles will need to be halved or quartered; small ones can be left whole. Trim away any bruised tops, scraping the stems and cutting away the bottoms. Wipe them two or three times before draining them on a dish cloth.

If using morels, trim away the bottom of the stem and split the mushroom lengthwise in half. Again, wipe them before draining on a cloth.

For oyster mushrooms, cut away the thick stems. Wipe them carefully all over with a damp paper towel. If the mushrooms are large, then simply tear them into strips.

Untie the prepared birds, setting aside the liver and heart from each. Place a sprig of thyme, piece of garlic, a heaping teaspoon of butter, and some salt and pepper into each cavity. Season the outside, replace the piece of back fat and re-tie the partridges.

The livers and hearts can now be chopped coarsely and set aside.

For the toast, melt the butter and add the finely chopped shallots. Cook for a few minutes, without browning, until softened; remove them from the heat and allow to cool. When the shallots are cold, mix the chopped livers and hearts with them. If you are using *foie gras*, smooth to a purée and add to the mixture. If not, add 2–3 oz (50–75 g) of chicken liver or canned *foie gras pâté*. Season with salt and pepper. The topping for the toast is now ready.

Heat a roasting pan with some peanut oil. Place the seasoned birds in the pan on one leg side. Add a heaping teaspoon of butter and cook for 2–3 minutes until well browned. Turn over onto the other leg and repeat the same cooking time. Now, turn each bird breast-side down to seal for another 2–3 minutes.

Turn the birds onto their backs and roast in the preheated oven for 6 minutes. If they are particularly plump, roast for an extra 1–2 minutes.

Remove from the oven and place the birds upside-down onto a clean serving plate, so all juices run into the breasts. Keep the roasting pan with all the juices. Let the birds rest for 6–8 minutes.

Spread the toast topping onto the bread using all of the mixture, and cut the slices into triangles.

OPPOSITE
*Roast Partridges on Toast with
Wild Mushrooms*

Put the roasting pan over a medium heat and place the triangles, bread-side down, in the sediment and oils left in the pan. Pan-fry the breads for a few minutes to crisp and absorb all of the flavors. Now, remove the bread triangles, place them on a baking pan, and finish them, topping-side-up, under a medium broiler. Toast for a few minutes, heating the mixture through.

Heat a large frying-pan or wok. Add a tablespoon of oil, and when it is very hot, add the chanterelle mushrooms and the morels, if using. Toss in the pan for about a minute before adding the remaining mushrooms. (If using a bag of mixed mushrooms, simply fry them all together.) Add a heaping teaspoon of butter and season with salt and pepper. Cook for 2–3 minutes.

Warm the game stock, adding the Madeira to taste. This sauce will now have a very thin consistency. For a slightly thicker sauce and stronger flavor, reduce by half. The sauce is now ready.

The partridges can now be untied and the fat and the legs removed and trimmed to a neat finish. Remove the breasts. The skin of the breasts can be left on or removed. In a sieve, press each carcass to allow all the juices to run through and into the game sauce for extra flavor.

Place the toast triangles in bowls or on plates. Point them towards the top of the plate. Place the two breasts side by side on top of the lower part of the triangle. The legs can now be placed with thigh towards the top, recreating the shape of the bird. Spoon the mixed wild mushrooms around the breast and legs and finish with the sauce on top of the mushrooms. The dish is now ready to serve.

Note: *Mashed Potatoes* (page 124) go very well with this dish.

The toast trimmings left over when the triangles were cut can be warmed to eat separately.

Roast Pheasant with Bacon-braised Barley and Whiskey Cream Sauce

Pheasants, probably the most popular sporting birds, are native to Asia, and were spread throughout Europe by the Romans. During the Roman occupation of Britain, pheasants were kept and fed for the chase, much as gamekeepers on large estates do with game birds today. Their season is between October 1st and February 1st; those shot between December and January have the best flavor. There are both cock and hen pheasants to choose from. The cock is a large bird with enough meat for four servings. The hen is smaller with a much more delicate taste. If using the hen, which I prefer, one bird will provide only two servings.

Pheasants eat grains, particularly preferring barley, so the association in a dish seems obvious. The flavor of the barley is heightened by the addition of bacon. For extra texture I have fried breadcrumbs (a classic accompaniment to roast pheasant), and sprinkled the crumbs over the barley giving a crispy crunch on the palate. The delicious combination of enriching the cream sauce with whiskey, is a nod to Scotland where so many pheasants are bred. For maximum taste, use a single malt rather than a blended whiskey.

SERVES 4

2 oven-ready hen pheasants
4 juniper berries, lightly crushed
2 fresh thyme sprigs
Melted butter, for brushing pheasants
Cooking oil
2–3 slices of white bread, crusts removed and broken into crumbs
Salt and pepper

For the Barley

6 oz (175 g) strips of bacon
4 oz (100 g) pearl barley
2 tablespoons (25 g) butter, melted
1 onion, finely chopped
2½ cups (600 ml) *Chicken Stock* (page 33)
1 tablespoon chopped fresh parsley

For the Sauce

1 small carrot, roughly chopped
2 shallots, roughly chopped
2–3 cup mushrooms, quartered
8 tablespoons whiskey
1¼ cups (300 ml) *Chicken Stock* (page 33)
    or water
⅔ cup (150 ml) heavy cream

Season the cavity of each bird and place 2 juniper berries and a sprig of thyme inside. Brush the birds with butter and season well with salt and pepper. These can now be refrigerated until needed.

Cut the bacon strips into ¼ in (5 mm) dice. The pearl barley can now be rinsed under cold running water. Heat the butter in a saucepan. Add the chopped onion and bacon. Cook over a medium heat, allowing the bacon to take on a slight color. Add the pearl barley and cover with 2½ cups (600 ml) of the chicken stock. Bring to a simmer and cook gently for 30–40 minutes until the barley is tender. During its cooking time, the barley will have swollen, becoming soft and absorbing the stock and the bacon flavor. While the barley is cooking, the pheasants can be roasted.

Preheat the oven to 375°F/190°C. In a roasting pan, heat 2 tablespoons of the cooking oil. Scatter in the carrot, shallots, and mushrooms for the sauce in the pan, leaving enough room in the center to roast the pheasants. Place the birds on one side, allowing them to seal and become golden brown. Turn the birds over. After they've browned, turn the birds on their backs and roast in the preheated oven for 12–15 minutes. After 12–15 minutes, turn the birds over and continue to roast for another 15 minutes.

Remove the pan from the oven and place it on top of the stove over a medium heat. Spoon 6 tablespoons of whiskey over the birds and turn them in the pan so that the whiskey covers all of them. Remove the birds, pouring any juices from inside the cavity into the pan. Let the birds rest, breast-side down (allowing any juices to run into the breasts) for 10–15 minutes.

During the resting time, the sauce can be made. Boil all of the juices, adding the 1¼ cups (300 ml) of chicken stock (water can replace the stock) and stirring well. The gamey residue will now be lifted from the pan. Allow the stock to reduce by half. Add the heavy cream and cook at a simmer for 6–8 minutes. The cream will slightly reduce giving a thick sauce consistency. Strain the sauce through a sieve, seasoning with salt and pepper. An extra splash of neat whiskey can be added, to heighten the flavor.

The breadcrumbs can be fried in cooking oil until golden and crisp. Season with a pinch of salt. (The crumbs can be fried in advance and warmed when serving the dish.)

Remove the breasts and legs from the hen birds. Sprinkle the remaining 2 tablespoons of whiskey onto the exposed meat of all four servings. The dish is now ready to serve.

Any impurities on top of the creamy whiskey sauce can be lifted off with a sheet of paper towel. Add the chopped parsley to the braised bacon-braised barley and sprinkle with the crisp crumbs.

The presentation of the dish is your choice. The barley and pheasant portions can be served in a large dish with the sauce offered separately, or all three components can be presented on individual plates.

Note: The vegetables in the roasting pan will have given extra flavor to the sauce. They can be served with the main course, a spoonful underneath the pheasant breasts and legs.

Armagnac can be used in place of the whiskey. Armagnac is a classic accompaniment to prunes, in both savory dishes and desserts. Chopped prunes can be added to the cream sauce and/or some of them roasted in the pan with the hens.

The roast pheasant can be served with the classic accompaniments to *Roast Grouse* on page 247.

Pheasant is best cooked after hanging for 7–8 days. This will give the bird a more gamey flavor rather than the chicken flavor to which it's often compared.

Pressed Guinea Fowl Terrine with Shallots, Mushrooms, and Bacon

The Romans introduced the guinea fowl to Britain, but after the Romans left, the bird seemed to disappear as well. Now, fifteen hundred years later, it has been reintroduced from West Africa, but it is only being domestically or commercially raised rather than living naturally as it does elsewhere in Europe. It is a game bird with the flavor of gamey chicken. Available all year round, it is at its best in early summer.

It is important to keep guinea fowl moist in whatever dish you happen to be making with them. The other ingredients here will help achieve that. I use a 5 cup (1.2 liter) terrine mold, which will require two birds. If you are using a 2 quart (1.75 liter) Le Creuset-type terrine, at least three birds will be needed. If a game terrine doesn't seem to be British, think again – pressed or potted meats, game, and fish became popular in Britain in the eighteenth century, and these were the British equivalent of the French pâté or terrine.

To bone a guinea fowl, simply follow the boning method for chicken, taking the breasts off, then skinning and boning the legs. You can replace the guinea fowl with chicken, if you wish.

SERVES 10–12

2 guinea fowl, cut up, boned, and skinned
2 small garlic cloves, crushed
Grated zest of 1 lemon
Small bunch of fresh basil
½ cup white wine
6 oz (175 g) piece of slab bacon
8 oz (225 g) shallots or pearl onions, peeled
8 oz (225 g) button mushrooms
10–12 strips of bacon
1 bay leaf
Salt and pepper

The breasts of the guinea fowl can either be left whole or split in two. Marinate all of the guinea fowl meat with the crushed garlic, lemon zest, basil leaves, and white wine. Let the birds marinate overnight to achieve maximum flavor.

Preheat the oven to 350°F/180°C.

Cut the piece of slab bacon into strips ¼ in (5 mm) thick and blanch them in boiling water for a few minutes. The shallots or onions must be blanched twice to take the rawness out of their flavor. Place them in cold water and bring to a boil before refreshing and starting again.

Trim the stems from the button mushrooms. Poach the caps in water (or chicken stock) for a few minutes until tender.

Line the buttered terrine with the strips of bacon, slightly overlapping and leaving the ends hanging over the edge of the pan to fold over the filled terrine. A few more strips of bacon may be needed to cover the top.

Take the guinea fowl pieces from the marinade and strain the marinade, keeping it to one side.

The guinea fowl, shallots, mushrooms and bacon pieces can now be seasoned and layered in the mold in no particular order, keeping a very rustic appearance to the dish. Pack the terrine well, overfilling the mold. Pour the strained marinade over all and fold the strips across the top, tucking in the bay leaf. The terrine can now be wrapped in parchment paper and foil.

Place the terrine in a roasting pan of hot water. Cook in the preheated oven for 50 minutes to 1 hour. A larger terrine will take 1¼ hours.

Remove the terrine mold from the oven and from the roasting pan. Let it rest for 30 minutes before topping with another terrine and a suitable weight (unopened cans will probably be enough). Refrigerate the terrine for several hours while pressing, preferably overnight, to guarantee a firm finish. After it has been pressed, the terrine is ready to turn out and slice.

This dish goes well with a chutney or relish – homemade *Piccalilli* (page 385) is a perfect choice.

Steamed and Braised Mallard in Parsnip Tarts

Mallard is a wild duck in season in Britain between September and the end of January. It is the largest of the wild duck family, and many varieties have been eaten in Britain since prehistoric times. You might have to order mallard from your butcher in advance. The recipe can be made using an available duck from the supermarket, but the cooking time will be longer.

This dish holds many exciting flavors and combinations. The pig's trotter sauce is quite unbelievable to eat, the sticky dice adding so much to the whole experience. This recipe requires a lot of work, but it's worth it. If you prefer, the trotters can be omitted. Simply serve the duck and parsnip tarts with a gamey red wine sauce.

SERVES 4

2 mallard ducks
1 bottle red wine
1 onion, sliced
2 strips of bacon, roughly chopped
Few juniper berries
Butter
2 strips of orange peel
Cooking oil
2¼–4 cups (600–900 ml) *Game Stock* (page 34),
    reduced to a *jus*, or *Veal Jus* (page 34)
All-purpose flour, for dusting
1–2 cooked pigs' trotters (page 220), including
    ⅔ cup (150 ml) trotter-cooking liquid
    (optional)
4 oz (100 g) *Buttered Spinach* (page 113)
Salt and pepper

For the Parsnip Tarts

12–14 oz (350–400 g) *Shortcrust Pastry*
    (page 364), with 1 teaspoon black pepper
Juice of ½ lemon
1 lb (450 g) peeled and cored parsnips, cut into
    ¾–1½ in (2–3 cm) pieces
4 tablespoons (50 g) butter
¼ cup (100 ml) water
½ cup (50 ml) heavy cream
Salt and pepper

Remove the legs from the mallard (these can be marinated for 24 hours with the red wine, onion, bacon, juniper berries, and orange peel). Split each bird in two, cutting away the wishbone and all bones surrounding the breast. The breasts should be left attached only to the breastbone; this allows them to keep their shape during cooking. The breasts can be seasoned with the skin left on and each wrapped individually in plastic wrap with a heaping teaspoon of butter. Keep them refrigerated until needed. The mallard carcasses and trimmings can all now be chopped.

Pan-fry the carcasses and bones in some oil until browned and place in a saucepan. Fry the onions and bacon in the same pan, scrapping up any residue. Add to the bones with the juniper berries and orange peel before pouring in the red wine. Bring to a simmer and reduce by half. Add the game *jus* and bring to a simmer.

Season the mallard legs and dust them with flour. Heat a clean frying-pan with a little cooking oil and pan-fry until well browned on both sides. Place the legs in the game *jus* and simmer gently for 45 minutes–1 hour.

The legs will now be very tender and full of red wine flavor. Remove from the *jus* and trim away any protruding bones from the thighs. Place to one side. The *jus* can now be strained through a fine sieve. Check the consistency and flavor. The *jus* does not need to be too thick, just full of duck and red wine taste. Season with salt and pepper. The legs can be cooked well beforehand and simply re-heated when needed in the *jus*.

To make the pastry shells, follow the recipe on page 364, adding the black pepper to the flour before binding with the butter.

Butter and season four 4 × 1 in (10 × 2.5 cm) pastry rings. Line the rings with pastry, leaving the excess hanging over the sides. Line each with waxed paper, and fill with pie weights or dried beans. Refrigerate for 15 minutes before baking in a preheated oven at 400°F/200°C, for 20–25 minutes until golden. Remove the waxed paper and the weights. The over-hanging edge can now be cut away, leaving a straight and neat finish.

For the parsnip purée tart filling, add the lemon juice to the cut parsnips. Melt the butter in a heavy-bottomed pan. When it bubbles, add the parsnips and water. Now, slowly cook the parsnips until they have become very tender and begin to break down. This will take 25–30 minutes.

Bring the cream to a boil and add to the parsnips. Season with salt and pepper (a pinch of nutmeg can also be added) and process to a smooth purée. For the ultimate smooth finish, push the purée through a fine sieve.

The trotter meat, if using, can now be cut into ¼ in (5 mm) dice. If using trotter liquid (also optional), mix with ⅔ cup (150 ml) of the game-and-red wine cooking *jus*. Check for seasoning. The mallard legs can be re-heated in the remaining game *jus*. If they are cold, they will take at least 30 minutes over a very gentle heat. This keeps them very moist and tender.

The breasts can now be placed in a hot steamer and cooked for 10–12 minutes. Ten minutes will cook the breasts medium-rare and 12 minutes, medium. After they are cooked, remove them from the steamer and let them rest, still wrapped in plastic wrap, for 5 minutes.

Re-heat the game/trotter sauce and add the diced trotter. The pastry shells can be re-heated in a warm oven.

Microwave or pan-fry the buttered spinach. Spoon it among the four tartlets. Top each tartlet with hot parsnip purée (which, if made in advance and refrigerated, can also be microwaved), totally filling the tarts. Place the parsnip tarts in the center of the bowls or plates. Remove the plastic wrap and the skin from the breasts, cut them away from the bone, and carve each into 3–4 slices. Arrange the slices on top of the tarts, leaving enough space to position the legs, which will have taken on a rich color and glaze from the sauce. Spoon the game/trotter sauce around the tarts and serve.

OPPOSITE
Steamed and Braised Mallard in a Parsnip Tart

Note: Any excess parsnip purée should be passed separately. Any remaining game sauce can be frozen. It will keep for up to 3 months in the freezer – a sauce packed with flavor, ready to be used.

Game Stew or Pie

For centuries, all sorts of wild birds have been featured in stews and pies – the more common ones, such as pigeons, partridge, grouse, wild duck, and less familiar ones, such as capercaillie, ptarmigan, and woodcock. Venison, too, was made into stews and covered with pastry, and venison pasties made on the same principle as Cornish pasties, have been popular since Tudor times.

This recipe is for a mixed game pie. The game – pheasant, partridge, and wood pigeon – are first going to be slowly braised for 2–2½ hours, giving the meat a melt-in-the-mouth texture. After it is cooked, the stew can be served immediately or be allowed to cool completely before being topped with the puff pastry and baked to create a pie.

For maximum taste, the game should first be marinated for 24 hours. I prefer to take the meat off the bone, apart from the partridge or pheasant drumsticks. I also leave the squab legs on the bone.

SERVES 6–8

1 cock pheasant
2 partridges
2 squabs
Pinch of ground allspice
Butter
5 cups (1.2 liters) game *jus* made from *Game Stock* (page 34)
1 tablespoon red wine vinegar, preferably Cabernet Sauvignon
1 tablespoon red currant jelly
Salt and pepper

For the Marinade

4 strips of orange peel
1 teaspoon black peppercorns, lightly crushed
1 teaspoon juniper berries, lightly crushed
1 bay leaf

Bottle of red wine, preferably claret
4 tablespoons brandy
⅔ cup (150 ml) port
2 large carrots, peeled and cut into ¾ in (2 cm) cubes
4 celery sticks, cut into ¾ in (2 cm) pieces
8 oz (225 g) pearl onions, peeled
8 oz (225 g) cremini or button mushrooms
Sprig of thyme

For the Pie (optional)

1 lb (450 g) *Quick Puff Pastry* (page 365)
1 egg, beaten
Coarse sea salt

Remove the legs and breasts from the birds. Pheasant and partridge legs can be split, taking the thighs from the drumsticks and boning them. The drumsticks can now be trimmed and the skin removed. The squab legs can simply be trimmed and also skinned. Remove the skin from the breasts. The pheasant breasts can now be cut into three pieces. Cut the partridge breasts in two and leave the squab breasts whole.

All the meats can now be placed in a bowl. Use the carcasses to make the *Game Stock* (page 34).

For the marinade, place the orange peel, peppercorns, juniper berries, and bay leaf into a saucepan. Pour the bottle of red wine over them and boil until reduced by half. While the wine is reducing, the brandy can be poured over the meats and stirred well so all has been coated. After the wine has reduced, remove the pan from the stove and add the port. Allow the mixture to cool until barely warm. Add the chopped vegetables, pearl onions, mushrooms, and thyme to the meats and

then cover with the boiled wine and port. Marinate in the refrigerator for 24 hours. It is important to turn the game from time to time to achieve maximum flavor.

After 24 hours, preheat the oven to 275°F/140°C. Drain the meat and vegetables from the marinade, keeping the wine to one side. Lightly pat the game dry with paper towels. Season with salt, pepper, and allspice.

Heat a frying-pan with a heaping teaspoon of butter and fry half of the meat, sealing and browning on all sides. Transfer the sealed meat to a braising pan. Pour a small ladle of the marinade wine into the frying-pan. This will dissolve all residue and juices. Strain the mixture over the sealed meat. Wipe the pan clean and repeat the same ladling process, further dissolving any flavors with the wine and adding all to the braising pan. The vegetables (from the marinade) can now be quickly fried in the pan. Add to the meats, pouring the remaining wine on top. Bring to a simmer and pour the game *jus* on top. Return to a simmer. The stew can now be braised in the preheated oven, covered with a lid, for 2–2½ hours.

The stew will be beautifully rich and very tender. Remove the orange peel and the thyme stems. To bring the sauce to a good consistency, strain it into a pan and bring to a simmer, skimming off any impurities. If the sauce is too thin, thicken with cornstarch or arrowroot stirred in a drop of port. Check for seasoning with salt and pepper.

Warm together the red wine vinegar and red currant jelly and add to the sauce. Pour the finished sauce back over the game and vegetables. The stew is now ready to serve. If you wish to turn it into a pie, let it cool completely.

Preheat the oven to 400°F/200°C. The pastry can now be rolled into a shape large enough to cover the chosen pie dish. Just 12 oz (350 g) may be

OPPOSITE
Marinade for Game Stew or Pie

needed, depending on the size of dish used. Brush beaten egg around the edge of the dish. Cut a thin strip of pastry and press around the edge, then also brush this edge with egg. Having a pastry border to seal the pastry lid on completely will keep the pastry in place, preventing it from shrinking. Press the lid on well, sealing tightly to the pastry border. Brush well with the beaten egg and sprinkle a little coarse sea salt on top. Let it rest for 15 minutes before baking in the preheated oven for 40–45 minutes.

The pastry will now be rich, golden, and crispy. It is best to present the whole pie on the table with all the meat and vegetables sealed inside.

Note: If the stew is made into a pie, add enough of the sauce/gravy to cover the meat and vegetables generously, serving any remaining sauce separately.

Roast Fillets of Hare Wrapped in Ham with Port and Walnuts

The hare is native to Britain, the one animal that escaped the stringent game laws passed throughout the centuries. A poacher – a man who was often trying to feed his starving family – could be beheaded for taking a deer or pheasant, but the hare was always available. Hare as a meat was slightly looked down on by the middle and upper classes, since it was considered a food of the poor.

A hare is not the same as a rabbit. It is larger, and has two main features that immediately help you tell them apart: the hare's long legs and the length of its ears. The meat is a lot darker than the chicken-like color of rabbit, and is almost as deep and rich as venison. When buying hare, look for a younger animal, which will be more tender in flavor, and less tough and leathery. Hare doesn't need to be hung for too long: just 2–3 days will be plenty, allowing enough time for the meat to relax.

The ham used in this recipe can be either Prosciutto (an Italian salted and air-dried ham), or Bayonne (a French ham, cured with wine and often slightly smoked). Either can be bought loose from gourmet food shops (see Suppliers, page 400). If neither can be found, strips of bacon, lightly pounded between sheets of plastic wrap to make the slices thinner and to prevent shrinkage during cooking, can also be used.

The hare is not going to be marinated in this recipe. Marinating is a wonderful process but it can sometimes dominate the flavors of the meat. For this dish, I want the natural flavors of the hare and ham to work together.

SERVES 4

2 saddles of hare, filleted, boned, and bones chopped
4 slices of Prosciutto or Bayonne ham
Salt and pepper
12 walnut halves, to garnish

For the Sauce

Chopped saddle bones
Walnut oil (or cooking oil)
1 onion, chopped
1 carrot, chopped
2 celery sticks, chopped
1 tablespoon all-purpose flour
1¼ cups (300 ml) *Chicken* or *Game Stock*
    (page 33 or 34) or water
Sprig of thyme
1 bay leaf
Few juniper berries, crushed
¼ cup (25 g) walnuts, chopped
½ teaspoon pink peppercorns or 6 black
    peppercorns, lightly crushed
1 tablespoon red wine vinegar, preferably Cabernet
    Sauvignon
½ cup (120 ml) port
1 teaspoon red currant jelly

Preheat the oven to 400°F/200°C.

Trim the fillets of any sinews. Place the Prosciutto or Bayonne ham slices in pairs next to each other, slightly overlapping by ½ in (1 cm), on plastic wrap.

Press two fillets of hare together and place on the ham slices. Roll and wrap the fillets well, giving the impression of one thick loin. Seal in plastic wrap

and refrigerate. Repeat the same process with the remaining two fillets.

To make the sauce, fry the chopped bones in a roasting pan on top of the stove, using a tablespoon or two of walnut or cooking oil. When the bones are browned, add the chopped vegetables and roast in the preheated oven for 20 minutes. Remove from the oven, pouring off any fat from the pan. Sprinkle the bones with the flour, return them to the oven, and bake for another 5–6 minutes. The bones and vegetables can now be transferred to a saucepan.

Heat the roasting pan, pouring in the stock or water. This will dissolve any flavors left in the pan. Add the thyme, bay leaf, juniper berries, chopped walnuts, and pink peppercorns to the bones in the saucepan. Now add the red wine vinegar and the port; bring the mixture to a simmer and reduce by half. Add the stock from the roasting pan and return to a simmer. The stock can now be cooked for 30 minutes at a low simmer. After 30 minutes of simmering, pass the stock through a fine sieve. Any impurities or fat floating on top of the sauce can be lifted using a sheet of paper towel.

This will give you plenty for the four servings. Add the red currant jelly. This sauce will have a good hare flavor, but if it's too thin, it can be thickened with a pinch of arrowroot or cornstarch moistened with port.

To roast the hare, unwrap the fillets from the plastic wrap. Three or four strings can now be tied loosely around each pair of fillets and the ham slices.

Heat a roasting pan with some walnut or cooking oil. Season the meat with a grinding of pepper. Fry the fillets, browning the ham all around. This will take 3–4 minutes. Place the pan in the preheated oven and cook the fillets for 8–10 minutes, keeping the fillets pink. Halfway through the roasting process, turn the fillets over to achieve an even browning. Remove the fillets from the pan and let them rest for 5 minutes.

Add the walnut pieces to the sauce. The string can now be cut away from the fillets and each piece cut into four, giving two medallions per serving. Spoon the sauce and walnuts around them and serve.

This dish goes very well with any of the following – buttered *Curly Kale* (page 105), *Gratin of Grated Turnips* (page 112), or creamy *Mashed Potatoes* (page 124).

White Pudding

White pudding as it is known in Britain bears little or no relationship to black pudding; it contains no blood, with the oatmeal they both contain being the only connection. It is also known traditionally as "mealie pudding." Its basic ingredients are oatmeal, beef suet, and onions – not the most exciting of combinations.

The recipe I include here, however, is more along the lines of the French *boudin blanc*, having a white-meat base, such as chicken, veal, rabbit, or pork. Here, the oatmeal has been replaced with breadcrumbs.

After it's poached and cooked, the sausages can be cooled and refrigerated, which means they can be made in advance. When you're ready to serve them, simply pan-fry or broil them gently, and serve as an appetizer or main course. *Mashed Potatoes* (page 124) and mustard are good with them, or *Applesauce* or *Cumberland Applesauce* (page 44 or 47). A simple white pudding salad makes a delicious appetizer, with a wholegrain mustard dressing the perfect accompaniment.

MAKES APPROX. 8–10 SAUSAGES

Butter
5 oz (150 g) shallots, finely chopped
6 oz (175 g) chicken breast half, diced
6 oz (175 g) pork back fat, diced
4 oz (100 g) lean shoulder of pork, diced
1 cup (200 ml) heavy cream
2 thick slices of white bread, crusts removed and crumbed
2 eggs, beaten
½ teaspoon cornstarch
Salt, pepper and freshly grated nutmeg
Sausage skins, enough for 8–10 lengths of 6 in (15 cm)

For the Cooking Liquid

2½ cups (600 ml) milk
2½ cups (600 ml) water

Because the sausage skins have been preserved in salt, they will need to be well soaked and rinsed in cold water. These can then be squeezed dry and cut into 6 in (15 cm) lengths. Tie a knot in one end to prepare the skins to be filled.

Melt a heaping teaspoon of butter in a saucepan. Add the shallots and cook, without browning, until tender. Remove from the heat and allow them to cool completely.

Pass the meats and back fat three times through the fine blade of a meat grinder, or purée them in a food processor and then push through a fine sieve.

Warm half the cream and add to the breadcrumbs. Keep this mixture at room temperature.

In a bowl over a pan of ice, season the ground meats with the salt, pepper, and nutmeg. Add 1 egg at a time, mixing it in well. As the egg is being stirred in, the mixture will return to a gelatinous

BELOW
White Pudding

form. Add the second egg and mix again. Add the cornstarch to the shallots and stir into the meat. Stir in the crumbs and cream mixture before adding the remaining heavy cream. Re-check the seasoning.

The sausage skins can now be filled. This can be simply achieved by using a piping bag and plain nozzle. Place the skin over the nozzle and pull to the knotted end. Pipe in the sausage mixture and as you do so the skin will fill and extend naturally. Leave up to 1¾ in (4 cm) of excess sausage skin – which then provides space for shrinkage during cooking. Tie the other end.

The sausages can now be pricked in 3–4 places. Season the milk with salt and pour the milk and water into a saucepan. Put the sausages into the liquid and heat it slowly, not allowing it to rise above 180°F/82°C. Cook for 15 minutes before removing from the stove and allowing the sausages to cool in the liquid.

The sausages can now be removed from the liquid. If serving immediately, dry and brush them with butter before pan-frying gently or broiling until golden brown. Otherwise, the puddings can be refrigerated until needed.

Note: The skin can be removed, if preferred, before pan-frying or broiling. Make an incision with a sharp knife along the length of the sausage. The skin will now easily peel away.

Other flavors can be added to the sausages – freshly chopped herbs (sage or thyme work particularly well), diced sweet peppers, grated lemon zest, and mustard seeds.

Slow-honey-roast Duck

Domestic ducks were once a very familiar sight in Britain, scratching around in the farmyard alongside the chickens. Many larger houses or villages would have a pond on which ducks could swim, offering another source of fresh meat.

For this recipe, I have adopted the slow-roasting cooking method often used in the old days. The duck is basted every so often with honey to give the skin a crisp texture and a golden color. The meat becomes so tender, with such a full flavor, that you'll want to eat more and more of it. For this reason, it's best to allow half a duck per person. *Mashed Potato Sauce* (page 125) goes perfectly with this dish.

SERVES 2

2½–3 lb (1.25–1.5 kg) duck
1 teaspoon crushed white peppercorns
2 teaspoons coarse sea salt
5 heaped tablespoons honey

Preheat the oven to 325°F/160°C. The duck-breast skin should first be scored four or five times, only cutting into the skin itself, not into the meat. Put the duck in a small roasting pan. Sprinkle the peppercorns and the salt over the duck, pushing the salt into the skin. Spoon the honey over the duck, making sure it is completely covered. Place the duck in the oven.

After the first half hour of cooking, baste the duck with the honey and duck residue in the roasting pan. Let it slow-roast for another 30 minutes. The salt sprinkled over the duck will draw the excess water and fat from the skin itself and this will, obviously, collect in the roasting pan.

After the second half hour, remove the duck from the roasting pan and from one corner of the pan, carefully pour off as much fat as possible; the fat will be floating on top of the honey in the pan. Replace the duck in the pan, baste with the honey residue, and return to the oven. The duck can now be left to slow-roast, basting every 15 minutes for another hour.

The duck has now been slowly cooking for 2 hours. Remove the duck once more from the pan and again pour off any excess fat. Baste the duck with the honey and return to the oven. During the last half hour of cooking, baste the duck every 5–10 minutes. The honey will now have reduced and become very thick, glazing the duck even more.

OPPOSITE
Slow-honey-roast Duck

After the 2½ hours are up, remove the duck from the oven and from the pan. If the honey glaze still seems to be a little thin, simply boil it in the pan to reduce it to a thick, coating consistency. Pour it over the duck and let the duck rest for 15 minutes.

Remove the legs, along with the breasts, making sure they are left whole. Place the breast and leg for each serving on plates, spooning a tablespoon of honey and any residue over each one. The slow-roast duck will be well done throughout; the meat will have become very tender and moist, melting nicely as you eat it.

BELOW
Fillet of Venison Wellington

Fillet of Venison Wellington

Wellington is a dish usually associated with fillet of beef, but I've tried it with venison and it works equally well, having the extra benefit of a stronger, gamey flavor. Venison is one of the healthiest and most nutritious foods available. Even though it is a "red" meat, it is lower in fat, higher in protein, and contains fewer calories than most other red and white meats. "Venison" is the name given to deer that have been killed and hung. There are five or six species of deer available in Britain – the varieties sold for meat are roe, fallow, or red deer. In France, roe is considered to be the ultimate venison meat (called *chevreuil*), since it is the youngest and the most tender. Fallow deer follows next in popularity, but I consider it to be equal to roe. Fallow has a slightly stronger flavor and also gives you a larger saddle fillet, which will still holds a good, pink finish while the pastry crust is baking. The largest of the three types of deer meat is red deer. It often requires a longer hanging period in order to tenderize the meat. In the US, farm-raised red deer from New Zealand are available in some butcher shops and supermarkets. (Check with your state's game commission about deer hunting.)

Ask your butcher to bone the venison for you and trim the fillet of all sinew; have the bones chopped to be used to create a game sauce. This recipe can, of course, be made using beef fillet. If you decide do for this, simply increase the cooking time by 15–20 minutes.

SERVES 4

12 oz–1 lb (350–450 g) *Quick Puff Pastry*
  (page 365)
1–1½ lb (450–675 g) boned loin of venison
  from a saddle deer, preferably fallow
4 tablespoons (50 g) unsalted butter
4–6 thin *Pancakes* (page 82)
1 egg, beaten
Salt and pepper

For the Stuffing

8 oz (225 g) mushrooms, finely chopped
1 onion, finely chopped
2 strips of bacon, finely diced

1 garlic clove, crushed
Pinch of chopped fresh sage
Pinch of chopped fresh thyme
2 tablespoons (25 g) unsalted butter
½ cup (50 g) shelled chestnuts, chopped
½ cup (25 g) fresh white breadcrumbs
1 teaspoon chopped fresh parsley
1 large chicken breast half, skinned and ground
    or very finely chopped
1 egg, beaten
Salt and pepper

For the Sauce

Venison bones (optional)
2½ cups (600 ml) *Red Wine Sauce* (page 48)
1–2 teaspoons cranberry jelly

To make the stuffing, cook the mushrooms on their own in a pan until almost dry. Cook the chopped onion, bacon, garlic, sage, and thyme in the butter for a few minutes without browning. Let this mixture cool. Add the chestnuts, breadcrumbs, and parsley. Season the chicken with salt and pepper; gradually add the egg and mix until firm to the touch. Stir in the mushrooms and the bacon mixture and check for seasoning. The stuffing can be made up to two days advance and kept refrigerated until needed.

The sauce can also be made in advance. If you have the venison bones, preheat the oven to 425°F/220°C. Roast the bones in the preheated oven for about 30 minutes until browned. Add them to the reduction for the red wine sauce before adding the veal *jus*, then cook in the normal way. After the sauce has been pushed through a sieve, a delicious venison flavor will have developed. Stir in the cranberry jelly to give the sauce a slightly sweet taste.

Roll out the pastry until large enough to wrap the venison and approximately ⅛ in (3 mm) thick. Let it rest in the refrigerator.

Season the venison and fry in the butter in a hot pan until browned but not cooked. Let it cool.

To make the Wellington, lay two or three pancakes along the center of the pastry and spread with three-fourths of the stuffing to cover them. Place the fillet on top and spread with the remaining stuffing. Fold the pancakes around the meat and place the other two or three on top. Brush the edges of the pastry with beaten egg and fold over to enclose the meat and stuffing. Trim off any excess pastry and turn the package over onto a buttered roasting pan. Let them rest in the refrigerator for 30 minutes.

Preheat the oven to 425°F/220°C.

Brush the pastry with a little more beaten egg and roast in the preheated oven for 20–25 minutes. This timing will leave the meat still pink inside. Let it relax for 10–15 minutes.

Now, it's time to carve the Wellington. Cut one thick slice or two thinner slices per serving and serve with the rich venison sauce.

Note: A potato accompaniment is not essential for this dish since you have a pastry border. However, if you are a potato fan, I suggest you serve buttered new potatoes with perhaps some green beans.

See also
Roast Chicken Sandwich (page 274)
*Traditional Roast Turkey with Sage, Lemon, and
Chestnut Stuffing with all the Trimmings*
(page 327)

Picnics

The *Oxford Dictionary* defines the word "picnic" as "a fashionable social event in which each party present contributed a share of the provisions." I don't know about you, but I feel the research for this description must have been done many years ago. How times change! Today, I think of a picnic as an eating outdoors event, the "hamper" usually provided by the host. Having said that, a picnic *does* seem to bring family and friends together, with everybody helping prepare the food – so the dictionary could be correct.

We think of picnics and food eaten in the open air as one and the same thing, but this was not always the case. The origin of the word itself are fairly obscure, but it probably derives from the French "*pique-nique*," the terms appeared around the same time, the late seventeenth century. The Pick-Nick Club was formed by a group of fashionable Londoners, who used to meet in each others houses to enjoy selected items of food and to provide various types fo entertainment. The idea obviously spread. In 1802, *The London Times* clarified the new fashion: "A Pic Nic supper consists of a variety of dishes. The Subscribers to the entertainment have a bill of fare presented to them, with a number against each dish. The lot he draws obliges him to furnish the dish marked against it, which he either takes with him in his carriage, or sends by a servant."

By 1815, only thirteen years later, the concept became so popular that picnics were given – out of doors – to celebrate Napoleon's defeat at Waterloo. Since then, "picnic" has firmly meant a meal eaten outside.

But people have always eaten under the sky – eating in the fields while bringing in the harvest, eating in the woods while out hunting, and when the fish were not biting, fishermen would munch picnics on riverbanks. It is said that Henry VIII and Anne Boleyn ate pasties when they went a-Maying, and Queen Victoria enjoyed some simple foods in the deer forests around Balmoral, washed down by a dram or two. These picnic meals were purely for convenience, however, not taking too much time away from the primary, and most important, object of the expedition, the sport itself. Lady Harriet St Clair, in *Dainty Dishes* (published in 1862), gives the following advice for a shooting breakfast: "Gentlemen usually prefer eating this about the middle of the day, in the open air, with their fingers, in order that they may lose no time; so it is not generally necessary to send knives and forks or tablecloths; but you must take care, in order not to make them angry, that the luncheon is there at the right time and place." It's interesting that this "eating event" was the means of introducing the first "convenience" foods, provided to fill a gap and not interfere with the main event. The fashionable picnics of today make appearances at the most elegant events. Whether it's a day at Ascot, the Henley Regatta, or at the Glyndebourne opera, the classic picnic hamper, often takes priority over the actual event.

Many times, meals away from home were a necessity. When traveling by stagecoach or, later, by railway, food was not provided and was unreliable at the various stops (then as now, unfortunately), so the answer was to take a home-prepared meal that was portable – in other words a picnic. Charles Dickens would take picnics with him as he traveled around the country giving readings of his works. Railway excursion picnics – traveling by rail to a particular location, laden down with picnic baskets, rugs, parasols, friends, and bottles of wine – were hugely fashionable during the Victorian era.

Whatever the reason for a picnic, the food must be portable and sturdy enough to withstand travel. The original and best-known picnic dish must be the British meat pie or pasty, vegetables and gravy encased in their own crisp, crunchy pastry case. Cornish pasties or their Scottish counterpart, Forfar bridies, are perfect, as well as the traditional English veal and ham or bacon and egg pies. And, of course, sandwiches are popular. In *Jeeves and the Old School Chum* (*Very Good, Jeeves*, P. G. Wodehouse), Bingo waxes lyrical about what Jeeves has packed in the picnic basket: "There's ham sandwiches," he proceeded, a strange, soft light in his eyes, "and tongue sandwiches and potted meat sandwiches and game sandwiches and hard-boiled eggs and lobster and a cold chicken and sardines and a cake and a couple of bottles of Bollinger and some old brandy…" Despite this over-abundance, Bertie felt he had to add, "And if we want a bite to eat after that, of course we can go to the pub."

You'll find plenty of ideas for your next picnic within this chapter. Creating time to make homemade pork pies, or any of the other traditional British picnic foods presented here, is really worth every minute and every mouthful. You feel such pride when presenting a picnic hamper, knowing it contains mostly homemade things – the races at Ascot will hardly be noticed! But take a warning from something that happened to me many years ago when we were planning a family and friends picnic. A friend telephoned to ask what sort of sandwiches we should have. I replied, "ham, cheese, egg, with, tomato, cucumber, pickle, etc." Off we go and lunchtime arrives. We all delve in and find one ham, one cheese, one egg, along with one tomato, one cucumber and one plain pickle! Guess which sandwich that particular friend had to eat...

Another outdoor eating event is the barbecue. Although not a long-standing British tradition, it has become a very popular summer custom, one that can provide a delicious meal at a low cost. The barbecue also falls under the picnic heading, but one that provides hot cooked food. The food is transported raw and then cooked over charcoal *in situ*, whether in someone's backyard or on the beach perhaps. The backyard barbecue idea originated in the US and is popular in Australia and South Africa – it definitely has something to do with the climate! But the basics of cooking in the open air over charcoal are certainly not new. These methods date from prehistoric times since the discovery of fire.

Whether you choose a picnic or a barbecue, I do hope your hamper has room for one of the following recipes.

Cornish Pasty

The pasty has been a staple food in Cornwall for centuries, and it often went by different names: "tiddy oggy" was one and "hoggen" another, meaning a version without potatoes. Almost any food at one time was fitted into a pasty crust, including meat, fish, vegetables, eggs, or fruit, sometimes savory at one end of the pasty and sweet at the other. I'm not sure that such a combination would be accepted today, but I have been offered chocolate pasties before. I prefer to eat and cook the classic recipe, one that I stick close to here.

Legend has it that if a Cornish pasty was dropped 100 feet down a tin mine without the pastry breaking, a good pasty had landed. Thereafter the pasty could be broken open and the meal enjoyed. I don't suggest you try that with this recipe, but the pastry used here will stay crisp while it encases lots of rich and tender flavor.

SERVES 4

1¾–2 lb (750–900 g) *Puff* or *Shortcrust Pastry* (page 365 or 364)
8 oz (225 g) beef skirt steak, sliced into very thin strips (approximately 2–3 × ¾ in/6–8 × 2 cm)
1 medium potato, peeled and thinly sliced
1 large onion, peeled and thinly sliced
1 small rutabaga, peeled and thinly sliced
2 tablespoons (25 g) butter
1 egg, beaten
Salt and pepper

Roll the pastry between ⅛–¼ in (3 mm and 5 mm) thick. Cut disks approximately 8 in (20 cm) in diameter. Season the meat and vegetables separately with salt and grindings of pepper. Melt the butter and trickle it over the vegetables. The meat can now be layered to one side of the pastry between individual layers of potatoes, rutabaga, and onion, leaving a border of pastry to seal. For a better finished shape, carefully arrange the vegetables in a domed fashion.

Brush the border of the pastry with the beaten egg. Fold the pastry over and seal. The edge can now be rolled and pinched from one end to the other, giving a rope effect, or simply cut to your desired shape. Place the pasties on a greased baking pan and brush with more egg. It's now best to refrigerate before baking.

Preheat the oven to 400°F/200°C, place the pasties in the oven and bake for 15–20 minutes until golden brown. Now, reduce the oven temperature to 350°F/180°C and continue to cook for 30–35 minutes. The homemade Cornish pasties are now ready to serve.

Pasties are best served piping hot, straight from the oven. If you happen to be in Cornwall, why not have a foaming mug of local "scrumpy" to go with them?

Note: For an even more peppery flavor, black pepper shortcrust pastry can also be used (page 261).

I also love to eat pasties with either a splash of Worcestershire sauce or a spoonful of *Piccalilli* (page 385).

The amount of pastry might seem large; this is necessary, however, to obtain a securely sealed pasty and allow for a rope finish, if desired.

Roast Chicken Sandwich

The Earl of Sandwich (see page 372) would have approved of this – well-seasoned and moist roast chicken sandwiched between slices of good-quality crusty bread; this becomes almost a complete meal in itself.

The choice of bread is very important when making any type of sandwich. I prefer to use an uncut whole wheat or grain loaf. Slices from these breads have a good texture and taste that enhance the filling. You will notice the bread is not buttered in this recipe. Butter has been replaced with the cooking juices for maximum flavor. For the ultimate eating experience, the sandwich is best served warm.

MAKES 4 ROUNDS

4 lb (1.75 kg) roasting chicken
4 tablespoons (50 g) butter, softened
1–2 tablespoons cooking oil
8 slices of good-quality bread, preferably whole wheat or multigrain

BELOW
Roast Chicken Sandwich

Coarse sea salt and pepper
½ of a head of iceberg lettuce
4–5 tablespoons homemade *Mayonnaise* (page 49)
    or commercial mayonnaise, to bind
Squeeze of lemon juice (optional)

Preheat the oven to 400°F/200°C. Brush the chicken with the butter and season well with salt and pepper. Place a roasting pan with the cooking oil over a medium heat. Cook the chicken for 6–7 minutes until it becomes a golden color. Turn the chicken over to color the other side.

Now, turn the bird on its back, place in the preheated oven, and roast for 50 minutes. During the cooking time, it is important to baste with the fat and juices in the pan every 10–15 minutes. To check that the bird is cooked, pinch the leg between thumb and forefinger: the meat should give, feeling tender. The maximum time the chicken will need is 1 hour.

Remove the chicken from the oven and from the roasting pan and let it rest for 20–30 minutes. Any fat and juices left in the roasting pan can now be strained into a small bowl. It's these juices that I will be "buttering" the bread with, not wasting a single taste.

After the resting time, remove the legs and their skin, removing the meat from the bones. All of the dark meat can now be shredded finely with a sharp knife. The juices and fat saved in the bowl can now be stirred together, ready to brush onto the bread. If there seems to be a lot of fat, then before mixing, spoon away some of it to leave equal amounts of fat and juices. This is purely optional, but it adds extra flavor to the sandwich.

Mix the mayonnaise with the shredded chicken and season with salt and pepper. Brush the slices of bread with the fat and cooking liquid. Spread the shredded meat and mayonnaise mixture onto four of the slices. Shred the iceberg lettuce finely and season it with a few granules of coarse sea salt and fresh pepper (a squeeze of lemon juice can also be added to the lettuce for extra bite).

Divide the shredded lettuce among the covered slices. Now, the breasts can be carved. Either slice while still on the bone or remove the meat before cutting. Lay a few slices per serving onto the lettuce. Place the other slice of bread on top and the sandwich is finished. Apply a little pressure on top and cut each sandwich in half.

The "perfect" roast chicken sandwich is ready to serve.

Variation

A quick, lower-fat mayonnaise can be made for a healthier sandwich. The fat/juices on the bread slices will have to be omitted.

Take a scant ⅔ cup (140 g) of fromage frais (fromage blanc is a very low fat version), 1 teaspoon of Dijon mustard and 1 teaspoon of lemon juice. Mix all three ingredients together, season with salt and pepper, and the healthy mayonnaise is finished. An egg yolk can be added, for a richer color and flavor. This recipe can be substituted for any mayonnaise used throughout the book.

Extras for the Sandwich Filling

Any of these can be used, individually or all together, to give a different flavor to the sandwich. Mix your choice of ingredients with the mayonnaise.

½ small onion, grated
1 teaspoon English, Dijon or wholegrain mustard
1 teaspoon chopped fresh tarragon
2–3 scallions, finely shredded

Coarse Pork Pâté

There is really very little difference between French pâtés and terrines and English potted meats. The word "*pâté*" means paste and that is virtually what potted meat is, meat reduced to a paste so that it can be kept in a pot. This recipe derives from many traditions. It's cooked in a style usually associated with the French confit (meaning "preserved'). It is then shredded and covered with its own fat, rather like the French *rillettes*, but potted meats were also covered with fat, usually clarified butter, for precisely the same reason – to preserve the meat.

The 1 lb (450 g) of lard is for poaching the pork. Very little of it will actually be used to finish the dish, so please don't be put off.

This recipe has very few ingredients, but when

they are combined for the pâté, they deliver a lot of flavors. If accompanied by a good homemade chutney (see the Preserves chapter, page 388) and crusty bread or hot toast, you'll have a delicious taste experience.

SERVES 6–8

1 lb (450 g) lard for cooking
2 lb (900 g) skinned and boned pork belly, cut into 4 pieces
2 garlic cloves, peeled
1 bay leaf
Fresh thyme sprig
1¼ cups (150 ml) *Chicken Stock* (page 33, optional)
Salt and pepper

Preheat the oven to 350°F/180°C.

Melt the lard in an ovenproof saucepan or dish. Add the four pork pieces, with the garlic, bay leaf, and the sprig of thyme. Bring to a simmer, cover with a lid, and cook in the preheated oven for 1–1½ hours.

After an hour has passed, check the pork by piercing with a knife. The meat must be so well cooked that it feels it will almost fall apart. If it isn't ready, continue to cook for the last 30 minutes.

After it has cooked, remove the meat from the lard and transfer it to a bowl. Discard the bay leaf and thyme. The garlic can simply be crushed with the back of a knife and added to the pork pieces.

Shred the pork with a fork. The paté will be smoother the finer the pork is shredded.

Strain the fat from the pan and add a tablespoon at a time to the paté along with the chicken stock, if using. The stock will guarantee a moist finish. Five to six tablespoons of each should be plenty. Season well with salt and pepper.

The pâté will now be soft and damp in texture; this is perfect since it will become firm when it's cold. It's absolutely vital the shredding and finishing of the pâté is carried out while the pork is still warm because it will absorb all of the juices and flavors.

Now, divide among six or eight ⅔ cup/150 ml ramekins or press into a dish holding 2½ cups (600 ml). Spoon a small amount of warm fat on top of each so that it is barely covers. This will seal in all of the flavors and become a preserving layer. Refrigerated, the pâté will now keep for up to 1 week.

Remove from the refrigerator 1–2 hours before serving. This will allow the pâté to come closer to room temperature and make it softer to eat.

Note: 2–4 oz (50–100 g) of prunes soaked in Armagnac can be chopped and added to the pâté after it is shredded. Adding a little Armagnac also increases the flavor.

Meatloaf

The basic idea of meatloaf is a very old one. In the Middle Ages, people would pound various meats together with spices and other flavorings before stiffening the mixture with eggs and breadcrumbs and then baking it. The recipe was probably taken to America by the Pilgrim Fathers, and it has since come back to Britain as the seemingly unique American "meatloaf."

A meatloaf is useful since it can be served hot or cold, providing lots of flavor at both temperatures. It's as a cold dish that it found its way into our picnic hampers. The loaf ingredients can actually be shaped many different ways, known then by different names such as meatballs or "savory ducks."
I use the mixture as the filling for my homemade sausage rolls, see opposite.

I cook this loaf in a standard 8½ x 4½ inch (22 x 11 cm) loaf pan, which can be lined with bacon strips or the bacon can be simply diced and folded into the rest of the ingredients. If you are using this recipe for meatloaf, then the bacon will have to be finely diced and added to the meat mixture or omitted all together.

SERVES 6–8

10–12 strips of bacon
12 oz (350 g) pork belly, skinned and boned
6 oz (175 g) lean pork shoulder
4 oz (100 g) pork fat
2 onions, chopped or minced
2 slices of white bread, crusts removed, soaked in milk and then squeezed of excess
Finely grated zest of 1 lemon
1 egg, beaten
Pinch of ground allspice
Pinch of freshly grated nutmeg
1 teaspoon chopped fresh marjoram or thyme

1 teaspoon chopped fresh sage
1½ tablespoons of Worcestershire sauce
Butter, melted
Salt and pepper

Preheat the oven to 350°F/180°C and select a 8½ x 4½ inch (22 x 11 cm) loaf pan. If lining the loaf pan with the bacon, then simply lay the strips in, slightly overlapping them and leaving the ends hanging over the edge of the pan. The bacon can be stretched using the flat side of a knife, to lengthen them. The pork belly, shoulder/cheeks and pork fat can now all be ground in a food processor or a meat grinder. The bacon should be diced and added to the ground meats, if not used to line the pan.

Obviously, if you are buying all of the meat from your butcher, you can ask for the meat to be ground. Ask for the meat to be ground once, giving the meat a somewhat coarse texture.

If you are grinding the meat yourself, here are a couple of tips to make the job easier. Cut all three kinds of meat and the fat into ½–¾ in (1–2 cm) dice. Make sure the meat and the machine's attachments are very cold. In fact, at the point of almost freezing, the meat will glide through the machine. If ground at room temperature, the meat becomes soft and gets caught. If cut small, the meat can be ground in a food processor; don't overgrind, however. Be sure to process in small quantities, making the job a lot easier for the machine.

Now, mix all of the ingredients except the butter with the meats. This can be done easily with an electric mixer. Check for seasoning, adding Worcestershire sauce to increase the flavor.

Press the mixture into the loaf pan evenly, and if you have lined it with bacon, fold the strips over. Brush with a teaspoon of melted butter and bake in the preheated oven for 1½–1¾ hours. After it has cooked, the loaf will come away from the sides of the pan.

Let it stand for 10–15 minutes before turning out. If cooked for serving cold, then let it cool in the pan. After it's cold, turn out and wrap with plastic wrap until needed.

Note: As a main dish, meatloaf goes very well with *Onion Gravy* (page 50) and creamy *Mashed Potatoes* (page 124).

If using the onion gravy, add any juices from the loaf; this keeps from wasting flavors.

Diced dried apricots can be added to the gravy.
Applesauce (page 44) is a good accompaniment to meatloaf.

Any excess mixture can be shaped into patties, pan-fried, and served on a bun with fried onions.

This recipe will make 20–25 sausage rolls.

Sausage Rolls

Homemade sausage rolls seem to have become an annual event at British Christmases, but they used to form part of afternoon and high teas and are typical for a packed lunch or picnic. They are very simple to make and will give you a lot of self-satisfaction as you watch your friends enjoy the results.

The filling has been made from bought sausage with a few other flavors to help it along. The *Meatloaf* mixture opposite can also be used, for a totally "homemade" experience.

BELOW
Sausage Rolls

1 lb (450 g) commercially made sausage
1 onion, finely chopped or grated
Finely grated zest of ½ lemon
1 heaped teaspoon of mixed chopped fresh thyme
    and sage
8 oz (225 g) *Quick Puff* or *Flaky Pastry* (page 365)
1 egg yolk, mixed with 2 teaspoons milk
Salt, pepper and freshly grated nutmeg

Preheat the oven to 400°F/200°C.

Mix together the sausage, onion, lemon, and chopped herbs. Season with the salt, pepper, and nutmeg. This can now be refrigerated to firm while the pastry is being rolled.

Roll out the pastry thinly (about ⅛ in/2–3 mm) on a floured surface into three long strips approximately 4 in (10 cm) wide.

The sausage mixture can now be shaped, using your hands, into three long links, preferably 1 in (2.5 cm) thick. If the meat is too moist, then dust it with flour.

Place each "sausage" on a pastry strip, ¾–1½ in (2–3 cm) from the edge of the pastry. Brush the pastry along the other side nearest the sausage with the egg yolk. Fold the pastry over the meat, rolling it as you do so. Where the pastry meets, leave a small overlap before cutting away any excess. After being rolled all along, cut each into 2 in (5 cm) sausage rolls.

The sausage rolls can now all be transferred to a greased baking sheet. Lift them carefully, making sure that the seal is on the bottom when placed on a baking sheet. The rolls can be left as they are, or 3–4 cuts with scissors can be made along the top. Brush each with the remaining egg yolk before baking in the preheated oven for 25–30 minutes.

After they are baked, golden, and crisp, remove from the oven and serve them warm. Alternatively, allow the rolls to cool on a wire rack and keep in a tightly covered jar or airtight plastic container.

Note: Many additions can be added to the sausage mixture. My favorite is to add 2 oz (50 g) of chopped prunes. Cut soft prunes into a small dice. Soak in a tablespoon of Armagnac (optional) and add to the mixture. Pork and prune sausage rolls are simply sensational. Other additions might be chopped scallions, chopped walnuts, or chestnuts. Or boil cider with the onions, reducing until dry. Cool, add, and you have pork and cider rolls.

Vegetarian Cheese and Onion "Sausage" Rolls ⓥ

These are a lovely vegetarian alternative to our very homely *Sausage Rolls* (page 277). They consist of simply cheese, onions, and pastry. The pastry has been made with the addition of vegetarian suet, giving the rolls a new texture.

Some of the filling might ooze out during the cooking, so the rolls might not have a "neat" finish, but the flavor is fantastic.

Individual cheese and onion rolls are delicious to serve as part of a picnic or for afternoon tea.

For the Pastry

1¼ cups (175 g) self-rising flour
Pinch of salt
3 oz (75 g) shredded vegetarian suet
5–6 tablespoons cold water

For the Filling

6 oz (175 g) strong Cheddar cheese, grated
1 medium onion, finely chopped
Salt and cayenne pepper

Preheat the oven to 425°F/220°C.

Sift together the flour and salt. Mix in the suet. Add enough of the cold water to create a pliable dough. Divide the dough into two pieces. On a floured surface, roll into two strips 12 x 4 in (30 x 10 cm). Brush water around the border. Mix together the grated cheese and onion and season with salt and cayenne pepper.

The filling can now be spooned onto the two pastry strips up to the moistened edge. Roll up as for two long jelly rolls, and slice each into four or five slices, giving a total of eight to ten little rolls. Place on a waxed paper-covered pan, keeping the sealed edge on the bottom.

Bake in the preheated oven for 15–20 minutes until golden brown and crispy. The cheese and onion rolls are delicious served cold but are even better served warm because the cheese is still soft and melting.

Note: Lots of other cheeses can be used. The Cheddar can be mixed with half Stilton and the onion replaced with scallions. Chopped raisins also go well with the cheese and onion. Another flavor I like to add is chopped tarragon or mixed herbs. They all give an extra perfume to the finished rolls.

Gruyère Cheese, Leek, and Mushroom Flan ⓥ

This is my favorite flan recipe, one that's full of textures and lots of flavors. Cheddar cheese also works well for this recipe. A tasty accompaniment to offer is the *Spicy Tomato and Mint Relish* (page 381).

SERVES 8–12

1 large onion, sliced
2 oz (50 g) mushrooms, sliced
3 tablespoons (40 g) unsalted butter
1½ tablespoons peanut or vegetable oil
1 medium leek, shredded and washed
2 eggs
1 egg yolk
1¼ cups (150 ml) heavy cream or milk
4 oz (100 g) Gruyère or Cheddar cheese, grated
Cayenne pepper (optional)
6 oz (175 g) *Shortcrust* or *Puff Pastry*
  (page 364 or 365)
Salt and pepper

Preheat the oven to 350°F/180°C.

Butter a 8 in (20 cm) flan pan or a flan ring and baking sheet.

To start the filling, cook the sliced onion and mushrooms in 1 tablespoon of the butter and ½ tablespoon of the oil for 5–6 minutes until tender. Let it cool. The shredded leek can now be blanched by plunging into boiling salted water for 1 minute. This will tenderize the leek without making it too soggy. After the minute, drain in a colander and allow it to cool naturally without running under cold water.

In a bowl, beat the eggs and the egg yolk together, then add the cream or milk and set to one side. Melt the remaining butter and oil together until blended, then let it cool.

Mix the grated cheese with the eggs and cream and fold in the onion, mushrooms, and leek along with the cool butter and oil mixture. Season with salt and pepper

and a little cayenne, if using. The mixture can be made the day before it's needed since it keeps very well.

Roll out the pastry and line the flan pan or ring, leaving any excess pastry overhanging the edge; after it has cooked, the excess pastry can be carefully cut away to give an even finish. Refrigerate it for 20 minutes. Line the pastry with waxed paper and fill with baking beans or pie weights. Bake blind in the preheated oven for 15–20 minutes, then allow it to cool. Remove the beans/weights and paper.

BELOW
Gruyère Cheese, Leek, and Mushroom Flan

Reduce the oven temperature to 325°F/160°C. Pour the filling mixture into the pastry base and cook in the oven for about 35–40 minutes until the flan just sets. The tart should brown during cooking. If it starts to over-brown, lightly cover with foil or waxed paper. The flan is best left to rest for 20–30 minutes before serving because this will help set the texture of the filling, creating a creamy taste.

Homemade Pork Pie

The British have been making pies since the Middle Ages at least. The raised "coffin" casing was to protect the meat inside from the extreme heat of the fire, and usually was not eaten. However, as the art of making pastry developed, many pie recipes did also, and the pork pie became a tradition. It was perfected at Melton Mowbray, and the original recipe contained, some anchovy essence.

A lot of dishes, such as this one and *Corned Beef* (page 189), seem like hard work, and you might think there is no point in going to all this trouble when there are so many bought varieties available. The reality is that both recipes are relatively simple. And there is one thing that eating a bought pie can't give you - that is the personal satisfaction of knowing you've made it.

I use pork shoulder and back fat for this recipe. Pork belly can also be used, maintaining the same total weight. The filling must be made before the pastry, since hot water crust has to be molded while still warm. To finish the pie, a homemade pork jelly can be made using pigs' trotters. Alternatively, homemade chicken stock can be used and set with leaf or powdered gelatin; 1 oz (25 g) per 2½ cups (600 ml) stock will guarantee a good setting consistency.

SERVES 8–12

2 tablespoons (25 g) butter
2 large onions, finely chopped
1 teaspoon chopped fresh sage
1 teaspoon chopped fresh thyme
1 teaspoon ground mace
1 teaspoon English mustard powder
A blend of ¼ teaspoon cinnamon, ¼ teaspoon
    nutmeg, a pinch each of cloves, ginger, and
    ground coriander

2 lb 2 oz (1 kg) trimmed shoulder pork
    (or pork belly)
6 oz (175 g) pork back fat (or pork belly)
Salt and pepper

For the Jellied Stock

3 pig's trotters or 2 ham hocks
1 onion
1 carrot
2 celery sticks
Few black peppercorns
Sprig of fresh thyme
1 bay leaf
2 quarts (1.8 liters) water
1 oz (25 g) gelatin (or 2 leaves), if needed for
    5 cups (1.2 liters) stock

For the Pastry

⅔ cup (150 ml) milk
⅔ cup (150 ml) water
6 oz (175 g) lard
6 cups (675 g) all-purpose flour
1 teaspoon salt
1 egg, beaten, to glaze

The mold used for this recipe is a loose-bottomed or spring-form pan approximately 8 in (20 cm) in diameter and 2½–3 in (6.75–7.5 cm) deep.

First, make the jellied stock. Place all of the ingredients except for the gelatin, in a saucepan and bring to a simmer. Cook for 3 hours, before straining the stock through a sieve.

The stock can now be boiled and reduced to 2½–4 cups (600–900 ml). Refrigerate the reduced stock until cold and firm. If the jelly is still a little too liquid, add 1 or 2 leaves of gelatin to the stock.

Now, make the filling. Melt the butter in a saucepan. After it bubbles, add the chopped onions and cook for a few minutes, without browning, until they begin to soften.

Remove the pan of onions from the stove and add the sage, thyme, mace, mustard, and spices. Let the filling cool. While this is cooling, the pork shoulder and back fat can be chopped into ¼ in (5 mm) rough dice. The meat can also be ground in a food processor or a meat grinder. Dicing will, however, always maintain the maximum moistness in the meat. Mix the cooked onions with the chopped pork, seasoning well with salt and pepper. Refrigerate until needed.

Now, make the pastry. Preheat the oven to 425°F/220°C. Grease the spring-form pan and place it on a baking sheet. Bring the milk, water, and lard to a boil. Sift the flour with the salt into a bowl, forming a well in the center. Pour in the hot lard liquid and stir into the flour to form a dough.

Knead lightly by hand and finish to a smooth dough. Keep a quarter of the pastry warm to one side, then work or roll the rest of the pastry on a lightly floured surface until just large enough to fill the mold and approximately ¼ in (5 mm) thick.

Place the pastry into the pan and work by hand, gently pushing it out to make it fill to just above the top of the mold. Trim the edges.

Fill the pastry with the pork filling, packing it in just above the top. Fold the pastry around the top onto the mixture and brush with the beaten egg. Roll out the remaining pastry to the same thickness and place it on top of the pie, pressing the edges together and cutting away any excess. Using a ½ in (1 cm) plain metal piping nozzle, cut a cross in the center, pressing the nozzle in to create a hole and leaving it in place. The pie can now be decorated, if desired, with pastry trimmings. The border can also be pinched with a fork to give a simple patterned edge. Brush the pie with the beaten egg.

Bake the pie immediately in the hot oven for 30 minutes. The oven temperature can now be reduced to 375°F/190°C and the pie cooked for another hour. After the pie becomes a golden brown, gently cover with foil to prevent the pastry from burning.

At this point, the pie can be checked, inserting a skewer through the nozzle. The skewer should be hot and clean when removed. If not, continue to cook for another 15–20 minutes.

After it's cooked, lift the pie from the oven and relax for 15 minutes before removing from the spring-form pan. Brush the pastry with the beaten egg. Return to the oven for another 15–20 minutes until the pie has a golden glaze.

Remove from the oven and allow the pie to rest for 30 minutes. The pie filling will have shrunk slightly during the cooking process, leaving a space to be filled with the gelatin.

Using a measuring cup and funnel, pour a little of the thickened stock into the pie. This will be absorbed slowly by the meat, giving it a moister finish. Repeat this process until the pie has cooled. Now, refrigerate before adding enough more cold gelatin to fill the pie. Any remaining gelatin can simply be frozen, ready for your next pork pie. After you've tasted the results, you'll realize it really was worth every minute you put into it.

Note: It's best to make the pork pie at least 48 hours before serving. This will give the filling time to mature, with all the spices flavoring the pork stuffing.

For a richer, golden jelly, the pig's trotters can first be browned in a hot pan along with the vegetables. Now, simply follow the rest of the recipe method.

The homemade *Piccalilli* on page 385 goes very well with this dish.

See also

Arbroath Smokie and Cream Cheese Pâté (page 89)
Boiled and Baked Ham (page 211)
Cheddar Apple Cake (page 344)
Corned Beef (page 189)
Cucumber Sandwiches (page 373)
Egg Sandwiches (page 372)
Haslet (page 212)
Jam Sandwiches (page 374)
Pressed Ox Tongue (page 216)
Scotch Eggs (page 73)
Smoked Salmon Rolls (page 374)
Watercress and Cream Cheese Sandwiches (page 373)

Desserts

This chapter will be many people's favorite, since we all seem to love desserts. The British have quite a sweet tooth, and I believe because of that, the British "pudding" tradition is second to none. The word "pudding" should actually be used only for rich foods that are normally baked or steamed. Many recipes in this chapter fall under this category – *Ale Cake*, *Steamed Upsidedown Pudding*, *Blackberry and Apple Pudding*, *Apricot and Almond Pudding* and *Sticky Toffee Pudding*, for instance. The other recipes are "styled" desserts – trifles, fools, syllabubs, fruit pies, tarts – and really fall under the "desserts" category.
Here they all are, under one heading, creating a mixture of textures and flavors to excite your tastebuds.

Honey was the earliest sweetener in the British diet and it continued to be used long after sugar – from tropical sugar cane – was introduced. Originally very expensive, sugar could be afforded only by the rich. It was brought in by the spice ships beginning in the fourteenth century and was considered to be as precious as spices. Like spices, sugar was used in almost every kind of recipe which previously had called for honey, not only sweet pottages of almond milk, dried fruit, and eggs, but in meat, poultry, and fish dishes, too. Sugar was actually used as a kind of spice, possibly to counteract the saltiness of preserved meat or fish or the acidity of vinegar or verjuice. (In the Middle Ages, sour flavorings such as verjuice, the juice of unripe grapes, were used a great deal in cooking before citrus fruit and juice became common.)

Toward the end of the seventeenth century, when the use of spices declined in cooking, the consumption of sugar rose, possibly to compensate for the lack of spice. Sugar had also become much cheaper to buy because it was now being grown in some of the British colonies. Tea, coffee, and chocolate were the new drinks of this time, and because they were naturally rather bitter, sugar came to play a great part in their consumption. Because of these developments, the eighteenth century became the heyday of the English dessert tradition, when the idea of "dessert" as a separate course originated.

Sweetness also came from fruit, particularly from dried fruit. The Romans had brought in many fruit trees, among them apples (as opposed to the native crab apples), pears, plums, and cherries, plus many that could only grow well in sheltered places in England such as grapes, peaches, apricots, and figs. Very few fruits of these were actually eaten raw because it was believed that raw fruit was bad for your health and digestion. Everything was dried to be cooked in pies and other desserts with sugar and spices, or made into preserves. This continued until the eighteenth century. Dried fruit such as raisins were imported and used abundantly in cooking by the wealthy. Poorer people ate them for special occasions such as Christmas in pies and pottages.

Most traditional British fruit-filled desserts and cakes are a result of this association of festivity with dried fruit. The multitude of suet desserts which became so popular took over the role of the thick pottages of earlier times, probably providing much the same sort of high calorie satisfaction. The fact that they contained meat fat or suet is a reminder of the medieval mixing of savory and sweet; the present day mince pie is a classic example – it was once actually made with meat. The rice and milk desserts of today are a sweet version of the medieval frumenty, also cooked in milk. The sweet pie tradition grew from the medieval pastry "coffins" which once contained meats and spices, and putting cloves in an apple pie is a classic example of this. Bread, too, once used as a trencher (plate) or to thicken sauces, played its part in sweet things as well. Many famous British puddings are bread based – summer pudding, queen of desserts, apple charlotte, and many more, including, of course, bread and butter pudding. And because of England's rich dairy produce, many classic creamy puddings developed, and they were included in the "banquet course" which crowned sixteenth century feasts.

Menu planning and cooking today have changed greatly. Balancing textures and flavors throughout the meal is extremely important; often the eating experience is built around the grand final course. Sometimes I like to invite friends in for a drink and a snack and then deliberately surprise them. Most expect a savory dish, but now and then I offer them a chocolate flan, or steamed cake with custard, or sherry trifle, or bread and butter pudding. This changes the whole evening and it becomes the focal point with everyone feeling comfortable eating the "pudding" because it's the only course.

I hope this chapter will put you in a similar mood, offering you a good range of choices to make.

PAGE 282
Afternoon Tea Pudding (page 320)

Ale Cake with Golden Syrup Cream

Cakes made using ale or beer are a strong part of the British tradition. There's a porter or stout cake in Ireland, for instance. Use your choice of ale here – a light one will give you a milder flavor, but a strong stout like Guinness will make it richer.

One of the secrets to serving this cake at its absolute best is to bake it, let it rest and relax for 30–40 minutes, and then serve it barely warm. As the syrup cream is spooned on top, it begins to melt, almost turning into a sauce.

MAKES A 6–7 IN (15–18 CM) CAKE

8 tablespoons (100 g) butter, softened
½ cup (100 g) dark soft brown sugar
1 egg, beaten
⅔ cup (100 g) mixed dried fruit e.g. raisins, currants, and golden raisins
2 cups (225 g) all-purpose flour
Pinch of ground cinnamon
Pinch of ground nutmeg
Pinch of ground ginger
⅔ cup (150 ml) ale
Butter, to grease the pan

For the Syrup Cream

1 tablespoon golden syrup
5 tablespoons heavy cream

These quantities will fill a 6–7 in (15–18 cm) deep cake pan. Preheat the oven to 350°F/180°C.

Cream together the butter and sugar. Slowly beat in the egg and then fold in the dried fruit. Sift the flour with the spices and fold into the cake mixture. The ale can now be added slowly until the mixture has reached a thick liquid consistency.

The cake pan can now be greased with butter and the bottom lined with waxed paper. Spoon the cake mixture into the pan, smoothing across the top with a spatula.

Bake in the preheated oven for 1 hour before testing with a sharp knife, which should come out clean. If the cake isn't done yet, then continue to bake, testing every 5–10 minutes. It should not be dry but barely moist.

After the cake has cooked, let it stand in the pan for 15 minutes before turning out. Now, let it rest for another 15–20 minutes until barely warm.

To make the syrup cream, whisk the syrup and cream together to a "lightly-whipped" stage. You can increase the amounts to your choice.

The ale cake is now ready to serve.

Raspberry Cranachan

This Scottish speciality, sometimes known as "cream crowdie," was originally a gruel made from oatmeal and water; the name "crowdie" was then applied to fresh cheese (sold as such today). The name "cranachan" became associated with an oatmeal cream and raspberries were added. Cranachan was traditionally served at festive times, particularly All Saints' Eve, when it contained charms – a ring for marriage, a coin for wealth, or a tiny horseshoe for good luck. These charms are definitely found in this finished recipe: you'll have a marriage of textures, a wealth of flavors – and good luck to you if you try to eat it all yourself.

SERVES 4

1 cup (100 g) medium oatmeal
2 tablespoons raspberry jam or 1 tablespoon of Crème de Framboise liqueur (optional)
2 tablespoons water (to thin the jam)
1¼ cups (300 ml) heavy cream
2 teaspoons superfine sugar
2–3 tablespoons (or more) whiskey
6 oz (175 g) fresh raspberries
Confectioners' sugar, for dusting

Toast the oatmeal until it's completely golden brown. Let it cool. If using the raspberry jam (this can be used to flavor the cream or dribbled through the cranachan), warm it with the water. After the jam has dissolved, strain through a tea strainer/sieve. This now has a "jam *coulis*" consistency.

Whisk the heavy cream, superfine sugar, and whiskey together until lightly whipped. Fold in the toasted oatmeal. Divide half of the raspberries among four glasses. Spoon a little of the "jam *coulis*" or liqueur, if using, over each.

Half-fill each glass with cranachan cream before placing the remaining raspberries on top. Spoon more "jam *coulis*" or liqueur on top of the raspberries before topping with the remaining cranachan mixture.

Smooth the top of each cranachan cream. The juicy raspberries are now set beneath and between the whiskey oatmeal cranachan.

To finish, dust each pudding with confectioners' sugar just before serving. The desserts can be served immediately or refrigerated until needed and dusted with confectioners' sugar when ready to eat.

Note: Other fruit can also be used: cooked rhubarb goes beautifully with the oatmeal cream. Oranges can also be used, flavoring the cream with marmalade or an orange liqueur.

BELOW
Raspberry Cranachan

Scottish Fruit Tart with Whiskey

This is a typical British tart, its Scottish origins betrayed by the addition of whiskey. The enclosure of dried fruit in pastry is very similar to the Scottish black bun, a cake made especially for New Year's. This tart would be perfect for Christmas, New Year, or any time of the year.

If you're not a fan of whiskey you can omit it from the recipe and replaced with the juice of a lemon. The whiskey can be passed separately after it's whipped into the heavy cream or custard.

The sweet shortcrust pastry includes the finely grated zest of a lemon, which enhances the flavor of the pastry and adds to the finished result.

MAKES AN 8 IN (20 CM) TART

12 oz (350 g) *Sweet Shortcrust Pastry* (page 364)
Finely grated zest of 1 lemon

For the Filling

½ cup (100 g) dark brown sugar
8 tablespoons (100 g) butter
1 tablespoon golden syrup
2 medium eggs, beaten
Grated zest of 1 lemon
⅓ cup (100 g) currants
⅓ cup (50 g) golden raisins
⅓ cup (50 g) raisins
½ cup (50 g) walnuts, chopped
2 tablespoons whiskey (or juice of 1 lemon)

After the pastry has been made with the addition of grated lemon zest, let it rest, refrigerated, for 20 minutes before rolling.

Roll the pastry about ⅛ in (2–3 mm) thick and line an 8 in (20 cm) springform pan, pressing gently into the edge for a neat finish. Leave untrimmed and refrigerate for another 20 minutes.

Preheat the oven to 400°F/200°C. The top edge of the pastry can either be left hanging during cooking to trim after it has baked or be pressed and "pinched" finish for a decorated edge.

Line the springform pan with waxed paper, fill with baking weights or dried beans, and cook in the preheated oven for 15–20 minutes.

Remove from the oven and lift the paper and weights or beans from the tart shell.

For the filling, reduce the oven temperature to 375°F/190°C.

Gently melt the sugar, butter, and golden syrup in a saucepan. Remove from the heat and whisk in the beaten eggs. Add the lemon zest, fruit, walnuts, and whiskey or lemon juice. Mix the ingredients together well and spoon it into the pastry shell.

This can now be baked for 20–25 minutes. Remove the pastry from the oven and let it relax. This tart tastes delicious warm or cold, with heavy cream, custard, or ice cream.

Apricot and Almond Pudding

Apricot and almond trees were introduced by the Romans to Britain, where, like figs and peaches, they grow well in warm, sheltered areas. Almonds were once used, ground or as milk, in many medieval dishes to thicken and to add flavor. Here I have combined them in a delicious pudding.

The apricots are gently cooked before being placed in a soufflé dish. The cake layer, almost like a frangipane mixture but lighter, is spooned on top and then it is baked in the oven. After it is cooked, the pudding is turned out and covered with the remaining soft cooked apricots.

This dish goes well with thick cream or custard.

SERVES 6–8

2 lb (900 g) fresh apricots, halved and stoned
A heaping teaspoon of butter
¼ cup (50 g) superfine sugar
2 tablespoons apricot jam

For the Sponge

3 large eggs, at room temperature
½ cup (100 g) superfine sugar
½ cup (50 g) all-purpose flour
1½ cup (175 g) ground almonds

Butter and flour a soufflé dish. Preheat the oven to 375°F/190°C.

Cut each apricot half into three pieces. Melt the butter in a large saucepan, and when it bubbles, add the apricots. Cook and stir for 2 minutes before adding the superfine sugar. Continue to cook for another 2 minutes and then remove from the heat. Add the apricot jam and let the apricots cool. They are not completely cooked but will finish cooking inside the pudding.

Spoon two-thirds of the apricots into the bottom of the buttered and floured soufflé dish.

Break the eggs into a warm mixing bowl, add the sugar, and beat until thickened to a thick ribbon (sabayon) stage. Sift the flour with the ground almonds and fold gently into the sabayon.

BELOW
Scottish Fruit Tart with Whiskey

When they are completely blended, spoon the mixture over the cooked apricots.

Bake for 35–40 minutes until the top is firm to the touch. Remove from the oven and let the pudding rest for 10 minutes.

During this resting time, the remaining apricots can be warmed and cooked until tender. Turn the pudding onto a presentation plate, topping with the warmed apricots. It is now ready to serve along with custard or cream.

Baked Egg Custard Tart

The British have been making custard since someone thought of mixing eggs and milk together over heat. In Tudor times, custard was used as a filling for pastry "coffins," sometimes with fruit added – in fact the word "custard" comes from "crustade," a pastry container or crust.

Baking egg custard tarts brings back pleasurable memories for me. I always looked forward to devouring one or two of them when I got home from school. Once you've tried this recipe, I'm sure you won't forget the experience.

The quantities listed here are an extravagance – lots of egg yolks and cream that make for a deliciously rich dessert. The cooking times are a guide. If the tart seems to be almost liquid when you test it, simply continue to cook it at the same temperature, checking every 5–10 minutes until set.

Since eggs have different cooking times and ovens differ, the tart could take almost double the time given. When checking to see if the tart is cooked, gently shake the pan. A stiff wobble will indicate that the tart is ready.

At the end of the recipe, I have given amounts needed to fill a 10 × 2 in (25 × 5 cm) flan ring (12–16 servings). Another recipe featured in the book that goes well with the custard tart is *Nutmeg Ice Cream* (page 309).

SERVES 8–12

(makes an 8 in/20 cm tart)

9 oz (250 g) *Sweet Shortcrust Pastry* (page 364)
½ nutmeg, grated, or ½ teaspoon ground nutmeg (optional)

For the Filling

2¼ cups (500 ml) heavy cream
¼ cup plus 1 tablespoon (75 g) superfine sugar
8 egg yolks
Grated nutmeg

To spread the nutmeg flavor throughout the whole dish when making the sweet shortcrust pastry, grate the nutmeg into the flour before mixing with the other ingredients. Preheat the oven to 350°F/180°C.

When the pastry has been made, roll it out and line an 8 in (20-cm) greased flan ring (any excess pastry can be left hanging over the edge and trimmed after it has baked to guarantee an even finish). Line the unbaked pastry shell with waxed paper, fill with baking weights or dried beans, and bake for 15 minutes. After the pastry has cooked, remove from the oven, lifting out the paper and the beans or weights. Turn the oven down to 250°F/120°C.

To make the filling, bring the cream to a boil. Mix together the sugar and egg yolks. Pour the boiled cream onto the egg mixture and stir in well. Pass through a sieve, skimming any froth from the surface.

Pour the custard mixture into the baked pastry shell, grating fresh nutmeg on top of the custard surface. Bake for 30–35 minutes until the tart has barely set.

Remove from the oven and allow to cool to room temperature before serving.

Note: This dessert tastes best at room temperature with the eggs barely set which results in a soft and creamy texture. If refrigerated, the filling will become firm and slightly lose its full flavor.

Here are the amounts for a 10 × 2 in (25 × 5 cm) flan ring:

12 oz (350 g) *Sweet Shortcrust Pastry* (page 364)
1 whole nutmeg, grated, or 1 teaspoon ground
    nutmeg (optional)

For the Filling

17 egg yolks
1 quart (1.2 liters) heavy cream
Scant cup (190 g) superfine sugar
Grated nutmeg, for sprinkling

Use the same method of preparation as the smaller tart but extend the cooking time will need to to 45 minutes–1 hour.

OPPOSITE
Baked Egg Custard Tart

Roasted Figs with Brown Sugar Parfait

The Ancient Greeks were convinced the fig was such a healthy fruit that it became a major part of the athletes' diet in the original Olympic games. In Britain, because of the suspicion of raw fruit, figs were always eaten cooked and were most likely valued as medicine, thought to cure warts, leprosy, epilepsy, and constipation.

Now, people appreciate figs for their all-round usefulness. They have a flavor and texture that suit many desserts and savory dishes. In Italy, for instance, the Sicilian fig is served raw with *prosciutto*, the rich, soft, fruity flesh complementing the slices of cured meat so well.

Greek athletes might not have tasted this fig recipe, but it is one of the most delicious in this book. The hazelnut tuile cookies are shaped to fit beneath and above the parfait, giving the figs a base. It is not essential that you include the tuiles in this recipe, but they provide a crisp texture that balances the soft creamy parfait.

SERVES 6–8

For the Figs

12–16 figs (2 per serving)
4 tablespoons (50 g) butter
Confectioners' sugar
12–16 flat *Hazelnut Tuiles* (page 356),
    made to the shape of parfait
    (see method)

For the Parfait

4 egg yolks
¾ cup (100 g) dark brown sugar
3 tablespoons ginger syrup
    (taken from a jar of Chinese
    stem ginger)
1¼ cups (300 ml) heavy cream

For the Port Syrup
(makes 150–200 ml/5–7 fl oz)

⅔ cup (150 ml) port
½ cup (100 g) sugar
⅓ cup plus 1 tablespoon (100 ml) water
Juice of 1 lemon

ABOVE
Roasted Figs with Brown Sugar Parfait

Frozen Orange and Espresso Mousse

You will need 6–8 round, square or rectangular stainless molds. These are approximate sizes for each shape:

Round: about 3 in diameter × 1 in deep
(7–8 cm diameter × 2.5 cm deep)
Square: 3 × 3 × 1 in deep (7 × 7 cm × 2.5 cm deep)
Rectangle: 3 × 2 × 1 in deep
(7–8 cm × 4–5 cm × 2.5 cm deep)

A terrine can also be used to make the parfait but it will, obviously, take longer to freeze.

To make the parfait, whisk together the egg yolks and sugar in a bowl over simmering water to a sabayon stage (the mixture will have doubled in volume with a thick but light consistency). When it reaches this stage, remove the mixture from the heat. The sabayon must now be whisked continuously until cool. This is easy if you use an electric mixer.

Whip the cream to soft peaks. The ginger syrup can now be added to the cooled sabayon and the whipped cream folded in.

The molds can be placed on a waxed-paper-lined pan and filled with the parfait. Freeze for several hours to set.

To make the port syrup, boil all the ingredients together and cook to a syrup consistency. Check this by spooning some syrup onto a saucer. The sauce should hold a syrup consistency when it cools.

To roast the figs, preheat the oven to 400°F/200°C. Cut the figs in half, brushing each piece with the butter. Place on a baking sheet cut-side down and roast in the preheated oven for 4–5 minutes until soft to the touch.

Remove the figs from the oven, turn them over, and dust liberally with confectioners' sugar. These can now be glazed with a butane torch (page 11) or under a hot broiler.

To present the dish, remove the parfaits from their molds using a warm small knife, and place them on top of a hazelnut tuile cookie. Top with another tuile and arrange on dessert plates. The roasted figs can now be placed on top of the tuile and the syrup drizzled over or around them. The dish is now ready to serve.

Ice creams and iced desserts could not become part of the British "sweets" tradition until the nineteenth century, but as soon as making them became possible, they then became enormously popular at Edwardian and Victorian dinner parties, particularly the sorbet form.

Here, two flavored mousses in a very popular duo, orange and coffee, are frozen together on top of a coffee cake layer, the latter a texture and flavor borrowed from the *Gâteau Opéra* on page 315. Another borrowing is the rich chocolate ganache topping. The cake layer is required, but the ganache can be replaced with a last-minute dusting of cocoa powder and mixed chocolate shavings.

SERVES 9–12

For the Sponge Base

2 heaping teaspoons coffee granules
2 tablespoons hot water
3 egg yolks
4 oz (100 g) semisweet chocolate, melted
3 egg whites
¼ cup plus 1 tablespoon (65 g) superfine sugar

For the Orange Mousse

1¼ cups (300 ml) heavy cream
¼ cup milk
Finely grated zest of 1 orange
5 oz (150 g) white chocolate, chopped
8 egg yolks
2 tablespoons superfine sugar
2 tablespoons sour cream
1½ teaspoons extra grated orange zest
1 tablespoon Grand Marnier

For the Espresso Mousse

1¼ cups (300 ml) heavy cream
¼ cup milk
2 heaping tablespoons (50 g) finely ground coffee
5 oz (150 g) white chocolate, chopped
8 egg yolks
1 tablespoon superfine sugar
2 tablespoons sour cream
1 tablespoon Tia Maria

For the Coffee Syrup (makes ⅔ cup/150 ml)

1¼ cups (300 ml) strong fresh or instant coffee
⅔ cup (150 g) superfine sugar
Splash of Tia Maria liqueur (optional)

This recipe is made in the same form as the *Gâteau Opéra*, using a 10 × 10 in (25 × 25 cm) square or 10 in (25 cm) diameter springform pan. Preheat the oven to 350°F/180°C. Line the bottom of the cake pan with waxed paper and lightly grease.

Dissolve the coffee granules in the hot water. Mix the egg yolks into the coffee, adding the melted chocolate. Whisk the egg whites and sugar to soft peaks and fold into the chocolate mixture.

Pour the mixture into the cake pan and bake in the preheated oven for 10–12 minutes until just firm. Allow the cake to cool.

To make the orange mousse, pour half of the heavy cream, the milk, and the zest from 1 orange into a saucepan and bring to a boil. Remove from the heat and add the chopped chocolate. Stir until the chocolate has melted.

Whisk the egg yolks and superfine sugar together to a thick ribbon (sabayon) stage. Add the chocolate and orange cream mixture, and cook in a bowl over simmering water until you have a thick-

BELOW
Frozen Orange and Espresso Mousse

cream consistency. Pour the custard through a fine sieve and whisk until it is cool.

Whisk the remaining ⅔ cup (150 ml) heavy cream, the sour cream, ½ teaspoon orange zest and the Grand Marnier to a soft peak. Fold into the cooled orange custard. The mousse can now be spooned on top of the cake layer and frozen.

While the orange mousse is freezing, the espresso mousse can be made. Pour half of the cream, all of the milk, and the ground coffee into a saucepan and bring to a boil. Remove from the heat and add the chopped white chocolate.

Whisk the egg yolks and superfine sugar to a thick ribbon (sabayon) stage. Add the chocolate and coffee cream mixture and cook in a bowl set over simmering water until you have a thick-cream consistency. Pour through a fine sieve and whisk until cool.

Whisk the remaining ⅔ cup (150 ml) heavy cream, sour cream, and Tia Maria to a soft peak. Fold into the cooled coffee custard. The espresso mousse can now be spooned on top of the frozen orange mousse.

Return to the freezer until completely set. After it has frozen, the mousse can be removed from the pan and topped with a thin layer of chocolate ganache (see *Gâteau Opéra*, page 315). For this recipe only half of the recipe will be needed.

To make the coffee syrup, put the coffee and sugar in a pan and bring to a boil. Cook until reduced by half. Allow the syrup to cool. For a liqueur coffee syrup, add a splash of Tia Maria.

It is best to cut and divide the mousse into servings while it's still frozen, using a hot knife (return the portions you're not serving to the freezer until needed). Before serving, transfer the dessert from the freezer to the refrigerator for 15–20 minutes. This removes the completely frozen texture from the dessert, making it slightly softer, without losing the frozen edge. Serve with the coffee syrup, warm or at room temperature.

This dessert also goes very well with *Bittersweet Chocolate Sauce* (page 323) or heavy cream. Nine to twelve servings is quite a large recipe; the ingredient quantities cannot be reduced without spoiling the consistency and texture of the mousses, however.

Warm Port and Fig Broth with Cream Cheese Ice Cream

Apicius, the great Roman gourmet, preserved figs in honey, and he force-fed his pigs with figs and mead (a honey wine) to fatten them and to improve the flavor of the meat. This combination of port and figs into a fruit-soup dessert is a delicious one, the luxurious fruit cooked in the imported wine that has become so associated with Britain.

Figs and port work together so well with cream cheese ice cream to finish the dish that I'm sure you won't need to be force-fed.

SERVES 6

For the Fig Broth (makes about 2½ cups/600 ml)

8 fresh figs (Black Mission), quartered
1¼ cups (300 ml) port
1 cup (250 ml) water
Scant 2 tablespoons (20 g) sugar
½ cinnamon stick
2 teaspoons lemon juice

For the Cream Cheese Ice Cream

1¼ cups (400 ml) heavy cream
¼ cup (50 ml) milk
4 egg yolks
¼ cup (60 g) superfine sugar
6 oz (175 g) cream cheese

To Serve

6–9 fresh figs, halved
Port Syrup (page 289, optional), or 2 tablespoons (25 g) butter and ¼ cup (25 g) confectioners' sugar

First, make the ice cream. Boil together the cream and milk. While the cream is heating, whisk together the egg yolks and sugar until they form thick ribbons. You can use an electric hand mixer to do this.

Beat the cheese until smooth. Pour the boiled cream and milk onto the cream cheese, stir until smooth, and then mix with the whisked egg yolks.

Cook in a bowl set over simmering water, stirring until the custard coats the back of a spoon. (Do not let it boil or the eggs will scramble.) Strain through a sieve. Let the mixture cool, stirring from time to time to prevent a skin from forming.

When the mixture is cool, churn it in an ice cream freezer in two batches if necessary. (If you don't have an ice cream maker, see Note, page 309.) Either method will take approximately 20 minutes to the point of thickening and increasing in volume. Do not churn it until completely frozen because this will curdle the mixture, causing a slightly grainy texture.

Pour the ice cream into a container and place it in the freezer to finish setting. Repeat the same churning process for the second batch.

Now, make the fig broth. Place all of the broth ingredients in a saucepan. Bring to a simmer and cook slowly until the quantity has reduced by a third.

Remove the cinnamon stick, pour into a food processor, and blend until smooth. Pass through a fine sieve. The fig broth is now ready.

Two or three fig halves will be plenty per serving for the fig garnish. There are two methods for cooking the garnishes.

1.   Remove the stems and place the figs in the port syrup (it is best to make the syrup slightly thinner than mentioned in the recipe). Simmer for a few minutes until the figs have become tender.

2.   Butter the fig halves and place them on a baking sheet, face-side down. Bake in a preheated oven at 400°F/200°C, for 4–5 minutes before removing from the oven. Turn the figs and dust with confectioners' sugar. These can now be glazed with a butane torch, (page 11) or under a hot broiler.

To present the dish, warm the fig broth and spoon into bowls. Place 2–3 fig halves in each bowl. Shape the cream cheese ice cream (creating a scroll or using a scoop), and present on top of the warm figs or serve in a separate bowl.

Note: *Fig Rolls* (page 360) go very well with this dish.

Iced Vanilla Parfait with Nutmeg Clotted Cream and Caramelized Apples

Vanilla and nutmeg are two flavors used in bread and butter pudding, and that dessert was the inspiration for this parfait. The beauty of serving ice cream such as a parfait as the main part of a dessert is that it can be prepared and frozen well in advance. The caramelized apples can also be made in advance, ready to be re-warmed for serving.

Using vanilla beans will give a natural flavor, with the small black seeds running through the mixture. You can replace the beans with 2 teaspoons of vanilla extract if you wish.

Here, I make the parfait in a terrine or loaf pan, but you can make individual parfaits. Another way of presenting the parfait is to freeze it in teacups. The apples can then be presented on top with the cream.

SERVES 6

6 egg yolks
¾ cup plus 1 tablespoon (175 g) superfine sugar
2 vanilla beans, split and scraped, or 2 teaspoons of vanilla extract
2 cups (450 ml) heavy cream
⅔ cup (150 ml) clotted cream
Freshly grated nutmeg
3 Granny Smith apples
Butter
Light brown or superfine sugar

Line a 1 quart (1.2 liter) terrine or loaf pan or six 2½ × 2½ in (6 × 6 cm) rings with waxed paper.

Whisk together the egg yolks, sugar, and vanilla bean seeds or the extract in a bowl over simmering water until doubled in volume or reaches a thick ribbon (sabayon) stage. Remove from the heat and continue to whisk until cool (this can be done with an electric mixer).

Lightly whip the heavy cream until it reaches a soft peak stage. Fold into the sabayon and pour into the lined loaf pan or into individual rings. The parfait can now be frozen until set. The freezing process will take a minimum of 2–3 hours.

The split vanilla beans, if using, can be cut into long thin strips. These will be used to decorate the dish.

Finely grate between ¼ and ½ teaspoon of nutmeg into the clotted cream (more can be added if you wish). Refrigerate to set the cream, making it easier to shape.

Peel the apples and cut into quarters. Cut away the core and split each quarter in two. This now gives you 24 apple wedges, 4 per serving.

Place the wedges in cold water and bring to a boil. Drain and dry the apples. When ready to serve, pan-fry the apples in melted butter, adding a teaspoon or two of the sugar you've chosen; this will begin to caramelize. Add 1–2 tablespoons of water, turning the caramel into a thick syrup.

Another method is to sprinkle the apple wedges with superfine sugar (confectioners' sugar can also be used) and caramelize it under a hot broiler or using a butane torch (page 11) just before serving the dessert.

To serve the parfait, turn out the rings and place apple wedges on each plate with the nutmeg clotted cream, shaped between two spoons.

Note: A sponge cake layer can be used in the individual molds or be placed on top of the terrine. When the dessert is cake layer becomes the base. Use the recipe for the cake from the *Sherry Trifle* (page 312) for this purpose. Simply spread the cake mixture ½ in (1 cm) deep into a suitably sized baking pan.

Cranberry and Walnut Tart

Cranberries are actually native to Europe, although they are now associated with America. In the form of cranberry, they have become the traditional accompaniment to roast Christmas turkey in Britain. Another popular use for them is in a relish or chutney, normally served with game birds or venison, and in pies.

The sharp bite of fresh cranberries also lends itself well to these walnut tarts, which basically resembles the sweet, nutty pecan pie everyone loves. The tart is garnished with cranberries warmed in a mixture of orange juice and cranberry jelly.

SERVES 6

½ lb (225 g) *Sweet Shortcrust Pastry* (page 364) (1 lb/450 g will be needed for individual rings)
3 tablespoons (40 g) butter
½ cup (100 g) superfine sugar
⅓ cup (50 g) light brown sugar
⅓ cup (50 g) dark brown sugar
175 g (6 oz) golden syrup
1 teaspoon vanilla extract
Pinch of salt
2 whole eggs
1 egg yolk
1 cup (100 g) chopped walnuts
1 cup (100 g) fresh cranberries
Confectioners' sugar, sifted, to decorate

For the Cranberry Compote

2 cups (225 g) fresh cranberries
Juice of 1 orange
¼ cup (50 g) superfine sugar
1–2 tablespoons cranberry jelly

This recipe will fill a springform pan or six 3½ in (9 cm) diameter individual tart rings.

Preheat the oven to 400°F/200°C. Line the pastry cases with the sweet pastry, waxed paper, and baking weights or dried beans.

Blind-bake the pastry in the preheated oven for 20 minutes. Remove from the oven and let it cool. Turn the oven down to 315°F/160°C.

Melt the butter in a saucepan, allowing it to reach a nut-brown stage. Mix together the superfine sugar, light and dark brown sugars, and the golden syrup. Stir the mixture into the nut-brown butter off the heat.

The vanilla, salt, whole eggs, and egg yolk can now be added. Allow the mixture to cool. When the mixture has cooled, spoon it into the tart case(s). Mix together the chopped walnuts and the

cranberries and sprinkle over the tart(s). Bake in the preheated oven for 40–45 minutes for the large tart and just 20 minutes for individual ones. Let the tart(s) rest before removing from the springform pan or individual tart rings.

The tarts are best served warm, but can also be served at room temperature.

To make the compote, place the cranberries, orange juice, and sugar in a saucepan and bring to a simmer. Lift the cranberries from the pan.

Add the jelly to the liquid and bring to a simmer. The consistency needs to be syrupy; the sauce can either be reduced or more jelly added to achieve this. Allow the sauce to cool slightly before mixing the cranberries back in.

The cranberry compote will be at its best served warm. To serve, place small spoonfuls of compote around the rim of the plate and sift a little confectioners' sugar over it.

Note: Vanilla ice cream (see *Nutmeg Ice Cream*, page 309 or store-bought) goes very well with this dish.

Steamed Lemon Pudding with Easy Lemon Sauce

This recipe belongs to Marguerite Patten who wrote *Puddings and Desserts*, published in 1963. At thirteen years old, it was the first pudding I had ever cooked, and I followed the recipe from her book. The book belonged to my mother, originally, but I am pleased to say it's mine now.

This recipe is a great example of how classic recipes never die. More than thirty years later and it tastes just as sensational! Thank you for the recipe,

OPPOSITE
Cranberry and Walnut Tart with Vanilla Ice Cream

Marguerite, and also for the inspiration it gave me to want to cook.

This recipe will fill a 1 quart (1.2 liter) pudding mold.

SERVES 6–8

16 tablespoons (225 g) butter
¾ cup plus 1 tablespoon (175 g) superfine sugar
Zest and juice of 2 lemons
4 eggs
2 cups (225 g) self-rising flour, sifted
Pinch of salt

For the Easy Lemon Sauce

Zest and juice of 2 lemons
Water
¼ cup (50 g) superfine sugar
1 heaping tablespoon arrowroot mixed with
    1 tablespoon of water

You will need a 1 quart (1.2 liter) pudding mold, buttered and floured.

To make the cake, cream together the butter, sugar, and lemon zest until light and fluffy. Add the eggs, beating in one at a time until mixed well. Mix together the flour and salt and beat into the butter mixture. Add the lemon juice. Spoon into the prepared mold, cover lightly with buttered foil, and steam on a rack in a hot steamer for 1¼–1½ hours.

The sauce can be made about 5 minutes before the pudding is ready. Pour the juice from the lemons into a measuring cup and fill it with water to reach 1¼ cups (300 ml). Pour into a saucepan with the zest and superfine sugar and bring to a boil. When it is boiling, whisk in the arrowroot. Return to a simmer and cook for 2–3 minutes.

After the pudding is cooked, remove it from the steamer and let it stand for a few minutes. Remove the foil and turn out onto a plate, gently shaking the mold to help the pudding along. Pour some of the sauce on top. Cut into servings and pass the remaining sauce separately.

Steamed Upsidedown Blackberry and Apple Pudding

Steamed desserts are direct descendants of the desserts that used to be wrapped in cloths and suspended in cooking pots. Apples have always been a favorite ingredient, and their combination with blackberries – which begin to ripen at the same time of the year – is very traditional. The combination usually appears in pies, where the fruit is encased in sweet pastry, but here I have steamed a light lemon and cinnamon cake layer on top of the fruit. When it is cooked, the pudding is turned out upsidedown. I always save some of the "topping" to finish the dish, making the dessert even fruitier.

SERVES 6

4 Granny Smith apples, peeled, cored, and halved
Butter
¼ cup (50 g) superfine sugar
2 cups (225 g) blackberries
1 tablespoon blackberry jam

For the Sponge

8 tablespoons (100 g) unsalted butter
⅔ cup (150 g) superfine sugar
4 eggs
1 egg yolk
1¼ cups (200 g) self-rising flour
¼ teaspoon ground cinnamon
Finely grated zest of 1 lemon
1–2 tablespoons of milk, if necessary

Butter and flour a 1 quart (900 ml) pudding mold or six ⅔ cup (150 ml) molds.

Quarter each apple and then cut these in half, forming eight wedges. Now, halve these also, cutting through the middle, creating chunks of apples.

Melt 1 teaspoon of butter in a saucepan, and add the apples and superfine sugar. Cook for 2–3 minutes before adding the blackberries and blackberry jam. Mix well and remove from the heat. Let the mixture cool.

To make the cake, beat the butter and sugar together until the sugar has dissolved and the mixture is fluffy. This stage can be easily done with an electric mixer.

Beat together the eggs and egg yolk. These can now be slowly added while whisking the butter. Beat them completely until the mixture is light and fluffy.

Sift the flour with the cinnamon and the lemon zest until completely incorporated, adding the milk as necessary to create a thick liquid.

Spoon half of the apple and blackberry mixture into the pudding mold(s). Top with the cake mixture and cover with waxed paper or aluminum foil, with a fold in the center to create space for the rising pudding. Place in a steamer or on a trivet in a saucepan, cover with a lid, and steam. Individual desserts will take 35– 40 minutes and a large pudding 1–1¼ hours. Add more water if necessary during cooking.

BELOW
Steamed Upsidedown Blackberry and Apple Pudding

When cooked, remove the pudding(s) from the steamer and cool for 5 minutes before turning out. During this resting time the remaining blackberry and apple mixture can be re-heated.

After turning out the pudding(s), spoon the extra fruit on top, allowing the mixture to tumble onto the plate.

This dessert tastes wonderful with heavy cream or custard, as do almost all steamed puddings.

Sticky Toffee Apple Pudding

Toffee apples were always a treat on Guy Fawkes Night when I was a child. The crunchy boiled sugar surrounding the apple was very enticing. These days I'm not sure I could eat one of those, but the toffee flavor does go well with apples, so here is a recipe giving you exactly that.

The toffee flavor can be as sticky as you want it to be. It is created by dark brown sugar cooking and caramelizing around the outside of the suet pastry, while the apples cook inside it.

SERVES 6

For the Suet Pastry

1½ cup (175 g) self-rising flour
Pinch of salt
3 oz (75 g) beef or vegetable suet
⅔ cup (150 ml) water or milk
4 tablespoons (50 g) unsalted butter
2 tablespoons–⅓ cup (25–50 g) dark brown sugar

For the Filling

1½ lb (675 g) Granny Smith apples, peeled and quartered
4 tablespoons (50 g) butter
½ cup (75 g) light brown sugar
2–3 tablespoons lemon juice

To make the pastry, sift together the flour and salt. Add the suet, stirring in the water or milk. The dough can now be mixed to create a smooth consistency. Wrap it and let it rest for 20 minutes.

Spread the butter around a 1 quart (900 ml) pudding mold and sprinkle with the dark brown sugar. The more evenly sprinkled, the better the toffee flavor will be. Roll out three-fourths of the pastry and line the mold with it.

Halve the apple quarters once more into eight slices per apple. These can now also be halved to shape into rough chunks.

Melt the butter. When it bubbles, add the apples and cook for 1–2 minutes. Add the sugar and lemon juice and remove the pan from the stove. Let the mixture cool. When the mixture is cool, spoon it into the pudding mold.

Roll the remaining fourth of the pastry and place on top of the pudding, sealing the edges well. This can now be covered with folded waxed paper and foil and tied with string, if necessary. Steam over boiling water for 1½–1¾ hours, topping up the hot water if necessary.

When the pudding is done, remove it from the steamer and rest it for 5 minutes before turning out.

Serve the sticky toffee apple pudding now with custard, thick cream, or vanilla ice cream.

Syllabub

One of the most famous British desserts, the syllabub is related to a number of others such as posset, flummery, and Atholl Brose. The original syllabub was a mixture of fresh milk and a sweet wine popular in Britain during Elizabethan times that was imported from Sillery, a *grand cru* village in Champagne. The milk was squeezed straight from a cow into a bucket of "Sille" wine, creating a fine froth. "Bub" was Elizabethan slang for a bubbling drink – hence "sille bub."

Syllabub, at first, was drunk rather than eaten with a spoon. It is said that Charles II was so fond of it that he kept cows in St James's Park so that if he got thirsty while walking, the cows could be milked directly into a bowl of wine!

Recipes for syllabub haven't changed much from the original. All of them still use lemon, sugar, whipped cream, and sweet wine, sherry, or brandy – depending on which part of the country you come from. There are many different versions. The syllabub mixture is left to settle for several hours, by which time the alcohol and cream will have separated, creating the classic syllabub consistency.

SERVES 4–6

½ bottle of sweet white wine or ⅔ cup (150 ml) sweet sherry
¼ cup (50 g) superfine sugar
Peeled rind and juice of 2 lemons
4 tablespoons brandy
1¼ cups (300 ml) heavy cream

If using the sweet wine, bring it to a boil with the sugar and reduce it by half. When it has reduced, remove the mixture from the stove and add the lemon rind. After it's cool, add the lemon juice and brandy, cover with plastic wrap, and let it stand for several hours or for an even stronger flavor – overnight. If using sweet sherry, follow the above method but without reducing by half, only warming through before adding the rind.

When the mixture has infused, strain it through a sieve. The heavy cream can now be whisked until thickened and the wine poured slowly in until all of it has been absorbed. It is important to keep the cream softly whipped. Spoon into serving dishes and chill for several hours. You may find the wine syrup will almost separate from the cream as it rests in the bottom of the dishes.

This dessert almost has the texture of an Irish coffee with the thick cream on top.

Note: This syllabub goes very nicely with fresh raspberries placed in the bottom of the serving dishes. The fruit then becomes marinated with the sweet wine and brandy.

Jam Roly-poly

This is a classic example of a British steamed pudding made with suet, but it is rolled with a filling rather than being cooked in a pudding mold. If you had this dessert during your schooldays like I did, it would stay with you for life. The gooey texture of suet pastry absorbing and oozing strawberry jam, along with the flavor of fresh vanilla custard: need I say more? Here is the recipe.

SERVES 6

2 cups (225 g) self-rising flour
1 teaspoon baking powder
Pinch of salt
Finely grated zest of 1 lemon or orange (optional)
5 oz (150 g) vegetarian or beef suet
¼–⅔ cup (100–150 ml) milk
About ½ cup (150–175 g) strawberry jam
Custard Sauce (page 324), to serve

Sift together the self-rising flour, baking powder, and pinch of salt. Add the grated zest of lemon or orange, if using, along with the suet, and crumble together with your fingers to a breadcrumb consistency.

The milk can now be added, a little at a time, until a soft texture has formed, without allowing the dough to become sticky. Wrap it in plastic wrap and allow it to rest for 20–30 minutes.

The suet dough can now be rolled into a rectangle, approximately 12 × 8 in (30 × 20 cm). Spread the jam onto the pastry, leaving a clear ½ in (1 cm) border.

Now, brush the border with water or extra milk before rolling it like a jellyroll. Pinch at either end to seal the jam inside. The roly-poly can now be wrapped very loosely in waxed paper, followed by loose foil. Tie at either end.

The pudding can now be steamed for 2 hours, adding more water during the cooking time, if necessary. After it has cooked, unwrap it, slice, and serve the pudding with the custard.

Note: The orange or lemon zest is an optional extra, but either adds an extra flavor and bite to the dish. Orange marmalade, lemon curd, or mincemeat can also be used as a filling in place of the jam.

Baked Raspberry Desserts

The raspberry is one the best tasting berries, and it grows very well both wild and cultivated in Scotland. The berries used to always be baked into crumbles and pies, never served uncooked as they are served today. Here, I use them in a baked pudding. Baked desserts were introduced in the early seventeenth century as an alternate way of cooking a traditional pudding mixture other than boiling it in a pudding bag. Baking a pudding tended to be more of a rich man's method since the fuel for ovens was more expensive than that for a cooking pot.

These desserts are baked in individual soufflé serving dishes. They are larger than the standard ⅔ cup (150 ml) ramekins. The beauty of this recipe is that it's so easy to make: all the ingredients (except the raspberries) are puréed in a food processor, poured into the molds, and baked – it couldn't be simpler.

SERVES 4

1 cup (225 g) fresh raspberries
4 eggs
½ cup (50 g) all-purpose flour
½ cup (50 g) ground almonds, or hazelnuts
2 tablespoons (25 g) butter, melted
Scant 3 oz (65 g) superfine sugar
¼ cup plus 1 tablespoon (150 ml) heavy cream
Finely grated zest of 1 lemon
Confectioners' sugar, for dusting

Preheat the oven to 375°F/190°C and butter four soufflé dishes.

Purée all the ingredients (except the raspberries) together in a food processor until smooth. Warm the soufflé dishes in the oven. After they are warmed, divide the raspberries among the dishes and pour the pudding mixture on top.

BELOW
Jam Roly-poly

Bake them immediately for 30–35 minutes (maximum 40 minutes) until golden brown. The mixture will have almost souffléd in the dishes, creating a light cake-like pudding. Remove from the oven and dust each dish with confectioners' sugar.

The dessert can now be served with lightly whipped cream or a lemon custard (see Variation on *Custard Sauce*, page 324).

Note: Other fruit can be used in this dessert; try a mixture of summer berries particularly.

Strawberry Cheesecake Jelly Roll

The sponge for jelly roll is normally a basic Genoise, where a thick frothy texture is created with the eggs and sugar (sabayon) before folding in the flour. This recipe is a little different; the eggs are separated, then the whites are whisked to a meringue consistency and folded into the cake mixture at the last minute. The texture is lovely to eat, but when being rolled up, the cold sponge sometimes cracks. But that's the beauty of homemade dishes – the flavors come first and who cares if the sponge is broken!

SERVES 6–8

Strawberry Jam (page 387), for spreading
Confectioners' sugar, for dusting

For the Sponge

4 large eggs
¼ cup (50 g) superfine sugar
½ cup (50 g) all-purpose flour

For the Cream

1 tablespoon (15 g) superfine sugar
4 oz (100 g) cream cheese
1¼ cups (150 ml) heavy cream, lightly whipped

For this recipe you will need an 7 x 11 in (18 x 28 cm) jelly roll pan, buttered and lined with waxed paper. Preheat the oven to 350°F/180°C.

Separate the eggs. The yolks in one bowl can be mixed with the superfine sugar and whisked to a thick (sabayon) consistency. Sift the flour into the egg-yolk mixture and fold it in.

In another bowl, whisk the egg whites to a soft peak stage. Add a few tablespoons to the egg yolks, beating in well. The remaining whites can be gently folded into the cake mixture.

Pour the mixture into the lined pan and bake in the preheated oven for 12–15 minutes. After the cake has cooked, remove it from the oven and cover with a damp cloth to prevent it from cracking.

The cheesecake cream can now be made while the cake layer cools. Beat the sugar into the cream cheese until the sugar has dissolved and creamed. Gently fold in the lightly whipped heavy cream. The mixture can now be refrigerated for 20–30 minutes to firm it slightly.

After the cake layer has cooled, remove the cloth. Place a sheet of waxed paper on a small chopping board and the board over the cake layer. Now, simply turn the jelly roll pan over and lift it off carefully. If the waxed paper lining the pan attaches to the cake, carefully peel it away.

The strawberry jam can now be spread onto the sponge, leaving a ½ in (1 cm) clear border.

Spoon cheesecake cream over the jelly and then carefully roll it up using the waxed paper. Remove the paper and lightly dust with confectioners' sugar.

The strawberry cheesecake jelly roll is now ready to serve.

Note: The seeds from a freshly scraped vanilla bean can be added to the cheesecake mixture for a fuller flavor.

Gooseberry Sherbet

Fruit-flavored water ices, known as "sorbets" to the French and "sherbets" to the Arabs, have been known since the thirteenth century. They were invented by the Chinese, brought to Europe by Marco Polo, and perfected by the Italians. Apparently the first water ices in England were

Rhubarb Tart

created by Charles I's Italian chefs, but it took another few centuries before sorbets or ice creams became common in the British tradition.

"Sherbets" are not, however, the same as "sorbets." A sorbet is made from fruit purée mixed with sweet stock syrup and that's basically it, while a sherbet uses those ingredients plus milk and egg white, giving it a fluffy-like finish. Almost any other fruit, fresh or frozen, can replace the gooseberries. Since few farmers grow them, gooseberries rarely appear at markets in the US. Buy them for making this recipe whenever you have the opportunity.

SERVES 4–6

1 lb (450 g) fresh or frozen gooseberries
1 cup (250 ml) stock syrup (see Note)
1 cup (250 ml) milk
1 teaspoon lemon juice
1 egg white

Wash the fresh gooseberries, put them in a saucepan with the sugar syrup, and bring to a simmer. Cover and cook gently for 3–4 minutes or until the fruit is tender. Remove from the heat and let the fruit cool. Now, purée the gooseberries in the syrup and strain them through a sieve. Stir in the milk and lemon juice, then pour the mixture into an ice cream machine, and begin to churn. It will take between 20–25 minutes to reach a thick, nearly set stage. When ready, whisk the egg white to soft peaks and add it to the mixture. Store the sherbet in the freezer until needed – or serve it immediately.

Note: If you do not have an ice cream maker, freeze the sherbet before adding the egg white, whisking every so often to break the ice crystals. After it has frozen, put it into a food processor and purée it. Then, fold in the beaten egg white and re-freeze.

For a stock syrup, bring 1¼ cups (300 ml) water and 1 cup (225 g) superfine sugar to a boil. Simmer for a few minutes until the sugar has completely dissolved and thickened the water. Cool and keep refrigerated. This makes 2 cups (450 ml).

RIGHT
Gooseberry Sherbet

Rhubarb is native to northern Asia, and the plant did not reach Britain until the sixteenth century. It was used medicinally at first, and was not valued as a food until at least the eighteenth century.

Homemade fresh fruit tarts are so seductive, the juicy fresh fruits on top of a delicious homemade pastry cream (*crème pâtisserie* in French) in a crisp pastry shell. They really are very delicious. For rhubarb, I like to use sweet shortcrust pastry. This provides a crumbly texture needed to balance the cream and soft texture of the fruit.

The pastry shell and the cream will work as foundation for a tart made with almost any fruit – fresh berries such as raspberries, blackberries, strawberries, as well as for apricots, plums, nectarines, or peaches.

SERVES 6–8

10–12 oz (300–350 g) *Sweet Shortcrust Pastry*
    (page 364)
1¾–2 lb (750–900 g) fresh rhubarb
¼–½ cup (60–75 g) superfine sugar

For the Pastry Cream
(makes approx. 2 cups/500 ml)

4 egg yolks
¼ cup plus 1 tablespoon (75 g) superfine sugar
Salt
1 tablespoon (25 g) cornstarch
1¼ cups (300 ml) milk

1 vanilla bean, split and scraped,
    or 2 teaspoons vanilla extract
2½ tablespoons (35 ml) heavy cream
2 tablespoons (25 g) unsalted butter

Preheat the oven to 425°F/220°C.

Roll the pastry on a floured surface to approximately ⅛ in (3 mm) thick, and use it to line a springform pan of 8–9 in (20–25 cm) diameter and 1–1½ in (2.5–3.5 cm) deep. To guarantee a clean finish with no shrinking of the pastry, it's best to let the excess pastry hang over the edge of the pan. (After it is baked, this can be cut away with a sharp knife.) Prick the bottom of the pastry with a fork, and refrigerate it for 20 minutes before baking.

Line the pastry shell with waxed paper and fill with baking weights or dried beans. Blind-bake in the oven for 20–25 minutes until crisp and golden. Remove from the oven, take out the beans or weights, and trim the overhanging pastry. Let it cool. Reduce the oven temperature to 350°F/180°C.

To prepare the rhubarb, first peel it if slightly tough and stringy. Now, cut it into ¾–1¼ in (2–3 cm) pieces and place in a roasting pan. Sprinkle with the sugar, place in the oven, and cook for 10–15 minutes or until tender. Remove from the oven and let it cool. The rhubarb can now be carefully spooned from the pan, and any juices brought to a boil and reduced to a syrupy consistency. The rhubarb is now ready to use.

For a different finish, place the cooked rhubarb on a baking pan, lightly dust with confectioners' sugar and glaze under a hot broiler or with a butane torch (page 11). This will give the fruit slightly bittersweet caramel taste and color. Let it cool.

Meanwhile, make the pastry cream. Cream together the egg yolks and the superfine sugar in a bowl. Add a small pinch of salt and the cornstarch. Bring the milk to a boil with the split and scraped vanilla bean (or extract) and pour into the egg-yolk mixture. Return the mixture to the pan, bring back to a simmer and cook for a few minutes, making sure it doesn't boil. Add the heavy cream and the butter and then pass through a sieve. Press a piece of waxed paper or plastic wrap onto the surface to prevent a skin from forming. Let it cool. The fresh, vanilla-flavored pastry cream is ready to use. (Grated citrus fruit zests can be added to the milk for a different flavor.) You will need approximately 1¾ cups (400 ml) of the pastry cream; the remainder will last well in the refrigerator for 3–4 days.

When all the components are cold, the tart can be assembled. Spread the pastry cream into the pastry shell, and fill to approximately ½ in (1 cm) deep. Now, place the fruit on top, either carefully arranged on the cream or merely spooned over in a more rustic fashion. Brush the syrup over the rhubarb for a more flavorful finish. The tart is now ready to enjoy, with the tender fruit and rich cream balanced by the crumbly pastry.

Note: The quantities for this pastry cream recipe can be halved for a shallow mold. After it has cooled, any remaining cream can be refrigerated for 3–4 days or used as a foundation for individual fruit tarts.

Queen of Desserts

This is also known as *Manchester Pudding*. It is another combination of custard ingredients and breadcrumbs, and, significantly, Mrs Beeton called it *Queen of Bread Puddings*. You could use breadcrumbs as here, or a vanilla flavored cake and jam, which is a delicious variation. What is essential, though, is the meringue topping. This is a very sweet pudding, one you'll want to eat plenty of but might regret doing so afterward.

2½ cups (600 ml) milk
Grated zest of 1 lemon
4 tablespoons (50 g) unsalted butter
¼ cup (50 g) superfine sugar
2 cups (100 g) fresh white breadcrumbs
6 egg yolks, beaten
4 tablespoons *Strawberry Jam* (page 387)

For the Meringue

4 egg whites
1 cup (225 g) superfine sugar

Preheat the oven to 350°F/180°C. Butter six 3 in (7.5 cm) soufflé dishes or one 2 quart (1.75 liter) dish.

Mix the milk and zest in a pan and bring to a boil; remove the pan from the heat and let the mixture stand for 15 minutes. Remove the zest and add the butter and sugar. Bring back to a simmer and remove from the heat. Mix in the breadcrumbs, allow the mixture to cool slightly, and then stir in the yolks. Pour the mixture into soufflé dish(es) placed in a roasting pan filled with hot water three-fourths up the sides of the dishes. Bake for 30–40 minutes until set. When the desserts have barely set, remove them from the oven and from the water bath; let them rest for 10 minutes.

Increase the oven temperature to 450°F/230°C. Spoon the jam over the tops of the desserts. To make the meringue, whisk the egg whites with the sugar until they form firm peaks. Pipe or spoon the meringue over the top of the desserts and return them to the hot oven, or place them under a preheated broiler for about 6–8 minutes until golden brown. The "queen of desserts" is now ready to serve.

Variation

Baked vanilla cake (see *Lemon and Vanilla Sponge Cake*, page 341)
Strawberry Jam (page 387)
4 eggs
¼ cup plus 1 tablespoon (75 g) superfine sugar
1¼ cups (300 ml) milk
1¼ cups (300 ml) heavy cream
1 vanilla bean, split (optional)

For the Meringue

4 egg whites
1 cup (225 g) superfine sugar

Preheat the oven to 325°F/160°C and prepare six 3 in (7.5 cm) soufflé dishes or one 2 quart (1.75 liter) soufflé dish.

Split the cake into three layers and sandwich together again with the strawberry jam. Cut into ½ in (1 cm) squares and divide these among the soufflé dishes or arrange them in the bottom of the large dish.

Whisk the eggs and sugar together and add the milk, cream, and the scraped-out seeds of the vanilla bean, if using. Strain through a sieve and pour on top of the cake squares. Place the molds in a roasting pan three-fourths filled with hot water and cook in the preheated oven for 30–40 minutes until the custard has barely set. Remove from the oven and the water bath and let them rest.

Increase the oven temperature to 450°F/230°C.

To make the meringue, whisk the egg whites with the sugar until they form firm peaks. Pipe or spoon the meringue over the top of the desserts and return them to the hot oven for about 6–8 minutes until golden brown.

Now, those are two ways to make this pudding: it's up to you to decide which one to use.

Bread and Butter Pudding

Yet another variation on a custard with bread and butter dessert has become another British classic. It was always a good way of using up stale bread with milk, sugar, and eggs, but this sometimes result in an overcooked, dry, and tasteless pudding, giving it a bad reputation. The recipe below will give you a quite different dish, something with an almost cake-like texture with thick fresh custard oozing out

OPPOSITE
Bread and Butter Pudding

between the layers. I use only the egg yolks and half milk and heavy cream, making the dessert a little more expensive, but once you've tried it you'll never want to make it any other way.

SERVES 6–8

12 medium slices of white bread
4 tablespoons (50 g) unsalted butter, softened
8 egg yolks
¾ cup plus 1 tablespoon (175 g) superfine sugar
1 vanilla bean or a few drops of vanilla extract
1¼ cups (300 ml) milk
1¼ cups (300 ml) heavy cream
1 oz (25 g) golden raisins
1 oz (25 g) raisins

To Finish

Superfine sugar

Grease a 2 quart (1.75 liter) pudding mold with butter.

First, butter the bread, then remove the crusts and cut the bread in half diagonally to create triangles. Whisk the egg yolks and superfine sugar together in a bowl. Split the vanilla bean, if using, and place in a pan with the milk and cream, or add the vanilla extract. Bring the milk and cream to a simmer, then pass through a sieve onto the egg yolks, stirring all the time. You now have the custard.

Arrange the bread in layers in the prepared mold, sprinkling the golden raisins and raisins in between the layers. Finish with a final layer of bread

without any fruit on top (fruit tends to burn if it's the top layer). The warm egg mixture can now be poured over the bread and cooked immediately, but I prefer to let the custard soak into the bread for 20 minutes before cooking. This allows the bread to take on a new texture and have the flavors permeate all the way through.

Preheat the oven to 350°F/180°C.

After the bread has been soaked, place the dish in a roasting pan three-fourths filled with warm water. Lightly cover with buttered foil and place in the preheated oven. Cook for about 20–30 minutes until the pudding begins to set. Because using egg yolks and not whole eggs, the mixture cooks like a fresh custard and only thickens; it will not become firm.

When the custard is ready, remove it from the water bath, sprinkle liberally with superfine sugar to cover, and glaze under the broiler under medium heat. The sugar will dissolve and caramelize and you may find that the corners of the bread start to burn a little. This will provide a bittersweet taste and it looks beautiful. The bread and butter pudding is now ready to serve. When you take that first spoonful, you will see the custard barely seeping from the dish – a new British classic at its best.

Note: Freshly grated or ground nutmeg can be sprinkled between the layers for an extra spicy flavor.

Bread and Butter Pudding Ice Cream

You all know how much I like bread and butter pudding, so turning it into an ice cream might seem a little out of character – but not at all. When you eat this ice cream, you taste all of the original recipe's flavors.

The ice cream is finished with caramelized Melba toast, which represents the crisp glazed topping of the classic bread and butter pudding.

SERVES 6–8

For the ice Cream

1 cup (250 ml) heavy cream
1 cup (250 ml) milk
1 oz (25 g) raisins
1 oz (25 g) golden raisins
1 vanilla bean, split
¼ teaspoon freshly grated nutmeg

For the Crumbs

2 cups (100 g) fresh white breadcrumbs
2½ tablespoons (40 g) light brown sugar

For the Custard

6 egg yolks
¼ cup (50 g) superfine sugar

To Serve

Caramelized Melba toasts (see Note opposite)
Custard Sauce (page 324, optional)

Preheat the oven to 350°F/180°C.

Bring all of the ingredients for the ice cream to a simmer. Remove from the heat and allow to infuse for 20–30 minutes.

Meanwhile, mix the crumbs with the light brown sugar and spread them on a baking sheet. Roast for approximately 10 minutes, then remove the sheet from the oven. The crumbs and sugar will begin to solidify: break them down again into crumbs and return to the oven for another 5 minutes. Remove from the oven and break to crumble them. Place to one side.

Cream together the egg yolks and sugar. Remove the vanilla bean from the cream mixture and strain the cream into the yolks, keeping the dried fruit to one side. Whisk the egg mixture with the cream and return it to the saucepan ora bowl placed over simmering water. Cook the custard over a low heat until it thickens and coats the back of a spoon. Add the reserved fruit and allow it to cool.

When it is cool, stir the roasted crumbs into the mixture. Now, churn the ice cream in an ice cream maker for 20–25 minutes until it has thickened and increased in volume. Pour it into a bowl and allow it to finish setting in the freezer.

To serve, place a triangle of caramelized Melba toast on top of a scoop of the ice cream. You could also trickle a little custard sauce around it to represent the custard that flows out of a baked bread and butter pudding.

Note: Use 3 × 1¾ in (7.5 × 3.5 cm) rings to make individual ice creams.

This ice cream can also be made without a machine. When the custard is ready for churning, place the mixture in a large bowl and freeze until well thickened. Now, beat it, keeping a blended consistency, re-freeze, and repeat this process every 15–20 minutes until almost set. Leave it to freeze completely.

To make caramelized Melba toasts, toast sliced bread on both sides. Then remove the crusts and split the slice through the middle. Cut each piece into two triangles. Dust heavily with confectioners' sugar and place them under a broiler at a low setting. The sugar will slowly caramelize and the bread will toast. After they are golden with burned tinges of sugar, your Melbas are ready.

White Chocolate Coffee Ice Cream

Coffee and chocolate were introduced at almost simultaneously to Britain. Coffee in particular became a passion, with coffee houses opening all over London (actually these were the origin of many of the present-day London men's clubs). Both white chocolate and ice cream are much later inventions, but the combination is one that works so well, with the infusion of the fresh coffee beans working behind the white chocolate.

This is lovely to serve on its own as an accompaniment to almost any chocolate dessert, in particular, the *Gâteau Opéra* on page 315.

MAKES 2½ CUPS (600 ML)

2 oz (50 g) whole fresh coffee beans
5 oz (150 g) white chocolate, chopped
2¼ cups (550 ml) milk
4 egg yolks
2½ tablespoons (40 g) superfine sugar

To achieve the maximum flavor from the beans, place them in an airtight container with the white chocolate. Keep this in a warm place for 24 hours and the coffee flavor and aroma will be absorbed by the chocolate.

Bring the milk to a boil. While it is heating, whisk the egg yolks with the sugar until thick, frothy, and falling from the whisk in thick ribbons. Pour the milk onto the egg "sabayon" and cook in a bowl set over simmering water, stirring until the "custard" is beginning to thicken. Pour this over the chocolate and coffee beans, stir until the chocolate has melted, allow it to cool, and strain through a sieve. The ice cream mixture can now be churned in an ice cream maker (in two batches if necessary) not allowing it to freeze completely. A thick, creamy consistency will be enough; this will guarantee a smooth, silky finish.

This process will take 20 minutes per batch. Pour the ice cream into a suitable container and put it in the freezer to finish setting. If you don't have an ice cream maker, see Note for previous recipe.

Nutmeg Ice Cream

Nutmeg is a spice that has had a long relationship with Britain's cooking – bread and butter pudding immediately comes to mind. Here I've used it in an ice cream, and it will work well with many dishes, from something as simple as a baked apple to my *Baked Egg Custard Tart* on page 288.

If you substitute a fresh vanilla bean (or a few drops of vanilla extract) for the nutmeg, you will have a wonderful vanilla ice cream.

MAKES 3–4 CUPS (750–900 ML)

1¼ cups (300 ml) heavy cream
1¼ cups (300 ml) milk
1 nutmeg, freshly grated
6 egg yolks
¾ cup (175 g) superfine sugar

Mix together the cream and milk in a saucepan. Add the grated nutmeg and bring slowly to a boil. While the cream mixture is heating, whisk the egg yolks and sugar together until pale and light. Pour the hot cream slowly into the egg mixture and stir until well blended. Cook in the bowl over a pan of simmering water, stirring until the custard coats the back of a spoon. (Do not let it boil or the eggs will scramble.) Strain through a sieve, then let it cool, stirring from time to time to prevent a skin from forming.

You will need to churn the ice cream in an ice cream maker in two batches. Pour in the first half and churn for 20 minutes until it has thickened and increased in volume. Repeat with the second batch. It's important not to churn it until it is completely frozen or it will take on a curdled, slightly grainy texture. Pour the ice cream into a container and put it in the freezer to finish setting. This will guarantee a lovely silky-smooth consistency.

Note: If you don't have an ice cream maker, see Note, page 309.

Clotted Cream Ice Cream

Clotted cream is a speciality of Devon, Cornwall and Somerset. The warm, very fresh milk is left to settle in a wide pan until the cream – which is lighter than the rest of the milk – rises; then it is heated very slowly until the cream has formed a crinkled layer on top of the milk. This cream is carefully skimmed off and enjoyed as part of the British tradition of cream tea with scones and jam.

Here, I've used the richness of clotted cream in an ice cream, which is the one used in the *Afternoon Tea Pudding* on page 320. It's a pudding that everyone should try, warm griddle scones topped with toffeed strawberries and a scoop of this clotted cream ice cream – a new experience. The ice cream also goes well with all summer berries and with the classic *Summer Pudding* (page 313), as well as with any hot steamed puddings.

MAKES APPROX. 3 CUPS (750 ML)

1⅔ cups (375 ml) milk
½ cup plus 1 tablespoon (125 g) superfine sugar
5 egg yolks
½ cup plus 1 tablespoon (125 g) clotted cream

Bring the milk to a boil. Whisk together the superfine sugar and the egg yolks until the mixture forms rich, thick ribbons (sabayon). This can be easily achieved in a food processor or with an electric mixer. Pour on the hot milk and stir well. Now, cook the mixture in a bowl set over a pan of simmering water, stirring, until the custard coats the back of a spoon. Remove from the heat and add the clotted cream.

When the clotted cream mixture is cold, churn it in an ice cream maker in two batches, if necessary, allowing approximately 20 minutes for each. The ice cream will now have increased in volume, holding a thicker consistency. Repeat the same process for the next batch. It's important not to churn it until it is completely frozen or it will take on a curdled, slightly grainy texture. Pour the ice cream into a container and put in the freezer to finish setting.

Note: The quantity of clotted cream can be increased to give you a richer flavor.
If you don't have an ice cream maker, see Note, page 309.

Bakewell Tart Ice Cream

The historic Bakewell tart is said to have originated at the Rutland Arms in Bakewell, Derbyshire. Because the almond filling is very similar to a frangipane, some claim it was created by an Italian cook, but the British were equally experienced in baking with ground almonds. The tart is a cross between a cake and pudding and can be served for dessert or for afternoon or high tea. It was a challenge to simulate that taste in an ice cream – but the recipe works. All the flavor is here. Crisp pastry tartlets, raspberries bound in their own *coulis*, almond ice cream, and a touch of lemon water icing – the Bakewell classic in a completely new form.

SERVES 6

½ recipe *Sweet Shortcrust Pastry* (page 364)
1 cup (225 g) fresh raspberries
⅔ cup (150 ml) raspberry *coulis* (see Note opposite)

1¼ cups (300 ml) heavy cream
1¼ cups (300 ml) milk
1 cup (100 g) ground almonds
8 egg yolks
½ cup plus 1 tablespoon (125 g) superfine sugar
¼ cup (50 ml) Amaretto (almond liqueur)

For the Lemon Water Icing

Finely grated zest and juice of ½–1 lemon
1–1¼ cups (100–150 g) confectioners' sugar

Preheat the oven to 400°F/200°C. Grease six 4 × ½–1 in deep (10 cm diameter × 1–2.5 cm) tartlet pans.

First, make the ice cream. Bring to a boil the cream, milk, and almonds. Whisk the egg yolks, sugar, and Amaretto until ribbons form. Pour the cream mixture over the eggs and cook in a bowl over simmering water until it coats the back of a spoon. Let it cool. Then strain through a sieve and churn it in an ice cream maker for 20–25 minutes. When it has thickened and increased in volume, pour into a container and freeze until set.

While the ice cream is churning, roll the pastry to ⅛ in (3 mm) thick and use it to line the tartlet pans. Then line the pastry shells with waxed paper and baking weights or dried beans and blind-bake for 15–20 minutes, until crisp and golden. Remove the weights and let it cool.

Make the lemon water icing just before you assemble the tarts by whisking the lemon juice and zest into the confectioners' sugar. Strain out the zest if you prefer a smoother finish.

To build the tart, pipe or drizzle a little lemon icing across the plate, then spoon a little into the bottom of each pastry shell. Place the shells in the center of the plates on top of the icing. Stir together the raspberries and the *coulis*, then divide the mixture either warmed or left cold, among the tartlets. Now, scoop the almond ice cream on top of the raspberries and drizzle with more icing.

Note: To make a raspberry *coulis*, place 1 lb (450 g) fresh raspberries, 1 cup (4 oz) confectioners' sugar, ⅓–⅔ cup

(85–150 ml) water, and a squeeze of lemon juice in a saucepan. Heat gently for 5 minutes. Remove from the heat and mix thoroughly to a purée, then strain through a fine sieve.

The fresh raspberries in the *coulis* can be replaced by a high-quality raspberry jam.

Sticky Toffee Pudding Ice Cream

Sticky toffee pudding is a first-rate dessert, and this variation on the theme is up there with the stars. I serve it in a glass goblet, with a toffee sauce poured over it.

SERVES 6–8

2 cups (500 ml) heavy cream
2 cups (500 ml) milk
1 cup plus 1 tablespoon (200 g) dates, chopped
12 egg yolks
½ cup (100 g) superfine sugar
1 × 14 oz (394 g) can condensed milk, made into toffee (see Note)
1½ cups (250 g) dried sugar dates (see Note), chopped into small dice

Boil the cream and milk with the chopped dates. Whisk the egg yolks and sugar until they form ribbons. Pour the boiled cream onto the egg mixture and whisk it in. Cook over a pan of simmering water until it coats the back of a spoon.

Add the softened condensed milk toffee, stirring until it is well mixed. Let it cool, then pass through a sieve and discard the dates. Now, churn the mixture in an ice cream maker until it has thickened almost to the setting point.

For the last few turns in the machine, add the dried sugar dates. Pour into an airtight container and put in the freezer to finish setting. This ice cream goes beautifully with toffee-cream sauce (see Note), or melted rich bought toffees. Warm sauces are best with this dessert.

Note: This ice cream makes a delicious accompaniment for crumbles, pies, and steamed desserts.

If you can't get dried sugar dates, which are available in some gourmet food stores, replace with Medjool dates.

To make toffee from condensed milk, simply put the unopened can in a deep saucepan, cover with cold water, bring to a boil, and boil for 3 hours. Keep the pan totally covered with water. After 3 hours, remove the pan from the heat and allow the can to cool while still immersed in water. The toffee is now ready for use but can be kept refrigerated until the expiration date on the can. When you open it, you will find a rich golden-brown toffee waiting to be served.

For a toffee-cream sauce, simply whisk in some heavy or light cream – about 1 cup plus 1 tablespoon (250 ml) per can of toffeed sweetened condensed milk.

BELOW
Sherry Trifle

Sherry Trifle

The name "trifle" actually comes from the word meaning something of little importance, and it was applied to the pudding in around the sixteenth century when sweet things as part of a "banquet" course all had frivolous names. In the beginning, custard was poured over wine-soaked macaroons or ratafia sweet cookies and then covered with a syllabub. The recipe has taken on many variations over the years, but as with most other things, I like old-fashioned simplicity, and my recipe here has plenty of taste and texture without all the extras.

There are two options for making the custard layer in this dessert. For a store-bought mix variety, follow the recipe here. For a homemade version, use the *Pastry Cream* recipe featured on page 305.

SERVES 4

For the Cake Layer

3 eggs
¼ cup plus 1 tablespoon (75 g) superfine sugar
⅔ cup (75 g) all-purpose flour
40 g (1½ oz) unsalted butter, melted

For the Syrup

½ cup plus 1 tablespoon (125 g) superfine sugar
⅔ cup (150 ml) water
3–4 tablespoons sweet sherry, to taste

For the Custard Sauce

2½ cups (600 ml) milk
2 oz (50 g) powdered custard mix
¼ cup (50 g) superfine sugar

For the Filling and Topping

Strawberry Jam (page 387) or raspberry jam
⅔–1¼ cups (150–300 ml) heavy cream, whipped, to taste

Preheat the oven to 375°F/190°C and grease and line an 8 in (20 cm) springform pan or flan ring on a baking sheet.

To make the cake layer, whisk the eggs and sugar in a bowl over a pan of hot water until the mixture has doubled in bulk has become light and creamy. Remove from the heat and continue to whisk until cold. Gently fold in the flour and melted butter. Pour the mixture into the lined springform pan or the flan ring and bake in the preheated oven for 15 minutes. Turn out and allow it to cool.

To make the syrup, boil the sugar and water together for about 2 minutes to form a syrup, then add the sherry – more than the amount listed if you want a stronger flavor.

To make the custard sauce, stir some of the milk into the custard mix in a pan. Bring the remaining milk to a boil in another pan. Pour this onto the custard mix, whisking all the time. Return to the heat and bring back to a boil. The sauce will thicken as you stir it. Add the sugar, cover with buttered waxed paper, and allow it to cool.

Split the cake in half horizontally and spread jam on both pieces. Place one half in a bowl and sprinkle half the sherry syrup over it. Place the other half of the cake on top and again soak with the sherry syrup. Pour the custard on top and allow to set in the refrigerator. When the cake has soaked, spoon the whipped cream on top (the amount is up to you) and serve.

Note: You can also make individual trifles in 4 in (10 cm) soufflé dishes. Bake little cakes to fit or cut cake to fit and then assemble in exactly the same way.

Spotted Dick

This recipe – with its peculiar name – is a typical example of an early roly-poly boiled pudding made with suet (the relic of the savory). I've never been quite sure about the name, which also went by the names "Spotted Dog" or "Plum Bolster," but always very sure about the taste. It was one of those desserts I would look forward to at school when it lunchtime came. The moist dough dotted with currants or raisins and topped with loads of custard (usually lumpy) was a real treat. Here's a modernized recipe for you to enjoy. The dessert can be served with thick cream or custard and it also goes very well drizzled with honey or golden syrup.

SERVES 6–8

2⅓ cups plus 1 tablespoon (300 g) all-purpose flour
1 teaspoon (10 g) baking powder
5 oz (150 g) shredded suet
¼ cup plus 1 tablespoon (75 g) superfine sugar
⅔ cup (100 g) currants
Finely grated zest of 1–2 lemons
¾ cup–¾ cup plus 1 tablespoon (185–200 ml) milk

Mix together all the dry ingredients with the currants and lemon zest. Pour in ¾ cup (185 ml) of the milk and stir together, adding more milk if necessary to give a binding/dropping consistency. The wetter the mixture, the moister the cake. Roll the mixture into a 6–8 × 2 in diameter (15–20 × 5 cm) cylinder, wrap it in buttered waxed paper, with a fold to allow space for the sponge to rise, and tie the paper at both ends. Put it in a hot steamer and cook for about 1 hour.

Remove the paper and slice the pudding into servings. I find it's best to cut the slices approximately 1 in (2.5 cm) thick for a good texture.

Spotted Dick goes very well with *Custard Sauce* (page 324).

Note: Try replacing ⅔ cup (50 g) of flour with ½ cup (50 g) of cocoa, and add some chocolate chips and orange zest. Or replace the sugar and half the milk with 5–6 tablespoons of golden syrup.

Summer Pudding

Another Great British pudding using bread originated much later than the others, during the eighteenth century. It was called "hydropathic pudding" at first because it had been designed for nursing-home patients who were not allowed the rich pastry desserts of the time.

I've listed the amounts and varieties of fruit below, but, of course, the beauty of this dish is that the choice of berries is entirely up to you, so use whatever berries are available. You need about 3 lb (1.4 kg) of them altogether. If there is some of the fruit mixture left over, it can be kept for a few days and served with ice cream.

SERVES 8–10

Approx. 3 lb (1.4 kg) mixed berries e.g. raspberries, strawberries, blackberries, red currants, or blueberries
2 tablespoons *crème de framboise* liqueur (optional)
1 loaf of white bread, thinly sliced
Clotted or whipped heavy cream, to serve

For the Raspberry Purée

1 lb (450 g) fresh or frozen raspberries
½ cup (50 g) confectioners' sugar

For the Sugar Syrup

1¼ cups (300 ml) water
¾ cup (175 g) superfine sugar

Lightly butter a 1 quart (1.5 liter) mold or eight ⅔ cup (150 ml) individual molds. Trim and wash all the berries and let them drain.

To make the raspberry purée, simply purée the berries and sugar together in a blender and then push them through a sieve.

BELOW
Summer Pudding

To make the sugar syrup, simply boil the water and sugar together for a few minutes to a clear syrup. Let it cool.

Mix half of the raspberry purée with the sugar syrup and bring to a simmer. Add the berries and *crème de framboise*, if using, to the sauce, then remove from the heat and let the mixture rest. The fruits should have all softened but will still have kept their shape. When cool, pour some of the syrup into a separate bowl.

Remove the crusts from the bread and cut each slice into thirds, keeping a disk shape for the bottom. Dip these in the reserved raspberry syrup and line the mold(s) with the soaked bread, overlapping slightly with each slice. When the the mold(s) are lined, fill with the berries and a little of the sauce and cover with more bread. Cover the mold(s) with plastic wrap and then with a plate, pressing down with a weight; leave the mold(s) in the refrigerator for a few hours or preferably overnight.

Mix the remaining raspberry sauce with a little of the remaining pudding juices until you have a sauce consistency. Turn out the summer pudding(s) onto a plate (or plates) and spoon the finished raspberry sauce over them. Decorate with the remaining berry mixture, the sauce, and the clotted or whipped cream.

Gâteau Opéra

A French name and a French concept, but I couldn't resist including this gâteau, which is a chocoholic's dream with lots of layers and lots of chocolate.

There are quite a few ingredients involved but the dessert is relatively simple to put together. It's made in a 10 in (25 cm) square cake pan and served as a dessert, but you can make it in a large round pan and present it as a cake.

A scroll of white chocolate and coffee ice cream is placed on top of the cake and a trickle of coffee syrup is used to finish the dish.

The sponge cake is going to be cooked in three separate 10 in (25 cm) square pans. This guarantees that all the cake layers are equal in thickness and have a smooth finish. The layers will then be stacked in the cake pan, spreading the ganache and cream in between. If you only have the one pan, then bake in three batches. Each layer will take only 12 minutes to bake.

SERVES 9–12

For the Chocolate Sponge

4 heaping teaspoons coffee granules
¼ cup plus 1 tablespoon (85 ml) hot water
9 egg yolks (3 per layer)
10 oz (275 g) semisweet chocolate, melted
9 egg whites (3 per sponge)
¾ cup (185 g) superfine sugar

For the Chocolate and Hazelnut Ganache

13 oz (375 g) semisweet chocolate, chopped
1 cup (225 ml) heavy cream
4 tablespoons Frangelico hazelnut liqueur (optional)
4 oz (100 g) Nutella hazelnut paste
4 egg yolks
¼ cup (50 g) superfine sugar
1 cup (225 ml) heavy cream, whipped to soft peaks

For the Coffee Buttercream

2 medium eggs
½ cup plus 1 tablespoon (150 g) superfine sugar
4 tablespoons water
10 tablespoons (150 g) softened butter, at room temperature
2 tablespoons strong coffee flavoring (Camp)

For the Finishing Ganache

7 oz (200 g) semisweet chocolate
8 tablespoons (100 g) unsalted butter
¼ cup (50 ml) heavy cream

For the Coffee Syrup

1¼ cups (300 ml) strong fresh or instant coffee
½ cup plus 1 tablespoon (150 g) superfine sugar

To Serve

White Chocolate Coffee Ice Cream (page 309)

Preheat the oven to 350°F/180°C. Grease and flour three 10 in (25 cm) square, cake pans.

For the cake layers, dissolve the coffee granules in the hot water and remove from the heat. Beat the egg yolks into the coffee, then stir in the melted chocolate.

Whisk the egg whites and superfine sugar to the soft-peak stage. Fold the meringue into the chocolate mixture. Divide equally among the three pans (or spoon in a third of the mixture if only one pan is available). Bake in the preheated oven for 12 minutes. Allow the layer(s) to cool. Remove the cake and line another cake pan with waxed paper. One of the layers can now be placed in the bottom.

Now, make the chocolate and hazelnut ganache. Melt together the chocolate, the liquid heavy cream, the liqueur (if using), and the Nutella.

Whisk the egg yolks and sugar together until the mixture trails off the whisk in ribbons. Stir the egg into the chocolate, then gently fold in the whipped cream. Let the mixture cool, stirring occasionally until it has reached a spreading consistency.

For the coffee buttercream (this is the second of the spreads for the gâteau), whisk the whole eggs in an electric mixer to a ribbon (sabayon) stage.

Boil the sugar and water together to the "soft ball" stage – 240°F/117°C. When the mixture reaches this temperature, pour into the egg sabayon and continue to whisk until cool (room temperature).

The softened butter can now be added gradually along with the coffee flavoring, to finish the buttercream.

To assemble the gâteau, divide the amounts of chocolate ganache and the coffee buttercream into halves. Spread the first half of the chocolate onto the cake in the pan.

Refrigerate to set a little before spreading the first half of the buttercream on top. Also refrigerate to set.

Another layer can now be placed on top of the buttercream. Repeat the same process – chocolate ganache, coffee buttercream, and cake layer –

remembering to let the dessert set between each spread. Refrigerate to set.

Now, make the finishing ganache. This will be used to spread across the top of the gâteau, giving it a shiny smooth, chocolatey finish. Make sure all the ingredients are at room temperature before you start to prevent the mixture from separating.

Melt the semisweet chocolate and butter together gently. Stir in the heavy cream. This can now be cooled to a spreading consistency before topping the cake. Let it set.

BELOW
Gâteau Opéra with
White Chocolate Coffee Ice Cream

Finally, make the coffee syrup. Boil the coffee and sugar together to reduce by half. Cool to room temperature and the syrup is ready.

Remove the pan and the Gâteau Opéra is now ready to serve. It is best served close to room temperature, keeping the creams smooth. The gâteau can be cut into 9–12 squares. Place the squares on dessert plates and top each with a scroll of white chocolate coffee ice cream and a trickle of coffee syrup.

Note: When spreading the creams on the sponges, a thickness of only ¼ in (5–6 mm) of each per layer will be needed. If you have buttercream leftover, it can be used to cover and fill almost any other cake.

Any ganache not used in this gâteau can be rolled into balls and dusted with cocoa powder or dipped in melted chocolate, forming homemade chocolates.

The cake layers, after they have slightly cooled, can be lightly rolled between sheets of plastic wrap, keeping the thickness at ¼ in (5–6 mm), to make them completely flat and smooth.

It is not essential but, if prepared and finished in this way, trim the edges to fit the pan size.

For an extra touch, decorate the dessert with a bought chocolate "twig."

Burned Cream or Crème Brûlée

Of the two names, the French sounds more inviting than the English but apparently, "burned cream" has been made in England since the seventeenth century, and it could be much older than that. It is the good old traditional British custard. The caramelized sugar topping was said to have been invented by a chef at Trinity College, Cambridge.

It can be served cold (refrigerated), but I really do believe that the best way to eat "burned cream" is at room temperature. The custard is barely at the setting point and it releases its full vanilla flavor. If refrigerated, it tends to set completely, becoming over-chilled and not as flavorful. The choice is yours.

SERVES 6

8 egg yolks
¼ cup (50 g) superfine sugar
2½ cups (600 ml) heavy cream
1 vanilla bean, split, or a few drops of
    vanilla extract
Confectioners' sugar

Preheat the oven to 350°F/180°C.

Mix the egg yolks and sugar together in a bowl. Bring the cream to a boil with the vanilla bean, if using. Remove the bean and scrape the seeds into the cream (or add vanilla extract). Now, whisk the cream into the egg yolks and sugar. Place the bowl over a pan of hot water and heat until the custard begins to thicken, stirring all the time, until it reaches the consistency of light cream.

Now, pour the custard evenly into six 3 in (7.5 cm) ramekins or molds. Place these in a roasting pan and add warm water until it comes three-fourths up the sides of the molds. Bake in the oven until barely set, about 20–30 minutes. To test, remove one of the molds from the water after 20 minutes and shake gently. There should still be a slight movement in the center of the custard. If it is still runny, put it back in the oven and check after another 5 minutes. Remove the custards from the oven and allow them to cool. I prefer to serve the custards at room temperature, so I don't put them in the refrigerator.

To finish the *brûlées* after they have cooled and set, sprinkle them with confectioners' sugar. If you have a butane torch (page 11), use it to achieve a quick and even glaze. If not, then brown them under a preheated hot broiler, having the molds as close as possible to the heat. As the sugar is heating, it will bubble and start to brown. More sugar may need to be added and then continue to brown until deep golden. The *brûlées* are now ready to serve.

Variation

You can make chocolate *brûlées* by simply adding grated chocolate to the mixture before putting it into the ramekins. About 4 oz (100 g) semisweet chocolate should be enough for this recipe – but, of course, if you prefer it stronger, simply add more. The *brûlées* can be glazed with confectioners' sugar, but I think they are better when topped with chocolate shavings.

Nutty Apple Crumble

Jane Grigson suggested that crumbles may have originated in America, the idea of a streusel cake topping having been brought by Austrian Jewish immigrants. This may be so, but cooked fruit topped with pastry or breadcrumbs is familiar in the British tradition. Wherever and whenever it originated, the crumble is very much part of the history of British food, and is a particular favorite served as part of the Sunday dinner with lots of homemade custard.

This crumble has a new twist. The crumble topping is cooked separately, giving it a very crunchy finish. Almonds are included for a coarse nutty crunch. The apple filling is simple – Granny Smith apples, a heaping teaspoon of butter, some sugar, and, to give another flavor, the finely grated zest of a lemon. A pinch of cinnamon can also be added to either the apples or the crumble.

SERVES 6

For the Apples

2 lb (900 g) Granny Smith apples
2 tablespoons (25 g) butter
¼ cup (50 g) superfine sugar
Finely grated zest of 1 lemon

For the Crumble

8 tablespoons (100 g) butter
1½ cup (175 g) all-purpose flour
½ cup (75 g) light brown sugar
½–¾ cup (50–75 g) chopped almonds

Preheat the oven to 400°F/200°C, if cooking the crumble immediately.

To make the crumble topping, rub the butter into the flour. When it has a breadcrumb texture, add the sugar and almonds. The mixture can now be re-rubbed until it becomes coarse and lumpy. Sprinkle it onto a baking pan and bake it in the preheated oven for about 15–20 minutes, turning occasionally.

The topping should now be crunchy and golden. When it reaches this stage, remove it from the oven and let it cool. Keep the topping in an airtight container and used whenever within 48 hours.

Any fruit filling can now be cooked, cooled, and then re-heated with this topping.

To cook the apples, peel and quarter them and cut each quarter into three wedges. Remove the core and cut each wedge in half. Melt the butter in a large saucepan and when it bubbles, add the apple pieces. Cook for a few minutes and then add the superfine sugar and lemon zest. Cook the apples over a medium heat until softened and tender. This will release some of the apple juices, giving a sweet apple purée surrounding the chunks. The cooking time will be between 10 and 15 minutes (20 if the chunks are particularly big).

Spoon into a buttered 1 quart (1.5 liter) serving dish. The apples can now be allowed to cool or topped immediately with the crumble topping and finished in the preheated oven for 15–20 minutes. If allowed to cool, simply spoon the crumble on top when needed, and bake for up to 30 minutes. The apples can also be microwaved and then topped with the warmed crumble mixture.

This dessert tastes its best with fresh *Custard Sauce* (page 324) or heavy cream.

Note: The almonds can be omitted from the recipe.

Blancmange

The word "blancmange" derives from the French *blanc-manger* meaning "white food." The dish was first recorded in the fourteenth century in a cookbook compiled by chefs in the court of Richard II. At that time, it was a bland pottage or soup containing ground boiled capon, sugar, cooked rice, and almond milk, and it was decorated with red aniseeds or blanched almonds. The recipe changed over the years, as did the name, and by the seventeenth century, like many British dishes evolved, the blancmange had become sweet, losing all its savory connections apart from the setting agent, a stewed calf's foot (now, of course, commercial gelatin is used).

Here is a basic recipe, but many other flavors can be added to create new tastes and textures. For instance, hazelnuts are often used to replace the almonds, and you could add chocolate or raspberry purée for a completely different taste.

SERVES 4

1¼ cups (300 ml) milk
Thinly peeled rind of 1 lemon
¼ cup (50 g) superfine sugar
½ cup (50 g) ground almonds
3–4 leaves gelatin, soaked in cold water
⅓ cup (60 ml) brandy
1¼ cups (300 ml) heavy cream
1 vanilla bean (optional)

If using the vanilla bean to increase the flavor, split it lengthwise and place it in the milk with the lemon peel. Bring the milk to a simmer, remove from the stove, add the sugar and the almonds and let the mixture stand to infuse for 1 hour.

After the flavor has infused, pass the milk through a sieve. The vanilla bean can now be scraped, adding the rich vanilla seeds to the sweetened lemon milk. The soaked gelatin leaves or the softened powdered gelatin can now be warmed in a few tablespoons of the milk. After the gelatin is dissolved, add it to the blancmange foundation. The brandy can now also be added to the milk. As the gelatin mixture cools, it will begin to thicken.

When the gelatin mixture becomes cold, but hasn't yet set, lightly whip the cream and fold it into the mixture. The blancmange can now be spooned into four ⅔ cup (150 ml) pudding molds (or serve it directly from ramekins). Refrigerate for 2–3 hours until completely set before turning out of the molds.

The blancmange is ready to serve on its own with its fresh lemon and almond flavor. If you want a richer finish, a warm (or cold) raspberry *coulis* (see Note to *Bakewell Tart Ice Cream*, page 311) will make the perfect accompaniment. Raspberries have always held a very close relationship with lemon and almonds, so the *coulis* goes very well with them.

Fresh raspberries can be used to garnish the dish.

Note: The gelatin quantity is listed as 3–4 leaves. Three leaves provide gentler and softer setting, the dessert barely holding its own weight. Four guarantees a firm setting.

Raspberry *coulis* can also be added to the mixture, creating a fresh fruit flavor and color. Simply follow the recipe omitting half of the amount of milk and replacing it with raspberry *coulis*. Finish the raspberry blancmange as instructed in the method above.

When using the fresh scraped vanilla bean in the blancmange, the seeds will fall to the bottom of the molds as the pudding sets. When turned out, the blancmange will have a black speckled top. The vanilla flavor still runs through the complete dessert, and it looks as good as it tastes.

BELOW
Blancmange

Afternoon Tea Pudding

Afternoon tea is a uniquely British institution (see page 366), and so is a Cornish cream tea, so I decided to combine the two here in a pudding. Warm scones, clotted cream, and strawberry jam are many peoples' favorites, but announcing such a dessert for your next dinner party might make some guests wonder if you have partaken one or two glasses too many. But when you present this dessert, they will be delighted with the result: a griddle scone topped with warmed sweet strawberries and clotted cream ice cream.

SERVES 4–6

1 lb (450 g) fresh strawberries
½ cup (50 g) confectioners' sugar
3 tablespoons water
2 tablespoons (25 g) butter
2 teaspoons light brown sugar (optional)

To Serve

1–2 warm *Griddle Scones* per portion
   (page 362)
Clotted Cream Ice Cream (page 310)

Chop 1 cup (100 g) of the strawberries and place in a saucepan with the confectioners' sugar and water. Bring to a simmer and cook for 4–5 minutes before pushing through a sieve. This forms a strawberry sauce to roll the rest of the strawberries in after they are pan-fried. A teaspoon or two of strawberry jam can also be added while the berries simmer, giving the sauce a richer flavor.

The remaining strawberries can either be left whole if they are small or halved if large.

Melt the butter and when it bubbles, add the remaining strawberries. Cook over a relatively high heat for 1–2 minutes, warming through and allowing to soften slightly.

The light brown sugar, if using, can now be added. This will caramelize, giving you toffeed strawberries. Pour in the sieved strawberry sauce, and they are ready to serve.

The warm griddle scones can now be presented on plates, topped with the strawberries and clotted cream ice cream. This dish is beautiful and absolutely delicious. The plate can be decorated with a dusting of confectioners' sugar and a sprig of mint to create color.

Note: Almost any fruit can be used in this recipe. All berries – raspberries, blackberries, and so on – will work well. Fresh plums, apricots, peaches, and other fruit also go beautifully with the clotted cream ice cream.

Rhubarb and Apple Charlotte

No one is quite sure why this eighteenth-century British dessert is called a "charlotte." It was probably to honor the new bride of George III, Charlotte Sophia of Mecklenburg-Strelitz. Tender fresh fruit is surrounded by a casing of crisp, baked bread slices. It's traditionally made with apples alone, but I have added rhubarb for extra flavor. The rhubarb is slightly cooked before the pudding is baked, allowing the juices to mix with the apples, turning into a rhubarb syrup/sauce to offer with the crispy finished charlotte.

Fresh cream, custard, or ice cream go well with this dish.

SERVES 6

1 lb (450 g) stale bread (approx. 12–18 slices)
Softened butter, for spreading

For the Fruit Filling

1 lb (450 g) fresh rhubarb
4 tablespoons (50 g) butter
¼ cup plus 1 tablespoon (75 g) superfine sugar
3 Granny Smith apples

Preheat the oven to 425°F/220°C and have ready six 3–3½ × 2 in (7–8 × 5 cm) individual metal pudding molds or a 5 × 2½–3 in (12.5 × 6–7 cm) Charlotte mold.

OPPOSITE
Rhubarb and Apple Charlotte

Cut six bread disks to fit the bottoms of the molds, and six to fit the tops (if using a large mold, simply cut 2 disks).

Cut away the crusts of the remaining slices and slice into approximately 1 in (3 cm) strips.

Butter all of the bread on one side only. Place one disk, butter-side down, in the base of each mold. The strips can now be placed, butter-side against the mold, slightly overlapping all the way around.

To make the fruit filling, peel the rhubarb, if stringy, and cut into ½ in (1 cm) chunks. Melt half of the butter in a large saucepan, and when it bubbles, add the rhubarb. Turn the fruit pieces in the pan for 1 minute before adding ¼ cup (50 g) of the superfine sugar. Continue to cook for another minute. The rhubarb can now be strained in a colander or large sieve, allowing the sweet juices to collect in a bowl.

While draining the rhubarb, the apples can also be prepared. Peel, core, and cut each apple into eight wedges. The wedges can now be cut in half, leaving chunky pieces.

Melt the remaining butter in a saucepan, adding the apples when the butter begins to bubble.

Cook for 2 minutes before adding the remaining sugar. Continue to cook for 1–2 minutes. Let the mixture cool.

The rhubarb will have now drained. Take a fourth of the actual fruit pieces and mix with the juices that have collected. These can now be brought to a simmer and the rhubarb cooked until tender. When it is tender, purée in a food processor and push through a sieve. You now have a fresh rhubarb syrup to serve with the charlottes.

When both fruits have cooled, gently mix them together. Now, taste the mixture for sweetness. If the flavor is too tart, add a sprinkling of superfine or confectioners' sugar. (A pinch of ground cinnamon can also be added.)

Divide the mixture among the molds, then top with the lids. Any excess bread at the sides should be folded over, keeping the lids in place.

For individual charlottes, bake in the preheated oven for 20 minutes; a large charlotte will take twice as long – 40–45 minutes.

After they have cooked, turn out the charlottes onto plates to reveal the crispy golden finish. Spoon the rhubarb syrup around them and serve.

BELOW
Baked Apple with Dates and Walnuts

Baked Apples with Dates and Walnuts

Until fairly recently, raw fruit was considered to be unwholesome and looked upon with suspicion. Most fruit – even the humble apple from the sixteenth century onward was cooked and served with digestive spices. The old-fashioned baked apple is a classic example, and it's a basically good idea that simply needs a little help. Usually it's an apple scored around the middle, cored, filled with sugar, butter, and a pinch of spices, and then cooked with a little water until tender. Here, I've adorned it a little more.

Dates, walnuts, and apples are a delicious combination. I have also added grated apple to the mixture, which helps bind the other flavors. My favorite dates to use are the Californian-grown Medjools. These are dried dates with a thick wrinkled flesh and a buttery toffee flavor. They are more expensive, but worth it.

SERVES 4

3 large apples (Golden Delicious or
   Granny Smith)
1½ tablespoons (25 g) light brown sugar
6–8 dates, preferably Medjool
10 walnut halves, scraped clean and roughly
   chopped
Pinch of ground cinnamon
2 tablespoons (25 g) butter

Optional Extras

2 tablespoons crème fraîche or heavy cream
1 egg yolk
Calvados, to taste

Preheat the oven to 400°F/200°C.

Split two of the apples horizontally through the middle. The halves can now be cored. Place in a buttered ovenproof dish, sprinkle with a little of the sugar, and bake in the preheated oven for 10 minutes.

While baking, the remaining apple can be peeled, cored, and coarsely grated. The dates can be halved and pitted before being cut into thin strips.

Mix together the grated apple, dates, and chopped walnuts, adding the pinch of cinnamon. The optional extras can now also be added to the mixture, if desired. A a tablespoon or two of Calvados will be plenty for this amount.

Spoon the grated apple mixture into and on top of the par-baked apples. Sprinkle with the remaining sugar and top each with a heaping teaspoon of the measured butter. Lower the oven temperature to 350°F/180°C. Finish baking the apples for another 25–30 minutes. During the baking, apple juices mingling with the sugar can be used to baste the apples to intensify the flavor.

After they are cooked, remove the apples from the oven, trickling each with the natural sweetened juices. Extra-thick cream will be all the apples need to complete the dish.

Bittersweet Chocolate Sauce

Chocolate recipes began to appear in cookbooks at the beginning of the eighteenth century, but they used the raw material rather than the processed. The semisweet and bittersweet chocolates the British enjoy today did not appear until at least 100 years later, made at first by Mr Fry and then by Mr Cadbury.

This sauce goes very well with all sorts of desserts, in particular, with sorbets and ice creams.

MAKES APPROX. 2 CUPS (500 ML)

10 oz (300 g) bittersweet chocolate, chopped
10 tablespoons (150 g) unsalted butter
¼ cup plus 1 tablespoon (75 ml) heavy cream

Mix all of the ingredients together in a bowl over simmering water until the chocolate has completely melted. Stir well. This sauce should be served warm.

Note: This recipe also works using semisweet or milk chocolate.

Light cream can be used to replace the heavy cream, and the amount doubled for a richer finish.

Custard Sauce or Creme Anglaise

Eggs and milk have always been freely available in Britain, so their early combination in a smooth, sweet sauce, whether to be poured into or baked in pastry, was perhaps inevitable. Custard sauce, king of the classic British sweet sauces, is the ideal accompaniment to baked or steamed desserts, stewed fruit, and sweet pies and tarts. The French so associated custard with the English that they distinguished it with the name *crème anglaise*.

This fresh custard sauce can act as a foundation for many different flavors such as lemon, orange, rum, and coffee. You must be careful not to boil the sauce because boiling scrambles the egg yolks in the cream mixture. The fresh vanilla bean is optional and can be omitted when using other flavors.

You can easily halve the amount of this recipe.

MAKES 3 CUPS (750 ML)

8 egg yolks
¼ cup plus 1 tablespoon (75 g) superfine sugar
1 vanilla bean, split (optional)
1 ¼ cups (300 ml) milk
1 ¼ cups (300 ml) heavy cream

Beat the egg yolks and sugar together in a bowl until well blended. Scrape the insides of the vanilla bean, if using, into the milk and cream; add the bean, and bring the mixture to a boil. Place the bowl over a pan of hot water and whisk the cream into the egg yolks and sugar. As the egg yolks cook, the custard will thicken. Keep stirring it until it starts to coat the back of a spoon, then remove the bowl from the heat and the bean from the custard. Stir the sauce occasionally until cool, to prevent a skin forming, or cover with waxed paper while it cools. Serve the sauce warm or cold.

The custard can be warmed back up in a bowl set over a pan of hot water, but never let it boil. If that happens, the sauce will separate.

Variations

For a lemon custard, add the zest of 2 lemons to the milk and cream when heating. After the custard has thickened, add the juice of 1 or more lemons to taste. Strain through a sieve.

For an orange custard, add the zest of 2 oranges as for the lemon custard, but no juice. Try adding a few drops of Grand Marnier or Cointreau instead.

For a rum custard, add rum to taste at the end of the cooking process; adding a spoonful or two of coconut milk also gives extra flavor.

For a coffee custard, replace the vanilla bean with 2 teaspoons of freshly ground coffee. After the custard is ready, strain it through a sieve.

BELOW
Baked Rice Pudding

Baked Rice Pudding

Most of the traditional, nursery-style milk desserts are Victorian, but many have their origins in much earlier dishes. The grain desserts, such as tapioca, sago, and rice, have developed from the wheat frumenty of the fourteenth century; like many other sweet dishes, they were originally savory. It took a while for rice to be accepted, but once it was, it was baked with milk, butter, and spices for a rich rice pudding that is little different from the classic of today. Street vendors in the eighteenth century would sell bowls of grain which had been boiled to a jelly and then served with some sugar, spices, and butter. The natural jellied liquid of boiled grain is still the basis of many local recipes, including the Welsh *llymru*, which was anglicized to "flummery." Another version was Atholl Brose, a strong and delicious combination of oatmeal and liqueur popular at New Year in Scotland.

This is a very basic recipe, but it has more than plain, basic flavor, and with it you can be as sensible or decadent as you like. The pudding can be made completely with milk. As you can see, I've been an extravagant and used half light cream. The light can be replaced by heavy cream for an even richer finish. The cream content, whether heavy or light, can be halved and substituted with extra milk. For a very thick baked rice pudding the cooking time can be increased to 2–2½ hours, but the time quoted here keeps the rice slightly thinner and, I think, more enjoyable.

SERVES 4–6

½ cup plus 1 tablespoon (100 g) short-grain pudding rice
2 cups (450 ml) milk
2 cups (450 ml) light cream
¼ cup (50 g) superfine sugar
2 tablespoons (25 g) butter, unsalted
Freshly grated nutmeg

Preheat the oven to 350°F/180°C and butter a 1 quart (1.5 liter) baking dish. Wash the rice and place in the dish. Heat the milk and cream together and pour over the rice. Sprinkle the sugar over the rice and stir it in. Dot with the butter and grate fresh nutmeg over the top. Bake for 10 minutes. After the 10 minutes reduce the oven temperature to 300°F/150°C and bake for another 1 hour 20 minutes–1 hour 30 minutes.

The pudding will become golden brown on top, with rich creamy rice pudding underneath. This goes beautifully with a dollop of homemade ice cream.

See also

Apple and Blue Cheese Tart or Pie (page 67)
Christmas Pudding (page 333)
Christmas Scotch Pancakes (page 334)
Rich Warm Chocolate Cake (page 349)
Tuile Cookies (page 356)
Warm Spiced Pineapple Cakes (page 394)

A Festive Christmas

It's December and the big annual Christmas event is upon us. It's that part of the year when everyone spends far too much money and there are too many guests invited to dinner. Imagine, the kitchen looks like a bomb hit it and everyone is crowded around the table.

I hope the recipes here, accompanied with some hints and tips on how to attack the day, will take all that pressure away and leave you with lots of flavors to simply enjoy. Before we get to my suggestions here's a brief history.

December has been a time for celebration since the very earliest times. In northern Europe, the "heathen" Scandinavians worshiped their gods, Odin and Thor among them, and celebrated the winter solstice in a feast that lasted for twelve days. The Christmas word "Yule" comes from the name of this solstice festival. In southern Europe, the Romans held their Saturnalia in December, an orgy of feasting and drinking in honor of the god Saturn (god of agriculture and vegetation), and gifts were exchanged. As Christianity spread throughout Europe during the first centuries after Christ, converts were persuaded to dedicate their winter festival to Christ instead of to their pagan gods – one reason why the arbitrary date of December 25th became Jesus' supposed birth date.

And since then, December 25th and the "twelve days of Christmas" have been important in the Christian calendar, although many of the traditions associated with Christmas still have roots in pagan practices. The Yule cake which stems from the Norse tradition of offering sweet cakes to the gods, the burning of a Yule log in the hearth, and perhaps even the lighting of spirits poured over Christmas pudding are relics of early fire worship. Bringing greenery such as holly and mistletoe into the house is a reflection of pagan tradition as well, although the prickly holly soon came to symbolize the Crown of Thorns. All this disturbed the Church, which wanted Christmas to be a time of religious fasting and reflection instead of a time of apparently irreligious feasting and revelry. In fact, when the Puritans came to power in 1642, they actually "banned" Christmas! They believed that the spices and fruit included in traditional festive foods such as mince pies and puddings inflamed passions.

With the Restoration in 1660, Christmas became again a time of feasting in England and elsewhere.

But in Scotland, the influence of the religious reformer, John Knox, was so great that Christmas was not properly recognized until as late as the 1950s. (A Scottish friend of mine remembers her father going to work on Christmas Day, for the Scots' major celebration was – New Year, or Hogmanay, and still is.) It wasn't until the Victorian era that Christmas became as it is in England today; Prince Albert was very influential in this, introducing many German ideas. He popularized Christmas trees decorated with symbols such as apples (the "fruit of the Tree of Knowledge') and candles, the forerunners of our present-day electric lights. Christmas cards, fire crackers, and Father Christmas became features of the festival at this time, although Christmas cakes, puddings, and mince pies had long existed, relics of the celebratory pottages and pies with the dried fruits and spices of centuries before.

The featured food of early Christmases used to be brawn, a jellied loaf that was usually made from a wild boar's head. Swans, cranes, and peacocks were also eaten by the rich on feast days, but they were notoriously tough, and it must have been a relief when the fleshier and more tender turkey was introduced from the Americas in the sixteenth century. This large bird soon became popular, and large flocks were raised in the grain-rich region of East Anglia – as they are today – and marched to London, the main turkey market, often wearing small shoes to protect their feet. Until then, farmyard geese had been the more common celebratory food. The geese, too, were taken to London on foot, but they had their feet tarred, since they could not be shod – thus the expression "to shoe a goose," meaning a waste of effort (or a wild goose chase).

Stuffings using breadcrumbs, shredded meat, herbs, and spices had been part of the British tradition since very early on, so the newfangled turkey was treated in the same way as other birds. A sharp sauce had long been associated with birds, both domestic and wild; while goose had its apple or sorrel sauce, turkey soon became associated with cranberries, probably an American influence (although wild cranberries are native to Europe). The lightly spiced bread sauce eaten in Britain with Christmas turkey – and also with game birds – is a direct reflection of the medieval habit of thickening sauces with breadcrumbs.

Then there's the "Christmas pud," of course, which which is a direct descendant of the Great British pottage via the classic British steamed pudding. This particular type of pudding is thought to have become associated with Christmas because George I – who was later known as the "pudding king" (and sung about in the nursery rhyme, "Georgie-Porgie, pudding and pie') – is said to have had it at his first Christmas meal in this country. During the Victorian era, alcohol was added, as well as trinkets (similar to *Twelfth Night Cake*, page 343), and butter sauces, spiked with rum, port or brandy, became traditional accompaniments.

So now you know a little of the Christmas history, let's move on to the cooking for the actual event. Cooking Christmas dinner for possibly a dozen family and friends can cause stress that no one needs. So how do you make the event an easy one? As with all cooking, the answer lies in the preparation, and, of course, in keeping the dishes simple to make as well as amazingly delicious. The recipes in the following pages are all beloved British classics, but I have given them a twist. The flavors are like pulling a Christmas cracker: there's something in there to excite you and take you by surprise.

IMPORTANT CHRISTMAS POINTS TO REMEMBER

Before the Day

1 It's best to serve a cold appetizer (if offering a three-course menu) that can be prepared at least 24 hours in advance.

2 The stuffing for the turkey should be made no earlier than 24 hours before stuffing the turkey. On Christmas day, stuff the turkey just before it goes into the oven. If you have extra stuffing, roll it in buttered foil and cook it separately.

3 Turkey stock made from giblets or veal *jus* can be made up to two days in advance.

4 All vegetables can be prepared on Christmas Eve.

5 If making homemade cranberry sauce, you can make it up to a week in advance and keep it refrigerated.

6 Any brandy or rum butters can be made well in advance and frozen.

7 Homemade rum sauce or custard can be made a day in advance.

On Christmas Day

1 Pre-cook vegetables such as carrots, green beans, broccoli, cauliflower, or Brussels sprouts in the morning. These can be refreshed in iced water, buttered, seasoned, and placed in covered serving dishes. Microwave to re-heat when needed. Or plunge them into boiling water to re-heat (about 1 minute) and then season and butter.

2 If using, make the *Homemade Bread Sauce* (page 43).

3 The roast turkey can be covered with bacon strips, which will crisp beautifully during the roasting time.

4 Thirty to forty minutes before the turkey should be finished cooking, place the potatoes in the oven.

5 When the turkey has cooked, remove it from the oven and from the roasting pan. Cover with foil and let it rest for 30 minutes.

6 Place the parsnips in the oven after the turkey has been removed (they usually take 20–30 minutes). The potatoes can also continue to cook during the 30 minutes' of resting time for the turkey.

7 Meanwhile, finish the gravy in the roasting pan using the prepared stock or its alternative.

8 Cook the chipolata sausages and bacon.

9 Re-heat vegetables and sauces when needed.

10 The main course is then ready to serve with little panic.

11 The Christmas pudding can be microwaved in separate servings, or steamed for 2 hours previously.

Happy Christmas dining!

Traditional Roast Turkey with Sage, Lemon, and Chestnut Stuffing and all the Trimmings

Here we have what is usually the biggest "roast" of the year. The secret to success with a roast turkey is to keep it moist and juicy. Often I hear that the bird has been roasted for up to 6 hours, or even throughout the night! It's purely because of the size and volume of the bird that we try to be "safe" and leave it for another hour just to be sure.

Since a 3½ lb (1.6 kg) chicken takes only 50–60 minutes to roast, multiply that by three and for a 10 lb

(4.5 kg) turkey. You don't need a calculator to work out the rest. Most people, however, roast it for twice that long, causing the meat to have a dry and coarse texture to the meat. For a 10–12 lb (4.5–5.4 kg) bird, the cooking time is 3–3½ hours and, if you're a little nervous, then 4 hours is maximum.

So that's the main point; the rest is all about organized trimmings: crisp bacon, pork chipolatas, the chestnut stuffing (this one is also flavored with lemon and apple to increase flavors and texture) and a delicious gravy to finish the whole experience.

I've also included a recipe for homemade cranberry sauce. If you're not a fan of cranberries, you can just add a teaspoon or two of cranberry jelly to the gravy for a sweeter finish – the flavor works very well. And, of course, you can serve the roast with *Bread Sauce* (page 43).

So here's the recipe for our main event.

SERVES 6–8

For the Cranberry Sauce

1 lb (450 g) fresh cranberries
1 cup (100 g) sugar
Juice of 2 large oranges
½ teaspoon very finely chopped shallots
½ cup port

For the Turkey

10–12 lb (4.5–5.4 kg) fresh turkey, giblets and neck
    removed
4 tablespoons (50 g) butter
1 small onion (optional)
Salt and pepper

For the Stuffing

Butter
2 large onions, finely chopped or grated
Grated zest of 2 lemons (juice may also be needed)
1 heaping tablespoon chopped fresh sage
1½ lb (675 g) pork sausage
4–6 oz (100–175 g) roasted chestnuts, chopped
    (page 332)
2 apples, grated
2 cups (100 g) fresh white breadcrumbs
2 eggs
Turkey liver (optional)
Salt, pepper and ground mace

For the Gravy

2–4 tablespoons (15-30 g) all-purpose flour
    (optional)
2½ cups (600 ml) turkey stock, made from roasted
    giblets boiled in water and reduced, or
    Chicken Stock (page 33) or 2 cups (450 ml)
    Veal Jus (page 34) or alternative (page 11)
Butter

For the Garnishes

Strips of bacon
Chipolata sausages

The cranberry sauce can be made at least two or three weeks in advance. Simply place all the ingredients in a pan and bring to a simmer. Cook gently for 10–15 minutes until the cranberries are just beginning to break. After they are cooked, refrigerate until needed. Heat gently before serving.

    The stuffing can be made up to 24 hours in advance, giving the mixture time to relax and the flavors to mingle.

OPPOSITE
Traditional Roast Turkey

Do not add the eggs or stuff the mixture into the turkey until just before roasting on Christmas day.

    Melt a heaping teaspoon of butter and cook the onions, for a few minutes until they begin to soften. Add the lemon zest and sage and remove from the heat and allow the mixture to cool. Then, add the onions to the sausage along with the chestnuts, apples, and breadcrumbs. Season with salt, pepper, and a pinch of mace. The eggs can now also be added as a binder to hold the mixture together. Check for seasoning.

    It's now time to taste the stuffing. If the lemon has been lost among all of the other flavors, then add a squeeze or two of the juice to heighten all the flavors. If the turkey liver is to be added, then cut it into dice and quickly pan-fry in a heaping teaspoon of butter. Let it cool before folding into the stuffing mixture. The turkey neck cavity can now be filled with the stuffing, folding any excess skin under. This not only helps flavor the bird but also helps keep it in a good shape.

    Before stuffing, here's a quick tip on how to improve the flavor of your roast turkey. Gently release the skin from the breast and push extra seasoned and softened butter between the meat and skin. As the turkey roasts, the butter melts and bastes it. After filling the neck cavity, pull the skin underneath and seal with a toothpick or two. Any remaining stuffing can either be wrapped and rolled in buttered foil or spooned into a suitable ovenproof dish. Either can be baked for 20–30 minutes while the turkey is roasting.

    If you choose to cook an onion with the bird, then simply quarter it and place inside the body cavity.

    To roast the turkey, a 10 lb (4.5 kg) bird will take 3 hours and every additional 2 lb (900 g) of weight will need another 30 minutes (for example, a 14 lb/6.5 kg bird will take 4 hours). The bird will then need to rest for 30 minutes. This relaxes the meat, making it even more tender and, at the same time, leaves the oven free to finish roasting the potatoes and parsnips. Cover the turkey with foil and let it rest for up to 45 minutes; it will still retain its heat.

    Preheat your oven to 400°F/200°C. If you plan on eating dinner at 1:30 p.m., then, for a 14 lb (6.5 kg) bird you will need to place it in the oven at 9:00 a.m. (or 8:45 a.m. for extra roasting and free oven time).

    Place the turkey in a large roasting pan, brush the breast with butter, and season it with salt and pepper.

The strips of bacon can either be cooked separately (see below) or they can be arranged on top of the bird at this point. Place the pan in the oven and cook at this temperature for 30 minutes. After a half-hour has passed, baste with the fat that has melted in the pan. The breast and legs will have taken on a golden tinge. Cover the turkey completely with foil and reduce the oven temperature to 350°F/180°C. The bird should now be basted every 20 minutes until half an hour before the end of its cooking time, when you should begin roasting the potatoes. At this point, remove the foil and bacon (which can be crisped separately) and continue to cook and baste the turkey to a rich, deep golden finish. To check that the bird is cooked, pinch the thigh/leg and if it "gives," the turkey is ready.

Place the turkey on a large platter and totally cover it with foil to retain the heat.

The fat can now be poured carefully from the pan and used to roast the parsnips or pan-fry the Brussels sprouts. (It can also be refrigerated and kept to stir-fry turkey for paella or risotto.)

While the turkey is resting, finish cooking the vegetables, along with the chipolatas and bacon. The amounts of these two ingredients are really up to you. The minimum you need is 1 strip of bacon and 1 sausage per person. It's always good, however, to have extra for second helpings.

The chipolatas can be cooked in the turkey fat that you've poured from the roasting pan, which will give even more flavor and help enhance the finished flavor. They can be either broiled, roasted, or pan-fried to a golden brown. It's best to cook the sausages during the resting time of the roast turkey; they only take about 15 minutes.

There's a choice for cooking the bacon too: the strips can either be broiled until crisp or laid over the turkey breasts to protect the bird during cooking. The latter contributes to the finished flavor of the turkey as the bacon fat melts over the skin.

If the bacon is still a little soft after it has been removed from the turkey, simply place it on a baking pan and finish in the oven or under a hot broiler.

To make a gravy that has a thick consistency, pour off the fat, add the flour (using 4 tablespoons/30 g will give you a thicker gravy) and stir into the sediment left in the roasting pan. Now, add the stock, water or veal *jus*.

Bring to a simmer and cook gently for a few minutes. Season with salt and pepper and strain through a sieve. The gravy can now be finished with a heaping teaspoon of butter just before serving.

The turkey will have rested to a warm stage, and the meat will be totally relaxed, moist, and tender. Served with the hot gravy, the turkey is now at its best.

Note: A 14 lb (6.5 kg) bird will allow second helpings for 6–8.

There are two other ways to make gravy. You can add turkey stock (made from frying or roasting the giblets) or chicken stock to the residue taken from the roasting pan to make a basic gravy. Or you can simply add veal *jus*/gravy or alternative (page 11) to the roasting pan.

Roast Loin of Pork with an Apricot and Sage Stuffing

This roast is a good alternative to the classic Christmas turkey. The loin is filled with a moist, slightly sweet and savory stuffing in keeping with Christmas style. But, actually, this roast is good at any time of the year.

Pork often becomes drained of all its juices during roasting. But stuffing the roast provides a beautiful moist center and totally changes its texture. The loin is for this roast should be bought on the bone and "French-trimmed" or "crown roast," which means that you can see how many servings you have by the number of bones neatly exposed above the meat.

For this recipe, I like to use a six-bone cut, which will give you the same number of very generous portions. It's also important to ask your butcher to remove the "chine" bone. This is the central piece that connects the cut to the opposite loin. After this has been removed, you will be able to cut between each bone without any problems.

Another feature of this recipe is the finished glaze. The rind skin is removed and cooked separately to provide the crackling. When the loin is nearly roasted (approximately 15–20 minutes before the end of its cooking time), honey is spooned over the roast and the meat is basted every 5 minutes. As the loin cooks, the honey thickens to a deep caramel color, leaving a rich glaze over the roast. The residue in the pan can also be used to flavor the gravy.

1 × 6-bone loin of pork, "French-trimmed" or
    prepared for a crown roast (see recipe intro),
    with skin removed for the crackling
4 strips of bacon
2–3 tablespoons cooking oil
Salt and pepper
All-purpose flour, for dusting
½ cup (100 g) honey

For the Stuffing

2 oz (50 g) chicken livers
4 shallots or 1 onion, finely chopped
1¼ cups (300 ml) dry cider
2 oz (50 g) wild or button mushrooms,
    cut into small dice
Butter
Cooking oil
8 oz (225 g) pork belly (including 2 oz/50 g
    of belly fat or pork sausage), finely ground
    or processed in a food processor
2 eggs
3 oz (75 g) ready-to-eat dried apricots,
    cut into ¼ in (5 mm) dice
5–6 sage leaves, chopped
1 cup (50 g) fresh white breadcrumbs

For the Gravy or Cream Sauce

½ cup white wine or ⅔ cup (150 ml) cider
⅔–1¼ cups (150–300 ml) *Veal Jus*/gravy (page 34),
    (or ⅔ cup (150 ml) *Chicken Stock* (page 33)
    plus ⅔ cup (150 ml) heavy cream)

The chicken livers are best soaked in milk for 24 hours in advance. This draws the bitter flavor from the livers, giving them a fresher taste. After they've been soaked, dry them on paper towels.

Pierce the loin through the center of the meat and from end to end using a long, sharp carving knife. Make this cut approximately 2 in (5 cm) deep, creating a cavity to fill with the apricot and sage stuffing. Now, refrigerate until needed.

For the stuffing, place the shallots or onion in a saucepan with the cider. Bring to a boil and allow to reduce until almost dry. Let the mixture cool.

The mushrooms can now be quickly pan-fried in a small teaspoon of butter until softened. Season with salt and pepper and let them cool.

Heat a frying pan with a little cooking oil. When it is hot, add a heaping teaspoon of butter and fry the livers for 1–2 minutes on each side, seasoning them with salt and pepper. Let them cool and then either finely chopped or purée them in a food processor. If you are grinding your own pork, also grind the livers, using a fine blade. Place the ground pork in a bowl over a container of ice. This will keep the meat firm and makes it easier to mix. Season with salt and pepper before mixing in the chicken livers. Add one egg at a time, beating each one in thoroughly. The mixture should be bound together and firm.

Now, mix in the cold shallots, the mushrooms, and the apricots along with the chopped sage and breadcrumbs. Check for seasoning, adding more if necessary.

Pan-fry a spoonful of the mixture (like a mini-burger) to check that the flavor is right for you. Fill a piping bag with the mixture, making sure it has a piping hole at least 2 in (5 cm) diameter. Insert the tip of the piping bag into the cut at one end of the loin and squeeze until the cavity becomes full. Be as generous as possible to give plenty of filling. Any excess stuffing can be rolled in buttered foil, creating a log shape, and baked for 20–25 minutes in the oven. Then, you'll have extra stuffing to pass with the dish.

Place 2 strips of bacon over each end of the loin and tie with string to hold them in place. The fat on the loin can be scored with a sharp knife before gently tying between each bone to keep its neat cylinder shape. When it is filled, the loin is best refrigerated for a few hours before roasting.

Preheat the oven to 400°F/200°C.

To roast, heat a large roasting pan with the cooking oil. Season the meat with salt and pepper. When it is hot, seal both ends of the loin in the pan, giving a golden brown finish. (To prevent the bacon from sticking to the pan, lightly dust both ends in all-purpose flour.) Next, seal and brown the fat side on a medium heat. When the meat is totally golden brown, place the roast on top of the bones in the roasting pan, put the pan in a preheated oven, and roast for 50 minutes–1 hour, basting with the fat in the pan every 10–15 minutes. The skin removed for crackling can simply be scored with a sharp knife, salted well, placed in a separate pan and put directly into the oven. As the loin is roasting, the crackling will become very crisp.

For the last 15–20 minutes of the roasting time, remove the loin from the oven, pouring out any excess fat. Return the loin to the pan and cover the golden brown roast with the honey. Continue to roast, basting every 5 minutes. The honey will become thicker and cover the roast with a rich glaze.

Remove the pork from the pan and let it rest. The roasting pan can now be heated on top of the stove, boiling any honey left on the bottom. As this reduces (make sure it doesn't burn) it becomes even thicker; spoon some over the resting loin. Now, add the white wine or cider to the pan and mix well with any sediment left in the pan. Add the *jus*/gravy, if using, and bring to a simmer. Skim away the fat from the sauce, season with salt and pepper, and strain through a fine sieve. The gravy is now ready.

If you're making a cream sauce rather than a gravy, add the chicken stock after the cider has reduced. Boil and reduce by half before adding the cream and then bring the sauce to a simmer. Season and strain, and the sauce is then ready.

It's important that the pork has at least 15–20 minutes" resting time before you remove the string and carve between the bones. The rich, moist stuffing will be revealed as you cut through the first slice. It not only looks sensational, but tastes that way too. The stuffed loin can now be served passing the gravy or cream sauce separately.

Note: Two wonderful accompaniments to serve with this dish are *Hazelnut Mashed Potatoes* (page 126) and *Broiled Baby Leeks* (page 97).

Chestnuts

Imagine it's Christmastime, and you are shopping on London's Oxford Street. As you approach a small street brazier, coals aglow, you pick up that classic aroma of roasted chestnuts. It's odd that chestnuts are rarely roasted at home; they are mainly used for chestnut stuffings. But there you are trying to carry far too many packages, and these wonderful roasted chestnuts

suddenly take priority. After you've peeled one, the first bite releases a slightly bittersweet taste, but then you find the tender texture all the way through.

When buying chestnuts to cook at home, make sure to choose rich and shiny ones that feel heavy for their size to guarantee a better result. It's also an idea to buy a few more than needed – there always tends to be a dud or two no matter how well you select them. Chestnuts appear in the markets in the fall and winter – when the nuts mature – which is why they've probably become associated with Christmas. If you pick them yourself in the country, be sure to choose the sweet variety, which comes in casings with long, very prickly spines (like a sea-urchin). The inedible buckeye (or horse-chestnut) – which produce the "conkers" kids play with in England – comes in a casing with shorter, stubbier spines.

Chestnuts can be cooked by three basic methods – boiling, roasting, or broiling. Whichever you choose, you should first make a slit/cross into the shell on two sides of the chestnut, cutting through the bitter-tasting skin surrounding the flesh.

To roast them, arrange on a baking sheet, sprinkle with a little water and cook for 15 minutes in an oven preheated to 400°F/200°C.

To broil, preheat the broiler to hot and broil the chestnuts for about 15 minutes.

To boil, simply cover the chestnuts with cold water, bring to a boil, and cook for 5–6 minutes. Turn the heat off, and leave the chestnuts in the liquid.

Peeling cooked chestnuts is very easy if they are still warm, so remove a few at a time to peel them. The skin surrounding the flesh should also be removed. Now, they are ready to use in the stuffing on page 329, or perhaps with the Brussels sprouts in the recipe on page 106.

If all of this seems to be too much work, then I suggest you use a can of vacuum-packed chestnuts. These are available from supermarkets or gourmet food stores. There's no peeling; these only need chopping.

Other chestnuts available for savory dishes or desserts are canned, unsweetened purée; canned, sweetened purée/*crème de marrons*; sweet and rich *marrons glacés*; and canned chestnuts in syrup – another *marrons glacés* variety.

Christmas Pudding

Rich puddings have always been part of culinary tradition in Britain. A plum pudding – the original name for the Christmas pudding, containing lots of prunes (rather than plums) – was as essential to many people as roast beef. It was the German kings in Britain who really popularized puddings such as these, and Prince Albert made them part of the Christmas feast.

In medieval times, a pudding called "hackin" was made from meat, usually shin of beef, stewed with raisins, currants, prunes, sugar, spices, claret, and lemon juice. This was then thickened with either sago or breadcrumbs. All of these flavors were mixed and cooked in pig or sheep intestines. I promise this recipe is nothing like that. In the seventeenth century, puddings began to be cooked in pudding cloths, and by the nineteenth century, the meat had dropped out of the recipe, although the suet remained.

The traditional day for making the pudding was the 30th November – St Andrew's Day or Stir-up Sunday. (The latter name comes from the Anglican prayer book reading for that day: "Stir up, we beseech Thee, O Lord....") Everyone in the family would stir the mixture, from east to west in honor of the wise men who traveled in that direction. I prefer to make my puddings in August, or even earlier, giving them more time to mature. I leave the mixture raw in the refrigerator for up to a week, stirring it from time to time. After they are cooked, the puddings must be kept in a cool place until they are served on Christmas day.

MAKES 3 x 2 LB (900 G) PUDDINGS

2 cups (225 g) all-purpose flour
1 teaspoon baking powder
3 cups (225 g) fresh white breadcrumbs
8 oz (225 g) shredded suet
1 cup (100 g) ground almonds
2¼ cups (500 g) dark brown sugar
½ teaspoon ground cloves
¼ teaspoon ground coriander
¾ teaspoon ground ginger
¾ teaspoon grated nutmeg
½ teaspoon cinnamon
6 oz (175 g) pitted prunes
6 oz (175 g) carrots, peeled

1¼ lb (750 g) mixed currants, raisins, and golden raisins
2 oz (50 g) chopped candied citrus peel
2 apples, peeled, cored, and roughly chopped
Juice and grated zest of 1 orange
Juice and grated zest of 1 lemon
5 eggs
⅓–⅔ cup (100–150 ml) rum
4 tablespoons molasses
4 tablespoons golden syrup
1¼ cups (300 ml) stout

Sift the flour with the baking powder. Add the breadcrumbs, suet, ground almonds, dark brown sugar, and spices. Grind the prunes and carrots together through a medium blade and add to the mixture with the dried fruit, mixed peel, apples, and the lemon and orange zests. Beat the eggs and stir them into the pudding mixture, with the lemon and orange juice, rum, molasses, golden syrup, and stout. You should now have a pudding mixture of approximately 7 lb (3 kg) in total weight. It will have a reasonably moist and loose texture, but if it appears dry, add some more stout and rum. Then taste it to check for full flavor and richness. If it's bland, add some more spices to liven it up. Now, the uncooked mixture can be refrigerated for up to a week to mature.

To cook the puddings, butter and lightly flour three 2 lb (900 g) pudding molds. Fill each three-fourths full with the mixture, cover with a circle of waxed paper, and then cover with baking parchment, muslin, or foil and tie it on firmly with some space left to give the pudding room to rise. Steam over boiling water for 4–6 hours (6 hours will make the puddings even richer). Don't forget to check the water level from time to time, adding more water, if necessary.

Let the puddings cool before refrigerating or storing them in a cold, dark place.

To serve the puddings on the Big Day, they will need a minimum of 1 hour of steaming (preferably 1½–2, which will make them richer), to return them to a tender pudding texture. I like to serve rum or brandy-flavored *Custard Sauce* or *Crème Anglaise* (page 324) with Christmas pudding, along with lots of cream – it is Christmas!

Christmas Pudding Fritters with Cranberry Ice Cream

After a generous serving of the Christmas dinner, the rich fruity pudding always ends up being served in thin slices. So what do you do with the remaining two-thirds or half of the pudding? Here's the answer: turn them into crispy fritters. This is a wonderful dessert made from simple Christmas leftovers. The cranberry ice cream is a great way to use the cranberry sauce that wouldn't otherwise be finished. Offering hot, crispy fritters with homemade ice cream is the perfect present for any guest.

The number of servings depends on the amount of pudding you have left over.

For the Cider Batter
(to coat a maximum of 20 fritters)

2 cups (225 g) self-rising flour, sifted
¼ cup (50 g) sugar
1¼ cups (300 ml) cider
Cooking oil, for frying

For the Cranberry Ice Cream (to serve 4–6)

Approx. 1 cup (200 g) leftover cranberry sauce
1–1¼ cups (200–250 g) custard, made from a
    packaged mix
⅔ cup (150 ml) heavy cream, lightly whipped

Whisk the cranberry sauce into the custard. Gently fold in the whipped cream and place in a container suitable for freezing. This can now be placed in the freezer for 3–4 hours, after which the ice cream is ready.

Preheat the cooking oil to 350°F/180°C. An electric fryer is good to use for temperature control.

For the fritters, break down and roll the leftover pudding into balls approximately ¾ in (2 cm) in diameter. Roll in a little of the flour and pierce with toothpicks.

Mix together the sifted flour with the sugar. Whisk in the cider and the batter is made. Dip the balls into the thick batter and gently lower 6–8 at a time into the oil, allowing the batter to soufflé and float. After they are golden and crisp, the fritters are ready to take out. Drain on paper towels. Three fritters should be ample per serving. Fry more if needed and serve with a scoop of the homemade cranberry ice cream.

Christmas Pudding Scotch Pancakes

This dessert idea is not a classic yet, but I hope it will become one in the future.

The pancakes in the recipe contain many Christmassy flavors, but they have a much lighter finish than a conventional pudding. They can be made a few hours in advance, while the turkey is roasting, and then be re-heated in the oven, or you can microwave them.

The beauty of this dish is that you can have as many or as few pancakes as you like. I suggest four to five per serving. Along with them, I like to serve a vanilla and raisin syrup, a rum-flavored custard, and lots of extra-thick cream.

This recipe will give you 25–30 pancakes.

SERVES 5–6
For the Pancake Batter

3 cups (350 g) self-rising flour
¼ teaspoon ground cloves
½ teaspoon ground ginger
½ teaspoon grated nutmeg
½ teaspoon cinnamon
½ cup (75 g) mixed currants and golden raisins
1½ oz (40 g) glacé cherries, chopped
1 oz (20 g) candied citrus peel, chopped
3 tablespoons (40 g) unsalted butter
1 cup (225 ml) milk
3 eggs
⅔ cup (150 g) sugar
Butter or oil, for frying
Pinch of salt

For the Vanilla and Raisin Syrup

4 oz (100 g) raisins
⅔ cup (150 ml) water
¼ cup (50 g) sugar
Juice of 1 lemon
1 vanilla pod, split

To Decorate

Confectioners' sugar, sifted
Holly leaves

To Serve

Rum custard (see Note)
Heavy cream

Sift the flour, adding the spices, fruit, glacé cherries, and candied peel. Melt the butter and whisk into the milk with the eggs, sugar, and the pinch of salt. Whisk the butter into the flour mixture and the batter is ready.

To cook the pancakes, heat a non-stick frying-pan and brush it with butter or oil. The batter can now be spooned into the pan, allowing 2 tablespoons per pancake. These will take approximately 2–3 minutes before they are ready for turning. To help time the turning, look for small bubbles appearing on the surface. This tells you they are ready to turn. After you've turned them, cook for 2 minutes before removing from the pan. In a large pan, 4–6 pancakes can be cooked at the same time. When all the pancakes are cooked, keep covered with a dish towel to prevent them from becoming dry.

To make the vanilla and raisin syrup, mix all the ingredients together and simmer for 10 minutes. Remove the vanilla bean and purée in a food processor. Push through a sieve. The bean can now be scraped and the seeds added to the syrup. The syrup is now ready.

To serve, warm the pancakes and stack them on each plate, allowing four to six per serving. Spoon the warm rum custard around them, and drizzle the warm raisin syrup over the top. Now, finish the dessert with a spoonful of thick cream. The plate can now be decorated with a dusting of confectioners' sugar (to create the snow effect) and a holly leaf. The Christmas pudding pancakes are now ready to serve.

Note: If you have family or friends who are not fans of dried fruit, then keep some of the batter plain and simply serve Scotch pancakes with rum custard.

The lemon juice in the vanilla and raisin syrup can be replaced with rum or brandy for an even richer Christmas finish.

To make a quick rum custard, use a purchased custard mix and flavor it with rum. Simple, quick, easy, and tasty. To thin it slightly, add a little light or heavy cream.

You can use heavy cream or whipped cream for this recipe.

BELOW
Christmas Pudding Scotch Pancakes

Christmas Cake

Christmas cake is a prime example of a British enriched bread or cake made for celebrations over the centuries. It's packed with dried fruit, nuts, and other flavors, including a number of spices. Christening cakes, wedding cakes, and at one time birthday cakes all used to be made on the same basic principles.

This is a fruit cake that holds such a moist richness that once you have tasted it, you'll find yourself cooking it more than one celebration a year.

MAKES ONE 8 IN (20 CM) CAKE

16 tablespoons (225 g) unsalted butter
1 cup (packed) (225 g) light brown sugar
2¼ cups (250 g) all-purpose flour
Pinch of ground cinnamon
Pinch of ground cloves
Pinch of ground coriander
Pinch of ground ginger
Pinch of grated nutmeg
Pinch of salt
4 large eggs
½ cup (50 g) ground almonds
½ cup (50 g) chopped almonds
Juice and finely grated zest of 1 lemon
Finely grated zest of 1 orange
2 tablespoons marmalade
1 tablespoon molasses
4 tablespoons brandy
1 lb 2 oz (500 g) currants
7 oz (200 g) golden raisins
7 oz (200 g) raisins
3 oz (75 g) glacé cherries
2 oz (50 g) mixed candied peel
Brandy, to finish

For this recipe, you will need a 8 in (20 cm) round or square cake pan. The pan should be lined with two layers of waxed paper; this helps prevent the cake from burning during its cooking time.

Preheat the oven to 275°F/140°C.

Cream together the butter and brown sugar until fluffy. Sift together the flour, spices, and salt. Beat the eggs together and add them a little at a time to the creamed butter and sugar. It's important to mix them in slowly to make sure the eggs are emulsified with the butter and will not curdle. If the mixture does begins to curdle, then sprinkle in some of the flour to stop the mixture from separating completely.

The sifted flour and ground almonds can now be gently worked into the mixture. Add the chopped almonds, zests, marmalade, molasses, lemon juice, and brandy. To finish, fold in the fruit and candied peel.

The Christmas cake mixture can now be spooned into the lined cake pan, spreading evenly. Bake in the preheated oven for approximately 3–3½ hours.

After the first 30 minutes, cover the top of the cake with a double thickness of waxed paper. This will help prevent the top of the cake from becoming too dark. Pierce the paper to release the steam created.

To test that the cake is done, press the center; if it feels slightly springy and does not hold the impression, then your cake is ready. Another way to test is to insert a small knife or skewer. The cake should be moist but with no uncooked mixture showing.

After the cake is done, remove it from the oven and let it stand in the pan for 45 minutes before turning out onto a wire rack and letting it cool.

When it's cool, make small holes in the cake with a skewer or a small knife and sprinkle a spoonful or two of brandy on top. This will be nicely absorbed by the cake, giving a rich and moist finish. Now, wrap the cake in waxed paper and store it in an airtight cake tin or plastic container. The brandy-soaking can be repeated every 4–5 days, giving the cake time to absorb the brandy flavor and to mature, making it increase in richness.

The cake is wonderful as it is, but it can, of course, be finished in the classic way with marzipan and icing.

Homemade Mincemeat and Mince Pies

This is Delia Smith's recipe, so many thanks to her for allowing me to include it. This is the best mincemeat I've ever tasted, and as she says, once you've made it and tried it, you'll never again revert to store-bought.

Mincemeat and the pies made with it are echoes of the savory-sweet pies of medieval times actually made with shredded meat. This continued until quite recently – one of Mrs Beeton's recipes for mincemeat called for 1 lb (450 g) of beef and a pint of brandy. Nowadays, all that we are left with in a savory sense is the beef suet (you can now buy vegetarian suet).

Mince pies have always been a favorite of mine – at least since making them with *this* mincemeat. You can make half the recipe if you prefer.

MAKES APPROX. 6 LB (2.75 KG)

For the Mincemeat

1 lb (450 g) Granny Smith apples, cored and chopped small (no need to peel them)
8 oz (225 g) shredded suet
12 oz (350 g) raisins
28 oz (225 g) golden raisins
8 oz (225 g) currants
8 oz (225 g) whole mixed candied peel, finely chopped
1½ cups (packed) (350 g) soft dark brown sugar
Juice and grated zest of 2 oranges and 2 lemons
½ cup (2 oz) whole almonds, cut into slivers
1 teaspoon nutmeg
½ teaspoon cloves
½ teaspoon ground coriander
¾ teaspoon ground ginger
1 teaspoon ground cinnamon
Nutmeg, grated
6 tablespoons brandy

For the Mince Pies

Sweet Shortcrust Pastry (page 364)
Milk, for brushing
Confectioners' or superfine sugar, to decorate

Combine the above ingredients, except the brandy, in a large mixing bowl, mixing them together thoroughly. Then cover the bowl with a clean cloth and leave the mixture in a cool place overnight for 12 hours so the flavors have a chance to mingle and develop. After that preheat the oven to 225°F/120°C, cover the bowl loosely with foil, and place it in the oven for 3 hours.

Then remove the bowl from the oven and don't worry about the appearance of the mincemeat, which will be positively swimming in fat. This is how it should be. As it cools, stir it from time to time; the fat will coagulate and instead of it being in tiny shreds it will encase all the other ingredients. When the mincemeat is cold, stir in the brandy. Pack in clean, dry jars, cover with waxed paper disks, and seal. It will keep in a cool, dark pantry or cupboard indefinitely, but it is best used within a year of making.

To make mince pies, line small tart pans or Yorkshire pudding molds with thin disks of the sweet shortcrust pastry. Spoon in some mincemeat, a tablespoon or two depending on the size of the pan. Brush the edges of the pastry with milk, then top with pastry lids. Chill them before baking.

Preheat the oven to 400°F/200°C. Brush the tops of the pies with milk, and bake for 25–30 minutes, depending on size. When the pies are crisp and golden, remove and allow them to rest for 5 minutes before placing on a wire rack to cool. The pies can be sprinkled with sugar during their last 5 minutes in the oven, or dusted with confectioners' sugar when they are cooled.

The mincemeat traditionally includes three spices to symbolize the gifts brought to Jesus by the three wise men. The pies were once made in oval shapes to represent the manger. And if you eat twelve pies between Christmas Day and Twelfth Night, you will guarantee twelve whole months of good fortune.

Note: Vegetarians can make this mincemeat happily, using vegetarian suet.

See also

Bread Sauce (page 43)
Buttered Brussels Sprouts (page 106)
Classic Roast Potatoes (page 238)
Creamy Bubble and Squeak Soup with Crisp Bacon (page 29)
Roast Parsnips (page 95)

Cakes, Sweetened Breads, and Baking

Although there are not many famous
breads that originated in Britain, the
number of traditional enriched breads,
cakes, and sweet "biscuits" is immense.
Why this should be so, I'm not sure,
but it could have something to do,
with the peoples' national sweet tooth.
In fact it's said Britons like sweet
things so much that they had to invent
an extra meal at which to enjoy them
– afternoon tea.

Early breads were hard and flat, made from whatever grain was local, then ground, and baked on hot flat stones by the fire. Later, a flat metal griddle or "girdle" was suspended over the fire for "baking" bread. The word "griddle" is thought to come from the name for hot stones in the Celtic language, *greadeal*, and the use of the implement is common to all the Celtic countries, from northern France to Ireland and Scotland. Today, the northern "bannock" or "oatcake" is the closest equivalent to that early bread.

The leavening or rising power of "barm," consisting of fermented liquor containing airborne yeasts, was discovered early on, allowing a lighter bread to be baked, either directly on hot hearthstones or in the trapped hot air under a clay dome set over the stones – the earliest oven. Ovens were not common, however, and for centuries small, plain, yeasted and non-yeasted breads continued to be the most prevalent. The much later sweetened descendants of these are drop scones, pancakes, crumpets, muffins, and Welsh "pikelets."

Breads of this type continued to be made at home. But breads which needed to be baked in an oven were taken to the manorial oven or to a public baker. The rich class would have white breads made from the finest wheat flour. This was the "manchet" for eating, whereas the "trencher" (a slice of bread used as a plate) was a less fine, brown bread. These trenchers were always a few days old, so would have been fairly hard and more able to absorb fats and liquids. By the end of the sixteenth century, wooden and metal plates had been introduced – as well as the fork – so the trencher "plate" was discontinued. Bread was still used, though, as "sops" to soak up the soup left in the bottom of the bowl, or as sippets, little pieces of bread or toast arranged on top of or around a dish. Breadcrumbs were, and still are, mixed into sauces as thickeners, and into sausages, stuffings, drinks, and desserts.

The poor, however, had to make do with the husks of wheat in their inevitably coarser brown bread, or use other local grains such as rye and barley. These two grains contained much less natural gluten than wheat so were dense, dark, and hard, making a less digestible product.

For special occasions from the Middle Ages on, basic doughs were often enriched by honey, spices, and/or dried fruit, and these ingredients mark the beginnings of tea breads, loaves, and buns – as well as of cakes. In later years, eggs and butter were often added to the dough, the beaten eggs allowing enough air to be incorporated without the addition of yeast. When chemical leavening agents were introduced in the nineteenth century, many yeast-risen doughs were abandoned.

The earliest sweet "biscuits" were rusks – pieces of baked bread put back into the oven to dry out. Later, finer mixtures were used and baked or dried in an oven. "Biscuits" like these were cut into animal and human shapes and known as "fairings" since they were sold at local fairs.

The baking tradition in Britain seems to have been at its strongest in the north and west and in Ireland. This may be because these areas were furthest from outside influences, including France and elsewhere, and recipes and traditions were able to be retained. For instance, high tea, a tradition that is quite rare in the south, demands a variety of baked goods. But also, the fuel needed for baking was more plentiful in the north than in the south, and this was another contributing factor. The glory of English cakes, however, is entirely due to the gentry's adoption of the new meal – afternoon tea (see page 366 for how it began and for recipes associated with the occasion). Sticking to this chapter you'll find many flavors and "classic" cakes such as parkin, simnel, lardy, and Twelfth Night, all included alongside many others.

Happy baking!

PAGE 338
Homemade Malt Loaf (page 350)

Lemon and Vanilla Sponge Cake

Sponge cakes were made with vigorously beaten eggs along with sugar and flour. They date from before the nineteenth century, when chemical leavening agents were introduced. The Victorians added butter to a sponge mixture, resulting in the Victoria sponge recipe. This is a combination of many old methods, giving a lighter and softer finish to the cake, a perfect one to offer for afternoon tea. The lemon and vanilla are flavors that are wonderful together, and the rich but light finish is a dream to eat. The sponge mixture can also be made into cup cakes.

The top is glazed with a lemon glaze – simply lemon juice mixed with confectioners' sugar and spooned over the top. Another way to make the taste extra lemony is to split the cake in two and fill with lemon curd. The curd can have its strong flavor softened by folding in a tablespoon of lightly whipped cream.

MAKES ONE 8 IN (20 CM) CAKE OR 18–22 LITTLE CAKES

1 vanilla bean, split lengthwise6 eggs
⅔ cup plus 1 tablespoon (175 g) superfine sugar
    (preferably flavored with vanilla)
1⅓ cups plus 1 tablespoon (175 g) all-purpose flour,
    sifted
4 tablespoons (50 g) butter, melted
Finely grated zest of 2 lemons
Juice of 1 lemon

For the Icing

1 tablespoon lemon juice
6 tablespoons confectioners' sugar

For this recipe, you will need an 8 in (20 cm) diameter, deep, round or square cake pan, lined with buttered waxed paper; or make 18–22 mini-muffin sized cakes in paper cases. Preheat the oven to 400°F/200°C.

Scrape all of the vanilla seeds from the bean. Add them to the eggs with the superfine or vanilla sugar in a bowl over a pan of hot water. Whisk until the mixture has at least doubled in volume, making sure the hot water does not come in contact with the bowl. The yolks and sugar will become thick, light, and creamy. Remove the bowl from the heat and continue to whisk until cold, thick, and forming ribbons.

Lightly fold in the flour, melted butter, lemon zest, and juice. Pour the mixture into the cake pan or mini-muffin pans and bake for 25–35 minutes for the large cake or 12–15 minutes for the small ones. Test with a skewer, which should come out clean if the sponge is ready. Remove from the oven and allow the cake(s) to rest in the pan(s) for 10–15 minutes before turning out upside down onto a wire rack. Let the cake(s) cool.

To make the icing, warm the lemon juice and pour into a bowl. Mix the confectioners' sugar into the juice a tablespoon at a time until the mixture begins to coat the back of a spoon. More confectioners' sugar can be added for a thicker finish. The icing can now be spooned on top of the cake(s).

Note: If filling with lemon curd, it's best to split and fill the cake(s) before icing.

BELOW
Lemon and Vanilla Sponge Cakes

Simnel Cake

Simnel is a traditional British cake made during Lent, and for a while the cake became associated with the fourth Sunday of that period – "Mothering Sunday." Many years ago, young women away from home, probably in service, were allowed home to visit their parents on that day, and they would take this cake with them as a gift. It's basically a rich fruit cake baked with a layer of marzipan running through it and topped with almond paste. Traditionally, it is garnished with eleven small marzipan balls which are lightly toasted to a golden brown and arranged in a circle on top of the cake. These balls represent the eleven faithful disciples.

MAKES AN 8 IN (20 CM) ROUND CAKE

1¾ cups plus 1 tablespoon (225 g) all-purpose flour
¼ teaspoon ground nutmeg
¼ teaspoon ground ginger
Pinch of ground cloves
Pinch of ground coriander
½ teaspoon ground cinnamon
Pinch of salt
12 tablespoons (175 g) butter
1 cup (175 g) light brown sugar
3 eggs, beaten
1 tablespoon golden syrup, warmed
1 cup (175 g) golden raisins
1 cup (175 g) currants

BELOW
Simnel Cake

⅓ cup (50 g) glacé cherries, chopped
¼ cup (50 g) mixed peel, chopped
2–3 tablespoons brandy
Milk, if necessary
1 lb 5 oz (600 g) marzipan
1 tablespoon warmed apricot jam, strained
1 egg, for glazing

Grease and double-line an 8 in (20 cm) diameter, deep, round cake pan with waxed paper. Preheat the oven to 325°F/170°C.

Roll one third (200 g) of the marzipan into an 8 in (20 cm) disk.

Sift the flour with the spices and salt. Cream together the butter and brown sugar until light and fluffy. The eggs can now be beaten one at a time into the butter mixture. Add the golden syrup along with the sifted flour. Add all of the fruit and brandy. The cake mixture should not be too thin. If it seems too thick, thin with a spoonful of milk. Spoon half the cake mixture into the lined pan. Smooth it out evenly, making sure there are no air bubbles. Place the marzipan disk on top. Pour the remaining cake mixture over the marzipan and smooth it out.

Because of the long cooking time it's best to wrap and tie brown paper around the pan. The cake can now be baked in the preheated oven for 1½–2 hours. After 1½ hours, check every 10 minutes by pressing in the center; the cake should feel firm when it's ready. (Do not test the cake with a skewer. The warm marzipan will give the impression the cake is not cooked.) When the cake is done, remove it from the oven and let it rest for 30 minutes. Turn it out onto a wire rack. The cake must be completely cold before topping with more marzipan.

When the cake is cold roll another one third (200 g) of marzipan into an 8 in (20 cm) disk. Brush the top of the cake with the warm, strained apricot jam. Place the marzipan disk on top and trim around it for a neat finish. The top can now be score-marked for a criss-cross pattern or you can leave it plain. Brush with some of the beaten egg and place it under a preheated broiler to toast it to a light golden brown.

The remaining third (200 g) of the marzipan can now be shaped into eleven small balls. Place the balls on a baking sheet, brush with egg, and glaze them also under the broiler. Place the balls on top and the simnel cake is ready. The cake can now be left as it is or finished with a ribbon tied around it with some small marzipan flowers or leaves arranged on top. Happy Easter!

Twelfth Night Cake

Twelfth Night, January 6th, is the last night of the Christmas feast in Britain, and long ago there were always festivities before the work of the New Year began in earnest. This cake – similar to a Christmas cake – was made as part of the celebration. Often a bean was baked into the cake mixture, and whoever was given the slice containing the bean was named "King of the Bean," signifying good luck was theirs for the coming year.

The cake is usually covered with royal icing, but I prefer to keep it plain or to cover it with a fondant icing, the recipe included here. This whole recipe is very quick and easy to make. I've also added chopped dates to give the mixture a fuller fruit flavor, but if you prefer not to use them, simply replace their weight with extra dried fruit.

MAKES AN 8 IN (20 CM) CAKE

12 tablespoons (175 g) butter
⅔ cup plus 1 tablespoon (175 g) superfine sugar
3 eggs, beaten
1⅓ cups plus 1 tablespoon (175 g) all-purpose flour
¼ teaspoon ground cinnamon
¼ teaspoon freshly grated nutmeg
1 cup (175 g) currants
1 cup (175 g) golden raisins
1 cup (175 g) dates, preferably Medjool, chopped
½ cup (50 g) blanched almonds, chopped
4 tablespoons brandy

For the Fondant

¼ cup (50 ml) warm water
3 cups (350 g) confectioners' sugar, sifted

This recipe requires an 8 in (20 cm) round or square cake pan. The pan needs to be greased and double-lined with waxed paper. Preheat the oven to 325°F/170°C.

Cream the butter and sugar together until light and fluffy. Add the eggs one at a time, beating them into the sweet butter mixture.

Stir in the flour and spices, followed by the fruit and the chopped almonds. Mix the ingredients together well, adding the brandy.

Spoon the mixture into the cake pan, smoothing and leveling the top. The cake can now be baked in the preheated oven for 1 hour. Check to see if the cake is ready by inserting a skewer or small sharp knife into it; if the skewer comes out clean, the cake is ready. If not, return it to the oven and cook for another 30 minutes. It's important to keep an eye on the cake while it's cooking. If it's becoming dark, cover with foil to prevent it from burning.

Let the cake cool in the pan for 20–30 minutes before turning out onto a rack.

For the fondant icing, sift the confectioners' sugar into a large bowl. Stir in the warm water a little at a time until the sugar has reached a thick, coating consistency.

Most cakes are decorated on the bottom, turning the cake upside down for that flat finish. This cake is best left sitting on its base, with the fondant poured on top. I like to have the fondant just falling around the sides and not completely covering the cake.

Note: Classically, the top is decorated with glacé cherries and angelica.

Cheddar Apple Cake

Cheddar is one of the most famous British cheeses, and often, especially in the north, it is baked in pies along with apples. This recipe is from the West Country, however, so try to buy a mature English Cheddar from that region. The cake is not thick, it's more the depth of Italian *focaccia*

bread. After the cake is baked, the cheese is sprinkled on top and the cake is either returned to the oven or or placed under the broiler to melt the cheese. Easy to make, the cake is best eaten while still warm with the cheese at its melting best. You can also serve it at teatime or take it to a picnic. The amount of cheese is up to you. The more that is melted on top, the richer the cake.

MAKES AN 7–8 IN (18–20 CM) CAKE

1¾ cups plus 1 tablespoon (225 g) self-rising flour
Pinch of salt
Pinch of freshly grated nutmeg
8 tablespoons (100 g) butter
Approximately 2 medium-size (225 g) apples, preferably Granny Smith, peeled and grated
2 tablespoons (25 g) sugar
1 small egg or ½ large egg, beaten
2–4 oz (50–100 g) Cheddar cheese, grated

This can be baked in an 8 in (20 cm) cake pan or flan ring. Grease the pan and preheat the oven to 350°F/180°C.

Sift the self-rising flour with the salt and nutmeg. Rub the butter into the flour, creating a breadcrumb-like texture. Mix the apples with the sugar and stir into the flour. Add the beaten egg and mix into a dough.

This can be rolled to fit in the pan, or transfer the dough to the pan and press into the edges with your fingers; the mixture should be ¾–1¼ in (2–3 cm) thick. Place in the preheated oven and bake for 40–50 minutes until barely firm.

The grated cheese (the amount that suits your personal taste) can now be sprinkled on top and returned to the oven to melt, or finished under the broiler. Allow to cool slightly, serving barely warm.

Note: Fresh herbs can be added to the cake mixture. Chopped sage or tarragon are two flavors that go well with cheese and apples. Two teaspoons of either will be enough.

OPPOSITE
Chocolate Molasses Cake

Chocolate Molasses Cake

Layer cakes can be the most basic of sponge cakes, held together with jam and whipped cream. Delicious they are, too, but this recipe which is Scottish in origin, is even more delicious. The addition of cooking oil and molasses makes it very moist and rich. (In Ireland, a chocolate layer cake is made with mashed potatoes.)

I fill the cake with a chocolate buttercream. To balance the richness of this cake, I add a layer of lightly whipped fresh cream – extravagant to the point of indulgence.

MAKES AN 8 IN (20 CM) CAKE

For the Sponge Layers

1⅓ cups plus 1 tablespoon (175 g) all-purpose flour
½ cup (50 g) cocoa powder
1 heaping teaspoon baking powder
1 heaping teaspoon baking soda
2 tablespoons molasses
2 eggs
⅓ cup (75 g) superfine sugar
⅔ cup (150 ml) milk
⅔ cup (150 ml) vegetable oil

For the Chocolate Filling

6 oz (175 g) semisweet or milk chocolate, chopped
⅓ cup (80 ml) heavy cream
2 tablespoons (25 g) butter

For the Cream Filling

⅔ cup (150 ml) heavy cream, lightly whipped

For this recipe you will need two 8 in (20 cm) layer cake pans, the bottoms lined with waxed paper and then buttered and floured. Preheat the oven to 325°F/170°C.

Sift together the flour, cocoa powder, baking powder, and baking soda. Add all the other sponge ingredients and whisk to a smooth consistency.

Divide the mixture between the two pans and bake in the preheated oven for 20–25 minutes. After they have just become firm, remove the layers from the oven and let them rest for 10 minutes before turning out and cooling on wire racks.

To make the filling, melt the chopped chocolate with the heavy cream in a bowl over a pan of warm water. After the chocolate has melted, add the butter and remove from the heat.

As this mixture cools it will also thicken. After it is cool, spread it onto the bottom sponge layer, before being topped with the lightly whipped cream and then the remaining sponge layer placed on top. The chocolate molasses cake is ready to serve.

Sally Lunn Cake or Bread

Sally Lunn is a famous teacake that's yeast leavened. The name is said to come from the lady herself, a pastry chef from Bath in the eighteenth century who sold the cakes on the street. Another story says the cake was French in origin and that when its name, "Soleil Lune" ("the sun and moon") was cried in the streets, the people in the West Country heard it as "Sally Lunn." Who knows?

One thing have found about Sally Lunn is that there are many different recipes. I've tried more than I can even remember. In the West Country, one of the

favorite spices is saffron, and this is included in most of the recipes. Florence White's *Good Things in England* (1932) says that the cake should only be made with clotted cream, never butter. That prove here is a West Country recipe. The simplicity of this recipe makes it easy to prepare. After it has cooked, the cake is split into three layers while still warm and finished with clotted cream.

So here is the recipe. It's made either with lemon zest to add another flavor, or with mixed spices. I like to use all. You can use either dried or fresh yeast; the method for using fresh is included after the recipe.

MAKES A 6 IN (15 CM) ROUND CAKE

1 teaspoon sugar
2 tablespoons warm milk (tepid)
1 teaspoon dried yeast
1¾ cups plus 1 tablespoon (225 g) all-purpose flour
1 teaspoon salt
Finely grated zest of 1 small lemon
½ cup (120 ml) heavy cream, at room temperature
2 eggs, beaten

To Glaze

1 tablespoon milk
1 tablespoon sugar

If Filling the Cake

Softened butter and/or clotted cream

All you will need for this recipe is a 6 in (15 cm) round cake pan 2½–3 in (7–8 cm) deep. If you have a non-stick pan, simply grease it. If not, then line it with waxed paper and grease the paper.

Stir the teaspoon of sugar into the warm milk. Sprinkle in the dried yeast. Let it stand for 10–15 minutes until a thick froth (2 cm/¾ in deep) has formed.

Sift together the flour, salt, and spices, if using. Add the grated zest of the lemon. The yeast mixture, heavy cream, and eggs can now all be added. This will have a thick batter consistency, barely firm enough to form a "bun" shape.

After the batter or dough has been shaped into a suitable ball/bun, place in the prepared pan. Cover and let it rise in a warm place until it reaches to the top of the pan. This will take 1–1½ hours. Preheat the oven to 400°F/200°C.

The cake can now be baked in the oven. This should take about 15–20 minutes until it has a rich golden color. Boil the milk and sugar together for the glaze, and while the cake is still in its pan, brush the top. This will leave a rich shine. Let the glaze settle for 5–10 minutes and then remove the cake from the pan. The traditional way to finish the Sally Lunn is to split it into three layers and spread them with clotted cream or butter. Reassemble and serve while still warm.

I prefer to serve it as a baked "bun" to be sliced and accompanied by butter or cream for the guests to help themselves. It tastes best served on the day it is has been baked. After that, the texture becomes very dry and then it needs to be toasted and buttered in order to taste good.

Note: To use fresh yeast, simply crumble ⅓ oz (10 g) of it into the warm milk and sugar. When it reaches a smooth liquid stage it's ready to use.

Lardy Cake

If you happen to be on a diet, lardy cake is not for you, for it's a delicious bread dough flavored with lots of sugar and spices and then rolled around pork fat. It's traditionally made in Wiltshire, probably because it's a pig-raising county where there is always plenty of lard. It was made as a special celebration cake, usually at harvest time. It's very good to offer at

BELOW
Lardy Cake

teatime, and to taste at its best, it must be served, within a day of being made.

The cake is usually made with lard alone, but I like to use half butter. Don't be put off by the thought of eating a pork-fat cake because the butter balances the taste. Lardy cake is certainly something you wouldn't make very often, but when you do, you'll wish you'd made two. Simply double the recipe and freeze one cake, well wrapped in plastic wrap, for up to a month.

Elizabeth David says that lardy cake, like cigarettes, should carry a Government health warning. She's not far wrong, but the warning should be followed by my words of advice: "Please try at least once."

MAKES AN 8 IN (20 CM) CAKE

1 teaspoon dried yeast
½ cup (120 ml) milk, warmed
1 teaspoon sugar
1¾ cups plus 1 tablespoon (225 g) all-purpose flour
¼ teaspoon salt
¼ teaspoon ground cinnamon
¼ teaspoon ground nutmeg
¼ teaspoon ground ginger
Pinch of ground cloves
Pinch of ground coriander
1 egg, beaten
Flour, for dusting
½ cup (100 g) lard, chilled and diced
8 tablespoons (100 g) butter, chilled and diced
½ cup (100 g) sugar
⅓ cup (50 g) currants
⅓ cup (50 g) golden raisins

This recipe requires an 8 in (20 cm), round, deep, greased cake pan.

Stir the yeast and teaspoon of sugar into the warm milk. Let it rest for 10–15 minutes in a warm place until a thick, frothy consistency is achieved.

Sift the flour, salt, and spices together in a bowl. Make a well in the center. Mix in the yeast along with the beaten egg, forming a sticky dough.

Dust a surface with flour and knead the dough for about 10 minutes until you have a smooth,

elastic dough. Return it to the bowl, dust with flour, and let it double in volume. This will take approximately 1 hour in a fairly warm place.

The dough can now be punched down and placed on a fresh floured surface. Now, roll the dough into a rectangle, approximately 10 x 6 in (25 x 15 cm). Mix the lard and butter, ½ cup (100 g) sugar, and the fruit and divide the mixture into three equal batches. Sprinkle one of these across the top two-thirds of the rectangle. Fold over the uncovered third onto the middle piece. Now, fold the remaining third on top. This makes a three-layered square of dough. Now, it's best to press down and seal the exposed edges with a rolling pin. Turn the dough once to the left and re-roll into the rectangular shape, repeating the same sprinkling of fats and fruit and then folding. Turn left once more and repeat for the final time.

The finished layered dough can now be rolled slightly larger to fill the cake pan. Place the dough in the pan, folding the corners under to fit. Cover with a damp dish towel and let the dough rise until doubled in size. This will take 50–60 minutes. Preheat the oven to 400°F/200°C.

The dough can now be scored with a sharp knife, crossing through the middle to create several diamonds. Bake in the preheated oven for 25–30 minutes until golden brown.

After the cake has cooked remove it from the oven and turn out onto a wire rack. Leave it upside-down so the melted fats are distributed through the cake. The lardy cake is now ready to serve.

Note: The maximum cooking time for the cake will be 35 minutes.

When making the layered dough, refrigerate it for 15 minutes before re-rolling if it seems to be too warm and the lard and butter are becoming too soft.

If you want to use fresh yeast, use ⅓ oz (10 g) for the recipe. Simply crumble the yeast and stir it into the warm milk and sugar. After it reaches a liquid stage, it's ready to use.

OPPOSITE
Rich Warm Chocolate Cake

Rich Warm Chocolate Cake

In the late seventeenth century in London, "chocolate houses" were established only for drinking chocolate. It wasn't until much later, in the nineteenth century, that chocolate was formed into bars and used commonly in cooking.

I prefer to serve this chocolate cake as a dessert served warm with extra-thick cream rather than as an afternoon-tea cake, but it can be served either way.

It is best to use a bittersweet chocolate to achieve the maximum taste.

MAKES AN 8 IN (20 CM) CAKE

8 oz (225 g) bittersweet chocolate
8 tablespoons (100 g) unsalted butter
½ cup (100 g) superfine sugar
3 eggs, separated
2 tablespoons (25 g) all-purpose flour, sifted
Pinch of salt

Grease and line an 7–8 in (18–20 cm), springform pan. Preheat the oven to 350°F/180°C.

Chop the bittersweet chocolate and mix with the butter and sugar in a stainless steel bowl. Melt them together over a bowl of barely simmering water. When they are melted, remove from the heat. The chocolate needs to be at a warm room temperature.

The egg yolks can now be whisked together and slowly added to the chocolate and butter mixture. Whisk the egg whites to soft peaks. Fold the sifted flour and salt into the chocolate mixture before whisking in a quarter of the egg white. The remaining egg white can now be gently folded in.

Pour into the lined cake pan, making sure the batter is evenly smoothed. Bake in the oven for 30–35 minutes until firm.

Let the cake stand in the pan for 15–20 minutes before carefully removing. The warm chocolate cake is now ready to serve.

Heavy cream or vanilla ice cream goes well with this cake. For chocolate lovers, *Bittersweet Chocolate Sauce* (page 323) can also be offered.

Homemade Malt Loaf

Slices of malt loaf topped with lots of butter are a great favorite of mine. Malt loaf is one of those Great British traditions that the British seldom make at home, but always buy ready-made from the store to go with a hot drink for afternoon tea.

This recipe calls for a malt extract (see Suppliers, page 400), which gives the loaf a very rich flavor and keeps it moist. You can also use two-thirds extract mixed with one-third molasses.

This is a loaf that needs to mature to reach the moist texture of a traditional malt loaf. When it has cooked and cooled, it should be wrapped in baking parchment and kept for a minimum of 2–3 days in an airtight container. Here's the recipe.

MAKES A 2 LB (900 G) LOAF

8 tablespoons malt extract
⅓ cup (75 ml) hot strong tea
1⅔ cups (175 g) whole wheat flour
1 teaspoon baking powder
½ teaspoon salt
¼ teaspoon ground cinnamon
¼ teaspoon ground nutmeg
¼ teaspoon ground ginger
Pinch of ground cloves
½ cup (75 g) raisins
½ cup (75 g) golden raisins
1 egg

Butter an 8 x 4 x 2½ inch (900 g) loaf pan and line it with waxed paper. Preheat the oven to 275°F/140°C.

Mix the malt extract with the hot tea and let it cool. Place the flour with the spices in a bowl along with the fruit, egg, and malt, and tea. Mix the ingredients well together before spooning into the lined loaf pan.

Bake in the preheated oven for 1¼–1½ hours. Pierce with a skewer, and if it comes out clean, the loaf is ready. Let it stand for 10 minutes in the pan before turning out onto a wire rack. When the loaf is cold, wrap as explained in the recipe introduction.

You must have patience to wait for this loaf, it tastes best in 2 or 3 days, sliced and buttered.

Note: As an optional extra, include the grated zest of ½ orange.

Parkin

This is a type of gingerbread that is made in the north of England and Scotland, and it includes a proportion of oatmeal as well as molasses and golden syrup. There are a number of forms but, generally, in England, it is made into large cakes, and in Scotland, into small cakes and cookies. The history of the name is not known – it may have simply come from someone's family name.

In Yorkshire parkin is served on Bonfire Night, November 5th. Guy Fawkes was a Yorkshireman, and a dialect calendar published 300 years after his execution in 1606 states: "Th' children's all lukkin" forrad to th' plot an' parkin."

MAKES AN 8 IN (20 CM) SQUARE CAKE

¾ cup plus 1 tablespoon (100 g) self-rising flour
½ teaspoon ground cinnamon
½ teaspoon ground ginger
Pinch of ground cloves
¾ cup (75 g) oatmeal
¾ cup (175 g) dark syrup (or ½ cup/100 g golden syrup and ¼ cup/50 g molasses)
8 tablespoons (100 g) butter
½ cup (100 g) light brown sugar
1 egg, beaten
1 tablespoon milk

This parkin mixture will need an 8 in (20 cm) square cake pan. Preheat the oven to 275°F/140°C.

Sift together the self-rising flour, salt, ginger, nutmeg, and spices. Mix in the oatmeal.

The dark syrup (or golden syrup and molasses), butter, and sugar will have to be melted all together in a saucepan. Heat together carefully, barely allowing it to melt but not to simmer or boil.

Stir the syrup mixture into the dry mixture and blend together. Add in the egg and milk to create a soft, almost liquid consistency. Pour the mixture into the greased pan. Bake in the preheated oven for 1¼ hours until firm in the center.

After it has cooked, let it stand in the pan for 30 minutes before turning out. After it has cooled, the parkin can be served immediately. If kept in an airtight pan, however, the cake will mature with age, like a good wine. Leave it for a minimum of 2 weeks, and a whole new texture will be created; for even more flavor, leave it for 3 weeks.

Note: The grated zest of 1 orange can be added to the mixture, giving a slightly tangy finish.

BELOW
Parkin

Lemon Syrup Loaf

This delicious lemony and golden syrupy loaf is a classic example of an enriched bread served as a tea bread. It is very simple to make and wonderful to eat, which is why it very rarely lasts longer than the day on which it has been baked!

MAKES A 900 G (2 LB) LOAF

12 tablespoons (175 g) unsalted butter
¾ cup (175 g) superfine sugar
3 eggs
1¼ cups plus 1 tablespoon (225 g) self-rising flour
Finely grated zest of 1 lemon
2 tablespoons milk
6 tablespoons lemon juice
3 tablespoons golden syrup

For this recipe you need an 8 x 4 x 2½ inch (900 g) loaf pan, buttered and lined with waxed paper. Preheat the oven to 350°F/180°C.

Cream together the butter and sugar until light and fluffy. Lightly beat the eggs and slowly whisk them into the butter mixture.

Sift the flour and fold in along with the lemon zest. Fold in the milk and then half the lemon juice.

Spoon the batter into the lined pan and spread to level it. Bake in the preheated oven for 45–50 minutes until firm to the touch.

Warm together the remaining lemon juice and golden syrup. Remove the cake from the oven and pierce several holes in the top with a skewer. The lemon and golden syrup can now be slowly spooned over the loaf, allowing it to be absorbed by the sponge.

Once all has been added and the sponge has cooled, remove from the pan. The cake is now ready to serve. The loaf can be sprinkled with confectioners' sugar for a sweet dusted topping.

Note: It may seem as though a lot of liquid is being added when pouring over the lemon and syrup; after the loaf is cool, however, the cake will have a moist/sticky finish.

Banana and Golden Syrup Loaf

Bananas were carefully and competitively cultivated in early greenhouses by the gentry in the mid-eighteenth century – along with pineapples, guavas, mangoes, and so on. It was only when steamships could speed the highly perishable fruit to its destination that the general population began to know them. The first shipments of bananas – from the Canaries – docked in England in 1882. One of the banana shipping companies was started by a Mr Fyffe, and the name is familiar in Britain still.

This recipe is very simple, and it's great for using up over-ripe bananas. The golden syrup flavor working with them makes the loaf richer, and it develops a wonderful, soft texture.

MAKES A 900 G (2 LB) LOAF

1¼ cups plus 1 tablespoon (225 g) self-rising flour
8 tablespoons (100 g) butter, softened
4 ripe bananas, mashed
¼ cup (50 g) dark brown sugar
4 tablespoons golden syrup
4 eggs

This recipe will fill a buttered and greased 8 x 4 x 2½ inch (900 g) loaf pan. Preheat the oven to 350°F/180°C. Simply mix all of the ingredients together until well combined.

Spoon into the lined pan and bake in the preheated oven for 50–55 minutes. The loaf can be tested by piercing with a skewer. The loaf is baked when the skewer comes out clean.

Remove the loaf from the oven and let it rest in the pan for 10 minutes before turning out and allowing to cool.

Note: For a nutty finish, ½ cup (50 g) of chopped walnuts, hazelnuts, or pecans can be added to the above recipe.

OPPOSITE
Banana and Golden Syrup Loaf

Hot Cross Buns

The origin of the hot cross bun is unknown, but some say it dates from early, even pagan, times, when the small round shape represented the sun, the cross dividing it into four parts for the seasons. Breads bearing crosses were commonplace, though, right up until the Reformation in the sixteenth century, usually to guard against evil spirits and bad luck. In the Middle Ages the strongest and most effective bread was that made on Good Friday. It was suspended from the ceiling to guard the household until the next Easter. Perhaps it was this Good Friday loaf that began the Easter association of the bun with a cross on it.

Whatever the case, hot cross buns have now become an annual treat. And I'm delighted because I love them straight from the oven, hot and sticky, or toasted and dripping with butter.

A piping bag with a small plain tube (½ in/1 cm diameter) will be needed to pipe the cross.

MAKES APPROX. 12 BUNS

¼ cup (50 g) superfine sugar, plus 1 teaspoon
½ cup (125 ml) water, warmed
½ cup (125 ml) milk, warmed
1 tablespoon dried yeast
3¾ cups (450 g) all-purpose flour
1 teaspoon salt
¼ teaspoon ground cinnamon
¼ teaspoon ground nutmeg
¼ teaspoon ground ginger
Pinch of ground coriander
Pinch of ground cloves
⅓ cup (50 g) currants
⅓ cup (50 g) mixed peel
4 tablespoons (50 g) melted butter
1 egg, beaten

For the Cross

4 tablespoons all-purpose flour
1 tablespoon superfine sugar
3–4 tablespoons water

For the Sticky Glaze

2 tablespoons sugar
2 tablespoons water

Stir the teaspoon of superfine sugar into the warm water and milk. Add the dried yeast, cover the mixture, and leave it in a warm place until a thick frothy surface (about ¾ in/2 cm deep) has appeared. This will take about 15–20 minutes.

Sift the flour, salt, and spices into a warm bowl, adding the ¼ cup (50 g) of sugar, currants, and mixed peel. Make a well in the center and pour in the melted butter, egg, and yeast mixture. Stir the dough to mix and work into a sticky ball.

Now, knead and work the dough on a clean surface until smooth and elastic. This will take 8–10 minutes. Place the dough in a clean bowl, cover with a damp kitchen towel, and let it rise in a warm place for 45–60 minutes until doubled in volume.

Now, punch down the risen dough to its original size. The mixture can now be divided into 12 pieces and shaped into round buns. Place the buns on a greased baking sheet (two sheets may be needed), leaving some space between each for rising. Now, cover again with the dish towel and let rise once more for 35–45 minutes until doubled in volume. Preheat the oven to 425°F/220°C.

While the buns are rising, the piping dough can be made. Mix the flour with the sugar and water to a smooth paste. This can now be placed in the piping bag with the plain tube. Remove the towel from the buns, and with the back of a small knife, indent a cross shape on each bun. The piping dough can now be piped into the indentation in each bun.

Place the buns in the preheated oven and cook for 15–18 minutes until they are golden brown and sound hollow when tapped underneath.

While the buns are cooking melt the sugar for the glaze in the water over a low heat. As soon as the buns are removed from the oven, brush with the glaze. Place on a wire rack to cool.

Note: If you prefer to use fresh yeast, 1 oz (25 g) will be needed. Simply crumble the yeast into a small bowl and cream with the warm milk and water. Continue with the recipe, adding the melted butter.

OPPOSITE
Hot Cross Buns

Tuile Cookies

Even though "tuile" is a French name, cookies such as these did exist in the British tradition. Wafers were small sweet breads made in an iron mold held over the fire on a long handle and were often rolled into a curl after baking. These were the predecessors of the modern British brandy snap, a cookie virtually indistinguishable from the tuile. (Interestingly, wafer irons were taken to America by the first settlers, and the American waffle tradition was born.)

Tuiles are often used as containers for serving ice cream or sorbet, and they are also served as petits-fours. They can be made in almost any shape – a basic curved disk, a leaf, swan, triangle, twist, and many other shapes. (Use a stencil cut from a plastic container lid.) For a large circular tuile you will need a 4–4¾ in (10–12 cm) diameter disk. For petits-fours, a 2½–3 in (6–8 cm) disk will be just right.

To shape a tuile into a cup, place it while warm over the bottom of muffin pan cups. For a curved shape, drape it over a rolling pin.

Tuiles will stay crisp for up to 48 hours if they are kept in an airtight container. Mixture not used immediately will keep, refrigerated, for 7–10 days.

Basic Tuile Cookies

MAKES 15–18 LARGE OR 30–35 SMALL TUILES

2 egg whites
¾ cup (75 g) confectioners' sugar, sifted
⅓ cup plus 1 tablespoon (50 g) all-purpose flour, sifted
4 tablespoons (50 g) unsalted butter, melted

Preheat the oven to 350°F/180°C.

Place the egg whites in a bowl. Add the sifted confectioners' sugar and whisk for 10–15 seconds. Add the flour, gently pour in the melted butter and mix to a smooth paste.

To bake the tuile cookies, spread the mixture, using your shaped stencil if needed (see introduction left), on baking parchment, leaving space between each for them to spread. Bake for 8–10 minutes until golden brown and beginning to bubble on the tray. Remove from the oven and shape the tuiles while they are still warm. When they are cool and crisp, they are ready to eat.

Hazelnut Tuiles

MAKES APPROX. 16 LARGE OR 30 SMALL TUILES

2 egg whites
2 tablespoons (25 g) superfine sugar
1 cup (125 g) all-purpose flour
1 cup (125 g) ground hazelnuts
1½ tablespoons hazelnut oil

Preheat the oven to 350°F/180°C.

Lightly whisk the egg whites and superfine sugar to a froth. Add all of the remaining ingredients and mix to a paste. Spread as described in the basic recipe (left) and bake for 5–8 minutes until lightly golden. Remove from the oven and complete shaping while still warm.

Sesame Seed and Orange Tuiles

MAKES 5–6 LARGE OR 10–12 SMALL TUILES

4 tablespoons orange juice
2 tablespoons (25 g) sesame seeds
2 tablespoons (50 g) superfine sugar
¼ cup (25 g) all-purpose flour
Finely grated zest of 1 orange

Preheat the oven to 350°F/180°C.

Bring the orange juice to a boil and reduce by half. Let it cool.

When the juice has cooled, mix all the ingredients together. Spread and bake as in the basic recipe (see left), shaping while still warm.

Brandy Snaps

9 tablespoons (125 g) unsalted butter
¾ cup (125 g) light soft brown sugar
½ cup (125 g) golden syrup
4 teaspoons lemon juice
1 cup (125 g) all-purpose flour
1 teaspoon ground ginger

Preheat the oven to 375°F/190°C.

Place the butter, sugar, golden syrup, and lemon juice in a saucepan and stir over a moderate heat until the butter melts and the sugar has dissolved. Remove the pan from the heat. Sift the flour and ginger into the pan and mix to a smooth paste. Allow the mixture to cool completely.

Roll into balls the size of a quarter and press them onto a greased baking pan. Keep a space between each one or you will finish up with one vast brandy snap. Bake for 8–10 minutes. Allow the brandy snaps to relax for a few seconds, then mold them to the shape desired (see introduction, page 356). If the snaps cool before you can finish shaping them, place them back into the oven to become warm again.

Ginger Cookies

Ginger was one of the most common spices available in Britain, so it was used a lot in many regional specialities such as *Parkin* (page 350), which is actually a form of gingerbread. Gingerbread was first made as a cookie, baked slowly until crisp, and then cut into various shapes. The cake type of gingerbread developed only in the eighteenth and nineteenth centuries when leavening agents such as soda were introduced.

These cookies taste even more delicious if you add some chopped pecans or dates – or both. If you are using dates or nuts, simply stir them in with the evaporated milk.

1¾ cups plus 1 tablespoon (225 g) all-purpose flour
¼ teaspoon salt
2 teaspoons baking soda
1 heaping teaspoon ground ginger
½ teaspoon ground cinnamon
4 tablespoons (50 g) unsalted butter
⅔ cup (100 g) light brown sugar
½ cup (100 g) golden syrup
1 tablespoon evaporated milk

Sift together the flour, salt, soda, and spices. Heat the butter, sugar, and syrup until dissolved. Let the mixture cool. When it has cooled, mix it into the dry ingredients with the evaporated milk to make a dough. Chill for 30 minutes.

Preheat the oven to 375°F/190°C and grease two baking sheets.

Roll out the cookie dough to about ¼ in (5 mm) thick and cut into strips, circles, or even gingerbread men. Place on the baking sheets, allowing a little space to spread. Bake in the preheated oven for 10–15 minutes. Remove from the oven. Let them cool slightly on the baking sheet before transferring to a wire rack.

Note: An additional teaspoon of ginger can be added for a stronger ginger flavor. Gingerbread men often enjoy being "dressed" with currant eyes and buttons.

Cheddar and Pecan Cheese Crackers

Flavored with grated Cheddar and rolled in chopped pecans, these cheese crackers would be perfect to serve with your cheese course or to enjoy with other accompaniments, such as grapes, apples, celery, and so on. The pecans give the crackers an added crunch.

4 oz (100 g) Cheddar cheese, grated
8 tablespoons (100 g) butter
½ teaspoon cayenne pepper
1 cup plus 2 tablespoons (150 g) all-purpose flour
½ cup (50 g) chopped pecan nuts

Preheat the oven to 350°F/180°C.

Cream together the Cheddar cheese and butter. Add the cayenne pepper and flour, mixing to a firm dough. The mixture can now be rolled into a log, approximately 2 in (5 cm) in diameter and rolled to coat in the chopped pecans. Refrigerate to firm.

The log can now be cut into round or oval slices (⅛ in/3 mm thick).

Place the crackers on a baking sheet lined with parchment or waxed paper. Bake in the preheated oven for 12–15 minutes. Let them cool slightly before transferring to a wire rack.

Stilton and Sesame Seed Crackers

Again, a very British cheese mixed with sesame seeds to make a pungent cheese crackers for a savory snack or to accompany a cheeseboard. Almost any other cheese can be grated and used to flavor the crackers.

MAKES APPROX. 40 CRACKERS

¾ cup plus 1 tablespoon (100 g) all-purpose flour
8 tablespoons (100 g) butter
¼ teaspoon cayenne pepper
4 oz (100 g) Stilton cheese, grated
2–4 tablespoons (25–50 g) sesame seeds

Preheat the oven to 350°F/180°C.

Rub the flour, butter, and cayenne together.

OPPOSITE
Cheddar and Pecan Cheese Crackers and
Stilton and Sesame Seed Crackers

Add the grated Stilton cheese and mix to a firm dough. Roll into a log, approximately 2 in (5 cm) in diameter, and then roll in the sesame seeds. Refrigerate to firm the log.

When the log is chilled and set, cut into disks or oval shapes approximately ⅛ in (3 mm) thick. Place on a baking sheet covered with parchment or waxed paper and bake in the preheated oven for 12–15 minutes.

Let the crackers cool for a few minutes on the pan before transferring to a wire rack. They are now ready to serve.

Shortbread Cookies

Shortbread is a delicious and buttery example of the rich Scottish baking tradition. There are various regional types, the most famous, perhaps, Edinburgh's "petticoat tails," a round cake cut into wedges to resemble the hooped petticoats of long ago. Shortbread is perfect for afternoon tea. It is often featured at Hogmanay or New Year celebrations, along with an oatmeal drink called "Atholl Brose," and a rich dried fruit cake encased in pastry called "black bun" – and, of course, whisky.

MAKES 16–24 COOKIES, DEPENDING ON SIZE

16 tablespoons (225 g) unsalted butter
⅓ cup (75 g) superfine sugar
2¾ cups (350 g) all-purpose flour
2 teaspoons (15 g) cornstarch

Preheat the oven to 350°F/180°C and grease and line a baking sheet.

Cream together the butter and sugar until light and fluffy. Sift the flour and cornstarch together and work into the butter mixture. Roll out the dough to approximately ¼ in (5 mm) thick and, using a pastry cutter, cut into cookies. Alternately, cut the dough into strips. Place them on the baking sheet and bake in the preheated oven for 20–25 minutes until golden brown. Let them cool on a wire rack. The cookies are delicious sprinkled with superfine sugar.

Lightly roll the shortbread mixture into a circle about ½–¾ in (1–2 cm) thick and 8 in (20 cm) in diameter and place it in a flan ring. Mark it into eight pieces and prick all over with a fork before cooking. It will take about 30–35 minutes to bake in the preheated oven.

Fig Rolls

Dried figs were introduced to Britain many centuries ago, and they were used in many medieval pottages and in sweet and savory pies. Fig rolls are a more recent combination of dried fig purée and pastry, wonderful with a mug of tea to accompany a dessert.

This is not quite the classic cookie, however. Here the fig purée still runs through the center but there are two different pastries to wrap it in. One is flavored with ground almonds while the other contains light brown sugar, providing two different textures, both complementing the rich fig filling.

MAKES APPROX. 15 ROLLS

For the Filling

1 cup (200 g) ready-to-eat dried figs
⅔ cup (150 ml) water
⅓ cup (50 g) dark brown sugar
2 oz (50 g) ladyfingers, crumbled

For the Brown-sugar Dough

2 cups (250 g) all-purpose flour
¾ teaspoon baking powder
½ cup plus 1 tablespoon (90 g) light brown sugar
9 tablespoons (125 g) butter
1 egg
1 tablespoon milk (optional), to finish
3 teaspoons superfine sugar (optional), to finish

For the Almond Dough

3 cups (375 g) ground almonds
¾ cup plus 1 tablespoon (185 g) superfine sugar
1¼ cups (185 g) confectioners' sugar
2 eggs
2 teaspoons lemon juice

For the filling, place the figs and water into a saucepan, bring to a simmer, and cook it 10 minutes. Add the sugar and continue to cook until the liquid has almost evaporated. Purée the mixture and allow it to cool. Then stir in the ladyfinger crumbs. Roll the mixture into a log 12 in (30 cm) long. To make handling easier, cut into two 6 in (15 cm) pieces.

Next, make the brown sugar dough (this is the outside dough). Rub together the flour, baking powder, sugar, and butter to a crumbly texture. Add the egg and mix to form a dough. Wrap it in plastic wrap and chill for 30 minutes.

Now, make the almond dough. Mix together the ground almonds and the sugars. Beat an egg, add it with the lemon juice to the almond mixture, and work to a firm paste. Dust the work surface with confectioners' sugar and roll the almond dough 12 in (30 cm) long and wide enough to roll around the fig log. Beat the remaining egg and brush the paste. Cut into two 6 in (15 cm) pieces. Place a fig log on top of each and roll. Chill.

Lightly flour the work surface and roll the brown sugar dough to 12 in (30 cm) long and wide enough to cover the first dough. Again, cut it into two 6 in (15 cm) pieces. Brush each piece with the remaining egg and place a wrapped fig roll on top. Cover the roll with the dough. Press the rolls slightly to take on the classic shape, then cut, making seven or eight rolled cookies from each. Press a fork on top of each and draw it across to create a channel effect. Refrigerate for 15–20 minutes. Preheat the oven to 350°F/180°C.

Keep the cookies plain or brush them with milk and sprinkle with superfine sugar. Bake for 20–25 minutes. Remove from the oven; cool on wire racks.

Golden Oatcakes

Oatcakes – also known as "bannocks" – are a typical example of the earliest types of bread cooked in Britain – flat and hard, shaped and cooked on the hearthstone or on a flat griddle. They were once made with oats and water alone. I've added some golden syrup, giving the cakes a golden edge and a delicious toffee flavor.

The oats used here are rolled oats, which have been steamed and then flattened, making them quicker to cook. (Cooked cereal made with rolled oats will only take 10–12 minutes to make, for instance.) Rolled oats are very good for oatcakes, hence their use here. If you can find a source for jumbo oats use them for a nuttier finish.

MAKES 10–14 OATCAKES

8 tablespoons (100 g) butter
2 tablespoons or ¼ cup (50 g) golden syrup
¼ cup (50 g) light brown sugar
½ teaspoon baking soda
⅓ cup plus 1 tablespoon (50 g) self-rising flour
2 cups (225 g) rolled oats

OPPOSITE
Fig Rolls

Preheat the oven to 350°F/180°C.

Melt the butter, golden syrup, sugar, and baking soda in a saucepan over a gentle heat. It's important this is not allowed to get too hot, just barely melting.

Sift the self-rising flour into a bowl and mix with the rolled oats. Pour the syrupy butter into the bowl and mix well.

The oatcake mixture can now be shaped and rolled into 10–14 balls. Place on a greased baking pan and flatten with your hand; then cook in the preheated oven for 12–15 minutes. When they are golden brown and firm, remove from the oven and transfer to a wire rack. Let them cool before storing in an air-tight container.

Note: These oatcakes are delicious to offer at teatime, coffee-time – any time. They are delicious with ice cream.

Homemade Crumpets

Crumpets, which appeared in the later seventeenth century, fit into the category of tea cakes. The name is thought to come from the Middle English *crompid*, meaning to bend or curl into a curve, which is what homemade crumpets tend to do. They are very closely related to the Welsh "pikelet," which is still found in the Midlands, the west of England, and Wales. Muffins are also related, but few exist now in the British tradition – although they are very popular in America (where the British took them). And crumpets are not too different from drop or girdle/griddle scones.

Toasted crumpets are a favorite with my sons, Samuel and George, butnot at teatime, although that's when I remember having them. My sons want crumpets at breakfast – and it's always toasted with butter and huge scoops of jam, washed down with a big mug of tea.

Watching the "bubbled" look develop in the pan is quite amazing. And to eat them straight from the pan with lots of butter is a very delicious experience. Whether having them at breakfast or afternoon tea, here's the recipe.

MAKES APPROX. 20 CRUMPETS

3¾ cups (450 g) all-purpose flour
1 teaspoon (15 g) salt
1 teaspoon (15 g) fresh yeast
2½ cups (600 ml) warm water

Sift together the flour and the salt. Mix the yeast with a few tablespoons of the warm water. Whisk three-fourths of the remaining warm water into the flour and then add the yeasty liquid. Cover and let it rest in a warm place. When the mixture has risen, check the consistency. If the batter is very thick, thin with the remaining water. The batter should now be left to stand for 8–10 minutes.

Warm a non-stick frying-pan over a low heat. Grease some crumpet rings or small tartlet rings and rub the pan with butter.

Place the rings in the frying-pan and pour in some of the batter until half-full (¼–½ in/5 mm–1 cm deep). Cook over a low heat until small holes appear and the top has started to dry. The bottom of the crumpet will now be golden and it can be turned over and cooked for another minute. The crumpets can now be buttered and served.

Note: The crumpets can be cooked without turning: simply cook until the tops are completely dry.

The finely grated zest of 1 lemon can also be added to the batter to give a lemony bite.

If fresh yeast isn't available, use 2 teaspoons dried yeast. Mix with the flour and the salt, add the water, and let the mixture rise as above.

Griddle Scones

These scones are great to serve at Sunday teatime with butter, jam, and cream. The ingredients are usually already in the cupboard, and they take no time to make and cook. This recipe will give you about 20 scones; you can halve the recipe, but I'm sure you'll eat 20. You can make a great variety of scones by adding other flavors. I like to make them with the finely grated zest of lemon, but orange or lime can also be used. Chopped apple can be added with a pinch of ground cinnamon, or you can even

ABOVE
Homemade Crumpets

make them Christmassy with the addition of glacé fruit. They can also be served as a dessert with fresh fruit and creamy sabayon – or in the Afternoon Tea Pudding on page 320. And one last suggestion – serve them as soon as possible after they are cooked.

MAKES APPROX. 20 SCONES

3¾ cups (450 g) self-rising flour, plus extra for
 dusting
Pinch of salt
4 tablespoons (50 g) unsalted butter, plus extra for
 frying
4 tablespoons (50 g) lard
1 cup (175 g) currants or golden raisins
Grated zest of 1 lemon
1 cup (100 g) superfine sugar
2 eggs
2–4 tablespoons milk

Sift and mix the flour with the salt, then rub in the butter and the lard. Fold in the currants or golden raisins, lemon zest, and sugar. Make a well in the center and add the eggs and milk, mixing in the flour to form a soft dough. The dough can now be rolled out to ½ in (1 cm) thick and cut into 2½ in (6 cm) rounds, or molded by hand into ½ in (1 cm) thick individual scones.

Heat a frying-pan or griddle and cook over a medium heat in a little butter for 5 minutes on each side until golden brown. The scones are now ready to serve.

Variation

The scones go very well with griddle strawberries. These are simply strawberries cooked on a hot stove-top griddle, giving a slightly bitter tinge that is then balanced with a dusting of confectioners' sugar. I like to serve these with crème fraîche to finish the dish.

For a richer scone, use 8 tablespoons (100 g) unsalted butter for the 4 tablespoons (50 g) lard.

Shortcrust Pastry and Sweet Shortcrust Pastry

The first pastries in England were probably hot-water crusts, but a variety of them have been used over the years. Both of the pastries here share a basic method: the difference is the sugar. Obviously, use the unsweetened for savory tarts and flans and the sweetened in open fruit tarts and other sweet pastries. The latter pastry contains sugar, but it also differs in that I've added an extra egg yolk for a richer finish. You could use water instead, but this recipe has the maximum flavor. Either superfine or confectioners' sugar can be used, but I have found that confectioners' sugar gives a richer, smoother consistency. The choice is yours.

FOR SHORTCRUST PASTRY (MAKES 14 OZ/400 G)

1¼ cups plus 1 tablespoon (225 g) all-purpose flour
Pinch of salt
10 tablespoons (150 g) cold butter, chopped
1 whole egg
2 tablespoons (25 ml) water

FOR SWEET SHORTCRUST PASTRY (MAKES 450 G/1 LB)

1¼ cups plus 1 tablespoon (225 g) all-purpose flour
Pinch of salt
10 tablespoons (150 g) cold butter, chopped
⅓ cup plus 1 tablespoon (75 g) superfine sugar
1 egg yolk
1 whole egg

For the basic shortcrust pastry, sift the flour with the salt. Rub the flour and butter together to a crumbly texture. Add the egg and water together and mix briefly to a smooth dough. Wrap in plastic wrap and refrigerate for 30–60 minutes before rolling and using.

To make the sweet pastry, sift the flour with the salt. In a bowl or cold work surface quickly rub in the butter until the mixture resembles crumbs. Stir the sugar into the flour mixture, then add the egg yolk and egg. Work everything together and refrigerate for 30–60 minutes before using.

Note: When blind-baking a pastry-lined flan case or ring, line with waxed paper and fill with pie weights or dried beans. This applies to all the pastry recipes.

For a different flavor, add the finely grated zest of 1 lemon or the seeds from a vanilla bean to the flour mixture.

Quick Puff or Flaky Pastry

We usually think of puff pastry as a French invention, but in the sixteenth century, the British were making rich butter pastes – flour mixed with butter, sugar, rose-water, and spices which were interleaved with more butter. It was given the name "puff pastry" in 1605, and used mainly for making sweet tarts and the precursors of vol-au-vents.

Making puff pastry in the traditional way cannot really be beaten. This recipe, however, is a lot quicker and does bring you very close to it. The resultant pastry can be used in any recipe needing puff pastry. Any not used will freeze very well.

MAKES 750 G (1¾ LB)

20 tablespoons (300 g) butter, chilled
3¾ cups (450 g) all-purpose flour
1 teaspoon salt
About 1 cup (200–250 ml) cold water

Cut the chilled butter into small cubes. Sift the flour with the salt. Add the butter, gently working it into the flour but not totally it breaking down. Add the water, mixing to a pliable dough, still with pieces of butter showing.

Turn onto a floured surface and roll as for classic puff pastry, into a rectangle (approximately 18 X 6 in/45 X 15 cm). Fold in the right-hand one-third and then fold in the left-hand side on top. Let the dough rest for 20 minutes. The pastry now needs to be rolled three times in the same fashion, resting it for 20 minutes between each turn.

The quick puff/flaky pastry is now ready to use.

Note: A richer version of this pastry can be made with a higher butter content and with the addition of the juice from 1 lemon. Simply follow the above recipe, only adding ¾ cup (175–225 ml) of water with the juice.

Puff pastry can also be bought ready-made.

See also

Christmas Cake (page 336)
Homemade Mincemeat and Mince Pies (page 336)
Homemade Pork Pie (page 280)
Saffron Bread (page 397)
Sausage Rolls (page 277)
Vegetarian Cheese and Onion "Sausage" Rolls (page 278)

Afternoon and High Teas

The tradition of "afternoon tea" is the epitome of what is "British," a way of eating that is completely unique to Britain. The custom features a wonderful selection of light and delicious food, with warm scones, homemade jams, and clotted cream dominating the spread. A number of reasons are responsible for its development.

The first is the introduction to Britain in the late sixteenth century of what was then a new drink – tea. Catherine of Braganza, the wife of King Charles II, is said to have been very enthusiastic about tea-drinking. It was then mostly green tea from China, and during the next 200 years or so, the drink was to take over in popularity from home-brewed ale and the other imported drinks, coffee and chocolate. At first, tea was a drink for the rich, since the leaves were not cheap (one reason for all the rather expensive tea accessories – silver teapots, caddy spoons, sugar tongs, and so on). Served at breakfast and after dinner, it later became the drink of choice at the new pleasure- or tea-gardens which opened in and around London (most famously at Vauxhall, Ranelagh, and Marylebone) in the late eighteenth century. In the mid-nineteenth century, when tea was planted in India and later Ceylon (Sri Lanka), tea, by now usually black, became cheaper and more available to everyone. Some people considered tea a harmful drug and were horrified by the amount drunk by all classes of people. A commentator in the late 1750s wrote: "When will this evil stop? . . . Your very *Chambermaids* have lost their bloom, I suppose by *sipping tea*." It is actually thought that milk began to be put in tea in order to dilute the effects of tannin. Tea-drinking had become the British national habit by then, however, as it is to this day.

Another reason the tradition of "tea" developed relates to the changing pattern of mealtimes. Before the seventeenth century, peoples' lives, including their mealtimes, were dominated by the sun. They rose and breakfasted at sunrise, ate a dinner – the main meal of the day – some hours later, and then ate lightly before going to bed not long after the sun set. Following the introduction of oil lamps, wealthier people could extend their days, getting out of bed later, and staying up longer at night. Breakfast was taken later in the morning, and the dinner hour began to slide from about midday toward evening, the distance between them became longer and longer.

Lunch did not exist as a separate meal, so there was a need for the occasional snack. Hunger, apparently, was what drove Anna, the seventh Duchess of Bedford, to order some mid-afternoon slices of bread and butter as well as some macaroons and other small cakes and cookies. Her friends learned of her new habit and approved of it, and by the mid-nineteenth century, afternoon tea had become a fashionable and popular way of eating and entertaining. The choice of foods became broader, with sandwiches enclosing thin slices of cucumber, potted meats, or fish (or Gentleman's Relish, for the men), and tiny sausage rolls, muffins, rich fruit or seed cakes, and cookies were added.

The working population, however, still had their dinner around midday, and the meal they ate when work was finished, from five to seven o'clock, became known as "high tea." It was followed, at around ten in the evening, by "supper." High tea was fairly substantial, consisting of dishes that could be cooked slowly all day while the members of the household were at work, and also of foods that could be cooked quickly upon returning from work. Irish stew and Lancashire hotpot are examples of long-cooked dishes. Quicker dishes might include chops, bacon, sausages, "Toad in the Hole," preserved fish, salads, pies, and cold or potted meats with pickles. These would be followed by bread, butter, and a variety of sweet cakes, all washed down with plenty of tea. Supper would consist of tea, bread, and butter, perhaps some cheese, and a few small cakes. Because high tea and supper both survive mostly in the north of England and Scotland, it is said that many specialties of regional baking have been preserved there rather than lost.

Afternoon tea was a meal to be enjoyed at home, and it was a leisurely affair. High tea was more a meal of necessity, but it, too, was home-based. "At homes" started off as tea parties, and various other "meals" based on tea came into being, such as family tea, nursery tea, then church teas, and sporting teas. The strawberries and cream associated today with teatime at Wimbledon and other sporting events have their origin in the "subtleties" served at the tea-gardens in the Georgian era. And the height of the tea craze must surely have been the *thé dansants* – "dancing teas" – enjoyed in many hotels in Edwardian times, now being reintroduced. In the late nineteenth century, the first public snack and sandwich bar and the first tea-rooms opened, both in Glasgow. Thackeray described these new phenomena as "... fifty separate ways of spoiling one's dinner."

This chapter might not give you fifty ways but it does give lots of nice ways of spoiling your dinner. These recipes all suit the time of taking tea and would be good at many other times, too, whether you are looking for a substantial high tea or a lighter afternoon tea. They range from some hearty, hot, and savory dishes that are very much in the "high tea" tradition, such as the *Cumberland Sausages* (page 368) and *Toad in the Hole* (page 370), to more delicate and "ladylike" morsels such as *Cucumber Sandwiches* (page 373), among others. When trying these recipes, I hope you'll find all the reasons how and why this occasion has stayed with the British for so long and enjoy the tradition of teatime.

Pork Sausages

The word "sausage" actually comes from the Latin, *salsicius*, prepared by salting, which in turn comes from *salsus*, meaning "salted." Sausages have been eaten in Britain since Roman times. The Anglo-Saxons developed their own varieties, and the Normans introduced French creations, among them the pure pork sausage, the black pudding made with blood, and the *andouille* which is an entrail sausage known in England as "chitterlings."

More or less every country in the world has a variety of sausages to offer, both fresh and dried or smoked, but what about the Great British sausage? There are a number of choices – the Yorkshire, Oxford, Cumberland, Cambridge, and country pork sausage – and they are served for breakfast, lunch, high tea, and dinner. At first the sausages would have been dried, and then possibly smoked, but now they are cooked them from fresh meat.

This is my recipe for pork sausages. I use the classic cut associated with sausages – the shoulder – but also add pork cheek which has a wonderfully lean texture and a rich pork taste. Since I first put this recipe together, I've tried replacing the meat and pork fat with a piece of pork belly. This works well because pork belly has a good but not excessive fat content. If

you use 2¼ lb (1 kg) of pork belly and mix it with 5–7 oz (150–200 g) pork fat, you will have a perfect balance of fat for a good pork sausage.

The sausage skins should be readily available from your butcher shop. The skins will have been salted to preserve them and keep them fresh. Before using the skin, soak them in cold water running water. To be completely sure of cleaning them well and taking out all the salt, run the water through the actual skin. Now, dry them before using.

I always cut 10 inches (25 cm) lengths of skin, tying a knot in one end before filling. This then leaves you with 2–3 inches (5–8 cm) to spare. During cooking, this will shrink around the filling, but the sausage will not burst because of the extra space you have.

MAKES APPROX. 16 SAUSAGES

2 lb (900 g) boned shoulder of pork
4 pigs' cheeks, trimmed (optional)
8 oz (225 g) pork back fat, trimmed of rind
1 onion, very finely chopped
2 tablespoons (25 g) unsalted butter
¼ teaspoon chopped fresh thyme
¼ teaspoon chopped fresh sage
1 garlic clove, crushed (optional)
Pinch of ground mace
2 slices of white bread, crusts removed
    and crumbled
1 egg, beaten
Worcestershire sauce
Salt and pepper
About 4½ yards (4 meters) sausage skins, well
    washed
2–4 tablespoons (25–50 g) lard, for frying

To make grinding easier, always cut up the meats and fat finely before grinding. Also, make sure they are well chilled so they can then be ground very easily. Grind the pork shoulder, cheeks, and back fat (or belly and fat) through the medium blade of a meat grinder; this will give you a medium-coarse finish. If you prefer a finer sausage and smoother texture, then pass through the grinder once or twice more.

Sweat the chopped onion in the butter with the herbs and garlic (if using) for 2–3 minutes until soft. Let the onions cool. Then mix the onion with the ground pork. Season with salt, pepper, and the ground mace. Add the breadcrumbs and the egg. A few drops of Worcestershire sauce can now be added to finish the sausage mixture, being careful not to overdo it so the Worcestershire sauce doesn't dominate flavor.

I always make a small sausage patty and pan-fry it at this stage. Taste it to see if you have the right flavor, in particular for mace and the seasonings.

Now, fill the sausage skins while the sausage mixture is at this temperature and workable. Here's a tip for filling. Use a ½ in (1 cm) piping bag with a plain nozzle. Only half-fill the bag. This gives you more control. If it's overfilled, you can almost break your hand trying to squeeze the meat out of it.

Take the skin and pull it back to the knot; place the skin over the end of the piping tube and squeeze. After the skin has been filled to the size of a standard sausage, remove the bag, and make sure to push the sausage meat further in to give a firm, plump shape. Push out any air left in the remaining skin and then tie at the end. Repeat the process with the remaining sausages. Place the sausages in the refrigerator for at least 30 minutes before cooking.

The sausages can be broiled or pan-fried. I prefer to pan-fry. With this cooking method you have total control of the heat. Melt the lard in a warm frying-pan, place the sausages in the pan, and fry gently, letting them take on a golden color. The excess skin will quickly shrink around the sausage. Extreme heat will burst the sausage. I never prick the sausage skin – I really can't see any point in it. The casing is there to hold all of those flavors and juices in. If released, the meat will be left very dry.

Beautifully and slowly cooked sausages will take 15–20 minutes – well worth waiting every second.

These sausages taste delicious for breakfast, lunch, or dinner. I can't resist eating homemade sausages (or any sausages for that matter) with *Mashed Potatoes* (page 124) and *Onion Gravy* (page 50). Another great accompaniment is *Braised Split Peas* (page 117).

Note: The shoulder and cheeks can be replaced with 2 lb 6 oz (1.1 kg) of pork belly, reducing the pork fat amount to be added to 5–7 oz (150–200 g).

Cumberland Sausage

This is probably one of the most famous British sausages, thought to be the meatiest of them all. Some butchers in Cumberland actually claim they are made with 98 percent pork. But there are a number of people who feel that the real Cumberland has long disappeared. The sausages were once made from a special breed of pig that is said to have died out in 1960.

The most recognizable feature of Cumberland sausage is that it is not twisted into individual sausages, but made into long lengths, sometimes of several feet, and then, traditionally, rolled like a Catherine wheel. You buy it by the length rather than by weight, and it is twisted and cut off for you. Another speciality of the sausage is its seasoning, which is made up of several spices: 1 percent ground cayenne pepper, 1 percent ground nutmeg, 24 percent ground white pepper, and 74 percent fine salt, to be precise. For every 1 lb (450 g) of meat, you will need ½ oz (15 g) of this seasoning.

If you are going to try making these, it's probably best just to pipe two or three long sausage links and roll them into Cumberlands. These can then be pan-fried, broiled, or baked.

MAKES 2–3 GOOD-SIZED CUMBERLANDS

1 lb (450 g) lean shoulder pork, cut into rough dice
9 oz (250 g) pork belly, rind removed, cut into rough dice
4½ oz (125 g) rindless pork back fat, cut into rough dice
2 cups (100 g) white breadcrumbs
1 teaspoon chopped fresh thyme
1 teaspoon chopped fresh sage
1 teaspoon chopped fresh rosemary
2–3 yards (2–3 meters) sausage skins, soaked and washed in water
Butter, lard, or cooking oil, for frying

OPPOSITE
Cumberland Sausage

For the Cumberland Sausage Seasoning

2 teaspoons salt
1 teaspoon ground white pepper
Pinch of freshly grated nutmeg
Pinch of cayenne pepper

The meat can be ground to your choice, since the Cumberland sausage has always come in different textures, depending on where it has been made.

For a medium texture, grind once through a coarse disk and then through a medium disk. This breaks the texture a little more, giving it a finer consistency. Mix in the breadcrumbs, seasonings, and herbs.

The skins are ready to be filled. The easiest way is to follow the method used for *Pork Sausages* (page 367), using a piping bag and tube. After they've been made, refrigerate the sausages for at least 30 minutes before cooking.

To bake, preheat the oven to 350°F/180°C. Brush the sausages with butter and place in a roasting pan. The sausages can now be baked for 25–35 minutes, basting with the butter. After they are ready, cut them into separate servings.

To pan-fry, heat a frying-pan with a teaspoon of lard or of cooking oil. Place the sausages in the warm pan. Fry them gently until golden (this will take 12–15 minutes). Turn the Cumberlands over and cook for another 8–10 minutes.

To broil, brush with butter and place under a medium-hot broiler. Cook for 8–10 minutes on each side and then serve.

A bowl of *Mashed Potatoes* (page 124) and classic *Applesauce* (page 44) will go very well with this dish. Or there's also a recipe for *Cumberland Applesauce* (page 47), that has an extra spicy touch, perfect for this recipe.

Note: Individual, smaller-sized sausages can also be made.

Toad in the Hole

It's not known when batter puddings – Yorkshire pudding being the most famous – developed, but it must have been inspired by economy. During spit-roasting, a pan was put below the meat to catch the juices and fats, and these were used to baste whatever was roasting. Sometimes these fats were used to cook smaller food items, and it must only have been a matter of time before a batter was poured in to make a crisp wrapping for the meat and also to make the meat go further. The recipe for Yorkshire pudding was first written down in a cookbook in 1737 (see page 237 for my recipe), although it had probably long existed, and "Toad in the Hole" must have developed afterwards.

The original "toad" in the hole wasn't made with sausages but strips of fresh or leftover meat. Sausages were substituted at some point, and they have become the classic of today. The "toad" can be baked in a roasting pan, baking dish, or individual pans of about 4 in (10 cm). If making individual "toads", there may be some batter left over, so just bake it in separate pans for extra "Yorkies."

You can use any sausages you like. The homemade *Pork Sausages* on page 367 are excellent, or choose good-quality bought pork, lamb, or beef sausages.

SERVES 4

8 sausages
4 tablespoons cooking oil or lard/drippings

For the Batter

1¼ cups (175 g) all-purpose flour
Pinch of salt
1 egg
1 egg white
1-1¼ cups (250–300 ml) milk

For making four individual "toads" – use 4 in (10 cm) pans ¾ in (2 cm) deep – or make one "toad" in a small roasting pan or ovenproof dish. Preheat the oven to 425°F/220°C.

The batter can be made as far in advance as 24 hours. This gives it time to relax totally and changes the consistency; just before using, quickly re-whisk it. This is not essential, however; the timing is up to you – in fact, the batter can be made and used immediately, but I do suggest a minimum rest of 30 minutes. Sift the flour with the salt. Add the egg and the egg

OPPOSITE
Toad in the Hole

white. The egg white will give extra height to the batter. Whisk in 1 cup (250 ml) of the milk; this will give you a very thick batter. To check the correct consistency, simply lift a spoon in and out: the batter should hold and coat the back of the spoon. If it seems to have thickened too much, add the remaining milk. The batter can now be used or allowed to rest. If resting it, check the consistency again before use, adding a little extra milk if required.

If using individual pans, put a little of the cooking oil/fat into a frying-pan and divide the rest of it among the small pans. Heat these in the oven. The sausages can now be quickly fried for a minute or two to seal in the flavor and to begin browning. Then transfer them to the individual pans, ready for the batter.

If using a roasting pan or ovenproof dish, simply heat half of the oil/fat and brown the sausages on top of the stove, adding the remaining oil/fat.

To cook the "Toad in the Hole," the fat and sausages should be very hot and almost at a smoking stage. Pour in the batter mixture to come three-fourths of the way up the sausages. Place in the preheated oven and bake individual "toads" for 20–25 minutes until well risen and rich in color. Large "toads" in a roasting pan or ovenproof dish should be cooked for 35–45 minutes.

The "toads" are now ready to serve. For me, the best accompaniment is *Onion Gravy* (page 50). I like to spoon some gravy into the cooked individual "toads" or ladle it over servings of the large "toad" on the plates.

Instead of gravy, fried onions can be served. Simply take a large sliced onion and pan-fry in a trickle of oil for 8–10 minutes until well browned. Add a heaping teaspoon of butter and a pinch of light brown sugar. Cook for another minute or two before seasoning with salt and pepper.

The onions are now ready to serve. And as accompaniment to "Toad in the Hole" serve cooked and buttered garden peas.

Mini Toad in the Holes

Here's an alternate "Toad in the Hole" dish. These are simple to make and great to serve as canapés at a party.

1 • recipe batter (page 370)
Butter
3 onions, finely chopped
1 tablespoon light brown sugar
½ cup red wine
1 lb (450 g) pork sausages
Salt and pepper

You will need 3 non-stick mini-muffin pans with 12 holes each.

Follow the recipe on page 370, using the same cooking method and amount of batter. When the puddings are cooked, remove them from the oven and keep warm. Heat a frying-pan or wok. Add a heaping teaspoon of butter and when it bubbles, add the chopped onions. Shallow-fry until deep brown in color. Add the sugar and red wine, bring to a boil, and reduce the mixture until almost dry. Season with salt and pepper.

Remove the skin from the sausages and roll it into small balls, ¼–¾ in (1–2 cm) in diameter. Now, shallow-fry the balls of sausage for a few minutes until they are completely golden brown.

Make a hole in the Yorkshire puddings and spoon a little onion into each. Place a hot sausage ball on top of each, leaving a domed finish. The canapés are ready.

Note: To make 36–40 mini "toads," follow the *Yorkshire Pudding* recipe (page 237) for the increased batter quantity.

Egg Sandwiches Ⓥ

Sandwiches are said to have been invented when the eighteenth-century Earl of Sandwich could not bear to leave the gaming tables to eat, and ordered his dinner to be brought to him. He was given meat slices between two slices of bread and a new form of British eating was born. Sandwiches are actually a very British idea, and they have become universally popular eating for packed lunches, picnics, and afternoon tea.

Egg (or "egg salad") sandwiches are, without question, one of the most popular features of afternoon tea. I'm not quite sure why; maybe because it's one of those fillings we rarely make at home. They are best made with thinly sliced white or brown bread – a thicker slice of bread is likely to allow the bread flavor to dominate that of the egg. Hard-boiled eggs are bound with mayonnaise, which moistens the texture. If the eggs have been soft-boiled (see below), the creamy yolk will be enough.

For a very soft egg yolk, place eggs in cold water and then boil for 3½–4½ minutes. Run under cold water for 3–4 minutes and then peel and mash with a fork to a spreadable and creamy consistency.

MAKES 4 SANDWICH ROUNDS

4 hard-boiled eggs (page 81)
Salt and pepper
1–2 tablespoons *Mayonnaise* (page 49, or store-bought)
8 thin slices of white or brown bread

There's no butter listed in the ingredients. If you'd rather use butter instead of mayonnaise, however, using softened butter spread thinly will give a creamy finish.

Lightly mash the eggs with a fork to break down the whites and to mix them with the yolks. Don't over mash so the eggs won't lose texture and balance with the mayonnaise. When the eggs are broken down, season with salt and pepper. Add the mayonnaise and spread onto four slices of the bread, but not right up to the edges since these will be cut away with the crusts. Top with the remaining bread slices.

Trim off the crusts and cut the sandwiches from corner to corner into four small triangles. Or you could cut the sandwiches into three or four strips.

Other classic egg-sandwich ingredients are mustard and watercress. These can be added to the sandwich, giving a warm spicy bite to the total flavor. Use watercress or try adding ½–1 teaspoon of Dijon mustard to the mayonnaise. English mustard can be too strong for the egg flavor.

Note: If you are entertaining with these homemade egg sandwiches, it's best to make at least one and half times or even twice as many as you expect to need – everyone loves them and wants more.

Anchovy is another flavor added to eggs for sandwiches. Take 2–3 canned fillets and crush them to a paste. Then mix the paste with the mayonnaise or butter before spreading.

Watercress and Cream Cheese Sandwiches ⓥ

Watercress, with its peppery fresh flavor, was popular for afternoon tea – and nursery, family, and high teas as well. Here I have mixed it with cream cheese for a moist and tasty sandwich filling.

MAKES 4 ROUNDS OF SANDWICHES

1 bunch of watercress leaves, picked off the stems
2 tablespoons (25 g) butter, softened
4 oz (100 g) cream cheese
8 thin slices of whole wheat or brown bread
Squeeze of lime or lemon juice
Salt and pepper

Rinse the leaves before picking and shake off any water left on them. The watercress leaves can be completely picked, using only the leaves, but I prefer the bite and texture gained by including the stems.

Mix the softened butter with the cream cheese and spread onto the eight slices of bread.

Add a squeeze of lime or lemon to the watercress, season with salt and pepper, and divide among four slices of bread. Top with the remaining bread slices, cut away the crusts, and divide each round into four triangles.

Cucumber Sandwiches ⓥ

Cucumber, sliced very thinly, is a familiar and traditional sandwich filling, made famous by the lack of cucumbers in Oscar Wilde's *The Importance of Being Earnest*. The butter can be replaced with the healthy *Mayonnaise* (see Variation, page 49). A very thin spread is all that will be needed.

MAKES 4 ROUNDS OF SANDWICHES

Butter, for spreading
8 thin white or brown bread slices
40–48 thin slices of peeled cucumber
Salt and pepper

Butter each slice of bread. It's best to work the butter to a creamy consistency to guarantee a thin spread.

The cucumber needs to be sliced 20–30 minutes before the sandwiches are going to be made. After slicing them, sprinkle ¼ teaspoon of salt onto the cucumber. Place the slices in a stainless-steel colander or sieve. It's important not to use aluminum – this will give a metallic taste caused by a reaction with the salt. Let them stand, probably won't need to be "drained" from the cucumber.

After 20–30 minutes, taste one of the slices. They probably won't be over-salty and so will not need to be rinsed; if too salty for your taste, however, then quickly rinse under cold water, and shake them off well. Place the slices slightly over-lapping on top of four of the bread slices. Season with a grinding of pepper and top with remaining bread. Cut off the crusts of the bread and cut into squares, triangles, or strips.

Note: The seed center of the cucumber can also be removed. Take ½ small cucumber, peel, and halve lengthwise. Now, slice thinly and salt, drain, and finish as above.

For an extra "bite" in a cucumber sandwich, add a few sprinkles of vinegar – malt, white, or red wine vinegar can be used – to the cucumber before placing the slices on the bread.

Smoked Salmon Rolls

Rolls were used for holding sandwich fillings from early times. "Bridge" rolls were actually made for bridge players who, like the Earl of Sandwich, couldn't bear to leave the table. The "rolls" here, however, are pieces of bread rolled up around a spicy filling of smoked salmon and horseradish.

MAKES 4 SANDWICH ROLLS

4 slices of thin brown bread
4 slices of smoked salmon
½ recipe healthy *Mayonnaise* (see Variation,
    page 49) or softened butter
¼ –½ teaspoon creamed horseradish

To make the bread even thinner, flatten each slice by rolling with a rolling pin. Now, cut the crusts off. Add the horseradish cream to the mayonnaise and spread onto each slice, not quite to the edge for a neater finish. Place a slice of smoked salmon on top of each

and then roll as for a jelly roll. These can now be served as they are or sliced into ½ in (1 cm) "Catherine wheel" pieces.

Jam Sandwiches ⓥ

One last sandwich we should not forget is the British Jam Sandwich. If you use one of the homemade preserves from the next chapter (page 386–390), the idea – probably long a favorite at nursery teas – won't appear so old-fashioned.

Lightly spread a slice of white bread with softened butter, and spread the jam over it before covering with another slice. Cut the crusts off the bread and serve.

Note: Here's an idea that originated during the *nouvelle cuisine* trend of the 1970s and 1980s. If making strawberry jam sandwiches, lightly grind some fresh black pepper onto one of the buttered slices before finishing the sandwich. The pepper gives a little fiery bite to excite the strawberries. It would certainly be a bit different to offer strawberry jam sandwiches *au poivre*.

Jam Omelette ⓥ

The British dish similar to the French omelette, introduced to England in about the late sixteenth century was more like scrambled eggs in concept. Later, though, the omelette made as it is in France became known, and various savory versions became popular in Victorian and Edwardian times, including *Omelette Arnold Bennett* (page 71).

Sweet omelettes were enjoyed as well, and homemade jam was the favorite filling. If you're ever out of ideas, or you simply want something sweet and quick to make, then here is the perfect snack. After it's made and turned out, the omelette is dusted with confectioners' sugar and marked with a hot skewer to garnish and give a bitter-sweet flavor. A large spoonful of extra-thick cream (always a nice extra) spooned on top adds the final touch.

MAKES 1 OMELETTE

3 eggs, beaten
1 tablespoon (15 g) butter
1 tablespoon *Strawberry Jam* (page 387), warmed
Confectioners' sugar

The skewers can be heated directly on the stove burner used for cooking the omelette. Obviously, a gas stove will give you the open flame to heat the skewers. If you have an electric stove, place the skewers under a hot broiler.

Warm a 6–8 in (15–20 cm) omelette pan on the stove. While the pan is warming, crack the eggs into a bowl and whisk with a fork.

When the pan is hot, add the butter. As the butter melts and becomes bubbly, pour the eggs into the pan. They will take only 3–4 minutes to cook.

To keep the omelette light, keep the eggs moving by shaking the pan and stirring them with the fork. This will prevent them from sticking and browning. (If your omelette becomes golden brown, it has over-cooked. The natural yellow of the eggs indicates the most

tender finish to the dish.) You will soon have a scrambled look and consistency to the eggs.

Allow the eggs to set on the bottom for 5–10 seconds, then remove from the heat before spooning the warmed jam into the center. The eggs will still be moist and not completely set in the center. Holding the pan at a downward angle, slide and tap the omelette toward the edge, folding it over as you do so. Turn out onto a plate and shape under a cloth to give a cigar shape. Dust generously with confectioners' sugar and mark a criss-cross pattern with the hot skewers.

The omelette is now ready to serve, filled with strawberry jam and holding a souffléd texture. This makes it a dream to eat, with every mouthful melting.

BELOW
Jam Omelette

Homemade Scones (v)

Although most of us think that scones are Scottish – the Stone of Scone, for instance – the word apparently comes from the Dutch word *Schoonbroot*, or "beautiful bread." Scones have become one of the most popular afternoon and high tea cakes, and form part of yet another British speciality, the cream tea. Still warm from the oven, they are spread with homemade preserves and then topped with clotted cream. Wonderful!

MAKES 8–10 SCONES

2 cups (225 g) self-rising flour
1 teaspoon baking powder
Pinch of salt
2 tablespoons (25 g) superfine sugar
4 tablespoons (50 g) unsalted butter
⅔ cup (150 ml) milk
1 egg, beaten, or all-purpose flour, for brushing or dusting

Preheat the oven to 425°F/220°C.

Sift together the flour, baking powder, and salt into a bowl. Stir in the sugar, add the slightly softened butter, and rub it into the flour, creating a fine breadcrumb consistency. Add the milk, a little at a time, working to a smooth dough. Let the mixture rest for 10–15 minutes before rolling.

Roll the dough on a lightly floured work surface until ¾ in (2 cm) thick. Using a 2 in (5 cm) pastry cutter, cut the dough, using one sharp tap and not twisting the dough as you cut. Twisting the scone mixture will result in an uneven rising.

After they are cut, the scones can be either brushed with the beaten egg for a shiny glaze, or dusted with the flour for a matt finish.

Place the scones on a greased baking pan and bake in the preheated oven for 10–12 minutes until golden brown. Allow them to cool slightly and serve while still warm.

Note: An extra 4 tablespoons (50 g) of butter can be added to make richer scones. ⅓ cup (50 g) mixed golden raisins and currants can be added for fruity scones. The sugar can be omitted for plain savory scones. 2 oz (50 g) of grated Parmesan or Cheddar cheese can be added along with a pinch of English mustard for homemade cheese scones. Freshly chopped thyme can also be added to savory scones.

After the scones have been cut, the trimmings can be rolled and re-cut until all of the dough has been used.

OPPOSITE
Homemade Scones

See also

Banana and Golden Syrup Loaf (page 352)
Cauliflower Cheese with Crisp Parmesan Crumbs (page 68)
Cheddar Apple Cake (page 344)
Chocolate Molasses Cake (page 345)
Cornish Pasty (page 273)
Griddle Scones (page 362)
Homemade Malt Loaf (page 350)
Homemade Pork Pie (page 280)
Lardy Cake (page 347)
Lemon and Vanilla Sponge Cakes (page 341)
Lemon Syrup Loaf (page 352)
Parkin (page 350)
Strawberry Jam (page 387)
Saffron Bread (page 397)
Sally Lunn Cake or Bread (page 346)
Sausage Rolls (page 277)
Shortbread Cookies (page 359)
Simnel Cake (page 342)
Vegetarian Cheese and Onion "Sausage" Rolls (page 278)
Welsh Rarebit (page 178)

Preserves
and Pickles

Until a few hundred years ago, people
in Britain – and all over the world –
relied on preserved food in order to
survive the winter months. Perhaps the
earliest known form of preservation
was *chuño*, the "freeze-drying" of
potatoes by the Incas in
Chile about 1000 years ago.
In northern Europe, meat animals
would have to be killed in autumn,
for there was little fodder on which to
feed them over winter. Some of the
meat – of cattle, sheep, and pigs – was
eaten fresh, but the bulk was salted,
brined, and/or smoked to preserve it.
The British bacon tradition is a
direct result of this
form of preservation.

Fish was also preserved by smoking or salting, not only for a supply of winter food but, also, to allow them to be transported inland from the coast.

Vegetables and fruit weren't as easy to preserve, but it is from them that the popular and common British preserves of today are descended. Legumes as well as grains could be dried, and from early times these were life-sustaining in winter pottages. In Tudor and Stuart times, vegetables, herbs, and nuts were pickled to provide winter salads, garnishes, and flavorings for meat and fish. Mushrooms, cucumbers, and beets, along with parts of vegetables and flowers – among them borage and violet flowers, nasturtium leaves, samphire, and broom buds – were pickled in verjuice, the medieval forerunner of vinegar. This preservative was made from the sour juice of unripe grapes or crab apples (although the flavor of verjuice is thought to have resembled a sharp cider more than it did a vinegar). A mushroom pickle, made with a variety of spices, might be the ancestor of the present-day mushroom ketchup; the liquid was sometimes used as much as the vegetable because of its piquancy. Following the development of trade with India – and later the influence of the years of the Raj, vegetable and fruit chutneys and other Indian pickles became popular as accompaniments to meat, and many condiment recipes were invented and copied. I've included homemade *Piccalilli* (page 385) and *Mango Chutney* (page 388) in this chapter.

Dried fruits were imported from abroad for the desserts and pies that are so much part of the British tradition. Fruit was not often dried in Britain because areas of fruit-growing did not have long periods of sunny, hot dry weather or much cheap fuel. Instead of drying, fruit was preserved in sugar – thus the development of the traditional British jams, jellies, and marmalades.

Fruit was also brandied, candied, and boiled down to form thick, sweet pastes which were cut into cubes, rolled in powdered sugar, and eaten as a Turkish delight might be today. These pastes were also served as fruit cheeses or "marmalades" to accompany meats. Quince was the favorite, or original, variety of marmalade, the idea introduced from Portugal, but many other fruits were also used. Citrus fruit was not used until later, and even then, marmalade had to be cut with a knife rather than being soft enough to spoon. Softer sets of fruit and sugar became popular in Elizabethan times, and were known by the slang word "jam." Fruit was also preserved in fruit curds and butters, pickles, sauces, and vinegars. When you think of how short a season most fruits have, workers of the land must have been very, very busy preserving food for the winter.

Making homemade pickles and jams brings a sense of accomplishment and satisfaction. Watching the preserves develop in the pan is very exciting, with the texture and taste changing all the time as the ingredients bubble on the stove. I love giving and receiving homemade jams and pickles as presents; somehow no commercially-made products will ever match them. Hopefully, this chapter will help you with your Christmas gift list.

PAGE 378
Spicy Tomato and Mint Relish (page 381)

Spicy Tomato and Mint Relish

Relishes are actually quick pickles, and they are great with all kinds of meat. This tomato relish goes with lamb particularly well. Serve it instead of red currant jelly or mint sauce with roast lamb. It also goes well with *Shepherd's Pie Fritters* (page 185).

For a tomato relish with a background flavor of apples, simply omit the mint. This variation will become a great favorite with roast pork.

MAKES 2–2½ CUPS (450–600 ML)

Butter
1 onion, finely diced
1 garlic clove, crushed
Pinch of cinnamon
Pinch of nutmeg
Pinch of ginger
1 Granny Smith apple, peeled and diced
2 tablespoons sherry or white-wine vinegar
1 tablespoon light brown sugar
1 tablespoon tomato purée or ketchup
10 tomatoes, blanched, seeded and flesh diced or
    1 × 14 oz (400 g) can of chopped tomatoes,
    drained
1 teaspoon chopped fresh mint
Dash of Worcestershire sauce
Dash of Tabasco sauce
Salt and pepper

Melt a heaping teaspoon of butter and, when it begins to bubble, add the chopped onion and garlic. Cook for a few minutes until softened. Add the spices and diced apple and cook for another minute. Add the vinegar and sugar and bring to a boil. Reduce the mixture until almost dry. Add the diced tomatoes along with the ketchup or purée (ketchup will help the acidity and provide a spicy finish). Cook for a few minutes. Season with salt, pepper, Worcestershire sauce, and Tabasco and remove from the heat. Stir in the chopped mint. Drain the relish through a sieve, saving all of the tomato juices. These can now be reduced to a thick syrup consistency. Stir the syrup into the relish to strengthen the flavor of the chutney. The relish can be served slightly warmed or cold. It will keep for a week if refrigerated.

Note: To sterilize the jars, place them in a large saucepan, cover with cold water, bring to a boil, and boil for 15 minutes. Carefully remove them with tongs and allow to dry. After the jars have been filled, covered, and sealed, you can sterilize them again: place the jars on a wire rack or cloth in a large pan and almost cover them with water. Bring to a boil and boil for 15 minutes. Remove the filled jars from the pan, dry them, and cool.

Pickled Limes

Limes were introduced to Britain in the late seventeenth century, and using their juice in punches quickly became popular. They were also pickled. The particular pickling mixture here is Indian in influence, using green chilies, mustard seeds, ginger, star anise, and fenugreek.

Star anise is a star-shaped "pod," the fruit of an evergreen tree related to the magnolia growing wild in China and Japan. The whole pod is fragrant with a strong smell of aniseed mixed with liquorice. Inside each of the star's petals is a small oval, light brown seed, and a spoonful of them is needed here.

Fenugreek should be mentioned also, the seed and leaves of which are used, fresh or dried, in Indian cooking. It is an ancient herb, used medicinally by the Greeks and Egyptians. A member of the pea and clover family, the seeds are found in tiny pods, and they are small, square-shaped, and dusty yellow in color. To capture their curry-like flavor they must always be roasted, making sure they do not burn, which makes them very bitter.

These pickled limes are featured in the trout dish on page 145, mixed with pan-fried new potatoes, but they can also be served with curries or added to stir-fried spicy chicken. To capture the full flavor and to preserve the limes, the recipe must be made at least 4 weeks in advance of using.

MAKES A 1 LB/1 QUART (450 G/800 ML) JAR

6 limes, washed and cut into 6 wedges, trimming
    away any central excess pith from each wedge
¼ cup (50 g) salt
1 tablespoon yellow mustard seeds
1 teaspoon fenugreek seeds

Seeds from 2 star anises
4 small fresh green chilies, split, seeded and finely
chopped
½ cup (100 g) light brown sugar
1 tablespoon ground ginger
4 tablespoons water

In a stainless-steel colander (do not use aluminum because it reacts with citrus fruit and salt), sprinkle the limes with the salt. Place over a bowl, cover, and let them stand for 24 hours.

Place the mustard seeds, fenugreek, star anise seeds, and chilies in a frying-pan and dry-roast on top of the stove over a medium heat. Cook until the seeds begin to brown and pop.

Pour off the liquid from the limes and place them in a saucepan. Add the sugar, ginger, and water; bring to a boil and cook until the sugar has dissolved.

Mix the lime wedges with the dry-roasted spices and chilies. Pack them into a sterilized jar (see Note, page 381), making sure the limes are pressed in together firmly. Pour the sugar mixture on top, covering the limes as much as possible.

Seal the jars and store them in a cool place, or refrigerate, for at least 4 weeks before using. The limes will keep, refrigerated, for a minimum of 6 months.

Pickled Damsons

Damsons, related to plums, grow well all over Britain, but they are difficult to find in the US. Occasionally they appear at farmers' markets in late summer. Available in England during the months of September and October, they rarely ripen enough to eat as fresh fruit so they are traditionally made into jams, cheeses, and pickles. They are also used to make apple and damson crumbles or pies. Make this recipe whenever you are fortunate enough to find some to buy, or substitute tart plums. Pickled damsons go well with cold or warm ham, game, and pies (especially pork pies), served cold or slightly warmed.

This recipe is made with red-wine vinegar, but white-wine, cider, or malt vinegar can also be used. The fruit can be marinated in the vinegar overnight, but to increase the flavor and to develop the taste, they should be pickled at least 2–3 weeks in advance.

All the "spices" – cinnamon, ginger, lemon, orange, and cloves – are extras; adding them will give you a more flavorful result. A substitute for them is allspice, replacing the spices called for with half a dozen lightly crushed allspice berries will give a similar flavor. Note: If you can find a source for preserving sugar, using it will result in a clearer jelly.

MAKES APPROX. 7 LB (3 KG)

4½ lb (2 kg) damsons, or use 4½ lb tart plums
1¼ cups (300 ml) red-wine vinegar
2¼ lb (1 kg) sugar (see Note, above)
Walnut-sized piece of fresh ginger
Peeled rind of ½ lemon
Peeled rind of ½ orange
Piece of cinnamon stick
3–4 cloves

Remove the stems from the damsons, wash, and prick them with a fork. Peel and halve the ginger, if using, and tie it in muslin cloth, along with the other spices (including orange and lemon rind). Place the spice bag in a large saucepan along with the vinegar and sugar. Bring to a boil, stirring until the sugar has dissolved. After the mixture reaches at this syrup stage, add the damsons and bring to a simmer. Cook gently for 2–3 minutes, making sure the damsons are not broken but are becoming tender.

Remove the fruit carefully with a slotted spoon and arrange on baking pans to cool.

While the damsons are cooling, return the syrup to a boil. This now needs to be boiled for 5–8 minutes, until thickened and syrupy.

Place the fruits in warm, sterilized jars (see Note, page 381). While the syrup is still hot, strain it into the jars filled with the damsons. Cover with lids and let the jars cool. The pickled fruit should now be kept in a cool dark place for a minimum of 2–3 weeks before using. After being opened, the pickled damsons will keep, refrigerated, for a minimum of 6 months.

Note: This recipe can also be used with plums. The plums can be left whole or halved with pits removed. If you have halved the plums, place them in a pan and bring them to a simmer in the syrup, removing them immediately to prevent the plums from breaking up too much.

Plum or Damson Cheese

This is a highly traditional way of making a "fruit cheese" – a very thick sweet fruit purée. There's actually no cheese in the recipe. It is called "cheese" because of its consistency, basically a very thick, solidly-set purée. After it is made and set in suitable jars – jars from which you can release the jelly whole – it is left to mature for 6 months or more. Most "fruit cheese" will keep for up to 2 years. When it is served, the jelly is turned out of the jar and sliced. The jelly will go with many things from buttered toast for tea to cream cheese as a dessert. In the eighteenth century, fruit cheeses were eaten by themselves with a fork, or were served with cold meats, as we would serve a chutney or relish today.

The volume of the fruit is greatly reduced in cooking. In many old recipes, 1 lb (450 g) of sugar is boiled with the same weight of fruit. When cooked to the "cheese" stage, this loses most of its fruit flavor, becoming intensely sweet. Depending on the fruit, ½–¾ cup (100–175 g) of sugar per 1 lb (450 g) fruit is plenty, and leaves you with a more intense fruit flavor. Note: If you can find a source for preserving sugar, using it will result in a clearer jelly.

MAKES 2½ LB (1.2 KG)

4½ lb (2 kg) plums or damsons
1 lb 2 oz (500 g) sugar

The plums or damsons must first be baked in a slow oven (300°F/150°C) for approximately 50–60 minutes until soft. Transfer to a saucepan and bring to a slow boil. Cook briefly until the juices begin to thicken. Take the pan off the heat and remove the pits. The fruit can now be pushed through a sieve.

Add the sugar to the sieved fruit and bring to a boil. Allow the mixture to cook and reduce until very thick, making sure the fruit does not stick. To test the consistency, pull a spoon across the bottom of the pan. For a "cheese," a cleared trail should be left through the fruit. At this stage the fruit may have started to crystallize around the edge of the pan. If it is at a thick-cream stage but too soft to hold a trail, the fruit purée can be removed to set in jars and will become a "fruit butter" with a softer texture instead of a "fruit cheese."

When the fruit is thick enough, lightly brush the inside of sterilized jars (see Note, page 381) with peanut oil which allows the "cheeses" to turn out more easily when you serve them. Pour the purée into the jars, screw on the lids, and let them cool. As mentioned in the recipe introduction, the jars should be left for at least 6 months (up to 2 years), refrigerated, before opening. After they have been opened, the cheese will last about a month, refrigerated.

Pickled Shallots or Onions

These must have been one of the earliest and, considering how popular they are today, possibly the best-loved of all pickles. They are a perfect accompaniment to cold meat; you can't have a traditional "plowman's lunch" of bread and cheese without pickled onions.

Shallots have a fuller flavor than onions, but either will give good results. It's important that whichever you choose, they all are the same size.

Shallots or onions can be pickled hot or cold. The hot method takes less time to make and infuse to get the pickled results. Cold pickling, however, will give a crisper finish. I'll give you both methods to play with; both are very flavorful. I use cider vinegar since the flavor works very well with the oniony taste. Either white-wine or malt vinegar will also provide a good, basic flavor.

Cold Pickling

3 quarts (2.4 liters) water
1 cup (225 g) salt
2¼ lb (1 kg) small shallots or onions, skin left on
2½ cups (600 ml) spiced vinegar (page 385)

Mix together half of the water with half of the salt.
The shallots or onions can now be left in this brine,
unpeeled for a minimum of 12 hours.

The shallots or onions can now be drained and
peeled. Place in a fresh brine, using the remaining
amounts of water and salt. These should now be left
to stand for 3 days.

Drain and place the shallots or onions in
sterilized pickling jars (see Note, page 381). Pour the
cold vinegar and spices over them, making sure the
they are covered (more vinegar can be added if
needed.) Cover, seal, and for the best results, leave
for 3 months before serving. After they've been
opened, they will last for up to a year, refrigerated.

Hot Pickling

2¼ lb (1 kg) small shallots or onions, unpeeled
½ cup (100 g) salt
2½–4 cups (600–900 ml) spiced vinegar (see right)

Cover the shallots or onions with water and boil in
them for 2–3 minutes, drain, and peel. Roll them in
the salt and let them dry-marinate for 24 hours.

After 24 hours, wash the onions well. Cover
with the spiced vinegar and bring to a boil. Cook for
6–8 minutes before spooning them into sterilized jars
(see Note, page 381). Pour the spicy vinegar on top
and cover. The pickled shallots or onions will be best
served after a minimum of 2 weeks to 1 month.
After they have been opened, they will last for up
to a year, refrigerated.

OPPOSITE
Piccalilli with *Boiled or Baked Ham* (page 211)

SPICED VINEGAR (MAKES 2½ CUPS/600 ML)

2½ cups (600 ml) cider vinegar
1 teaspoon mustard seeds
1 heaping teaspoon allspice berries
8 cloves
8 black peppercorns
½ cinnamon stick
½ teaspoon coriander seeds

Place all in a saucepan and bring to a boil. This can
now be used immediately for "hot pickling" or left
to cool for "cold pickling."

Piccalilli

A recipe of 1694 has the title "Pickle Lila, an
Indian Pickle," and describes vegetables
preserved in a brine and vinegar sauce flavored with
spices, among them mustard seed and turmeric.
Piccalilli is much the same today and very easy to
make. There are also many variations that you can
try – different vegetables, mustards, and vinegars.

This "relish" is delicious with cold meats, pâtés,
cold pies, and terrines. It goes well with oily fish,
such as mackerel and herrings, its acidity working
against the oils to provide a good, clean taste.

MAKES APPROX. 3 LB (1.25 KG)

1 cauliflower
3 large onions
8 large shallots or 16 onions
1 cucumber
2½ cups (600 ml) white-wine vinegar
1¼ cups (300 ml) malt vinegar
¼ teaspoon chopped dried chili
1⅔ cups (350 g) superfine sugar
2 oz (50 g) English mustard powder
1 oz (25 g) ground turmeric
3 tablespoons cornstarch
Salt and pepper

Cut the cauliflower into small florets. Peel and cut the shallots or onions into ½ in (1 cm) dice. Place in a bowl, sprinkle with 2 tablespoons (25 g) of salt, and let them stand for 24 hours. Afterwards, rinse the vegetables in cold water and dry.

Peel and seed the cucumber and cut it into ½ in (1 cm) dice. Sprinkle with a little salt and let it stand for 10–15 minutes. Rinse in cold water, then dry and add to the shallots or onions and cauliflower.

Boil the two vinegars together with the chili and then let the liquid cool for 30 minutes. Strain through a sieve and discard the chili.

Mix together the sugar and remaining dry ingredients in a bowl. When the vinegar is cool, mix a little of it with the dry ingredients. Bring the bulk of the vinegar back to a boil, pour it into the sugar mixture, whisking until it is all blended together. Bring this mixture back to a boil and cook for 3 minutes, then simply pour it over the vegetables and mix well. Let it cool. The piccalilli is now ready and can be put into sterilized jars (see Note, page 381). Serve at once or keep refrigerated for up to a month.

Lobster or Shellfish Oil

This oil takes 2 weeks of infusing before you have the best result – but it's worth it. It holds a rich color and flavor from the lobster and is a wonderful finish to many dishes, such as *Lobster Omelette "Thermidor"* (page 75) and *Lobster Bisque Soup* (page 23). After it is made, infused, and strained, the oil will keep for several months, refrigerated.

MAKES 1¼ CUPS (300 ML)

¾ cup (350 ml) olive oil
1 small carrot, chopped
1 small fennel bulb (or ½ medium), chopped
1 celery stick, chopped (optional)
2 shallots, chopped
12 oz–1 lb (350–450 g) crushed lobster shells
⅓ cup (85 ml) brandy
½ tablespoon chopped fresh flatleaf parsley
½ tablespoon chopped fresh tarragon
1 garlic clove, crushed
1 teaspoon tomato purée
1 small sprig of thyme
1 bay leaf
1 star anise
2–3 coriander seeds, crushed

Warm 2 tablespoons of the olive oil in a large saucepan. Add the chopped carrot, fennel, celery (if using), and shallots. Cook until barely softened.

Heat a frying-pan until piping hot. Add a touch of olive oil and quickly fry the lobster shells until they have taken on a full, rich red color.

Add the brandy, flambé it, and reduce until almost dry. The lobster shells can now be transferred to the saucepan with the vegetables and cooked for 3–4 minutes. Add all the remaining ingredients, including the rest of the olive oil. Stir well and gently cook over a low heat for 1½–2 hours. Let the mixture cool.

Pour into a suitable container, cover, refrigerate, and infuse for two weeks. After infusing, re-warm the oil and pour through a fine strainer, preferably lined with muslin to leave you with approximately 1¼ cups (300 ml) of rich red lobster oil. After it has been opened, the oil will keep refrigerated for several months.

Note: Crab or shrimp oil can also be made using the above recipe.

Rowan Berry Jelly

The scarlet berries of the rowan tree that grows in the north of England and Scotland make a jelly that is a traditional accompaniment or "tracklement" for game, particularly roast grouse and venison (pages 247 and 270). The berries have a sweet–sour flavor that works very well with most game birds. Rowanberries are rarely available in markets, even in England, but people pick them wherever they grow wild to have the opportunity to make this jelly.

Strawberry Jam

MAKES 1¾–2 LB (750–900 G)

4½ lb (2 kg) ripe rowanberries
Approx. 1 quart (1.2 liters) water
1 lb (450 g) sugar to every 2½ cups (600 ml)
    of juices

Place the picked rowanberries in a deep pan, adding just enough water to cover them. Bring to a boil and cook until softened. This should take just 10–15 minutes; any more and the flavor of the fruit might become bitter.

To extract the maximum flavor, lightly mash the berries and then strain through a fine sieve or muslin jelly bag. It's best to allow the fruit to drain naturally (if so, leave for 24 hours). The jelly bag can be helped along by squeezing to allow a little of the purée through but this causes a slightly cloudy finish.

Whichever method you choose, when the berries are completely drained, measure the amount of juice. Add to it 1 lb (450 g) of sugar per 2½ cups (600 ml). I normally prefer to reduce the sugar quantity to 1⅔ cups (350 g). To give a less sweet flavor to the fruit. Rowanberries have a fairly low pectin content, however, and consequently do not gel so easily. If you make the jelly with less sugar, it will take longer to boil and reduce.

After the sugar has been added to the juice, bring to a boil and cook until it reaches a set-up point. This normally takes about 20 minutes. Check it every 5–6 minutes by spooning a tablespoon of the hot mixture onto a cold saucer. If the jelly becomes set, it is ready to be poured into hot, sterilized jars (see Note, page 381).

This jelly keeps between 2 and 3 months, improving in flavor from week to week.

Note: When boiling the jelly, any impurities rising to the top should be skimmed off.

While the berries are at their first and second stages of cooking, fresh herbs can be added. Thyme, marjoram, or savory all work very well. Simply tie an herb bunch in muslin; this can now be added and used in both stages. Discard it once the jelly is ready to set.

Britain is famous for its strawberries, so here is the way to make jam using these lovely, flavorful berries. Other berries, such as raspberries, blackberries, blueberries, and currants can also be used.

The recipe also works with larger soft fruit, such as ripe cherries, plums, peaches, and apricots. Most of these hold a medium quantity of pectin, the natural substance found in the cells of fruit and released by the natural acids also present, and by cooking the fruit in sugar.

The proportion of sugar to fruit is important in jam-making. The normal ratio is equal amounts of each, which helps the pectin to reach its setting point and preserves the jam. I often feel this leads to a too sweet jam with a minimal fruit flavor. By reducing the sugar to three-fourths of the fruit amount, the fruit flavor becomes more apparent and still allows the jelly to set up. The sugar can also be reduced to half the fruit amount. This then creates a thick syrup rather than a jam, but it does work well with many dishes because of the strong fruit flavor. Any jams

BELOW
Strawberry Jam

made with a lesser amount of sugar should be kept refrigerated, giving the jam a longer life. Whatever amount of sugar used, I suggest you use some bought pectin to guarantee a jellied finish.

Small berries, such as raspberries and blackberries, can be left whole, or half the amount can be lightly mashed to give a thicker consistency to the jam. Larger berries should be cut or mashed, while small ones should be left whole. Plums, apricots, and peaches are best cut into wedges.

Two methods follow, each giving great results.

MAKES 3¼ LB (1.5 KG)

2¼ lb (1 kg) fresh strawberries
Finely grated zest and juice of 1 lemon
2¼ lb (1 kg) or 1½ lb (750 g) or 1 lb 2 oz (500 g)
  jam sugar (containing pectin)

Method 1

Mash half the amount of berries in a large saucepan. Add the lemon zest, juice, sugar, and remaining berries and bring to a boil. (It's important to use a large saucepan because this allows the jam to boil rapidly without boiling over.) The jam can now be cooked for 3–4 minutes for a fairly thin consistency. If you prefer a jellied-style jam, boil for 8–10 minutes. Skim away any frothy impurities as it cooks. After it has cooked, let it cool slightly before spooning into suitable containers or sterilized jars (see Note, page 381).

Method 2

Place the sugar, zest, and juice in a large pan and bring to a simmer. Add the berries (left whole if not too big) and stir in carefully. Bring the mixture to a boil and cook for 3–4 minutes for a thin consistency. If you prefer a jellied-style jam, boil for 8–10 minutes and skim off any impurities. You now have a rich, shiny jam with the strawberries still holding their shape. Let the jam cool slightly before spooning it into containers or sterilized jars (see Note, page 381).

Mango Chutney

When mango pickles were first introduced to Britain, the idea was applied to cucumbers, peaches, and melons in an attempt to recreate the flavors. After the years of the Raj, Britain could import the necessary mangoes, and people began to make chutney themselves.

This is a chutney I love to spoon onto a spicy curry. Curries are now part of British life, so it is important to include this recipe. Usually, mango chutney is bought ready-made and the curry is the dish you make at home. Next time you have a curry dinner, the chutney part of it will be homemade.

MAKES APPROX. 4 LB (1.75 KG)

6 mangoes, not too ripe
1 lb (450 g) light brown sugar
2 teaspoons ground mixed spice
Good pinch of ground turmeric
½ teaspoon cayenne pepper
3 cooking apples, peeled, cored, and chopped
2 onions, finely chopped
4 garlic cloves, finely crushed with 1 teaspoon salt
3 cups (750 ml) malt vinegar
2 oz (50 g) finely grated fresh ginger

Peel the mangoes and then cut either side of the seed, giving you two thick slices of the fruit. Cut the opposite ends of the mango away from the edge of the seed. Any remaining fruit should be scraped off into a bowl. Cut the large slices into thick strips or chunks. Stir the sugar, spices, turmeric, and cayenne into the mango. This should now be left for a few hours to marinate.

Next, place all the ingredients in a large saucepan, bring to a simmer, and cook for 1½ hours, stirring from time to time for even cooking and to prevent it from sticking. The mango will become soft and cooked through, leaving a thick syrup. If the chutney seems to be too thin, simply increase the heat to reduce it more to make a thicker consistency. Let the mixture rest for 20–30 minutes before ladling into sterilized preserving jars (see Note, page 381).

Cool the jars and store in a cool place. The chutney can be served days after cooking, but it tastes best left to mature only a few for several weeks. After it has been opened, it will last for up to 3 months, refrigerated.

Homemade Red Currant Jelly

Red current jelly and mint sauce are two flavors commonly offered as accompaniments to lamb. They are very traditional, originating from the idea that you serve a meat with something it may have fed on or that grew nearby. Dorothy Hartley in *Food in England* is even more specific, saying red currant should be served only with sheep raised in valleys, since the berry's flavor is too strong for the more delicate mountain sheep. In my opinion, this homemade red currant jelly goes well with all lamb dishes.

MAKES 1½–2 LB (750–900 G)

3 lb (1.5 kg) freshly picked red currants
1⅔ cups (350 g) sugar for every 2½ cups (600 ml) juice

Place the red currants in a saucepan and barely cover them with water. Bring to a boil and then reduce the heat and simmer for 25–30 minutes until the currants have become overcooked and mushy.

Strain them through a fine sieve or muslin bag into a bowl and allow them to drain naturally. This will draw out all of the flavor and color from the fruit. After several hours, when the dripping has stopped, measure the amount of juice. For every 2½ cups (600 ml) of juice, add 1⅔ cups (350 g) of sugar. (Normally, the quantity is 1 lb/450 g sugar to 2½ cups/600 ml of juice but I find this too sweet and sickly. Red currants have a high pectin level and the 1⅔ cups/350 g of sugar will be plenty.) Boil the sugar with the juices and simmer for 10 minutes. The jelly is now ready to pour into hot, sterilized jars (see Note, page 381). After it is cold, the jelly will set. When the jelly is opened, it will keep refrigerated for up to 6 months.

Note: The flavor can be changed slightly with the addition of the grated zest of 1 orange and 2–3 tablespoons of port. This will give you an even richer jelly with an orange tang.

Candied Orange

This is basically candied orange peel, cooked in a sweet syrup to calm the bitter flavor of the pith and zest. I use it as a garnish for the *Scallops with Broiled Black Pudding à l'Orange* (page 147), but it goes well with many other dishes, sweet and savory.

MAKES 2 ORANGES

2 oranges, each cut into 8 wedges
1 cup (200 ml) water
1 cup plus 2 tablespoons (225 g) superfine sugar

After the orange wedges have been cut, the flesh can be used for another purpose, leaving the peel with the pith and outside zest.

Place the orange zest "petals" in a saucepan, cover with cold water, and bring to a boil. When it's at a boiling point, drain off the liquid and refresh the orange peel under cold water.

Repeat the same process, until the peel has been blanched five times.

Bring the measured water and sugar to a boil. Add the "petals" and poach gently for 1½ hours. Let them cool in the syrup. Left steeped in the cooking syrup, the orange peel will last for several months.

To use as a garnish, cut the orange into ⅛ in (3 mm) dice.

Note: The candied orange peel can be used in many dishes. Dice and add to steamed puddings, flavor a bread and butter pudding, garnish a mousse, or sprinkle over ice cream.

Orange Marmalade

The best oranges to use because of their strong bitter flavor and high pectin content are Seville, in season from late December/early January until late February. Almost any variety of orange or other citrus fruit – lemon, lime, grapefruit – can be used in this recipe, however.

How did marmalade get its name? There are several stories. Until the seventeenth century, a fruit preserve was made from quince, known in Spain and Portugal as *marmalada* and *marmelo*, hence the name "marmalade." Later, oranges took the place of quince, but the name stayed the same. Another story has to do with the voyage of Mary, Queen of Scots, from France to Scotland to claim her throne. She became seasick, and one of her maids, who was making a dish of bitter oranges for her, said, "*Marie est malade,*" which sounds a bit like marmalade. Who knows which is true!

The pectin in citrus fruit is held in the pith and seeds, so don't throw them away. The sugar content in marmalade is twice the amount of the fruit in order to balance the bitterness of the peel.

MAKES 2¼–3½ LB (1.25–1.5 KG)

1 lb (450 g) oranges
Juice of 1 lemon
5 cups (1.2 liters) water
2 lb (900 g) sugar

Wash and scrub the oranges to remove any artificial dyes. Halve the oranges and squeeze out the juice into a large pan, keeping any seeds and membrane. Now, cut the orange shells in half and cut away and discard the white pith. How conscientiously you do this really depends on how bitter you prefer your marmalade to be. Put the seeds and membrane in a piece of muslin and tie it into a bag. Cut the peel into thin or thick strips and place it in a saucepan with the orange and lemon juice and the water. Tie the bag to the pan handle and submerge it in the water.

Bring it to a simmer and cook for 1–1½ hours, until the peel is tender and the liquid has reduced by half. Remove the muslin bag, squeezing out any juices, and discard it. Add the sugar and stir over a low heat until it has dissolved. Now, bring the marmalade to a boil, skimming away any impurities and stirring from time to time. Cook for 10 minutes. While the marmalade is boiling, chill a saucer, for testing the setting point.

After 10 minutes has passed, spoon a little marmalade onto the saucer and chill it. It should set-up as a jelly and wrinkle when moved with a spoon, but if it does not, continue to boil for another 5 minutes and then re-test. Remove from the heat and skim off any impurities. Let it stand for 15–20 minutes. Stir it to spread the peel, then ladle into sterilized jars (see Note, page 381), cover, and seal. Store in a cool, dark place. After it has been opened, it can be kept refrigerated for up to 6 months.

Note: For a "warmer" taste, ⅓–½ cup (50–60 ml) of brandy, whiskey, Cointreau, or Grand Marnier can be added at the end of the cooking time. Or you can add 2–3 oz (50–75 g) of freshly grated ginger with the orange peel for a spicy finish.

OPPOSITE
Orange Marmalade

Spices and Flavorings

Although spices themselves have been used by the British since very early times, there are few *native* British spices. Coriander seeds from a Mediterranean plant were found at a Bronze Age site in Britain. The Romans introduced many spices as well as herbs vital to their cooking, among them pepper, ginger, and mustard. After the Norman Conquest, more spices were introduced, both French and Arab, and the returning Crusaders, too, brought back many of the spices they encountered in the East. These included cinnamon, cassia (Chinese cinnamon), cardamom, nutmeg, mace, and cloves, and all were incorporated into medieval cooking sometimes in alarming amounts. They brought back other imports too, such as almonds, almond milk, and dried fruit. But these foods from all those years ago were not as basic to Britain as their image has led us to believe.

It has been claimed that this early British passion for spices developed because of the need to disguise too salty or off flavors by creating very pungent tastes. But people who could afford to buy spices – for they were very expensive in those early times – would have been able to eat fresh meat and fish frequently. It is more likely that they simply enjoyed the taste the spices could give, or that it was fashionable (I like to think it was the former). These spices and herbs were not just used in cooking; they played a very big part in medicinal products too. Their quality would not have been of the best, because of the long journey from their countries of origin – their aroma and strength of flavor would have diminished. It is likely that many medieval dishes that would be very hot today using *fresh* spices would have been merely piquant then.

London was the center of the spice trade in Britain, and very early on, around 1180, the trade was organized by the Guild of Pepperers, one of the earliest London guilds. In the fourteenth century this became the guild of Grossers or Grocers (from *grossarii*, dealers who buy and sell in the gross). Wealthy people all over the country used spices in most of their cooking – in soups, pies, sauces, meat and fish dishes, and in puddings, both sweet and savory. In *Food and Drink in Britain*, C. Anne Wilson describes a typical recipe for stewed beef: it "recommends the addition of cinnamon, cloves, maces, grains of paradise, cubebs, minced onions, parsley, sage, and saffron. The stew was thickened with bread steeped in broth and vinegar, with extra salt and vinegar added at the last for good measure. The final instruction, 'and look that it be poignant enough,' seems redundant." I'd agree with that – you certainly wouldn't need to be searching for flavors!

Imported spices remained expensive for a very long time, although pepper and ginger were quite common (perhaps one reason why dried ginger is used in many regional British cakes and sweet breads). Mustard was cheap and popular because it could be cultivated in England – primarily in East Anglia, where, much later, a Norwich mustard company was founded by one Jeremiah Colman. It was used in many sauces and served with fresh and salted fish and meat and with "brawn" (a meat terrine). Saffron, too, was planted in East Anglia, where it gave its name to a town, Saffron Walden, and it is one spice that hasn't changed its relative price – as expensive then as it is now.

The discovery of the New World in the sixteenth century brought chilies, vanilla, and allspice to Europe and eventually to Britain, and they, too, were incorporated into much of British cooking. Some spices began to be sold as mixtures, hot or mild, as you might buy curry powder; a type of pre-prepared curry powder was in fact available in the late-eighteenth century, although curries were not to become a British passion until after the days of the Raj. A number of spices were used whole – cinnamon and nutmegs, for instance – and the clove-pierced onion so vital for British bread sauce was in use by the 1660s, a borrowing from the French.

As spices diminished in price after the seventeenth century – mainly due to wider cultivation and availability – it seems that they began to lose their importance in northern European cooking. Pickles, preserves, desserts/puddings, cakes, and sweet breads still relied on them to a certain extent, but they were not added automatically to every meat or fish dish. The fact that sugar was now cheap, too, may have played a part in this. In fact, the spiced liquid from pickles was often used instead of the spices themselves, and at the end of the eighteenth century, the first bottled sauces were sold commercially, the origin perhaps of the British passion for tomato ketchup, brown sauce, and Worcestershire sauce, the most famous of all.

At the beginning of the twenty-first century, the British actually seem to have returned to their medieval tastes, and they are now cooking with a broad selection of spices. Indian recipes and restaurants, a reminder of the years the British spent on the subcontinent, keep the British familiar with many of these. But Britain is also host to many other nationalities and their particular spices and flavors – Thai lemongrass, for instance. A number of these spices are being enthusiastically incorporated into a new style of "Great British" cooking. But whenever people are cooking with spices, it is important to learn from the early lessons – spices should be used to lend flavors, enhancing the main ingredients, but never used to mask or overpower a natural taste.

Curry Powder

People were able to buy mixtures of ground spices as long ago as the eighteenth century, although these spices were expensive. Today, there are many good-quality curry powders and pastes available on the market, all carrying different strengths to suit the curry of your choice. The recipe below is a mixture that I frequently use. As I say about cooking generally, there's nothing like making it yourself. This spice mixture will give you a well-flavored medium-hot curry.

MAKES ABOUT 1 OZ (25 G)

2 teaspoons cumin seeds
2 teaspoons cardamom pods or seeds
1 tablespoon coriander seeds
½ teaspoon ground ginger
½ teaspoon ground turmeric
½ teaspoon paprika
½ teaspoon chili powder
¼ teaspoon ground cloves

The cumin, cardamom, and coriander can all be "roasted," as for *Garam Masala* (page 396). Simply place in a dry frying-pan over a medium heat and roast until they brown and become aromatic. Let them cool. They can now be ground to a powder in a coffee grinder or blender. Shake through a fine sieve or tea-strainer and mix with all of the remaining spices. This powder will keep well in an airtight container in a dark place.

Curry Cream Sauce

I use this sauce for *Smoked Eel Kedgeree* (page 162), and also for *Curried Eggs* (page 396). The curry powder is the homemade one on the left, but it can be replaced with a bought medium-hot powder, such as Madras.

MAKES APPROX. 2–2½ CUPS (500–600 ML)

1 teaspoon of butter
1 large onion, finely chopped
2 garlic cloves, crushed
1 tablespoon curry powder (left) or ready-made Madras curry powder
1¼ cups (300 ml) *Chicken* or *Vegetable Stock* (page 33 or 36)
1¼ cups (300 ml) heavy cream
⅔ cup (150 ml) coconut milk
Squeeze of lime juice (optional)
Salt

Melt the butter and add the chopped onion and garlic. Cook over a medium heat without browning for 5–6 minutes. Add the curry powder and continue to cook for another 6–8 minutes, stirring occasionally. Add the vegetable or chicken stock and bring it to a simmer. Allow the sauce to cook at a fast simmer to reduce the stock by half. This will increase its total flavor. Add the heavy cream and return to a simmer. The mixture can now be cooked for 10–15 minutes. Add the coconut milk, bring to a simmer, and the sauce is ready. Season with salt, adding a squeeze of lime, if using, to heighten the total taste. After it's cooked, strain through a sieve for a smooth sauce.

Note: To thicken the sauce, simply simmer the stock but do not reduce. Instead take 1 teaspoon of arrowroot and moisten with a tablespoon or two of the cream. Whisk the arrowroot into the stock and return to a simmer. It's best to use light cream here, because the sauce will be thickened from the arrowroot. Cook according to the recipe, finishing with the coconut milk and a squeeze of lime.
For a slightly sweet finish, a tablespoon of *Mango Chutney* (page 388) can be added. If limes are unavailable, substitute lemon juice.
This recipe gives you a mild sauce; increase the curry powder from 1½–2 tablespoons for a hotter finish.

Curried Eggs

During the years of the Raj, many culinary concepts came to be adopted by British households. The "memsahibs," British wives of the men serving in the tropical subcontinent, would attempt to get their Indian cooks to make dishes in the Anglo-French style so prevalent at home, but inevitably, Indian spices and other less familiar ingredients would creep in. The British acquired a taste for these adaptations, and they brought the ideas back to Britain, where Mrs Beeton was to devote a whole chapter in one of her books to the art of Indian cooking.

European curries bear little resemblance to the Indian originals. Authentic curry was a sauce (the Hindi word *kari* means "sauce") working as a relish, not a complete dish. Its purpose was to enhance bland foods, such as rice or the wheat pancakes known as "chapattis." It was used much as tomato ketchup is by the British today, as an extra flavor to heighten tastes. A pre-medieval "curry" might have consisted of eggplant, onions, and probably lentils, flavored with cardamom, cumin, coriander, and turmeric. If you wanted it hotter, then there might be the addition of white pepper and mustard seeds. Whatever the case, most "curries" would have been diluted with coconut milk or yogurt. The hot chilies included in today's curries were not, in fact, introduced to India from tropical Central America until the sixteenth century. So in this recipe we are using a *kari* sauce, made with the "modern" chili flavor.

The eggs, classically, are served with plain boiled rice. This always works well, but a good braised rice will give you even more flavor.

SERVES 4

8 large eggs
2½ cups (600 ml) *Curry Cream Sauce* (page 393)
2 teaspoons chopped cilantro (optional)

Preheat the oven to 350°F/180°C. Boil the eggs for 7–8 minutes. These can now be run under cold water for a few minutes. Shell carefully and split in half lengthwise.

OPPOSITE
Warm Spiced Pineapple Cakes

They can now be laid in an ovenproof dish. Bring the curry sauce to a fast simmer, reduce by a quarter to thicken slightly and pour over the eggs. Cover with foil and bake in the preheated oven for 15–20 minutes.

After the dish is warmed through, remove the foil and sprinkle with the chopped cilantro if using. Serve with rice of your choice.

Note: To heighten the taste of the rice or sauce and to provide a sweeter finish, add a spoonful of raisins.

Warm Spiced Pineapple Cakes

Pineapple may not seem particularly British, but in the eighteenth century, English gardeners led Europe in pineapple growing. The gentry competed with each other to raise them in "stove houses," buildings heated by Dutch stoves, the ancestors of our modern greenhouses. The public became so passionate about the fruit that wrought-iron gates and fences were topped with pineapple shapes, which can still be seen to this day. But pineapple did not become truly common until the late nineteenth century when steamships brought the fruit from the West Indies.

Pineapples always make me think of the Caribbean, and two of the spices being used in this dessert originate from there – allspice from Jamaica and nutmeg from Grenada. After the pineapples have been cut into disks to fill the molds, the trimmings can be chopped and made into a sorbet (recipe provided on page 396). The pineapple sorbet is an optional extra but it does bring a lively contrast of flavors and textures, and it uses up all the pineapple trimmings too. I have also included a pineapple caramel sauce just to spoon over the dessert. So here are lots of different flavors and textures to enjoy.

SERVES 8–10

2 medium pineapples, peeled, "eyes" removed
    with the tip of a carrot scraper
Peanut oil, for frying
Superfine sugar for caramelizing

For the Sponges

1 cup (125 g) Brazil nuts
18 tablespoons (250 g) butter
1 tablespoon clear honey

1 cup (150 g) all-purpose flour
½ teaspoon salt
½ teaspoon baking powder
½ teaspoon each of ground cinnamon, nutmeg,
    freshly grated ground ginger, ground allspice,
    and ground black pepper
1 cup (200 g) sugar
6 egg whites

For the Pineapple and Caramel Sauce
(makes about 1¼ cups/300 ml)

½ cup plus 1 tablespoon (125 g) sugar
⅓ cup plus 1 tablespoon (85 ml) water
¼ cup (50 ml) heavy cream
⅓ cup plus 1 tablespoon (85 ml) pineapple juice

For the Pineapple Sorbet (optional)

2 cups (225 g) pineapple trimmings
⅔ cup (150 ml) syrup (page 312), replacing the
    water with bought pineapple juice
Juice of ½ lemon
White rum, to taste (optional)

This recipe will fill eight to ten 3 × 2 in (7.5 × 5 cm) small rings or one large 10 in (25 cm) springform pan.

The pineapple is going to be cut into disks to fit the individual molds. Do this by cutting vertically on either side of the core, giving two large half-cylinders to use for the disk. There will, obviously, be some flesh left on the core, which can be cut away and chopped to use in the sorbet mixture.

After the "sides" have been cut from both pineapples, cut them horizontally into ½ in (1 cm) thick slices; 4–5 disks will be needed from each half-cylinder. Any trimmings can now be chopped for the sorbet mixture. If using one large cake pan, disks can still be cut or simply halved through the center of the pineapples, cutting lengthwise and removing the core. Now, cut into enough half-moon slices to fill the bottom of the pan.

The disks can now be pan-fried in a little oil on one side only to create a golden caramel finish. When these starting to brown, add a pinch or two of superfine sugar to finish the caramelizing of the fruit. Place caramel-side down in the individual rings or the springform pan. Let them cool.

Preheat the oven to 325°F/160°C and toast the Brazil nuts before rubbing off the skins. Grind the nuts to a medium-fine texture in a food processor. Then place the butter in a saucepan over a medium heat, melting it and cooking until lightly brown in color. At this stage, remove from the butter from the heat and stir in the honey. Sift the flour, salt, pepper, baking powder, and all the spices together. Add the sugar and Brazil nuts, stirring in the honey butter.

Whisk the egg whites to a soft-peak stage and fold into the cake mixture.

Pour the mixture onto the caramelized pineapples and bake in the preheated oven for 35–40 minutes. The small cakes will be just firm to the touch. If baking a large cake, the cooking time will be extended by 10–15 minutes.

They are now ready to be turned upside-down out of their molds or pan to show the caramelized pineapple slices. Or, you can allow to cool, refrigerate them and then microwave when needed. The cake(s) will keep for 2–3 days, if refrigerated.

To make the sauce, first boil the sugar and water together until they reach a golden caramel color. The heavy cream and pineapple juice can also be boiled and then poured into the caramel. Mix well before straining through a sieve. The sauce is ready to serve.

To make the sorbet, chop all the pineapple trimmings and place them in a saucepan with the syrup. Bring to a simmer and cook for a few minutes until the pineapple has softened. Add the lemon juice and rum to taste, if using. Allow the mixture to cool before churning in an ice cream machine (see Note, page 309). The freezing process will take 20–30 minutes.

To serve, re-heat the cake(s) if necessary. Spoon the sauce around or over the dessert and place a scoop of pineapple sorbet, if using, on the side.

Note: The recipes can be halved to make 4–5 individual cakes or to fill a small 6½–7 in (17–18 cm) springform pan.

Garam Masala

Garam masala was a mixture of spices put together originally to "perk" people up – to prepare them for hard winter's work. It is a "hot" spice and it sets people's appetites in India for hot dishes. It has since become a very varied mixture of spices for different dishes, some hotter than others.

The spice mixture does not have to be used only for Indian curry dishes; it will liven up vegetarian risottos, pancakes, ratatouille, lentils, and most tomato-based dishes as well as cream and yogurt sauces. This recipe is a combination that will suit all of these. After it's made, keep it in an airtight container in a dark place and use it whenever needed. Of course, you can buy garam masala ready-made, but the aromatic smell and flavor when you make it yourself is wonderful.

MAKES ABOUT 2 OZ (50 G)

2 tablespoons coriander seeds
2 tablespoons cumin seeds
1 teaspoon cardamom seeds
1 cinnamon stick
2 bay leaves
1 tablespoon black peppercorns
2 teaspoons cloves
½ teaspoon freshly grated nutmeg
¼ teaspoon ground mace
¼ teaspoon ground ginger

Dry-roast all the ingredients, except the nutmeg, mace, and ginger, in a dry skillet over a medium heat until they darken slightly and become aromatic. Let the mixture cool, then add the remaining spices and grind them to a powder in a coffee grinder or by using a mortar and pestle. Store the blend in an airtight jar.

Saffron Bread

Saffron's rich, orange-colored strands are the stigmas of *Crocus sativus*, the saffron crocus. Saffron is the most highly flavored and expensive spice in the world. While writing this book, the price ranged from $95 to $110 for 1 oz (25 g). This makes it about $1600 a pound (450 g). The reason for this expense is that each plant will contribute only three stigmas. It's harvested by hand, and to make 1 oz (25 g) of it, 13,000 stigmas are needed.

This is a spice that has been with us since many centuries BC, and it has been used not only as a flavoring but also in perfume making, in medicines, and as a dye. It's thought that saffron was introduced to Britain by the Romans (as were so many other herbs and spices), and it was the Arabs who re-introduced the spice to medieval Europe. The word saffron actually comes from the Arabic for "yellow."

Saffron for some time was quite an important crop in England. The town of Saffron Waldon in Essex grew the crocuses whose stigmas produce the spice, as did the town Stratton in Cornwall, until only a hundred or so years ago. In the fifteenth century, anybody found "abusing" the spice in Germany would have been burned and buried.

Most of the world's saffron today comes from Spain where it grows on the central plains of La Mancha. The stigmas are put through a grading process based on length (the best are up to 2 in/5 cm), depth, and strength of color. Powdered saffron can also be found. This is a cheaper product and must be checked carefully because similarly colored tumeric is often added as filler. If you can find the Selecto label on a container of saffron, it will always be a safe choice.

Because of its strength, only a small amount of saffron needs to be used in recipes. To get the best results, the strands must first be infused with warm water. Many old recipes will tell you to do this 24 hours in advance but this isn't really necessary. It's best to take the amount required and pour a little hot water (1–2 tablespoons) over it. This can now be left to steep and infuse for 1 hour. A quicker alternative is to break the threads down using a mortar and pestle. Pour the warm water over this and leave for 10–15 minutes. Steeping for 1 hour will always give stronger results.

The saffron bread, below, is a sweet tea bread, best served sliced and spread with butter.

MAKES A 2 LB (900 G) LOAF OR
2 × 1 LB (450 G) LOAVES

1 teaspoon saffron strands
2 tablespoons warm water
4 teaspoons dried yeast
⅔ cup (150 ml) warm milk
¼ cup plus 1 tablespoon (75 g) sugar
4 cups (450 g) all-purpose flour
½ teaspoon salt
¼ teaspoon ground cinnamon
¼ teaspoon freshly grated nutmeg
12 tablespoons (175 g) butter, diced

1 cup (175 g) mixed dried fruit
⅓ cup (50 g) mixed candied citrus peel, chopped

The saffron should first be steeped in the 2 tablespoons of warm water as explained in the introduction.

Stir the dried yeast into half the milk along with 1 teaspoon of the sugar. This can now be left to froth for about 5–10 minutes.

Sift the flour, salt, and spices together in a mixing bowl and rub in the butter. Add the remaining sugar and all dried fruit and mixed peel. Make a well in the center, pouring in the yeast and saffron mixtures.

Mixing by hand, gradually stir the flour into the liquids. As you are mixing, add the remaining milk until a soft, but not too sticky, dough is formed. The dough can now be kneaded for 10–15 minutes for an elastic, smooth finish. Cover with a damp dish towel and let the dough rise in a warm place for about 3-4 hours.

When it has doubled in size, knead and punch down the dough. This can now either be placed into the well greased 8 x 4 x 2½ inch (900 g) loaf pan or divided into two pieces to be placed in the two 1 lb (450 g) loaf pans.

Cover and let them double in size once more. This will take 2–3 hours.

Preheat the oven to 375°F/190°C. Bake the large loaf for 50–60 minutes and the 2 small loaves for 40–50 minutes.

To check whether the bread is done, tap on the bottom of the loaf; a hollow sound will tell you it's ready. Now, remove the bread from the pan(s) and cool on a wire rack.

Note: To give the bread a shiny finish, boil a tablespoon of sugar with a tablespoon of milk and as soon as the bread is out of the oven, brush it with the glaze.

If fresh yeast is available, crumble 1 oz (25 g) into the sugar and milk as for dried yeast. When it is stirred, it will become thick and smooth – ready to use in the recipe.

OPPOSITE
Saffron Bread

See also

Gingerbread Cookies (page 357)
Iced Vanilla Parfait with Nutmeg Clotted Cream
(page 294)
Lemon and Vanilla Sponge (page 341)
Mango Chutney (page 388)
Nutmeg Ice Cream (page 309)
Parkin (page 350)
Piccalilli (page 385)
Pickled Limes (page 381)
Spicy Scrambled Eggs (page 81)
Spicy Smoked Haddock Saffron Soup (page 18)

Bibliography

Cold Smoking and Salt Curing Meat, Fish and Game, A.D. Livingston, The Lyons Press, 1995

Curries and Bugles: A Memoir and Cookbook of the British Raj, Jennifer Brennan, Periplus Editions, 2000

How To Cook, Delia Smith, DK Publishing Inc., 2001

D'Artagnan's Glorious Game Cookbook, Little, Brown and Company, 1999

Encyclopedia of Herbs and Their Uses, Deni Brown, DK Publishing, Inc., 1995

Food and Drink in Britain:From the Stone Age to the Nineteenth Century, C. Anne Wilson, Academy Chicago Publishing, 1991

Fabulous Food, Gary Rhodes, DK Publishing, Inc. 2000

Food and Feast in Tudor England, Alison Sim, Palgrave, 1998

Food in History, Reay Tannahill, Crown Publishing, 1995

Great British Cooking: A Well-Kept Secret, Jane Garmey, Harper Collins, 1992

Irish Traditional Cooking: Over 300 Recipes from Ireland's Heritage, Darina Allen, Trafalgar Square, 1998

Larousse Gastronomique, Crown Publishing, 1988

A Little Book of English Teas, Rosa Mashiter, Chronicle, 1995

The Midieval Cookbook, Maggie Black , Thames and Hudson, 1996

The New Cooking of Britain and Ireland: A Culinary Journey in Search of Regional Foods and Innovative Chefs, Gwenda Hyman, John Wiley & Sons, 1995

An Omelette and a Glass of Wine, Elizabeth David, The Lyons Press, 1997

On Food and Cooking: The Science and Lore of the Kitchen, Harold Mcgee, Collier Books, Inc., 1997

Rhodes Around Britain, Gary Rhodes, West 175, 1998

Seeds of Change: Six Plants That Transformed Mankind, Henry Hobhouse, McClellan and Stewart, 1999

Seven Centuries of English Cooking, Maxine de la Falaise, Grove Press, 1992

Suppliers

The British Shoppe
catalog available
800-842-6674
www.thebritishshoppe.com
45 Wall Street
Madison, CT 06443
Gourmet foods from Britain

Browne Trading Co.
catalog available
800-944-7848
www.browne-trading.com
260 Commercial Street
Portland, ME 04101
Good selection of fresh and smoked fish, including Finnan Haddie

D'Artagnan
catalog available
800-327-8246
www.dartagnan.com
280 Wilson Avenue
Newark, NJ 07105
Specialist game and poultry supplier, stocks

Dean and Deluca
catalog available
877-826-9246
www.dean-deluca.com
8200 E. 34th Street Circle,
North Building 2000
Wichita, KA 67226
Extensive selection of specialty foods

King Arthur Flour
catalog available
800-827-6836
www.kingarthurflour.com
P.O. Box 876
Norwich, VT 05055
Baking supplies and specialties

Old World Venison Company
320-749-2197
www.upstel.net
21564 100th Avenue
Randall, NM 56475
Farm-raised red deer available

Index

Page numbers in *italic* refer to illustrations